Retailing

Retailing

J. Barry Mason

Morris L. Mayer

Hazel F. Ezell

all of
Graduate School of Business
College of Commerce and Business Administration
The University of Alabama

1988
Third Edition

Business Publications, Inc.
Plano, Texas 75075

The first two editions of this text were published
under the title, *Foundations of Retailing*.

Acquisitions editor: *John R. Weimeister*
Developmental editor: *Rhonda K. Harris*
Production manager: *Bette Ittersagen*
Production editor: *Ann Cassady*
Copyediting coordinator: *Jean Roberts*
Designer: *Stuart Paterson*
Artist: *Alice Thiede*
Compositor: *Carlisle Communications, Ltd.*
Typeface: *10/12 Times Roman*
Printer: *Arcata Graphics/Halliday*

ISBN 0-256-05815-6

Library of Congress Catalog Card No. 87–72015

Printed in the United States of America

1 2 3 4 5 6 7 8 9 0 H 5 4 3 2 1 0 9 8

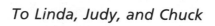

To Linda, Judy, and Chuck

Preface

For the career-oriented student, few topics are more exciting and dynamic than retailing. Studying the subject paves the way for the most diversified career opportunities available in the marketplace of the 1990s and beyond. Our third edition has been designed to reflect the dynamics of retailing and to make study of the field more rewarding for both students and instructors.

APPROACH OF THE TEXT

This text uses a "how-to" approach within the context of strategic retailing. We address all questions likely to be asked by a person interested in a retail career as an owner, a manager of an enterprise, or an employee who is uncertain of future directions. Answers to the questions we raise are stated from a pragmatic, how-to point of view, but we have not sacrificed the conceptual and analytical foundation necessary for a complete introduction to the field. The approach we have taken assumes no prior knowledge of retailing. Thus, the material is presented in simple, straightforward language. With our assumption of "no prerequisites needed," we have defined all terms carefully. We also provided many real-life examples to illustrate the points in the text.

The book has a strong career focus which provides students the opportunity to learn more about the world of retailing, regardless of whether they will ever be employed in a retail setting.

The stage is set in the first chapter. The excitement of retailing today is captured in this introductory chapter. The strategic framework of the book is presented in Chapter 2.

The objectives of this text are to ask and answer questions about:

— What a person needs to know before making a decision (either careerwise or investmentwise) about retailing.
— Key strategic decisions in a successful retail strategy.
— What must be considered to plan for situations over which management has no control, in other words the external environment of retailing.
— The ways a person can ensure that operations will be profitable.
— Now to evaluate profitability (as determined by accounting and control systems).
— Whether retailing is a viable career (or investment) in your future.

This book is written from the point of view of the student who is asking questions about retailing as a career and as a possible future business venture. After studying the book, the student will know the opportunities, problems, challenges, and success potential of operating a retail business or working for someone else who does.

This book presents the broad spectrum of opportunities that exist for the aspiring retailer. What types of stores are out there? Large ones like J. C. Penney and small ones like your local 7-Eleven; fancy ones like Neiman-Marcus and no-frills operations such as Marshalls and T. J. Maxx all exist successfully.

Where will the action in retailing be during the 1990s? The small, secondary markets look good to many strategic planners. Will the outlying regional malls in metropolitan areas still be attractive investments? What about downtown (the central business district)?

Which names are part of the big retail action? Nordstrom, The Limited, Macy's, Dayton-Hudson, May, and Federated are well known in upscale general merchandise. What action can we expect from the big national general merchandise chains—Sears and Penney's? A good question! Will Macy's Herald Square Store continue to challenge Bloomingdale's in New York? Watch The Limited for smart fashion strategy and market segmentation, the exciting festival malls like Riverwalk in New Orleans and the open-air fashion centers proliferating the urban landscape, B. Dalton books, deli departments in superstores, and upscale fancy food emporiums for at-home dining, the vast proliferation of computer hard- and software in all kinds of outlets, and much more!

What does all this diversity mean to the student? Many choices for different types of careers exist—choices in type of retailing, location, size, and degree of dynamics. Many types of skills are needed. Retail organizations need people to manage all functions that exist to serve the customer. This edition incorporates all these aspects.

ORGANIZATION OF THE TEXT

The book flows in a logical sequence since each topic fits into a planned framework. Part 1 of the framework, Structural Dynamics and Strategic Planning, discusses what retailing is like today (Chpater 1) by quickly initiating you into the retailing fraternity! Chapter 2 introduces students to the essence of strategic planning as a way of defining the purposes of the firm and deciding how to compete. Part 2 introduces students to the environmental factors affecting retail strategy development, including the key legal and public policy issues (Chapter 3), the critical dimensions of the economic and social environments (Chapter 4) and the new technology (Chapter 5).

Part 3 introduces students to selecting markets in which to compete. Chapter 6, asks and answers critical questions about the consumer, followed by concepts of lifestyle merchandising in Chapter 7. Part 4 introduces students to the resources needed to compete, including issues in financing and organizing a business (Chapter 8), and franchising as a way of owning and operating a retail firm (Chapter 9). Chapter 10 presents the key issues in the location, site, and building decisions, and Chapter 11 introduces students to critical issues in the recruiting, selection, training, and motivation of employees.

Part 5, positioning for competitive advantage, is a critical part of the text and introduces students to expense planning (Chapter 12); buying and inventory management (Chapter 13); determining retail prices (Chapter 14); physically handling and securing merchandise (Chapter 15); layout and merchandise presentation (Chapter 16); keys to successful selling (Chapter 17); advertising, sales promotion, and publicity (Chapter 18); and sales-support services (Chapter 19).

Part 6, consisting of Chapters 20 and 21, provides the tools for evaluating competitive actions, including the elements involved in developing control systems and in developing an accounting system. The text ends with Chapter 22 which provides an overview of trends, social dimensions, and prospects that affect retailing, followed by a comprehensive careers appendix to help students make better decisions about the many facets of a career in retailing.

SOME OTHER THINGS ABOUT THE BOOK

We have tried to make this book interesting and to reflect the excitement of retailing. Some of the premier retail firms in our country have provided excellent photographs. Study Aids in many chapters provide additional substance to enlighten the topics. The introductory retailing capsule at the beginning of each chapter and the two cases at the end of each chapter also bring a high degree of realism to the material.

HOW TO STUDY RETAILING WITH THIS BOOK

Look carefully at the first page or two of each chapter. This information is valuable. It lists topics covered in the chapter and spells out the specific chapter learning objectives. If you can answer the questions raised on these pages, you're making progress. It's a good preview and review.

Each chapter includes discussion questions to make you think about what you've read and to test your memory and understanding of the chapter. Practice problems are given in some chapters so you can check your understanding of skills explained in the book. Always work the problems. Each chapter also includes two cases. These cases let you confront a real situation to make a decision or to judge someone else's actions. These cases are fun and good learning experiences.

This edition offers another outstanding plus—a student Learning Resource Guide—which can be of great value in studying retailing. Its self-examinations let you test your knowledge, additional short cases let you apply your logic, and selected readings broaden your knowledge of the subject. The Learning Resource Guide will make learning more challenging and give you confidence in your mastery of retailing topics.

In addition to the key terms highlighted in the beginning of each chapter, important definitions have been added to the end of each chapter.

ACKNOWLEDGMENTS

Colleagues who have taught the book for the past several years have given us valuable suggestions for improvements. People from both the business world and the academic world have been valuable in assisting us throughout this experience.

Our sincerest appreciation is extended to the following people who graciously assisted in the preparation of the manuscripts for one or more editions: Gemmy S. Allen, Mountain View College; Mark I. Alpert, University of Texas at Austin; Ronald Bernard, Diablo Valley College; Martin R. Clayman, University of Tulsa; Jerry A. Cooper, Southern Oregon State College; Wilma S. Greene, The University of Alabama; Blaine Greenfield, Bucks County Community College; Larry G. Gresham, Texas A&M University; James Healey, Chabot College; Judith S. Leonard, Eastern Kentucky University; Richard O. Leventhal, Metropolitan State College; Michael F. O'Neill, California State University, Chico; Elisabeth K. Ryland, Farmville, Virginia; Robert H. Solomon, Stephen F. Austin State University; Robert Stephens, University of Tennessee at Martin; and Robert E. Witt, University of Texas at Austin.

The following business firms have been generous with their time and materials. We extend our gratitude to: the A&P Company, Aronov Realty, Dillards, IBM, Macy's, National Cash Register, Parisian, The Jewel Companies, J. C. Penney Company, Inc., Carter Hawley Hale, The May Company, Sears, K mart, The Doody Co., Neiman-Marcus, Mercantile Stores, and The Fannie Farmer Company.

J. Barry Mason
Morris L. Mayer
Hazel F. Ezell

Brief Contents

Contents

Structural Dynamics and Strategic Planning

The size and complexity of retailing become quickly apparent when one thinks about its structure. The millions of retail outlets in the United States today generate billions of dollars in annual sales. All of us are familiar with such giants as Sears, Wal-Mart, and J. C. Penney. Yet small, independent retail and franchised outlets far outnumber the larger, well-known chains.

The number of retail outlets continues to increase at a much faster rate than the population. As more and more markets have become saturated with retail stores, competition has become increasingly strong. The development of strategic plans in retailing as the essence of competitive strategy thus has become as important as merchandising skills in recent years. Retailers are now more careful about choosing the markets in which they compete, as well as the competitive strategies and marketing mix variables they use. Market segmentation, market positioning, and other strategies essential to competing effectively have become highly refined skills.

Chapter 1 reviews the essence of marketing structure to help students understand the complexity, excitement, and dynamic nature of retailing. Chapter 2 provides an overview of the ingredients of retail strategy development and is designed to help students understand how retailers develop strategies for competing in today's marketplace.

1

Retailing Today: The Structure as It Is and as It Might Be

Madison and Fifth Avenues

"On the avenue, Fifth Avenue," the parade marches up and down the street, not only at Easter but every day of the week. The heart of "the" avenue is about one and one-quarter miles extending from 34th to 59th streets, and this piece of real estate proclaims the "optimism and enterprise that is New York." The best example of shopping along Fifth Avenue is in its great fashion department stores. Many have disappeared over the years (De Pinna, Best & Co., and Arnold Constable to name only a few), but the choices still include Saks, B. Altman, Bergdorf Goodman, and Lord & Taylor. What else does the street offer to the constantly surging traffic? The shops of the three-block-wide Rockefeller Center; Gucci (no longer closing for lunch), with the famous silk scarves and the well-known signature or initial-adorned bags and belts; Bijan, the Beverly Hills menswear retailer that admits potential customers only after making an appointment to show the amazing luxury items in the shop (such as a chinchilla bedspread); Botticelli which offers leather footwear in the classic style of master craftsmen from the 16th century to the 21st; and the world-renowned jewelers, Tiffany and Cartier, for the epitome in quality accessories.

Fifth Avenue today is challenged by Madison Avenue, one block to the east, for the upscale fashion market in Manhattan. "Madison is an avenue for devotees of perfect proportion—an international boulevard in miniature. . . . Shops, galleries, salons, restaurants in brownstones and vintage apartment houses,

Based on "Shopping" by Rosie Barraclough, in *Guestinformant*, New York, 1984–85 Edition, pp. 33–84.

few of them rising above three stories, crowd the pavements to create a dollhouse of delight, of treasure and temptation which demands a stroller's pace, a connoisseur's attention to detail.'' The world's most famous couturier empires have homes on Madison Avenue—Sonia Rykiel, Emanuel Ungaro, Gianni Versace, Missoni, Jager, Armani—all of whom join Yves St. Laurent's Rive Gauche boutique which is the ultimate in elegance and drama.

*T*he retailing capsule depicting Fifth and Madison Avenues in New York City suggests the dramatic and changing character of retailing in that great mecca of shopping activity. The profile also directs attention to New York as the most dynamic, exciting, and challenging microcosm of trend-setting retailing in the world. We can think of no better framework to ''set the tone'' of this text than to introduce retailing à la New York. We are not suggesting that mid-America replicate New York, but we are using the nation's largest city to demonstrate innovativeness within the retailing structure and to focus on the constant change within the structure.

The first chapter in any book, just as the first lecture in a class or the first meeting of a new organization, sets the tone for all that follows. We find our topic dynamic, exciting, and challenging and want to share our enthusiasm with you. After reading this chapter, you will be able to:

1. Relate retailing to the marketing discipline.

2. Place retailing within the channel of distribution.

3. Explain and describe the current retail institutional structure.

4. Discuss how retailing is classified and described quantitatively.

5. Review the explanations of institutional change.

Before profiling New York, we must introduce some essential terms that will be valuable throughout this chapter. **Retailing** consists of all activities involved in the sale of goods and services to the ultimate consumer. A retail sale occurs whenever an individual purchases groceries at a supermarket, a videocassette at a record store, a meal at McDonald's, a haircut at a barbershop, or a membership in a health spa. Not all retail sales are made at a place of business. Direct home sellers such as Mary Kay Cosmetics, Tupperware, and Avon are examples of nonstore retailing, as are the mail-order firm L. L. Bean and vending machine operators.

In 1985 the American Marketing Association defined **marketing** as the process of planning and executing the conception, pricing, promotion, and distribution of ideas, goods, and services to create exchanges that satisfy individual and organizational objectives. Retailing is the final part of that process; they are inseparable.

Structure is the arrangement of parts, elements, or constituents considered as a whole rather than a single part. So, when we talk about the *retailing structure,* we are discussing *all* of the outlets (organizations, establishments) through which goods or services move to the retail customer (ultimate consumer). The structure is a complex system which can be classified in various ways to help understand its components.

Retailing thus is a part of marketing from a process point of view and is a complex structure from an institutional perspective. Finally, retailing is primarily carried on by organizations who are middlemen in the **channel of distribution**. Channels of distribution are interorganizational systems through which products/commodities or services are marketed. Figure 1–1 presents a diagram of the place of retailing in the classic marketing channels of distribution.

STRUCTURAL DYNAMICS—URBAN RETAILING— NEW YORK CITY—A CASE STUDY OF LOCATIONAL STRUCTURE OPTIONS

One of the ways to classify the retail structure is by location. Our focus on New York (Manhattan) is actually locationally framed. Figure 1–2 is a guide to the discussion of urban retailing and is in fact an outline of the first section of this chapter. The first part is New York oriented; the second part is concerned with urban retailing outside of New York.

Our beginning is shown in Figure 1–3 which is the retailing center of Manhattan. Our discussion follows from south to north on the island and describes the following parts of the city which offer differing lifestyles and strategic opportunities for retailing:

1. Lower Manhattan, including:
   a. Battery Park City.
   b. Tribeca (Triangle below Canal).

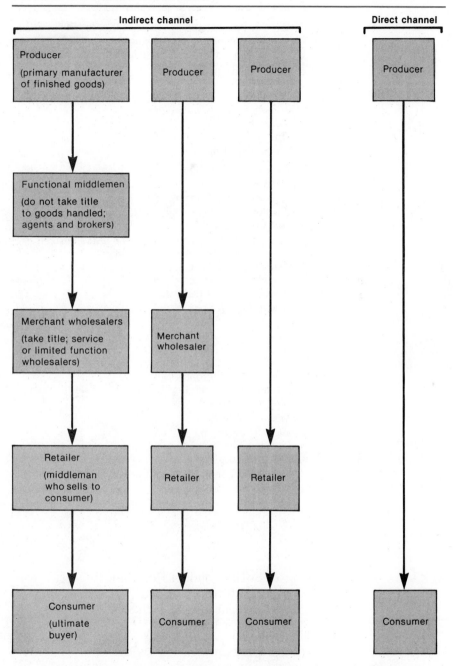

Indirect channel --Involves the use of intermediaries between producer and consumer.
Direct channel --Allows the movement of goods or services directly from producer to consumer.

New York City (Manhattan)
  The central business district ("downtown"; the once dominant retail location in an urban area; an area in transition; still important shopping area, offices, eating establishments, financial institutions)
      Theater District
      Midtown

  Other shopping areas, outside the CBD
      Lower Manhattan
      The neighborhoods
      Upper West Side

Mid-America (outside Manhattan)
  The old ones
      El Paseo, Santa Barbara, Calif.
      Stanford Shopping Center, Calif.
      The Country Club Plaza, Kansas City, Mo.

  The classic revitalized urban centers—the festival markets
      Faneuil Hall Marketplace, Boston, Mass.
      Harborplace, Baltimore, Md.
      Union Station, St. Louis, Mo.
      Riverwalk, New Orleans, La.
      The Jackson Brewery, New Orleans, La.
      The New/Old Post Office, Washington, D.C.

  The new inner-city mixed-use developments
      Crown Center, Kansas City, Mo.
      Triad Center, Salt Lake City, Utah
      Eaton Center, Toronto, Can.
      Renaissance Center, Detroit, Mi.
      Water Tower Place, Chicago, Ill.

  The downtown malls
      Denver, Colo.
      Portland, Ore.

  The mega (super) malls
      Riverchase Galleria, Birmingham, Ala.
      West Edmonton Mall, Can.

            c. SoHo (South of Houston).
            d. Southstreet Seaport.
          2. The neighborhoods including:
            a. Lower East Side.
            b. Greenwich Village.
            c. East Village.
          3. Theater District, including:
            a. Herald Square (Macy's).
            b. Herald Center.

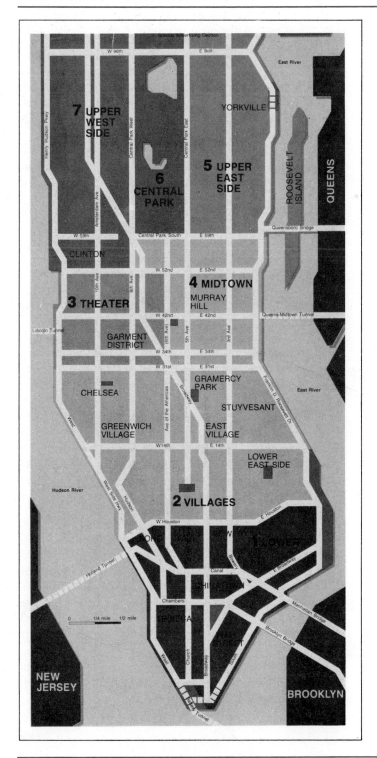

4. Midtown, including:
    a. Fifth and Madison Avenues.
    b. Trump Tower.
5. Upper West Side, including:
    a. Amsterdam/Columbus Avenues.

*Lower
Manhattan*

At the southern tip of Manhattan is the newest, most exciting, and perhaps the next "choicest" neighborhood in New York—Battery Park City.[1] The planned community was conceived for landfill (created partly from digging the foundations of the World Trade Center nearby), and is a $4 billion, 92-acre development which will eventually accommodate 31,000 workers in 6 million square feet of office space, and 30,000 residents in as many as 14,000 apartments. One of the office towers' developers is planning 13 restaurants and up to 100 stores. The early residents may face long trips for bare necessities, but as the development grows, residents and retailers will be offered remarkable opportunities.

Tribeca and SoHo

To fully understand the dynamics within urban retailing today, **gentrification** as a phenomenon must be recognized. The term refers to the return of the "gentry" (defined today in part as the well-bred, upwardly mobile young middle-class professional), a movement spurred by an epic shortage in rental housing wherein tens of thousands of middle-class urban-oriented consumers move into sagging neighborhoods that are being and have been spruced up. In Lower Manhattan, Tribeca and SoHo represent badly deteriorating neighborhoods of the 1970s which have become excellent examples of gentrified areas within the city.[2] The areas noted have become homes for many artists, photographers, and designers, and the retail structure has responded by offering French, Mexican, Italian, and just plain American restaurants, cafes, saloons, or bars and some of the city's most unusual shops. Industrial buildings have been beautifully converted into lofts for living, selling, and showing of the art of the area. The response has been ideally suited to the lifestyles of the neighborhoods, and the renovations have attracted many tourists to enjoy the new offerings.

South Street Seaport

Finally, in this Lower Manhattan area is South Street Seaport, which is a revitalization of the historic Seaport district. Blocks of century-old buildings have been restored as a center of retailing and culture. The redevelopment has been spearheaded by the Rouse Company, the creators of the new town of Columbia, Maryland, and the remarkably successful waterfront projects of Faneuil Hall Marketplace in Boston and Harborplace in Baltimore. Rouse's philosophy is based on a mix of techniques that combines historic buildings with stylistically sympathetic new construction and an intense concentration of shops and restaurants.[3] See Exhibit 1–1 for a description of the South Street Seaport District.

South Street Seaport is a revitalization of the historic Seaport district of lower Manhattan. Blocks of century-old buildings have been restored as a center of commerce and culture. A new office tower is rising near the waterfront. And a new pier pavilion will extend into the East River.

1. Schermerhorn Row was first developed by Peter Schermerhorn in 1811 as a series of counting-houses, where merchants received goods brought on ships. Today, you will find merchandise from around the world, restaurants, and the South Street Seaport Museum Visitors' Center.

2. The Museum Block is a group of new and renovated buildings. Here you can discover the Seaport Gallery, restaurants, specialty shops, the Trans-Lux Seaport Theater, and the exhibits of the South Street Seaport Museum—a rich introduction to the history of the Seaport district. Plus Cannon's Walk, an interior courtyard lined with more fine shops.

3. The Fulton Market Building is a thriving marketplace where you will find three stories of market goods, specialty foods, restaurants, and cafes. At street level, merchants have stocked their stalls with the freshest fish, meats, poultry, eggs, and baked goods. On the second level, you'll discover Beekman Market's 22 pushcarts, with handmade goods and crafts. So you can do your shopping for the week. Or for a very special occasion.

4. Pier 16 in the East River is the docking site of historic sailing vessels. The South Street Seaport Museum maintains the four-masted bark *Peking*, the *Ambrose Lightship*, the three-masted *Wavertree*, and the schooners *Lattie G. Howard* and *Pioneer*.

5. Pier 17 will be the site of the new Pier Pavilion at the foot of Fulton Street. The three-story glass and steel pavilion extends into the East River, with new shops and restaurants for you to visit. Its public promenades open vistas of the Brooklyn Bridge and the historic ships at Pier 16.

6. Seaport Plaza is a 34-story office tower with more Seaport shopping on the first two levels.

| *The Neighborhoods* | As we move further north from the section known as Lower Manhattan, we are in the part of this land called the neighborhoods. The Lower East Side (see Figure 1–2) and the East Village are two distinct, though overlapping communities separated by complex sociological differences of class, history, and style.[4] It is said that nowhere have the tensions and dramas of gentrification been displayed more starkly than in this area where a rent-controlled apartment can lease for $115 a month while in the same building one which is not controlled goes for $700. While gentrification provides exciting opportunities for retailing enterprise, the phenomenon likewise creates severe social displacements of those low-income people forced out of areas when renovation is followed by high rents and middle-class residents. Just as in other sections, the harbingers of gentrification are the art galleries. Next come the retailers to serve the new lifestyles. So it is in the East Village where major retailers are moving in to serve the new gentry. Experts say that the art galleries bring the fancy restaurants and that plays a big role in making another upper-class neighborhood. The future is uncertain at the time of writing, but predictions are that this is another example of the retailing structure adjusting to serve new markets; as the market changes, so will the structure. |

Greenwich Village

The Village is a block north of SoHo and is where the artists used to live before the environment they created attracted the gentry with their high rents. The arts moved to SoHo and its new lifestyles while Greenwich Village today offers some of the city's chicest specialty boutiques and antique stores nestled among beautiful turn-of-the-century architecture on narrow, tree-lined streets.

Theater District and Midtown

If there is a Central Business District (CBD) in Manhattan, it would have to be identified as the two areas known as the Theater District and Midtown. The venerable and currently exciting Macy's Herald Square is in the center of the CBD. Joining Macy's at this location in 1985 (along with the now-vanished Gimbels), is the 300,000-square-foot, vertical shopping mall, *Herald Center*. The center is located in a totally renovated property most recently inhabited by the beleaguered Korvette's and before that, by Saks, 34th Street. The center comprises 10 levels of 140 shops. Each level is designed to mirror the ambiance of one of the city's neighborhoods. (See Figure 1–4 for a description of Herald Center.) When he was closely involved with the project, Stanley Marcus was heard to say that this spot may be the busiest crossroads in America with 39.4 million subway riders annually entering or leaving the two nearby 34th Street stations, and 105,000 commuters arriving daily at Penn Station. Additionally, there are an annual 15.5 million visitors to the Empire State Building, Madison Square Garden, and the theater district. Also, 3 million people a year are expected to visit the new Javits Convention Center—all "in the neighborhood." One hears conflicting reports about the new vertical center; the jury is still out. Whatever the verdict, Herald Center represents retailing at its most exciting, and perhaps risks and rents at their most exorbitant, levels.

Since we have profiled Fifth and Madison Avenues in our capsule at the beginning of this chapter, we shall highlight Trump Tower as Midtown's example of New York's retailing today. How does one describe Trump Tower? Six shopping floors (The Atrium) of chrome and mirrors and peach-colored marble topped by a 56-story block of apartments; an 80-foot waterfall cascading down on one side of the central atrium; a peach-colored piano in the extravagant lobby played daily by a tuxedoed pianist playing up-beat tunes? We simply settled on Figure 1–5, which indicates the retailers who offer romance and luxury in 41 shops from around the world, 365 days a year.

Upper West Side

We could write reams about this "first of the gentrified" neighborhoods of New York. When one says "Columbus Avenue" today, it means rebirth of a major part of the city. The renovation of the Upper West Side did not happen overnight. It all probably started with the development of Lincoln Center at 60th Street which opened in 1969. The center became a catalyst for development along Columbus Avenue going north (on the map, Figure 1–3, Columbus Avenue is just East of Amsterdam). The examples of gentrification in the East Village and SoHo are recent compared to the Upper West Side development during the late 1970s and early 1980s, but the impacts

FIGURE 1–4

THE ATRIUM AT TRUMP TOWER

La Lingerie	Addison on Madison
Lina Lee for Men	Boehm
Brècy of Paris	MCM
Stefan Mann	Elan Home Fashion
Eastern News Service	Saity Jewelry
DDL Foodshow	Bottega del Vino
Cartier	Lina Lee
Norman Crider Antiques	Botticellino
Andrea Carrano	Arras 2 Gallery
Pineider	Mondi
Bruestle	Asprey
Kenneth Jay Lane	Harry Winston Petit Salon
Elan Flowers	Charles Jourdan
Pascal Morabito	Fila Boutique
Fred Leighton	Ludwig Beck
Galeria Cano	Amazoni
Giorgios-Pappas	Napoleon
Optica	Saity
Chocolaterie Corné Toison D'or	Loewe
Buccellati	Martha
Terrace Five	Bonwit Teller

A bouquet of shops at Fifth Avenue and Fifty-Seventh Street, New York

are similar. The same opportunities for serving markets through innovative retailing exist. The Upper West Side, as is true of SoHo and perhaps the East Village, provide the retailing future for New York. The enormous investment opportunities in a Herald Center and Trump Tower will occur from time to time, but the smaller entrepreneur cannot associate with such opportunities. And retailing *is* a business for small investors.

"Mid-America" or What's Going on Outside of New York?

As noted, the focus on New York is the best example of urban retailing we know. But it is important for students to realize that many intriguing developments are going on all over the world. Our focus is North America (we do have several interesting examples from Canada) and the Central City (refer again to Figure 1–2).

The "Old" Ones

For those who believe that inner city developments are of recent vintage, we introduce you to reality. Please do not be confused by our "Mid-America" designation; that does not mean a central location within our continent, but rather a state of mind that suggests actions outside of areas like New York and Los Angeles. It is difficult to select from all the developments in our country those that reflect the "most" or the "best." Consequently, we admit our selections are based on personal knowledge and biased selectivity. Our choices are good ones; they are not necessarily representative of all that is

FIGURE 1–6

STATE ST. ARCADE

EL PASEO: A PUBLIC TRUST

El Paseo has been fortunate that its succession of owners loved its beauty and recognized its importance and that additions and alterations over the years have left its character essentially unchanged.

In 1971 Mrs. Irene Fendon and her children, then owners, presented El Paseo in memory of husband and father, Thaddeus Suski, to the Santa Barbara Trust for Historic Preservation. This generous gift perpetuates El Paseo for the enjoyment of Santa Barbarans and their guests. Any surplus income is used to further restoration of the Royal Presidio of Santa Barbara, a major project of the Trust.

SHOPS • STUDIOS • GALLERIES • RESTAURANTS

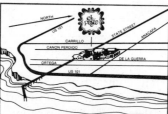

SHOPS · STUDIOS · GALLERIES · RESTAURANTS

SANTA BARBARA TRUST FOR
HISTORIC PRESERVATION
P.O. Box 388, SANTA BARBARA, CALIFORNIA 93102

MODELS: LA BELLE

SANTA BARBARA

out there. We have aimed for geographic dispersion and, frankly, we chose those which were interesting and reflect retailing today in the central city.

El Paseo. Santa Barbara is a jewel in the crown of Southern California, and El Paseo is a diamond that shines in that setting. El Paseo is a vintage, central business district shopping center. Some say it is the oldest center of its type in America, but such claims are difficult to substantiate. "Over 50 years ago it was said that if one lingered long enough at El Paseo he would surely meet everyone of importance in Santa Barbara—and not a few from the world as

Stanford Shopping Center

well. It is still true. They come to browse among the 32 shops, studios, galleries, and restaurants; to meet a friend for lunch; to buy fine jewelry or antiques, handsome leather goods, homemade fudge, a bottle of wine, a collectible toy, or a rare first edition."[5] The creation of El Paseo in the 1920s set the pattern for rebuilding State Street (see Figure 1–6) after a 1925 earthquake, and the charming adobe construction has directly influenced the growth of Santa Barbara's renowned Mediterranean architecture.

Stanford Shopping Center. One of the most successful urban shopping developments is the Stanford Shopping Center, adjacent to Stanford University in Palo Alto, California. The 30-year-old center is not an enclosed, "weatherized" mall but an open air regional center with over 135 national, regional, and local tenants. The layout and architecture take advantage of the magnificent California weather, and the planting and ambiance create a magic shopping experience. Figure 1–7 indicates the center's layout and the tenant mix. The center has recently welcomed Saks-Fifth Avenue and the West Coast's most exciting fashion retailer, Nordstrom's, to join Neiman-Marcus, Macy's, and Emporium as up-scale anchors serving an affluent market.

The Country Club Plaza. Our final visit to a vintage center is truly mid-America—Kansas City, Missouri. From our biased point of view, we believe that The Plaza is the nation's most innovative, different, beautiful shopping development, vintage or otherwise. "To describe The Plaza to someone who

RETAILING TODAY

Retailing today takes place primarily in shopping malls—regional, community, and neighborhood; suburban and inner-city; fully enclosed and open air. The tenants are department store anchors and specialty stores offering almost anything customers desire. Stores may be owned by mammoth national chains, modest regional groups, or small local independents. Merchandise is imported or domestic, private labeled or nationally branded, dear or inexpensive. We present it for you here as a sample of your times!

Above: Carson Pirie Scott & Co. in Chicago. (Courtesy of Carson Pirie Scott & Co. and Robert Keeling.)

Right: Dillard's at Eastland Mall in Tulsa, Oklahoma.
(Courtesy of Dillard's.)

J. Riggings, one of United States Shoe's portfolio of stores. (Courtesy of The U.S. Shoe Corporation.)

Above: Wicker is an important category today. (Courtesy of Aronov Realty.)

Right: Interest in sporting goods coincides with today's emphasis on fitness. (Courtesy of Aronov Realty.)

A cosmetics demonstration. (Courtesy of Aronov Realty.)

Stuffed animals. (Courtesy of Aronov Realty.)

Tabletop items. (Courtesy of Aronov Realty.)

Shoe buyers assemble the finest in style, quality, and color. (Courtesy of Mercantile Department Stores.)

THE MERCHANDISE

What's hot in merchandise changes quickly in retailing. Two current high-traffic, highly profitable categories are cosmetics and women's shoes.

The craze for stuffed animals explains the displays in many stores, and tabletop items are ever popular.

Polo by Ralph Lauren. (Courtesy of Dillard's.)

Above: Esprit, a name for today. (Courtesy of Dillard's.)

Left: Clothing for women who appreciate classic quality. (Courtesy of Mercantile Department Stores.)

STORES WITHIN STORES

Designer names, boutiques, shops within shops—all describe today's efforts to assist customers in satisfying their wants and needs. Two important names—Ralph Lauren's Polo and Esprit—make statements in dramatic ways through layout, design, color, mix, fixturing, and general presentation.

Retailers often develop private brand suits. (Courtesy of Aronov Realty.)

Dayton Hudson's private label, Boundary Waters, has gained excellent acceptance. (Courtesy of Dayton Hudson Department Store Company.)

Boundary Waters products. (Courtesy of Dayton Hudson Department Store Company.)

PRIVATE LABELS

Some organizations base their strategy on offering the most well-known national brands; others carefully develop their own private labels in strategic attempts to differentiate themselves with their own brands. Generally, however, retailers offer customers both options.

WHERE TODAY'S MERCHANDISE IS FOUND— THE MALLS!

Tenants lease space from shopping center developers and become part of an environment within which many things happen. The retailer has control over the "shell" leased, and the center becomes to customers a place of excitement—an experience to savor. Many shoppers visit the mall merely to browse. Others may have a shopping objective, such as purchasing a pair of shoes. Some visitors may come to meet friends at the food court for refreshment and conversation. Clever mall managers offer entertainment and leisure activities, which helps the mall replace the "town center" of yesterday.

A shopper scans shoe selections.

A mall's lunch area can draw many visitors.

Ice skating at center court.

(All photos courtesy of Aronov Realty.)

Entertainment at center court.

Above: *Shopping can be fun.*

Left: *The atrium is an important design element in some modern malls.*

Wendy's. (Courtesy of Wendy's.)

Sister's. (Courtesy of Wendy's.)

Pizza Hut and Friends. (Courtesy of PepsiCo., Inc., 1987. Reproduced with permission.)

Pizza Hut delivers, too. (Courtesy of PepsiCo., Inc., 1987. Reproduced with permission.)

FAST FOOD IS RETAILING, TOO!

An integral part of the retail tenant mix in today's shopping environments is food—fast, convenient, and tasty. Franchising offers many entrepreneurs opportunities to get into business. Here are some well-known names from the fast-food world. Fast-food outlets may be part of shopping malls or freestanding. Fashion abounds in food offerings, as well as in apparel and home furnishings.

hasn't experienced it is an exercise in frustration, because, above all, it's a feeling . . . it's a matter of style, a pocket of panache and lovely impressions that even long-time residents don't take for granted."[6] It all began in 1922 as The Country Club Plaza, an idea of the J. C. Nichols Co. It is difficult to believe that this shopping city in the middle of a major U.S. city was the vision of the developer so many years ago. The Plaza is an exhilaration of foundations, sculpture, fine stores, painstakingly cared-for landscaping, tree-lined boulevards and festive events. Because of strict planning by management, the Plaza has been free of unsightly commercial structures for well over 60 years. The architectural motif is of Spanish origin and is dominated by red-tiled roofs, imported filigree ironwork, ceramic plaques and organte towers, and murals, art, and sculpture from everywhere. Over 150 stores (see Figure 1–8 for the layout) offer everything "imaginable from diamonds to door knockers, paintings to pantry items, high fashion from the biggest names in the world, and unique things you simply won't find anywhere else. Restaurants . . . from jeans-casual to *très elegant*, indoors and out. Entertainment ranging from quiet piano bars and intimate club jazz to huge . . . free concerts featuring the renowned Kansas City Philharmonic Orchestra, big band, country, rock, and stars from every reach of the performing arts."

The Plaza is a fixed-use development[7]—55 acres including world-class hotel accommodations, transient and regular apartment rates, and condo dwelling. The Plaza demonstrates the nature of successful urban retailing as well as any we know.

The Classic Revitalized Urban Centers—The Festival Markets

Rouse is the name that has become closely tied to inner-city revitalization as noted earlier in this chapter in relation to South Street Seaport. The company is the focus of this section because of its contribution to the phenomenon of festival markets—the urban opportunity of the present and recent past.

Faneuil Hall Marketplace. Perhaps the most famous of the Rouse developments is Faneuil Hall Marketplace in Boston which consists of three 19th century market buildings adjacent to Faneuil Hall.[8] (The first phase opened in 1976.) The Marketplace occupies 6.5 acres, and each building is over 500 feet long and 50–65 feet wide. The *Quincy Market* has resumed its historic use in 86,000 square feet of retail space as a food market. It features a variety of restaurants, delicatessens, sidewalk cafes; meat, poultry, fish, cheese, vegetable, and fruit stands; gourmet food stores; and food-related specialty shops. The *Bull Market* is a group of merchants and artisans selling select wares from small carts and stands under the canopies. The *South Market* building is revitalized and leased for mixed retail and office use with 46 retail stores in six floors containing 167,000 square feet, 76,000 for retail use. The *North Market* building is also leased for mixed retail and office use in 114,000 square feet, 59,000 for retail use. More than 155 merchants occupy space in the three buildings, not counting the pushcart operators in the Bull Market.

FIGURE 1–8

Children's Apparel					
Melart's	D-116	Hastings	D-88	Hobbies/Sports/Toys	
		L'Uomo International	D-122	Eddie Bauer	M-355
Ladies' Apparel		Polo–Ralph Lauren	C-11	Games & Things	D-128
Alain Manoukian*	C-611	Ports International	H-148	Ingear	H-157
Ann Taylor	M-353	Shirtique	L-214	Kits Cameras	D-121
Banana Republic	D-120	Tannery West	F-181	Nature Company	C-6
Benetton	N-313	Tearney's	C-36	Thinker Toys	F-196
Casual Corner	N-305	Tennis Man	D-129	Home Furnishings	
Cielo*	C-601	Beauty Hair		The Best of All Worlds	D-132
Contempo Casuals	D-91	Great Expectations	L-232	Brass International	H-150
Daisy	M-361	The Haircut!	M-387	The Company	F-183
Eddie Bauer	M-355	i. Natural Cosmetics	H-151	The Hammock Way	L-200
Foxmoor Casuals	D-113	Books		Harrison's Silversmiths	L-208
The Gap	L-228	B. Dalton Bookseller	D-101	Just Closets	N-309
Grace Muchmores	N-325	Books, Inc.	M-359	Laura Ashley	C-12
Hastings	D-88	Electronics/Music		Malke-Sage Galleries	L-210
Lanz of California	D-74	Radio Shack	D-73	Scandia Down Shops	D-71
Laura Ashley	C-12	Wherehouse Records	F-194	Taylor & Ng	H-149
The Limited	D-82	Fabrics		Jewelry	
Livingston's	C-18	In Material	D-68	Beadazzled	F-189
Page Boy Maternity	M-371	Flowers		Concepts*	C-600
Parklane	L-218	Blossoms Flower Shop	F-199	Gleim the Jeweler	D-119
Peck & Peck	F-186	Food		Granat Bros.	F-185
Polo–Ralph Lauren	C-11	Caravansary	N-321	Jewel Tree	H-152
Ports International	H-148	Cocolat	N-315	Johnson & Co. Jewelers	D-111
St. Tropez	M-369	Cookie Habit	L-238	Shreve & Co.	N-329
Shelly's Tall Girl	D-131	Eat-Rite Nutrition Center	F-198	Tom Wing & Sons	C-10
Shirtique	L-214	La Baguette	F-170	Whitehall Company	M-367
Stuart's Apparel	D-126	La Foret	H-145	Leather Goods	
Talbot's*	C-607	Le Fromage	L-248	Edward's Luggage & Gifts	C-7
Tannery West	F-181	See's Candies	D-123	Major Stores	
Tearney's	C-36	Stanford Delicatessen	D-83	Emporium-Capwell	
Tennis Lady	D-129	Sweet Dreams	A-3	I. Magnin	
Victoria's Secret	C-14	Yogurt Village	L-220	Macy's	
				Neiman-Marcus	
Men's Apparel		Gifts/Specialty		Nordstrom	
Abrams Formal Attire	M-394	The Best of All World's	D-132	Saks Fifth Avenue	
Aca Joe	F-187	The Company	F-183	Restaurants	
Alain Manoukian*	C-611	Crabtree & Evelyn	A-4B	Food Service	
Banana Republic	D-120	Great Gift Ideas	L-240	Bravo Fono	D-99
Barcelino	M-351	Harrison's Silversmiths	L-208	Caravansary	N-321
Benetton	N-313	Just Cards	F-168	Gaylord India	N-317
Eddie Bauer	M-355	Paper World	D-136	The Great Hot Dog	L-204
The Gap	L-228	Primavera	C-16	Experience	
Grodins	F-180	The Tinder Box	F-188	Happi House	L-244

FIGURE 1–8 (concluded)

L'Escale	C-5	1st Nationwide Savings	M-395	Byron's Shoes	C-9
Mama's	M-379	Pack & Send	L-236	C. H. Baker	H-155
McDonald's	F-190	Pan American Airlines	M-385	Florsheim Shoes	D-124
Pedro's	A-2	Perspectacles—	D-102	Florsheim Thayer	D-130
The Perfect Recipe	D-76	Optometrist		McNeil	
Sandy's Kitchen	H-153	Phototime—1 Hour Photo	D-138	Johnston & Murphy	C-15
		The Tailor Maid	C-616	Joyce-Selby Shoes	N-301
Services		United Airlines	M-385	Kramar's Shoes	D-110
American Express	M-393	World Savings & Loan	N-345	**Variety Stores**	
Bank of America	M-383	**Shoes**		Norney's	D-80
The Cobbler Shoppe	M-391	The Athlete's Foot	L-206	Woolworth's	F-172
Crocker National Bank	M-399				

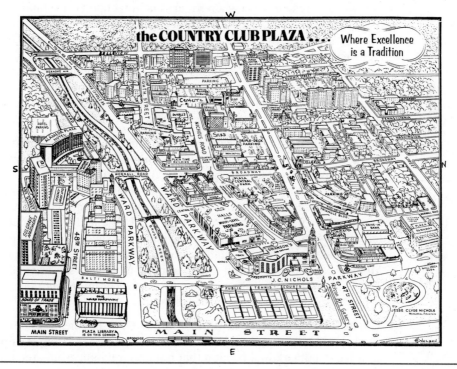

Harborplace. Baltimore's reputation over time was that of a dull, blue-collar town with a fancy hospital (Johns Hopkins) and little else. It has been reported that the Rouse Company's revitalized Inner Harbor now draws more visitors annually than Walt Disney World. For 30 years after World War II, the Inner Harbor was a stagnant, commercially ignored backwater of Chesapeake Bay. It has been transformed into the tastefully planned Harborplace, the glittery retail core actually modeled after Faneuil Hall Marketplace. Some assume that Baltimore was reborn in July 1980 when Harborplace opened, but the city actually began to turn itself around in the

1950s. The revitalized downtown is the product of a continuing effort by a group of executives, planners, and politicians, and the Rouse development is a part of an urban renewal effort that has been under way for over 30 years.

Union Station. The largest adaptive reuse project in the United States is Rouse's Union Station in St. Louis. In September 1985 the ornate Union Station with its magnificent steel train shed, abandoned by Amtrak in 1978, was opened after having been restored and turned into a complex of restaurants, promenades, 80 shops, and a 550-room hotel. Under the far end of the shed, a boat pond and a beer garden are housed. The project cost $135 million.[9]

Riverwalk. The latest Rouse festival opening was in New Orleans on the Labor Day weekend of 1986 when Riverwalk burst upon the retailing scene with its 180,000 square foot contemporary specialty retail-dining-entertainment center with vast glass walls overlooking the Mississippi River. The development is conveniently located at the foot of major downtown New Orleans thoroughfares, Canal and Poydras streets. "With the mighty Mississippi as a backdrop, Riverwalk's visitors can enjoy indoor and outdoor cafes, food stands, unique retail kiosks, entertainment, local, regional, and international foods, and distinctly merchandised stores."[10]

The Jackson Brewery. Again New Orleans, but not Rouse! In 1984, the castle-like landmark Jax Brewery at famous Jackson Square and the Mississippi River was restored and opened to the shopping public as the Jackson Brewery. The festival center is a six-level dining-entertainment-shopping complex housed in a building that dates from 1891, and the renovated Brewhouse retails its exterior Romanesque Revival quality. The interior is centered by a beautiful 100-foot glass atrium. The success of Jackson Brewery is emphasized by the fact that in August 1986 a sparkling new addition, the Millhouse, was opened and is linked by walkway to the original structure. The Brewery is a retail showplace with over 60 different shopping and dining experiences in 65,000 square feet of space.

The New/Old Post Office in Washington, D.C. Like the other developments cited in this section, the Old Post Office is yet another example of preserving an urban landmark in a fashion that not only revitalizes an area but pays its own way. Completed in 1899, the Old Post Office is the capital's oldest federal building, in height second only to the Washington Monument. The building stands today because of intense campaigning by a local preservationist group, D.C. Preservation League. Nancy Hanks, chairwoman of the National Endowment for the Arts, led the fight to preserve the Old Post Office building. After her death in 1983, Congress designated the Old Post Office as the "Nancy Hanks Center." The Pavilion offers 35 specialty shops, seven restaurants, and free entertainment daily on The Pavilion Stage. "The real estate is breathtaking. Glowing Victorian brass fittings, red oak woodwork, and frosted glass set off the Pavilion, a graceful three-level gallery in a vast sunlit atrium that rises 215 feet and has a floor two thirds the length of a football field."[11]

The New Inner-City Mixed-Use Developments

Crown Center. It may be surprising to the person outside the Midwest that perhaps the most successful inner-city development is in Kansas City, the home of the previously discussed Plaza. Crown Center is a $500 million, 85-acre "city-within-a-city" that is being developed with private capital by Hallmark Cards, Inc. just 10 blocks from the heart of downtown Kansas City. The project is expected to be completed by 1990 and now includes a 660,000-square-foot office complex; a 10-acre landscaped central square for community events; the 730-room Westin Crown Center Hotel; the 733-room Hyatt Regency Kansas City; a 400,000-square-foot shopping center including a six-theater cinema; approximately 20 restaurants and lounges; a full-service bank; a savings and loan facility; a children's art center adjacent to the Hallmark Visitors Center; a 250-unit residential community of high-rise condominiums and mid-rise apartment and recreational areas; a secondary 600,000-square-foot office complex; and structured parking for nearly 5,000 cars. On completion, Crown Center is expected to serve a daytime population of 75,000 and a resident population of 8,000.[12]

Triad Center. Salt Lake City has Triad Center, which consists of restaurant, shopping, office, residential, retail, hotel, entertainment, and recreational space. At completion Triad Center will also include two 35-story business towers and two world-class hotels with a total of 1,000 rooms. Salt Lake City also has Z.C.M.I. Center, which is an outgrowth of Zions Cooperative Mercantile Institution, the first department store in the Far West. Across the street from Z.C.M.I. on the central business district's main shopping street is Crossroads Plaza, which consists of four floors of shops, department stores, boutiques, restaurants, movie theaters, a massive sports complex, commercial offices, and eight levels of parking.

Eaton Centre. Toronto has the world famous Eaton Centre, a 15-acre site that highlights the 10-level flagship store for the T. Eaton Company, Limited, Canada's largest retailer. The complex contains over 300 shops totaling 550,000 square feet and two six-sided office towers. A shopping street, 860 feet long, is topped by a glass arch 90 feet above the street level, suggestive of the famous Galleria in Milan, Italy.

Renaissance Center. Perhaps the most infamous of the inner city, mixed-use developments is Detroit's Renaissance Center (Ren Cen). The development is described as "a bundle of skyscraping glass tubes consisting of a 73-story, 1,424-room hotel, convention halls, four office towers, four movie theaters and a big circular mall . . . of shops, boutiques, restaurants, glitter, and Muzak-drenched confusion."[13] The center was built to lure shoppers back to a dying downtown, but it has been a financial disaster since its opening in 1977 primarily due to the fact that the center is located a mile and a half from the CBD. The occupancy rate of shopping space as well as office space has been dismal. We cite Ren Cen to illustrate that not all such investments are successful.

Water Tower Place. In stark contrast to Ren Cen is Water Tower Place on the "Magnificent Mile" in Chicago. The development rises 74 stories and was opened in 1976. In addition to the Atrium Shopping Mall which is anchored by Lord & Taylor and Marshall Field's and includes 125 stores, shops, and boutiques, as well as 11 restaurants, there is a bank; 200,000 square feet of corporate and professional office space; the 22–story, 450–room Ritz-Carlton Hotel; and 40 floors of luxury condominium residences and below-ground parking. Water Tower Place takes its name from the nearby Old Chicago Water Tower. The shopping mall takes in some $480,000 a day, and one out of every two shoppers is from outside Chicago.

The Downtown Malls[14]

It has been reported that downtown malls were a fad in the 1960s and the 1970s. It is estimated that more than 150 exist in the United States today. Many cities developed downtown malls. Money was available, and cities typically introduced trees, foliage, concrete sculpture, playgrounds, and fountains as a means of attracting people downtown. Many of these efforts failed to meet expectations. They have not in themselves been able to guarantee a vital retail area. The following examples are reported as successes, however.

Denver. The 16th Street Mall in Denver created a tremendous amount of controversy when it was built. Critics predicted that it would be the death of Denver. Proponents thought it was what the downtown needed to regain a foothold in the retail market. In 1986, the general consensus was that it has been a success. There are some problems, of course. Buses leak oil, and lunch-hour crowds make it hard for shuttle buses to get through. But the safety record is good, and outdoor cafes and vendors have managed to coexist on the renovated pedestrian part of the mall. The trip from end to end takes less than three minutes; in rush hours, about five minutes. The mall shuttle system was finished in 1984. The mall, which is 80 feet wide and has two 10-foot bus lanes, replaced a main downtown street. There are transfer stations at each end of the 4,000-foot mall where passengers get off regular city buses and get free transfers for the mall shuttles.

Portland, Oregon. The city actually has two malls, an 11-block stretch of two parallel streets. Each street used to carry five lanes of traffic. Now there are two bus lanes and a car lane on each street with expanded sidewalks, plantings, kiosks, and outdoor cafes where the other two lanes used to be. Every fourth block sees the car lane disappear so that cars are only used for pickups and deliveries.

Throughout the nation, cities are still redesigning downtown malls— Memphis, Tampa, Des Moines, Minneapolis, San Antonio, Cedar Rapids, Iowa. Champaign is tearing one up; some are adding more sophisticated transit systems; others are just developing in the 1980s.

The Mega (or Super) Malls[15]

The Riverchase Galleria. This venture, reportedly the largest mixed-use project in the United States, is in Birmingham, Alabama, and features a 1.5 million-square-foot mall plus a 17-story, 250,000-square-foot office building and a 330-room hotel. The shopping center's most visible feature is a 90,000-square-foot skylight which the trade says is the largest in the world. The $6 million, 10-story-high skylight spans almost half the length of the development. The anchor tenants are Rich's (225,000 square feet), J. C. Penney (140,000), Macy's (240,000), and the two locally based department stores, Pizitz and Parisian, with 135,000 and 123,000 square feet, respectively. The mall contains 188 specialty shops and a 14-restaurant food court.

The West Edmonton Mall. Located in Canada, this is the world's largest indoor shopping center. Four expatriate Iranians have spent more than $1 billion on the mall, which covers the equivalent of 108 football fields, has 817 shops and 11 department stores, streets fashioned after the Champs-Elysées and Bourbon Street, a fleet of submarines cruising a man-made lake, carnival rides, Siberian tigers, an aquarium filled with sharks and dolphins, and its own hockey arena. It is estimated that some 8 million visitors walk through the mall's 57 entrances annually. The Ghermezians (developers) say that they do not make money on the entertainment, but on the retail sales. The entertainment, however, brings in the people. The Canadian success is sprouting a U.S. branch when, in the spring of 1987, development of another super mall began in Bloomington, Minnesota. The project is planned to be twice the size of the West Edmonton Mall.[16]

At this point we conclude our discussion of retail structural dynamics focusing on urban America. The prior discussion was locationally based. The next section, continuing to accomplish the chapter's objectives, completes the alternative methods of classification of the structure.

ALTERNATIVE WAYS TO CLASSIFY THE RETAIL STRUCTURE

The retailing structure can be classified in many ways, including type of merchandise offered, ownership, and geographic location, among others, as shown in Figure 1–9. Classifying the retail structure aids understanding of retail evolution, growth, and change. These classifications are also used by government officials analyzing the impact of retailing on the economy, and managers developing strategies for increasing profits. Analysis of the size, growth record, and future outlook of the various components of the structure can enable management to evaluate the competitive position of the firm's outlets. Analysis and classification of the structure are the first steps in making predictions about the changes in the institutional makeup of retailing.

FIGURE 1–9   ALTERNATIVE WAYS FOR CLASSIFYING RETAIL STRUCTURE

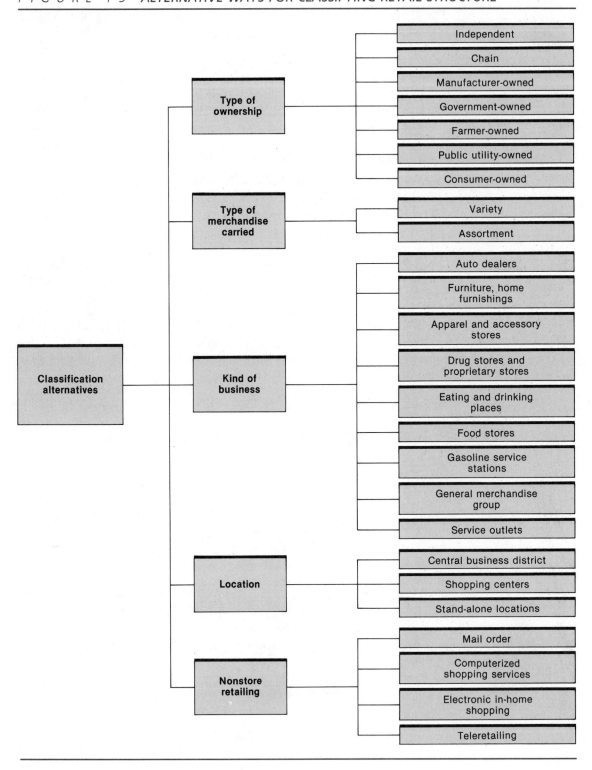

RETAIL TRADE FAILURES, 1984 AND 1985

	1984 Number	1985 p Number	Failure Rate per 10,000 Listed Concerns	
			1984	1985 p
Retail trade				
Building materials and garden supplies	772	787	97	99
General merchandise stores	214	206	75	70
Food stores	1,281	1,300	96	96
Automotive dealers and service stations	1,321	1,383	77	80
Apparel and accessory stores	2,027	1,807	180	161
Furniture and home furnishing stores	1,531	1,410	122	112
Eating and drinking places	3,579	3,335	158	145
Miscellaneous retail trade				
Drug and proprietary stores	147	139	41	38
Liquor stores	214	204	74	70
Used merchandise stores	98	143	43	61
Sporting goods	461	379	127	102
Bookstores	80	64	94	72
Stationery stores	84	87	102	104
Jewelry stores	275	211	116	87
Hobby, toy and game shops	90	79	117	100
Camera and photographic supply stores	54	61	147	171
Gift, novelty, and souvenir shops	283	311	78	82
Luggage and leather goods stores	14	17	85	102
Sewing, needlework and piece goods	90	75	72	60
Nonstore retailers	186	181	104	97
Fuel and ice dealers	39	42	35	38
Other retail stores	947	1,197	105	127
Total miscellaneous retail trade	3,062	3,190	89	90
Total retail trade	13,787	13,418	113	108

p = Preliminary.
SOURCE: Tiziana Mohorovic, ed., *The Business Failure Record* (New York: Dun & Bradstreet, 1985), p. 8.

Type of Ownership

The most common classification is based on ownership. The *independent* operator with a single store dominates retailing in terms of numbers of outlets and accounts for approximately 83 percent of all retail establishments. Sales by single-unit establishments constitute 53 percent of total retail sales. These independents tend to be small businesses operated by family members. Failure rates among small, independent retail stores are high, and such failures can be attributed to inexperience, incompetence, or other management shortcomings (see Table 1–1).

A **chain** (or multiunit organization) is characterized by (1) the sale of similar merchandise in more than one outlet, (2) a similar architectural format, (3) centralized buying, and (4) common ownership.

Whether an independent, single store or a chain, retail stores can also be classified as follows:

Manufacturer owned—Some manufacturers practice *forward integration*; that is, they own their retail outlets. Examples are Firestone retail outlets and manufacturer-owned gasoline outlets such as Texaco.

Government owned—The most typical example of government-owned outlets is state-owned stores that sell liquor for consumption off the premises. Military commissaries or post exchanges are also examples.

Farmer owned—A limited number of retail outlets are operated by farmers, often as seasonal roadside establishments. Open-air markets are experiencing a resurgence across the nation. They are, in effect, direct marketing outlets (see Figure 1–1).

Public utility owned—For many years, public utilities have sold stoves, refrigerators, and other types of appliances to boost the consumption of natural gas or electricity. In times of energy shortages, retail sales of appliances decline.

Consumer owned—**Consumer cooperatives** are retail stores owned by consumers and operated by a hired manager. Co-ops have not been important in the U.S. structure because the advantages of membership have been important only in isolated instances where the population has some strong reason—often social—for wanting to associate for mutual benefit.

Type of Merchandise Carried

Retail establishments may also be classified by the variety and assortment of their merchandise. Their size, location, and merchandising methods are often dictated by the lines of merchandise they offer.

Variety refers to the number of lines of merchandise carried, hence the term *variety store*. **Assortment** refers to the choices offered within a line. Another way to look at these terms is that *variety* can be thought of as the width of a store's selection of merchandise whereas *assortment* is the depth of a store's selection, including sizes, colors, and types of materials. Figure 1–10 illustrates the concept of width and depth.

Nonstore Retailing

Nonstore retailing stated in the positive is *direct retailing*. This method of distribution includes (1) mail order, (2) telephone shopping, (3) door-to-door (direct selling), and (4) vending machines. The direct method of retailing accounts for some 10 percent of retail sales with store outlets responsible for about 90 percent.

Mail Order

Historically, mail-order retailing thrived in nonurban areas where consumers had few shopping alternatives. Mail-order operations today, however, also serve the specialty needs of urban areas. They include general merchandise mail-order specialists (such as Sears) and novelty retailers (such as Sunset House). More than 9,000 businesses use mail order to market their products. Mail-order sales volume exceeds $32 billion. Sears is by far the largest firm, followed by J. C. Penney. Mail-order sales with company credit cards exceed $320 million annually. Mail-order goods bought with travel and entertainment credit cards cost more than $110 million annually.

Department store

Width →

Dresses/Shortalls	Sleepwear	Blankets	Crib Accessories	Sheets	Diapers
Feltman Brothers Imperial Oshkosh Healthtex	Carters Healthtex	Carters	Cothran Collection	Carters Dundee	Birdseye

Depth ↓

Specialty store

Width →

Dresses/Shortalls	Sleepwear	Blankets
Feltman Brothers Imperial Florence Eiseman Dior Monday's Child Snips and Snails	Fusen Usigi Asorba Wibbies Sara's Prints	Imperial Feltman Brothers Boston Weavers

Depth ↓

Discount store

Width →

Dresses/Shortalls	Sleepwear	Blankets	Sheets	Diapers
Buster Brown Healthtex	Carters Healthtex	Carters	Dundee	Pampers

Depth ↓

Telephone Shopping

Telephone shopping has also become increasingly popular. General merchandise enterprises such as Sears maintain catalog desks at their local retail outlets. Telephone shopping has become increasingly important since more women work outside the home. Computerized shopping sources and electronic in-home shopping experiments show promise.

Door-to-Door (Direct Selling)

The variations of the house-to-house canvassing (such as Avon) include party-plan selling (such as Tupperware and Mary Kay) and home calls made after advance prospecting over the telephone. Such successful big ticket

FIGURE 1–11 THE MARGIN-TURNOVER CLASSIFICATION

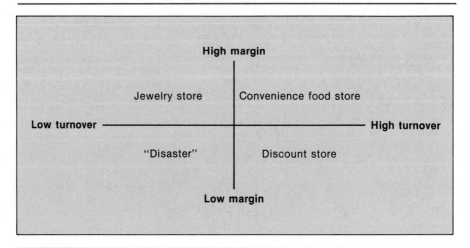

items as vacuum cleaners and encyclopedias (e.g., Electrolux and Britannica) have been successfully demonstrated and sold in homes for many years. The direct-selling industry is in transition because of changing environmental conditions, such as the large number of women now in the work force. Direct sellers are investigating other avenues of reaching the consumer, including telemarketing and catalogs.

Vending Machines

Sales by vending machines total more than $14 billion for products ranging from coffee to cigarettes. Machines are typically located in workplaces and public buildings.

The Margin-Turnover Classification

The margin-turnover framework for the retail structure may be applied to all types of outlets.[17] The framework is useful in strategy formulation rather than in data reporting and analysis. Data simply do not exist for the structure on the basis of margin and turnover; it is a conceptual framework that can be most helpful.

Margin is defined as the difference between the cost and the selling price or as the percentage markup at which the inventory in a store is sold, and **turnover** is the number of times the average inventory is sold in a given year.

Figure 1–11 diagrams four quadrants, defined by margin and turnover, into which any retail outlet can be placed. The outlets can then be described in terms of store-level retail strategy, as shown in Figure 1–12. The key elements are types of merchandise sold, varieties and assortments, services, price level, type of personal selling, type of promotion, complexity of organizational structure, and location requirements.

PROTOTYPES OF THE MARGIN-TURNOVER APPROACH TO THE CLASSIFICATION OF RETAIL INSTITUTIONS

Low margin–high turnover
  Merchandise presold or self-sold
  Few services or "optional charge" services
  Isolated locations
  Simple organizational characteristics
  Variety large, assortments small
  Prices below the market
  Promotional emphasis on price

High margin–low turnover
  Merchandise sold in store
  Many services
  Cluster locations
  Complex organization
  Variety smaller, assortments larger
  Prices above the market
  Promotion institutional and merchandise-oriented

F I G U R E   1–13   *EMPLOYMENT BY INDUSTRY, 1984*

Employment Field	Number Employed (000)
Construction	6,665
Finance, insurance, real estate	6,750
Manufacturing	20,995
Mining	957
Retailing	17,767
Transportation and public utilities	7,358
Wholesaling	4,212
Public administration	4,768
Total	105,005

SOURCE: *Statistical Abstract of the United States* (Washington, D.C.: U. S. Government Printing Office, 1986), p. 404.

MEASURES OF THE IMPORTANCE OF RETAILING

Employment

Retailing is one of the nation's largest employers. Approximately 17 million persons work in the retailing sector, compared to approximately 20 million in manufacturing (see Figure 1–13). Retailing employment is forecast to reach 22 million by 1990.[18] The number of women in retailing will undoubtedly increase absolutely, particularly at the executive levels. With the continuing increases in hours opened, part-time employment will continue to be a substantial percentage of total employment.

FIGURE 1–14 TOTAL RETAIL TRADE (in millions of dollars)

	1976	1977	1978	1979
Retail trade, total	657,375	725,212	806,773	899,116
Durable goods stores, total	217,805	248,638	280,417	306,353
Nondurable goods stores, total	439,570	476,574	526,356	592,763
General merchandise group	81,756	93,948	103,165	109,345
General merchandise stores	74,557	86,853	95,878	101,455
Department stores	65,651	76,909	84,399	89,239
Variety stores	7,199	7,095	7,287	7,890
Apparel group	33,717	35,565	41,050	44,603
Men's and boy's wear stores	6,535	6,943	7,421	7,654
Women's apparel, accessory				
stores	13,382	13,458	16,075	17,498
Family and other apparel stores	7,224	8,055	8,648	9,495
Shoe stores	5,033	5,650	6,649	7,760
Furniture and appliance group	30,021	33,168	36,692	42,253
GAF, total†	N.A.	N.A.	205,763	223,007
Automotive group	129,754	149,952	167,896	178,581
Gasoline service stations	51,949	56,468	59,709	73,301
Lumber, building materials, hardware	27,933	33,214	38,512	44,121
Eating and drinking places	57,211	63,276	71,724	81,990
Food group	147,972	157,941	174,842	197,322
Drug and proprietary stores	21,620	23,196	25,404	28,230
Liquor stores	12,357	12,967	13,563	15,120

*Computed by Standard & Poor's.
†GAF represents stores which specialize in department store types of merchandise.
R = Revised. N.A. = Not available.
SOURCE: Department of Commerce.

Sales

Retail sales levels across the United States are proportionate to the population. Historically, retail sales have increased approximately three times as fast as income. Some markets clearly grow more rapidly than others, however. The fastest growing markets include Southern California; Tampa–St. Petersburg, Florida; Ft. Lauderdale–Hollywood, Florida; and such northeastern locations as Norfolk–Virginia Beach–Portsmouth, Virginia.

The top 10 markets in the United States account for more than 22 percent of total retail sales. The top 10 markets include Los Angeles, Long Beach, and San Francisco–Oakland, California; New York City; Chicago; Philadelphia; Detroit; the Boston metropolitan area; the Washington, D.C. area; Dallas–Fort Worth and Houston, Texas.

Figure 1–14 shows the level of retail sales over the past 10 years. Wide differences in levels of growth are evident. Growth rates ranged from a low of 2.2 percent for variety stores to 11.1 percent for family and other apparel stores.

1980	1981	1982	1983	1984	1985	Percent change 1984–85	10-Year Growth Rate*
959,561	1,041,327	1,072,065	1,174,298	1,293,062	1,373,941	+ 6.3	+ 8.6
298,973	325,068	336,712	396,493	465,798	514,207	+ 10.4	+ 9.5
660,588	716,259	735,353	777,805	827,264	859,734	+ 3.9	+ 8.1
113,905	125,378	128,745	139,386	152,913	159,456	+ 4.3	+ 7.5
105,994	117,050	120,408	130,762	143,818	150,557	+ 4.7	+ 8.0
93,190	103,519	107,163	116,562	129,054	134,744	+ 4.4	+ 8.2
7,911	8,328	8,337	8,624	9,095	8,899	− 2.2	+ 2.2
48,102	53,044	55,281	60,384	65,103	69,673	+ 7.0	+ 8.5
7,557	7,799	7,694	7,962	8,327	8,336	+ 0.1	+ 2.6
18,483	20,443	21,981	24,484	27,094	28,121	+ 7.5	+ 9.2
10,956	12,379	13,802	15,435	16,597	18,332	+ 10.5	+ 11.1
8,430	9,464	9,142	9,794	10,335	10,857	+ 5.1	+ 9.1
44,058	44,147	46,530	54,689	61,843	68,112	+ 10.1	+ 9.1
236,331	258,180	265,420	291,734	322,258	342,521	+ 6.3	—
164,365	182,443	193,215	232,750	278,534	312,793	+ 12.3	+ 9.6
93,811	102,763	97,148	98,862	99,464	100,767	+ 1.3	+ 8.9
43,279	44,147	43,803	51,483	60,207	64,933	+ 7.8	+ 9.4
89,924	97,969	104,427	114,684	124,541	131,035	+ 5.2	+ 10.1
219.493	235,423	245,346	254,878	270,430	282,198	+ 4.4	+ 7.8
30,707	33,730	36,152	40,050	43,174	46,014	+ 6.6	+ 9.0
16,799	17,615	18,057	19,014	18,157	17,802	− 2.0	+ 5.1

Number of Outlets

Approximately 1.9 million retail outlets exist in the United States, a number that has varied little since 1929. However, the average sales per retail establishment increased significantly during this period, partly because of inflation and partly because of increasing economies of scale.

RETAIL STRUCTURAL CHANGE

Figure 1–15 illustrates selected changes in the retail institutional structure which have occurred during the past 100 years. We indicate the period of fastest growth for each type of institution, the stage in the life cycle of each store type, our own reasonable explanation for the development of each type, and an example of each. The table provides a framework for the discussion that follows.

No single theory can explain the evolution of all types of retail outlets.

FIGURE 1–15 SELECTED CHANGES IN RETAIL INSTITUTIONAL STRUCTURE

Institutional Type	Period of Fastest Growth	Period from Inception to Maturity (years)	Stage of Life Cycle	Examples of Explanatory Hypotheses	Representative Firms*
General store	1800–40	100	Declining/obsolete	Retail accordion	A local institution
Single-line store	1820–40	100	Mature	Adaptive behavior	Hickory Farms
Department store	1860–1940	80	Mature	Dialectic process	Marshall Field's
Variety store	1870–1930	50	Declining/obsolete	Adaptive behavior	Morgan-Lindsay
Mail-order house	1951–50	50	Mature	Adaptive behavior	Spiegel
Corporate chain	1920–30	50	Mature	Adaptive behavior	Sears
Discount store	1955–75	20	Mature	Adaptive behavior, dialectic process	K mart
Conventional supermarket	1935–65	35	Mature/declining	Dialectic process	Winn Dixie
Shopping center	1950–65	40	Mature	Adaptive behavior	Paramus
Cooperative	1930–50	40	Mature	Adaptive behavior	Ace Hardware
Gasoline station	1930–50	45	Mature	Dialectic process	Texaco
Convenience store	1965–75	20	Mature	Retail accordion	7-Eleven
Fast-food outlet	1960–75	15	Late growth	Dialectic process	McDonald's
Home improvement center	1965–80	15	Late growth	Retail accordion	Lowes
Super specialists	1975–85	10	Growth	Retail accordion	The Limited
Warehouse retailing	1970–80	10	Maturity	Wheel of retailing	Levitz
Computer store	1980–	?	Growth	Retail accordion	Computerland
Electronics superstores	1982–	?	Growth	Retail accordion	Circuit City Stores
Off-price retailer	1980–	?	Growth	Dialectic process	Burlington Coat Factory

* These firms are representative of Institutional types and are not necessarily in the stage of life cycle specified for the Institutional group as a whole.

At best, the existing theories discussed are descriptive and perhaps somewhat explanatory. Certainly they are not *predictive* of institutional change. Also they are not applicable without modification outside the retailing structure of the United States.

THEORIES OF RETAIL INSTITUTIONAL CHANGE

The Wheel of Retailing

The *wheel of retailing* hypothesis, developed by Harvard University professor Malcolm McNair, is the best-known explanation for changes in the structure (see Figure 1–16). McNair's theory states that new types of retailers enter a market as low-margin, low-priced, low-status merchants. This is the *entry phase*. Gradually, they add to their operating costs by providing new services and improving their facilities in the *trading-up phase*. Over time, they become high-cost merchants and are vulnerable to new types of competition which enter the marketplace as low-cost, no-frills competitors.

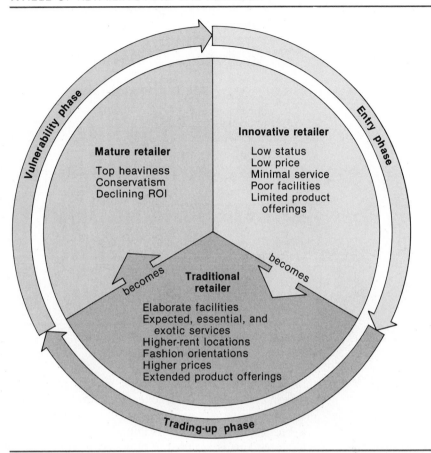

SOURCE: Dale Lewison and Wayne Delozier, *Retailing* (Columbus, Ohio: Charles E. Merrill Publishing, 1982), p. 37.

The theory has been criticized because not all institutions begin as low-margin outlets with few services. Department stores, for example, did not follow this model; however, other types of institutions have followed it.

The Retail Accordion

An alternative explanation for changes in the structure is the concept of the **retail accordion**. Proponents of the theory argue that changes in the merchandising mix, not prices and margins, are a better explanation for changes in retail institutional structure than the wheel of retailing. The accordion theory is based on the premise that retail institutions evolve over time from broad-based outlets with wide assortments to outlets offering specialized, narrow lines. Over time the outlets again begin to offer a wide assortment,

Chapter 1 Retailing Today: The Structure as It is and as It Might Be   **31**

FIGURE 1–17   *THE DIALECTIC PROCESS*

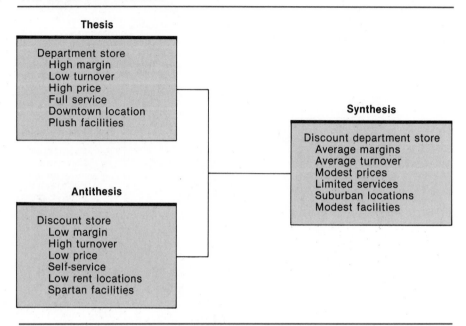

SOURCE: Dale Lewison and Wayne Delozier, *Retailing* (Columbus, Ohio: Charles E. Merrill Publishing, 1982), p. 37.

thus establishing a general-specific-general pattern. This evolution suggests the term *accordion*, which reflects a contraction and expansion of merchandise lines.

For example, modern retailing in the United States began with the general store. This is a one-stop outlet with wide assortments of merchandise. Then came the urbanized department stores, more specialized than the general store. As urbanization continued, **single-line** and **specialty** stores (e.g., bookstores, drugstores) emerged. More recently, the single-line and specialty stores added complementary lines. For example, grocery stores over time added faster-moving merchandise to the traditional lines. Some stores added small appliances, convenience-food items, and paper products. In some instances full lines were added. Many supermarkets now offer nonfood items such as drugs and cosmetics, and discount stores offer a variety of soft goods.

The Dialectic Process

The **dialectic process** as an explanation for changes is based on the adage, "If you can't beat them, join them." For example, as shown in Figure 1–17, the **department store** was originally developed as an institution offering both hard goods and soft goods, a wide array of services, and attractive surroundings (*the thesis*). The challenging institution (*the antithesis*) was the discount store. The discount store offered merchandise similar to that of the department store, but in unattractive, low-cost surroundings and without services such as credit and delivery. The promotional or discount department store (the *synthesis*) then emerged as a blend of the strengths of both the department store and the discount store. K mart is an example of a promotional department store.

Adaptive Behavior/ Natural Selection

The *adaptive behavior* explanation states that institutions evolve when environmental conditions are conducive. **Natural selection** suggests that the retailing institutions that can most effectively adapt to economic, competitive, social, technological, and legal/political environmental changes are the ones most likely to prosper or survive.

The **shopping centers** of the late 1950s and the 1960s were seen as the ultimate answer to serving the needs of consumers living in suburbia, an example of adaptive behavior of retailing institutions. The **variety store** is often cited as an institution that failed to adapt to changing environmental conditions and today is virtually absent from the retailing scene.

Summary

This section of the chapter has presented theories developed to explain changes in retail structure. Each theory is different, but together they provide a more comprehensive understanding of the evolution of retail structure. This is true of both past changes and those which are likely to occur in the future.

Retailing is an exciting, dynamic world where challenges and opportunities are abundant. The focus of this chapter was innovations in retailing. Chapter 2 discusses strategic management with an eye on future innovation.

CHAPTER HIGHLIGHTS

—— New York (Manhattan) is a microcosm of urban retailing, and an analysis of the major retailing clusters within the city serves as a focus for understanding retailing today in America.

—— To understand the dynamics within urban retailing today, gentrification must be recognized and understood. The phenomenon is the return of upwardly mobile, young, middle-class professionals to sagging neighborhoods which are being and have been revitalized.

—— The dynamics of retailing can best be understood by analyzing its structure. Structural analysis also helps illustrate the strategies by which retailers compete in the marketplace.

—— The retailing structure can be classified in many ways, including location, margin and turnover, ownership, and type of merchandise carried. The margin-turnover classification is particularly useful in strategy formulation.

— Retailing is the third largest employer in the nation with more than 17 million employees. Retail sales levels are distributed across the United States in proportion to the population. Approximately 1.9 million retail outlets exist in the United States. The number of outlets has not increased significantly since 1929. During this time, however, the average sales per retail establishment have grown significantly.

— The retail institutional structure is dynamic. Institutional types appear to follow a pattern of evolution, but no single theory explains the evolution of all types of retail outlets. The existing theories are, at best, descriptive and perhaps somewhat explanatory.

— The wheel of retailing is based on the premise that (1) institutional innovations penetrate the retail system on the basis of price appeal; (2) the new institution's lower prices are achieved through a reduction in operating costs made possible by eliminating store services and frills; (3) after establishing itself in the system, the new institution engages in a process of trading up; and (4) trading up results in new institutional innovations in retailing.

— An alternative explanation for retail structural change is that retail institutions evolve from broad-based outlets with wide assortment patterns to specialized narrow lines and then return to the wide-assortment pattern. This evolution suggests the term *accordion*.

— The dialectic model of structural change is based on the premise that retailers mutually adapt in the face of competition from "opposites." Thus, when challenged by a competitor with a differential advantage, an established institution will adopt strategies and tactics in the direction of that advantage, thereby negating some of the innovator's attraction.

— Natural selection and adaptive behavior are essentially the same. The latter states that institutions evolve when environmental conditions are conducive. The former suggests that the retail institutions that can most effectively adapt to environmental changes are the ones most likely to prosper or survive.

— The various theories differ, but in combination, they provide a comprehensive understanding of the evolution of the retail structure. This is true of both past changes and probable future changes.

KEY TERMS

Assortment The depth of a store's selection of merchandise, such as sizes and colors.

Catalog showroom A type of retail outlet that customers visit to purchase articles described in catalogs mailed to their homes. Such organizations feature self-service, checkout lanes, discount prices, and a large assortment of gift and jewelry merchandise.

Chain A type of outlet characterized by the sale of similar merchandise in more than one outlet, a sim-

ilar architectural format, centralized buying, and common ownership.

Channel of distribution Interorganizational system through which products, commodities, or services are marketed.

Classification dominance A situation in which an outlet has an extensive variety and assortment of a particular line of merchandise.

Consumer cooperative A type of retail store owned by consumers and operated by a hired manager. The stores are operated on the "one person, one vote" principle, regardless of the number of shares of stock held. Prices are competitive, and members benefit at year-end by receiving dividends based on the dollar amount of purchases they made during the year.

Convenience store A type of retail outlet, primarily in food, which features long hours, self-service, narrow assortments, higher prices than conventional outlets, and convenient locations.

Cooperative A type of voluntary chain that may be headed by either a wholesaler or a retailer. The co-op provides purchasing and operating economies of scale to independent retailers and/or wholesalers which they could not obtain by working alone.

Corporate chain A type of retailing institution characterized by central ownership and central control over all retail units, including control of profit planning, losses, and merchandising.

Department store A type of retail institution featuring a wide variety and assortment of merchandise, supplementary services, high prices, and high margins.

Dialectic process A theory of change in retail institutional structure based on the premise that retailers mutually adapt in the face of competition from "opposites." When challenged by a competitor with a differential advantage, an established institution will adopt strategies and tactics in the direction of that advantage, thereby negating some of the innovator's attraction.

Gentrification The movement of upwardly mobile, young, middle-class professionals to previously deteriorating neighborhoods which have been rehabilitated.

Life cycle The stages through which retail institutions evolve, including innovation, growth, maturity, and decline or stagnation.

Limited-assortment store A type of retail food outlet that features 500 to 800 fast-moving, limited assortment items.

Margin The percentage markup at which inventory is sold.

Marketing The process of planning and executing the conception, pricing, promotion, and distribution of ideas, goods, and services to create exchanges that satisfy individual and organizational objectives.

National chain department stores Outlets offering extensive customer service, store credit, and brand merchandise, which are part of nationally administered marketing programs. Strong emphasis is also placed on store brands.

Natural selection A theory of change in institutional retailing structure based on the premise that the retailing institutions that can most effectively adapt to environmental changes are the ones most likely to prosper or survive.

Nonstore retailing The sale of merchandise other than through retail stores. Examples include door-to-door sales, catalog sales, telemarketing, and direct marketing by the use of television or other media.

Off-price retailing The everyday sale of medium-to-high-quality brand-name products at deep discount prices.

Retail accordion A theory about institutional change based on the premise that retail institutions evolve from broad-based outlets with wide assortments to specialized narrow lines and then return to the wide-assortment pattern.

Retailing Consists of all activities involved in the sale of goods and services to the ultimate consumer.

Shopping center A cluster of retail outlets under a single roof. They collectively offer an assortment of varied goods that satisfies most of the merchandise needs of consumers within convenient traveling times of their homes or places of work.

Single-line store A retail outlet specializing in the sale of one product line of merchandise, such as family shoes.

Specialty store An outlet specializing in the sale of one item in a product line. An example is a store specializing in athletic shoes.

Structure (retail institutional) All of the outlets through which goods or services move to the retail customer.

Traditional department store A type of retail outlet offering a wide array of hard and soft goods, full service, and high margins. Such outlets typically serve a local market and offer extensive customer service, store credit, and brand merchandise.

Turnover The number of times the average inventory in a store is sold in a 12-month period.

Variety The width of a store's selection of merchandise.

Variety store A type of retail establishment selling a wide variety of merchandise in the low price range. Such outlets are frequently referred to as "five and dime" stores, although merchandise is usually sold above these ranges.

Warehouse retailing A type of retailing that consists of five strategic elements: (1) a very large, low-cost facility; (2) emphasis on wholesale-type operating approaches in materials-handling technology; (3) maximum use of vertical space in merchandise display; (4) an exceptionally large on-premise inventory; and (5) few customer services.

Wheel of retailing A theory about institutional structure change based on the premise that institutional innovations in retailing penetrate the system on the basis of price appeal and gradually trade up over time in terms of store standing, quality, store services, and prices.

DISCUSSION QUESTIONS

1. Relate the following concepts retailing, marketing, retailing structure, and channels of distribution.
2. Describe the types of neighborhoods found in New York City. What is the importance of gentrification to the dynamics of Manhattan? What is the reason for the focus on New York City? Discuss the "Mid-America" retailing dynamics.
3. Why is it important to classify the retail institutional structure?
4. Discuss the margin-turnover classification model. Give an example of the type of institutional outlet that may exist in each of the four quadrants of the model.
5. What are the differences in the operating characteristics of a low-margin/high-turnover retail firm and a high-margin/low-turnover one?

6. Describe the classification of retail institutions based on ownership, type of merchandise, and kind of selling approach (i.e., nonstore).
7. How might the owner of an existing store benefit from a study of the retail structure in a given market area?
8. Is it likely that a universal model for explaining retail institutional change will be developed? Explain your answer.
9. Describe these theories of change in the retail structure: the wheel of retailing, the retail accordion theory, the dialectic process, and the adaptive behavior/natural selection model.
10. Discuss several institutional innovations that may hold the key to future success in retailing.

APPLICATION EXERCISES

1. Draw a map of the major streets in your local community. Choose a starting point and locate all the various types of shopping areas. Classify each one by type of location; plot them all on the map you draw. Include only major streets on which major retail opportunities exist.
2. Select either the downtown (CBD) or a shopping center (preferably a regional one) or both in your local community. Walk the area; list every tenant; describe each type of store in as many ways as you can. Make any necessary assumptions to do this job.
3. Take a careful look at the CBD in your town. Describe what is happening in the core and on the fringe. What do you think will happen in the near and distant future to that part of the city? Give your reasons.

CASES

1. The Hypermarkets

Bob Majors had just returned from Cincinnati where he was very impressed with Biggs, a European-based hypermarket. As the owner of a large shopping mall chain, Bob decided to investigate the possibility of establishing a hypermarket in the Southeast. Bob has called his management team together to discuss this idea and is encountering some dissension. Joe Williams, Bob's operations manager, feels that the public will not react favorably to a 250,000-square-foot store. Joe admits that

he has few facts to back his conclusion. Bob Majors has commissioned Joe to research and report on the major differences between the European hypermarket and the American shopping mall. In addition, Joe is to analyze these differences and to assess whether the concept is working in Cincinnati and will work elsewhere.

Assume you are Joe. Come up with some answers.

2. Cohoes and the Competition

Over the years, department stores such as Macy's and Marshall Field's and specialty stores such as Saks-Fifth Avenue and Sakowitz virtually controlled the retail apparel business where customers demanded quality and convenience and paid for them. A natural outgrowth of this business was the discount phenomenon. It offered no-frills shopping, self-service, and sterile ambiance such as in the K marts and Woolcos which peaked in the 1950s and 1960s. The discount houses usually carried goods of lower quality, and discounted prices to serve their less affluent target market.

In 1983, an explosive retailing phenomenon appeared which combined the quality goods of department and specialty stores with the plain atmosphere of the discounters. The explosion referred to is **off-price retailing**. Examples of this genre are not new—Filene's basement and Loehmann's Inc. are over 50 years old. But the explosion in the number of stores is recent. We now hear of Marshalls, T.J. Maxx, and Cohoes. Off-price retailing is characterized by aggressive purchasing, buying goods near the end of the season, or buying irregulars, samples, and garments that have been overproduced. With such a strategy, sometimes the inventories are not deep and many items are not always available.

Cohoes? You may never have heard of the name. A family name? No. The name of an obscure New York town is now famous among a new breed of consumer buying discounted ego-intensive merchandise; a $400 Trigere coat for $270; a $409 Ralph Lauren man's suit, $340; a $1,700 Judith Leiber handbag, $1,270; $40 Opium perfume, $32; an $11,900 Piaget Pole watch, $8,900.

Analysts say that Cohoes has merged the value of the discounter with the service, atmosphere, inventory depth, and modishness of Bloomingdale's and Neiman-Marcus. Productivity is the secret to the success of this firm. Cohoes produces $600 per square foot, the **traditional department store**, $115, and the "classic" off-price apparel store, $105. Respectively, each of these retail types is earning 6 percent, 2.4 percent, and 4 percent profit after taxes. The difference between Cohoes and its off-price cousins is that Cohoes has nothing but the latest presented with flair and full service, all priced for less.

Questions

Discuss the place of the different types of retailing outlined in this case by viewing them in the present, the immediate future, and the long term. Focus your reactions on Cohoes and off-price retailing in general.

ENDNOTES

1. Carter Wiseman, "The Next Great Place: The Triumph of Battery Park City," *New York*, June 16, 1986, pp. 33–41.
2. See *Guestinformant*, pp. 152–65, for more.
3. Carter Wiseman, "Waterfront Wonderland," *New York,* July 4–11, 1983, pp. 37–39.
4. Craig Unger, "The Lower East Side," *New York*, May 28, 1984, pp. 32–41.
5. Santa Barbara Trust for Historic Preservation, "El Paseo," a brochure.
6. Plaza Merchant's Association, "The Plaza, An American Original," a brochure.
7. A mixed use development can include, in addition to retail properties, office buildings, hotels, and apartments.
8. Fact Sheet, Faneuil Hall Marketplace Inc., Boston, Mass., a brochure.
9. See "New Gilded Age Grandeur," *Time*, September 2, 1985, pp. 46–47; and Edgar Cheatham and Patricia Cheatham, "Crescent City Soundings," *Sky*, September 1986, pp. 55–67.
10. Cheatham and Cheatham, "Crescent City Soundings," p. 61.
11. J. D. Reed, "Capital Success in Washington," *Time*, October 17, 1983, pp. 85–86; and "Washington's Newest Tradition, The Pavilion at the Old Post Office," a brochure.
12. Information from Steve Doyal. Crown Center Redevelopment Corporation.
13. Wolf Von Eckardt, "Drawing a Blank Downtown," *Time*, April 4, 1983, p. 61. Also see Susan Dentzer with Richard Manning, "Hard Times for Ren Cen," *Time*, January 24, 1983, p. 56.
14. John Branston, "Malls: Urban Fad of 1970s Raises Questions for '80s," *The Commercial Appeal*, Memphis, Tenn., September 4, 1986, pp. A1, A8.
15. Jeff Atkinson, "Mega-Mall Riverchase Galleria Exceeds Developer's Expectations," *Shopping Center World*, June 1986, pp. 38–43.
16. Gordon M. Henry, "Welcome to the Pleasure Dome," *Time*, October 27, 1986, p. 75.
17. Ronald Gist, *Retailing: Concepts and Decisions* (New York: John Wiley & Sons, 1968), pp. 37–40.
18. U.S. Department of Labor, *Employment and Projections for the 1980s*, June 1977.

2

Strategic Retail Management

Ramada and Holiday Inns Focus on the Business Traveler

During the past 10 years the guest mix of most motels has changed from 60 percent leisure and 40 percent business to the reverse. Some motel executives were unsure about how to respond to such changes. Ramada Inn and Holiday Inn, however, responded to the changes and developed strategies designed to attract the business traveler.

Holiday Inn underwent a massive repositioning effort in an attempt to attract the business traveler. When it was founded in the 1950s, Holiday Inn's mission was to serve passersby—mainly families on vacation. About 95 percent of its guests were such individuals. Today, however, nearly 97 percent of Holiday Inn's customers have reservations. As the family vacationing market continued to shrink, Holiday Inn began to focus its efforts on serving the needs of business travelers. As part of the strategy to meet the needs of this market, Holiday Inn now builds most of its newer facilities in downtown or suburban airport locations.

Ramada Inn also launched a program to change from its leisure-traveler, cut-rate orientation to a new position as a motel for the business traveler. The strategy required building new motels, modernizing old ones, and conducting an expensive advertising campaign featuring Ramada as a midpriced motel catering to the needs of business travelers. The strategy has worked—on a typical night, more than 70 percent of Ramada's customers are now business travelers.

Based on Laurel Leff, "Changing Trends in Motel Marketing," *Marketing Communications*, May 30, 1983, pp. 57–63; and "The New 'Inn' Places for Business Pleasure," *Dun's Business Month*, March 1984, p. 64.

*T*he preceding profile illustrates the concept of strategic planning in two service retail organizations. **Strategic planning** includes defining the overall mission or purpose of the company, deciding on objectives that management wants to achieve, and developing a plan to achieve these objectives. Ramada and Holiday Inns observed marketplace alterations that required a strategic change for the organizations to continue to prosper and grow. Management in both firms redefined the purpose of their organizations as that of serving business travelers. Pricing, promotion, and physical facility plans were then developed to support this new mission.

The purpose of this chapter is to focus on the issues surrounding strategic planning in retail organizations. These issues serve as the framework for the content and organization of this text.

After reading this chapter, you will be able to:

1. List the steps involved in strategic retail planning.

2. Interpret the concept of an organization's mission statement.

3. Explain the difference between long-range and short-range objectives.

4. Evaluate the issues involved in a situation analysis.

5. Discuss factors involved in selecting markets in which to compete.

6. Explain how retailers obtain resources needed to compete.

7. Review the components of retail positioning strategy.

8. Describe several strategic options available to retailers.

9. Discuss the issues involved in the evaluation and control of a retail operation.

FIGURE 2–1 STRATEGIC PLANNING

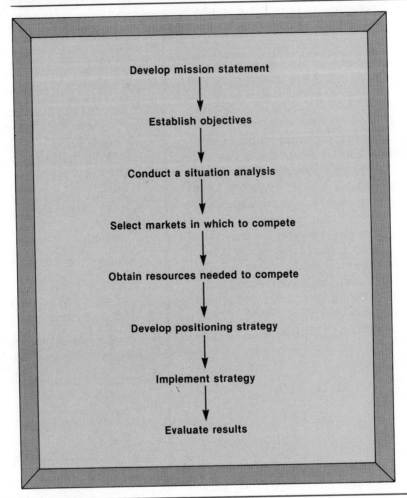

Figure 2–1 illustrates the steps involved in strategic planning. The plan begins with a statement of the mission or purpose of the organization. Objectives that management wants to achieve are then established. An analysis of internal strengths and weaknesses and external threats and opportunities is then undertaken to help management decide on the best way to carry out the organization's mission and to achieve its objectives. Markets in which to compete must be selected, and resources needed to compete must be obtained. A positioning strategy that outlines how the organization will compete in serving the needs of chosen markets is developed. The strategy must then be implemented. Finally, results must be measured and evaluated to ensure that the strategy is working.

FIGURE 2–2   INGREDIENTS OF A MISSION STATEMENT

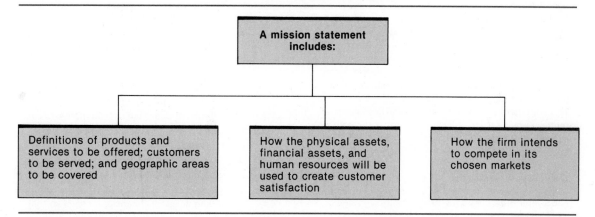

DEFINING THE MISSION OR PURPOSE OF THE ORGANIZATION

Management begins the planning process by identifying the organization's mission or purpose. The **mission statement** tells what the firm intends to do and how it plans to do it. Figure 2–2 outlines the ingredients of a mission statement. A statement of mission or purpose normally includes:

1. Definitions of products and services to be offered; customers to be served; and geographic areas to be covered.
2. How the physical assets, financial assets, and human resources will be used to create customer satisfaction.
3. How the firm intends to compete in its chosen markets.

Exhibit 2–1 outlines the mission of J. C. Penney Company and its strategy for carrying out the mission. The mission statement indicates the types of products/services to be offered, the markets to be served, and how the firm plans to compete. The character of the organization and its key activities are readily evident. The mission statement provides a clear sense of direction for the organization and distinguishes the firm from all others.

Mission statements often reflect an organization's values or corporate culture. **Corporate culture** establishes the values of greatest importance to the organization. These are values on which emphasis is constantly placed. Often these values reflect the personal goals of top management. A firm's values are often stated in the company motto, as shown in the following examples:

McDonald's: (QSCV) Quality, Service, Convenience, and Value. This slogan is emphasized to all employees as they are brought into the organization.

Company Mission

Our mission at J. C. Penney has changed little since Mr. Penney founded the Company in 1902: It was, and is, to sell merchandise and services to consumers at a profit, primarily but not exclusively in the United States, in a manner that is consistent with our corporate ethics and responsibilities.

This statement covers our current activities and potentially many others. It includes stores and catalog, as well as our financial services, drugstore, and European operations.

Corporate Objectives

Objectives express the kind of company we want to be—within the framework of the Company mission. At the corporate level, objectives tend to be broad and primarily financial. Each division has its own objectives, which are consistent with and support those of the Company.

In setting corporate objectives, we are guided by two concepts. The first is *leadership*. We are one of the world's largest retailers, a unique presence in consumer markets, an innovator—in short, a leader. We recognize that leadership does not necessarily equate with size. It does equate with our ability to fulfill the needs and expectations of all those who have some stake in our activities as a Company.

Stakeholders (or constituencies) are the second basic concept for setting objectives. Our principal stakeholders are *customers, associates, suppliers, investors, government,* and the *public* at large. If we serve these "constituencies" to their satisfaction, we will earn a reputation for outstanding value with commensurate goodwill and financial rewards. Our reputation will give us access to the resources required for profitable growth: human, material, financial. We compete with all other enterprises for these resources.

In accordance with these concepts of leadership and stakeholders, we have developed the following corporate objectives:

1. To achieve and maintain a position of *leadership* in the businesses in which we compete.

2. To be a positive force that enhances the interests of our *customers, associates, suppliers, investors, government,* and the *public* at large.

3. To be an attractive *investment* for our shareholders and creditors, and for this purpose:

   a. To achieve a *return on equity* in the top quartile of major competitors for the Company as a whole and for each operating division.

At the present time, this will require us to achieve an after-tax return of 16 percent.

   b. To achieve consistent growth in *earnings* at a rate required to meet or exceed the return on equity objective.

To achieve the 16 percent ROE from our current level will require a consistent earnings growth rate of approximately 15 percent.

   c. To maintain consistency and growth in *dividend* payout through increased earnings.

At the current time our objective is a payout of 33 percent of net income.   .

   d. To maintain a *capital structure* that will assure continuing access to financial markets so that we can, at reasonable cost, provide for future resource needs and capitalize on attractive opportunities for growth.

Specifically, we will maintain a minimum of A1/A+ ratings (Moody's/Standard & Poor's) on senior long-term debt and the A1/P1 ratings on commercial paper.

   e. To ensure that *financing* objectives governing the amount, composition, and cost of capital are consistent with and support other corporate objectives.

All performance objectives will be reviewed at least once a year and, if necessary, revised to reflect the results required to be in the top quartile of our major competitors.

Capital Resource Allocation

J. C. Penney Stores and Catalog, the two largest operating divisions, are currently the principal users of capital resources. As they achieve their objectives, they will become net providers of capital for future Company growth.

As funds become available for other purposes, they will be deployed where they can achieve the highest rate of return consistent with the Company's mission and financial objectives.

Funds will be made available for expansion or improved profitability where they generate the highest rate of return in excess of the cost of capital and where they support corporate objectives and strategies.

Our principal base of operations today is J.C. Penney Stores and Catalog. In these businesses we have become an important presence in the marketplace. We have more store space in premier shopping malls than any other retailer in America and we are the second largest catalog retailer, using the most mod-

EXHIBIT 2-1 (continued)

ern facilities. For many years to come the Company's results will largely depend on the performance of these two divisions.

These facts determine the base from which we can capitalize on trends in the environment. These trends include:

— Slower population growth.

— A more predominantly adult population.

— Disappearance of "under-stored" markets.

— Intensified competition caused by and in part resulting from consolidations that leave fewer, larger, financially stronger, and more professionally managed retailers—all fighting for market share.

— Rapidly rising costs of doing business in part due to inflation.

We expect these trends to continue.

An age shift in the population should favor general merchandise retailing. Adult consumers will be a larger, faster growing population segment than either younger or older age groups. By 1990 nearly half our population will fall between the ages of 25 to 44. They will have relatively high discretionary incomes and spend heavily on apparel and home furnishings.

The rising number of working women provides further opportunities to serve the shopping needs of career women both through stores and nonstore retailing such as catalog.

Retailing is so competitive, however, that prices tend to rise much more slowly than costs. This challenges our industry to raise productivity in order to use all our assets more intensively. To achieve this end, we will need to make full use of technology.

During the balance of the decade, J.C. Penney Stores will complete the positioning evolution into department stores, with J.C. Penney becoming the only national department store chain. Catalog will continue its rapid growth and its evolution in line with our department store direction. Opportunities to leverage our investment in technology and other capabilities by marketing them to others will continue to be addressed.

Major elements of our Company operating strategies are:

— To capitalize on existing resources, such as management skills, knowledge, consumer franchise, physical plant, and financing capacity.

— To monitor continually the changing lifestyles, wants, needs, and desires of our target consumers.

— To improve productivity of existing assets in each division.

— To combine strong, central, strategic planning with disciplined creative management at the market and unit level.

— To strive for the minimum corporate overhead required to achieve corporate objectives.

— To capitalize on technology for improving productivity.

— To maintain a competitive edge in compensation.

— To be a leader in competitive management pay practices that will attract and retain the most highly qualified and productive management team.

— To assure that objectives and strategies are based on the realities of the environment and agreed assumptions about trends.

The primary focus of our repositioning strategy is the broad middle-income consumer segment. Key elements of our actions to build our competitive posture in satisfying this consumer segment are:

— Developing a compelling reason to shop at J. C. Penney by entity and store. The several elements of value—selection, service, fashionability, quality, price, shopping environment, and other factors— provide the ingredients for differentiating ourselves from department and specialty store competition.

— Fine-tuning our positioning by entity and store. An individual entity or store's positioning will be more focused than the Company-wide target. Company merchandise offerings and merchandising support will be broad enough to allow a specific store to tailor its merchandise assortments to its customer base.

— Determining pricing and promotional strategies for items, with less reliance on total line or store price-off events.

— Balancing merchandise offerings across the good/ better/best spectrum so as to enhance selection. Assortment emphasis of specific stores will differ depending on the consumers in their market.

— Developing branding strategies by entity and subdivision that make appropriate use of private, national, and designer labels to enhance our competitive position.

EXHIBIT 2–1   (concluded)

Corporate Ethics and Responsibility
The manner in which we work toward Company objectives will be consistent with the seven principles of the "Penney Idea."
In keeping with these principles, we acknowledge our societal and environmental obligations and will

continue to fulfill our responsibilities in such areas as community involvement, contributions, energy conservation, minority economic development, resource recovery, and equal employment opportunity.
We will operate within the letter and spirit of the J. C. Penney Statement of Business Ethics.

Wal-Mart: Managers wear buttons that say, "We care about our people." Sam Walton, the founder, believes that it's important for everyone to be involved and believes that his best ideas often come from clerks and stockboys.

Mary Kay Cosmetics: "You can do it." Mary Kay Ash, the founder, uses this slogan to inspire confidence in her salespeople. She believes that anyone who has the confidence and persistence to try, can be a hero.[1]

SETTING OBJECTIVES

Management's task, after agreeing on the mission statement, is to establish objectives. **Objectives** are statements of results to be achieved. Objectives may include profitability, sales volume, market share, or expansion results that the firm wants to accomplish.

Management normally sets both long-term and short-term objectives. Long-term objectives are usually set for five or more years, while short-term objectives are set in one-year or two-year time frames. Long-term objectives indicate results the organization must achieve to remain successful over time. Short-term objectives, on the other hand, are designed to measure at regular intervals how well the organization is meeting its long-term objectives.

Good objectives are measurable, are specific as to time, and indicate the priorities for the organization. Examples of well-stated and poorly stated objectives appear in Table 2–1.

CONDUCTING A SITUATION ANALYSIS

Once objectives are set, management must decide on a plan for achieving them within the context of the firm's mission. This plan is based on an analysis of strengths and weaknesses of the organization and threats and opportunities in the environments. This assessment of internal strengths and weaknesses and external threats and opportunities is referred to as a **situation analysis.**

EXAMPLES OF WELL-STATED AND POORLY STATED OBJECTIVES

Examples of Well-Stated Objectives	Examples of Poorly Stated Objectives
Our objective is to increase market share from 15 percent to 18 percent in 1989 by increasing promotional expenditures 15 percent.	Our objective in 1989 is to increase promotional expenditures.
Our objective for 1990 is to earn aftertax profits of $5 million.	Our objective is to maximize profits.
Our objective is to open three new units by 1990 in each of the following states where the chain presently has no units: Tennessee, Georgia, and Florida.	Our objective is to expand by adding units to the chain.

Internal factors evaluated in the situation analysis are those variables largely under the control of store management. Such factors include financial resources, management skills, sales force composition, product lines carried, and the reputation of the firm with customers.

External factors analyzed in the situation analysis are those over which store management has no control. The external environments on which management focuses in the situation analysis are discussed in Chapters 3, 4, and 5 of the text. Chapter 3 focuses on the legal and public policy situation. The economic and social environments are covered in Chapter 4, and the technological environment is the topic of Chapter 5. Management studies trends in these environments and determines whether the trends pose threats or opportunities, or have no relevance for the organization.

The result of the situation analysis suggests markets in which to compete. Management may "stay the course" and make only minor adjustments in strategy. In other instances, as in the case of Ramada Inn and Holiday Inn, major changes may be made in markets served and in strategies for serving the new markets.

DECIDING ON MARKETS IN WHICH TO COMPETE

The ultimate value of the situation analysis is that it helps the firm identify and capitalize on the opportunities available to it. Such an analysis aids store management in identifying markets that offer strong opportunities for growth and profitability and in avoiding markets that appear undesirable.

Screening criteria are useful tools for identifying markets that are most compatible with the firm's resources and skills, as well as threats and opportunities from external environments. Typical criteria are shown in Table 2–2 and include such factors as the growth potential of each likely market, the investment needed to compete, and the strength of competition. The possible markets are evaluated by deciding on the importance of each factor to management and how each possible market ranks on each factor. Mul-

MARKET ALTERNATIVES PROFILE ANALYSIS

Critical Market Factors	Importance to Management	×	Attractiveness of the Market Based on the Factor Evaluated	=	Total Score
Future growth potential	2		1		2
Present size	6		4		24
Investment required	5		6		30
Strength of competition	4		5		20
Ability to meet the needs of the market	1		3		3
Profit potential	3		2		6
	1 is most important		1 is most attractive to management		85

tiplying the importance of each factor by the attractiveness of the market on that characteristic yields a score for each factor. The sum of factor scores for each possible market indicates to management the most attractive markets.

Exhibit 2–1 provides an example of how such an analysis shaped strategy development at J. C. Penney. Penney's management identified slower population growth, intensified competition because of mergers, more professionally managed retail outlets, and saturated markets as forces affecting the organization's future and adjusted strategy accordingly. Management chose to compete in more affluent consumer markets rather than in its traditional blue-collar market.

The markets that management decides to serve are referred to as **target markets**. As shown in Figure 2–3, retail managers may follow one of three approaches in selecting target markets: aggregation, extreme segmentation, and partial segmentation.

Aggregation

Aggregation as an approach to target market selection assumes that most consumers are alike in their needs and wants. Retailers following such an approach do not recognize varying demand curves for different groups of consumers. Such retailers focus on the common dimensions of a market. They attempt to attract the broadest possible number of buyers by relying on mass advertising and by appealing to the universal theme of low price. Examples of retailers following such an approach are warehouse food stores and discount department stores such as K mart and Wal-Mart.

Extreme Segmentation

In an **extreme segmentation** approach, retailers concentrate on a very narrowly defined market segment. The emphasis is on personalized service and depth of product lines. Numerous examples can be given of specialty operations that follow this approach to target market selection. Ted E. Bear

FIGURE 2–3   APPROACHES TO SELECTING TARGET MARKETS

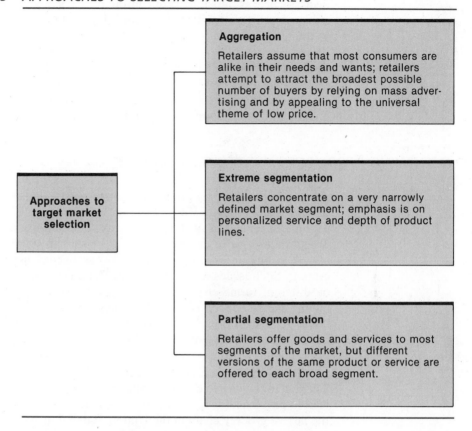

Approaches to target market selection

Aggregation

Retailers assume that most consumers are alike in their needs and wants; retailers attempt to attract the broadest possible number of buyers by relying on mass advertising and by appealing to the universal theme of low price.

Extreme segmentation

Retailers concentrate on a very narrowly defined market segment; emphasis is on personalized service and depth of product lines.

Partial segmentation

Retailers offer goods and services to most segments of the market, but different versions of the same product or service are offered to each broad segment.

and Company sells nothing but teddy bears; Murder Ink is a bookstore that carries only mystery books. The Forgotten Woman specializes in large-sized women's clothing. In the maternity wear market are firms such as Mothercare and Lady Madonna.

Partial Segmentation

In a **partial segmentation** approach to target market selection, retailers offer goods and services to most segments of the market, but different versions of the same product or service are offered to each broad segment. A department store, for example, may have separate clothing departments for juniors, budget-conscious shoppers, and high-income, fashion-conscious consumers. A record shop may carry a full line of records to cater to the diverse musical tastes of consumers.

Once retailers have chosen markets in which to compete, a plan must be developed for attracting targeted consumers. The basis for such planning is a thorough understanding of those consumers—their behavior, values, motives, and expectations. Especially important is an understanding of the decision process customers go through in making merchandise and store choice decisions. Because of the importance of this topic, a separate chapter in the text is devoted to a discussion of buyer behavior. Chapter 6 focuses on the consumer as a problem-solver and highlights a number of different issues related to the behavior of consumers. Chapter 7 provides an in-depth look at consumers by focusing on living patterns of customers. Understanding the lifestyles of consumers helps retailers better understand their merchandise and store preferences and their shopping behavior.

OBTAINING RESOURCES NEEDED TO COMPETE

As part of the planning process, retailers must evaluate the alternatives for owning a business as well as avenues for entering a retail business. For example, a retail firm can be operated as a sole proprietorship, a partnership, or a corporation. To enter retailing, a person can start his or her own business, can buy an existing business, or can become part of a franchise operation. Such issues are the topics of Chapters 8 and 9. Chapter 8 focuses on different forms of ownership, issues in buying a retail business, determining capital needed for a new business and sources of needed funds, and issues related to organization structure. Because franchising is one of the fastest growing segments in retailing today, a separate chapter, Chapter 9, is devoted to a discussion of franchising as a retail business concept.

Store location is a crucial element of retail planning and is the topic of Chapter 10. Failure to consider the strategic importance of store location can lead to problems for retail organizations. For example, until 1973 A&P was the largest grocery chain in the United States. Since that time, however, the chain has experienced continual problems and major losses. One of the problems for A&P was that it failed to follow its customers and build suburban stores during the 1950s and 1960s when competitive chains were doing so. By the time the chain decided to locate in suburban areas, the best locations had already been taken by competitors.[2] Wal-Mart is an illustration of the successful role store location can play in strategy. Sam Walton, founder of Wal-Mart, realized that there was a market for discounters in small towns—his rivals were concentrating on locating in urban areas. Beyond that, he understood the importance of getting merchandise to the stores from the chain's distribution warehouses. To be successful in the small, out-of-the-way locations, he needed the same efficient merchandise delivery methods of his big-city counterparts. He got these efficiencies by locating his stores in clusters.

Human resources are just as vital to the success of a retail operation as are financial resources and physical facilities. As you will see in Chapter 11, the human resources plan must be consistent with the overall strategy of the retail organization. You will also learn that human resources management involves a variety of issues such as recruiting, selecting, training, compensating, and motivating personnel and that it is essential that these activities be managed effectively and efficiently.

DEVELOPING A POSITIONING STRATEGY

After markets in which to compete are selected and resources needed to compete are obtained, a positioning strategy is developed. A **positioning strategy** is a plan of action which outlines how the organization will compete in chosen markets and how the firm will differentiate itself from other organizations competing for the same customers.

An example of positioning is Rudy's Sirloin Steak Burgers, an up-scale, fast-service restaurant serving 100 percent sirloin on a bun. The restaurant is "positioned between sit-down, full-service, and liquor-serving places such as Bennigan's and TGI Friday's on the high end and fast-food strongholds such as McDonald's, Burger King, and Wendy's on the low end."[3]

The importance of developing a positioning strategy must be stressed, especially in an era when competition in retailing is fierce. The critical nature of positioning is indicated in the following quote:

> In an era of cutthroat retail competition, few if any strategic responses are more critical to a retailer than positioning: identifying—and then occupying—an available position in the market. . . . Occupying an available position involves selling the store, not just the merchandise. A store becomes the "brand" with all marketing variables—merchandise mix, ambiance, personnel, advertising, pricing policy—coordinated to reinforce what the firm stands for, why it exists. In brief, occupying a position requires that the retailer's *reason for being* is clearly and powerfully defined in the prospective customer's mind and in the mind of management and personnel. An effective positioning strategy can contribute greatly to a retailer's success. In a cluttered marketplace, the well-positioned retailer is distinctive; it is a first-choice outlet.[4]

The positioning strategy involves the use of retailing mix variables. The **retailing mix** consists of all variables that can be used as part of a positioning strategy for competing in chosen markets. As shown in Figure 2–4, the retailing mix variables include product, price, presentation, promotion, personal selling, and customer services. Issues related to the retailing mix variables are included in Chapters 12–19 of the text.

Let's use Wendy's hamburger chain to illustrate how the retailing mix variables play a critical role in positioning efforts within target markets. Wendy's target market is white-collar professionals, aged 18 to 34, who have above average education and above average income. Wendy's positioning strategy in this target market is to offer a superior quality product at a premium price in attractive surroundings. The blend of some of the retailing mix variables in support of this positioning strategy is as follows:

FIGURE 2–4 VARIABLES OF THE RETAILING MIX

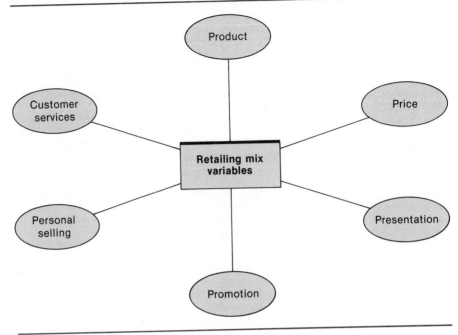

— *Product variable:* fresh, domestic ground beef, never frozen, served hot off the grill and fixed the way people want—any of 256 different ways. The product offering also includes taco salad, a chicken sandwich, a line of hot baked potatoes, and other additions.

— *Price variable:* above the competition and in harmony with a premium product in an attractive, restaurant-like setting.

— *Presentation and customer service variables*: upgraded exterior and interior design. Enlarged dining areas with greenhouse windows. Drive-in window order options and late night hours.

— *Promotion variable*: a consistent theme emphasizing that "Wendy's Is Better." Initially based on a "Hot 'n Juicy" theme to emphasize their unique product attributes, now replaced with a broader theme of "Wendy's Has the Taste" to reflect a campaign aimed at broadening consumer perceptions of Wendy's offering.[5]

STRATEGY IMPLEMENTATION

A sound strategy is no guarantee of success if it cannot be successfully executed. To implement a firm's desired positioning effectively, every aspect of the store must be focused on the target market. Merchandising must be

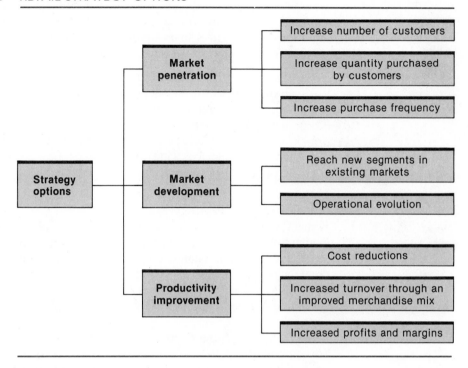

single minded; displays must appeal to the target market; advertising must talk to it; personnel must have empathy for it; and customer service must be designed with the target customer in mind.

Our purpose in this section of the chapter is to show how the retailing mix variables can be blended in implementing a store's positioning strategy. While space does not permit an extensive discussion of strategy options, we believe that those discussed will show how retailers implement strategy within target markets. The strategy options to be discussed include market penetration, market development, and productivity improvement. The range of options within each strategy is shown in Figure 2–5.

Market Penetration

Retailers following a strategy of **market penetration** seek a differential advantage over competition by a strong market presence which borders on saturation. Such a strategy is designed to increase (1) the number of customers, (2) the quantity purchased by customers, and (3) purchase frequency.

Increasing the Number of Customers
Strategies designed to increase the number of customers have worked well for a number of retail operations. One such firm is K mart. K mart has

aggressively sought a strong market presence by adding new stores in areas where it seeks market dominance. Further, K mart has modified its in-store offerings in an effort to increase the number of customers in the stores.[6] Additional aspects of K mart's penetration strategy have included use of the retailing mix variables to ensure:

1. The lowest price lines and the lowest prices within the market area.
2. Extensive width and depth of consumer goods such as health and beauty aids and housewares.
3. Aggregate convenience including location, parking, hours, and ease of purchase; features such as supermarket-like front ends, total merchandise display, wide aisles, easy-to-see-and-locate merchandise groupings, shopping carts, and usually a single display floor.

Increasing the Quantity Purchased

K mart is also trying to get customers to spend more money while they are in the store. Much of K mart's effort in this area has been on improved store layout and merchandise presentation. Management has attempted to create an atmosphere that is conducive to free spending. Departments have been relocated within the stores. New display fixtures that provide shelf space and more attractive presentation of merchandise have been added.[7]

Increasing Purchase Frequency

Toy supermarkets such as Toys-R-Us, Child World, and Lionel Leisure have been quite successful in implementing strategies designed to increase purchase frequency. The keys to the success of these firms include: (1) a complete selection of toys year-round; (2) customer knowledge that when they buy a toy at such outlets at Christmas they will find a good selection after Christmas to accommodate returns; (3) stable year-round lines plus merchandise categories with seasonal appeal in spring and summer, such as juvenile furniture, bicycles, gym sets, and family pools; (4) a huge inventory; (5) low prices; (6) minimum service; and (7) wide aisles.[8]

Basically these firms offer items that sell year round. Toys in the low to medium price ranges, often with strong licensed-character affiliations such as the Smurfs and Care Bears, provide sales day in, day out. High-impulse items like peg-boards, die-cast toys, and hobby kits lead to high customer traffic. The firms capitalize not only on birthdays and Christmas but also on other holidays and special occasions like Valentine's Day, Easter, Halloween, and back-to-school.

Market Development

A strategy of **market development** focuses either on attracting new market segments or completely changing the customer base. Market development normally involves bolder strategy shifts, more capital, and greater risk than a market penetration strategy. Examples of market development efforts include (1) reaching new segments and (2) operational evolution.

Reaching New Segments

Wendy's and Arby's fast-food restaurant chains provide examples of firms that have followed a strategy of attracting new segments in existing markets. Wendy's, for example, has looked beyond the heavily saturated hamburger market and added a salad bar, chicken sandwiches, breakfast items, and hot baked potatoes with different fillings. Such menu additions help Wendy's attract new segments of the market—consumers who are looking for something nonfried, less filling, lower calorie, and more nutritious than many traditional fast-food offerings.

Arby's introduced a menu targeted to children in an attempt to increase its share of the family market. Youngsters can order the Arby's Adventure Meal, which comes with "R.B.," a robot that is the firm's first children's character.[9]

Operational Evolution

Operational evolution means changing competitive strategy over time by focusing on a new target market and developing a business concept different from the existing one. This strategy is different from that of increasing the customer base as previously discussed because it involves changing, rather than adding customers to, the customer base.

Spiegel, Inc. provides an example of a firm that has followed a strategy of operational evolution. Spiegel, for many years, focused on lower-income, rural, mail-order shoppers as its target market. Management then made a major strategic decision to position the organization as a fashion catalog retailer of women's apparel and home furnishings. The new target market is fashion-conscious, sophisticated, working women, as shown in Exhibit 2–2. This market consists of women 25 to 54 years of age with annual household incomes of at least $34,000. The firm's new strategy included higher prices, a change in the merchandise mix, expanded customer services and self-improvement programs for women, and increased advertising to the target market.

Productivity Improvement

The strategy of **productivity improvement** focuses on improved earnings through cost reductions, increased turnover through an improved merchandise mix, and increased prices and margins. Productivity improvement often occurs in firms in the mature or declining phases of their life cycles. During these stages, strategies requiring major infusions of cash are not acceptable to management. Rather, the emphasis is on squeezing as much profit as possible from the operation. The strategy is more a refinement of existing strategies than a dramatic new way of doing business.

Cost Reductions

Some retailers concentrate on cost reductions as a competitive weapon in increasing productivity. A key to such a strategy often is to increase self-service to hold down labor costs. Reducing store hours, making better use

"I DON'T GO TO THE TOP FRENCH DESIGNERS. THE TOP FRENCH DESIGNERS COME TO ME."

"In my 9-to-5 role as a film producer, I do a lot of running around.

So in my other role (you know, the one as a *real* person) I prefer to do as little chasing around as possible.

Which is precisely why I'm addicted to the Spiegel Catalog.

With Spiegel, I get the same French designers I'd find at a better boutique: Anne Marie Beretta, Azzedine Alaïa, Jean Charles de Castelbajac, Jean Claude de Luca. Over 200 designers in all.

But Spiegel sends them right to my home. Office. Anywhere. And if I change my mind about *anything*, they pick it up. Free.

Which leaves me the time to chase after bigger, better things—like Rover and Ripley here."

Spiegel

ALL STYLE. ALL SERVICE. ALL SATISFACTION.
To get your copy of the new Spiegel Fall Catalog, mail $3 with the attached card. Or call, toll-free, 1 800 345 4500, and ask for Dept. 041.

SOURCE: Courtesy of Spiegel Incorporated, Chicago, Illinois, HCM Agency.

of part-time help, and cutting back on customer services are other actions that can be taken to reduce costs.

In an effort to reduce costs, Montgomery Ward has reduced sales help to increase employee sales per hour. Renovation expenses have been minimized through use of modular departments, fewer merchandise departments, and the use of less expensive display fixtures.[10]

Improved Merchandise Mix

Many department stores have attempted to improve productivity by increasing their turnover through a better merchandise mix. In the past, department stores carried everything from wristwatches to kitchen sinks. Now many department stores are reducing the number of lines carried. They are dropping such lines as appliances, toys, tools, health and beauty aids, books, and sporting goods. Management has realized that consumers have no special inclination to shop for these products at department stores. Rather, department stores are now focusing on fashion apparel, jewelry and other accessories, and cosmetics—goods that enjoy high margins and relatively quick turnover. Fashion is where department stores perform best, and fashion goods are the lines department store managers are now committed to promoting.[11]

Price and Margin Increases

Price and margin increases can be a key element in productivity-based strategies. Higher-than-normal prices may be possible on low-visibility items or infrequently purchased products. Charging for services such as delivery or installation may also be feasible. Lowes Home Improvement Center, for example, charges a fee for delivery of merchandise. Adding high-margin items to the merchandise mix, as is done by superstores, is a further dimension of such a strategy.

EVALUATING AND CONTROLLING OPERATIONS

Once a strategy is implemented, managers need feedback on the performance of the new strategy. Some types of information are needed on a routine, ongoing basis to help management determine whether objectives have been met. Chapters 20 and 21 of the text focus on several types of control systems which help management assess the success of operations.

The effectiveness of the long-term competitive strategy of the firm, however, must also be evaluated periodically. Such an evaluation covers all elements of the plan, as shown in Table 2–3. This type of evaluation guarantees that the firm's plan does not degenerate into fragmented, ad hoc efforts that are not in harmony with the overall competitive strategy of the business. Management can also use the process to decide what changes, if any, should be made in the future to ensure that the combination of retailing mix variables supports the firm's strategy.

T A B L E 2–3 EVALUATING COMPETITIVE STRATEGY

Merchandising plan
1. What is the growth pattern of existing merchandise lines?
2. Is the merchandise line portfolio balanced? Should merchandise lines be added or deleted?
3. Should product line breadth or depth be modified?
4. What is the strength of the individual brands carried?
5. Are the merchandise lines properly positioned against the competition and in support of the marketing plan?
6. Does the firm have an adequate open-to-buy plan?
7. Are adequate inventory controls in place?

Pricing plan
1. What are the profit margins on the merchandise lines carried? Are they increasing or decreasing? How do they compare to those of competition?
2. Are the pricing policies, including price lines (at, equal to, or above the competition) appropriate for each target market?
3. Does pricing have a primary or secondary role in the marketing plan?
4. Is a realistic system for planned markdowns in place?

Advertising and sales promotion plan
1. Are the objectives for advertising and sales promotion clearly stated? Do they support the marketing plan?
2. Is the media mix supportive of the marketing plan?
3. Are budgets adequate to accomplish the objectives? How are budgets established?
4. Are the creative strategies compatible with the marketing plan?
5. Does the firm have weekly, monthly, and seasonal plans for such activities in place?

Distribution and sales support plan
1. Are customer service levels such as on warranties and repairs satisfactory? What weaknesses exist?
2. Are mail and telephone sales programs compatible with the overall marketing plan?
3. Are the after-sales delivery programs, if any, compatible with the marketing plan?
4. Are the credit programs offered cost effective? Should credit options be added or deleted?
5. Is the breadth and intensity of market coverage satisfactory for a firm with branches or multiple outlets?

Financial plan
1. Is a profit analysis possible, including a break-even analysis and analysis of ROI and leverage?
2. What are the profit margins by merchandise line? Are they increasing or decreasing? How do they compare to the competition? Compare with trade statistics where possible.
3. Does the firm have a sound accounting and information system?
4. What are the trends in such indicators as return on assets, earnings per share, and net profits?

Physical facilities plan
1. Is adequate emphasis placed on space productivity?
2. Is flexible fixturing used whenever possible?
3. Does signing provide adequate information to shoppers?
4. Do the atmospherics support the other elements of the marketing plan?
5. Is merchandise arranged for easy cross-selling whenever possible?

The retail information system
1. Does the merchandise information system provide the information needed for key operating decisions?
2. Is a sound, competitive shopping system in place?
3. Is someone in the firm responsible for evaluating environmental trends that can affect the continuing success of the firm?
4. Are the financial and merchandising ratios of the firm regularly compared to comparable trade statistics?

Human resources plan
1. Does the firm have the talent to execute its marketing strategies?
2. Is the firm adequately staffed?
3. Are the firm's selection and recruiting efforts and training programs adequate?
4. Are the firm's pay scales adequate? Are opportunities for promotion available? Are performance appraisals and feedback occurring?
5. If several outlets exist, are personnel decisions centralized or decentralized?
6. Are disciplinary procedures in place?
7. Do union/management relations receive adequate attention?

CHAPTER HIGHLIGHTS

— The beginning point in developing a strategic plan is identification of the organization's mission or purpose. The mission statement tells what the firm intends to do and how it plans to do it. The mission statement often reflects the firm's values or corporate culture.

— Objectives are statements of results to be achieved. Management normally sets both long- and short-term objectives.

— The retailer's plan for achieving objectives within the context of the mission statement is based on an analysis of the strengths and weaknesses of the organization and threats and opportunities in the environments. Such an analysis is called a situation analysis.

— The situation analysis helps store management identify markets in which to compete. The markets that management decides to serve are referred to as target markets. Retailers may follow one of three approaches in selecting target markets—aggregation, extreme segmentation, and partial segmentation.

— Retailers must develop a plan for attracting targeted consumers. The basis for such planning is a thorough understanding of those consumers. Retailers thus must understand the decision process consumers go through in making merchandise and store choices as well as a variety of other issues related to buyer behavior.

— As part of the planning process, retailers must evaluate the alternatives for owning a business as well as the avenues for entering a retail business. The planning process also involves store location decisions. A human resources plan that is consistent with the overall strategy of the firm must also be developed.

— The retailer must develop a positioning strategy. The positioning strategy is a plan of action that outlines how the organization will compete in chosen markets and how it will differentiate itself from other organizations competing for the same customers. The positioning strategy is developed through a combination of the retailing mix variables. These variables include product, price, presentation, promotion, personal selling, and customer services.

— A sound strategy is no guarantee of success if it cannot be implemented successfully. The retailing mix variables must be blended appropriately in implementing a store's positioning strategy.

— Some strategy options available to retailers include market penetration, market development, and productivity improvement. Market penetration includes strategies designed to increase (1) the number of customers, (2) the quantity purchased by customers, and (3) purchase frequency. Market development strategies focus on either attracting new market segments or completely changing the customer base (operational evolution). A strategy of productivity improvement focuses on improved earnings through cost reductions, increased turnover through an improved merchandise mix, and increased prices and margins.

Once a strategy is implemented, managers need feedback on how the organization is performing based on its strategy. Some types of information are needed on a routine, ongoing basis to help management determine whether objectives are being met. However, the effectiveness of the long-term competitive strategy of the firm must also be periodically evaluated.

KEY TERMS

Aggregation An approach to target market selection whereby retailers assume that most consumers are alike in their needs and wants.

Corporate culture The values of greatest importance to the organization.

External factors In a situation analysis, variables over which store management has no control.

Extreme segmentation An approach to target market selection whereby retailers concentrate on a very narrowly defined segment of the market.

Internal factors In a situation analysis, variables that are largely under the control of store management.

Market development A strategy option which focuses either on attracting new market segments or completely changing the customer base.

Market penetration A strategy option whereby retailers seek a differential advantage over competition by a strong market presence that borders on saturation.

Mission statement A statement that indicates what a firm plans to do and how it intends to do it.

Objectives Statements of results to be achieved.

Operational evolution Changing competitive strategy over time by focusing on a new target market and developing a business concept different from the existing one.

Partial segmentation An approach to target market selection whereby retailers offer goods and services to most segments of the market, but different versions of the same product or service are offered to each broad segment.

Positioning strategy An action plan that outlines how the organization will compete in chosen markets and how the firm will differentiate itself from other organizations competing for the same customers.

Productivity improvement A strategy that focuses on improved earnings through cost reductions, increased turnover through an improved merchandise mix, and increased prices and margins.

Retailing mix Those variables—product, price, presentation, promotion, personal selling, and customer services—that can be used as part of a positioning strategy for competing in chosen markets.

Situation analysis An assessment of internal strengths and weaknesses and external threats and opportunities.

Strategic planning Defining the overall mission/purpose of the company, deciding on objectives that management wants to achieve, and developing a plan to achieve those objectives.

Target markets The markets that management decides to serve.

DISCUSSION QUESTIONS

1. Indicate the steps involved in developing a strategic plan.
2. What is meant by an organization's mission statement? What does this statement normally include?
3. What is the difference between long-term and short-term objectives?
4. What is a situation analysis? Which factors are evaluated in such an analysis?
5. What is the ultimate value and use of a situation analysis?
6. Differentiate between the following approaches to selecting target markets: aggregation, extreme segmentation, and partial segmentation.
7. Explain the relationships between target markets, positioning strategy, and the retailing mix.
8. Discuss each of the following strategy options: market penetration, market development, and productivity improvement.
9. How is evaluation of the short-term results of a retail operation different from evaluating the effectiveness of the firm's long-term competitive strategy?

APPLICATION EXERCISES

1. Your text indicates the mission statement of J. C. Penney. Visit your school library and find mission statements of other retail operations from their annual reports.
2. Visit several different types of retail stores in your community and ask store managers to define the store's target market. Indicate which approach to target market selection—aggregation, extreme segmentation, or partial segmentation—each store is following.
3. Select at least three fast-food operations in your community. Indicate each firm's target market and positioning strategy and discuss how the elements of the retailing mix are combined in implementing the positioning strategy.

4. In the text you read about fast-food restaurants reaching new segments in existing markets through additions to their menus. Investigate other types of highly competitive retail businesses. Look for the strategies they use to develop new markets. Some possible areas for study are movie theaters, videocassette outlets, and home computer stores.
5. Find as many examples as you can of firms following the strategy of market penetration. Summarize your findings and draw conclusions, such as which firm is doing the best job of penetration and why.

CASES

1. Avon Re-Do Isn't Cosmetic

The 1980s have not been good to Avon Products, the New York–based company that depends on 1.4 million women to sell its fragrances and cosmetics on a one-to-one basis. Four consecutive years of flat or declining sales have forced Avon management to reevaluate the company's position in the marketplace.

The problem in the 80s, according to Kurt Sanger, director of skin care products marketing, is that Avon tried to appeal to an upscale customer that its distribution system does not reach. Avon tried to appeal to the women who were helping create two-income families with more money to spend on discretionary items. In 1982, for example, Avon introduced its first designer fragrance. They also tried expensive packaging and higher price points for other products. In skin care, Avon replaced a line of treatment products called Envira with a new line called Pure Care. The idea was to position Pure Care against Estée Lauder's Clinique line, which is sold in department stores. The new Pure Care line was priced at the same level as Clinique products and higher than its predecessor Envira products.

The result of these changes was a loss of 30 percent of the customers who had previously purchased the Envira line. They would not trade up to the higher priced products. Of Avon's core customers, 65 percent have household incomes of $35,000 or less and 50 percent earn $25,000 or less. This is a consumer who is very price conscious.

The Avon company is now trying to get back to basics and recapture its core customers. Pricing has been pulled back to make the Pure Care line comparable with the mass-marketed Almay line of products. New products are being tested and will be offered at prices that are in line with the Avon target audience's budget. Advertising also will appeal directly to this customer.

Questions
1. Explain how the changes that occurred in Avon's strategy illustrate the concept of operational evolution.
2. What were the reasons Avon began to focus on upscale, higher income consumers?
3. Why was Avon's attempt to change its target market and positioning strategy unsuccessful?
4. What actions are being taken by Avon to recapture its core customers?

Adapted from "Avon Re-Do Isn't Cosmetic," *Chicago Sun-Times*, September 1, 1986, p. 49.

2. Wellpet: Felix and Fido Create Its Niche

Wellpet is a new chain of pet nutrition centers based in California. The chain is going head-to-head against supermarkets and independent pet food and supply stores. The owner, Robert Bartlett, claims that consumers would rather purchase their pet food and supplies at Wellpet than at the supermarket. He claims that the new chain is focusing on consumer needs that no one deals with—pet nutrition and care.

Unlike a typical pet store, Wellpet does not carry animals. Instead, the chain stocks a combination of supermarket-type pet foods, premium meat-based pet foods, pet toys and supplies, and pet-related general merchandise geared to the pet's human counterpart (schnauzer-emblazoned coffee mugs).

Although the merchandise mix may be familiar to pet owners, it's the store design and quality of customer service that creates the allure. Bartlett points out that the average pet store is dark, smelly, and unsophisticated. The Wellpet store, on the other hand, is friendly and spotlessly clean. The store design is a cross between a country store and a supermarket. A wood veneer pathway guides cus-

tomers through the store. Wooden fixtures add a quality image. Lightboxes with transparencies of heartwarming scenes shine through the windows at night.

Store clerks gladly indulge customers by listening to their stories of animal antics. Inside the store, large information panels with graphics tell customers about pet nutrition and other aspects of pet health. According to Bartlett, this information "adds credibility to what we're saying—that is, we're not just a food store. We care about nutrition in relation to your pet; we understand it."

Questions
1. Which approach to target market selection is being followed by Wellpet?
2. How would you define Wellpet's target market?
3. Describe Wellpet's positioning strategy and how the variables of the retailing mix are combined in implementing this strategy.

Adapted from "Wellpet: Felix and Fido Create Its Niche," *Chain Store Age Executive*, September 1986, p. 4.

ENDNOTES

1. Terrence Deal and Allan Kennedy, *Corporate Culture* (Reading, Mass.: Addison-Wesley Publishing, 1982), p. 40.
2. "A&P Looks Like Tengelmann's Vietnam," *Business Week*, February 1, 1982.
3. "Rudy's Courts Gourmet-Burger Lover," *Advertising Age,* December 10, 1984, p. 61-S.
4. Leonard L. Berry, "Retail Positioning Strategies for the 1980s," *Business Horizons*, November-December 1982, p. 45.
5. "Wendy's Aims to Get Better with Its BEST," *Advertising Age*, April 30, 1984, p. 4.
6. "To K mart, Home Gyms Are Profitable Exercise," *Advertising Age*, May 21, 1984, p. 78.
7. Charles W. Stevens, "K mart Stores Try New Look to Incite More Spending," *The Wall Street Journal*, November 26, 1980, p. 29.
8. "Founder Lazarus Is a Reason Toys-R-Us Dominates Its Industry," *The Wall Street Journal*, November 21, 1985, p. 1.
9. "Arby's Aims New Push at Kid's Market," *Advertising Age*, May 30, 1983, p. 3.
10. James E. Ellis, "Mobil May Finally Say 'So Long' to a Mending Montgomery Ward," *Business Week*, November 3, 1986, p. 34.
11. Anthony Ramirez, "Department Stores Shape Up," *Fortune*, September 1, 1986, pp. 50–52.

Environmental Factors Affecting Retail Strategy Development

The retail strategies discussed in Chapter 2 are not developed in a vacuum. Rather, the strategies emerge after a careful analysis of both the internal and external environments facing the firm.

The environments discussed in Chapters 3, 4, and 5 are of obvious importance in shaping retailing strategies. Important are consumer demographics, cultural differences between consumers, differing lifestyle patterns, and the effects of the economy on consumer behavior. Similarly, interest rates, energy costs, and both inflation and deflation affect the strategies of retailers.

Legal and public policy issues also influence strategy development. Raising the legal drinking age to 21, for example, has created major problems for bars and restaurants. Various federal and state laws affect all dimensions of the retailing mix, including promotion, pricing, products, and customer services decisions.

One of the most dramatic impacts on retail operations in recent years has been the changing technology of retailing. The microcomputer has revolutionized the way in which retailers keep track of inventory and make decisions about when and what levels of merchandise to stock. Additionally, video text, interactive home-shopping networks, and instore electronic sales aids are posing both new challenges and opportunities for today's retailers.

3

The Legal and Public Policy Situation

Gourmet Ice Cream Company Fights for Store Freezer Space

Ben & Jerry's Homemade, Inc. has become more than a little ice cream maker with a loyal local following. The Burlington, Vermont, company's superpremium, that is to say, awfully rich, ice cream is found in some New England supermarket freezer cases beside national brands marketed by billion-dollar corporations. The six-year-old company's sales this year will top $4 million; a new factory is in the works.

Even this modest amount of success isn't without its problems, though, because companies already established in a market rarely welcome competition. More aggressive ones often use their market dominance to keep upstarts from elbowing onto grocery shelves.

So it is that inexperienced ice cream marketers Ben Cohen and Jerry Greenfield are getting a lesson in big-league competition from a giant, Pillsbury Co., whose Haagen-Dazs Ice Cream Co. subsidiary dominates the superpremium, or gourmet, ice cream market.

Mr. Cohen was surprised by Haagen-Dazs's reaction to his product's slight inroads, he says. According to a lawsuit that Ben & Jerry's filed against Pillsbury in the U.S. District Court in Boston, Haagen-Dazs told some New England distributors earlier this year that they had to drop other superpremium ice cream brands or lose Haagen-Dazs.

Reuben Mattus, creator of Haagen-Dazs, who remains chairman after selling it to Pillsbury

Source: Sanford L. Jacobs, "Gourmet Ice Cream Company Fights for Store Freezer Space," *The Wall Street Journal,* December 17, 1984, p. 37. Reprinted by permission of *The Wall Street Journal,* ©Dow Jones& Company, Inc., 1984. All rights reserved.

last year, knows the importance of distributors who stock and deliver goods to retail outlets.

"I had to go and break into the market myself," Mr. Mattus says. "Ben & Jerry's", he says, "can put out their own trucks like I did in California in 1971."

As for Pillsbury, a spokeswoman says it prefers "exclusive dealing" with distributors so they don't carry directly competitive products. "It is difficult for a distributor to fully, equally, and fairly represent two similar products," she says, adding, "We think it is in Ben & Jerry's best interest to have a distributor represent them solely."

Ben & Jerry's response, however, was to file suit, alleging that the dominance of Haagen-Dazs made its attempts at exclusive dealing with distributors a violation of federal antitrust law. The company also complained to the Federal Trade Commission, whose Boston office is investigating.

*T*he legal wrangle between Ben & Jerry's Homemade, Inc. and Haagen-Dazs illustrates the legal complexities that can affect retailing. Government regulations are among the most persistent issues facing retailers. Local, state, and federal laws influence virtually every aspect of business. The regulations are intended to: (1) keep competition at a high level, (2) protect consumers from unfair business practices, and (3) give consumers enough information to make wise buying decisions.

After reading this chapter you will be able to:

1. Explain the meaning of restraint of trade.

2. Discuss unfair methods of competition.

3. List trade regulation rules.

4. Describe regulations affecting pricing, promotion, distribution, and products sold.

5. Discuss legal issues in credit.

This chapter examines broad legal areas of importance to retailers. These areas are: (1) regulations constraining growth, (2) unfair competition, (3) Federal Trade Commission regulations, and (4) laws affecting the retail mix, including pricing, promotion, distribution, the product, credit, and methods of selling. We also review the importance of ethical standards and social responsibility in day-to-day operations.

WHAT ARE THE REGULATIONS CONSTRAINING GROWTH?

The oldest regulations constraining growth are the antitrust laws. The philosophy behind the regulations is that more rigorous competition and better customer service are likely if all firms must compete aggressively to survive.

What Is Restraint of Trade?

Restraint of trade means:

1. Putting pressure on suppliers to prevent them from selling products to competitors.
2. Acquiring other retail firms in an effort to lessen competition or to create a monopoly.
3. Trying to fix the prices of goods sold. In other words, retailers cannot agree to stop price competition among themselves.
4. Underselling other retailers to gain control of a market. This prevents a large chain, for example, from lowering prices to drive smaller competitors in one area out of business, while the chain maintains high prices in its other areas.

Key Restraint-of-Trade Laws

The key restraint-of-trade laws are (1) the Sherman Act, (2) the Clayton Act, and (3) the Federal Trade Commission Act.

The Sherman Act

The **Sherman Act** (1890) was the first law passed to maintain competition. The law makes every action to restrain trade illegal. The possible forms of trade restraint are almost limitless. However, they most frequently include price-fixing, dividing markets among competitors, forcing suppliers to provide a retailer with the exclusive right to sell merchandise in a given area, or suppliers requiring retailers to purchase a variety of products in order to get the one product they really want. These activities are illegal when they create a monopoly or substantially lessen competition.

The Clayton Act

The **Clayton Act** (1914) is more specific in its restrictions than the Sherman Act. It declares certain practices illegal even if they do not actually restrain trade or do not constitute a monopoly or an attempt to monopolize. Further, the practices are illegal even if they do not actually injure competition. Practices violate the Clayton Act if they might lessen competition or tend to create a monopoly.

The Federal Trade Commission Act

The **Federal Trade Commission Act** (1914) created an independent agency, the **Federal Trade Commission (FTC).** The Commission's duty is to help enforce the Clayton Act and other antitrust laws. The FTC has the power of investigation and the power to issue cease and desist orders. Other acts or practices not in violation of the Sherman or Clayton Acts may be restrained by the FTC as unfair methods of competition.

The Federal Trade Commission is primarily concerned with interstate commerce. The philosophy behind its enforcement is that by removing various restraints to trade, prices will be kept at reasonable levels. Stronger price competition and better consumer service are likely to occur if all firms must compete with one another to survive. Recent actions by the FTC led to lower prices for eyeglasses and contact lenses, for example. FTC actions have also helped permit advertising by such professionals as attorneys, CPAs, and physicians.

Retailers are too frequently involved in court cases involving restraint of trade, as seen in the opening capsule. Toys-R-Us similarly charged that General Mills and Federated Department Stores tried to keep its Kids-R-Us off-priced apparel chain from selling Izod merchandise. Toys-R-Us contended that such a move, if successful, would lessen competition and monopolize distribution channels for children's clothes.[1] Similarly, Jerrico Inc. was charged in a federal court suit with unreasonably restraining competition in the sale of fish products by seeking to monopolize the purchase of products for distribution to Long John Silver's franchise restaurants.[2]

Mergers and Acquisitions

The restraint of trade laws also affect the efforts of retailers to use mergers and acquisitions as growth strategies. *Mergers* and *acquisitions* are terms often used interchangeably. The terms mean the combining of two companies into one organization by issuing stock or using some other method to pay for the assets of the merged or acquired business. Mergers between two competitors (horizontal mergers) are particularly risky from a legal point of view since the courts often view such actions as attempts to eliminate competition.

Mergers and acquisitions occur for a variety of reasons. A company may desire to add new products or services, to reduce dependence on an existing merchandising strategy, or to offset seasonal fluctuations in the present business. Sales growth is more rapid in an acquisition than in a start-up, and management avoids risks inherent in starting a new business. Examples of recent transactions include the acquisition of Lane Bryant by The

Limited, the acquisition of Marshall Field's by B.A.T., Inc., and the acquisition of Rich's Department Stores of Atlanta by Federated Department Stores. Retailing is currently being restructured as a result of mergers and acquisitions.

WHAT ARE TRADE REGULATION RULES?

Trade regulation rules are guidelines issued by the FTC which must be followed in selling certain products or services. The rules are issued as guidelines for specific industries and are not laws passed by Congress. For example, *retailers selling items by mail* must state the delivery dates for the items. If merchandise cannot be delivered by the stated time, the buyer can cancel the order.

The FTC also requires door-to-door sellers to identify themselves as salespersons before entering a person's home, and to allow three days for the customer to decide whether to cancel an order.

Mispricing and advertising out-of-stock food items are other areas covered by trade rules. Retailers are required to have enough of the advertised item to meet a "normal" level of demand. Mispricing is also prohibited.

Other agencies can issue trade rules. For example, the Food and Drug Administration (FDA) has established rules concerning *posting or advertising prescription drug prices.*

LAWS AFFECTING THE RETAILING MIX

Pricing is one of the key elements of the retailers' marketing plan. Pricing decisions affect profitability and market share, and can also serve as an advantage over competition if used properly. On the other hand, cutthroat pricing by certain retailers can drive smaller or less efficient firms out of business.

Price-fixing is always illegal. Management cannot agree with competitors on the price at which items will be sold. The practice is illegal under the Sherman Act and the Federal Trade Commission Act.

Price

What Is Horizontal Price-Fixing?

Horizontal price-fixing is the agreement between competing retailers on the price of identical merchandise. Horizontal price-fixing occurs far too frequently. For example, a federal grand jury indicted Waldbaum and Stop and Shop Companies for allegedly conspiring to fix the price of grocery and meat products in Connecticut and Western Massachusetts.[3] Retailers engaging in price-fixing may be prosecuted under the Sherman Act or the FTC Act.

What Is Vertical Price-Fixing?

Vertical price-fixing is often referred to as resale price maintenance. Vertical price-fixing occurs when manufacturers set minimum prices at which their products must be sold. While "fair trade legally imposed" is no longer law, "resale price maintenance" as a philosophy cannot be legislated away. Many manufacturers continue to stress "suggested retail prices" and encourage dealers to maintain these prices.[4]

Various charges of vertical price-fixing have been brought in recent years. For example, Cuisinarts, Inc., was fined $250,000 when it didn't contest antitrust charges that it conspired with retailers to fix the retail price of its food blenders. Similarly, Russell Stover was found guilty by the FTC of violating antitrust laws in trying to control the resale prices of its candies.

What Is Predatory Pricing?

Predatory pricing is the setting of prices to try to drive competition out of business. Varying retail prices by community is illegal if: (1) management cannot justify the practice on the basis of its costs and (2) management is trying to get rid of competition. The FTC enforces this regulation.

What Are Sales below Cost?

Several states have laws that do not allow the sale of items at less than their cost. These laws usually cover such product lines as milk and dairy products, cigarettes, or gasoline. Some states allow sales below cost if they are necessary to meet the price of a competitor.

What about Price Discrimination?

The ***Robinson-Patman Act (1936),*** *enforced by the FTC, is the primary law regulating* ***price discrimination.*** Not all price discrimination is illegal under the Robinson-Patman Act, but management should be prepared to justify price differences. These are the key areas to watch out for:

Like Grade and Quantity. Price differences to various retailers are legal when (1) differences exist in the cost of manufacturing or delivery and (2) the differences do not lessen competition.

The Good-Faith Defense. A supplier can charge a differing price to various retailers if done "in good faith to meet an equally low price of a competitor or the facilities furnished by a competitor." Services or facilities offered by a supplier must, however, be available to all retailers on "proportionally equal terms."

Management cannot legally force a supplier to knowingly grant a price lower than that given to competition, unless it can be justified as above.

As a guide, price differences between retailers cannot exceed the savings to the supplier. Also, the retailer and the supplier must be able to justify the price difference based on cost savings.

Promotion

False advertising allowances by suppliers to lower the cost of goods sold to retailers are illegal. Also, misleading advertising is illegal. FTC regulations affect all media advertising, promotional items sent through the mail, price lists, and similar promotional material. Retail ads cannot make false or misleading claims about prices, the value of goods, or guarantees. McDonald's, Burger King, and Wendy's, for example, fought an extensive legal battle over the truthfulness of claims made by Burger King. The latter claimed its burgers were superior to those of McDonald's and Wendy's.

Also, Section 2-E of the Robinson-Patman Act states that any services such as advertising furnished to a retailer by a supplier must be available to all retailers on a proportionately equal basis. The law is designed to ensure that such allowances or services are not a disguised form of reduced price to a few customers. The Federal Trade Commission, for example, investigated alleged anticompetitive behavior at Federated Department Stores. Federated allegedly induced suppliers to give larger advertising allowances to Federated than to competitors.[5]

The Mail Order Consumer Protection Amendment of 1983 gave the U.S. Postal Services broadened powers to issue cease-and-desist orders against a business that makes fraudulent advertising claims in the print media and uses the postal service in the advertising.[6]

Management must be prepared to prove the truth of their advertising claims. Advertisers can be required to submit data to the FTC to support claims about a product's safety, performance, or quality. Large national retailers with private-label products have to run corrective ads if the FTC finds their advertising misleading. For example, Sears ads stated that the Lady Kenmore dishwasher eliminated the need for prerinsing. The FTC found the claim was not substantiated, and the courts upheld its finding.[7] The Wheeler-Lea Act of 1938 extends Section 4 of the Federal Trade Commission Act and prohibits practices that might injure the public. The Act gives the FTC authority over the false advertising of food, drugs, cosmetics, and therapeutic devices.

Management cannot employ "bait and switch" advertising. With bait and switch, goods are advertised at a very low price. The retailer then tries to "switch" customers to a higher-priced item when they come to the store. Sears was found guilty of this practice in selling sewing machines.

Finally, state laws prohibit interstate liquor shipments through the mail, which keeps liquor manufacturers from capitalizing on telemarketing or mail-order sales.

Distribution

Exclusive dealing can cause problems for a retailer. **Exclusive dealing** occurs when a supplier requires that a retailer not sell a competitor's products. Under Section III of the Sherman Act, this practice is illegal when it lessens competition. Exclusive-dealing agreements, when made in good faith, can help both the retailer and the supplier: the retailer may get a more stable source of supply; the supplier gets a sure market for its merchandise.[8]

Exclusive territories may be a problem. **Exclusive territories** are created by suppliers who limit the areas in which a retailer can sell a product. In return, the supplier agrees not to sell to any other retailer in the defined areas. As a result, retailers probably give more time and attention to merchandise they sell under such an agreement. Many such agreements are illegal, however. Probably the surest way for a supplier to avoid violating the law is to use an agency distribution system. In this system, the supplier keeps title to the merchandise until it is sold by the retailer.

Congress has passed a law legalizing territorial exclusive franchising in the soft-drink industry. The law stipulates, however, that the product must be in substantial and effective competition with other products of the same general class before the practice will be permitted under the antitrust laws.

Also, **dual distribution,** in which wholesalers operate retail outlets, is not per se illegal. However, the courts have yet to fully define legal practices in this area. Manufacturers watch this type of distribution closely to make sure that wholesalers are not selling to independent retailers at high prices and then undercutting them by reselling merchandise at lower prices through their own retail outlets. Independent gasoline retailers contend that company-owned gasoline stations engage in such practices, often with devastating results.

Retailers cannot try to unfairly eliminate competitors. Big "anchor" stores in shopping centers cannot legally say which other tenants may locate in the center. They also cannot restrict the marketing practices of smaller tenants. The FTC obtained agreements with such retail firms as Federated, Gimbels, May Department Stores, and Sears, stopping them from engaging in such practices.

The Product

Unsafe consumer products are distributed in unacceptable numbers. Product tampering on supermarket shelves is a growing problem. Unfortunately, consumers are often unable to guard against the risks created by dangerous products. Both suppliers and retailers are being pressed to find better ways of informing consumers about these hazards.

Retailers have a specific responsibility under Section 15 of the Consumer Product Safety Act to monitor the safety of the products they sell. Management is required to report any information about product hazards to the Commission. They are also required to cooperate in product recalls.

Retailers also have a duty to warn consumers whenever they have knowledge of a dangerous condition of a product and when it appears unlikely that consumers will discover the danger for themselves. Management similarly can be held criminally negligent for selling certain products such as firearms to minors, gasoline in unlabeled containers, or liquor to intoxicated persons. Retailers can shift the burden of liability to themselves from the manufacturer by labeling products as their own.

Recall Systems

A recall system should be a critical part of store operating policies. The Food and Drug Administration (FDA) has expressed concern that retailers are often the weakest link in the recall chain simply because they are the last to be notified that an item should be pulled from the shelf.

Warranties

Retailers need to be careful about warranties. A warranty is a guarantee by a seller regarding the quality of performance of goods. **Express warranties** are in writing. The distinction between sales talk and **implied warranties** is often vague. Management has to carefully distinguish between puffery and promise in promotional efforts. Salespersons can establish implied warranties of fitness if they make specific performance promises about the product. Additionally, every sale, according to the Uniform Commercial Code, has an implied warranty of merchantability that the merchandise offered is fit for the purpose for which it is being sold.

The Magnuson-Moss Warranty Act (1975) is the major warranty law. This law applies to written warranties for merchandise. The law requires that warranty information is available *on the sales floor* for customers.

Many warranties are offered by a supplier. However, if a retailer offers a warranty for parts or labor, this also comes under the act. Retailers cannot require that a consumer use only a certain brand of replacement items before they will honor a warranty.

Retailers cannot be required to give a warranty, but they can be required to state that they have no obligation for repairs.

In summary, retailers are required to:

1. Give warranty information to consumers before they buy a product.
2. State warranty terms in "simple and readily understood language."
3. Establish a way to easily handle consumer complaints.

Montgomery Ward, for example, was found guilty by the FTC for not making warranty information readily available to consumers.

Management must make warranties available to consumers in at least one of four ways: (1) in text material near the product, (2) in a binder available for consumers; (3) on a product package, or (4) on a sign displaying the warranty text.

Weights and Measures Seal

Some businesses, such as supermarkets and gasoline service stations, are inspected by a representative from a bureau of weights and measures. The inspectors certify that the equipment is functioning accurately. A tag is then placed on the scales or pumps. Such equipment is also subject to periodic, unannounced inspections.

Fictitious Trade Name Registration

Some states require the fictitious name of a store to be registered with an appropriate agency within a set number of days after the business opens. This registration is necessary because the name of the firm may vary from the corporate name and often will not include the names of all owners or partners.

Credit

Consumer Credit Protection Act

Before 1969, the regulation of consumer credit was left largely to the states. However, in July 1969 the federal government entered the consumer credit field by passing the **Consumer Credit Protection Act,** commonly called the Truth-in-Lending Act. The law requires retailers to explain in easily understood language the dollar finance charge and annual percentage rate on merchandise they finance, the balance on which the charge is figured, the closing date of the billing cycle, and the rights and obligations of the customer.

Congress later passed a number of other laws affecting consumer credit, including the credit card provisions of the Truth-in-Lending Act, the Fair Credit Reporting Act, the Fair Credit Billing Act, the Equal Credit Opportunity Act, the Consumer Leasing Act, and the Fair Debt Collection Practices Act.

Fair Credit Reporting Act

The **Fair Credit Reporting Act** protects consumers' right to an accurate, up-to-date, and confidential credit report. Consumers have the right to obtain information about their credit records and to ask for a reinvestigation if the completeness or accuracy of any item in the record is questionable. Information must be given free of charge if the consumer has been denied credit within the previous 30 days.

Fair Credit Billing Act

The **Fair Credit Billing Act,** passed in 1975, sets up a billing dispute settlement procedure for "open end" credit and imposes certain other requirements on retailers to ensure fair and prompt handling of credit accounts.

The law also provides that a retailer may not be restricted by bank-card issuers from offering discounts for cash.

Equal Credit Opportunity Act

The **Equal Credit Opportunity Act,** passed in 1975, prohibits discrimination on the basis of sex or marital status in any aspect of a credit transaction. Later amendments expanded the act to prohibit discrimination based on race, color, religion, national origin, age, and receipt of income from public assistance programs.

Consumer Leasing Act

The **Consumer Leasing Act,** passed in 1977, applies to the leasing of personal property (such as automobiles and furniture) for more than four months and for which the total cost of transaction is under $25,000. The act requires the leasing company to make an accurate and detailed disclosure of all terms and costs in leasing contracts.

Fair Debt Collection Practices Act

The **Fair Debt Collection Practices Act** was passed in 1978. The intent of the law, which amends the Consumer Credit Protection Act, is to "eliminate abusive debt collection practices" and to protect the consumer from harassment and unfair collection procedures.

The most recent effort to further regulate consumer credit is a Federal Trade Commission Trade Regulation Rule, effective March 1, 1985, that restricts certain remedies used by lenders and retail installment sellers in consumer credit contracts. Its major provisions provide that:

1. A lender or retail installment seller in extending credit cannot require a consumer to sign a confession of judgment or secure any other waiver of the right to notice and the opportunity to be heard in court.
2. A customer cannot be required to provide a limitation of exemption from attachment on personal property.
3. A customer cannot be required to assign his or her wages unless this assignment is revokable at the will of the debtor.
4. A seller cannot misrepresent the nature or extent of cosigner liability to any person. To prevent such misrepresentation, a disclosure shall be given to the cosigner, prior to becoming obligated, including warnings stating, "If the borrower doesn't pay the debt, you will have to . . ." and "the creditor can collect this debt from you without first trying to collect from the borrower."[9]

Methods of Selling

Unordered Merchandise

Retailers are not allowed to ship merchandise that has not been ordered by the consumer. Consumers are not required to pay for items they do not order.

Push Money (PM)

Push money (PM) encourages the sale of certain merchandise by paying salespersons a bonus to sell the merchandise. This practice is not per se illegal. From management's point of view, allowing the use of push money paid by suppliers may cause some loss of control over their retail salespersons. On the other hand, the retailer may offer PMs to help move private brands and slow-moving merchandise.

Some forms of push money are clearly illegal. For example, payoffs by record distributors to disc jockeys are illegal. The FTC position is that this is a deceptive practice which leads consumers to believe that the records played the most often are the most popular.

Many states have so-called blue laws which prohibit the sale of various types of merchandise on Sunday. The laws have long been controversial because they are difficult to enforce and hamper the efforts of management to remain open seven days a week.

ETHICAL STANDARDS AND BUSINESS CONDUCT

The image of retailing as a whole suffers when any firm engages in unethical or questionable business practices. Such behavior should never be condoned by top management.

The allegations against retailers are numerous. Cartier, the world-renowned jeweler on Manhattan's Fifth Avenue, was indicted on 156 counts of falsifying business records. A probe by law-enforcement officials revealed that Cartier allegedly allowed some customers to supply false shipping addresses (out-of-state buyers are exempt from sales taxes). Investigators charged that Cartier sent empty boxes to the bogus addresses, but the jewels left the store in the customers' pockets.[10]

Bribery of buyers for retail stores has also been pervasive. TG&Y, a discount chain, filed charges against one of its buyers for taking bribes. Similarly, a health and beauty products buyer with Boston-based Stop and Shop companies faced similar charges, as did a buyer for Natco Industries, Inc., which operates men's apparel shops.[11]

Some retailers are including statements of ethical standards and business conduct as part of their corporate mission statements. The following is a part of the formal statement of mission and purpose for the Dayton-Hudson Corporation:

> The policy of the corporation is to maintain a consistently high standard of business conduct, ethics, and social responsibility. Individual employees are expected to demonstrate high levels of integrity and objectivity, unencumbered by conflicting interests in all decisions and actions affecting the corporation.
>
> Corporate policies governing the business conduct of employees will serve as a minimum standard of performance. Premier status requires exemplary behavior and attitudes—conduct befitting premier employees.

The unethical practices managers would most like to eliminate include gifts, gratuities, and bribes; cheating customers; unfair credit practices; and over-aggressive selling. Factors contributing to higher ethical standards include public disclosure and publicity.

EXAMPLES OF RETAILER SOCIAL RESPONSIBILITY IN SUPPORTING PROGRAMS TO LOCATE MISSING CHILDREN AND TO REDUCE CHILD ABUSE

Some of the companies that have joined in the child safety effort:

Bradlees, Braintree, Mass.—Strong Kids/Safe Kids; employee seminars.

The Broadway Southwest, Mesa, Ariz.—Childsafe, Easter event, ongoing ID program.

Diamond's, Tempe, Ariz.—Positive Parenting, Back-to-School Safely.

Foley's, Houston, Tex.—Child Protection Week.

Hess's, Allentown, Pa.—Child Awareness Day.

Jamesway, Secaucus, N.J.—"We Care" program.

K mart, Troy, Mich.—Shopping bags, ID card program.

Wal-Mart, Bentonville, Ark.—Child Safety Day.

Foodtown, Edison, N.J.—Shopping bags.

Shop-Rite, Elizabeth, N.J.—ID cards.

Trailways, Dallas, Tex.—Operation Home Free: bus transport for runaways.

Wendy's International, Dublin, Ohio—Free safety tips on calendars.

SOURCE: Reprinted from *Stores Magazine* August 1985, p. 17. © National Retail Merchants Association, 1985.

SOCIAL RESPONSIBILITY

Retailers must also exhibit thoughtful and sensitive behavior in their response to the expectations of society. Retailing suffers from a misperception that it is a profit-bound institution whose **social responsibility** is to stick to business. Retailers, however, are showing a renewed interest in social responsibility. The Dayton-Hudson Corporation has been one of the most active retailers in giving. Management contributes 5 percent of Dayton's annual pre-tax profits to community projects.

Efforts designed to locate missing children are another example of the social responsibility of retailers. The retailers' programs range from special events to ongoing programs to prevent child abduction or abuse. Activities include child-abuse awareness seminars, fingerprinting and photography programs, distribution of comic books written in cooperation with the National Committee for the Prevention of Child Abuse, printing pictures of missing children on products and bags, and distributing through retail outlets videotapes about the dangers of child abuse.[12] Examples of some of the programs are shown in Exhibit 3–1.

CHAPTER HIGHLIGHTS

— The key restraint-of-trade laws are the Sherman Act, the Clayton Act, and the Federal Trade Commission Act.

- Price-fixing is always illegal. Management cannot agree with competitors on the price at which items will be sold. Price-fixing may be either horizontal or vertical.
- Management cannot set prices so as to try to deliberately drive competition out of business. Some states also prohibit the sale of items at less than their cost.
- The Robinson-Patman Act regulates promotion practices of retailers. FTC regulations also affect all media advertising, promotional items sent through the mail, price lists, and similar promotional material. Retail ads also cannot make false or misleading claims.
- Retailers have a specific responsibility under Section 15 of the Consumer Products Safety Act to monitor the safety of the products they sell and to report any information about product hazards to the Consumer Product Safety Commission.
- The Magnuson-Moss Warranty Act is the primary warranty law affecting retailers. The law applies to written warranties for merchandise. Additionally, every sale, according to the Uniform Commercial Code, has an implied warranty of merchantability.
- The primary credit legislation affecting retailers includes the Consumer Credit Protection Act, Fair Credit Reporting Act, Fair Credit Billing Act, Equal Credit Opportunity Act, Consumer Leasing Act, and Fair Debt Collection Practices Act.
- Ethical behavior and social responsibility are becoming increasingly important issues for retailers. The image of retailing as a whole suffers when any firm engages in unethical or questionable business practices.

KEY TERMS

Clayton Act Declares certain practices illegal even if they do not actually restrain trade or do not constitute a monopoly or an attempt to monopolize.

Consumer Credit Protection Act An act requiring retailers to explain in easily understood language the dollar finance charge and annual percentage rate on the merchandise they finance.

Consumer Leasing Act An act requiring a leasing company to make an accurate and detailed disclosure of all terms and costs in leasing contracts.

Dual distribution A situation in which wholesalers also operate retail outlets.

Equal Credit Opportunity Act An act which prohibits discrimination on the basis of race, color, religion, national origin, age, sex, marital status, and receipt of income in any aspect of a credit transaction.

Exclusive dealing A situation in which a supplier prohibits a retailer from selling the products of a competitor.

Exclusive territories Territories created when suppliers limit the area in which a retailer can sell their products.

Express warranties Written warranties for products or services.

Fair Credit Billing Act An act establishing a billing dispute settlement procedure for "open-end" credit which also imposes certain other requirements on retailers to ensure fair and accurate handling of credit accounts.

Fair Credit Reporting Act Protects the consumer's right to an accurate, up-to-date, and confidential credit report.

Fair Debt Collection Practices Act An act designed to eliminate abusive debt collection practices and to protect the consumer from harassment and unfair collection procedures.

Federal Trade Commission An independent agency responsible for enforcing the Clayton Act and other antitrust laws.

Federal Trade Commission Act Legislation passed in 1914 to create the Federal Trade Commission for enforcing the Clayton Act provisions. The legislation prohibits "unfair methods" of competition as defined by the FTC and gives the FTC the power to prosecute violators.

Horizontal price-fixing An agreement among competing retailers on the price at which they will sell identical merchandise.

Implied warranty A provision of the Uniform Commercial Code which requires that all merchandise sold be fit for the purpose for which it is being sold.

Predatory pricing Setting prices to deliberately drive competition out of business.

Price discrimination Varying the prices charged to different retailers for identical merchandise without an economic justification for doing so.

Push money Money spent by suppliers to encourage the sale of certain merchandise by paying salespersons a bonus to sell the items.

Robinson-Patman Act (1936) The primary law regulating price discrimination. Not all price discrimination is illegal under the Robinson-Patman Act, but management must justify the different prices they charge to competing retailers.

Sherman Act The first law passed to maintain competition and to make every action to restrain trade illegal.

Social responsibility A belief by retailers that they have an obligation to society beyond making a profit and obeying the laws of the land.

Trade regulation rules Guidelines issued by the FTC which must be followed in selling certain products or services.

Vertical price fixing Often referred to as resale price maintenance, a situation in which manufacturers set minimum prices at which their products must be sold.

DISCUSSION QUESTIONS

1. Summarize the key restraint-of-trade laws and their impact on retail activities.
2. What are trade regulation rules? What are some retail activities covered by trade regulation rules?
3. What is meant by the term *predatory pricing*?
4. Why do some states have sales-below-cost laws that set prices below which it is illegal to sell certain merchandise?
5. What is meant by the term *good-faith defense*?
6. What is "bait and switch" advertising? Is this activity illegal?
7. What is meant by each of the following terms which relate to the distribution aspect of the marketing plan: *exclusive territories, exclusive dealing,* and *dual distribution*?
8. What precautions must a retailer take in advertising warranties on merchandise?
9. Review the key credit legislation of which the retailer must be aware.
10. Present arguments for and against this statement: Retailers have a social responsibility to society beyond making a profit and obeying the laws of the land.

APPLICATION EXERCISES

1. Visit the managers of two or three of the retail outlets in your city. Find out their major problems with government regulation. Which functions of the business seem most heavily affected? Does the manager think the regulations serve a useful purpose? Try to find out if the manager has an active affirmative action plan.
2. Shop at several stores for a major consumer durable such as a dishwasher. Ask to see the warranties for the several models in the store. Are the warranties readily available to shoppers? Are the salespersons careful in the statements they make about the warranties? In your opinion, are they making oral statements that go beyond the written statements? Summarize in writing your view of the stores in terms of their compliance with warranty regulations.

CASES

1. Discounters Fight Cuts in Their Supplies*

Not long ago, an eager bargain hunter could buy a Pioneer stereo receiver through a catalog showroom and save a good $100. But no more. Last June, Pioneer cut off distribution to all catalog showrooms, saying it wanted to thin out dealer ranks.

"Our product was overdistributed," explains Jack Doyle, president of Pioneer Electronics (USA) Inc. "When you have a product in too many places, it doesn't have much value to anybody," he adds.

Nonsense, say some discounters; Pioneer just wanted to get rid of the price choppers. "The end result is that consumers pay more" for Pioneer equipment, says Tracy Mandart, president of H. J. Wilson Co., a large catalog showroom dealer.

Many manufacturers besides Pioneer have choked off supplies to discounters in recent months, and the discounters are fighting back. They say cutting off a discount store constitutes price-fixing, violates antitrust laws, threatens the discount industry, and forces millions of consumers to pay higher prices in full-price stores.

Transshipping, in which discounters buy their merchandise from authorized dealers with overstock instead of from manufacturers, raises another issue in the discount pricing fight. "We don't terminate anybody for discounting," says Stephen F. Lichtenstein, secretary of Lenox Inc. But transshipping to unauthorized price-cutters "takes away control of our image," he adds.

"Our authorized dealers have magnificent displays, and they have people who are trained to discuss fine china," Mr. Lichtenstein says. Several other manufacturers have sought FTC permission to stop their dealers from transshipping.

Questions

1. Should manufacturers be allowed to terminate their relationships with authorized dealers who transship merchandise to unauthorized dealers? Why or why not?
2. Discuss the merits of exclusive distribution from the perspective of the manufacturer, the retailer, and the consumer.

Source: "Discounters Fight Cuts in Their Supplies," *The Wall Street Journal*, June 21, 1983, p. 37. Reprinted by permission of *The Wall Street Journal*, © Dow Jones & Company Inc., June 21, 1983. All rights reserved.

2. Thorp Finance Corporation and Alleged Deceptive Practices

It was the month before Christmas, and Katherine Snow, an unmarried mother, needed money. Subsisting on a monthly income of only $423, Ms. Snow sought help from Thorp Finance Corp., a consumer-loan company in Wisconsin.

Thorp agreed to lend Ms. Snow $126.72, but it also induced Ms. Snow to borrow $14.74 for credit life insurance, $73.44 for property insurance, and $202 for term life insurance. Finally, for an additional $24.50, Ms. Snow became a member of the Consumer Thrift Club offered by Thorp, entitling her to discounts on consumer products.

Ms. Snow would later say she didn't know she had purchased all the extras, financed at interest rates above 22 percent. "I bought more insurance than I borrowed money, if that makes any sense," Ms. Snow testified last year in circuit court in Dane County, Wisconsin, in connection with a lawsuit filed by the Wisconsin attorney general charging Thorp with "deceptive and unconscionable" sales practices.

Wisconsin officials say Ms. Snow was a victim of "packing," a lucrative practice in which a lender adds payments for "optional" insurance and other products to the amount of the loan without the customer's requesting them.

Indeed, many customers often don't want, need, or even understand the products they have purchased. Victims are frequently poor, unsophisticated, or so desperate for money that they will sign practically anything placed in front of them, law enforcement officials say.

Packing has been a common practice in many consumer loan operations, according to the former employees and customers. The company declines to discuss individual cases, but the general counsel for ITT Consumer Financial Corp., the corporate parent of Thorp, says: "Our company policy is crystal clear: Each customer is to understand the products they purchase and that the purchase of them is voluntary." Internal company memorandums, however, show that branch managers were ordered to sell certain amounts of insurance in connection with loans, or face disciplinary action.

Some former employees say they couldn't meet company goals without packing insurance that customers didn't want into loan agreements. Packing violates federal and many states' laws if lenders coerce borrowers into buying insurance from them as a condition for getting loans or if that insurance isn't fully explained.

Questions

1. What reasons exist for inducing consumers to buy such varied types of insurance and for financing the purchase of the insurance?
2. Why do consumers seek to borrow from small loan companies instead of dealing with more conventional financial institutions?
3. Are small loan companies justified in charging interest rates of 20 percent or higher to small loan customers? Present arguments for and against the practice.

ENDNOTES

1. "Toys- R-Us Charges Restraint of Trade," *Chain Store Age, General Merchandise Edition,* November 1983, p. 7.
2. "Jerrico, Inc., Four Others Named in Trust Suits Seeking $110 Million," *The Wall Street Journal,* February 24, 1983, p. 53.
3. Hal Taylor, "Waldbaum and Stop and Shop Indicted for Fixing Prices," *Supermarket News,* August 20, 1984, p. 1.
4. Mary Jane Sheffett and Deborah L. Scammon, "Resale Price Maintenance: Is It Safe to Suggest Retail Prices?" *Journal of Marketing* 49 (Fall 1985), pp. 82–91; Thomas R. Overstreet, Jr., and Allan A. Fisher, "Resale Price Maintenance and Distributional Efficiency: Some Lessons from the Past," *Contemporary Policy Issues* 3 (Spring 1985), pp. 43–54; Terry Calvani and James Lagenfeld, "An Overview of the Current Debate on Resale Price Maintenance," *Contemporary Policy Issues* 3 (Spring 1985), pp. 1–7; "Head of FTC Asks Repeal of R-P Act," *Supermarket News,* August 18, 1986, p. 1.
5. "FTC Reopens, Widens Probe of Federated Department Stores," *The Wall Street Journal,* October 29, 1984, p. 2.
6. Guy Adamo, "Mail-Order Law Successful in Crackdown on Deceptive Practices," *Marketing News,* August 16, 1985, p. 12.
7. "FTC Upheld in Sears, Litton Case," *Advertising Age,* May 24, 1982, p. 15.
8. For further reading, see William L. Trombretta, "Exclusive Dealing Contracts Require Caution by Health-Care Marketers," *Marketing News,* October 11, 1985, p. 27.
9. Reprinted from Dorothy Cohen, "New Consumer Credit Regulations Raise Questions of Effectiveness," *Marketing News,* April 12, 1985, p. 27.
10. "Cartier's Empty Box," *Time,* April 1, 1985, p. 59.
11. Frank Gilman, "Bribery of Retail Buyers Is Called Pervasive," *The Wall Street Journal,* April 1, 1985, p. 6; "Bribery of Buyers Called Easy Way to Do Business," *Supermarket News,* March 31, 1986, p. 1.
12. "Supermarket Chains Join in Quest for Missing Children," *Marketing News,* October 14, 1985, p. 22; "Protecting the Kids," *Stores,* August 1985, pp. 16–18.

4

The Economic and Social Environments

RETAILING CAPSULE

The Party at Mary Kay Isn't Quite So Lively Anymore

Call Carole Fischer, one of the Philadelphia saleswomen for Mary Kay Cosmetics, Inc., and you often get a tape-recorded message. In it, she breathlessly urges you to contact her through an answering service, "if it is indeed an emergency and your face may fall off before I get back to you." Lately, however, it is Mary Kay Cosmetics itself that is losing face.

Much of Mary Kay's success, like that of similar companies, depends on constantly replenishing its sales force, which now stands at more than 200,000 women and several hundred men.

The new people place big initial orders, generating nearly two thirds of Mary Kay's annual sales and healthy commissions for its sales directors. They also bring in other recruits. Without a successful recruiting program, outfits like Mary Kay, Avon Products, Inc., and Premark International's Tupperware face stagnant sales and declining profits and morale.

Students of the industry blame its problems on a number of factors: the increasing number of working women, which cuts into the number of available recruits and sales targets; the improvement in the economy which encourages women to avoid involvement in part-time sales and to shop for more expensive beauty products; and growing competition.

Portions quoted with permission from "The Party at Mary Kay Isn't Quite So Lively as Recruiting Falls Off," *The Wall Street Journal,* October 28, 1983, p. 1. Reprinted by permission of *The Wall Street Journal,* © Dow Jones & Company, Inc., October 28, 1983. All rights reserved. See also, "How Tupperware Hopes to Liven Up the Party," *Business Week,* February 25, 1985, p. 108; and "Avon Tries a New Formula to Restore Its Glow," *Business Week,* July 2, 1984, p. 46.

Some experts see more profound changes working against direct-sales concerns. Harry Davis, a professor of marketing at the University of Chicago, cites the changing relations of individuals within their own families and communities.

"The whole direct-selling approach operates by networks of relationships," he says, with women selling to their extended families, friends, and neighbors. But, Davis notes, "there has been a breakdown in some social ties" because of divorce, relocation, and changing lifestyles. He points out that party-plan selling continues to do best in close-knit working-class and ethnic areas, such as South Side Chicago neighborhoods dominated by Lithuanian and Polish Americans.

As the Mary Kay story shows, retailing is a very competitive business. Thousands of firms fail each year. The failures range from the smallest "mom and pop" operations to such giants as W. T. Grant and Woolco. Why is competition so fierce? Persons can get started in retailing without much money, most competing retailers carry essentially the same items, and most competing retailers operate in the same manner. Thus, retailers who don't accurately read warning signs can easily be wiped out. Retailers now face a competitive world characterized by saturated markets, rapid shifts in consumer moods, shifting value systems, an aging population, and rapid technological changes in the marketplace.

After reading this chapter you will be able to:

1. Evaluate the new consumer demographics.

2. Describe the mood of today's consumer.

3. Explain how changes in the economy affect retailing.

4. Discuss how changes in competition affect retailing.

ENVIRONMENTAL DYNAMICS

Retailers cannot always anticipate the rapid changes that can occur in the environments that can so vitally affect their future. Weather problems such as floods or blizzards can cost retailers millions of dollars in lost sales, and many of the losses are uninsured. Unforeseen rapid increases in interest rates led to many retail failures in the early 1980s. More recently, rapidly rising costs for liability insurance have driven some bars and nightclubs out of business.

Totally new forms of products or services can make some stores almost obsolete overnight. A few years ago, watches were sold mostly at jewelry stores. Today, they are sold in virtually every type of retail outlet. Video-cassette players and the low rental fees for the videocassette movies are threatening the future of movie houses.

Increased interest by consumers in fitness and health have led to the rapid growth of health spas and fitness centers. The continued acceleration in the number of working mothers has allowed Kinder-Care Learning Centers to become the nation's largest chain of day care centers, to expand its outlets to approximately 1,500 units, and to project sales and earnings growth at 30 percent per year well into the 1990s. Similarly, the growing number of two-income households has provided pressure to abolish Sunday closing laws and to keep retail stores open longer hours in the evening and on the weekend to meet the needs of working adults.

WHAT ARE THE NEW CONSUMER DEMOGRAPHICS?

Changes in the consumer demographics are critical since they affect the current and projected sizes of market segments. All of us have probably heard discussions of the buying behavior of Yuppies (young urban professionals). But changes in other population segments can be equally important in affecting retail strategy. The primary changes in the population include:

— Smaller households.
— Two-income households.
— Growth in suburbs.
— Changing age mixes.
— An older population.
— Regional growth.
— Growth in smaller communities.
— Mobility.
— Growth in subcultures and minorities.

Smaller Households

One- and two-person households now comprise 59 percent of all households. This group includes singles, widows, empty nesters, childless and unmarried couples, and younger couples planning to have children later. These small households are prime prospects for townhouses, condominiums, kitchen mini-appliances, and packaged goods in single servings. SSWDs (single, separated, widowed, and divorced) spend more money on travel and entertainment, but they save less and tend to buy more services.

Two-Income Households

Households with two or more wage earners account for more than 70 percent of all families.[1] They have more than two thirds of total family buying power. These households spend more for luxuries, though in many cases the second wage earners are working to pay off family debt. Working wives offer many markets for new services. They especially want products and services that offer them convenience and help save time.

Growth in Suburbs

The suburbs now account for more than half of all U.S. sales. During the past decade more Americans left such areas as New York and Chicago than moved into them. Younger and more affluent persons are the ones moving. Older and poorer consumers are left behind. Still, some evidence indicates that residential movement to central cities is again occurring as households start to restore older, elegant, larger homes in such areas.

Changing Age Mixes

The under-40 age group now constitutes the largest segment of the population and is dominated by baby boomers (persons born between 1946 and 1964) struggling to launch careers, establish families, and develop investment plans. The baby boomers are aging, however, and by the year 2000 the largest population segment will be persons 35–54 years of age, as shown in Figure 4–1.

Over the next 15 years the so-called baby boomers will swell the ranks of middle-aged Americans by more than 1 million a year. These persons are bringing with them changes in lifestyles, values, and outlooks. We are already seeing some such changes. At one time the idea of a 45-year-old rock star such as Mick Jagger or Tina Turner would have been absurd. Today no one thinks twice about the phenomenon.[2]

The baby boomers accept many traditional values of their parents such as a commitment to family and a patriotic attitude toward the nation. They also respect authority, but are more liberal than their parents on such issues as abortion, premarital sex, and the use of marijuana.[3]

Many of the baby boomers have college degrees and white-collar jobs, but have found that these attainments do not guarantee either affluence or financial security. The baby boomers making under $30,000 a year are a primary target for Levitt's Furniture Stores, discount clothing stores such as T. H. Mandy and Loehmann's, cosmetics companies such as Avon, the supermarket warehouse stores, and fast-food outlets such as Wendy's.

FIGURE 4-1 AGING AMERICANS

The United States will have 105.9 million households by the year 2000, a 22 percent increase from 1985. The breakdown by age of the head of the household (in millions) is:

	1985	2000	Change
Under 25	5.4	4.4	− 18%
25–29	9.6	7.8	− 19
30–34	10.4	10.2	− 2
35–44	17.5	25.3	+ 45
45–54	12.6	21.6	+ 71
55–64	13.1	13.9	+ 6
65–74	10.9	11.5	+ 6
75 and over	7.3	11.1	+ 52

An Older Population

The average age of the population in 1970 was 28 and in the year 2000 will be 35. These changes mean shifts in what is bought. People as a whole will be more conservative than today. The demand for health-related services will also rise.

A corollary to the older population is the increasing number of first children being born to older women. The number of births has been increasing steadily for the past 10 years because more women are of child-bearing age than in previous decades. The number of first births exceeds 42 percent, as high as it has ever been. The under-age-five segment of the U.S. population has soared 9 percent since 1980, in contrast to a 5 percent decline in the 1970s.[4]

Today's parents have more money to spend on children, and parents tend to spend more money on the first child than on subsequent children. Also parents are now buying things that historically have been beyond the means of most parents: educational toys, children's designer clothing, and imported strollers, for example.

Women today are likely to be part of two-career households, even after the baby is born. Such parents have very little discretionary time, accounting for the popularity of such stores as Toys-R-Us which provide a wide selection, a deep inventory, and discount prices on their toys. Company officials also believe the same formula will work in children's wear as they are now opening Kids-R-Us clothing stores at a fast pace.[5]

Although the number of births has risen, bigger families are not making a comeback. Typically, couples are having only one child. The irony, thus, is that in spite of the increasing number of babies being born, the U.S. birth rate is at an all-time low. Women today will have an average of only 1.8 children, 52 percent below the peak years of the baby boom and too low to maintain the current population. If present trends continue, deaths in the United States will exceed births by the year 2034. If the trend continues, the population will decline rapidly thereafter.[6]

Regional Growth	The Sun Belt and western states grew faster than other areas during the past decade. The West and South now have far more than half of the U.S. population. For example, these two regions accounted for 86 percent of U.S. population growth in the past decade. California, Texas, and Florida alone accounted for 35 percent of the total population gain during this period. Many Sun Belt and western states also have a higher birthrate because of their younger populations. The growth in the Sun Belt and the West did not occur largely because people were retiring and moving to those areas.[7]

Growth in the last half of the 1980s has been the highest on the east and west coasts, largely because of the depressed oil economy, farm foreclosures, and generally poor economic conditions in much of the South and Midwest.

Population density remains highest in the pocket of states east of the Mississippi River and north of the Mason-Dixon line. The 10 most densely populated states, based on the latest census, are: New Jersey, Rhode Island, Massachusetts, Connecticut, Maryland, New York, Delaware, Pennsylvania, Ohio, and Illinois, plus the District of Columbia. These states produce a higher dollar volume of retail sales per square mile than any other states.

Growth in Smaller Communities	The largest rate of growth continues to be in the smaller market areas—cities with populations of 50,000 to 200,000. On the average, these areas over the past decade had a population growth rate nearly four times that of the United States. Their retail sales' growth rate is one and a half times the national average.

Mobility	Today's shoppers are extremely mobile. Most households have at least two automobiles. Shoppers thus will travel considerable distances to shop at an appealing place either for specialty merchandise or for unique sensations as part of the shopping experience. Such a phenomenon has led to lower store loyalty than in the past. As many as 20 percent of the households in a community will move in a given year. Some of the moves are within a community, but many others are out-of-city moves. Such mobility means that consumers often look for recognized brand names and warranties that will be honored regardless of where they might live, thus, in many instances, favoring the national chains.

Growth in Subcultures and Minorities	Blacks and Hispanics are among the fastest growing market segments in the United States. Approximately 30 million black Americans live in the United States and represent over 20 percent of central city populations and approximately 20 percent of the population in the South. Blacks account for over 40 percent of the total population in cities such as Washington, D.C., Detroit, Birmingham, New Orleans, Newark, St. Louis, Atlanta, and Baltimore.

More than 12 million Hispanics live in the United States. The number exceeds 20 million if one includes illegal aliens. Hispanic Americans are expected to surpass blacks as the largest ethnic minority in the United States by the end of this decade. Los Angeles, with a population of almost 2 million Hispanics, is the world's second largest Mexican-American conglomeration after Mexico. New York surpasses San Juan in Hispanic population (1.3 million). The Hispanic population is also heavily concentrated in the Southwest and parts of the far West such as California.

Most of the growth in the under-21 population in the next decade will occur in the subcultures just mentioned. Such trends have major implications for the retail work force and for the merchandising strategies that will be necessary to serve these markets.

TODAY'S CONSUMER

Understanding shifts in ages and location of markets is not enough to help management plan for the future with confidence. Management also needs to understand how potential consumers of their products and services think and act. Changing consumer attitudes can be as important as changing economic conditions.

The Mood of the Consumer[8]

The current consumer mood can be described as "an age of . . . creativity, self-expression, and individualism." People are seeking a higher quality of life. Consider the following evidence:

— The growing consumer tendency to reject the artificial in favor of the natural, whether in ingredients, products, appearance, or behavior.
— The growing number of middle-aged adults refusing promotions because they would have to relocate.
— The appearance of books on the nonfiction, best-seller lists such as *Total Fitness, The Save Your Life Diet,* and *Overcoming Stress.*
— The march of females into the labor force, a trend only partly due to economic factors.
— Serious concern about appearance and fitness. People have become fanatical about jogging and bicycling.
— Preoccupation with status and personal achievements. Sales of Gucci, Cartier, and Yves St. Laurent products have grown rapidly.
— Commercials exploiting the drive for personal success are quite acceptable.

Because of these factors, today's consumers have been named the "Sensation Generation."

The Sensation Generation will pay a premium price for a premium sensation. For the Sensation Generation, a truly sensational experience is an experience they can touch or feel.

The Sensation Generation doesn't separate, it participates. People wind-surf, ride motorcycles, drive convertibles, climb mountains, and go on hair-raising roller coasters. Even walking can be sensational. They don't just play games; they participate in sensational fantasies such as "Dungeons and Dragons." Or they go to *The Rocky Horror Picture Show,* where the stars are the audience members.

To get a premium price, hotel lobbies must be sensational. Shopping malls must be sensational. The Sensation Generation represents some sensational marketing opportunities. Understanding the values of this generation can give a marketer a genuine competitive edge. West Edmonton Mall, located in Canada, is a good example of the response of consumers to the sensations of shopping. The mall is a 5 million-square-foot amusement shopping complex under glass—half theme park, half retail. Shoppers travel literally hundreds of miles, and some from foreign countries, just to experience the mall. Shopping is more than just a pastime in itself. It's a leisure and entertainment pastime as well.

One big, new value is really quite old. To this generation, "old-fashioned is new-fashioned." Old-fashioned things are suddenly modern, such as old townhouses, old railroad stations, old churches, old bridges, old toys, old clocks, old movies, old furniture, old styles, old cars, and old music.

The acquisition of the old-fashioned object is not in itself the goal. It is what the object represents. The new-fashioned generation seeks old-fashioned values and pursues them in many forms. An old-fashioned actor and actress are stars in an old-fashioned romantic movie. The new-fashioned generation loves it and gives them the Academy Award. The old big-band sound is the new sound. Dream cars are antique cars. Ralph Lauren designs "Rough Wear." Norman Rockwell is in. The "Woman of the Year" is Lauren Bacall. College kids stay up late to see the Marx Brothers, the Three Stooges, or Humphrey Bogart.

Old-fashioned ice cream, yogurt, hand-dipped chocolate confections, frilly nightgowns, fur coats, real wood furniture, clocks with hands, clothes made of wool, wine, bottled spring water, and leather boots all reflect old-fashioned values in a very modern world.

Many people are still terrified of technology. They are scared of synthetics. They are concerned about commercialism. Looking back is a way of fighting back.

So modern marketers have a big opportunity. Consumers are not saying, "Give me the old things." They are saying, "Give me the old values." Management who can demonstrate that modern products and services are consistent with or enhance these values have a way to capture a big share of the nation's heart.

Old-fashioned values in a new-fashioned world. These values can elect politicians. They can and do elect brands. Haagen-Dazs ice cream, Dannon yogurt, Calvin Klein jeans, Jack Daniel's whiskey, Seiko-Lasalle watches, Camel Lights cigarettes, Mondavi premium varietal wines, Bill Blass chocolates, and on and on.

Clearly, consumers are not turning their backs on money and what it can buy, but their priorities have changed. They know that money may not bring personal happiness. The quality of their lives today is at least as important as material gain.

No one knows how long this mood will prevail, but management needs to be aware of what's going on in the consumer's mind. Management has difficulty attracting a food-buying consumer who is concerned about health, nutrition, convenience, speed, cost, and gourmet cooking all at once.

WHAT ARE THE MAJOR CONSUMER SEGMENTS?

The things people value and their behavior patterns lead to diverse groups of consumers with different needs. The resulting consumer segments can be defined as follows, recognizing that some overlap does exist:

— The buy-for-one consumer.
— The stability-seeking consumer.
— The get-my-money's-worth consumer.
— The time-buying consumer.

The *buy-for-one consumer* represents the rapidly expanding number of single-person households comprised of divorced persons, people living alone, and single, elderly households. These persons spend their time and money differently. They seek food items packaged in single servings. They use utensils especially made for preparing meals for one person. They have more time for leisure and consequently spend more on entertainment and travel. They are prime targets for townhouses and condominiums, but poor markets for insurance.

Many of these persons are upwardly mobile professionals with high earning power and equally high expectations of the marketplace. They are good customers who expect quality products and quality service.

The *stability-seeking consumer* normally represents a blue-collar, middle-class household. Such people provide a good market for many products and services including durables such as recreation equipment and equipment for various do-it-yourself activities.

Stability-seeking consumers are somewhat overwhelmed by the rapid changes occurring around them. They seek (1) a return to yesterday (watching the "Lucy" TV program), (2) a return to nature (by buying indoor plants), and (3) life simplification (with hobbies and do-it-yourself activities that give them a sense of control over their destinies). This group of consumers readily responds to friendliness, personal attention, the hard work ethic, and the traditional American value and morality structure.

The *get-my-money's-worth consumer* is something of a consumer activist, an admirer of Ralph Nader, and a supporter of various social-activist causes. Persons of this type look for good values—though not always at the lowest price. They seek energy-efficient homes and appliances and look for durability. They substitute consumer labor for consumer costs. This group uses self-service gasoline stations and is willing to use inferior goods and services such as powdered meat extender and non–brand name products.

The *time-buying consumer* reflects the rapidly growing number of households with two or more incomes. More and more females are entering the labor force, either for self-fulfillment or because of economic necessity. Two-income households have an added pressure of time. The female often maintains the household in addition to a full-time job outside the home. Such households are prone to use telephone shopping services, to purchase well-known national brands, and to be receptive to such appliances as microwave ovens which save time.

WHAT ARE THE CHANGES IN THE COMPETITIVE ENVIRONMENTS?

Understanding Competition

Competition between retailers is a fact of life. The most familiar type of competition is **intratype competition.** Intratype competition is competition between two retailers of the same type, such as two drugstores. Most people are familiar with intratype competition since this is the model most frequently described in basic economics texts. Intratype competition is not limited to tangible goods retailers. Such competition can exist between hospitals, banks, financial institutions, churches, and educational institutions.

A second competitive model is **intertype competition** which is competition between different types of retail outlets selling the same merchandise. Intertype competition is one of the most familiar models of retail competition today. For example, Kroger Superstores compete with K mart in the nonfood lines sold by Kroger. Intertype competition is heavy in health and beauty aids, hardware products, and inexpensive glassware. Traditionally, health and beauty aids were sold primarily by department stores or drugstores; hardware in hardware stores; and glassware in variety stores.

Corporate systems competition occurs when a single-management ownership links resources, manufacturing capability, and distribution networks. The Limited is an example of corporate systems competition. They manufacture some of their merchandise, handle their own storage and distribution functions, and perform all management activities necessary for the sale of goods and services at the retail level.

Total systems networks can be formed either by backward or forward integration. In **forward integration,** a manufacturer establishes its own wholesale and retail network. Examples are Goodyear, Singer, and Sherwin Williams. **Backward integration** occurs when a retailer or wholesaler performs some manufacturing functions. Sears is an example. Sears began buying into suppliers in the 1920s when it expanded from an all-catalog store to a department store retailer and wanted a dependable source of supply.

The different types of competition do not exist in isolation. Retail firms in all channel structures face competition from retailers in any or all of the other systems. Also, our comments must be regarded only as broad generalizations about the nature of competition and the various types of channel systems because numerous exceptions exist.

The New Face of Competition

The competitive structure of retailing as a whole is undergoing rapid change. The changes are causing a rethinking of the concepts of retail competition and are also causing changes in consumer shopping habits.

Secondary Market Expansion. **Secondary market expansion** (expansion into small markets) is an increasingly attractive move. Thus, firms such as Wal-Mart typically face less competition, are able to pay lower wages, and face fewer zoning and other restrictions. Typically secondary markets are communities of 200,000 or fewer persons which are understored in terms of national competitors. They provide more viable markets than many of the major metropolitan markets which are already served by almost every major retailer.

Extremes in Establishment Types. The trend today can be described as diversity in retail outlets. Broad-based merchandising firms such as Lowes, with their home improvement centers and discount pricing, have made major inroads into the markets of traditional hardware stores. The other high-growth market, at the opposite end of the scale, is the specialty store which carries a deep assortment of a very specialized line, often limited to a concept or "look," as opposed to commodity types. One example is Open Country, shown in Figure 4–2. Other examples include Hickory Farms, Radio Shack, and Benetton. Their entire operations are programmed to a specific market segment, and they project a sharply defined image as a result.

Supermarket Retailing. The supermarket concept, long familiar in the food field, has been adopted by many other types of retailers. The key elements of **supermarket retailing** are (1) self-service and self-selection, (2) large-scale but low-cost physical facilities, (3) a strong price emphasis, (4) simplification and centralization of customer services, and (5) a wide variety and broad assortment of merchandise. This concept has been successful in many lines of trade including sporting goods (Sportmart), home improvement (Handy Dan), and furniture and housewares (Ikea).

The new face of competition can be illustrated in the context of food retailing. *Superstores* are 30,000 square feet or larger and have service departments not found in a conventional supermarket, including an on-premises bakery, a service deli, and a wine and cheese shop. A larger percentage of sales is in general merchandise than in a conventional supermarket.

Hypermarkets have sales as high as $40 million a year. They make heavy use of warehousing techniques and experience large average transactions sizes often associated with infrequent purchasing. They are the largest of any size of food store. The *combination stores* are a merger of two different

SOURCE: Courtesy of the Melville Corporation.

types of retailing operations. They maintain a drugstore atmosphere by means of a pharmacy. They also sell franchise cosmetics and have a strong health and beauty aids orientation. *Warehouse markets* have a strong warehouse orientation, strong price appeal, a limited general merchandise emphasis, a low operating expense ratio compared to conventional supermarkets, and limited customer service.

Limited-assortment stores are typically located near more conventional food stores. They have a merchandise assortment of less than 1,000 stock-keeping units, feature discount pricing, rely heavily on regional and house labels, and carry only a limited assortment of perishables. Talking about a supermarket really has very little meaning in the competitive environment we have outlined.

Shortening Life Cycles.   The life cycles for many types of retailing are becoming shorter. Department stores, for example, moved from a period of early growth to maturity in 80–100 years, while variety stores moved from accelerated growth in the 1930s to virtual oblivion as a type of institution by 1960. Other types of more recent retailing innovations such as video gamerooms covered the cycle from introduction to maturity in less than a decade.

Escalation of Price Competition.   Increasingly firms are ''buying'' a share of the market as a result of the intensified price competition emerging because of the struggle for market share. Thus, retailers projecting a strong price and value image are the ones most likely to increase their market share today.

Growing Importance of Power Marketing Programs. Many manufacturers now offer merchants comprehensive merchandising programs known as **power marketing programs.** The manufacturers seek superior results by offering the retailer a complete merchandising program. Suppliers handle everything from price to inventory to display. The result is that they establish strong market positions in their merchandise lines. L'eggs and American Greeting Cards are examples of such power marketing programs offered to retailers.

Market Saturation. Many people today believe the United States has too many stores. One author has observed that "it looks as if the country has finally got itself fully malled and chained."[9] Merchants with the wrong kinds of stores in the wrong kinds of places get hurt and are forced out of business.

Sales per square foot, when adjusted for inflation, are less than they were a decade ago. The result of such a situation has been a frenzy of competitive price-cutting. Most retailers can only look forward to stiffening competition and disappointing profits. Only the smartest merchandisers will be the exception to this situation. The Marketing Science Institute, in a recent publication entitled "Future Trends in Retailing," observed that "in 1990 dismal space productivity will continue to characterize American retailing."[10]

Department store retailers have gradually pushed their markups to 90–100 percent and gross profit margins to 45–50 percent in an effort to remain profitable in this intensively competitive market. Discount stores now have markups of 60 percent and margins of 30 percent. Overstoring is a threat to all retailers who haven't found the key to the shoppers' new taste for excitement, good quality, fair prices, and fashion. The signs of adjustment to overstoring are visible everywhere. Today, shopping centers are renting to retailers such as auto parts stores, exercise studios, and persons seeking office space. Until recently, shopping center developers would not lease to such individuals. The building of shopping centers also has dropped dramatically.

Some observers, however, see the problem not as one of overstoring but as one that has resulted from the failure of retailers to differentiate themselves from others in the marketplace, thereby making themselves unique and desirable to the customer. Some retailers are achieving success. One category of winners today is the power retailers. **Power retailers** include merchandisers such as The Limited, Inc. Such retailers have "such financial strength, marketing skill, and reasonably priced quality merchandise that they can bull their way into any market, however saturated, and make a profit."[11] Such merchants believe that the United States today is still understored in the types of stores that customers want and that the only overstoring is among retailers who don't give good service or good value.

The Increasing International Focus of Retailing. These days, large retailers often import directly from foreign countries. They do this to save money on the cost of the goods, but they sometimes have problems with delivery and

FIGURE 4–3

SOURCE: Courtesy of Wendy's.

poor product quality. Also, import restrictions are making it increasingly difficult for retailers to purchase merchandise from foreign suppliers.[12]

Supporters of limits on the imports of foreign merchandise were successful in getting the Federal Trade Commission to issue a country-of-origin labeling regulation. The new regulation requires retailers to tell their customers where their garments are made. Supporters of the regulation believe that it will limit consumer purchases of merchandise made in foreign countries.[13]

During the past decade, many foreign firms have purchased an interest in or bought control of major U.S. retailers. Several factors can explain the growth of foreign investment: the devaluation of the dollar, the size of the U.S. retail market, the stable U.S. political/legal environment, the U.S. labor and economic climates, and the advantages of real estate ownership associated with retailing.

Many retailers have expanded into U.S. markets by acquiring existing firms. For example, B.A.T. Industries of Great Britain acquired Marshall Field's, Saks-Fifth Avenue, and Gimbels stores in the United States. The Tinglemann Company of West Germany owns 51 percent of A&P Supermarkets. Such acquisitions are attractive because they provide for quick start-up and access to prime locations.

Joint ventures that occur when two firms combine to form a new organization are being used more frequently as a means of expanding in international markets. Also, Sears and K mart have arrangements with Japanese retailers such as Daiei to sell the organizations' private label U.S. goods. Still other outlets, such as McDonald's, Wendy's (shown in Figure 4–3), and Burger King, have franchised outlets in many foreign countries.

Some foreign firms have achieved notable success in U.S. markets. Esprit, the ready-to-wear apparel retailer, has outlets in Los Angeles and New Orleans as well as several successful stores in Hong Kong and Australia. Benetton, the Italian knitwear manufacturer, sells its clothing at retail in the United States through licensed stores. The number of Benetton licensed stores is projected to exceed 1,500 by 1990. Ikea, the Swedish furniture retailer, has opened an outlet in Philadelphia and has plans to open a variety of other outlets in the United States. The firm sells Swedish-designed furniture in "flat pack" kits that customers assemble at home. Finally, Laura Ashley, the British chain of women's fashions and home furnishings, also has a significant presence in the United States and has built its customer base primarily by using catalogs as an advertising tool.

CHAPTER HIGHLIGHTS

— The new family relationships can be described as less marriage, later marriage, and more divorce.

— The primary changes in the population of importance to retailers include smaller households, two-income households, growth of suburbs, changing family relationships, age mix changes, an older population, growth in the Sun Belt, and growth in smaller communities.

— In the mid-1980s the under-40 age group constituted the largest segment of the population and was dominated by baby boomers. By the year 2000 the largest population segment will be persons 35–54 years of age.

— Increasing numbers of first children are being born to older women. These women are likely to remain a part of two-career households, even after the baby is born.

— Sun Belt states and other states are growing faster than other areas. Population density, however, still remains highest in the pocket of states east of the Mississippi River and north of the Mason-Dixon line.

— The largest population growth is in smaller market areas, cities with populations of 50,000–200,000.

— The key consumer segments for this decade include the buy-for-one consumer, the stability-seeking consumer, the get-my-money's-worth consumer, and the time-buying consumer.

— Consumers are seeking products that are low in initial cost, resistant to obsolescence, durable, and energy efficient.

— The primary types of competition include intratype competition, intertype competition, and corporate systems competition.

— The competitive structure of retailing as a whole is undergoing rapid change. The changes include the following: secondary market expansion, extremes in establishment types, supermarket retailing, shortening life cycles, escalation of price competition, the growing importance of power marketing programs, and an increasing importance of the international dimensions of retailing.

KEY TERMS

Backward integration A development that occurs when a retailer or wholesaler performs some manufacturing functions.

Corporate systems competition A type of competition that occurs when a single management ownership links resources, manufacturing capability, and distribution networks. Examples include Sears and The Limited.

Forward integration A situation in which a manufacturer establishes its own wholesale and retail networks.

Intertype competition Competition between different types of retail outlets selling the same merchandise.

Intratype competition Competition among retailers of the same type.

Power marketing programs Programs in which manufacturers handle everything from price to inventory to display for a particular line of merchandise. An example would be merchandise programs for L'eggs and American Greeting Cards.

Power retailers Retailers with sufficient financial strength, marketing skill, and reasonably priced, quality merchandise to establish dominance in any market, however saturated, and make a profit.

Retail niching Marketing programs designed to offer customers something unique and thereby carve out a particular slice of the market.

Secondary market expansion Development of retail outlets in communities with 50,000–200,000 population.

Supermarket retailing A type of retailing characterized by self-service and self-selection, large-scale but low-cost physical facilities, strong price emphasis, simplification and centralization of customer services, and a wide variety and broad assortment of merchandise.

DISCUSSION QUESTIONS

1. Why is competition so intense in retailing today? Does this competitive intensity have an impact on retailers' needs to monitor and forecast environmental changes? Explain your answer.
2. Summarize the changes that are occurring in the demographic profile of consumers and households in our society, and the likely impact on retail operations.
3. Which geographical regions are experiencing population growth? Will these changes increase the probable success of a retail outlet in these areas? Why or why not? Does this mean that opportunities for retailing will not remain good in other parts of the United States? Discuss.
4. Summarize the information presented in the text with respect to changes in the values and lifestyles of consumers.
5. Such measures of change as the national unemployment rate and the rate of inflation may be misleading to a retailer. How can management avoid being misdirected by these indicators of change? What types of information would be useful at the store level? How can this information be obtained?
6. Summarize the information presented in the text relative to changes in the competitive environment. Explain how these changes are impacting retailing.

APPLICATION EXERCISES

1. Visit the central business district of your town and determine:
   a. The number of vacant stores.
   b. The particular types that are vacant.
   Discuss the factors leading to the vacancies. If the central business district in your town has been revitalized, how was it accomplished? How successful has it been?
2. Develop a sample of fast-food outlets, sit-down restaurants, coffee shops, and supermarkets and determine which of the outlets are offering breakfast menus. Compare and contrast the offerings and seek to identify the demographic characteristics of the primary customer base.

CASES

1. Is Sex Going out of Style?

Once synonymous with movie glamour, Hollywood Boulevard is now choked with runaways, prostitutes, and the occasional intrepid tourist. Nor has time been any kinder to Frederick's of Hollywood, which opened its doors in 1946. Feather boas, marabou slippers, and slinky lingerie designed to "show every curve" were dedicated to the theory that "fashions may change, but sex is always in style."

But Frederick's brand of sex isn't selling these days. Laments George Townson, the company's chairman and chief executive since May: "Today people perceive Frederick's as hard sensual, almost crossing the line in some instances to too sexual. Depending on which part of our operation you look at, we're either 5 years or 15 years behind the times."

Frederick's sexy image, once its best asset, is now its biggest headache. The company needs to open new stores, but some of the developers building luxury malls don't want Frederick's as a tenant. The message was so clear that since 1981 Frederick's has opened five stores under a new name—Private Moments. These 1,600- to 2,200-square-foot units are attempting to compete with the Victoria's Secret stores, the successful chain store/mail-order company owned by The Limited.

"Private Moments sells quiet sensuality and has a softer, more acceptable image," says Townson, who plans to open three more next year. But the look may be too low-key: The Private Moments catalog has been discontinued and the division is still in the red.

Frederick's needs Private Moments because its own 148 stores are merchandised the way they were 15 years ago: The decor runs from pink and burgundy to purple and aqua, and the shelves are piled high with edible panties in such flavors as passion fruit and tutti-frutti. What turned on their fathers and mothers, however, doesn't seem to do much for the younger generation of lingerie shoppers.

"To get new customers, we must change the look and feel of the stores and make them less hard and intimidating," says Townson. What he has in mind are more premises like the Westminster Mall store in Westminster, California. Since the recent remodeling there, sales are up 50 percent over last year. The renovated stores downplay the raunchy and stress such conventional and acceptable items as camisoles and beaded tops by displaying them in front where browsing customers can be seen through the windows. The rougher stuff is in the back where customers can look without being seen from the street.

In the back, customers can find one of Frederick's most popular sellers this holiday season: crotchless musical panties. When a tab is pulled, a computer chip plays different tunes like "Here Comes the Bride," "When the Saints Go Marching In," and a medley of Christmas tunes. The price is a scanty $8.

The company's famous catalog generates about 21 percent of sales—mostly to women—but this, too, suffers from a crudeness that seems out of place today. The catalogs feature drawings and photographs of chesty women in skimpy nylon nighties and push-up bras, as well as sex aids. Traditionally Frederick's advertised its catalogs in *Cosmopolitan, Glamour,* and *Penthouse.* Next year Frederick's will test-market a catalog without some of the X-rated items.

Townson faces a dilemma. If he cleans up the act, Frederick's becomes more respectable, but may lose its uniqueness. Acknowledges Townson, "We don't want to cripple ourselves by eliminating merchandise that does a good job for us." A strange twist, isn't it? One generation's daring is another generation's bad taste. In an era when sex has come out of the bedroom and into the living room, this pioneer of sexiness finds itself out of tune and out of step.

Questions

1. What changes are occurring in society which have caused Frederick's of Hollywood to fall behind the times?
2. What other factors do you believe have helped contribute to the consumer rejection of Frederick's of Hollywood's image?
3. Compare and contrast the marketing strategy differences between Frederick's of Hollywood, Victoria's Secret, and Private Moments.
4. What actions could Frederick's take to be more in line with the contemporary marketplace?

Source: Reprinted by permission of *Forbes* Magazine, December 30, 1985. © Forbes Inc., 1985.

2. Tupperware Aims at Keeping Abreast of Modern Times

Tupperware has discovered that the world is changing. Tupperware parties, traditionally daytime gatherings aimed at stay-at-home housewives, are on the verge of change. Soon Tupperware parties will be held in offices. They will be given during lunch hours and early and late in the day to fit work schedules. There will be more Tupperware parties for single men, working couples, and the affluent.

The new strategies are aimed at ending more than three years of declining profit at the company's former star performer. A two-year company investigation of Tupperware's problems showed "that (the) Tupperware (unit) was much more rigid than we thought." Not only had it failed to keep up with the times, but many of its incentive programs aimed at encouraging older dealers to recruit and train new dealers, were obsolete.

Besides trying to be more responsive to changing demographics, the company also is revamping its incentive programs aimed at getting experienced dealers to train new ones. It also is boosting its advertising and has introduced products that can be used in microwave ovens. The concern, however, said it wouldn't abandon its traditional parties or customers.

Questions

1. What other strategies should Tupperware consider? Should the firm, for example, open retail outlets?
2. What alternative strategies can you suggest for Tupperware parties? For example, should the dealers be encouraged to have 20-minute presentations at health clubs or during lunch hours at businesses?
3. Who is likely to be the target market for Tupperware? What trends in the environment have served to erode the traditional Tupperware customer base?

Source: Portions quoted with permission from *The Wall Street Journal*, May 3, 1985, p. 30. © Dow Jones & Company, Inc., May 3, 1985. All rights reserved.

ENDNOTES

1. Valerie Zeithaml, "The New Demographics and Market Fragmentation," *Journal of Marketing* 49 (Summer 1985), pp. 65–75.
2. "Measuring the Impact of the Baby Bust," *U.S. News and World Report,* December 16, 1985, p. 64.
3. "The Middle-Age Shape of Things to Come," *Money,* November 1985, pp. 66–68; also William Lazer, "Dimensions of the Mature Market," *The Journal of Consumer Marketing,* Summer 1986, pp. 23–34.
4. "A New Collar Class," *U.S. News and World Report,* September 16, 1985, p. 60.
5. *Sales and Marketing Management Update,* April 3, 1985.
6. "Bringing Up Baby: A New Kind of Marketing Boom," *Business Week,* April 22, 1985, pp. 58–62.
7. For further reading, see Gregory A. Jackson and George S. Masnick, "Take Another Look at Regional U.S. Growth," *Harvard Business Review,* March–April 1984, p. 77.
8. Quoted from Larry Light, "How To Win Share and Influence Profits," *Promotion Exchange,* September 1982, pp. 1–3.
9. Jeremy Maine, "Merchant's Woe: Too Many Stores," *Fortune,* May 13, 1985, p. 62; see also J. Barry Mason, "Redefining Excellence in Retailing," *Journal of Retailing,* Summer 1986, pp. 115–19.
10. Eleanor May, William Ress, and Walter Salmon, *Future Trends in Retailing* (Cambridge, Mass.: Marketing Science Institute, 1985).
11. "Store Wars: Is America Big Enough for All?" *Chain Store Age Executive,* August 1985, p. 15; Betsy Morris, "Smaller Fast Food Chains Brace for Shake-Out," *The Wall Street Journal,* May 31, 1985, p. 6.
12. "Block Those Quotas," *Stores,* September 1985, p. 45; see also, "Foreign Marketers Recruit U.S. Talent," *Marketing News,* March 13, 1987, p. 12; "Foreign Marketers Are Placing Products on Their Own Shelves," *Marketing News,* March 13, 1987, p. 12.
13. "Country-of-Origin Rules: NRMA's View," *NRMA AD–PRO,* June 1985, p. 5.

5

The New Technology of Retailing

RETAILING CAPSULE

Electronic Retailing Goes to the Supermarket

A variety of experiments are under way to entice consumers to make purchases via computer terminals and videodiscs. The timing may be right for the innovations because growth in the catalog showroom and the discount store business have slowed dramatically. In contrast, an extremely bright future for electronic systems is forecast by many analysts. A Touche Ross and Company retail consultant believes that by 1989 consumers may be spending $5 billion to $10 billion annually at some 50,000 videodisc-based kiosks.

The kiosks are designed to attract the hurried, cost-conscious shopper. All transactions necessary to complete a purchase occur on one touch-sensitive screen. By touching defined areas of the screen, the shopper uses "menus" to browse within a product category such as tools and to refine the search to the item in which he/she is interested. Accompanying text describes the price, size, and color of each item. Shoppers are then instructed on how to complete shipping and billing addresses and how to use a credit card to pay for the purchase. One firm, Compusave, dials up the machines each night and processes the orders. The orders are then shopped via United Parcel Service. The Compusave kiosks now offer 3,000 items in their catalog.

Source: Based on Marilyn A. Harris, "Electronic Retailing Goes to the Supermarket," *Business Week,* March 25, 1985, p. 78; see also, "Electronistore Debuts: Donnelley Enters Growing Retail Systems," *Marketing News,* May 24, 1985, p. 1.; "In-Store Retail Systems," *Marketing News,* May 24, 1985, p. 1; and "In-Store Retailing Goes Video," *Retail Technology,* October 1985.

LEARNING OBJECTIVES

*C*hanges in retailing technology are affecting virtually every dimension of the retailing outlet. Now available on a timely basis is detailed information which can aid retailers in making decisions ranging from merchandise elimination to credit authorization. The new technology has increased employee productivity, reduced losses due to cash register errors, and lowered losses caused by not having desired inventory in stock to meet customer needs. Other changes include new methods of merchandising presentation ranging from video kiosks, as discussed above, to home video shopping through such channels as the Home Television Network.

After reading this chapter, you will be able to:

1. Describe the impacts of the electronic cash register (ECR) and point-of-sale (POS) terminal on retailing.

2. Explain the meaning of the universal product code (UPC) for food retailers.

3. Evaluate the optical character recognition (OCR-A) system of merchandise marking in general merchandise retailing.

4. Discuss the importance of universal vendor marking (UVM).

5. Explain the meaning of electronic funds transfer systems (EFTS) to retailers.

6. Describe trends in videotex and electronic in-home shopping.

The video kiosk is one of the latest developments in the use of electronic technology in retailing. Retailers used mechanical cash registers for many years to ring up sales and make change. The original purpose of the cash register was to reduce employee theft by having cash under the control of one employee.

The first machines were really adding machines set on top of a cash drawer. A clerk pushed buttons and cranked an arm to enter information into the register. Later versions displayed the price of each item in large numbers for both the clerk and customer to read. Finally, mechanical registers printed a record of each sale and calculated the amount of change due.

The **electronic cash register (ECR)** was introduced in the 1960s. The ECR uses electric light beams to enter information at a very high rate of speed. Such equipment is used today in almost all retail stores. More and more ECRs are also used as part of a computer system to provide up-to-date reports for management.

The new electronic technology has brought about changes in (1) the way merchandise is marked, (2) the way money and credit are handled, and (3) the way the merchant works closely with a bank on a daily basis.

ECR equipment can calculate and process data at high speeds with great accuracy. The equipment also has the ability to store data and transfer information from one location to another.

Advances in electronic data processing for retailing have occurred more slowly than in many other areas of business. Various reasons exist for this slowness. First, the dollar investment in the equipment is high, particularly for department stores that carry thousands of **stock-keeping units (SKUs)**. Second, transactions are complicated, particularly in general merchandise retailing. Thus, not unexpectedly, the supermarket industry has made greater advances in use of data processing than other sectors of retailing have. Third, personnel problems still abound. People must be trained to work with the new equipment.

Recent advances in the technology, however, have brought prices down to the point where many outlets, including the smallest ones, can afford ECR equipment. And the electronic cash registers produce increased savings through better inventory management, reduction of underrings at the cash register, and higher labor productivity. A nationwide survey by Arthur Young and Company, as shown in Table 5–1, found that, overall, 80 percent or more of all retailers have one or more microcomputers in use.

UNDERSTANDING POS

A **point-of-sale (POS)** cash register (or checker terminal) is the key as an input device for many retailing systems. A POS device records a variety of information at the time a transaction occurs. The information is stored and can be called up at the end of the day or whenever it is needed. The system

T A B L E 5–1 MICROCOMPUTER USE IN THE RETAIL INDUSTRY

Average Number of Microcomputers Currently Installed	Sales			Type of Store				All Participants
	Under $100 Million	$100–$500 Million	Over $500 Million	Mass Merchandise Stores	Department Stores	Specialty Stores	Combination/Grocery Stores	
0	26%	5%	10%	13%	23%	12%	0%	13%
1–2	34	14	0	13	12	22	8	16
3–5	26	23	3	13	23	21	17	19
6–10	5	27	13	16	18	12	33	16
11–25	3	18	23	10	12	14	33	14
26–100	3	9	32	22	6	12	9	14
Over 100	3	4	19	13	6	7	0	8

SOURCE: *Retail MIS Expenses and Trends* (New York: Arthur Young & Co., 1985), p. 20.

Benefit	Initially Expected	Realized	Not Expected but Realized
Reduced inventory levels	58%	30%	26%
Increased inventory turn	63	26	16
Reduced markdowns	53	22	15
Increased gross margins	53	23	20

SOURCE: "Point-of-Sale '86: A New Study," *Stores,* November 1986, p. 89. Reprinted from *Stores* magazine © National Retail Merchants Association, 1986.

can reveal which merchandise, styles, and colors of various manufacturers are selling most rapidly.

The ability to identify slow- and fast-moving items is a key to good merchandise management.[1] Much information is available in an "exception report," which is a computer printout that identifies slow and fast sellers. Buyers must make quick merchandise decisions about these two extremes or "exceptions." All of the information necessary for such decisions is entered into the merchandise information system based on the original purchase order.

In one national survey, 75 percent of the retail respondents reported they had installed POS systems. The systems were the rule rather than the exception among all types of stores, with the lowest frequency of POS in smaller companies and specialty stores.[2]

Some retailers thrive on a large variety of merchandise, minimal inventory, and rapid turnover. The new systems allow frequent and up-to-date information on product sales rates, stock outages, sales patterns, and similar information which can be grouped for buyers by department.

Benefits include quicker completion of sales transactions, fewer cash register errors, and faster credit approval. The system also allows easier departmental interselling by store personnel. The merchandising and operating benefits and uses of POS systems are summarized in Tables 5–2 and 5–3.

Trends in Management Information Systems Development

The use of computers in building **management information systems (MIS)** is becoming increasingly important. *But a management information system is not just machines. It is the structure of people, equipment, and procedures necessary to gather, analyze, and distribute information needed by management.*

The uses of computers in an MIS context are shown in Table 5–4. Accounting and financial applications are the most frequent uses. For example, 62 percent of the surveyed respondents in a national study included payroll as part of their MIS, followed by general ledger systems, 58 percent;

Benefit	Initially Expected	Realized	Not Expected but Realized
Faster automation	74%	72%	27%
More accurate information	71	74	30
Additional sales information	68	71	28
Improved payroll and commission data capture	33	43	38
Reduced data entry	58	60	27
Reduced sales audit costs	55	59	27
Increased A/R cash flow	35	54	32
Reduced shrinkage	58	28	17
Reduced bad debt	37	45	26

SOURCE: "Point-of-Sale '86: A New Study," *Stores,* November 1986, p. 89. Reprinted from *Stores* magazine © National Retail Merchants Association, 1986.

accounts payable, 53 percent; sales reporting, 46 percent; and accounts receivable, 41 percent. The most rapidly growing applications include inventory control, point-of-sale (electronic cash register) systems, purchase order systems, stock replenishment systems, and open-to-buy control.[3]

Clearly, based on the above information, the computer provides important sources of information for retail managers. A look at some of the many applications of computer-based data today can help a retailer appreciate the potential of such information to management. Some of the key reasons for such a move are shown in Table 5–5, based on a national sample of general merchandise retailers. The reasons include SKU data capture, markdowns, layaways, merchandise credit and transfers, and such operational uses as bank credit card authorization and communications for a host computer.

Sales Reporting

One of the most useful retail reports is a daily sales report. This provides an analysis and count of departmental sales dollars and units. Figure 5–1 illustrates a daily sales report for the food service industry. In addition to a daily sales report, sales analysis reports can measure the sales performance of individual items by department or category within specified time intervals. As shown in Figure 5–2, unit price, units sold, extended dollar value, and percentage of items by sale are readily available.

The sales activities report can provide a much bigger picture of sales transactions and employee timekeeping activity to help increase sales in selected time periods (Figure 5–3).

Inventory Control

Merchandise on hand is another important area of information for retailers. Inventory ties up a large amount of a retail firm's capital, and retailers need

TABLE 5–4 TRENDS IN MIS DEVELOPMENT

	Sales			Type of Store				All Participants
	Under $100 Million	$100–$500 Million	Over $500 Million	Mass Merchandise Stores	Department Stores	Specialty Stores	Combination/ Grocery Stores	
Point-of-sale, ECRs, PCs	31%	24%	30%	35%	56%	20%	0%	28%
Distribution	6	24	26	35	19	9	27	20
Purchase order	9	17	33	28	13	15	27	20
Inventory control	22	31	33	41	44	13	46	29
Stock replenishment	9	26	19	21	19	15	27	19
Sales reporting	44	45	48	45	81	39	27	46
Open-to-buy control	13	31	33	35	63	11	9	26
Financial planning/ management	16	26	37	31	25	24	18	26
General ledger	56	60	59	72	63	50	46	58
Accounts payable	63	45	56	66	56	41	64	53
Accounts receivable	56	33	37	41	63	39	18	41
Credit management	25	14	22	24	38	15	0	20
Telecommunications	22	29	30	28	56	17	18	27
Payroll	63	57	70	69	75	57	46	62
Human resources	13	24	41	21	38	22	27	25
Unit control	13	14	26	24	19	17	0	18
Daily bank deposits	22	31	37	38	19	30	18	29
In-house credit	22	17	26	17	56	13	9	21
Third-party credit	9	24	19	14	25	17	18	18
Cieck approval	6	5	11	3	6	9	9	7
Timekeeping	3	12	22	10	13	7	36	12
Promo price lookup	6	17	19	24	0	11	18	14
Full price lookup	6	10	26	10	0	11	46	13
Price changes	19	29	33	17	31	28	46	28
Store receiving	9	17	30	21	13	15	27	18
Transfers	16	17	19	14	25	20	9	18
Rainchecks	0	5	4	7	0	0	9	3
Layaways	19	17	7	7	13	24	9	15
Bridal registry	3	10	0	0	19	4	0	5
Credit account payment	13	12	4	10	31	4	0	10
Labor scheduling	6	5	4	3	0	4	18	5
Electronic mail	0	2	7	7	6	0	0	3
Electronic fund transfers	0	5	4	3	0	4	0	3

SOURCE: *Retail MIS Expenses and Trends* (New York: Arthur Young & Co., 1985), p. 13.

Note: Since this is multiple response, data totals will not equal 100 percent.

T A B L E 5–5 **USES OF POS**

Merchandising Uses	Percent	Operational Uses	Percent
SKU data capture	84%	Communications to host	71%
Markdowns	66	Item description printing	66
Layaways	59	Bank card credit authorization	50
Merchandise credits	76	Report preparation	46
and refunds	40	Capture of commission data	44
Transfers	33		
Receipts	29		
Inventory	21		
Purchasing			

SOURCE: "Point-of-Sale '86: A New Study, *Stores,* November 1986, p. 89. Reprinted from *Stores* magazine © National Retail Merchants Association, 1986.

to know the composition of the inventory because merchandise outages can result in lost sales, and having too many wrong items will lead to excessive markdowns. Computer-generated reports are a highly efficient way to keep up with inventory and to answer the questions of what to buy, when to buy, how to buy, and from whom to buy.

Figure 5–4 illustrates a series of inventory analysis reports on an item-by-item basis for a retail liquor outlet. Such information can be developed each day to allow buyers to decide on how much to reorder or what to transfer between stores. It also shows a daily inventory analysis. This report indicates the day's sales, the number of items on hand, and the number of items to be purchased.

Sales Forecasting

Inventory data is necessary for forecasting sales. Analysis of previous sales levels can point out trends that can be a clue to future sales levels. Remember, however, that inventory reports can only show trends in past sales and cannot forecast the future.

Retailers have to temper sales reports with judgment to make them useful, but should not ignore the information and act on gut feeling. If there is a major strike in the community, sales will be higher in a future quarter than in the quarter that the strike occurs. If a retailer believes an area is going into recession, the forecast sales levels probably will be lower than computer reports indicate.

More complex reports are required in the detailed analysis of sales forecasts, including detailed sales analysis reports, salesperson productivity reports, and a retail inventory management report. Such information analysis can be used as a tool in merchandise management and should be viewed as part of a retail reporting system to control the business and improve profitability.[4]

FIGURE 5–1 DAILY SALES REPORT

Departmental Sales and Count*

An automatically printed report shows net sales and unit count for programmed departments. This report provides the information necessary to analyze the contribution of each menu item toward gross profit. Knowing sales by dollars and units per menu item also helps in the planning of additions to, or deletions from, the menu.

The report illustrated not only shows net sales and units for 70 categories, but also shows:

Net total sales for the combined 70 categories.
Net sales for two open departments.
Total net sales.
Gross sales total.

DAILY SALES REPORT		ITEM COUNT	REGISTER TOTALS	
START #52 PROGRAM CHANGE/RESET COUNTER CUSTOMER COUNTER/NO SALE	X	51	361	C
	X	621	22	C
Hamburger	X	112	39.78	1C
Deluxe Hamburger	X	61	35.99	2C
Double Hamburger	X	23	18.17	3C
Cheese Burger	X	74	36.26	4C
Double Cheese Burger	X	19	16.81	5C
Whopper	X	12	11.88	6C
Super Burger	X	8	7.92	7C
Beef	X	31	27.59	8C
Chili Burger	X	10	5.90	9C
Ribs	X	18	35.82	10C
Chicken	X	29	46.11	11C
White Chicken	X	5	8.45	12C
Dark Chicken	X	5	7.45	13C
Barrel	X	3	14.67	
Bucket	X	7	25.	54C
		11	5.50	55C
Mashed Potatoes	X	14	4.20	56C
Potato Salad	X	21	6.30	57C
Salad	X	32	16.00	58C
Bread	X	36	3.60	59C
Rolls	X	21	2.10	60C
Soup	X	3	.90	61C
Pie	X	32	14.40	62C
French Fries	X	123	36.90	63C
Iced Tea	X	41	6.15	64C
Hot Chocolate	X	6	.90	65C
Coffee	X	179	17.90	66C
Cola	X	312	62.40	67C
Milk	X	26	7.80	68C
Hot Tea	X	4	.60	69C
Orange	X	41	6.15	70C
NET PRESET SALES	X		926.09	71C
MISCELLANEOUS	X	3	11.85	72C
SPECIAL	X	1	4.50	73C
TOTAL NET SALES	X		942.44	74C
GROSS SALES	X		971.15	75C
	X			
CONSECUTIVE # / STORE & REGISTER # / DATE	X	2280	12 4/02/7-	

SOURCE: NCR Corporation, Dayton, Ohio.
*This report is for illustration only and does not represent the daily sales volume of an average fast-food restaurant.

Sales Analysis Report

This report enables management to measure sales performance of individual menu items by department or product category within certain time intervals. Unit price, quantity sold, extended dollar value, and percentage of sales by item are shown.

The sales analysis report provides management with the ability to track individual item sales, analyze product acceptance, and monitor advertising and sales promotional efforts.

```
X        SALES ANALYSIS REPORT          40
    ITEM      PRICE SOLD  $ VALUE    %
DEPT 0001
  DELX BRGR    .85   114    96.90   5.95
  CHZ BRGR     .60  1023   613.80  37.90
  DBL BRGR     .70    79    55.30   3.39
  HAMBURGR     .50   265   132.50   8.13
  SUPR BRGR   1.05    14    14.70    .90
    DEPT TOTALS     1595   913.20  56.09

DEPT 0003
  FISH SDW     .50    18     9.00    .55
  FISH BSK    1.65    43    70.95   4.35
  FISH PLT    1.95    67   130.65   8.02
  SHRIMP      2.50    12    30.00   1.84
  OYSTERS     3.15    19    59.85   3.67
    DEPT TOTALS      159   300.45  18.45




DEPT 0030
  COLA         .25   245    61.25   3.76
  COLA         .30   105    31.50   1.93
  COLA         .35    47    16.45   1.01
  CHOC SHK     .45    15     6.75    .41
  CHOC SHK     .65    63    40.95   2.51

    DEPT TOTALS      475   156.90   9.63

    REPT TOTALS     2325  1627.85
1200                            10:50PM
```

SOURCE: NCR Corporation, Dayton, Ohio.

FIGURE 5–3   SALES ACTIVITY REPORT

Activity Report

This report provides an in-depth picture of sales-transaction and employee-timekeeping activity during preselected time periods. Highlights of this report include:

1. Number of customer transactions.
2. Number of cashiers on duty.
3. Average check amount, customer count, and sales per man hour.
4. Number of bonus items sold.
5. Percentage of sales to total sales.
6. Employee hours and labor cost.

```
X              ACTIVITY REPORT           01
08:30AM - 10:00AM
   TRAN COUNT      14 BONUS 1          10
   NET SALES    36.21 BONUS 2           7
   AVRG CHECK    2.59 EMPLOYEES         6
   CASHIERS         2 LABOR HRS      2:02
   CSTMR/MNHR    6.90 LABOR COST     6.64
   SALES/MNHR   17.84 % OF SALES    18.34
10:00AM - 11:00AM
   TRAN COUNT     196 BONUS 1         113
   NET SALES   519.21 BONUS 2          90
   AVRG CHECK    2.65 EMPLOYEES         8
   CASHIERS         2 LABOR HRS     17:34
   CSTMR/MNHR   11.16 LABOR COST    72.16
   SALES/MNHR   29.55 % OF SALES    13.90
11:00AM - 11:15AM
   TRAN COUNT      49 BONUS 1          22
   NET SALES   163.13 BONUS 2           4
   AVRG CHECK    3.33 EMPLOYEES         8
   CASHIERS         3 LABOR HRS      6:00
   CSTMR/MNHR   24.50 LABOR COST    30.24
   SALES/MNHR   81.57 % OF SALES    18.53
11:15AM - 03:00PM
   TRAN COUNT     854 BONUS 1         125
   NET SALES  2528.10 BONUS 2         184
   AVRG CHECK    2.96 EMPLOYEES         6
   CASHIERS         5 LABOR HRS     77.88
   CSTMR/MNHR   43.17 LABOR COST   376.04
   SALES/MNHR  127.81 % OF SALES    14.87
```

SOURCE: NCR Corporation, Dayton, Ohio.

Managing Credit

The computer can allow retailers to handle two important elements of credit—credit authorization and credit control—more effectively. In **credit authorization,** retailers want to make sure a customer does not make purchases over an approved credit limit. Today, a salesperson will normally dial the credit authorization extension for the computer. After dialing in the customer's account number and the dollar amount of the sale, the salesperson receives an answer. The computer issues an OK for the sale or indicates that the customer will need to discuss the sale with the credit department.

Inventory Activity Report

This report provides store management with information relating to those items which have had activity within a specified period of time. The report provides vital data, such as current bottles on hand, sales by type of sale, inventory receipts, and adjustments.

Other Inventory Reports

Inventory On-Hand, Inventory Inquiry, Receiving, and Inventory Summary reports are always current and up-to-the-minute through the last completed transaction.

They provide these management benefits:

1. Complete inventory-on-hand listing.

2. A detailed record of inventory merchandise receipts.

3. Reports can be produced by any terminal within the store, whenever needed.

4. Reports provide store management with complete inventory price lookup control.

5. Management can selectively analyze the in-stock inventory level of any given item at any time.

6. Inventory data is in terms of bottles on hand and associated dollar value.

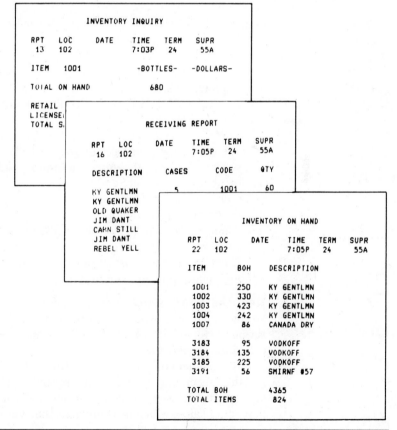

```
                INVENTORY ACTIVITY

RPT    LOC     DATE    TIME    TERM    SUPR
 23    102             7:15P    24     55A

          CUR     RET     LIC     TOTAL
ITEM      BOH     SALE    SALE    SALES

10001     150     200     100     300
10002     330      30      50      80
10003     423     500     200     700
10004     242      50      30      80

30183      95     125     225     350
30184     135      55      60     115
30185     225     220     190     410
30191      56      10      15      25

BOH              44,365
ITEMS             2,156
INV. RECEIVED    29,500
INV. ADJUSTED       225
RET. SALES       12,345
LIC. SALES       16,550
TOT. SALES       28,895
```

```
              INVENTORY INQUIRY

RPT    LOC     DATE    TIME    TERM    SUPR
 13    102             7:03P    24     55A

ITEM   1001          -BOTTLES-   -DOLLARS-

TOTAL ON HAND           680

RETAIL
LICENSE
TOTAL S.
```

```
              RECEIVING REPORT

RPT    LOC     DATE    TIME    TERM    SUPR
 16    102             7:05P    24     55A

DESCRIPTION    CASES       CODE      QTY

KY GENTLMN       5         1001       60
KY GENTLMN
OLD QUAKER
JIM DANT
CARN STILL
JIM DANT
REBEL YELL
```

```
                 INVENTORY ON HAND

RPT    LOC     DATE      TIME    TERM    SUPR
 22    102               7:05P    24     55A

ITEM      BOH       DESCRIPTION

1001      250       KY GENTLMN
1002      330       KY GENTLMN
1003      423       KY GENTLMN
1004      242       KY GENTLMN
1007       86       CANADA DRY

3183       95       VODKOFF
3184      135       VODKOFF
3185      225       VODKOFF
3191       56       SMIRNF #57

TOTAL BOH          4365
TOTAL ITEMS         824
```

SOURCE: NCR Corporation, Dayton, Ohio.

Credit control involves a series of issues, including tabulating outstanding credit by customers, mailing out monthly bills, and keeping up-to-date reports on delinquent accounts and those that need to be turned over to an attorney for collection. These can be readily generated using today's technology.

ITEM MARKING

Scanning or wanding are the most widely used methods of data entry at the point-of-sale terminal. As shown in Table 5–6, 25 percent of all respondents in a recent national survey indicated that they use either scanning or wanding for entering data at the point-of-sale terminal. Percentages range from a low of 12 percent in specialty stores to a high of 82 percent in combination/grocery stores.

Scanning has historically occurred primarily in supermarkets in which bar codes are read by a fixed slot scanner as shown in Figures 5–5 and 5–6. Wanding has been used primarily in general merchandise retailing. Many items in general merchandise retailing, such as apparel, cannot easily be passed over a fixed slot scanner. Rather, a **wand,** such as the one shown in Figure 5–7, is used to capture the information.

Scanning Technology Used

A variety of merchandise marking technologies are used as part of scanning/wanding systems. As shown in Table 5–6, the ones most frequently used are the UPC, OCR-A, bar coding, and magnetic coding.

The UPC

Most people are familiar with the small, black-and-white bars on supermarket items. These bars are the **universal product codes (UPCs)** that contain information about the product and the manufacturer (see Figure 5–8). These bar codes are passed over a ''scanner'' at the checkout, as shown in Figure 5–6. The information from the bar codes goes from the scanner into the POS system. Computers may then automatically update the store's inventory, ''look-up'' the price of the item in question, and print a receipt for the customer.

The UPC is the most popular form of general merchandise marking, although many retailers use multiple scanning technologies.

How Did It All Start? The idea of mechanizing the checkout has been around since 1920, when the founder of Piggly Wiggly stores introduced self-service.[5] He spent the rest of his life trying to develop an ''automatic'' store called the Keedoozle.

Today, checkout efficiency is critical. Checkers earn $6 or more an hour, and the ''front end'' accounts for approximately 40 percent of supermarkets' labor costs. Losses through misrings and cheating may run as high as 1.5 percent of sales, which is as much as the average supermarket makes before

T A B L E 5–6 DATA CAPTURE IN THE RETAIL INDUSTRY

	Sales			Type of Store				All Participants
	Under $100 Million	$100–$500 Million	Over $500 Million	Mass Merchandise Stores	Department Stores	Specialty Stores	Combination/ Grocery Stores	
POS system installed (percent of positive response)	62%	77%	94%	81%	100%	64%	92%	77%
Scanning/wanding used at POS terminal (percent of positive response)	17	15	45	24	18	12	82	25
Scanning technology used: (percent of those with scanning)								
OCR	0	0	31	33	33	25	0	18
UPC	75	100	69	83	33	50	100	77
Magnetic	0	20	0	0	33	0	0	5
Bar code	75	40	23	33	0	100	22	36
Other	0	20	0	0	0	25	0	5

SOURCE: *Retail MIS Expenses and Trends* (New York: Arthur Young & Co., 1985), p. 17.

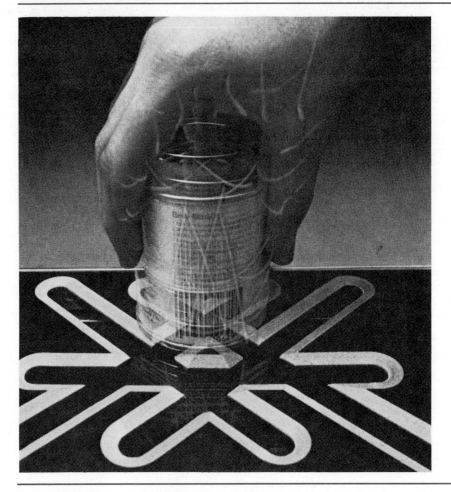

SOURCE: *Behavior Scan.*

taxes. And the checkout is not only a source of retailer dissatisfaction but, more importantly, a source of shopper resentment.

Potential Benefits to Consumer and Retailers. Tests of UPC scanner systems have revealed the following:

1. Improved *accuracy* of *checkout*.
2. Improved *customer satisfaction*. Speed, accuracy, quietness, and the detailed shopping tape are consumer pluses.
3. *Time and labor savings*. Some stores report productivity gains of up to 45 percent when item-price marking (no longer necessary since the price is carried in the computer) is eliminated. Even

(Courtesy NCR)

with price marking, other savings make scanner investment worthwhile.

4. *Improved inventory and financial control.*

Drawbacks to Faster Implementation. Scanning does have some disadvantages, including the following:

1. The full-scale switch to scanning represents an enormous dollar investment by a retailer.
2. Some people have failed to realize that scanner systems are not simply an improvement over previous technology but require entirely new operating procedures and management systems.
3. Some unions and consumer groups have opposed eliminating price marking, and legislation barring price elimination on packages has passed in some states and localities. This slows the implementation of scanning and makes retailers a bit hesitant to invest.
4. A relatively slow rate of coding (for other than national grocery brands) concerned retailers at first. They also had problems coding some items (e.g., produce) in hard-to-scan poly bags.

(Courtesy NCR)

5. Retailers have doubts about the new equipment (Is this the final version?), and they have found that certain colors are difficult to scan.

New Push to Scanning. A number of factors have pushed retailing into scanning, however:

1. Wages have risen quickly. Labor now represents over 67 percent of food retailing costs, up from 55 percent in the mid-60s. This has encouraged retailers to automate their operations.
2. Retail leaders are adopting the new technology on a large scale. The giants are heavily involved.
3. Many different kinds of products are being imprinted with the UPC by manufacturers. Other industries are interested in supermarket or chain drug distribution for their products. Some of the latest to organize for bar coding are the greeting card and long-playing record industries.

New Data Breakthroughs. Probably the greatest long-term benefit of scanning is its ability to generate totally new marketing information.

Scanners are providing retailers with:

1. The first ever accurate reading, item by item, of actual item movement at the point of sale.
2. Overnight, store-by-store readings of consumer buying behavior.

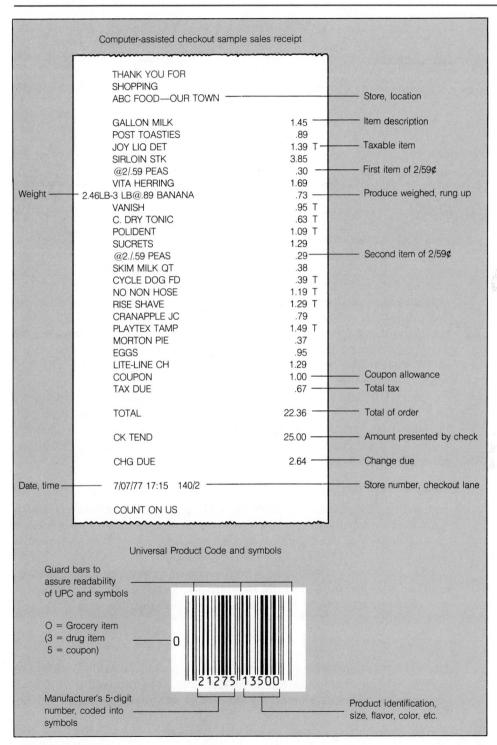

Computer-assisted checkout sample sales receipt

THANK YOU FOR
SHOPPING
ABC FOOD—OUR TOWN ———————— Store, location

GALLON MILK	1.45	Item description
POST TOASTIES	.89	
JOY LIQ DET	1.39 T	Taxable item
SIRLOIN STK	3.85	
@2/.59 PEAS	.30	First item of 2/59¢
VITA HERRING	1.69	
2.46LB-3 LB@.89 BANANA	.73	Produce weighed, rung up
VANISH	.95 T	
C. DRY TONIC	.63 T	
POLIDENT	1.09 T	
SUCRETS	1.29	
@2./.59 PEAS	.29	Second item of 2/59¢
SKIM MILK QT	.38	
CYCLE DOG FD	.39 T	
NO NON HOSE	1.19 T	
RISE SHAVE	1.29 T	
CRANAPPLE JC	.79	
PLAYTEX TAMP	1.49 T	
MORTON PIE	.37	
EGGS	.95	
LITE-LINE CH	1.29	
COUPON	1.00	Coupon allowance
TAX DUE	.67	Total tax
TOTAL	22.36	Total of order
CK TEND	25.00	Amount presented by check
CHG DUE	2.64	Change due

Weight ———— 2.46LB-3 LB@.89 BANANA

Date, time ———— 7/07/77 17:15   140/2 ———————— Store number, checkout lane

COUNT ON US

Universal Product Code and symbols

Guard bars to
assure readability
of UPC and symbols

O = Grocery item
(3 = drug item
 5 = coupon)   0

21275 13500

Manufacturer's 5-digit
number, coded into
symbols

Product identification,
size, flavor, color, etc.

C—Record keeping level
123—Classification (e.g., this is a panty within the lingerie department)
5025—Style (e.g., brief)
M9003—Color
07—Size (medium)

3. Fast, accurate feedback on test-market experiments.
4. Measurement of the effects of marketing and promotional activity.

OCR-A

***Optical character recognition (OCR-A)—*the A *identifies the style of the character—is a widely used format for general-merchandise marking.* It was the ticket-marking method initially recommended by the National Retail Merchants Association (NRMA). Sears uses OCR-A, and so do Montgomery Ward and J. C. Penney. The OCR tickets have been cheaper and more easily read by people than other scanning tickets (see Figure 5–9).

The OCR tickets are read with wands that are passed over the items (see Figure 5–7). Wand readers are important because most general merchandise (e.g., goods on hangers) is difficult to scan with a fixed scanner. Instead, a wand containing a light beam is moved across the tag. Electronically, the wand system is the same as a fixed scanner.

Other Types of Coding

Bar coding is a machine-readable merchandise-marking technology which has been developed by some equipment vendors such as NCR. Some large retailers have also developed bar coding systems to meet their own special needs.

Magnetic tape, another type of merchandise marking, produces a human-readable tape on which data are imprinted on a magnetic strip included as part of the pricing ticket. The information is read from the strip by the use of a wanding device.

Universal Vendor Marking

Universal vendor marking (UVM) is a standard vendor-created identification system. The need to mark the items when they are received at the store level can be eliminated largely by the use of such a standardized format;

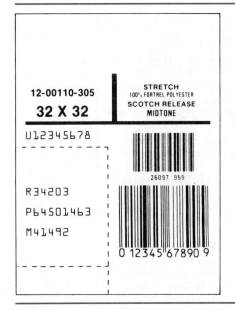

SOURCE: David Schulz, "Is UPC in Your Future?" *Stores*, September 1986, p. 36. Reprinted from *Stores* magazine. © National Retail Merchants Association, 1986.

indeed, much of the ticketing for Sears, Montgomery Ward, and J. C. Penney is now done at the vendor level.

The highest advances in labor productivity will not occur until at least 70 percent of all general merchandise is marked at the vendor level. Also, the differences between the OCR-A system and the UPC system are still being worked out. Supermarkets, for example, now carry nonfood items that cannot be read by scanners that only read the UPC. Consequently some manufacturers are experimenting with both UPC and OCR markings, as shown in Figure 5–10. The National Retail Merchants Association, as shown in Figure 5–11, endorses the dual marking technology as an interim step toward the eventual use of the Universal Product Code as the industry standard. The shift toward the UPC is a major change for general merchandise retailers who have joined OCR-A marking.

ELECTRONIC FUNDS TRANSFER

Most persons have read newspaper articles referring to a cashless, checkless society. Such a system may soon be upon us.

One of the advantages of an **electronic funds transfer system (EFTS)** is that, by using a terminal, a retail outlet can contact a bank to: (1) verify a customer's credit, (2) process credit card sales, (3) verify checks, and (4)

FIGURE 5–11

NRMA BOARD ENDORSES UPC

WHEREAS, the NRMA has previously endorsed a voluntary vendor source marking standard of OCR-A/UVM;

WHEREAS, the NRMA has determined that changes in industry conditions, needs and technological direction indicate that the Universal Product Code structure as administered by the Uniform Code Council is the preferable voluntary standard;

THEREFORE, be it now resolved that the NRMA now endorses Universal Product Code administered by the Uniform Code Council as the preferred voluntary standard, to be adopted by vendors who have not yet adopted a source marking technology. The NRMA will actively work with the Uniform Code Council to better accommodate general merchandise; and it is further

RESOLVED that for those vendors who have adopted OCR-A/UVM, the NRMA endorses a transition period of dual vendor souce marking embodying both Universal Product Code and OCR-A/UVM to be followed by the emergence of Universal Product Code only, at an appropriate time when industry conditions warrant. ∎

SOURCE: David Schulz, "Is UPC in Your Future?" *Stores*, September 1986, p. 42. Reprinted from *Stores* magazine. © National Retail Merchants Association, 1986.

shift money from the customer's account to the account of the merchant at the time of a sale.

Stores have a problem approving checks and collecting bad checks. A check guarantee card is helpful, but some stores are experimenting with customer-operated terminals. These eliminate the approval of checks by a third party in the store, as the customer gets the approval directly from the bank. An example of such a system offered by IBM is shown in Figure 5–12.

SOURCE: Courtesy of IBM Corporation.

The use of the **debit card** (a card that allows funds to be shifted from the customer's account to the merchant's account at the time of a purchase) is also being evaluated. Kroger has now installed in some stores experimental automatic bank-teller machines that allow the customer to move money directly from a bank account to Kroger's. Safeway has installed numerous similar machines in its outlets. Information on users of debit cards can be helpful to merchants in targeting promotional campaigns and thus can be a "plus" in the struggle for market share.

Clearly, retailers would like to reduce their "float" (the lag between the time a customer presents a check and the funds are deposited to the retailer's account). Automatic authorization of credit and electronic funds transfer from one account to another may soon eliminate float.[6]

Some problems still exist. Some customers do not like the instant switch of funds from their account to that of the retailer. They prefer to have several days before a check clears the bank. Some consumers simply do not trust computers, especially when it comes to their checking accounts.[7]

Many other changes are occurring in the way technology is used in retailing. Many involve customer communications, nonstore shopping, and similar activities.

Videotex

Videotex *is the label applied to all home information retrieval systems.* Estimates are that close to 10 percent of all households will have such capabilities by 1990.[8] Numerous large national retailers are experimenting with this technology.

There are uncertainties about exactly when home information shopping services will be widely used by consumers. It is not clear when the majority of households will be wired for cable television reception. Nor is it known when enough households will have home computer terminals. Cable connections and the number of computers are essential to make electronic shopping affordable. The basis for such activities is the two-way hookup between the consumer and an electronic merchant.[9] This allows the consumer to enter a purchase order into a central computer by pushing buttons on a home keyboard.

Retailers may be underestimating the potential impact of video technology on at-store retailing. The next generation of shoppers will have grown up with home computers and videogames. They will be literate in the use of the technology essential to electronic shopping. Touche Ross and Company believes that by 1989 consumers may be spending $5 billion–$10 billion annually in some 50,000 videodisc-based kiosks that allow buyers to view merchandise on a viewing screen, type in billing and shipping instructions, and pay for the merchandise by inserting a credit card in an automatic card reader.[10] Part of the success of videotex is also tied to future improvements in graphics to properly display fashion merchandise.

Videodisc Mail Order Catalogs

Sears has led the way in experimenting with video catalogs. The retailer has placed some of its catalogs on laser discs for in-home and at-store viewing. The discs with which they have experimented contain motion sequences plus color pictures. Product demonstrations, fashion shows, and footage from Sears TV commercials were part of their experiment.[11]

Cable Marketing

Retailers are responding slowly to cable marketing. One reason is their confusion about the choices and opportunities available. A bright future seems to exist for this technology, however.[12]

The cable experiments now underway allow retailers to transmit fashion shows, display housewares and sporting goods, and provide lengthy programs on how to use various products. The Home Shopping Network has experienced remarkable success in selling merchandise to shoppers by the use of cable and syndicated (noncable) TV and a toll-free number for ordering the merchandise offered for sale. Similarly, the details of the Cableshop program are shown in Figure 5–13. Consumers seem to be primarily interested in the availability of food products, apparel, and household appliances on a home shopping channel.

In-Store Video Sales Aids

Increasingly, retailers are turning to the use of in-store video to provide prerecorded answers to questions frequently asked by customers.[13] The devices increase productivity because they reduce the need for salespeople to provide basic information. For example, the Atari electronic retail information center exists in a variety of retail outlets. The device self-activates when customers come near the machine, and it allows customers to have hands-on experience with an Atari computer. The information center responds to the customers' button-pushed questions and provides answers by tailoring the video presentation directly to their needs. The device can keep an interested customer busy for up to 28 minutes. Additional examples include videotape demonstrations in the meat and fish departments and electronic advertising on handles of grocery carts in supermarkets. Still another mechanism senses when someone is close by and triggers a tape that begins playing a message. The electronic devices are so tiny that the speakers can be hidden inside a cigarette pack. Anheuser-Busch invested in disc players for six different brands on an experimental basis. When customers walk by six-packs of Bud Light, they hear a few notes of the brand's commercials and an announcer's pitch.[14]

The May Company of California also has an extensive in-store video program. A regular series of weekly tapes is produced by the communications manager. One week's tape may provide information about a costume design contest for Miss Piggy. The next one may feature specific merchandise offered by the store.

Dayton-Hudson, a leading department store headquartered in Minnesota, has a variety of such devices, including a touch-sensitive computer bridal registry. They also have experimented with a computerized Stork Club—a baby registry. Other stores experimenting with this new technology include Saks-Fifth Avenue and Jordan Marsh.

One of the latest dimensions of retailing to be affected by computer technology is discount grocery coupons. Shoppers in such cities as Los Angeles, Seattle, San Francisco, and New York can now get coupons easily and quickly from computerized machines that appear in grocery stores. Customers push buttons corresponding to their choices and the coupons are printed out. The coupons can then be redeemed at the checkout counter as usual. Preliminary studies indicate that as many as 50 percent of the shoppers use the coupons for products they ordinarily would not purchase.[15]

How to Cableshop.

Starting now, Peabody Cable TV subscribers have something nobody else in the world has.

A Cable TV Shopping Information Service that helps you be a more effective shopper because you'll be a more informed shopper.

You'll see messages about products and services brought to you by some of America's leading companies. Recipes and household hints. Product demonstrations and do-it-yourself ideas. News of local sales at supermarket, drug and department stores.

And using The Cableshop is as easy as one, two, three:

1. Select a message. Every month your Cable Entertainment Guide contains a special section listing all The Cableshop messages. Select the message you'd like to see. Note the code number next to it. Since your message may have already been selected, turn to The Cableshop channel (51) to see if it's listed.

2. Phone in your selection. Dial The Cableshop number: 532-4372. A recorded message will ask for your Cableshop User number (sent to all subscribers through the mail), and the code number mentioned above.

3. Sit back, relax and watch. Your message is now scheduled. Watch The Cableshop channel (51) for the exact time and channel it will be shown on.

Here's what you'll see on The Cableshop channel (51):

Time of Day
Cableshop Phone Number
Message Code Number
Message Title
Channel that Message will Appear On
Time it will Appear

The Cableshop is available 24 hours a day. And it's free to all Adams-Russell Cable TV subscribers. If you're a subscriber, you already have everything you need to take advantage of The Cableshop: a phone, a TV set, and your monthly Cable Entertainment Guide.

The Cableshop. A whole new way to go shopping before you go shopping.

The CABLESHOP
Stay Home and Shop Around.

— The cash register and the computer are two of the major electromechanical inventions in the history of retailing. New technology is affecting almost every aspect of retailing, including merchandise management, buying, pricing, promotion, location, operations, and personnel.

— The point-of-service (POS) terminal allows all sales data to be captured in the terminals at the point of sale and to be transmitted to a back-office system. The data can then be recalled for processing and analysis. The resulting data gives management timely, detailed information to help offset a decline in profit margins caused by such factors as lack of inventory control, rapid growth of credit, rising labor costs, and proliferation of merchandise.

— Keys to the acceptance of point-of-service terminals are the universal product code (UPC) in food stores and OCR-A in general merchandise retailing. These are machine-readable codes that allow greater productivity and efficiency at the point of service. The codes allow merchandise to be marked by the manufacturer and eliminate much of the retail-level marking.

— The use of electronic cash registers and POS systems is spreading rapidly. The electronic funds transfer system (EFTS) is making slower progress. An EFTS allows the automatic transfer of funds from the customer's account to that of the store. A final new area of promise is the use of electronic in-store video sales aids.

KEY TERMS

Credit authorization An electronic system that allows retailers to ensure that a customer does not make purchases over a preapproved credit limit.

Debit card A card that allows funds to be transferred from a customer's account to a merchant's account at the time of a purchase.

Electronic cash register A point-of-sale register that uses electronic light beams to enter information at a very high rate of speed.

Electronic funds transfer A system for the automatic transfer of cash from a customer's account to a retailer's account.

Management information system The structure of people, equipment, and procedures necessary to gather, analyze, and distribute information needed by management.

Optical Character Recognition (OCR-A) The A identifies the style of character. A ticket-marking method widely used for general merchandise marketing.

POS A point-of-sale terminal that records a variety of information at the time a transaction occurs.

SKU Stock-keeping units defined in such terms as size, color, and fabric for merchandise in inventory.

Universal product code (UPC) A standardized form of product marking for electronic reading of price and other information that is used for food and health and beauty aids.

Universal vendor marking A standard vendor-created identification system for marking merchandise items at the vendor level.

Videotex A generic term applied to all forms of home information retrieval systems.

Wand An electronic device that can be passed over items for reading machine-coded information.

DISCUSSION QUESTIONS

1. What are the advantages of the electronic cash register over mechanical cash registers?
2. Why have advances in the use of electronic data processing in retailing been slower than in many other areas of business?
3. What are the various ways in which the use of computer-based data has aided retail management?
4. What are some of the ways consumers benefit from the installation of POS equipment in a retail store?
5. What are some of the benefits to the retailer and the consumer of UPC scanner systems?
6. What is universal vendor marking and what are its advantages?
7. What are the advantages and disadvantages of a debit card to a retailer?
8. What are some of the technological advances occurring today which are impacting nonstore shopping?

APPLICATION EXERCISES

1. Interview the managers of a large department store, a local outlet of a supermarket chain, and a fast-food store. Determine the type of system (electromechanical cash registers, electronic cash registers, or POS) employed in each. How many terminals are there? Are there any plans to change the type of system currently used? Has this change occurred already? If they plan to change, what type of system will they go to? Why? What savings are associated with the change?
2. Electronic funds transfer systems (EFTS) are "hot" topics for management today in retailing. The impetus is perhaps coming from the banking community. Make contacts with local banks and see what is going on in your area relative to thinking and planning for the era of EFTS. What forms have EFTS taken in general? Then go to the retail community and see what the status of their knowledge is about the issue. If they are knowledgeable, pick their brains about future plans.
3. What is the state of technological advances in your local community? Do a careful survey of the state of adoption of POS systems in the area. Find out from management what equipment is being used; what functions are being performed by the equipment on hand; what are future plans for expanding functions or adopting the new technology in any form. Make a summary chart, comparing companies by kind of business.
4. Check in your area on the state of the art of technology in the specific area of vendor marking. At this time, what plans are being made for scanning in the stores? If plans are being made, when will implementation be accomplished? What problems are seen in the scanning process? How will the input be used? Do a convenience sample of customers to see what they know about vendor marking and how they react to the "non-human-readable" portion of the code in grocery stores. How do they react to the detailed tape received from the terminals? What are your general conclusions from such a study?

CASES

1. Catalog Goes Video to Tap VCR Boom

Now that many U.S. households own videocassette recorders, marketers of all kinds are trying to exploit the new technology. One of the first is a direct marketer in Brooklyn, New York, called Video-logue Marketing Corp., which promises to make catalog shopping come alive.

The company mails catalogs in the form of videotapes to VCR owners. Instead of just seeing pictures in a book, these consumers watch demonstrations of everything from an automatic potato peeler to a shower telephone and a cocktail-toting robot. Slinky models show off exercise equipment, and in a schmaltzy take-off of detective shows, a man in a trench coat explains how home-security devices operate.

"I see the VCR becoming an important adjunct to the catalog field as we figure out smart ways to use it," says Stan Rapp, chairman of Rapp & Collins, the direct-marketing subsidiary of Doyle Dane Bernbach International Inc. "It can dramatize products so much better than a catalog or brochure." For that reason, Murjani International Ltd. may produce a video catalog to hype its clothing line bearing the Coca-Cola logo.

Some marketing consultants, however, question whether people will spend 30 to 60 minutes watching an entire tape and then fiddle with the VCR controls to locate products they want to take a second look at. Catalog designers also note that a videotape has the capacity to show a very limited number of products and that the production costs of such a venture could be prohibitive. Videologue says its production expenses totaled about $160,000 for the 30-minute master tape; the cost to make each duplicate ranges from $8 to $10.

Other catalog companies have experimented with video technology, but to little avail. Sears put its 236-page summer catalog on laser videodiscs in 1981, but since then the market for home videodisc players has collapsed. Last year, the Sharper Image tried a catalog-sales program on cable TV. "We didn't move very many products," a spokeswoman says. "But a lot of people did call and ask for our printed catalogs."

Questions
1. Why are many shoppers hesitant to make purchases from a video catalog?
2. What are the types of products that can most easily be sold by the use of a video catalog?
3. What are the advantages of video catalog shopping over conventional in-store shopping?

Source: "Catalog Goes Video to Tap VCR Boom," *The Wall Street Journal*, July 25, 1985, p. 23. Reprinted by permission of *The Wall Street Journal*, © Dow Jones & Company, Inc., July 25, 1985. All rights reserved.

2. Shopping with E.C.

Morris and Cindy Mason received from Parisian the information presented in Exhibit 1.

Morris thought this was a particularly interesting idea since he was so busy, and Cindy would never give him any hints about what she wanted for Christmas. Wouldn't it be great if he really could get an "out-of-this world" suggestion from E.C.? He thought this was a cute idea, and decided at lunch one day he'd run by the mall and try it out. Going to the mall at lunch was a strange sensation to him, since he never thought of getting out of the CBD until dinner time en route to his suburban home. And once he left the office, no stopping for shopping. But he could grab a sandwich at the deli at the mall; that would save time.

At noon, Morris was interested to see several people standing by the terminal at the Parisian entrance, waiting to get their personal gift suggestions. He was a little concerned since he had to get lunch and still be back at the office for his 1 o'clock appointment. However, the pleasant young woman who was assisting customers with their electronic cataloging moved them through rapidly—by his calculations, about one per minute. So in five minutes he was answering several of the computer's questions displayed on the upright CRT: (1) What is your name? (2) How much do you want to spend and for whom? (3) From a list of famous names displayed on the CRT, who is most like your wife in dress and attitude?

In moments, the printout in Exhibit 2 appeared with suggestions.

Questions
1. What are the strengths and weaknesses of the Parisian E.C. concept?
2. What are the types of benefits Parisian should promote as part of the experiment?

In "Close Encounters of the Third Kind," actor Cary Guffey discovered other-worldly beings. Now he's made two new, out-of-this-world discoveries at Parisian...our new robot, "E.C.," and Alabama's first Electronic Christmas Catalog.

Instead of sending you a printed Christmas catalog, we've installed exciting Electronic Catalogs in all our stores to simplify your Christmas shopping. Now you can find the right gift for everyone on your list. Answer four simple questions about any person you're shopping for, and the Electronic Catalog will suggest three Out of This World gifts in a matter of seconds.

Count on Parisian this Christmas for great gift ideas...fine merchandise... a full staff of helpful people... free gift boxes with any purchase... and free postage and mailing anywhere in the United States on gifts purchased by December 4.

Come on in to Parisian and ask our Electronic Catalog for your personal gift suggestions... because Christmas at Parisian is Out of This World. Make Parisian your Christmas store now.

·P·A·R·I·S·I·A·N·

CHRISTMAS

EXHIBIT 2

OUT OF THIS WORLD

MORRIS,
HERE ARE THE GIFT SUGGESTIONS
YOU REQUESTED FOR YOUR WIFE:

LESLIE FAY DRESS

KAYSER LONG GOWN AND ROBE

AIGNER HANDBAG

AND WHY NOT CONSIDER
THIS GREAT STOCKING STUFFER:

MARVELLA REGISTERED PEARLS

THANKS FOR MAKING PARISIAN YOUR CHRISTMAS STORE!
WE HOPE THAT YOUR CHRISTMAS IS

OUT OF THIS WORLD

·P·A·R·I·S·I·A·N·

CHRISTMAS

ENDNOTES

1. For further reading, see "POS at NBO: Alterations Are Included," *Chain Store Age Executive,* January 1986, p. 88; and "Hands Off, System On," *Chain Store Age Executive,* January 1986, p. 94.
2. *Retail MIS Expenses and Trends* (New York: Arthur Young & Co., 1985), p. 17.
3. Ibid.
4. "POS Advances Address the Future," *Chain Store Age Executive,* January 1986, p. 82.
5. The material on the universal product code is either quoted or paraphrased from *Grey Matter* 48, no. 2 (1977), pp. 1–5, used with permission. See also "UPC Scanners Used on Nearly 12,000 Groceries as Over 70,000 Supermarket Items Bar Coded," *Marketing News,* October 24, 1986, p. 16.
6. Ruth Stroud, "Interlink Adds Retailers to ATM Card Uses," *Advertising Age,* April 29, 1985, p. 64.
7. "Customers Are Cool to Debit Cards Despite Growing Presence in Stores," *The Wall Street Journal,* August 20, 1985, p. 31.
8. "Cable TV: A Retail Alternative?" *Chain Store Age Executive,* August 1986, pp. 11–14.
9. "Video Text System Makes Use of Standard TV Set," *Marketing News,* May 24, 1985; see also "Liquor Store Uses Touch-Screen Technology," *Marketing News,* May 24, 1985, p. 28.
10. Marilyn A. Harris, "Electronic Retailing Goes to the Supermarket," *Business Week,* March 25, 1985, p. 78.
11. "Sears Steps into Future with Videodisc Mail Order Catalog," *Marketing News,* May 29, 1982, p. 1.
12. "Cable Marketing Options Confuse Retailers: Some Prepare for Future, Others Hang Back," *Marketing News,* November 27, 1981, p. 13.
13. Jesse Snyder, "Ford Adds Computer to Aid Sales to 'Yuppies'," *Advertising Age,* August 16, 1984; and "Boat Owners Choose Paint by Computer," *Marketing News,* May 24, 1985.
14. "To Snare Shoppers, Companies Test Talking, Scented Displays," *The Wall Street Journal,* June 12, 1986, p. 31.
15. "Coupons for the Computer Age," *Time,* February 3, 1986, p. 59; and Joe Agnew, "Home Shopping: TV's Hit of the Season," *Marketing News,* March 13, 1987, p. 1.

Selecting Markets in Which to Compete

Chapters 3, 4, and 5 reviewed the factors that affect retail strategy development. Part 3 of the text, which consists of Chapters 6 and 7, evaluates the behavior of consumers and how retailers can develop strategies compatible with that behavior. Consumers are problem solvers. As such, they must make decisions on when to buy, how to buy, where to buy, and how much to buy. Retailers must be aware of how consumers perceive their outlets in the context of these decisions, and of the factors that influence the image consumers have of their outlet.

The changing lifestyles of consumers also influence merchandising strategy. Consumers today place increasing emphasis on convenience over cost in buying decisions, no longer feel guilty about indulging themselves, and seem to be obsessed with health and fitness. Such trends present both challenges and opportunities to retailers.

6

Keys to Understanding the Consumer

Fashion Industry Courting Large Women, Offering Stylish Clothes in Big Sizes

If retailing is a measure of American trends, the large woman has arrived. Department stores court her, and designers allow their labels to grace a size 26 dress. Bloomingdale's in Manhattan recently moved its large-size department to the fashionable third floor from its budget fourth floor. *Vogue* magazine, a fashion arbiter, has scheduled its first section devoted to large women. "It's really been an explosion," says Ernestine Linn, president of a Carr Associates division that specializes in buying large sizes, which are then sold to retailers.

Until recently, even the basic sports and business clothes that were taken for granted by thin women were denied to large women. The industry stuck to the "bullet-proof polyester" variety designed for "camouflage," says Carole Shaw, editor of *Big Beautiful Woman* magazine. Companies stereotyped the large woman as "over 50, under 5 feet, with hundreds of children, who sat in front of TV and ate bonbons," says Ann Harper, 5 feet 9 inches, a size 18, who became one of the first professional "full-size" models when she was larger.

To Mr. Raphael Benaroya, president of The Limited's Sizes Unlimited, "the first real sign of recognition is that the market is beginning to have segmentation." Macy's opened a large-size designer shop next to its regular large-size department, and there are boutiques carrying large sizes, such as Manhattan's Ashanti, where prices range up to $1,600 for a leather jacket.

The growth of shops specializing in clothes for large women illustrates how retailers are responding to changing consumer needs. Stylish clothes for large women were a less attractive market segment when few females worked outside the home. The increase in dual-income households and the lifestyle changes that occurred as women entered the job market are providing the new retailing opportunities.

An old saying is, "Nothing happens until a sale is made." Sales can only occur when the retailer understands and responds to how consumers buy, what they buy, where they buy, and when they buy. After reading this chapter you will be able to:

1. Recognize the consumer as a problem solver.

2. Explain motives for shopping other than buying.

3. Discuss where consumers buy, how they buy, what they buy, and when they buy.

4. Describe the role of image in consumer buying decisions.

5. Discuss dissatisfied consumers and how to deal with them.

Keep in mind the following points about consumers and their shopping behavior when studying this chapter:

1. Consumers are problem solvers. The role of the retailer is to help them solve their buying problems.
2. Consumers try to lower their risk by seeking information before buying merchandise. They also seek information for reasons other than risk reduction.
3. Store choice and merchandise choice depend on such variables as location, image, hours, and price, which are under the control of the retailer.
4. Many other factors, such as store atmosphere and courtesy of sales clerks, affect the in-store behavior of consumers.

MOTIVES FOR SHOPPING

Consumers shop for reasons other than buying, as shown in Figure 6–1. Such reasons can be grouped into personal and social motives. Personal motives include role playing, diversion, sensory stimulation, physical activity, and self-gratification. Social motives include the desire for social experiences, peer group attraction, status and authority needs, the pleasure of bargaining, and being with others of similar interests. Careful planning by a retailer can induce shoppers to make purchases even when the primary purpose of the trip is social or personal.

Personal Motives

Typical personal motives for shopping are shown in Figure 6–1. Personal motives result from internal needs of the consumer that are distinct from the needs fulfilled by purchasing a good or service.

Role Playing

Consumers often engage in activities they perceive to be associated with their role in life. Familiar roles include those of housewife, student, husband, or father. For example, a husband may perceive that in his role he should purchase only high-quality gifts from prestigious outlets for his wife.

Diversion

Shopping often provides the opportunity to get a break from the daily routine. Simply walking through a shopping center can allow a person to keep up with the latest trends in fashion, styling, or innovation. Similarly, malls often schedule antique or auto shows in an effort to attract consumers.

FIGURE 6–1 MOTIVES FOR SHOPPING

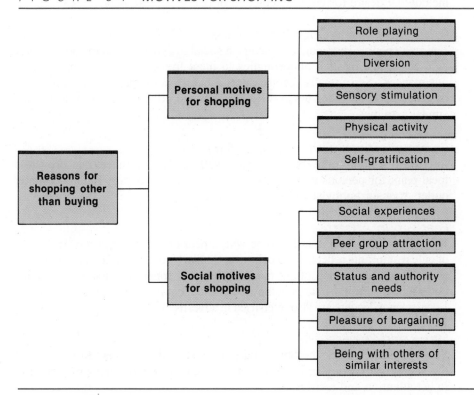

Physical Activity

Many people welcome the opportunity to walk for exercise in a safe, temperature-controlled environment. Some malls have organized walking and health clubs in response to such needs. The malls are opened for walking before the shops are opened for business.

Sensory Stimulation

Shoppers often respond favorably to background music, scents, and other types of sensory stimulation as part of the shopping process. Research has shown that customers feel more at ease, spend more time, and shop more often in a store that plays background music.

Self-Gratification

Shopping can alleviate loneliness or other emotional stress. Some persons also enjoy people watching while shopping.

Social Motives	Social motives for shopping are also illustrated in Figure 6–1. These motives include the desire for group interaction of one sort or another.

Social Experiences Outside the Home

For many people shopping has become a social activity outside the home. They take advantage of such opportunities to meet friends or to develop new acquaintances. Some malls feature special before-noon promotions especially designed to serve older persons. Others arrange cooking demonstrations and similar activities.

Communications with Persons of Similar Interests

Interest in a hobby may bring people together. Thus, retailers can provide a focal point for persons with similar interests or backgrounds. Retail computer outlets sponsor hobbyist clubs for such a reason.

Peer Group Attraction

Individuals may shop in order to be with a peer or reference group. Patronage of elite restaurants reflects such behavior. Similarly, one will often find teenagers at a record shop which offers music styles that appeal to their tastes. Some outlets have advisory boards composed of the most influential persons in a city. Local opinion leaders are also often used in advertising and promotion programs.

Status and Power

Some consumers seek the opportunity to be served and catered to as part of the shopping experience. Such an activity may be one of their primary ways to get attention and respect.

The Pleasure of Bargaining

Some persons enjoy the opportunity to negotiate over price. They get ego satisfaction as a result of bargaining.

A MODEL OF THE CONSUMER DECISION PROCESS

The decisions facing shoppers seeking to make a buying decision differ widely and depend on their past experiences with the merchandise to be bought. Many decisions, such as buying a loaf of bread, are routine because consumers have made similar purchases many times before. Other decisions, however, such as buying an automobile, may be difficult for some consumers because of their lack of experience or the risk of making a wrong decision.

When making other than routine purchases, the consumer normally goes through five decision stages, shown in Figure 6–2. The stages are: (1) problem recognition, (2) search for alternatives, (3) evaluation of alternatives, (4) purchasing decision, and (5) postpurchase behavior. Retailers can influence consumer choices and actions at each stage of the decision process.

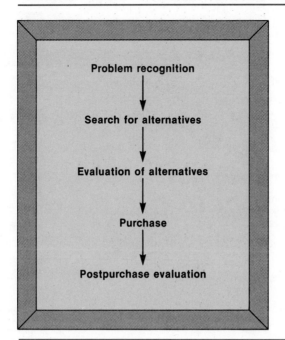

Problem recognition

↓

Search for alternatives

↓

Evaluation of alternatives

↓

Purchase

↓

Postpurchase evaluation

Problem Recognition

The decision process begins when the consumer perceives a difference between an existing and a preferred state of affairs. Sometimes, consumers may simply discover that they need to purchase gasoline for their automobile. Other things that may trigger problem recognition are a lack of satisfaction with an existing product or service, a raise, a spouse beginning to work (more money is now available), the need to purchase a gift for someone, or perhaps a change in dress fashions. Retailers can also trigger problem recognition through advertising, in-store displays, or the creative use of sight, sound, or smell.

Search for Alternatives

After problem recognition occurs, the consumer begins to seek and evaluate information, and may need up-to-date information about products, prices, stores, or terms of sale. The search for such data may be mental (the consumer draws on past experience) or physical.

The consumer may look for the merchandise or for the preferred store at which the purchase will be made. Consumers evaluate the store on the basis of factors important to them and choose the outlet that most closely matches these factors.

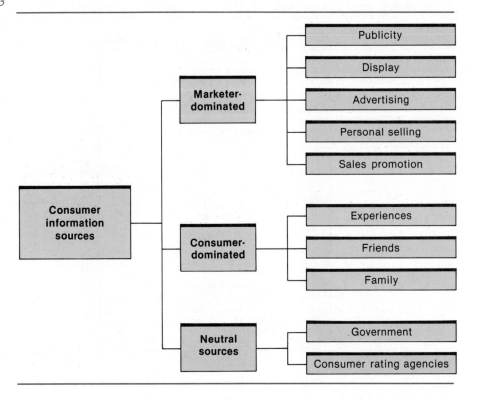

The retailer can make information available to consumers in a variety of forms to help them in their search. Consumers are normally exposed to (1) marketer-dominated sources, (2) consumer-dominated sources, and (3) neutral sources of information, as shown in Figure 6–3.

Marketer-Dominated Sources

Marketer-dominated information sources include advertising, personal selling, displays, sales promotion, and publicity. The retailer exercises control over their content. Typically, the retailer provides information on price, product features, terms of sale, and where the product may be purchased.

Consumer-Dominated Sources

Consumer-dominated sources include friends, relatives, acquaintances, or others. Consumer-dominated information is normally considered trustworthy. Satisfied consumers become especially important since they tend to talk to others about their shopping experiences.

Additional consumer-dominated sources of information are persons who are known and respected by their peers. Consumers are likely to respect information from such individuals. Retailers may therefore be able to utilize such groups as sports leaders, college class presidents, and other socially active persons to convey product and store information. Word-of-mouth information from such persons is likely to be received favorably.

Dissatisfied customers can also have a negative impact on an outlet. They often talk to many people about their bad experiences. Satisfied consumers typically are less vocal. Dissatisfied consumers in positions of influence can have a particularly damaging impact on an outlet because of the large number of people to whom they talk and because of their influence.

Neutral Sources of Information

Neutral sources of information are also likely to be perceived as accurate and trustworthy. Consumers Union is an example of an agency providing neutral information. Government rating agencies and state and local consumer affairs agencies also provide supposedly neutral information. Government agencies, for example, provide information on gasoline mileage for autos and energy efficiency ratings for appliances.

Typically, most information is provided by commercial sources even though consumers understandably may rely more on personal sources. Marketer-dominated sources may serve to create initial awareness while personal and neutral sources are used to help evaluate specific outlets or brands of merchandise.

Evaluation of Alternatives

After information is acquired, the consumer evaluates the alternatives available and assesses the options involved in a decision. Store and product attributes are used to compare outlets and merchandise. Examples of these attributes are shown in Table 6–1. Attribute importance varies among consumers. Knowledge of the importance of attributes is critical to management in helping consumers make choices compatible with their personal preferences. Product trial and

T A B L E 6–1 FACTORS INFLUENCING THE CHOICE OF MERCHANDISE AND THE CHOICE OF RETAIL OUTLETS

Factors Affecting Merchandise Choice		Factors Affecting Store Choice	
Product features	Service features	Store characteristics	Employee characteristics
Fashion	Credit terms	Hours	Knowledge
Brands	Installation	Layout	Friendliness
Quality	Accessories	Cleanliness	Helpfulness
Styles	Delivery	Displays	Courteousness
Colors	Layaway	Decor	
Assortments		Image	

demonstration, for example, is one way of reducing risk, as shown in Figure 6–4.

Six types of risks affecting store and merchandise choice decisions as consumers evaluate merchandise in terms of want satisfaction have been identified:

1. **Performance risk**—the chance that the merchandise purchased may not work properly.
2. **Financial risk**—the monetary loss from a wrong decision.
3. **Physical risk**—the likelihood that the decision will be injurious to one's health or likely to cause physical injury.
4. **Psychological risk**—the probability that the merchandise purchased or store shopped will not be compatible with the consumer's self-image.
5. **Social risk**—the likelihood that the merchandise or store will not meet with peer approval.

F I G U R E 6–4

Central to management objectives to broaden Carson Pirie Scott's market is a renewed emphasis on personalized service and individual attention as a way of reducing consumer risks of making a wrong buying decision. (Courtesy of Carson Pirie Scott. Photographed by Robert Kelling.)

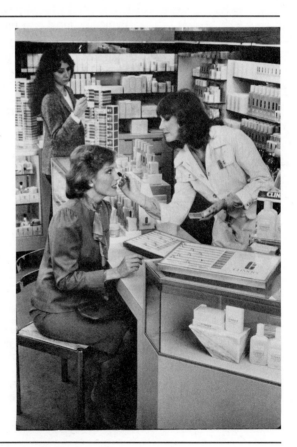

---

6. **Time-loss risk**—the likelihood that the consumer will not be able to get the merchandise adjusted, replaced, or repaired without loss of time and effort.[1]

The Purchasing Process

Choosing the store and the merchandise does not end the purchasing process. The consumer has to decide on the method of payment, accessories for the merchandise (such as a camera lens), whether to purchase an extended warranty, and delivery of bulky merchandise. Retailers often offer a variety of options designed to meet a diverse array of consumer preferences.

Post-Purchase Evaluation

Retailers need to reassure consumers after the purchase that they made the right decision. When making a major purchase, consumers are often afraid that they may have spent their money foolishly. A follow-up letter from the retailer or a phone call often can help reassure and satisfy the customer.

The level of consumer satisfaction also influences whether the store and its merchandise will be recommended to a friend. Retailers need to be sensitive to the uncertainties in the minds of the consumers, then work to alleviate their concerns.

UNDERSTANDING THE HOW, WHEN, WHERE, AND WHAT OF SHOPPING

Retailers probably can have the most influence on the behavior of consumers during the information search and evaluation stage of the decision process. An understanding of the *how, when, where,* and *what* of consumer shopping behavior can help retailers be responsive to consumer needs for information during their search and evaluation efforts.

The retailer needs to have the right merchandise at the right place, at the right time, and at the right price and quality to match consumer decisions on where to buy, what to buy, how to buy, and when to buy, as shown in Figure 6–5.

What includes consumer decisions on merchandise price and quality, whether to purchase store brands or national brands, and criteria used in evaluating merchandise. *When* includes decisions on such matters as time of day and day of week to shop. Similarly, *how* includes decisions on whether to engage in store or nonstore shopping. *Where* means the choice of a downtown location or a shopping center and the specific store.

Where Do Consumers Shop?

Shopping Centers

Consumers may choose shopping centers because children can be taken more easily to such places. Centers may be the best place to meet friends. Less walking is required and it is safer. Better store hours with a wider

FIGURE 6–5

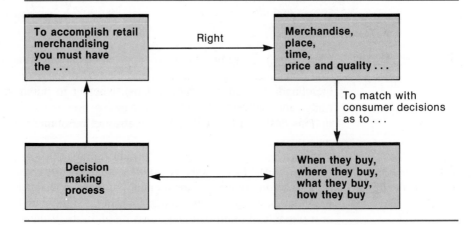

selection of merchandise may be available. The controlled climate of a shopping center often provides a social outing for shoppers who enjoy the festive atmosphere of the center or like to window shop as a way of keeping up with the latest trends in fashion.

Some people prefer shopping at "strip" shopping centers as opposed to the enclosed malls. Strip centers require less walking and generally involve less difficulty in shopping. Additionally, access is typically easier than to major enclosed malls.

Downtown

Some people prefer to shop downtown because of better delivery service, more convenient transportation, and the availability of nonshopping facilities, such as financial institutions. Others work downtown and find it convenient to shop there. Finally, some consumers, often those with lower incomes and no transportation, live near the downtown area and shop in the outlets closest to their homes.

Outshopping

Some consumers go out of town to shop (**outshopping**) because (1) the selection may be better ; (2) they may want to get out of town for a visit, including, perhaps, a good meal; (3) they may work out of town and do their shopping after work; and (4) store hours, store personnel, and services such as repair may be better in the other community.

Nonstore Shopping

Catalog and telephone shopping are the primary types of **nonstore shopping,** although at-home, personal selling of merchandise by firms such as Avon is also common. Nonstore shopping tends to be popular because it allows consumers to make purchase decisions at their leisure without leaving home. These shoppers seem to have higher incomes and higher education. Higher incomes allow them to make more discretionary purchases, and education often widens the opportunity for selling merchandise to these individuals. Because they have more education, nonstore shoppers often see less risk than other consumers in buying in a nonstore setting.[2]

Merchants can stress several important factors in nonstore purchases by consumers. Buying convenience allows consumers to make purchases in their homes. Good product guarantees are important in assuring consumers that risks in nonstore purchases are not unreasonable. The ease of credit-card buying offered by major merchants such as Sears also is a major factor in determining purchase decisions.

Choosing a Store

Consumers make decisions about stores at which to shop after deciding whether to shop downtown or at a shopping center if in-store purchases are to be made. The **image** of a retail outlet is important in such a decision. The major attraction characteristics include the merchandise, services offered, physical facilities, employees, and other shoppers. For example, consumers may be seeking a particular brand or quality of merchandise, specific services such as credit or delivery, an attractive outlet, courteous employees, and an outlet where consumers with similar lifestyles are likely to shop. All of these characteristics other than the characteristics of other shoppers are under the direct influence of retailers.

Research is often necessary to help management develop an understanding of the importance of these characteristics to shoppers. The information may help retailers do a better job of meeting consumer needs. One of the nation's foremost retailers is Neiman-Marcus. The firm has done an excellent job in developing a unique position in the minds of consumers by satisfying their needs. Indeed, Neiman-Marcus is known worldwide for its uniqueness. Some of the components of its mystique are shown in Exhibit 6–1.

The multiattribute model of consumer choice is one that is frequently used to help retailers understand the importance of various store features to consumers. The model can be applied as follows:

$$As = \sum_{i=1}^{n} B_i W_i$$

where

As = Attitude toward the store
B_i = Belief by a consumer that a store possesses a particular attribute
W_i = The weight or importance of the attribute to consumers
n = Number of attributes important to consumers in their choice of a store.

E X H I B I T 6–1   THE UNIQUENESS OF NEIMAN-MARCUS

The Neiman-Marcus Christmas Book has become one of the most popular and best-publicized Christmas books in the world. The catalogue is known for some of the most unusual and imaginative gifts, such as "His and Her" airplanes, Jaguars, and mummy cases. From the design of the cover to the originality of the merchandise, the Christmas book reflects the Neiman-Marcus belief in quality, good taste, and value.

Exclusivity . . . never daring to conform, Neiman-Marcus takes great pride in the ability to offer exclusive merchandise in many areas of the store. Look for the "Made Exclusively for Neiman-Marcus" label. This assures that the merchandise, whether it be a deck of cards displaying the Neiman-Marcus logo or an exclusively designed Russian lynx fur coat, will not be duplicated anywhere else in the world.

The precious jewelry department at Neiman-Marcus has been recognized as one of the largest and finest quality jewelry operations in the world. Besides the fact that many of the jewelry pieces are one-of-a-kind, Neiman-Marcus also designs in its own workroom. Other services offered include polishing, remounting, and jewelry appraisal. Expert guidance is offered with every purchase to ensure that each piece of jewelry will be enjoyed for years to come.

Many celebrities will frequent Neiman-Marcus due to its world-renowned reputation. We depend on our entire staff to extend a warm welcome. Employees should stay in their own department to allow the visitor time to shop without interference. In other words, let's extend the same courtesies to all our customers.

SOURCE: Courtesy of Neiman-Marcus.

Example: Assume that the four attributes shown in Table 6–2 are important in the consumer's choice of a store at which to shop. The *belief* about each attribute in store choice is rated on a scale of 1 to 3, with a score of 1 indicating high importance. Consumers rate the *importance* of each attribute on a scale of 1 to 5, with 1 reflecting a high degree of importance to consumers.

As shown in Table 6–2, the importance and belief scores are multiplied for each attribute and summed to develop a measure of the consumer's attitude toward each store being evaluated. Scores could range from 4 to 60 (3 × 5 × 4) with 4 being the most favorable score. Store attributes clearly vary in importance to consumers. For example, sporting goods stores may offer the widest selection of merchandise and the most qualified salespersons. Discount stores, on the other hand, offer little, if any, advice and only the fastest-moving items. However, their prices are likely to be lower than at other outlets.

Understanding Store Image

The model just shown is one way to determine a consumer's image of a retail outlet. *Image is the way consumers "feel" about a store.* The image is what people believe to be true about a store and how well those beliefs coincide with what they think it should be like. The image may be accurate. Or their image about a store may be quite different from reality. Knowing how consumers feel about an outlet is important in developing strategies for attracting them.

Attributes	Belief Weight (B_i)	Importance Weight (W_i)	Sum ($B_i \times W_i$)
Low price	2	3	6
Wide merchandise assortment	1	1	1
Courteous personnel	3	2	6
After-sale service	2	2	4
			17

$$As = \sum_{i=1}^{4} B_i \times W_i = 17$$

Why Think about Store Image?[3]

The retailer should be concerned about store image because the flow of customer traffic depends on it. Management may have what they think is the right merchandise, at the right price, in the right style, and in the desired size, color, and quality; but it is what the customer thinks of the price, the quality, and the service that is important.

Also important is the impression customers have of store employees. If they like the employees, they are more apt to have favorable impressions of what the store offers.

How Are Images Formed?

Specific features of a store provide the elements that make up its image. By examining each of the elements, management can determine the kind of image they want customers to have, as shown in Figure 6–6.

Price Policy. *A store's price line influences the way people think of its other aspects.* Therefore, prices must be consistent with the other elements.

A supermarket learned this fact when it installed carpeting. The plush floor covering created a high-price image. Customers felt that prices had gone up even though they had not.

Yet, it isn't always necessary for a store to give the impression that it is a "bargain center." A low-price policy can sometimes create an unfavorable image. Some customers feel that low quality goes with low prices and refuse to shop where they are promoted. Yet, other customers like bargain stores. The importance of price varies with the type of product, family income, and competitive offerings, to name a few of the considerations.

The sophisticated customer of the 1990s responds to the manner in which merchandise is displayed. (Courtesy Woodward & Lothrop)

Customers usually make up their minds about a store's prices from the store's advertising, displays, merchandising practices (such as stocking national brands), and location. They also rely on their impression of the store's pricing policies rather than on actual knowledge.

Two questions can be helpful in image building efforts:

1. What price do the customers expect to pay?
2. Do the customers consider price as important as quality, convenience, dependability, and selection?

Merchandise Variety. Image improves when customers find a product that they like but don't find in other stores. On the other hand, failure to carry certain items may give a retailer's whole product line a bad name. Similarly, when customers find one product in a store that displeases them, they are apt to become more critical of the rest of the offering. The key is in knowing the preferences of the customers.

Employees. Salespeople and other employees who are seen by customers affect the store's image. A negative impression is formed if the quality of a store's personnel is considerably above or below the educational level of most of its customers. Whether a store appeals primarily to professional or working people, salespeople should dress and speak in such a way that the customers feel comfortable talking to them.

These conversations, even though sometimes brief, determine whether customers regard the store as friendly and helpful, or impersonal and disinterested. A store may get a bad image because salespeople talk to each other rather than stepping up to greet customers. If customers have to ask for help, they may feel uncomfortable, as if they are interrupting a private conversation. In the same vein, a quality restaurant may suffer because of "chatty" waitresses. Customers want quiet and decorum when they dine by candlelight.

The Store's Appearance. What people see as they pass by the store is another important element in its image. Even people who never enter a store form an impression from its outside appearance. That impression may be the reason they don't break their stride when they go by the store.

Inside the store, the layout and the decor reinforce customers' impressions about the products and salespeople. For example, fixtures that are classic in design usually appeal to older and more conservative groups. Very plain, inexpensive-appearing fixtures help to build an image with young families whose incomes are limited. Low ceilings may make the store more personal, and indirect lighting usually makes the customer think of higher quality. Some color schemes are more masculine than others.

Type of Clientele. The image people have of a store may be determined by the type of people who shop there. Some people may view a particular store as one where professional people usually shop. They may think of others as stores where blue-collar workers usually shop.

Advertising. Advertising tells people whether the store is modern or old-fashioned, low-price or high-price, small or large. It also communicates other qualities of both a physical and psychological nature.

For example, when printed ads are full of heavy black print, customers get an image of low prices. Conversely, white space often connotes quality. A food store could improve its image by including a personal interest feature in its weekly ad of special prices. The outlet could feature a recipe, perhaps with the picture of the chef who originated it.

Changing the Store's Image

An image is a complex affair, and managers should not try to change a store's image without careful thought and planning. However, if a retailer is dissatisfied with the store image customers seem to have, three questions should be asked:

1. What kind of image will serve best in the existing market?
2. What kind of image does the store have now?
3. What changes can be made to improve the image?

A store cannot be all things to all people. In fact, one of the competitive strengths in retailing is that each store can be different. Many stores are successful because they specialize and their owner-managers build an image around the particular specialty.

Keeping the Image Sharp

Like the human face, a store's image does not stay bright by itself. Maintaining a store's image—regardless of the type—can be handled in the same way as other management problems. Managers should review the image periodically just as they periodically review financial statements. They can then find potential trouble spots and correct them before they get out of hand.

Listen to Customers
Management can ask customers what they like about a store and why they prefer it to others. Their answers give an idea of the strong points in the marketing mix and its image. They can also indicate what products and services should be advertised and promoted. A simple questionnaire such as the one shown in Figure 6–7 for Bradlees can provide very useful customer information.

All customers speak in sales. What they buy, or don't buy, speaks louder than words. Keeping track of sales by item can help to determine what customers like or don't like.

Customer complaints can help deal with reluctant customers—those who shop for one or two items they can't get elsewhere. In most cases, their reluctance is caused by the image they have of the store. Management can change that image only by learning its cause and making adjustments.

Management should also look at competitors. They can do some comparison shopping with the goal of trying to find out the strong points competitors use to create attractive images.

Listen to Noncustomers
Management often finds there are more people in their neighborhood who don't patronize them than who do. Why? Often only one or two aspects of an operation irritate and keep some people from having a good image of it. Because of a grouchy cashier, for example, potential customers may think poorly of the whole store.

FIGURE 6-7

Now It's Your Turn

We'd like to know what you think of our service, our merchandise, our personnel, and our appearance. We value your ideas and welcome your comments because we want to make Bradlees the kind of store you like to shop!

Please take a moment to rate us on each item indicated below. If there is anything else you'd like to add, we've included a space for your comments.

Rate Us

Please circle number that best applies to each category.

	Excellent	Very Good	Average	Below Average	Poor
Speedy Checkout	1	2	3	4	5
Availability of Sale Items	1	2	3	4	5
Raincheck Fulfillment	1	2	3	4	5
Employee Courtesy	1	2	3	4	5
Return Policy	1	2	3	4	5
Complaints Satisfactorily Resolved	1	2	3	4	5
Merchandise Quality	1	2	3	4	5
Regular (non-sale) Prices	1	2	3	4	5
Store Cleanliness	1	2	3	4	5
Restroom Facilities	1	2	3	4	5
Well Lit Parking Lot	1	2	3	4	5
Overall Rating of Bradlees	1	2	3	4	5
Compared to other Stores	1	2	3	4	5

Dear Karen: _____

_____
_____
_____
_____
_____
_____
_____
_____

Name _____
Street _____
City_____State _____
Zip _____
Home Phone_____Work Phone_____
Store Location_____
Date and Time of Visit _____

SOURCE: Courtesy of Bradlees.

Chapter 6 Keys to Understanding the Consumer

TABLE 6–3 COSTS IN SHOPPING AND BUYING

Cost of merchandise

Other monetary outlays
1. Parking fees.
2. Automobile gasoline and wear and tear.
3. Installation.
4. Credit.
5. Repairs.
6. Wrapping.
7. Babysitting fees.
8. Warranties.

Nonmonetary costs
1. Time away from other activities.
2. Waiting in line.
3. Comparison of merchandise between stores.
4. Comparison of alternative merchandise offerings.
5. Travel time.

Emotional costs
1. Frustration from out-of-stock items.
2. Dealing with surly or indifferent sales assistance.
3. Bargaining over price and terms of sale.
4. Concern over a wrong decision.
5. Effects of crowding.

How Do Consumers Shop?

The way in which consumers select products and services and the distance they will travel to shop also affect merchandising decisions.

The Costs of Shopping

Many consumers try to minimize the costs of shopping when making a shopping trip. The costs of shopping are money, time, and energy. *Money costs* are the cost of goods purchased and the cost of travel. *Time costs* include the time spent getting to and from the store(s), time spent in getting to and from the car, and time spent paying for merchandise. *Energy* costs include carrying packages, fighting traffic, parking, waiting in line, and various psychological costs as shown in Table 6–3.

Management can be responsive to these problems by having the proper store hours and by offering shoppers credit, delivery, and similar services.

Consumers are willing to travel farther for specialty goods than for either **shopping goods** or **convenience goods** because they believe the satisfaction they obtain from getting exactly what they want more than offsets the cost of the extra effort. Convenience goods are those items for which consumers are indifferent to brand name and will make a purchase at the most accessible outlet. Shopping goods are products for which consumers make comparisons between various brands in a product class. A specialty good is one for which a consumer exhibits a strong preference for a specific brand.

It is not possible to generalize as to what types of merchandise can be described as convenience, shopping, or specialty goods. Consumers view merchandise differently. What is a shopping good to one consumer may be a convenience good to another one. Typical examples of convenience, shopping goods, and specialty goods can be identified, however. Household salt is a convenience good for many shoppers. They will make the purchase at the nearest available outlet. Household durables or appliances are shopping goods for many persons. A lawnmower is an example of such a product. Consumers often do not have strong brand preferences for such an item. As a result they will compare price, warranties, and various features before making a purchase. Designer label merchandise such as Gloria Vanderbilt is a specialty good for many shoppers. Similarly, a Rolex watch may be regarded by many shoppers as a specialty good. They will travel considerable distances to purchase the item they want and will not compare alternative merchandise offerings.

Overall, less time is spent today in shopping than in the past. The reasons include: (1) advertising, which makes information more easily available, (2) the higher cost of gasoline, and (3) less time for shopping by women now working outside the home. Many shoppers do not visit more than two stores, even when buying items such as TV sets.

How Far Are Consumers Willing to Travel?

Most shoppers at corner food stores live within a half mile of the store. Shoppers usually will travel 10 minutes or so to shop for higher-priced merchandise. Typically, 75 percent of the persons traveling to a large shopping center live within 15 minutes of the center. However, shoppers will travel much farther to purchase specialty goods.

| What Do Consumers Buy? | *Price and brand are two major attributes that affect consumer purchases.* Price is important because it is often a measure of worth and quality. Brand is often relied on as a measure of quality. Other factors that are important in merchandise choice include open-code (freshness) dating, unit pricing, shelf displays, shelf location, and coupons. |

Price

Consumers ordinarily do not know the exact price of a merchandise item. But, they usually know within well-defined ranges. The higher-income consumer usually is less price conscious than the lower-income consumer seeking the same merchandise. The more of a shopper's income that is spent on an item, the greater price awareness there is likely to be. Also, price is not as important to the nondiscount shopper as to the discount shopper.

Brands

Some consumers purchase only well-known **national brands** of manufacturers such as Del Monte. This behavior helps them avoid bad purchases. But many consumers are now buying *nonbranded* items (or **generics**), such as paper products, hard goods, drugs, and liquor. Consumers can save up to 30–40 percent when making such purchases, through savings in packaging, advertising, and other marketing costs. They rely on the reputation of the store as an assurance of quality in buying the items. Some stores, such as Kroger, sell their own brands. These are known as **private brands.**

Private brands have been especially important to department stores and specialty stores in recent years. During much of the previous decade such outlets had relied heavily on designer labels such as Calvin Klein to help develop upscale, somewhat exclusive, images. However, as the sales volume of the designer labels leveled off as a result of the rather exclusive pattern of distribution through department and specialty stores, suppliers began selling the merchandise through mass market outlets such as K mart. The merchandise thus lost its exclusivity and in many instances was heavily price discounted. Department stores and specialty stores as a defensive strategy began developing their own private label brands to maintain desired margins on the merchandise and to protect the integrity of their image.

Open-Code Dating

Open-code dating means the consumer can tell the date after which a product should not be used, and food shoppers often use this information. The strongest users tend to be young consumers with higher incomes and higher levels of education, who live in the suburbs. The usage pattern for nutritional labeling is similar to that for open-code dating.

Unit Pricing

Unit pricing states price in such terms as price per pound or ounce. Shoppers use this information as a guide to the best buys. Here again, the younger, higher-income consumers are more likely to use the data. Brand switching often occurs when prices are stated on a per-unit basis.

Shelf Displays

Retailers tend to give the most shelf space to merchandise with the highest profit margins. Profits tend to drop, however, if managers shift store displays and layout too often. Point-of-sale materials, even simple signs, can increase item sales by as much as 100 percent. End-of-aisle and special displays can have even larger effects on consumer buying behavior. Today, with computerized cash registers, managers know exactly how often a product sells. As a result, they often will stock only the two or three best-selling brands in each product category. The subject of shelf space allocation is discussed in greater detail in Chapter 16 on layout and merchandise presentation.

Shelf Location

Shelf location is an important factor in influencing consumer purchase decisions. Consumers are most prone to purchase merchandise displayed at eye level. Merchandise located on the lowest shelves may present difficulties for elderly or infirm consumers, and merchandise on the higher shelves may be difficult for some individuals to reach. The ideal shelf location depends on the consumer. For example, merchandise directed primarily at children should be on a lower shelf level to establish eye contact.

Shelf location becomes especially critical for low-involvement products since consumers are likely to purchase the first item that catches their attention. Examples include cleaning supplies or paper products. Conversely, consumers are likely to make brand comparisons in a high-involvement product class, such as salad dressings, in which shoppers may compare products by content or number of calories. Shelf location may be a less critical factor for high-involvement products since consumers will make a more concerted effort to compare alternative offerings.

Coupons

Coupons can be used to draw new customers to a store and to increase purchases by regular consumers. They can also be used to offset the negative features of a store by drawing customers to a poor location. Nine out of 10 people redeem coupons during a year. The coupon users tend to have slightly higher incomes than the average household and normally have children. They are especially good customers for retailers. Trading stamps, rebate offers, and similar strategies also can be used to attract new consumers and to retain the loyalty of current customers.

When Do Consumers Buy? Sunday and 24-hour openings are attractive to many shoppers. Sunday is often the only time some families can shop together, and working wives are more likely to shop in the evenings and on Sunday. Ads such as shown in Figure 6–8 for Safeway reflect the increasingly busy **lifestyle** of today's consumers.

Many retailers do not like Sunday openings or long hours because they feel long hours drive up costs without helping profits. However, consumer preference for these hours and competitive pressures are making these openings increasingly common.

Retailers may experience great seasonal variations. Some retailers make one third or more of their annual sales in November and December. Spring dresses sell well just prior to Easter. Picnic supplies sell best in the summer, and ski equipment during the winter.

RESPONDING TO CONSUMER DISSATISFACTION[4]

Consumer complaints are a signal that all is not well in the business. Retailers should actively seek feedback from customers—what they like and don't like, how they can be better served, their satisfaction with store policies, and so forth. Unfortunately, too few stores do this.

It is too simple to say the customer is always right. Some consumers do not pay their bills. They shoplift, switch price tags, and so forth. Nor is the customer always wrong. Retailers sometimes use bad credit information, make errors in customers' accounts, and sell inferior merchandise.

FIGURE 6–8

24 reasons to shop at Safeway.

We're Open 7 a.m.
We're Open 8 a.m.
We're Open 9 a.m.
We're Open 10 a.m.
We're Open 11 a.m.
We're Open 12 p.m.
We're Open 1 p.m.
We're Open 2 p.m.
We're Open 3 p.m.
We're Open 4 p.m.
We're Open 5 p.m.
We're Open 6 p.m.
We're Open 7 p.m.
We're Open 8 p.m.
We're Open 9 p.m.
We're Open 10 p.m.
We're Open 11 p.m.
We're Open 12 a.m.
We're Open 1 a.m.
We're Open 2 a.m.
We're Open 3 a.m.
We're Open 4 a.m.
We're Open 5 a.m.
We're Open 6 a.m.
We're Open 7 a.m.

Now these Safeway locations are open to serve you 24 hours a day.

Evans & Downing, Denver • 1st & Steele, Cherry Creek • 14th & Krameria, Denver •
Parker & Dartmouth, Aurora • 80th & Wadsworth, Arvada • Arapahoe & Quebec, Englewood •
Highway 285 & Logan, Englewood • Colfax & Garrison, Lakewood • 84th & Federal, Westminster •
28th & Arapahoe, Boulder • Washington & Malley Drive, Northglenn

The Denver division of Safeway Stores used a lot of white space and the words "We're Open 24 Hours" to make its point that stores at certain locations are open 24 hours a day.

SOURCE: Printed with Permission of Safeway Stores, Incorporated © 1986.

How Do Consumers View Retailers?

Retailers rate weakest in communicating with consumers, in being interested in customers, in providing good value for money, and in speaking honestly about merchandise. Chains tend to rate highest in the quality of the job they perform; appliance and automobile repair services rank at the bottom of the list. The frequency of consumer complaints reported by the National Council of Better Business Bureaus and shown in Table 6–4 illustrates consumer dissatisfaction with various types of retail businesses.

Type of Business	Rank	Complaints		
		Number Received	Percent of Total	Percent Settled
Mail order companies	1	85,677	20.94%	72.7%
Home furnishing stores	3	10,457	2.56	68.0
Department stores	7	8,262	2.02	87.0
Apparel and accessory stores	14	4,756	1.16	68.7
Appliance stores	17	4,361	1.07	71.3
TV/radio/phono stores	18	4,074	1.00	69.9
Floor covering stores	26	2,943	.71	54.4
Jewelry stores	29	2,780	.67	70.2
Building material supply	60	1,070	.26	75.2
Music/record stores	64	912	.22	74.0
Chain food stores	73	550	.13	82.6
Drugstores	75	439	.11	80.2
Independent food stores	87	217	.05	76.4
Miscellaneous retail stores	Not listed	16,037	3.92	64.9

SOURCE: Reported in Robert Kahn, *Retailing Today,* May 1985, p. 3.

What's Being Done about Problems?

Retailer Responses

Freshness dates now appear on many products. Nutritional labeling is also being practiced. Unit pricing is another aid to the consumer.

Some stores provide in-store consumer consultants, consumer advisory panels, consumer affairs forums, buyer guides, employee training on consumer rights, and signs, sales notices, and applications in languages other than English when appropriate. The information often needed and how to provide it are shown in Figure 6–9.

Voluntary Action Groups

Voluntary action groups are organizations sponsored by an industry and designed to respond to consumer complaints about products or services sold by retailers. The groups also provide needed information to consumers to help them make important buying decisions. Such groups include the Major Appliance Consumer Action Panel, the Automobile Consumer Action Panel, and the Furniture Industry Consumer Action Panel.

Consumers also need to react responsibly to help avoid unnecessary problems in their capacity as consumers. Consumers are likely to have fewer problems with merchandise when they undertand how to operate the items they purchase, if they use proper care in handling the equipment, if they bring defective merchandise to the attention of retailers, if they are aware of their rights as consumers, and if they make comparisons before their purchases.

Better Business Bureaus

Better Business Bureaus serve a useful purpose in handling consumer problems at the local level. Complaints about false advertising and mislabeling of items are often taken to Better Business Bureaus. The bureau in each community is supported by dues from member firms. Membership is voluntary.

Many smaller communities do not have Better Business Bureaus. In such situations the function of monitoring business practices is usually carried out by local chambers of commerce. The chambers have codes of conduct which all ethical merchants are urged to follow, and chamber members work to help ensure that business licenses are not issued to firms engaging in questionable practices. They also sponsor seminars designed to remind members of unfair or questionable business practices that can alienate consumers.

A Philosophy of Action for Management

Retailers need to be alert to changing attitudes and demands of consumers and to practice better customer relations. The demands of consumers normally are not unrealistic. Customers simply want more, better, and honest information.

Retailers may need to do research from time to time to learn how customers feel about a store and its products. They should take a positive approach in dealing with customers. Most retailers do not want to make money by selling merchandise that may hurt customers or drive them away. Customers simply want such things as better labeling, honesty in advertising, and full information on credit terms.

Some retailers such as L. L. Bean make a special effort to advertise directly to consumers to tell them about their customer satisfaction programs. L. L. Bean, as noted in Figure 6–10, guarantees 100 percent satisfaction and will accept returns at any time for any reason. Bean will either replace the purchase or refund the purchase price and will pay all regular postage and handling charges.

CHAPTER HIGHLIGHTS

— Consumers go through a series of stages in making a purchase decision. The stages, for other than routine purchases, include problem recognition, information search, evaluation, the actual purchase decision, and postpurchase behavior. Retailers can influence consumer choices and actions at each stage of the decision process.

— Retailers can have the most influence on the behavior of consumers during the information search and evaluation stage. An understanding of the how, when, where, and what of consumer shopping and buying behavior can help retailers be responsive to their needs for information.

Consumers use consumer-dominated, marketer-dominated, and neutral sources of information in making store and product choices. Marketer-dominated sources include advertising, personal selling, displays, sales promotion, and publicity. Consumer-dominated sources include friends, relatives, acquaintances, or others. Neutral sources include government rating agencies and state and local consumer affairs agencies.

Consumers seek to minimize risks during the purchase evaluation stage. The risks they are seeking to avoid include performance risk, financial risk, physical risk, psychological risk, social risk, and time-loss risk.

Many consumers try to minimize the costs of shopping when making purchase decisions. These costs include money, time, and energy. Actual purchases by consumers are influenced by many factors, including price and brand, shopping aids such as open-code dating and unit pricing, shelf displays and shelf locations, coupons, trading stamps, and rebates.

Retailers also need to be sensitive to consumer concerns which often take the form of consumerism. Efforts at solving consumer dissatisfaction often start with the retailer from whom a purchase was made. In recent years, a variety of retailers have responded by including in-store consumer consultants, consumer advisory panels, consumer-affairs forums, buyer guides, and employee training on consumer rights.

KEY TERMS

Consumer-dominated information sources Information sources over which the retailer has no influence. Examples include friends, relatives, acquaintances, and others.

Convenience goods Those items of merchandise for which consumers are indifferent about brand names and which they will purchase at the most accessible outlet.

Financial risk The monetary loss from a wrong decision.

Generics Unbranded items such as paper products which are sold in many supermarkets.

Image The way consumers "feel" about a store or merchandise.

Lifestyles How consumers spend their time, what interests them, and how they view themselves.

Marketer-dominated information sources Sources of information under the control of the retailer. Examples are advertising, personal selling, displays, sales promotion, and publicity.

National brands The brands of a manufacturer such as Procter & Gamble which are sold through a wide variety of retail outlets.

Neutral sources of information Sources of information such as government rating agencies and state and local consumer affairs agencies which consumers perceive as trustworthy.

Nonstore shopping The purchase of merchandise by use of catalogs, telephone, or ways other than physically entering an outlet.

Open-code dating Information provided so that the consumer can tell the date after which a product should not be used.

Outshopping Traveling out of one's local area to make purchases.

Performance risk The chance that merchandise purchased may not work properly.

Physical risk The likelihood that a purchase decision will be injurious to one's health or is likely to cause physical injury.

Private brands Brands of merchandise which retailers develop and promote under their own label.

Psychological risk The probability that the merchandise purchased or the store shopped will be compatible with the consumer's self-image.

Shopping goods Merchandise for which consumers will make comparisons between various brands in a product class before making a purchase.

Social risk The likelihood that the merchandise or store will not meet with peer approval.

Time-loss risk The likelihood that the consumer will not be able to get merchandise adjusted, replaced, or repaired without loss of time and effort.

Unit pricing A situation in which price is stated in such terms as price per pound or ounce.

DISCUSSION QUESTIONS

1. Briefly describe each of the stages (steps) of the consumer decision process discussed in the text.
2. What are some of the reasons consumers might prefer to shop downtown? Why do some people prefer to shop in shopping centers?
3. What is the importance of image to the retailer? How does it affect the shopping behavior of consumers? Think of the two largest department stores in your community. How would you describe their images?
4. How does open-code dating and unit pricing information aid consumers in making purchase decisions? Develop a profile of those consumers who are the most likely to use these types of shopping information.
5. What are some of the things retailers can do to reduce each of the six types of risks discussed in the chapter?
6. Provide an example of each of the personal and social motives discussed in the chapter as reasons for shopping but not buying.

7. What are some of the things retailers can do to help consumers minimize the costs of shopping?
8. Discuss activities which you know are being undertaken by consumer groups and businesses in your area to help stop consumer dissatisfaction.
9. What are some retailers doing to help consumers buy more effectively?
10. Which roles do voluntary action groups and Better Business Bureaus play in helping to resolve consumer dissatisfaction?

APPLICATION EXERCISES

1. Visit a national supermarket in your community, a discount or warehouse grocer food outlet, and a 7-Eleven type of food store. Prepare a paper that points out the similarities and differences between the three types of stores. Write a brief summary of your thoughts about the image of each type of outlet. Describe the characteristics of the people you think are most likely to shop at each of the three outlets.

2. Briefly interview 10–15 of your fellow students. Find out their most recent dissatisfaction with a retail outlet. What action did they take, if any? What was the response of management to the situation if it was called to their attention? Will the situation cause the dissatisfied person not to shop at the outlet again? Write a short paper summarizing their experiences.

CASES

1. Foley's Answers Back: Chain's Customers Have the President's Ear

When Foley's male customers complained to John Utsey, president, about not stocking large sizes, big and tall shops for men suddenly appeared at Foley's.

The same thing happened when women wrote to the president saying they couldn't find small sizes. Petite shops soon become a standard.

It's all part of Foley's strategic plan to evaluate and improve sales productivity, while at the same time responding to consumer needs, all through the use of a sophisticated computer program.

Foley's, a Federated Department Store Division, operates 16 units in Houston, Dallas, San Antonio, and Austin. Like all other businesses in the Texas area, it has been suffering from an economy depressed by the plummeting prices of oil and gas. It has also seen the invasion of formidable competition in recent years, including Macy's, Marshall Field's, and Mervyn's, plus a slew of off-price chains and discounters.

In order to bolster declining revenues, Foley's, along with Garr Consulting Group, Marietta, Georgia, a subsidiary of Touche Ross, developed the Sales Floor Coverage Program. In the two years it's been in existence it has moved from its initial experimental stage to a full-time system.

Objectives of the program include:

1. Using postcards and face-to-face interviews to solicit 3,000 to 4,000 consumer comments per month.
2. Entering these comments into computers for immediate reaction, such as creating the big and tall shops and petite departments.
3. Using the computers to assign sales staff to various parts of each store during specific segments of the workday to match peak traffic flow.
4. Setting realistic sales goals for each employee, department, and store, with rewards to overachievers.

At the heart of the program are the customer comments. Comment cards are distributed at wrap desks and put in shopping bags. Comments are also solicited at semimonthly exit interviews. The results are tabulated and entered into in-store IBM PCs daily. The printouts reflect how many customers were greeted promptly in each store, whether the salesperson was pleasant or not, whether the store was adequately staffed or understaffed when the customer wanted to make a purchase. Each department in each store is evaluated.

When it initially began soliciting customer comments, Foley's found out what every customer with limited shopping hours already knows: when customers are eager to make a purchase, they can't find sales help.

"We found out that we weren't as good as we thought," says Gary Key, operating vice president of stores and customer service at Foley's. "We knew that (our) people were going to lunch at lunchtime, but we didn't know that there weren't any replacements on hand."

The Garr organization came in and literally counted the traffic in each store manually. It selected areas with high-density traffic flow and recorded the results every 30 minutes. Results were segregated by store departments and locations of the stores (shopping malls, downtown areas). Graphs plotted traffic patterns and staffing for each store. Often the graphs showed peaks and valleys of traffic flow and sales staffing not in sync with each other. All this resulted in changing the work schedules.

At the time, Foley's had mostly full-time salespeople on its staff, but after reading the results of the computer printouts and the graphs, management began to readjust the schedules. As many full-timers quit or retired, they were replaced with part-timers, people who were more than willing to work from 11 A.M. to 2 P.M. when the lunch crowd came storming in.

On the subject of the comment cards, Bob Oliver, senior vice president of stores, points out that Foley's planning called for it to take out a restaurant in one of the stores and replace it with a merchandise department. After the restaurant was eliminated, the howls that came in via the comment cards made management reassess the move and take steps to put it back. "As a result," says Oliver, "we spent a lot of money to rectify the mistake."

Executives at Foley's are enthusiastic about the consumer comment program. Every one of the cards that is sent in daily is read by Utsey, Oliver, and Key, who then pass them along to the store managers and most of the department people. Each of the thousands of cards is personally acknowledged by the 16 store managers. In one instance, one manager sent out 2,739 acknowledgments. Another sent out 1,718 in the same month.

Some of the comments are nice: "I think Foley's has the nicest salespersons," writes T. Taylor.

"It was good to find a selection of petite sizes," writes M. Biggers.

Some have a bone to pick: "Too hot—turn on your air conditioner! You lost a sale from me because I couldn't stand in the store long enough to shop for what I wanted. I'll go elsewhere to find what I need." This was unsigned.

Some have suggestions: "I stopped to shop because I saw some sheets that I would have loved to buy. However, your stores do not carry queen-size pillow cases and I will not buy king or regular cases," writes Theda Kelly. "These cases are manufactured. Why don't you carry them? Other stores do. So I shall go there."

According to Key, Foley's went into the program without an ultimate goal of reducing sales costs which, in fact, remained the same. It is among the lowest in the Federated Family of Chains.

"Today, Foley's has a leaner organization than we had five years ago, even though we've added four stores," says Key. "We have less corporate staff, less management people and support staffers."

"Our ultimate goal, our reason for being, is our desire to change the culture of the chain," says Oliver, adding, "We want to be a customer service organization. We're customer driven."

Questions

1. How can Foley's justify the costs of their new customer response programs including reinstalling the restaurant, for example?
2. How is it possible that a progressive retailer such as Foley's would be unaware that they were understaffed during peak sales periods and that they needed to add departments for big and tall men and petite shops for women?
3. Is the Foley program feasible for all retailers? Why or why not? What types of retailers would likely benefit the most from the Foley program?

Source: "Foley's Answers Back: Chain's Customers Have the President's Ear," *Chain Store Age Executive*, September 1986, p. 100. Reprinted by permission. Copyright by Lebhar-Friedman, Inc., 425 Park Avenue, New York, New York 10022.

2. Retailers Change Their Stores and Goods, Looking to Cash in on New Buying Habits

For years, the ServiStar hardware store in Gloucester, Virginia, was a real male bastion: dark, dank, and dirty. And why not? Men were just about the only customers.

But with women becoming bigger buyers of hardware-store items, ServiStar decided to change its image. Now the place is full of bright lights, chrome gridwork, and murals. "Some of the old guys come in here and kid us about being a disco,'' says Robert Fitchett, whose family owns the store, but ''our sales are up 33 percent in the past year.''

Retailers have a new tactic for responding to the changing buying habits of men and women: They're altering—often in subtle ways—their stores and merchandise. Hardware and auto-parts stores are remodeling to shed their macho image. Grocers sell soup cans on the higher shelves to suit men's height. And department stores are catering to women with color-coordinated TV and stereo sets.

The changes are not without some risks; some shoppers might find the steps sexist, playing to common but often mistaken stereotypes about women. The alterations do, however, signal a new direction for retailers. When more women began buying electronics products and more men started shopping for clothes a few years ago, merchants tried to lure these new shoppers mainly with advertisements. Now, many retailers are taking far more concrete steps.

Enough Reason to Change

"Advertising changed first and once that got enough people into the store, there was enough reason for merchandising to change,'' says Jack R. Terrazas, new products marketing manager for Hunter Fan Co., a ceiling-fan maker in Memphis, Tennessee.

Some of the changes are aimed at attracting men. For instance, Rich's, an Atlanta department store, holds two men's fashion shows a year and issues a men's catalog. Most of the changes though, are designed to attract women, whose purchasing power has grown more than men's.

Each retailing group has its own approach. Convenience stores, for example, are making subtle changes, such as offering salads and diet sandwiches. One chain, Wawa Food Markets, moved the produce and deli at 310 convenience stores farther from the beer, cigarettes, and snacks.

"We're doing this so women don't have to stand in line with the male construction worker,'' says Frederic Schroeder, marketing director for the Wawa, Pennsylvania–based chain.

Consumer electronics stores are making more noticeable moves. Tandy Corp.'s Radio Shack chain has remodeled 322 stores so far this year so they wouldn't look like hardware outlets anymore. Gizmos are being moved to the back, and assembled goods like radios and phones are being shoved up front.

The retailers making the most obvious efforts to woo women shoppers are auto-parts and hardware stores. Along with the major remodeling jobs, some hardware stores are putting in shopping carts, which they believe make women feel more comfortable. Chicago's Arlington Hardware store uses mock-ups to demonstrate how to operate drills, and its owner holds evening courses on home repairs. At a Bumper-to-Bumper auto-parts store in Fort Worth, Texas, portraits of women working on their cars decorate the walls.

"An auto-parts store isn't a typical place that a woman would feel good going into,'' says Larry Anton, president of the chain. "We hope the pictures personalize the store.''

The merchandise at hardware and auto-parts stores is changing, too. A programmable thermostat that controls furnaces is one example. The maker, Hunter Fan, boiled down the instructions to four steps and says the thermostat can be installed in 30 minutes with a screwdriver. (At least that was the average time it took 28 secretaries the company tested.)

"Nowadays, you can't design anything with just the man in mind or you won't turn it over,'' says Mr. Terrazas at Hunter Fan.

For the most part, such changes have helped retailers; a third of the 250,000 buyers of Hunter Fan's thermostat last year were women. "Five years ago, 95 percent would have been men and the rest would have been women buying them as gifts,'' Mr. Terrazas says. Tandy says sales are up 15 percent at its remodeled Radio Shack stores since last year; 35 percent of the store customers are women now, compared with 5 percent a decade ago.

Some of the changes are based on surveys, but many are pure hunches. Clearly, the moves are chancy, especially since retailers are assuming a whole sex prefers something.

Oppenheimer & Co., a brokerage firm, tried to draw female customers by opening a new office staffed with women a few years ago. The assumption was women felt more comfortable getting financial advice from other women. The idea died quickly.

"There was a backlash against all these things,'' says Barbara Lee, a financial consultant with Shearson Lehman Brothers Inc. "Women didn't like the idea that they were getting different information than men.''

Turning Off Customers

What's more, changes aimed at attracting a new group of buyers could turn off a store's traditional customers. That's one reason supermarket chains haven't made many major changes just to attract male shoppers, even though some industry estimates say men now account for as much as 40 percent of grocery sales, compared with 15 percent a decade ago.

Other retailers, though, say the risks are worth it. "I'm sure that when you make this drastic a change, you lose some male customers," says Robert Myers, Radio Shack's vice president and controller. "But we haven't lost any appreciable amount."

James Everett of Retail Planning Associates, a consulting firm in Columbus, Ohio, adds, "Redesigns tend to improve the reaction of women while men remain constant."

Some retailers reduce the risk by being cautious. Convenience-store chains, for example, say they're still trying just as hard as before to attract their main customer base of blue-collar men. Even the Bumper-to-Bumper auto-parts store isn't "too squeaky clean," chain president Mr. Anton says. "The nature of our business is still mostly men."

Questions

1. What factors are causing the changes in the who, where, and when of the store patronage decisions of shoppers today?
2. What are the likely risks consumers may fear in making buying decisions that are not part of their traditional roles as shoppers?
3. Why would some consumers be dissatisfied with store changes that are designed to appeal to new groups of shoppers? What steps could retailers take to lessen the dissatisfaction?

Source: Scott Kilman, "Retailers Change Their Stores and Goods, Looking to Cash in on New Buying Habits," September 8, 1986, p. 31. Reprinted by permission of *The Wall Street Journal,* © Dow Jones & Company, Inc. All rights reserved.

ENDNOTES

1. For further reading, see Karen Blumenthal, "Home-Buyer Warranties Can Cut Repair Outlays," *The Wall Street Journal,* July 24, 1985, p. 23; and Joshua Weiner, "Are Warranties Accurate Signals of Product Liability?" *Journal of Consumer Research,* September 1985, pp. 245–50.
2. George Moschis, Jac Goldstucker, and Thomas J. Stanley, "At-Home Shopping: Will Consumers Let Their Computers Do the Walking?" *Business Horizons,* March–April 1985, pp. 22–29.
3. Reproduced with modifications from Roger D. Blackwell, "Knowing Your Image," *Small Marketers Aids, No. 124* (Washington, D.C.: U.S. Small Business Administration); for further reading see C. J. Young, "Bijan Designs a Very Exclusive Image," *Advertising Age,* March 13, 1986, p. 18; "Jacobsons Cultivation Is the Personal Touch," *Advertising Age,* March 13, 1986, p. 22; and Michelle Bearden-Mason, "Borgata Builds Friendly Fortress in Arizona," *Advertising Age,* March 13, 1986, p. 13.
4. For further reading, see Monroe Friedman, "Consumer Boycotts in the United States, 1970–1980: Contemporary Events in Historical Perspective," *Journal of Consumer Affairs* 19, no. 1 (Summer 1985), pp. 96–117; also see Judith Langer, "Upscale Department Stores Often Provide Low-End Service," *Marketing News,* March 13, 1987, p. 17.

7

What Is Lifestyle Merchandising

RETAILING CAPSULE
Widening the Gap

The Gap, merchandisers of casual and active sportswear for men and women, has moved to change its image from a merchandiser of teenage jeans to an outlet in which people into their mid-40s feel comfortable shopping. The company is trying to change without losing its youth market, and their primary thrust has been to broaden their appeal to the 20–45-year-old customer in recognition of shifting age trends and lifestyles.

Management set out to change the image they projected by centering their media promotions on people in their mid-20s doing familiar things. The store avoided projecting the lifestyle either of the yuppie or of a hip teenager. The goal was to project a comfortable, easy, familiar look so that consumers could recognize that the Gap is for middle-America. For example, one catalog illustration shows a group of people under a canoe, rather than on a yacht. In recent years models in their catalog have aged from the initial teenage perception to a look that is over 25. In essence, management is trying to say that "We are for you, too. We were right for you in the 70s and we're right for you today."

The store decor and the merchandise presentations have also been changed to attract a broader market. Many of the stores, which until recently were painted bright orange, have been repainted white with pale coordinating gray. The table fixtures are pale gray formica, and the merchandise is now folded and stacked instead of being displayed on hangers.

Based on Jules Abend, "Widening the Gap," *Stores*, November 1985, pp. 95–99.

The ambiance of the store's visual advertising presents a sense of merchandise that is basic and almost homespun. The visual theme carries through from catalog to print to postcards and is restated with hang tags and brochures in-store.

*R*etailers are realizing that demographics alone do not allow them to adequately understand and serve a market. Astute executives are thus increasingly focusing on the attitudes, interests, and opinions of consumers as a way of supplementing demographic data. The way retailers adapt to changing consumer lifestyles is reflected in the strategy of The Gap, who responded to these trends by changing its merchandise mix, the decor of its stores, and its promotion.

After reading this chapter you will be able to:

1. Describe the changes in U.S. culture which affect the lifestyles of consumers.

2. Explain the techniques of lifestyle analysis.

3. List the benefits of lifestyle merchandising.

4. Discuss the role of lifestyle merchandising in the retail strategy mix.

Lifestyle concepts influence almost every dimension of merchandise presentation in retailing. The two key terms in this chapter are *lifestyle* and *psychographics*. **Lifestyle** is a customer's pattern of living as reflected in the way merchandise is purchased and used. **Psychographics** are the ways of defining and measuring the lifestyles of consumers.

Why has lifestyle merchandising become so important? We live in an age in which large differences exist in the behavior of people with similar demographic profiles. This diversity makes it hard to offer merchandise to consumers based only on an analysis of their age, income, and education. Instead, retailers need to know (1) how people spend their time, (2) how they spend their money, and (3) what they value, so that they can serve the customers better. Market segmentation based on lifestyle characteristics gives retailers a more realistic picture of the customers they want to serve.

THE EVOLUTION OF LIFESTYLE MERCHANDISING

Lifestyle retailing has grown in importance since the early 1970s. Previously, retailing had been characterized by a sameness in operations. Dominant merchants included Sears, Woolworth, A&P, and other retailers that were different only in degree. Managers could be shifted from one store to another across the country and would find few differences between the stores.[1]

The Marketing Concept

The marketing concept was developed in the early 1960s by packaged goods firms such as Procter & Gamble as a response to the lack of attention to the needs of consumers in merchandising decisions. The marketing concept involves focusing on consumer needs and integrating all activities of the store to satisfy the needs identified.

Retailers in the 1960s, even though insisting that "the customer is always right," often implemented the marketing concept only in the context of day-to-day operations, not in the context of the broader strategic dimensions of the store as discussed in Chapter 2. Refund policies, hours of operation, and customer service were developed with a consumer focus. Product lines, store location, style of merchandise, and other strategic issues still retained the sameness of earlier years, however.

The Positioning Concept

The concept of **market positioning** emerged during the early 1970s as the forerunner of contemporary lifestyle merchandising and as part of an effort to implement the marketing concept. Management began to tailor merchandising strategies to specific consumer segments. The segments to be served were defined, however, largely in terms of *demographics* such as age, income, and education.

Wal-Mart, a general merchandise outlet, was an early leader in positioning. The firm experienced rapid growth by serving small town and rural markets. Each dimension of store operations was geared to serve these markets. Other outlets, such as Toys-R-Us, experienced equal success by market positioning, again based on demographics, and by offering narrow but deep lines of merchandise to carefully defined consumer segments.

Lifestyle Merchandising

Retailers quickly realized that defining consumers in terms of demographics alone was not sufficient for fast growth. The concept of lifestyle merchandising thus evolved. *The new focus was on understanding and responding to the living patterns of customers rather than making merchandising decisions primarily on the basis of consumer demographics.*

The following examples illustrate the application of contemporary lifestyle merchandising:

ProCreation (Portland, Oregon) leases maternity clothes to pregnant working women. The firm charges $6.95 for fully lined two-piece wool suits or from $18–$25 a week for a full maternity wardrobe. The market for rental maternity clothing did not exist until large numbers of women entered the workplace and began to need a larger wardrobe as a result.[2]

Boston-based J. Bildner and Sons is a combination gourmet and convenience food store that is designed to accommodate busy lifestyles. Their clerks will even pick up laundry and deliver videos for their customers.[3]

Fizzazz Stores is operated by Murjani International, the licensee for Coca-Cola Clothes. Management has introduced what they call "The store of the 21st century—where clothes can be delivered almost as quickly as cash." Management's intention is eventually to operate Fizzazz on a 24-hour basis, letting shoppers select and order via a machine, pay via credit card, and receive their clothes the next day.[4]

A portfolio of lifestyle-oriented outlets is the latest trend in lifestyle merchandising. Management has recognized that a portfolio of lifestyle outlets is likely to be more profitable than focusing on the lifestyles of only one or two target groups. Even such a traditional mass merchant as K mart has opened a new lifestyle-oriented retailing firm called Designer Depot.

An example of a lifestyle portfolio is shown in Figure 7–1 for The Limited. Victoria's Secret offers designer lingerie for the fashion-conscious contemporary woman 25 to 45 years of age. Sizes Unlimited features special size apparel for women ages 25–50. Lane Bryant is the nation's leading retailer of medium-priced basic and intimate apparel designed for larger women, especially those over 25 years of age. The Limited Express offers popular-priced sportswear and accessories to fashion-oriented women aged 15–25 years. The Limited, probably the most widely known store in the portfolio, sells medium-priced fashion apparel to fashion-conscious contemporary women ages 20–40. The Limited management is experimenting with locating each of the different lifestyle stores side-by-side in shopping malls in such a way that each is accessible to the others through inside doors.

FIGURE 7–1   THE LIMITED, INC.—A PORTFOLIO OF LIFESTYLES

The Limited, Inc. is a growth company focused exclusively on women's apparel. The company's primary business is to provide fashion, quality, and value to the American woman through multiple retail formats:

Limited Stores.   There are 500 Limited stores in over 125 major markets throughout the United States. Limited stores sell medium-priced fashion apparel tailored to the tastes and lifestyles of fashion-conscious contemporary women 20 to 40 years of age. The majority of Limited stores are located in regional shopping centers with the remainder in key downtown locations.

Limited Express.   Distinguished by a unique store design and merchandise selection, Limited Express stores offer an exciting assortment of popular-priced sportswear and accessories designed to appeal primarily to fashion-forward women 15 to 25 years of age. Currently there are 45 Limited Express stores located in regional shopping centers in California, Texas, and the Midwest.

Lane Bryant.   Lane Bryant is the nation's leading retailer of women's special-size apparel. The 223 Lane Bryant stores specialize in the sale of medium-priced fashion, basic, and intimate apparel designed to appeal to the special-size woman, with particular emphasis on those over 25 years of age. The stores are located in regional shopping centers throughout the United States.

Brylane Mail Order.   The nation's foremost catalog retailer of women's special-size apparel and shoes,

Brylane Mail Order publishes five catalogs, each directed to a specific special-size customer. The catalogs include *Lane Bryant, Roaman's, Tall Collection, Nancy's Choice,* and *LB For Short.*

Victoria's Secret.   Through retail stores and a nationally distributed mail order catalog, Victoria's Secret offers European and American designer lingerie for the fashionable contemporary woman 25 to 45 years of age. The 12 stores are located in the San Francisco, Boston, Columbus, Dallas, Chicago, and New York metropolitan areas.

Sizes Unlimited.   This newly established division is an off-price retailer of women's special-size apparel. Composed of Sizes Unlimited and Smart Size stores, the division offers nationally known brand and private label merchandise designed to appeal primarily to women 25 to 50 years of age. The 77 stores are located in smaller shopping centers throughout the East and Midwest.

Mast Industries.   Mast Industries is a large, international supplier of moderate-priced apparel for fashion-conscious women. The Commercial Division employs a worldwide network of 150 contract production facilities to produce merchandise against specific orders from retailers, wholesalers, and manufacturers. Through sales offices in New York and Los Angeles, as well as a field sales force, the Wholesale Division supplies a wide variety of apparel products to department and specialty stores throughout the United States.

SOURCE: Roger D. Blackwell and W. Wayne Talarzyk, "Life-Style Retailing: Competitive Strategies for the 1980s," *Journal of Retailing* 59 (Winter 1983), p. 14.

WHY WORRY ABOUT LIFESTYLE MERCHANDISING?

Lifestyle analysis offers retailers: (1) a better opportunity to develop marketing strategies based on a lifelike portrait of the consumers they are seeking to serve, (2) the ability to partially protect the outlet from direct price competition by developing unique merchandise offerings that attract shoppers for reasons other than price, and (3) the opportunity to better understand the shopping behavior and merchandise preferences of customers.

Management can more accurately describe and understand the behavior of consumers when thinking in terms of lifestyle. Routinely thinking in terms of the activities, interests, needs, and values of customers can help retailers plan merchandise offerings, price lines, store layouts, and promotion programs that are tightly targeted. However, lifestyle analysis only adds to the demographic, geographic, and socioeconomic information retailers need to

EXHIBIT 7–1   NEIGHBORHOODS TELL LIFESTYLE

Mr. Thomas Stanley of Georgia State University is an expert on the lifestyles of the affluent. He offered these observations about the different lifestyles of the affluent in Atlanta, Georgia.

"We recently did a study of the old-money neighborhoods, areas like Buckhead in which the houses were built in the 1920s and 1930s—marvelous mansions," Mr. Stanley says. Much of the wealth in the area is "fifth and sixth generation, some of it going back to pre–Civil War."

Just outside the Atlanta city limits about five miles from the central business district, Buckhead residents "are white, Anglo-Saxon Protestant, conservative in their lifestyles, have trust funds, belong to a particular type of country club."

But in newer Atlanta communities such as the Dunwoody area, which has the highest income of any of the Atlanta neighborhoods, according to Mr. Stanley, residents are generally "hard-charging younger executives who live in very nice homes and who were not born here.

"They are 80 percent first-generation wealth, are very innovative in terms of changing styles, are more interested in having cable TV, are more likely to have videotex in their house or have a home [computer] terminal," he says.

Dunwoody houses were built in the 1960s and, even though the community's households boast higher incomes than Buckhead's, "the houses in Dunwoody are not in the league of the old mansions," Mr. Stanley says. "Dunwoody households are slightly lower in net worth [than are those in Buckhead]. There are a lot of millionaires there, but they haven't had that big hit yet."

Another significant difference between the old money and the new money is its source.

"Dunwoody people [who live about 15 miles from the center of Atlanta] are much less likely to work in Atlanta's central business district than are Buckhead residents," Mr. Stanley says. Dunwoody residents also are more likely to have sales positions, which has a significant impact on their lifestyles. They tend to be travelers and to frequent resources common to travelers.

"They do a lot of travel on the personal side as well as the business side because they build up travel coupons and they tend to have a regional or international interest. They want access to the airport, which is a key element in their lifestyles."

SOURCE: Portions quoted from "For the Rich, Home Is Where the Heart Is," *Advertising Age*, August 23, 1984, pp. 12–13. Reprinted with permission from *Advertising Age*. Copyright, Crain Communications, 1984.

serve markets effectively. Lifestyle analysis is not a substitute for this information. Rather, all the information sources taken together give retailers a richer view of their customers and help them recognize and serve consumer needs.

What Shapes Lifestyles?

We are all a product of the society in which we live. Very early, we learn concepts such as honesty and the value of money and these stay with us throughout our lives. These cultural influences, plus individual economic circumstances, produce consumer lifestyles—traits, activities, interests, and opinions reflected in shopping behavior. Individuals can be grouped into distinct market segments based on the similarities of their lifestyles, as shown in Exhibit 7–1.

Where Do Lifestyles Come From?

The lifestyles of consumers are rooted in their values. Values are beliefs or expectations about behavior shared by a number of individuals and learned from society. Some of these values do not change much over time, while others can change quite rapidly. The major forces shaping consumer values include family influence, religious institutions, schools, and early lifetime experiences.

Examples of changing household values in each decade since the 1950s are shown in Figure 7–2.[5] During the 1950s, most women did not work outside the home. The primary household emphasis was on money, home ownership, and material possessions. Television was beginning to make people more aware of trends around the world.

During the 1960s, the homogeneous value system of the United States began to fragment as the baby-boom generation questioned the existing social norms. Divorce rates soared, and antiwar, antiestablishment, and antigovernment protests became commonplace as the United States was torn by racial tension and families began to fragment.

During the 1970s, personal fulfillment emerged as one of the primary values of society. Women entered the work force in increasing numbers, and the divorce rate continued to accelerate. Society began to object to upward mobility and materialism, however, as primary life goals. Health foods, "natural products," and hand-crafted goods became popular with many segments of consumers, and retail outlets emerged to meet these needs. Inflation accelerated, as did advances in technology ranging from personal computers to videocassettes.

During the 1980s, consumers reassessed their personal values and goals. They again became interested in solving problems at the grass-roots levels. A greater personal tolerance across all segments of society has allowed advances in women's rights, workers' rights, and racial justice. Individuals are again focusing on their responsibilities in addition to their rights.

The values and lifestyles of the *future* to a large extent will be shaped by the teenagers who are now in high school or college and how they respond to trends and opportunities available to them. Likely examples of such values and lifestyles are shown in Figure 7–3.

A study of cultural and economic lifestyle influences such as those presented above offers some of the most important and interesting ways of understanding consumers. This information helps in serving them more effectively.

What Do We Know about Changing Cultural Patterns?

1. *Parents are spending less time with very young children.* For example, today more than 30 percent of preschool children are in day-care centers, a segment of retailing that will continue to grow very rapidly.

2. *The divorce rate remains high.* As a result, the value patterns of today's children are shifting. More children are being raised without fathers in the home. So, many children now learn some of their values from individuals other than family members.

3. *People move more often than in the past.* Thus, less influence comes from grandparents and aunts and uncles as part of the extended

FIGURE 7–2   SHIFTING CONSUMER VALUES IN THE UNITED STATES

The 1950s

1. Money, home ownership, and material possessions became important signs of social status.
2. Most families consisted of a married couple with a "working" husband and a "nonworking" wife.
3. Upward mobility and economic self-sufficiency were major goals.
4. Television brought people, places, and ideas from around the globe into family living rooms.
5. People were better housed, fed, and educated than ever before.
6. General Eisenhower, a wartime symbol of freedom and victory, was elected president.
7. In the midst of postwar conformity the rebellious "beat generation" shocked the establishment late in the decade with unconventional lifestyles.
8. Fads, from hula-hoops to pink bobby socks, were the norm. Everyone tried everything.

The 1960s

1. A once homogeneous value system began to fragment.
2. The baby boom generation questioned traditional social norms.
3. Between 1930 and 1960 the divorce rate doubled.
4. Self-awareness and self-understanding became important personal goals.
5. John Kennedy moved into the White House, and was assassinated almost three years later.
6. War in Vietnam escalated.
7. Antiwar, antiestablishment, antigovernment protests echoed across the land.
8. Racial tension rocked inner cities from Detroit to Los Angeles.
9. The hippie movement and its philosophy of peace, love, and understanding was born in San Francisco.
10. The family seemed to be torn apart—both literally and figuratively.
11. Religious cults and spiritual movements promised asylum from troubled times.

The 1970s

1. Personal goals of self-fulfillment became more entrenched.
2. "Me" values replaced traditional values.
3. Women began to reject traditional, stereotyped roles in the home. More women entered the work force while the divorce rate increased rapidly.
4. Upward mobility and materialism were rejected as desirable goals.
5. Health foods, "natural" products, and handcrafted goods flooded the marketplace.

6. The Watergate scandal made citizens question an already tenuous faith in "the American way."
7. Unemployment and inflation began to escalate.
8. Encounter groups and self-help books tried to explain America's social roller coaster.
9. Advances in technology transformed microcomputers, satellite dishes, videocassettes, and videodiscs into household items.

The 1980s

1. Economic realities are forcing Americans to reassess personal values and goals.
2. The demise of the "psychology of affluence" is making people more aware of the economy and the environment.
3. Diversity in family forms is now the norm.
4. The number of "latch key" children is growing.
5. Economic realities are bringing the return of "do-it-yourself" and bartering for goods and services.
6. Citizens are taking action on grass-roots issues.
7. Information is becoming a powerful economic resource.
8. The computer industry has rekindled the entrepreneurial spirit.
9. Tolerance and freedom have opened the door to women's rights, racial justice, worker rights, and social flexibility.
10. People are considering their responsibilities in addition to their rights.

The 1990s

1. What will you be doing in the 1990s?
   What kind of lifestyle will you have?
   What career options do you foresee?
2. What new things on the horizon would you like to integrate into your life?
3. How do you think your options will be affected by changing societal values, technology, and the economy?
4. Each life role presents options:
   a. As a family member, how will you balance individual needs with family relationships?
   b. As a business person, how will you balance "the bottom line" with developing human potential?
   c. As an individual, how will you find self-understanding and opportunities for lifelong growth?
   d. As an educator, how will you maintain the true basics of what you teach and yet change to accommodate new values and lifestyles?
   e. What are the *basics* that you would like to keep in your life?

SOURCE: "New Values and Lifestyles Implications," *J. C. Penney Forum,* September 1983, p. 10.

Chapter 7 What is Lifestyle Merchandising?

—— A unity or oneness of work and play
—— Free time anytime
—— Recognition as a creative person
—— Honor and affection more rewarding than money
—— Major societal commitments
—— Easy laughter, unembarrassed tears
—— Loving and in touch with self

SOURCE: "New Values and Lifestyles Implications," *J. C. Penney Forum*, September 1983, p. 27.

family. Many of today's young people lack "roots" and a sense of traditional family values.

4. *Religion is not important in many people's lives.* As a consequence, the moral standards of previous years are changing. People are
more prone to pursue pleasure and less likely to practice self-denial. Retailers are thus increasingly likely to feature advertising with a sexual
orientation.

5. *Schools are becoming more important in shaping values.* More
young people are staying in high school, and approximately half now go
to college. Young people are being exposed to a larger number of different
values than in the past and are more willing to experiment and try alternative lifestyles.

6. *Individuals in each generation have different experiences.* More
than 80 percent of consumers today were not alive during the depression
of the 1930s. Many have little awareness of World War II. Today's middle-
aged people grew up in an era of low-cost credit, plentiful jobs, job security, and loyalty to one's country and parents. Yet, these same people also
grew up with the Vietnam War and an energy crisis.

7. *Family size is decreasing and more single-person households are
being formed.* The smaller family sizes and the lifestyles accompanying
them are creating new merchandising opportunities. Such households
have more discretionary income and spend more on restaurants, educational products, and travel services. Their homes are typically smaller
than in the past and the furnishings also are smaller.[6]

8. *Single-person households reflect lifestyles that are not impacted
by family norms and the preferences of other family members.* Activities
are on a per-person basis as opposed to a household basis. Products and
services for such households are personalized rather than standardized.
Such retail services as health care, personal finance, and insurance are
now offered on a per-person rather than a per-household basis.

9. *The decline in the number of children is accompanied by an increase in adult-oriented lifestyles.* More and more adult-oriented programming is available to households through cable television and the networks.
The popularity of adult soap operas such as "Dallas" reflects this trend in
society, as do restaurants such as TGI Fridays.

10. *The yuppies (young, urban professionals) are getting older.* The number of people aged 35–44 has increased approximately 37 percent during this decade. The number of people aged 25–34 has increased almost as rapidly. Such households typically have two incomes, are well educated, and have the money to spend to support their lifestyle preferences.

These so-called yuppies are placing more emphasis on their households than they did when they were in their 20s. They are purchasing more expensive home furnishings and quality art, and are major consumers of services. Banks, stock-brokerage houses, and other financial institutions are rejoicing at the opportunity to serve these markets. These consumers are conspicuous in their consumption and are willing to spend heavily to support their lifestyles.

11. *The number of families earning more than $50,000 a year is growing at a rapid rate although they still comprise no more than 5 percent of the population.* Two thirds of those with incomes above $50,000 reside in the top 50 U.S. markets, concentrated primarily in Florida, Texas, the West Coast, and the Northeast.

Affluent buyers seek products and services that reflect their self-image and are interested in aesthetics as much as performance. From retailers, they seek the highest-quality merchandise that reflects prestige and fashion. They expect high-quality service and consultation.

Affluent dual-income households provide strong markets for luxury products such as satellite dishes, boats, and premium cars. Retailers such as Neiman-Marcus and Bloomingdale's are positioned to serve these markets.[7]

12. *No longer are the roles of the male and the female in the household as clearly defined as in the past.* Women are increasingly becoming buyers of financial services and other male-oriented products. Men are increasingly becoming purchasers of household products, and young adults of both sexes are learning how to manage households and to cope with problems of school and education. Retail promotions are increasingly universal in content and not targeted specifically to either males or females. Further, the California Supreme Court has ruled that "Ladies Day" discounts offered by many nightclubs, car washes, and other businesses are illegal because they perpetuate sexual stereotyping.[8]

13. *One of the most dramatic changes has been the effects of technology on consumer lifestyles.* The development of videocassette players led to the emergence of video outlets that specialize in the rental of movies and VCR equipment. Busy consumers are responding to the opportunity to view films at their convenience in the privacy of their homes rather than go to movie houses. Microwave ovens have led to changes in the types of foods eaten, and in-home interactive shopping offered by the Home Shopping Network and other cable services is beginning to redefine how and when consumers shop.

14. *Not all consumers are sharing in the affluence of some demographic segments.* Such consumers, as part of their lifestyles, are very responsive to coupons and other promotions. They use generic products, buy at flea markets and garage sales, are willing to accept less service in return for lower prices, and are active in seeking goods that last longer and require less maintenance. Such consumers are responsible for the growth of warehouse outlets for various types of merchandise.

15. *Self-involvement continues to be another trend in society.* Consumers are interested in being good to themselves. The result is a continuing growth in health club membership, in the popularity of aerobics centers and diet centers, and in retail outlets specializing in high-priced adult games.

16. *The more money people have to spend, the less time they have to spend it.* The most affluent households typically have two wage earners which means that they have little time for shopping. As a result, they are willing to pay for time-saving goods including lawn-care services and cleaning services. They also have been responsible for the rapid growth in deli operations in supermarkets and in downtown department stores. Such consumers also seek high-quality recreation because of the limited amount of time available to them. They are prone to go to fashionable ski resorts, theme restaurants, and expensive golf and tennis resorts.

Determining Consumers' Values

What have been the results of these forces in shaping the values of today's consumers? Consider the following:

1. Instant gratification.
2. Credit explosion.
3. The new theology of pleasure.
4. Life simplification.
5. Sexual revolution.
6. Changing concepts of time and leisure.[9]

Instant Gratification. Many people today prefer not to wait very long for anything. They want goods and services available when and where they need them. This preference partially explains the trend toward 24-hour store openings, for example.

The Credit Explosion. People used to think that consumers using credit did not know how to manage money, but today's young people do not think this way. They are not afraid to use credit; they look upon credit as a type of convenience, not as a debt.

The New Theology of Pleasure. Many people today think that if something brings pleasure, it is good. We have all heard the saying, "If it feels good, do it." Freedom and comfort are what people are looking for today in everything from clothes to automobiles and homes.

Life Simplification. People also want to simplify their lives. This explains the popularity of such things as self-cleaning ovens, microwave ovens, video-cassette recorders, and easy-to-clean products of all types. This move also accounts for the popularity of the many small electrical household appliances sold today.

Sexual Revolution. The values many people hold about the role of sex in their lives are changing quite rapidly. Sex is thus an important part of the creative strategies used by many retailers in selling merchandise. Many products are sold by showing how they appeal to the opposite sex. Such strategies have not been dampened by the AIDS scare.

HOW CAN MANAGEMENT SEGMENT MARKETS BY LIFESTYLE?[10]

The information used in **lifestyle segmentation** *is developed from consumer research.* Marketing researchers question consumers about the merchandise they purchased and their media habits, as well as their activities, interests, and opinions.

An Example of Clothing-Fashion Lifestyle Segments[11]

One research study yielded seven fashion segments which can provide a key to understanding how lifestyle segmentation can be used in a retail setting.

The seven segments are: leaders, followers, independents, neutrals, those uninvolved, negatives, and rejectors. A discussion of the profiles can help show the use of lifestyle analysis in merchandise planning.

Leaders. Leaders scored high on the factors of fashion leadership, interest, and importance. Their high scores on leadership set them apart from the other segments. They also demonstrated their strong involvement with mainstream (e.g., designer) fashion looks.

Followers. Followers exhibited a profile similar to leaders. This group is likely to pattern its behavior after the leaders.

Independents. Independents also are fashion aware, but have strong, anti-fashion attitudes. Independents are interested in fashion, but resent designers and other fashion experts dictating tastes to them.

Neutrals. The neutrals scored in the neutral range on all the fashion-oriented factors. This group does not regard fashion as particularly important, but neither are its members "antifashion."

Uninvolved. Their scores were all in the negative range. They showed a low desire for leadership and interest in fashion, gave a low importance to fashion, and had low antifashion attitudes.

Negatives. The negatives have no desire for leadership nor any interest in fashion. They do think it is moderately important to be well dressed, but perhaps this attitude stems more from the feeling that it is important to be "neat and clean" than "fashionably clothed." And they resent the "fashion establishment" telling people what to wear.

Rejectors. Their profile is similar to that of the negatives, except that they do not attach any importance to fashion, to the point of being unconcerned with what they wear.

Figure 7–4 is a further example of three lifestyle segments for dual-income households that emerged based on studies of families across the United States. As shown, the lifestyles of the three segments differ depending on whether the households have no children, young children, or older children.

How Does Lifestyle Merchandising Affect Marketing Strategies?

Idea-Oriented Presentations

Merchandise is often brought together from all areas of the store for its lifestyle appeal. Lifestyle merchandising breaks down departmental barriers. This approach allows salespeople to sell primarily to customers with similar lifestyles. Management seeks to group merchandise the way customers want to buy it, not the way the store thinks it is easiest to sell. Simply putting dresses into departments labeled better, moderate, and budget can help. Consumers match their lifestyles with the departments. Many complementary items are placed together to encourage multiple purchases. For example, all items of sporting equipment may be grouped in one department, women's accessories may be grouped in another, or furniture and accessories may be grouped in a single-room setting. Such efforts break down departmental rigidities, encourage multiple sales, and increase space productivity.

A similar concept is idea-oriented presentations as shown in Figure 7–5. Increasingly, merchants are using this concept to convey an idea by clus-

---

FIGURE 7–4 LIFESTYLES OF DUAL-INCOME FAMILIES

Traits	Dual-Income Families with No Children	Dual-Income Families with Young Children	Dual-Income Families with Older Children
Lifestyle and Priorities	Their lives are busy by choice. They do things both together and alone. Work and their spousal relationships are top priorities.	Their lives are hectic and rushed, as they juggle the demands of work and children. For women, children are the number one priority. For men, work is important, but the family also rates high.	Their lives are busy but manageable. Each family member pursues his/her own schedule. For many men and women personal time is a high priority. Family relationships are also important.
Attitudes Toward Work	Most of the women and all of the men derive personal satisfaction from work and are building careers.	Economic necessity forces the majority of women to work to provide additional income.	Women work for economic reasons, but career/job is taking on more personal importance. Men have accepted the dollar realities of their own careers/jobs and have a positive attitude toward their wives' working.

Traits	Dual-Income Families with No Children	Dual-Income Families with Young Children	Dual-Income Families with Older Children
Attitudes Toward Children	Most couples are still struggling with the question of whether or when to have children.	Their children dictate and dominate their lifestyle.	Parents are adjusting to the changing needs of their children as they go through the teenage years and become young adults.
Shared Home Responsibilities	There is an acceptance and shared practice of homemaking.	There is some sharing of homemaking tasks, but the primary responsibility for home and children remains with the women.	Men whose wives have recently gone back to work are making a concerted effort to share in some of the household responsibilities. Older children are helping out and are becoming more self-sufficient.
Financial Priorities and Savings	They spend on material goods and self-gratification (e.g., clothing, travel, and entertainment). Most savings are targeted for short-term goals.	Their main financial objective is to minimize debt. They spend for necessities and for maintaining their homes. They have little savings.	They are content with a moderate but comfortable standard of living. College expenses are the major financial concern and retirement is second. Most savings are for retirement.
Consumer Behavior	Some of these consumers shop in a hurry, while others use shopping as a leisure time activity. Many of them are looking for "the best," but they all want "to get a good buy."	This group of consumers has little time to shop. They want to "get in and get out" of a store quickly. Since money is tight for them, price is a strong factor in where they shop and what they buy.	The people in this group are conservative and informed shoppers. They want proven quality and durability. Some are struggling with their teenage children, who have different consumer values.
Community Involvement	They have little or no involvement in community activities.	They become involved in community issues only if there is a major threat to family or finances.	They are somewhat involved in community issues, especially when these issues affect family and home.
Life Satisfaction	They are satisfied for the present, but maintain their aspirations.	There are feelings of frustration primarily due to the pressures of time and finances. It is difficult to make the trade-offs between work and family responsibilities.	Men are basically content: their careers have peaked and their attention is directed more toward family/self. Women feel good about working, but still feel the pressure of home/family demands. Both are looking forward to the time when they can "do their own thing."

SOURCE: *Dual-Income Families* (New York: J. C. Penney Forum Publications, 1984), pp. 12–13.

*LEISURE-TIME, ACTIVE SPORTSWEAR FITS INTO THE PHYSICAL-FITNESS
LIFESTYLE OF THE 80S.*

(Courtesy The May Department Stores Company)

tering complementary items to motivate multiple purchases, but without the
extensive involvement of salesclerks. A typical example is the bath shop,
where the entire merchandise presentation is idea oriented. Customers find
all items related to the bath brought together from different merchandise
categories throughout the store.

Lifestyle Merchandise Classifications

One of the trends in merchandising for males is selling to "the better young
man," defined by the general merchandise manager of Saks-Fifth Avenue
as 18–25, and as "a fashion-aware young man in a college or university,
who doesn't have the budget yet for more expensive clothes." A representative of Carson Pirie Scott & Company says that this new category is an
attitude, a lifestyle type of selling that borrows from the excitement of wom-
en's ready-to-wear merchandise.

Some stores have opened separate shops with an updated, traditional flair, giving fashion direction with designer jeans by such names as Sasson. Levi Strauss's "98 Battery Street" collection is also popular. Saks-Fifth Avenue calls its better young man's shop the "Early On" and hopes to encourage men to purchase designer collections, such as Geoffrey Beene and Calvin Klein.

Super Specialty Retailing

The super specialists include such firms as Toys-R-Us, Topps & Trousers, The Proving Ground, Casual Corner, and The County Seat. Their exceptional profitability and rapid growth have made them formidable competitors for department/general merchandise stores and small independent retail operations.

The stores offer a limited assortment of contemporary merchandise aimed at specific segments, typically adults aged 18–35 with an interest in fashion.

Management is centralized, and the organizations are able to respond to market trends almost instantly. Personal service, breadth and depth in merchandise, and the ability to keep pace with fashion trends give these outlets a strong image relative to department stores and independent outlets.

Serving Customers with Unique Lifestyles

Information

Large retailers in such metropolitan markets as Miami, New York, and Los Angeles offer multilingual services to attract and serve foreign tourists. Many of these stores maintain lists of employees with foreign language abilities. Store directions and information pamphlets are sometimes printed in foreign languages. For example, Zayre Corporation prints a booklet outlining store policies in four foreign languages. Saks-Fifth Avenue has had its International Shopping Service for more than 50 years. The service is offered free to make shopping easy for tourists.

Shopping Services

Shopping services are becoming increasingly popular with working women. Customers make an initial visit to an outlet and provide retailers with essential measurements and other information needed to help make merchandise selection decisions for the customers. They can then call ahead and have several outfits assembled for their approval when they arrive at the store. Such services require creative talent by salespeople, but can lead to significant "plus" sales for the outlet.

Store Hours

Longer shopping hours are especially common in suburban areas where stores may be open late each night of the week and even on Sunday. Sunday and evening hours are less frequent in the central business districts. Increasing numbers of two-income households are likely to demand that retail outlets remain open in the evening and on Sundays to serve the needs of individuals who are unable to shop during "normal" store hours.

Effects on Retail Salespeople

Retail salespeople have to identify both with the items being sold and the lifestyle of the customer buying the items. Even store branches need to be tailored to the lifestyles of the customers living in that particular area. For example, the salesperson selling tennis equipment should ideally be an avid tennis player.

Better Promotion Efforts

Lifestyle merchandising is changing the media mix used by retailers. Lifestyle programming by various stations that offer sports, "middle-of-the-road" music, or all-news programs represent attempts to reach specific target audiences. Tightly defined media audiences are being sought by retailers today.

Visual Merchandising

Attractively displayed merchandise in harmony with a consumer's lifestyle increases that consumer's desire to buy. Lifestyle merchandising based on this psychology is a highly refined art. Promotional displays are likely to be strong, dramatic, and striking, and to support the theme of the other promotion efforts.

Creating the artistic environment so essential in lifestyle merchandising requires a unique blending of lighting, background, and props. All visual merchandising themes should start with what the customer wants and should communicate important merchandise information. These points are discussed in further detail in Chapter 16.

CHAPTER HIGHLIGHTS

— Retailers can more readily meet the needs of customers if they understand how people spend their time and money and what they value. The essence of this type of information is lifestyle analysis.

— Lifestyles are based on the values of people. The forces affecting consumer values are the influence of the family, religious institutions, schools, and early lifetime experiences.

— Retail management philosophies in meeting the needs of consumers have evolved gradually over time. Until the 1950s retailers were supply oriented. By the 1960s the marketing concept was introduced as a philosophy of management which required a total consumer orientation in all activities of the firm.

— Positioning as a strategy emerged in the early 1970s. Management began to target offerings to narrow groups of consumers defined in terms of demographics. By the mid-1970s, lifestyle merchandising emerged with an emphasis on the activities, interests, and opinions of consumers.

The latest evolution in marketing strategy is the development of a lifestyle portfolio of stores owned by a single organization, but with each store targeted toward the needs of a different group of consumers.

Understanding lifestyle merchandising is the key ingredient in marketing strategy.

KEY TERMS

Lifestyle A person's pattern of living as reflected in the way merchandise is purchased and used.

Lifestyle segmentation Dividing consumers into homogeneous groups based on similar activities, interests, and opinions.

Market positioning Developing a unique position in a market segment relative to other retailers by the use of merchandise, price, hours of operation, services offered, and a clear understanding of consumer demographics.

Psychographics Ways of defining and measuring the lifestyles of consumers.

DISCUSSION QUESTIONS

1. Define lifestyle and psychographics. What is the relationship of one to the other?
2. Summarize current social changes that are shaping American values and discuss the resulting effects on consumer behavior.
3. Why do you think more and more retailers are becoming interested in the concept of lifestyle analysis?
4. What is meant by the term *super specialty retailing?* What are some of the operating characteristics of super specialists?
5. Why is it important for the backgrounds of salespeople to match the lifestyles of the customers they will be serving?
6. What are some of the changes taking place in the groupings of merchandise in the retail firm?
7. What are retailers doing now to better serve customers with unique lifestyles?
8. Trace the differences among the following management philosophies: homogeneous retailing, retailing based on the marketing concept, and lifestyle retailing.

APPLICATION EXERCISES

1. Visit a mall or the CBD and identify as many stores as you can that represent lifestyle merchandising in action (e.g., The Gap). Discuss whether you feel management of the stores you identify need to be more alert to changes in lifestyles.
2. Visit several department and specialty outlets in your area. Describe examples of lifestyle merchandising you discover in your visits. Relate the strategy to the positioning you believe management is attempting.
3. *Your inside story.* What do you think of changing family forms? New lifestyles? Changing consumer behavior? Changing social norms? Complete the following sentences to discover how you feel about the new values and lifestyles. ("New Values and Lifestyle Implications," *J. C. Penney Forum*, September 1983, p. 3.)
   a. Today's consumer seems to value _____
   _____.
   b. Because of new economic realities, I have had to adjust my consumer behavior by _____
   _____.
   c. These new behaviors have changed my lifestyle by _____
   _____.
   d. In our society, some of the symbols that prove you "have made it" include _____
   _____.

e. My feelings about these symbols are _____.

f. When I hear the word *family,* I think of _____.

g. In the future the family will probably _____.

h. When I see children from single-parent families, I feel _____.

i. When I see children from families in which both parents have full-time careers, I feel _____.

j. When I see children from families in which the father works and the mother stays home, I feel _____.

k. When I hear the phrase "a woman's place is in the home," I feel _____.

l. In the future I think that more and more people will begin to value _____.

4. *If only I had.* . . . We express our values in the way we spend our time, our energy, and our money. As we go through the life cycle and as our circumstances change, we may find that our choices and perhaps our values change. Complete the following sentences. Then analyze your answers in relation to the lifestyle groups described in this chapter. What did you learn about your own lifestyle values? If you work with others, how can you use this model to help you understand them? ("New Values and Lifestyle Implications," *J. C. Penney Forum,* September 1983, p. 8.)

a. If only I had more time, I would _____.

b. If only I had more money, I would _____.

c. If only I had more energy, I would _____.

CASES

1. Penney Probes Lifestyles of Singles Market

J. C. Penney Co. is taking a fresh look at a potential target market—singles—and is posing some important questions about their lifestyles and habits.

Penney, through its consumer feedback program, conducted a study of this singles group, the never-married, the widowed, and the divorced, which numbers almost 77 million people—43.1 percent of the population 15 years or older.

What emerged were three issues for marketers to consider. First, being single is an acceptable lifestyle choice. Second, there are three basic types of singles' lifestyles—changing, focused, and settled—and a person will move from one to another as circumstances and attitudes change. Third, independence is a common value throughout all singles' lifestyles.

Donald Gordon, manager of Consumer Programs for Penney, said 12 focus groups, which included 100 people from Chicago, Denver, Houston, Los Angeles, and Washington, D.C. market areas, were the basis of the survey.

The goals were to increase understanding of the lifestyles of singles 25–39, whose incomes ranged from $17,500 to $50,000 for women, and from $25,000 to $50,000 for men.

In addition, he continued, the project attempted "to understand the values that underlie these lifestyles; to identify the changing needs and expectations of singles at home, at work, and in the marketplace; and to suggest some of the implications of the issues that the study surfaces."

For each of the three singles lifestyles groups, there were emphases on self, relationships, and career. Among the topics these groups addressed were their personal, career, and consumer choices.

Some of the characteristics of the three basic lifestyle groups as consumers were illustrated by their attitudes on eight issues.

The *changing singles* "buy to satisfy short-term needs; buy anywhere; and are concerned with fashion and price." Their approach to shopping is "sometimes impulsive, but willing to shop for the best price." This group reported "ads, signing, and friends were influences on buying behavior." They are the least brand oriented, most sales oriented, and least service oriented, although "return policy is important."

The *focused singles* (focused on self or career—those focused on children/relationships did not fit clearly in these categories) will generally "buy what they want, and shop primarily in specialty stores and better department stores." Their emphasis is on "fashion and quality," and they are described as "time pressured."

Some of the things that influence the buying behavior of the *focused singles* are "convenient location, appropriate selection, personal service, and knowledgeable salespeople." This group has a "strong interest in designer/national brands, which provide desired styling and quality, are least sale oriented, and are most service oriented."

The *settled single,* the survey indicated, buys "according to priorities in an overall plan, and selects stores for products and reputation." Quality and value are important to this segment. They are described as "planned shoppers." Sale ads for desired merchandise, and comparative price shopping are characteristic of their buying influences. They have "strong interest in national brands and private labels with proven quality and value, but wait for a sale in planned purchases. Postpurchase service and return policy are important."

Gordon pointed out, "While consumer feedback does not pretend to be a definitive study, it may be a starting point for anyone who wants to develop an understanding of singles' lifestyles." Some general features of the lifestyle types identified through the study are:

In terms of him- or herself, the *changing single* is building self-confidence; seeking life direction; adapting to single status; finding a new environment.

The *focused single* is concentrating on personal interests, avoiding commitments, and working for the money.

The segment described as *settled* has come to terms with being single and pursues interests for personal satisfaction.

Each of the groups is also distinguished by the types of relationships characteristic to them. *Changing singles* are considering marriage, contemplating parenthood, looking for relationships.

The *focused group* is committed to a relationship with an adult or child and tries to balance relationships with self and career.

The *settled group* has its social network in place and has resolved family relationships.

Where career is concerned, *changing singles* are seeking more—more challenge, more dollars, more satisfaction. Some are exploring a second career or considering their own businesses.

The *focused single* is committed to career—for advancement, money, or recognition.

Settled singles are secure in their jobs, have adequate income, feel satisfied with their careers, want to grow where they are.

Questions

1. Compare and contrast the lifestyles of the three types of singles identified: changing, focused, settled.
2. How do the shopping behaviors of the three groups mentioned differ?
3. What types of retailing strategies are likely to be the most successful in attracting these three groups of shoppers?

Source: Reprinted from *Stores* Magazine © National Retail Merchants Assoc., 1986.

2. The Spaghetti Pot

The Spaghetti Pot is one third the size of a typical Burger King or McDonald's. It has just five tables. Hours? Open from 4 P.M. to 9 P.M. Product mix? One entree—spaghetti! Only spaghetti!

What market is this small Southern California chain targeting? Not the customer who wants to sit down to a meal of burger, fries, and a drink, but the busy consumer who wants to eat at home without the pain (or time) involved in preparing the fare.

The director of marketing research at Campbell Soup says that "takeout" is the biggest opportunity of the 1980s. Several major corporations are investigating take-out operations. But the Spaghetti Pot is not a proven success yet. State health laws must

be satisfied, and it is not easy to do that and have the food stay warm from store to home. Management says that the food will remain warm without reheating for 40 minutes, but peaks at 20 minutes. In an area such as Los Angeles, that is not much time for the long-distance commuter.

The developer of the Spaghetti Pot concept came up with his idea after seeing how expensive it was to construct a conventional fast-food shop. The chain has 10 units and has sold another 130 franchises throughout the country at $30,000 each. The locations selected are in shopping centers near supermarkets and are designed to take only about two minutes to consummate the sale of the spaghetti,

2. Can you describe the typical Spaghetti Pot customer in terms of demographics as easily as lifestyles? Why or why not?
3. What are the potential problems with the concept in general and the Spaghetti Pot in particular?

ENDNOTES

1. This material is based on Jagdish N. Sheth, "Marketing Megatrends," *The Journal of Consumer Marketing* 1, no. 1 (Summer 1983), pp. 5–13.
2. *The Wall Street Journal,* November 14, 1985, p. 1.
3. Pat Sloan, "That Special Feeling: Retailers Race for New Ideas," *Advertising Age,* November 18, 1985, p. 1; "Off-Pricers Grab Growing Retail Market Share," *Marketing News,* March 13, 1987, p. 8.
4. Ibid.
5. This material is based on "New Values and Lifestyles Implications," *The J. C. Penney Forum,* September 1983.
6. "Solo Americans," *Time,* December 2, 1985, p. 41.
7. "Affluentials: The Class Mass Market," *Marketing Communications,* December 1983, pp. 17–21.
8. *U.S. News & World Report,* November 18, 1985, p. 87.
9. Some of this material is based on Roger D. Blackwell and W. Wayne Talarzyk, "Lifestyle Retailing: Competitive Strategies for the 1980s," *Journal of Retailing* 59 (Winter 1983), pp. 7–27.
10. For further reading, see Russell Haley, "Benefit Segments: Backwards and Forwards," *Journal of Advertising Research* 24, no. 1 (February–March 1984), pp. 5–22; see also, "System Profiles Neighborhood Lifestyles to Target New Markets," *Marketing News,* April 11, 1986, p. 21.
11. Jonathan Gutman and Michael Mills, "Fashion Lifestyles, Self-Concept, Shopping Orientation, and Store Patronage: An Integrated Analysis," *Journal of Retailing,* Summer 1982, pp. 75–81.

The Resources Needed to Compete

Thus far, the text has focused on the kinds of information retailers need to know before making decisions about both competitive and merchandising strategies. This section of the text, in contrast, focuses on the resources needed to compete. Chapter 8 focuses on sources of financing available to the retail firm and how changes occur in the organization of the firm over time. Chapter 9 provides an in-depth focus on franchising as a way of owning and operating a retail firm. Additional decisions of importance are the recruiting, selection, training, and motivation of employees, as discussed in Chapter 11. Personnel costs are one of the highest costs facing the retailer.

Another major issue is the choice of a location for the outlet. Location, site selection, and building decision are important because these decisions have such long-lasting effects on the profitability of the firm.

8

Financing and Organizing the Retail Firm

"You Know My Name"

It's after 6 P.M., and Sanitary Dry Cleaners of Laconia, New Hampshire, is closed for the night, but every time somebody comes to the door, proprietor Pamela Swenson or her husband, Paul, who happens to be visiting the store, jumps up and answers it. Who knows? It might be a new customer.

"There's this little lady about 75 years old who travels about a half-hour from Concord to do her dry cleaning with us," says Pamela. "She likes pleats down the side of her jacket, which most people don't, and we know she likes the plastic garment bags folded and stapled at the bottom because she's worried about dust. And we know what to talk to her about, so she likes spending a little time with us, chatting with us."

Pamela Swenson is one of the 3 million U.S women who now own and operate their own business. In 1982, anticipating college expenses for her two daughters, she decided it was time to start contributing to the family till. She bought Sanitary Dry Cleaners, which has a cleaning plant on the premises, from a neighbor.

Unfortunately, they got into the business when interest rates were running at about 14 percent. Says her husband, a local accountant, "In the beginning, we were just getting by with the note payments, and Pam kept asking me about a salary, and I kept saying, 'You're building equity.' But now she can take out a salary that's better than she could earn if she were working for somebody else in this area."

Reprinted by permission of *Forbes*, October 21, 1985. © Forbes Inc.

184

Nobody's going to get rich from Sanitary Dry Cleaners, but it's a living, and it has its triumphs. "There's another dry cleaner down the street," Pam says. "And it is much more convenient for one of my customers because it's just a block and a half away from where he lives, but he started coming in here. I asked him why and he said, 'I've been going to that other place for six months, and all I get is a hello when I walk in the door. You know my name'."

*M*any people share the Swensons' dream of owning their own business in spite of the long hours, the financial risks, and the fiercely competitive nature of retailing. They can get started in many ways. Examples include: Starting a business and operating as an independent organization, banding together with other retailers or wholesalers to have more power in buying goods while still operating as an independent business, or becoming a franchisee. Appendix A at the end of the chapter can be quite helpful in assessing the ways to begin a new venture.

After reading this chapter you will be able to:

1. Describe the risks and advantages of ownership.

2. Explain the differences between a sole proprietorship, a partnership, and a corporation.

3. Define the issues in buying a retail business.

4. Discuss the importance of planning in starting a business.

5. Estimate the operating capital needed for a new business and discuss possible sources of the funds.

6. Explain how to organize for profits.

Approximately 2 million retail businesses exist in the United States. Two thirds of these firms have less than four employees, and 90 percent are single-unit establishments. Clearly, most retail businesses are small by any standard. A person who wants to one day manage a family business or open a business may decide to start a retail career employed by a small firm. Higher quality and more specialized training is normally available in a chain organization.

Chains are often larger than independent firms. A **chain** is an organization that consists of two or more centrally owned units handling substantially similar lines of merchandise. Economies of scale are possible from such an arrangement. Specialized functions such as finance, accounting, buying, and legal services can be handled in one central location for all of the stores.

THE ADVANTAGES OF OWNERSHIP

Retailing offers more opportunities for ownership than virtually any other type of business. Read the newspaper on almost any day and you can probably find several retail businesses for sale. Also, many suppliers and bankers are glad to loan the funds to help people open their own firms; they will, however, probably want to see a cash flow plan as discussed later in this chapter and will need to understand the organization's planned business strategy. The Small Business Administration, an office of the U.S. government, is another source of possible funding.

Most retailing is local in nature so independent retailers can often compete successfully with large national firms. Store trading areas are small and the outlets are viewed as part of the local neighborhood. At the local level, small retailers can do things that a national firm cannot do. Most national firms do not vary their operations from town to town. Consequently, local merchants can offer unique merchandise lines, more specialized services, and more personal attention than are normally available from chain store merchants.

THE RISKS OF OWNERSHIP

Going-out-of-business signs are a part of every community, although few people voluntarily go out of business. Aspiring entrepreneurs should not be discouraged, however, from starting their own business if they are willing to take a risk, because the rewards can be large.[1]

Early Failure Is Likely

The first five years are the toughest for the business owner. Of the businesses that fail, more than 50 percent fail in the first five years, as shown in Table 8–1.

Research by the U.S. Small Business Administration has shown that the lowest retail failure rates are for funeral services and crematoriums; fuel

FAILURES BY AGE OF BUSINESS

Age in Years	Retail
One year or less	3.0%
Two	10.9
Three	16.3
Total three years or less	30.2
Four	13.2
Five	10.7
Total five years or less	54.1
Six	8.8
Seven	6.8
Eight	5.6
Nine	4.2
Ten	3.3
Total six to ten years	28.7
Over Ten Years	17.2
Total	100.0%

SOURCE: *The Business Failure Record* (New York: Dun & Bradstreet, Business Economics Department, 1985), p. 13.

and ice dealers; laundry, cleaning, and garment repair shops; drugstores; hotels; personal services such as secretarial services; and service stations, as shown in Figure 8–1.[2]

One study of retail failures revealed that: (1) the larger the size of the retail business, the greater the chances of survival; (2) the greater the degree of urbanization, the lower the rate of business survival; (3) retailers dealing in "big ticket" items had a higher chance of survival than retailers dealing in "small ticket" products; and (4) rates of survival were highest for corporations (50.8 percent), intermediate for partnerships (30.5 percent), and lowest for sole proprietorships (20.7 percent).[3]

What Are the Causes of Failure?

The most common reasons for failure are incompetence, unbalanced experience, lack of experience in the line, and a lack of managerial experience. Failure because of neglect, fraud, or disaster is unusual, as shown in Table 8–2.

STARTING A NEW BUSINESS

People interested in opening a new business can form a (1) sole proprietorship, (2) partnership, or (3) corporation. The advantages and disadvantages of each form of business are shown in Table 8–3. Management may also decide to purchase an existing business instead of starting a new one. The forms of business are the same whether starting a new business or buying an existing firm.

FIGURE 8–1 WHERE THE ACTION IS AND ISN'T

Fields for the faint at heart . . .

Industry	Failures per 100,000
Funeral services and crematoriums	10.9
Fuel and ice dealers	36.2
Laundry, cleaning, and garment repair	38.0
Drugstores	39.7
Hotels	40.4
Personal services (secretarial, consulting, etc.)	45.2
Service stations	46.2

SOURCE: Richard Greene, "Do You Really Want to Be Your Own Boss?" *Forbes*, October 21, 1985, p. 91.

TABLE 8–2 CAUSES OF RETAIL FAILURES

Underlying Causes	Percent
Neglect	.8
Fraud	.4
Lack of experience in the line	14.4
Lack of managerial experience	11.9
Unbalanced experience*	22.6
Incompetence	40.9
Disaster	1.0
Reason unknown	8.0
Number of failures	11,429
Average liabilities per failure	$203,792

* Experience not well rounded in sales, finance, purchasing, and production on the part of the individual in case of a proprietorship, or of two or more partners or officers constituting a management unit.

SOURCE: *The Business Failure Record* (New York: Dun & Bradstreet, Business Economics Department, 1985), p. 15.

TABLE 8–3 THE ADVANTAGES AND DISADVANTAGES OF EACH FORM OF OWNERSHIP

	Sole Proprietorship	Partnership	Corporation
Advantages	Easy to organize	Easy to organize	Limited financial liability
	Easy to dissolve	Greater capital availability	Easier to raise capital
	Owner keeps all profits	Combined management experience	Specialized management skills
Disadvantages	Unlimited financial liability	Unlimited liability	Complex government regulations
	Difficult to raise capital	Divided authority	Expensive to organize
	Limited life of firm	Hard to dissolve	Various tax disadvantages
	The business is based on the heartbeat of one individual		

| The Sole Proprietorship | The **sole proprietorship** is the most common form of ownership today. Everything belongs to the owner. |

The **sole proprietorship** is the most common form of ownership today. Everything belongs to the owner.

Being the sole owner of a business has several advantages. Such a business is the easiest to start, as less paper work is necessary and fewer restrictions exist other than for inspection or licensing. For example, (1) the owner is the boss; (2) the owner keeps all the profits; and (3) the owner decides on the goods to be sold, store hours, and so forth. The owner can go out of business very quickly, often simply by locking the door and hanging a sign in the window which says "closed."

Problems also exist. For example:

1. The full risk of loss is borne by the owner who can be forced to pay business debts out of personal assets.
2. The firm has limited borrowing power.
3. Qualified people may be hesitant about working for the firm.
4. Such a business can probably offer fewer fringe benefits to employees than could larger employers.
5. No one is legally able to make business decisions except the owner.

A Partnership

A **partnership** exists when two or more people jointly own a retail business. Partnerships can take various forms. For example, in a *general partnership* the partners share all of the responsibilities and benefits of the partnership, including profits and management authority. *Limited partners are persons whose input is limited to one area of the business.* For example, a lawyer may be a limited partner. The liability of limited partners is limited to their investment.

Silent partners likewise have limited liability. They are not active in the business, but are willing to allow their names to be used as one of the partners. Often, these partners are well known in the community and the use of their names is an asset to the firm. *Secret partners do not allow their names to be used.* They do not always have limited liabilities.

The disadvantages of partnerships shown in Table 8–3 make them less popular than other forms of organization, and the problems can be complicated when a firm has several partners. Partnerships often cease to exist when one of the partners becomes incapable of continuing in the business. Likewise, the unlimited liability for the debts of the business can be a drawback, as can the fact that the actions of any one partner are binding on the others.

Consequently, the articles of partnership are very important. They need to spell out carefully the roles of the partners, the ways for a partner to get out of the business, and what happens when one of the partners dies or becomes disabled.

A Corporation

A **corporation** *is a separate legal entity apart from the owners.* Thus, liability is limited to the amount that each individual stockholder has invested in the firm. Since management is separate from ownership, it may be easier for a corporation to attract strong managerial talent. It may also be easier to raise capital, either by issuing stock or through loans. Since corporations are often large and have greater earning power than sole proprietorships, they have easier access to borrowing money at favorable rates.

Again, some disadvantages exist. For example, earnings are taxed more heavily. Corporate earnings are taxed as well as dividends to stockholders.

Corporations may be either open or closed. **Closed corporations** are those owned by a few people, often a family, and persons outside the corporation cannot buy the stock on the open market. The stock value does not have a known market value and does not vary widely in price. **Open corporations** are those in which the stock of the firm can be purchased on the open market. Normally, only large retailers are open corporations.

A special form of corporation is the **Subchapter S corporation.** Under this arrangement, a business can be classified as a corporation, but taxed as a partnership. This arrangement has the advantage of limited liability and avoids the burden of double taxation placed on corporations. Various conditions must be met, including a limit on the number of stockholders. No more than 20 percent of the gross revenues from the business can be derived from interest, dividends, rents, royalties, or the gain on sale of securities. Most small businesses meet these provisions.

Chartering a corporation is easy to do, and most states have laws that standardize the process. Normally, at least three persons are needed to establish a corporation. These people are issued a corporate charter, which is a contract between the state and themselves allowing them to operate the business. The advice or counsel of an attorney should be sought on the details for such an arrangement.

BUYING A RETAIL BUSINESS

A person may decide to buy an existing business instead of starting a new one. Buying a retail business is a complex process. The potential buyer needs the help of professionals such as accountants, bankers, brokers, and attorneys on specific issues.

Deciding on the Type of Retailing

The type of retailing depends on the personal characteristics of the potential buyer, including personality, interests, experiences, and skills. The amount of financing available may also determine the type of business which can be purchased. The growth potential is also important. Information on the future prospects of the business can be developed by talking with executives in trade associations, bankers, suppliers, and others knowledgeable about the business.

| Identifying Potential Stores | Classified ads in a newspaper are a source of possible leads. Prospective buyers can also place "business wanted" ads in the newspaper. Persons specializing in buying and selling retail firms often can provide valuable assistance. The potential buyer needs to remember, however, that the broker represents the seller and gets a commission based on the sales price. |

Other potential sources of leads are suppliers, distributors, trade publications, and trade associations. Occasionally accountants or other management consultants may also be able to identify a business that is for sale.

| Evaluating the Business Opportunity | The potential buyer needs to determine the reasons a business is for sale. Old age, poor health, and pending bankruptcy are reasons that can be easily spotted. Other less obvious reasons include excessive competition, problems with creditors, excessive accounts receivable, or a pending lease loss. |

Assessing Earnings Potential

The potential buyer should look at past profits, sales, and expenses. Operating ratios should be compared with industry data provided by such sources as the National Retail Merchants Association, Dun & Bradstreet, and Robert Morris Associates before making an offer for a business. An independent accountant who specializes in retailing may need to analyze the profit and loss performance of the business over the past three to five years. The buyer should be wary of a seller who will not provide background information including financial statements, income tax returns, purchases, and bank deposits.

A detailed analysis will sometimes indicate that a business is not profitable. The potential owner must then make an assessment about whether it is possible to earn a profit from the business. Perhaps the person has better management skills, is willing to invest more time and energy, or has identified industry trends that make the business attractive to the near-term future.

Evaluating the Assets

The assets of the business should also be carefully considered. Independent appraisers should determine the dollar value of the inventory and its age, style, condition, and quality. Is the inventory compatible with the trading area of the store? How much inventory would have to be liquidated at a loss? What is the market value of the furniture and fixtures? Will they have to be replaced? Are the fixtures compatible with the business?

Accounts receivables should also be studied to determine their age, the credit standing of some of the larger customers, and the success of the firm in collecting past due accounts. Are too many of the credit customers slow in paying their bills? Would customers be lost if stricter credit requirements were established? Similarly, what is the condition of accounts payable? Are any lawsuits pending against the retailer?

The potential buyer should also determine if the lease is transferable. Also, what are the terms of the lease and how much time is left on the lease? Will mailing lists and customer lists be included as part of the sale? Is the business name included as part of the sale?

Finally, the potential buyer should check to determine whether the business has a good reputation and a satisfied clientele. Do the potential customers have a unique attachment to the present owner such that they might not continue to shop at the outlet if it is sold? Finally, any sales agreement should include a provision that keeps the seller from opening a similar business within the same market for a specified period of time.

THE CHARACTERISTICS NEEDED FOR SUCCESS AS AN OWNER/MANAGER[4]

Not all persons can succeed as the owner of a retail business. Retail owner/ managers need to be highly motivated to succeed. They need great energy and commitment and need to be prepared to overcome a lot of obstacles. In the face of setbacks they need to be able to "pick themselves up, dust themselves off, and start over again."

What Characteristics Are Essential to Success in Retailing?

The following is a list of questions and issues that may be helpful in deciding whether to open a retail business. In going through the list it is important to remember:

a. Not all successful people possess all of these characteristics in the same measure. An individual may be strong in some and not so strong in others. The more of them a person possesses, however, the more likely he or she is to succeed in retailing.
b. Many of the characteristics can be acquired if one sets out to do so with purpose.

Risk Taking
It may come as a surprise, but successful entrepreneurs prefer to take moderate rather than big risks. Moderate risks are defined as situations where the chances of winning are neither so small as to be a gamble nor so large as to be a certainty. Remember, though, that all business involves risk. If it didn't, everybody would be in it.

Dealing with Failure
The successful retailer can handle failure and setbacks. It is how the successful retailers handle failure and not whether they have experienced failure that counts.

Self-Confidence
The type of self-confidence useful in retailing is not necessarily being the life and soul of the party. Rather, the retailer needs to be self-reliant and

trusting in his or her ability when the going gets tough. Successful executives do not trust luck, nor do they believe that their own success or the success of others is due to luck.

Persistence and Determination

Persistence, determination, and the desire to overcome hurdles, solve problems, and complete the job are extremely important.

Setting Objectives

Successful retail owners set clear goals and objectives. What does this mean? A world of difference exists between setting out to sell more merchandise this year, and setting out to increase sales by 5 percent by the end of three months or 7 percent by the end of six months. Having clear objectives helps to concentrate effort and to achieve objectives, as noted in Chapter 2.

Attitude about Feedback

Some people look for feedback on how well they are doing and others prefer not to know. Successful retailers are continuously looking for feedback. They are as much, or more, interested in competing against their own standards, as they are in competing against other people.

Using Initiative and Taking Personal Responsibility

The successful retailer is likely to get frustrated if meetings or discussions drag on. More important, if the opportunity arises, they tend to take over running meetings and organizing the activities of the people. These are some of the characteristics of the successful retailer who likes to take on personal responsibility and who takes the initiative to solve a problem or provide leadership.

Using Resources and Services

While the retailer is self-reliant and likes to take charge, successful retailers are also good at knowing when they need help. Thus, self-reliance is important, but not to the exclusion of other sources of advice.

Living with Uncertainty

One of the characteristics of ownership is that there is risk involved and that it takes time to start a business. Both of these factors mean that the person who succeeds in retailing must be able to (1) live with uncertainty and (2) commit to something which, after a lot of effort, may still not bear fruit for a couple of years.

Drive and Energy

Successful retailers are generally recognized as having a high amount of energy and drive, and as possessing a capacity to work long hours.

Before considering starting and managing a retail business, the potential owner should critically examine the single overall factor more crucial to the business than any other—his or her personal characteristics. It is difficult to be realistic in a self-appraisal. However, the following guidelines might be of some help:

— What can the potential owner offer? Is the person prepared for lifestyle changes and a greater commitment to work?
— Can the person accept a lower standard of living initially?
— Can the person accept shorter leisure hours and make greater demands on family?
— What is the person's state of health? Will it stand up to the heavy stresses of business and longer working hours?

THE IMPORTANCE OF PLANNING[5]

In beginning the new business, proper planning is the most important ingredient in success, as discussed in Chapter 2. As stated earlier, half of all retail firms fail in their first five years. Effective planning will do more than anything else to help avoid becoming a part of this alarming failure rate. Success and planning go together. The owner/manager should:

1. Plan together with partners/associates.
2. Make performance expectations clear to everyone.
3. Provide for feedback on progress to keep plans on track.
4. Make plans goal oriented rather than activity oriented.
5. Remember that hard work is vital to success, but this should be accompanied by efficient work.

Five "Friends" Who Can Help Make It Go

The retailer can improve the chances for success by securing the services of these professionals: attorney, accountant, banker, insurance specialist, and professional consultants.

In planning the business, some basic questions also need to be considered:

— Why am I entering retailing?
— What business am I entering?
— What goods or services will I sell?
— What is my market and who is my consumer?
— Who is my competition?
— Can I compete successfully with my competition?
— What is my sales strategy?
— What marketing methods will I use?
— How much money is required?
— Where will the money come from?
— What technical and management skills do I need?
— Can I make just as much money working for someone else?

Answering these questions honestly and objectively will help ensure that the new businessperson is well on the way to building a successful business plan.

A quality business plan can be important in many ways:

1. A business plan provides the retailer a path to follow. It sets out goals and steps that allow the retailer to be in better control of steering the firm in the desired direction.
2. A business plan allows one's banker, accountant, attorney, and insurance agent to know clearly what the business is trying to do. A plan will give them insight into the situation so that they can be of greater assistance to the business.
3. A business plan can help the owner communicate better with the staff, suppliers, and others about operations and objectives of the business.
4. A business plan can help the owner develop better management skills and abilities. It can help management consider competitive conditions, promotional opportunities, and what situations are most advantageous to the new business. In short, a business plan will help the owner to make sound business judgments.

There are no set requirements as to the contents of the plan. The contents depend on the type and size of the business being started. The most important consideration is the quality of the plan, not its length. The plan should include all aspects of the proposed business. Any possible problem areas in starting the venture should be listed with possible methods of dealing with them. Bankers would rather know the problems before the business is started than down the road where possible solutions may be limited.

Suggested contents for a business plan are listed below. Each plan will be different and subject to variations of this list, but these suggestions will at least help to get started.

1. Summary of the mission of the retail firm—just a few paragraphs on what the owner is doing, and the plans for the future.
2. The retail industry in the community as a whole, the company, and its products or services. A paragraph on each.
3. Market research and analysis.
   a. Consumers.
   b. Market size and trends.
   c. Competition.
   d. Estimated market share and sales.
4. Marketing plan.
   a. Overall marketing strategy.
   b. Pricing.
   c. Sales tactics.
   d. Service.
   e. Advertising and promotion.

5. Management team.
   a. Organization.
   b. Key management personnel—who are they and what will they do?
   c. Ownership and compensation.
   d. Board of directors.
   e. Any supporting services.
6. The financial plan (you may need accounting help).
   a. Profit and loss forecasts.
   b. Pro forma cash flow analysis.
   c. Pro forma balance sheets.
7. Proposed company offering.
   a. Desired financing.
   b. Capitalization.
   c. Use of funds.
8. Overall schedule of activities for the next three years.

Further details on structuring a business plan are contained in Appendix A.

OPERATING CAPITAL NEEDED

After the business plan is developed, sources of capital must be obtained. The nature of retailing affects the types of capital needed. The main thing to do is avoid an early shortage of funds. Therefore, retailers need to begin by estimating the capital needed to open a business. Many have a tendency to underestimate the needed opening capital.

Retailers need to plan for two categories of costs: (1) *opening costs,* which are one-time costs such as the cost of fixturing and decorating; and (2) *operating expenses,* which are the estimated ongoing expenses of running the business for a designated time period. Examples of these costs are shown in Table 8–4. Operating expenses are shown in more detail in Table 8–5. The same expense categories exist in most retail businesses.

Developing a Cash Flow Forecast

Cash flow projections are helpful in planning for the opening and preparing for unforeseen difficulties. They are necessary when approaching a bank about loans.

A cash flow forecast is designed to predict when cash will be received by the firm and when payments need to be made. Cash inflow and outflow vary by type of retailer, especially for those that are seasonal and who stock merchandise based on varying seasonal sales levels.

Management can use a cash budget as shown in Table 8–6 to help estimate cash flow. Negative cash flow (when outlays exceed income) should be funded with the initial capital developed for the new venture. Retailers can base the projections on experience or on trade association statistics that

TABLE 8–4 OPERATING COSTS AND OPERATING EXPENSES FOR A TYPICAL RETAIL BUSINESS

Opening Costs	Operating Expenses
Inventory	Rent (including one month's deposit)
Fixtures and equipment	Taxes, licenses, and permits
Leasehold improvements	Advertising and promotion
(wiring, plumbing, lighting,	Legal and accounting fees
air conditioning)	Wages (including owner's)
Security system	
Exterior sign	

TABLE 8–5 TYPICAL EXPENSE CATEGORIES

Expenses
Wages (including owner's salary and payroll taxes)
Rent
Utilities
Advertising and promotion
Supplies
Depreciation
Insurance
Legal and accounting fees
Maintenance and repairs
Auto expense
Taxes, licenses, and permits
Miscellaneous

can be obtained from sources listed in Table 8–7, from trade magazines, and from their bankers. A retailer should ideally know approximately what the operating costs and the cash inflow will be before opening the business. A person should have enough money to cover all expenses for about six months. Management should be conservative if it is uncertain how much money is needed. They should borrow too much rather than too little, in order to avoid having to come back later for additional funds.

As shown in Table 8–6, anticipated cash sales for a jewelry firm in the first three months of operation are $53,000, $58,000, and $66,000 per month. Average monthly sales based on a sales forecast of $750,000 are $62,500 ($750,000 divided by 12). Management expects a $200 loss at the end of the first month, to break even at the end of the second month, and to show a profit at the end of December. December is traditionally a very strong month for jewelry sales. Conceivably the business could lose funds during the early part of the following year since 30 percent or more of jewelry sales typically are made the last three months of the year.

TABLE 8-6 PROJECTED CASH FLOW BUDGET FOR THREE MONTHS ENDING DECEMBER 19___

	October	November	December
Anticipated cash receipts			
Cash sales	$53,000	$58,000	$66,000
Payment for credit sales	2,000	4,000	4,500
Other income			
Total receipts	55,000	62,000	70,500
Anticipated payments			
Cost of merchandise	27,500	31,000	32,250
Payroll	20,000	21,000	21,500
Promotion	4,000	4,500	6,000
Sales commissions	1,200	1,300	1,600
Loans to be repaid	1,500	1,500	1,500
Maintenance	—	100	300
Utilities	600	600	700
Outside accounting and legal fees	400	2,000	1,300
Total	55,200	62,000	65,150
Expected surplus at end of month	(200)	—	5,350
Desired cash operating balance	2,000	2,000	—
Short-term loan needed	2,000	2,000	—
Cash available	—	—	5,350

Sources of Funds

One way to illustrate how merchants can get the capital needed is by the use of a scenario. Suppose that a son of the owner of Stein's jewelry store decides to go into business. He has worked for the family business for 10 years, in addition to part-time and summer work. He wants to be on his own, and his father has given his blessing.

Using the logic suggested earlier in the chapter, young Stein computes that he will need the following capital:

Operating expenses for six months	$175,000
Opening costs (fixtures, equipment, leasehold improvements)	50,000
	$225,000

Equity

Over the years Stein has saved and inherited enough to "comfortably" cover 45 percent of his capital needs. Thus, he needs an additional $123,750 ($225,000 × .55).

Suppliers

Stein's projected annual sales are $750,000. Assume a markup of 50 percent on retail and two merchandise turns per year. Retail markup is the difference between the invoice cost and the retail price. Merchandise turns are the

TABLE 8–7 **MAJOR RETAIL TRADE ASSOCIATIONS BY KINDS OF BUSINESS**

Kinds of Business	Trade Associations
Food stores:	International Federation of Grocers Association (IFGA)
	National Association of Convenience Stores (NACS)
	Food and Grocery Chain Stores of America (FGCSA)
Apparel and accessory stores:	Womenswear Retailers of America (WRA)
	National Association of Shoe Chain Stores (NASCS)
	American National Retail Jewelers Association (ANRJA)
Furniture, home furnishings, and equipment stores:	National Home Furnishings Association (NHFA)
	International Furniture and Accessories Association (AFAA)
	National Independent Furniture Retailers Association (NIFRA)
Building materials, hardware, and farm equipment dealers:	National Farm & Power Equipment Dealers Association (NFPEDA)
	National Retail Hardware Association (NRHA)
	National Lumber and Building Materials Dealers Association (NLBMDA)
General merchandise stores:	National Association of Variety Stores (NAVS)
	National Association of Discount Merchants (NADM)
	National Association of Mass Merchandisers (NAMM)

number of times the average inventory is sold and replaced in a given time period. On the basis of our assumptions, he can probably receive financing from suppliers of $31,875 based on the terms of sale of net 30 (invoice must be paid within 30 days to maintain a good credit rating) with no discount for early payment. The computations are as follows:

$$\frac{\text{Projected annual sales} \times \text{Percent markup}}{\text{Number of turns}}$$
$$= \frac{\$750,000 \times .50}{2}$$
$$= \$187,500 \text{ total cost of inventory for six months}$$

The $187,500 must be financed. With terms of 30 days in payment, Stein can probably get financing for one sixth (or 17 percent) of the inventory needed for one turnover period, which is six months (30 days is one sixth of the six-month turnover period based on two turns per year). Thus, the amount financed by suppliers will be:

$$\$187,500 \times .17 = \$31,875$$

Thus, Stein still needs \$91,875 additional capital (\$123,750 − 31,875 = 91,875).

Financial Institutions and Government

With his relatively healthy equity investment, Stein would probably have success in securing loans from banks to assist in financing inventory and accounts receivable as well as some fixed assets. The Small Business Administration, though often considered a difficult loan avenue because of the complexity of its process, is a source of government funds.

To continue the scenario, assume that Stein secured his permanent capital needs. His jewelry store has been in operation for some time. He has brought in additional partners as owners; he has increased his sales; his receivables have grown; and he needs more financing.

Stein can generate his capital needs to meet these new obligations from either internal or external sources. The major way to generate capital inside the firm is from profitable operations. His external sources of capital have been discussed above, except that once the business is profitable, he may be able to issue stock or perhaps bonds if the business is a corporation.

ORGANIZING

Decisions must also be made on how the retail firm will be organized. Most merchants are all-arounders. They do all jobs as the need arises, or assign tasks to various employees on a random, nonspecialized basis. Employees are extensions of the managers to carry out the tasks they lack time to attend to themselves. Small merchants don't think of setting up distinct functions and lines for the flow of authority, nor do they select specialists to handle each function. As a store grows, however, specialization becomes necessary.

Basic Organization Principles

Before discussing organization structure, certain management principles must be taken into consideration in organizing the firm. Four organization principles are important here. They are:

1. The principle of specialization of labor.
2. The principle of departmentalization.
3. The span-of-control principle.
4. The unity-of-command principle.

These four principles are reflected in the organization chart of the retail firm.

Specialization

Modern business organization is built upon the concept of **specialization.** More and better work is performed at less cost when it is done by specialists than when it is done by employees who shift from one job to another and who continually improvise.

Specialization is of two kinds: tasks and people. Specialization of tasks narrows a person's activities to simple, repetitive routines. Thus a relatively untrained employee can quickly become proficient at a narrow specialty. Because they develop routines and don't have to keep jumping from one job to the next, employees don't waste time and effort in a constant change of activity.

Specialization of people does not involve simplifying the job, but training a person to perform a certain job better than anyone else can. Training and experience improve the quality and quantity of the particular type of work.

In the smaller retail store, most of the specialization is of the second type; but in larger stores there is more and more need for narrow task specialization. For example, certain special records must be kept, and certain phases of merchandise handling must be done by a well-trained person.

Departmentalization

Management will probably find that they can use **departmentalization,** or group jobs into classes such as the following (each demanding a certain combination of skills for good performance):

— *Merchandising*—including buying and managing inventory for different groups of merchandise.
— *Direct and general selling and adjustments*—customer contact.
— *Sales promotion*—largely concerning advertising and display.
— *Accounting and finance*—records, correspondence, cash handling, insurance, and perhaps credit.
— *Store operation*—problems having to do with building, equipment, and safety measures.
— *Merchandise handling*—receiving, marking, storing, and delivering.
— *Personnel*—employment, training, employee benefits, and personnel records.

Recognizing the many functions to be performed in the firm doesn't mean a specialist is necessary for each of them. Management can combine some functions and delegate them, but management should look ahead and have an organization plan that provides for various specialized positions when they are needed.

Span of Control

Span of control addresses the question of how many subordinates should report to a supervisor. Generally, a supervisor's span of control should be small because an individual can work effectively with only a limited number

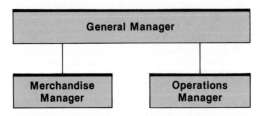

of people at one time. Span of control, however, depends on such factors as the competence of the supervisor and subordinates, the similarity of the functions to be performed, and the physical location of persons.

Unity of Command

The **unity-of-command** concept involves a series of superior/subordinate relationships. This concept states that no person should be under the direct control of more than one supervisor in performing job tasks. Thus, an employee should receive decision-making power from and report to only one supervisor. An unbroken chain of command should exist from top to bottom. Otherwise, frustration and confusion will occur.

How to Organize for Profitable Operations

The two functions that probably will be organized first are *merchandising* and *operations,* or store management. Such an organization would look like the one illustrated in Figure 8–2.

The merchandise manager has other functions in addition to being responsible for buying and selling. The person supervises and/or prepares merchandise budgets; handles advertising, displays, and other promotions; and is responsible for inventory planning and control.

The *operations manager* is responsible for building upkeep, delivery, stockroom(s), service, supplies, equipment purchasing, and similar activities.

As a store continues to grow in size, specialization of labor occurs. The organization structure may begin to look like the one in Figure 8–3.

As shown in Figure 8–3, the next managers who should be added are financial, promotion, and personnel managers. The financial manager, or controller, handles the finances of the firm and probably has an accounting background. The organization structure in Figure 8–3 is typical of most department stores. A food operation, however, performs the same functions as do all retail firms.

Trends in Organizing

The typical organization plan, illustrated in Figure 8–3, gives the merchandising manager responsibility for *both* buying and selling. After World War II, shopping centers were developed and downtown stores "branched" to the

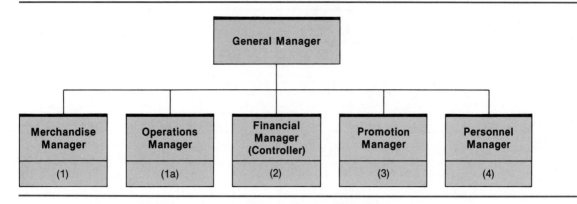

shopping centers. The merchandise manager became responsible not only for buying and selling merchandise in the downtown (main) store but also in the branches. This situation proved to be impossible. One merchandise manager could not be responsible for buying, supervising sales, and general management of the main store and the branch stores as well. So, a trend developed during this "branching" era to *separate* the buying and selling functions.

Separation of Buying and Selling

There are arguments for and against the separation of the buying and selling responsibilities in the organization. Those *opposing* the separation of the two functions argue that:

1. The buyer must have contact with consumers to be able to interpret their needs.
2. Those who buy merchandise should also be responsible for selling it.
3. It is easier to pinpoint merchandising successes and failures when the two functions are combined.

Those who *favor* the separation of the two functions argue that:

1. If the two functions are combined, buying is likely to have more importance than selling.
2. Buying and selling require two different types of job skills.
3. With technology, reports, and the like, it is not necessary for the two functions to be combined.
4. Salespeople can be shifted more easily under this arrangement.

The arguments against separating the buying and selling functions do not seem as strong as the counter-arguments. The branch-store problem seems to demand separation. Thus, the trend is to separate the two. Figure 8–4 shows a department store that is organized for the separation of buying

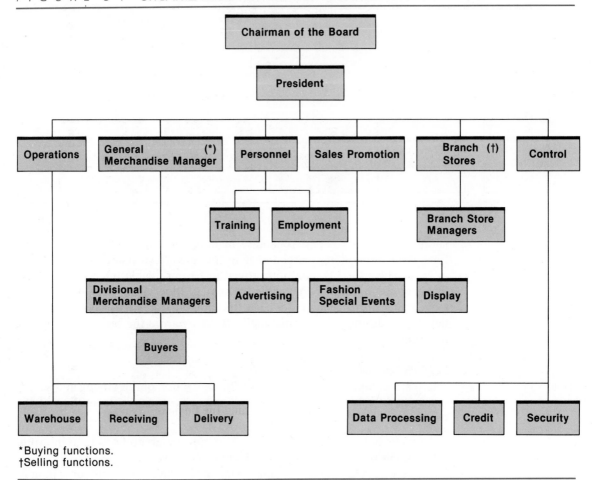

*Buying functions.
†Selling functions.

and selling. The general merchandise manager is responsible for buying, and the vice president for branch stores is responsible for selling.

Food stores could have faced the same conflict, but their expansion history actually solved their problems. Rather than branching, these companies expanded as chain-store organizations. No main stores exist in a chain organization. Buying and selling are always separated.

Chain-Store Organization

Certain features of a chain should be explained, since major differences exist between a chain organization and a branch-store arrangement. Some of the differences are as follows:

1. In a chain, responsibility is more centralized in the headquarters, or home office.

2. More divisions exist in a chain organization, such as real estate, transportation, warehousing, public relations, and legal divisions.
3. The chain organization has tighter supervision of store activities.
4. The chain probably has more reports for control purposes.

CHAPTER HIGHLIGHTS

— The important traits for success as a retail owner/manager include self-confidence, willingness to take risks, persistence and determination, initiative, a high level of drive and energy, and the ability to live with uncertainty.

— The most common reasons for failure in retailing are management incompetence, unbalanced experience, and the lack of experience in the line of trade. Failure because of neglect, fraud, or disaster is unusual.

— Many persons enter retailing by buying an existing business. Such persons have to decide on the type of business they want to buy based on their interests, skills, and experience as well as the financing they can arrange.

— Available opportunities for buying a business can be discovered by working with business brokers and realtors, by studying newspaper ads, and by contacts with trade sources.

— In making the decision on whether to buy a business, the potential buyer should determine the reasons the business is for sale, whether a profit is being earned, the operating ratios of the business as compared to industry averages, and the worth of the business assets.

— Capital is needed for two categories of cost in starting a business: (1) opening costs, which are one-time costs, and (2) operating expenses, which are the estimated ongoing expenses of running the business.

— Sources of cash include owners' equity, the credit available from suppliers, loans from financial institutions and government, and the sale of stock.

— Retailers have the choice of forming a new business as a sole proprietorship, a partnership, or a corporation. Also, they can operate as an independent firm or become part of a marketing system.

— Basic organizational principles are: specialization of labor, departmentalization, span of control, and unity of command.

— The two functions that probably will first be organized in a retail store are merchandising and operations, or store management.

KEY TERMS

Chain A retail organization consisting of two or more centrally owned units that handle similar lines of merchandise.

Closed corporation A corporation owned by a few people. Persons outside the corporation cannot buy the stock on the open market.

Corporation A group of people who obtain a charter which grants them collectively the rights, privileges, liabilities, and legal powers of an individual, separate and apart from the individual making up the group. The corporation can sell, buy, and inherit property. The corporation owns assets and is liable for the debts it contracts.

Departmentalization An organization principle that determines how jobs are grouped.

Open corporations Corporations in which the stock of a firm can be purchased on the open market.

Partnership A voluntary association of two or more persons to operate a retail outlet for profit as co-owners. The rights, responsibilities, and duties of the partners are stated in the articles of partnership.

Sole proprietorship A situation where the retail outlet is owned and operated by one person who has title to the assets and who is subject to the claims of all creditors.

Span of control A principle of organization that addresses the question of how many persons should report to a supervisor.

Specialization A principle of organization which states that the content of individual jobs should be narrowly defined.

Subchapter S corporation A situation whereby a business is classified as a corporation but taxed as a partnership.

Unity of command A principle of organization which states that no person should be under the direct control of more than one supervisor in performing job tasks.

DISCUSSION QUESTIONS

1. Why are the risks of business ownership so high today?
2. What are the major causes of retail business failure?
3. Evaluate the three forms of private business ownership (sole proprietorship, partnership, and corporation) in terms of the strengths and weaknesses of each.
4. What are the differences between the following terms: general partnership, limited partner, silent partner, and secret partner?
5. What is the difference between an open corporation and a closed corporation?
6. What are the advantages of a Subchapter S corporation arrangement? Must any special conditions be met for a corporation to be classified as a Subchapter S corporation? If so, what are they?
7. How does a retailer determine the amount of capital needed?
8. Describe the various sources of capital available to a retailer opening a new retail operation.
9. Discuss the following four principles of organization: specialization of labor, departmentalization, span of control, and unity of command.

APPLICATION EXERCISE

1. Visit four independent retail firms in your community that have opened in the last five years. Identify the factors that prompted the owner/manager to go into the business, the background of the owner prior to entering the business, the biggest mistakes the owner has made thus far, and the advice the owner/manager would offer to individuals contemplating opening a new retail business. Write a brief essay summarizing your findings.

CASES

1. Revolutionizing the Stagnant Floral Business

In the United States, the average person who buys flowers spends $10 on cut flowers per year. In contrast, the West German spends $58 per person and, because flowers cost much less in Germany, the $58 figure would be approximately $120 in this country.

When one considers the fact that the population in West Germany is 56 million and the population of the United States is 225 million, the potential here becomes most interesting.

The retail side of floral marketing has been characterized by tradition-bound situations as statistics show. The market has declined about one percentage point every few years. There are approximately 30,000 florists in the United States averaging about $150,000 annually in sales volume derived primarily (60 to 70 percent of sales) from arrangements ordered through catalogs or via phone. In other words, the florists operated on a format that was convenient for them, not for the consumer. Discussions about flowers and browsing through the offerings were the exception rather than the rule. The storage refrigerators seemed to be "off limits" to customers as they were difficult to get to and the storage facilities were intimidating to most customers. It was a rare situation to find floral offerings labeled with price, name, care, or handling. Clearly, flowers were "special occasion" purchases.

Mr. Jose Falconi of Southflower Market is reviving and revolutionizing a stagnant industry by recognizing its apparent lack of foresight and imagination together with its dearth of long-range planning. Falconi, after doing some research, decided that the time was right to change the way floral marketing had taken place in the past. So he put into practice his belief that fun and spontaneity could be put into the purchase of flowers. He also offered customers guaranteed variety, freshness, reasonable cost, and salespeople who were eager to help and answer questions. His concept was initiated on the unusually active and revived Columbus Avenue in New York. The store is long, narrow, and on a corner, and layout encourages smooth traffic flow. The only fixture in the store is a wrapping counter;

the flowers are the stars. Salespeople are carefully trained in all dimensions of the process of floral retailing. Southflower stresses retailer/customer communications to learn from the customers as much as possible as well as to give information.

Flowers are sold by the stem; special promotions have been planned; advertising has been limited to newspapers like *The New York Times,* but future plans call for more efforts in affluent demographic publications. Strong use of public relations has been effective. The New York store (now two) averages $1,000 sales per square foot. Seventy to 75 percent of the customers repeat purchases every week. A Lenox Square Atlanta store has been opened, and branches are planned for Fort Lauderdale, Houston, and St. Louis, plus plans for 40 more locations in the next five years. "The market niche has been identified, the need has been filled, the results are superb, and potential is great."

Questions
1. Review the material in the chapter on "Do You Have What It Takes to Succeed in Retailing?" What are the characteristics exhibited by Mr. Jose Falconi that are similar to those in the discussion?
2. Identify other types of retailing that have revolutionized traditional ways of doing business because a clever person thought of a better way of responding to consumer needs. What were the ingredients of their success?

Based on Carmella C. Maresca and Leslie R. Wolff, "Floral Chain Blossoms with Fresh Ideas," *Advertising Age,* July 12, 1982; "Flower Power," *Sky Magazine,* February 1987, pp. 11–16.

2. How Amway Caters to America's Dreams

Amway Corporation's estimated annual retail sales exceed $2 billion. Founded in 1959, Amway alone accounts for about 16 percent of all sales from direct selling. The firm competes successfully against the largest packaged goods marketers in the United States. Management's retailing formula pays little attention to media costs or store shelf space, yet generates 20 percent annual growth in revenues. For example, Amway spends roughly $5 million a year in advertising, primarily on recruiting distributors. In contrast, Procter & Gamble, with 10 times the sales, spends 130 times as much on advertising as Amway.

Amway has 750,000 distributors in the United States and more than 1 million worldwide. Distrib-

utors' primary mission is to sell the company's 350 household and personal care products. They also recruit future distributors on the Amway plan, who in turn can sell products. Distributors add to their own income whenever a person they have sponsored makes a sale. In other words, Amway's complicated commission structure rewards people for both their own sales performance and for those of the distributors they recruited.

Here is how the plan works. Amway distributors mark up wholesale prices on all products they sell personally by 30 percent. In addition, they receive a bonus based on their recruits' monthly sales. For example, with $7,500 in sales, direct distributors are eligible for a 25 percent performance bonus. They in turn pay distributors they have recruited smaller bonuses based on their sales level. Three percent is paid on $100 in sales, 6 percent on $300, and so on up to 25 percent.

Another secret of Amway's success is frequent motivational meetings. In weekly meetings, distributors learn about new sales and marketing plans and see product demonstrations. Monthly rallies draw thousands of distributors to a central point for more motivation and education.

Questions

1. Are each of the 750,000 Amway distributors retailers? List the reasons for defining the Amway distributor as a retailer. What reasons, if any, come to your mind which suggest that each of the distributors is not a retailer?
2. What are reasons for the popularity of such firms as Amway? What types of people are most likely to become Amway distributors?

Based on "How Amway Caters to 'America's Dreams'," *Advertising Age,* January 10, 1983, pp. M-4–M-5.

ENDNOTES

1. Richard Green, "Do You Really Want to Be Your Own Boss?" *Forbes,* October 21, 1985, p. 91.
2. For further information, see "Business Failures," *The Wall Street Journal,* March 25, 1986, p. 1.
3. Alvin Starr and Michael Massell, "Survival Rates for Retailers," *Journal of Retailing* 57 (Summer 1981), p. 93.
4. Adapted from Dennis Moynihan, Irish Productivity Center, *A Business of Your Own,* 1984.
5. Adapted from K. Mark Weaver, "The Importance of Planning," in *How to Start a Successful New Business* (Tuscaloosa: West Alabama Chamber of Commerce, undated).

APPENDIX A

CHECKLIST FOR GOING INTO BUSINESS

Thinking of starting a business? Ask yourself these questions.

You want to own and manage your own business. It's a good idea—provided you know what it takes and have what it takes.

Starting a business is risky at best. But your chances of making it go will be better if you understand the problems you'll meet and work out as many of them as you can before you start.

Here are some questions to help you think through what you need to know and do. Check each question if the answer is yes. Where the answer is no, you have some work to do.

Before you start

How about you?
Are you the kind of person who can get a business started and make it go? (Before you answer this question, use worksheet 1.) _____

Think about *why* you want to own your own business. Do you want to badly enough to keep working long hours without knowing how much money you'll end up with? _____

Have you worked in a business like the one you want to start? _____

Have you worked for someone else as a foreman or manager? _____

Have you had any business training in school? _____

Have you saved any money? _____

How about the money?
Do you know how much money you will need to get your business started? (Use worksheets 2 and 3 to figure this out.) _____

Have you counted up how much money of your own you can put into the business? _____

Do you know how much credit you can get from your suppliers—the people you will buy from? _____

Do you know where you can borrow the rest of the money you need to start your business? _____

Source: *Small Marketers Aid* no. 71 (Washington, D.C.: U.S. Small Business Administration), September 1977.

Under each question, check the answer that says what you feel or comes closest to it. Be honest with yourself.

Are you a self-starter?
- ☐ I do things on my own. Nobody has to tell me to get going.
- ☐ If someone gets me started, I keep going all right.
- ☐ Easy does it. I don't put myself out until I have to.

How do you feel about other people?
- ☐ I like people. I can get along with just about anybody.
- ☐ I have plenty of friends—I don't need anyone else.
- ☐ Most people irritate me.

Can you lead others?
- ☐ I can get most people to go along when I start something.
- ☐ I can give the orders if someone tells me what we should do.
- ☐ I let someone else get things moving. Then I go along if I feel like it.

Can you take responsibility?
- ☐ I like to take charge of things and see them through.
- ☐ I'll take over if I have to, but I'd rather let someone else be responsible.
- ☐ There's always some eager beavers around wanting to show how smart they are. I say, let them.

How good an organizer are you?
- ☐ I like to have a plan before I start. I'm usually the one to get things lined up when the group wants to do something.
- ☐ I do all right unless things get too confused. Then I quit.
- ☐ You get all set and then something comes along and presents too many problems. So I just take things as they come.

How good a worker are you?
- ☐ I can keep going as long as I need to. I don't mind working hard for something I want.
- ☐ I'll work hard for a while, but when I've had enough, that's it.
- ☐ I can't see that hard work gets you anywhere.

Can you make decisions?
- ☐ I can make up my mind in a hurry if I have to. It usually turns out OK, too.
- ☐ I can if I have plenty of time. If I have to make up my mind fast, later I think I should have decided the other way.
- ☐ I don't like to be the one who has to decide things.

Can people trust what you say?
- ☐ You bet they can. I don't say things I don't mean.
- ☐ I try to be on the level most of the time, but sometimes I just say what's easiest.
- ☐ Why bother if the other fellow doesn't know the difference?

Can you stick with it?
- ☐ If I make up mind to do something, I don't let *anything* stop me.
- ☐ I usually finish what I start—if it goes well.
- ☐ If it doesn't go right away, I quit. Why beat your brains out?

How good is your health?
- ☐ I *never* run down!
- ☐ I have enough energy for most things I want to do.
- ☐ I run out of energy sooner than most of my friends seem to.

Now count the checks you made.

How many checks are there beside the *first* answer to each question? _____

How many checks are there beside the *second* answer to each question? _____

How many checks are there beside the *third* answer to each question? _____

If most of your checks are beside the first answers, you probably have what it takes to run a business. If not, you're likely to have more trouble than you can handle by yourself. Better find a partner who is strong on the points you're weak on. If many checks are beside the third answer, not even a good partner will be able to shore you up.

Have you figured out what net income per year you expect to get from the business? Count your salary and your profit on the money you put into the business. _____

Can you live on less than this so that you can use some of it to help your business grow? _____

Have you talked to a banker about your plans? _____

How about a partner?

If you need a partner with money or know-how, do you know someone who will fit—someone you can get along with? _____

Do you know the good and bad points about going it alone, having a partner, and incorporating your business? _____

Have you talked to a lawyer about it? _____

How about your customers?

Do most businesses in your community seem to be doing well? _____

Have you tried to find out whether stores like the one you want to open are doing well in your community and in the rest of the country? _____

Estimated monthly expenses

Item	Column 1 Your estimate of monthly expenses based on sales of $ _____ per year	Column 2 Your estimate of how much cash you need to start your business (See column 3)	Column 3 What to put in column 2 (These figures are typical for one kind of business. You will have to decide how many months to allow for in your business.)
Salary of owner-manager	$	$	2 times column 1
All other salaries and wages			3 times column 1
Rent			3 times column 1
Advertising			3 times column 1
Delivery expense			3 times column 1
Supplies			3 times column 1
Telephone and telegraph			3 times column 1
Other utilities			3 times column 1
Insurance			Payment required by insurance company
Taxes, including Social Security			4 times column 1
Interest			3 times column 1
Maintenance			3 times column 1
Legal and other professional fees			3 times column 1
Miscellaneous			3 times column 1

Starting costs you only have to pay once — Leave column 2 blank

Item			Column 3
Fixtures and equipment			Fill in worksheet 3 and put the total here
Decorating and remodeling			Talk it over with a contractor
Installation of fixtures and equipment			Talk to suppliers from whom you buy these
Starting inventory			Suppliers will probably help you estimate this
Deposits with public utilities			Find out from utilities companies
Legal and other professional fees			Lawyer, accountant, and so on
Licenses and permits			Find out from city offices what you have to have
Advertising and promotion for opening			Estimate what you'll use
Accounts receivable			What you need to buy more stock until credit customers pay
Cash			For unexpected expenses or losses, special purchases, etc.
Other			Make a separate list and enter total
Total estimated cash you need to start with	$		Add up all the numbers in column 2

List of furniture, fixtures, and equipment

Leave out or add items to suit your business. Use separate sheets to list exactly what you need for each of the items below.	If you plan to pay cash in full, enter the full amount below and in the last column.	If you are going to pay by installments, fill out the columns below. Enter in the last column your downpayment plus at least one installment.			Estimate of the cash you need for furniture, fixtures, and equipment
		Price	Downpay-ment	Amount of each install-ment	
Counters	$	$	$	$	$
Storage shelves, cabinets					
Display stands, shelves, tables					
Cash register					
Safe					
Window display fixtures					
Special lighting					
Outside sign					
Delivery equipment if needed					
Total furniture, fixtures, and equipment (Enter this figure also in worksheet 2 under "Starting costs you only have to pay once")					$

Do you know what kind of people will want to buy what you plan to sell? _____

What do people who live in the area like where you want to open your store? _____

Do they need a store like yours? _____

If not, have you thought about opening a different kind of store or going to another neighborhood? _____

Getting started

Your building
Have you found a good building for your store? _____

Will you have enough room when your business gets bigger? _____

Can you fix the building the way you want it without spending too much money? _____

Can people get to it easily from parking spaces, bus stops, or their homes? _____

Have you had a lawyer check the lease and zoning? _____

Equipment and supplies

Do you know just what equipment and supplies you need and how much they will cost? (worksheet 3 and the lists you made should show this.) _____

Can you save some money by buying secondhand equipment? _____

Your merchandise

Have you decided what things you will sell? _____

Do you know how much or how many of each to buy with which to open your store? _____

Have you found suppliers who will sell you what you need at a good price? _____

Have you compared the prices and credit terms of different suppliers? _____

Your records

Have you planned a system of records that will keep track of your income and expenses, what you owe other people, and what other people owe you? _____

Have you worked out a way to keep track of your inventory so that you will always have enough on hand for your customers but not more than you can sell? _____

Have you figured out how to keep your payroll records and take care of tax reports and payments? _____

Do you know what financial statements you should prepare? _____

Do you know how to use these financial statements? _____

Do you know an accountant who will help you with your records and financial statements? _____

Your store and the law

Do you know what licenses and permits you need? _____

Do you know what business laws you have to obey? _____

Do you know a lawyer you can go to for advice and for help with legal papers? _____

Protecting your store

Have you made plans for protecting your store against thefts of all kinds—shoplifting, robbery, burglary, and employee thefts? _____

Have you talked with an insurance agent about what kinds of insurance you need? _____

Buying a business someone else has started

Have you made a list of what you like and don't like about buying a business someone else has started? _____

Are you sure you know the real reason why the owner wants to sell his/her business? _____

Have you compared the cost of buying this business with the cost of starting a new business? _____

Is the stock up to date and in good condition? _____

Is the building in good condition? _____

Will the owner of the building transfer the lease to you? _____

Have you talked with other businesspeople in the area to see what they think of the business? _____

Have you talked with the company's suppliers? _____

Have you talked with a lawyer about it? _____

Making it go

Advertising
Have you decided how you will advertise? (Newspapers—posters—handbills—radio—by mail?) _____

Do you know where to get help with your ads? _____

Have you watched what other stores do to get people to buy? _____

The prices you charge
Do you know how to figure what you should charge for each item you sell? _____

Do you know what other stores like yours charge? _____

Buying
Do you have a plan for finding out what your customers want? _____

Will your plan for keeping track of your inventory tell you when it is time to order more and how much to order? _____

Do you plan to buy most of your stock from a few suppliers rather than a little from many, so that those you buy from will want to help you succeed? _____

Selling
Have you decided whether you will have salesclerks or self-service? _____

Do you know how to get customers to buy? _____

Have you thought about why you like to buy from some salespersons while others turn you off? _____

Your employees
If you need to hire someone to help you, do you know where to look? _____

Do you know what kind of person you need?   _____

Do you know how much to pay?   _____

Do you have a plan for training your employees?   _____

Credit for your customers
Have you decided whether to let your customers buy on credit?   _____

Do you know the good and bad points about joining a credit-card plan?   _____

Can you tell a deadbeat from a good credit customer?   _____

A few extra questions
Have you figured out whether you could make more money working for someone else?   _____

Does your family go along with your plan to start a business of your own?   _____

Do you know where to find out about new ideas and new products?   _____

Do you have a work plan for yourself and your employees?   _____

Have you gone to the nearest Small Business Administration office for help with your plans?   _____

If you have answered all these questions carefully, you've done some hard work and serious thinking. That's good. But you have probably found some things you still need to know more about or do something about.

Do all you can for yourself, but don't hesitate to ask for help from people who can tell you what you need to know. Remember, running a business takes guts. You've got to be able to decide what you need and then go after it.

Good luck!

9

Franchising as a Way of Owning and Operating a Retail Firm

Gymboree Exercise Centers

Joan Barnes, a young mother of two, is the founder of Gymboree Exercise Centers for children. The Center is an example of how innovative entrepreneurs can develop a highly successful retailing concept. Mrs. Barnes still owns 50 percent of Gymboree Systems, and her personal net worth now exceeds $2 million.

The first Gymboree center was opened in a San Francisco suburb in 1977. The centers provide a fun way of limbering up the muscles of infants through light exercises. Twice a week for 45 minutes, children aged three months to four years, accompanied by their mothers, bounce, slide, climb, and roll on colorful, specially designed jungle gyms and trampolines to the rhythms of disco, folk, and Latin music. Parents gently move the arms and legs of the smaller babies in exercises called "boogies."

Revenue growth has exceeded 100 percent every year since 1980. A Gymboree franchise costs $12,000 for a single site. The franchisee can buy additional sites on a sliding scale down to a fee of $10,000 each for four or more units. The franchisee, in return for the fee, gets the right to use the company name and methods, an exclusive territory, and nine days of training. The franchisee also pays a royalty fee of 6 percent of revenues.

Based on Faye Rice, "How to Succeed at Cloning a Small Business," *Fortune*, October 28, 1985, pp. 60–61.

LEARNING OBJECTIVES

*T*he Gymboree Exercise Center retailing capsule illustrates how individuals with a promising new business concept can use franchising as a means for expanding a business by using other people's money. Franchising, which accounts for approximately one third of total retail sales in the United States, is such an important segment of retailing that we have treated the concept as a separate chapter.

After reading this chapter, you will be able to:

1. Discuss the importance of franchising in the U.S. economy.

2. Evaluate the advantages and disadvantages of becoming a franchisee.

3. Describe the primary types of franchise arrangements.

4. List the types of costs involved in becoming a franchisee.

5. Evaluate franchise opportunities.

6. Explain the items contained in a typical franchise contract.

7. Review legal restrictions on franchising.

8. Discuss trends and outlook for franchising.

A **franchise contract** is a legal document that enables a firm (the **franchisor**) to expand by allowing an independent businessperson (the **franchisee**) to use the franchisor's operating methods, financing systems, trademarks, and products in return for the payment of a fee. Franchisors may sell products, sell or lease equipment, or even sell or rent the site and premises.

Franchising is the fastest-growing segment of retailing in the United States and accounts for one third of all retail sales, as shown in Figure 9–1. The International Franchising Association says that annual sales by franchise companies will grow to $2.5 trillion by the year 2010, and by the year 2000 will account for one half of U.S. retail sales.[1]

Franchising as a business concept expanded rapidly following World War II. Many of the returning servicemen were entrepreneurs who saw franchising as a way to financial success. The major problem for many of them was their lack of business experience. Established retailers, as a result, began franchising their products and know-how. Franchises exist in virtually every line of trade today including lawn care, maid services, baby-sitters, dentists, tutors, funeral homes, dating services, skin care centers, and legal offices, among many others. Employment in franchising, including part-time workers and working proprietors, exceeds 5 million.[2]

Franchising has become a powerful force partly because economic factors have made growth through company-owned units difficult for many businesses. Therefore, by emphasizing independent ownership, franchising provides an effective method of overcoming such problems as shortage of capital, high interest rates, and finding and hiring competent employees.

ADVANTAGES IN BECOMING A FRANCHISEE

A number of advantages exist for franchisees as part of a franchising program. The advantages include training programs that teach the retailer how to operate the business. Also, such programs allow individuals to enter a business with no previous experience. Less cash is required to enter the business since the franchisor is often willing to provide credit to a prospective franchisee.

The purchasing power of the franchisor can result in lower costs and higher gross profits for the franchisee. The franchisee also benefits from the national advertising and promotion by the franchisor which exceeds the advertising of conventional independent businesses. Additionally, up-to-date merchandise assistance, displays, and other materials are prepared by the franchisor and distributed to franchisees.

An equally important advantage is the program of research and development that is designed to improve the product or service. Firms such as Wendy's and McDonald's have regular, ongoing programs of research designed to identify new menu additions to help increase the sales base. Franchisees also have access to a variety of fringe benefits such as retirement planning, hospitalization, and health insurance at lower rates than are available to independent retailers.

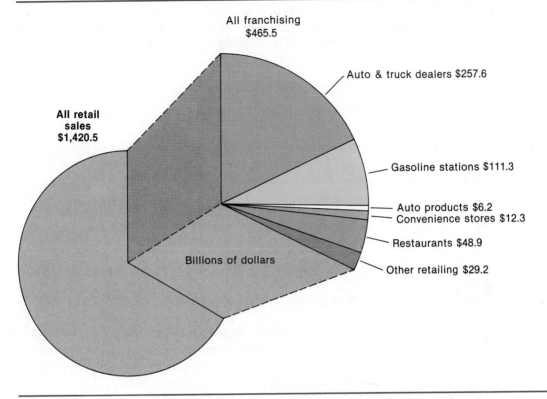

All franchising
$465.5

Auto & truck dealers $257.6

All retail
sales
$1,420.5

Gasoline stations $111.3

Auto products $6.2
Convenience stores $12.3

Restaurants $48.9

Billions of dollars

Other retailing $29.2

SOURCE: *Franchising in the U.S. Economy: 1983–85* (Washington, D.C.: U.S. Department of Commerce, 1985), p. 15.

The franchisor can also provide advice for handling special problems. Help is available in site selection, recordkeeping, taxes, and other issues. As a result, the failure rates for franchisees, around 4 percent, are lower than for nonaffiliated independent businesses.

DISADVANTAGES OF BECOMING A FRANCHISEE

Some disadvantages to franchising do exist. A major problem is the high cost of the franchise. Many franchisees feel they have to pay too much for supplies, in fees, and in other arrangements.

Also, the franchisee gives up flexibility in return for the right to a franchise. Operations are handled centrally at the corporate office, and cookie-cutter policies apply to all outlets. The rigidity that results from centralized operations can be detrimental to franchisees who face unusual local market conditions.[3]

Decisions on how profit is to be shared between the franchisor and the franchisee typically favor the franchisors because of their financial strength. However, the major complaint typically is the nature of the contract itself. Often franchisees do not understand the document. They also have problems in terminating a franchise. The conditions of termination typically favor the franchisor.

THE FRANCHISOR'S PERSPECTIVE

From the franchisor's perspective, the primary advantage in franchising is the opportunity to enjoy rapid expansion without decreasing the ownership or working capital of the company. However, one of the serious problems facing franchisors is finding management with the ambition and incentive to make a franchise a success. Still, the franchise system is often better than hiring employee/managers, since the franchisee has a financial investment in the outlet and can benefit directly from its profits.

LEGAL RESTRICTIONS IN FRANCHISING

Some contracts require a buyer to purchase specified products in order to obtain other desired products. Such contracts are illegal under Section 3 of the Clayton Act if a substantial portion of the sales is in interstate commerce and if the effect of the restraint is to lessen competition.

Some contracts tying the franchisee to the franchisor can be legal. For example, a service contract may be required in the sale or lease of a machine if the company's reputation depends on the operation of the equipment. Also, in some situations two products are required to be used jointly, and one will not function properly without the other. As a generalization, tying contracts have been found to be legal only in those situations in which the franchisors can prove that they are essential to the maintenance of quality.

TYPES OF FRANCHISES

Franchises are of two basic types. The first form is **product and trade name franchising,** such as by automobile dealers and gasoline outlets. The second form is **business format franchising** in which firms that have developed a unique method of performing a service or of doing business decide to make a profit by selling the rights to use the concept. The business format franchise is the arrangement followed by Holiday Inn, Avis, McDonald's, and Kelly Girl, among others.

TABLE 9–1   RANKING OF RETAIL FRANCHISES BY SALES

Kinds of Franchised Business	Sales ($000)	Number of Establishments
Total of all franchising	$422,830,992	441,181
Automobile and truck dealers	192,991,000	26,848
Gasoline service stations	103,121,000	136,570
Restaurants (all types)	38,691,594	67,528
Soft drink bottlers	16,200,000	1,568
Retailing (nonfood)	13,242,852	38,189
Hotels, motels, and campgrounds	12,426,747	6,806
Convenience stores	10,148,118	14,683
Automotive products and services	8,724,942	36,541
Retailing (food other than convenience stores)	8,595,540	15,208
Business aids and services	8,593,422	46,359
Rental services (auto-truck)	4,308,556	10,783
Construction, home improvement, maintenance, and cleaning services	2,700,227	17,512
Recreation, entertainment, and travel	1,003,872	6,515
Educational products and services	600,350	6,526
Rental service (equipment)	538,537	2,093
Laundry and dry cleaning services	255,870	2,937
Miscellaneous	688,365	4,515

SOURCE: *Franchising in the U.S. Economy: 1983–85* (Washington D.C.: U.S. Department of Commerce, 1985), p. 46.

Product and Trade Name Franchising

Product and trade name franchising began in the United States as an independent sales relationship between a supplier and a dealer with the dealer acquiring some of the identity of the supplier. Franchised dealers concentrate on one company's product line and, to some extent, identify their business with that company. Typical of this segment of franchising are automobile and truck dealers, gasoline service stations, and soft drink bottlers.[4] Together they dominate the franchise field, accounting for an estimated 73 percent of all franchise sales, as shown in Table 9–1.

Total sales by product and trade name franchises exceed $388 billion. Since 1972, however, the number of product and trade name franchises has decreased. For example, a net loss of almost 90,000 franchised gasoline service stations occurred between 1972 and 1983. The attrition rate is expected to slow in the next few years.[5]

Business Format Franchising

Business format franchising is characterized by an ongoing business relationship between the franchisor and franchisee that includes not only the product, service, and trademark but the entire business format. Such fran-

FIGURE 9–2

Wendy's—now open past midnight at most locations. Late-night operations improve sales and return on investment. (Courtesy of Wendy's International Inc.)

chises include a marketing strategy and plan, operating manuals and standards, quality control, and continuing two-way communications. Restaurants, nonfood retailing, personal and business services, rental services, real estate services, and a long list of other service businesses fall into the category of business format franchising. Business format franchising has been responsible for much growth of franchising in the United States since 1950 and will continue to offer excellent growth opportunities. Business format franchisees such as those shown in Figure 9–2 and 9–3 seem to exist on almost every street corner.

Annual sales of business format franchises exceed $150 billion. Such franchises are expected to reach $438 billion in sales by 1995, $705 billion by 2000, and $1.3 trillion by 2010. In contrast to product and trade name franchises, business format franchising is continuing to expand at a rapid pace.[6]

According to the U.S. Department of Commerce, large franchises, those with 1,000 or more units each, dominate business format franchising, with 55 companies accounting for 49 percent of all sales and for over 50 percent of all establishments. Of these large franchises, 13 operate restaurants and 10 are in automotive products and services.

FIGURE 9–3

Home cooking in a friendly environment characterizes the appeal of the 24-hour-service Toddle House. (Photograph by Robert Keeling)

SOURCE: Courtesy of Carson Pirie Scott & Company.

ELEMENTS OF AN IDEAL FRANCHISE PROGRAM

Successful franchises have a number of characteristics, as shown in Table 9–2, which can make the concept uniquely appropriate to the services field, the fastest-growing component of business format franchising.[7] The most essential ingredient for a franchising program is a line of merchandise with high gross margins. High margins are necessary to cover the annual franchise fee, operating expenses, and profits. Typically, fast-food and personal services (such as Gymboree, noted in the opening capsule) have sufficient gross margins to make franchising an ideal operating vehicle. The overriding advantage of a franchising program is the ability to quickly expand a store network with limited capital. Other advantages of franchising programs are often suggested, but these are often transitory.[8]

FORMS OF FRANCHISE ARRANGEMENTS

Product and trade name franchises and business format franchises can assume a variety of forms. The franchisor may sell individual franchises to

—— High Gross Margin—In order for the franchisee to be able to afford a high franchise fee (which the franchisor needs), it is necessary to operate on a high gross margin percentage. This explains the widespread application of franchising in the food and service industries.

—— In-Store Value Added—Franchising works best in those product categories where the product is at least partially processed in the store. Such environments require constant on-site supervision—a chronic problem for company-owned stores using a hired manager. Owners simply are willing to work harder over longer hours.

—— Secret Processes—Concepts, formulas, or products which the franchisee can't duplicate without joining the franchise program.

—— Real Estate Profits—The franchisor uses income from ownership of property as a significant revenue source.

—— Simplicity—The most successful franchises have been those which operate on automatic pilot: all the key decisions have been thought through, and the owner merely implements the decisions.

SOURCE: Philip D. White and Albert D. Bates, "Franchising Will Remain Retailing Fixture, but Its Salad Days Have Long Since Gone," *Marketing News,* February 17, 1984, p. 14. Reprinted by permission.

people who will develop each one. Alternatively, franchisors may sell **master franchises,** or **area-development franchises.**

Master franchisees buy the rights to an extensive geographic area but do not build and operate franchises. Rather, they divide the area into segments and sell the rights within the territory to individual franchisees. Franchisors often are attracted to the master franchise concept because it is easier for corporate management to work with one large franchisee than many small ones. Wendy's and Burger King, for example, have expanded rapidly by selling master franchises. People granted such franchises have substantial financial strength which increases their likelihood of success.

A second alternative is the area-development franchise. The franchisees purchase a large territory and in so doing open a large number of shops themselves.

Franchising Formats

Franchises can assume a variety of formats. In **mobile franchises,** business is done from a mobile vehicle. Snap-On Tools is an example of this type of franchise. **Distributorships** include systems where franchisees maintain warehouse stocks to supply other franchises. The distributor takes title to the goods and provides services to other customers. An example is Bear Brand Automotive Equipment.

Co-ownership and comanagement franchises are those in which the franchisor has an ownership interest in the operation. Examples include the International House of Pancakes and the Travelodge system. **Service franchises** are those in which franchisors license persons to dispense a service under a trade name. Snelling and Snelling, personnel agency, and H & R Block, tax service, are examples of this type of franchise.

Typically, a franchisee agrees to sell a product or service under contract and to follow the franchisor's formula. The franchisor is normally paid an initial fee for the right to operate at a particular location and a franchise fee based on monthly sales. The various costs involved in becoming a franchisee can include the following: the initial cost, the franchise fee, opening costs, working capital, premises expenses, site evaluation fees, royalties and service fees, and promotion charges. Each charge is briefly described below.

— *Initial costs*—franchisees typically must pay an initial sum for the right to operate under the terms and conditions of the franchise. The amount may be only a down payment with the remainder financed by the franchisor or from other financing sources.

— *Franchisee fee*—The right to use the trademark, license, service mark, or other operating procedures of the franchise.

— *Opening costs*—Payments for equipment, inventory, and fixtures.

— *Working capital*—The operating expenses needed until the business breaks even.

— *Premises costs*—The costs of building, remodeling, and decorating.

— *Site evaluation fee*—The charge by the franchisor to determine the market potential at alternative sites.

— *Royalties*—A continuing service charge or payment based on monthly gross sales. In return for the charge, the franchisor provides such services as product research, management advice, accounting services, inventory records, and similar activities.

— *Promotion costs*—A percentage of gross sales, normally 1 or 2 percent, to support local advertising and promotion.

Typical franchise fees are structured as follows:

Baskin Robbins: Franchisees pay about $120,000 for store design, construction, and equipment costs as well as a 10-year right to use the name. They also pay a royalty on ice cream of 68 cents per gallon.[9]

Wendy's: To be considered seriously for a franchise an individual needs $700,000 in credit and $150,000 in liquid assets. These funds allow the franchisee to lease or buy the land, the building, and the equipment; purchase supplies; and hire employees. Franchisees are charged a $20,000 franchisee fee, for technical assistance, for each restaurant. Wendy's also charges $40,000 to help locate a site and to construct a building. Franchisees pay 4 percent of gross sales as royalties.[10]

McDonald's: Franchisees invest from $275,000 to $400,000 to open a new outlet, depending on the design options. The money pays for the equipment within the store and entitles the franchisees to a 20-year operating license. Additionally, the franchisee pays fees generally totaling about 11.5 percent of annual gross sales in return for services that include training for

BUYING IN *(average amount required by a franchisor to start a new franchise, excluding real estate costs)*

Franchisor	Type of Business	Investment Cost
Aamco Transmission Inc.	Car transmission service shops	$101,000
Athlete's Foot Marketing Associates Inc.	Athletic shoe and clothing stores	$107,500 to $157,500
Command Performance	Haircutting and styling salons	$75,000 to $105,000
Dunkin' Donuts of America Inc.	Donut shops	$45,000 to $58,000
Entre Computer Centers Inc.	Computer stores	$125,000
Godfather's Pizza	Pizza parlors	$200,000 to $285,000
Gymboree Corp.	Play centers for preschoolers	$21,000 to $27,000
Jani-King Inc.	Commercial janitorial services	$6,500
Mail Boxes Etc. USA	Postal and business service centers	$46,000
Moto Photo Inc.	One-hour film processing labs	$160,000
Pier 1 Imports Inc.	Gift and home furnishings stores	$100,000 to $130,000
Southland Corp.	7-Eleven convenience stores	$37,075
Video Biz Inc.	Videotape movie rental shops	$55,000

SOURCE: U.S. Commerce Department, 1986.

management and crews, operating assistance, marketing, financial advice, and menu research.[11]

Computerland: Initial franchise fees are $75,000 with continuing revenues of 8 percent of gross sales paid each year.

Other examples are shown in Table 9–3.

IDENTIFYING FRANCHISE OPPORTUNITIES

Franchise opportunities are easy to identify. Choosing the right one is difficult. Intense competition exists among franchisors in attracting interested franchisees. Advertisements for franchise opportunities are common in many newspapers. Business fairs are also often held at which franchisors try to attract franchisees. Various publications such as the following are also good sources of information: *Franchising Opportunities Handbook*, published by the U.S. Department of Commerce; *Directory of Franchising Organizations*, published annually by Pilot Books; and the *Dow Jones-Irwin Guide to Franchises*. Periodicals that contain useful information include the *Continental Franchise Review, Franchising World, Franchising Today*, and *Franchise Newsletter*.

EVALUATING THE FRANCHISE AND THE FRANCHISE COMPANY

Federal Protection

Information about franchisors is available in a disclosure document required by federal law to be made available to interested buyers prior to purchasing a franchise. The Federal Trade Commission in 1979 issued a trade rule entitled "Disclosure Requirements and Prohibitions Concerning Franchising and Business Opportunity Ventures." The document spells out the information franchisors must provide to interested buyers at least 10 days before the buyer enters into a contract with the franchisor.

The disclosure document must include such information as the following: the amount of funds to be paid by the franchisee, the level of continuing payments to carry on the business, the franchisor's business experience, a list of persons with whom the franchisee is expected to do business, fees such as royalties and commissions to be paid to the franchisor, the litigation history of the franchisor and its executives, the restrictions placed on the franchisee's opportunity to conduct business, cancellation and renewal conditions of the lease, the number of franchises in existence and rate of termination, and financial information, including audited financial statements for the last three years.

State Legislation

State laws that require a franchisor to register franchise offers with state authorities also exist. They also require the franchisor to furnish the prospective franchisee with a disclosure statement prior to the signing of the contract. The state agency responsible for administering the disclosure laws reviews the financial statements, promotional materials, franchise contracts, and other material submitted as part of the offer. The franchisors may also be required to show that they can provide the financial assistance promised to a franchisee. The laws also contain provisions on the termination and renewal of franchises.

Evaluating the Company

The franchising company should have a good credit rating, a strong financial position, and a favorable reputation in the business community. The firm also should have been in business for a sufficient period of time to demonstrate expertise and the ability of its products or services to prosper in a competitive environment.

The local and national offices of the Better Business Bureau, the Federal Trade Commission field offices, and state attorney general offices should be contacted to determine the complaints, if any, about the franchise company and the resolution of the complaints.

Evaluating the Product or Service

Interested buyers should make sure the product or service has been tested in the marketplace before signing a franchise agreement. An independent investigation to determine the likelihood for the franchise's success in a local market is also in order. Equally important is an evaluation of the product warranties as part of the franchise agreement. The prospective buyer should understand the terms and conditions of the warranty, who is issuing the warranty, and the company's reputation for keeping its promises. The buyer should also determine the legitimacy of claimed trademarks, service marks, trade names, and copyrights.

Understanding the Franchise Contract

The franchise contract varies by franchisor. The contract is a legal document that specifies the rights and responsibilities of the franchisor. The advice of an attorney should be sought before signing the document. The critical areas to be considered in deciding whether to sign a franchise agreement are shown in Appendix A and include the nature of the company, the product, the territory, the contract, and assistance available.

All franchise contracts contain a variety of provisions to which the franchisee must agree. For example, the franchisee typically must agree to abide by the operating hours established by the franchisor. The franchisee often must also agree to use a standardized accounting system, follow companywide personnel policies, carry a minimum level of insurance, use supplies approved by the franchisor, and follow the pricing policies established by the franchisor.

The franchisor often retains the right to require the franchisees to periodically remodel their establishment(s) and to allow the franchisor to conduct unscheduled inspections. Territorial restrictions are typically stated in the contract agreement, and provisions for expanding into additional territories are carefully stated.

Some contracts impose sales quotas designed to ensure that the franchisee vigorously pursues sales opportunities in the territory. Most contracts also prohibit a franchisee from operating competing businesses and prohibit an individual whose franchise has been terminated from opening a similar type of business for a specified period of time.

Most franchise contracts cover a minimum period of 15 years. They typically contain provisions for termination and renewal of the contract, the franchisee's right to sell or transfer the business, and a provision for arbitration of disputes between the franchisor and franchisee.

Termination

Franchise contracts typically contain a provision for cancellation by either party on 30 to 60 days' notice. Normally franchises can only be terminated when the franchisee fails to meet the conditions of the franchise contract, including minimum payments required, sales quotas, and the need to keep the premises in good condition.

Renewal

The franchisor can refuse to renew the contract of any franchisee who does not fully comply with the terms of the contract, including maintaining required quality standards. Termination provisions give the franchisor substantial power over franchisees. As a result, many states have passed legislation that limits the right of a franchisor to terminate or refuse to renew a franchise.

Transferring a Franchise

The franchisee normally does not have the right to sell or transfer the franchise to a third party without the concurrence of the franchisor. The sale or transfer to a third party typically is not a problem, however.

Buy-Back Provisions

The franchisor often has the option to purchase a franchise unit or the inventory if the franchisee decides to sell. The buy-back provision is an advantage to the franchisee because it can provide a ready sale for the outlet.

Deciding on the price for the sale is often not easy. Some franchisors will offer a price that will only cover the value of the buildings and the equipment and will not consider payment for goodwill. *Goodwill is the price set for the intangible assets of a business including its future earning power and its condition at the time of the sale.* Franchisors often maintain that the goodwill of the business is reflected in the trademark or trade name.

Arbitration Provisions

The use of **arbitration** (the settlement of a dispute by a person or persons chosen to hear both sides and come to a decision) to settle disputes between franchisors and franchisees is growing slowly. Arbitration is faster and less expensive than litigation. Disputes can be settled in private without the glare of the courtroom.

Franchisee Associations

Some franchisees have established **franchisee associations** to represent individual owners in dealing with the franchisor. The purpose of joining together is to allow the franchisees to accomplish common goals and to exert greater power over the franchisor in resolving issues of concern to the individual franchisees. The franchisees as a group can also support needed legislation, exchange ideas, and generally work to strengthen their position relative to the franchisor.

TRENDS AND OUTLOOK[12]

Franchising can accurately be described as the "wave of the future." With long-term prospects for franchising extremely bright, growing numbers of smaller companies, operating in local or regional markets, are turning to franchising for new ways to distribute their goods and services. These new small franchising companies quickly react to changing market conditions and seek out new services and merchandising alternatives to broaden store appeal and attract greater patronage.

Continuing economic improvement, stable prices, a slower-growing population, and increased competition for market share are turning many large corporations and manufacturers to franchising, influenced by changing tastes of consumers and demographic shifts.

With rising costs of construction, marketing, and training, and with franchising enlarging its share of retail and service receipts, we will see an increased trend toward multiunit ownership by franchisees and the increased granting of rights to develop large regional areas. Larger franchisors will step up activity in acquiring existing chains for expansion instead of developing new, individual franchises.

Franchised restaurants of all types will continue to be the most popular sector of franchising. Casual theme restaurants designed to reflect a particular lifestyle or mood are finding increased acceptance in franchising, while restaurant franchisors associated with the popular "fast-food" concept will continue to show the greatest sales growth. Restaurant franchisors are moving toward more diversified menus including salad bars, fish, and poultry as personal health concerns influence increased consumption of such food items. The shift to ethnic foods is increasing. Significant penetration of foreign markets by restaurant franchisors will also occur during the next decade.

Franchisors confronted with static local markets are beginning to seek merger opportunities with franchisors in other sectors of the country, especially in the Sunbelt and western states where the population is on the rise and potential for growth is promising.

Business and personnel franchise services in particular are expected to continue to rise significantly for the next few years. Companies will need additional business and management consulting services to provide innovative marketing ideas geared to a better-educated and more affluent consumer in highly segmented markets. The trend toward specialized contract services is expected to continue, boosting such business areas as maid services, repair and home remodeling, temporary help, health care, carpet cleaning, and various maintenance and cleaning services.

Other areas in franchising that show signs of continued growth in the next few years are ice cream, yogurt, and popcorn outlets, home furnishing stores, security systems, automotive aftermarket services, travel agency operations, and video equipment sales and rental outlets.

International Markets

U.S. franchisors are currently operating in most major countries or are engaged in serious negotiations for the purpose of entering foreign markets, an indication that foreign nations have welcomed the entry of U.S. franchisors and that local laws and regulations have not been overly restrictive.

FIGURE 9–4 INTERNATIONAL FRANCHISING

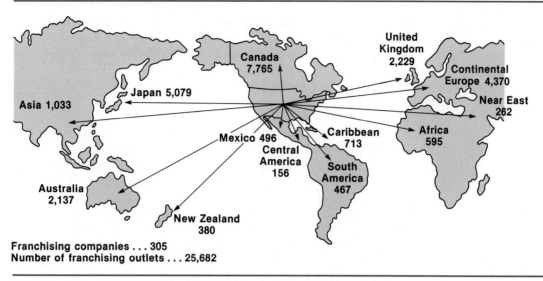

Franchising companies ... 305
Number of franchising outlets ... 25,682

SOURCE: *Franchising in the U.S. Economy: 1983–85* (Washington, D.C.: U.S. Department of Commerce, 1985), p. 7.

Franchising operations in foreign markets involve many of the same problems confronting other business ventures. Language difficulties, differences in customs, and sometimes unpredictable government decision making are examples of impediments all U.S. franchisors encounter when attempting to take advantage of opportunities in other countries.

Compared to other service sectors, the problems of franchise companies in international transactions are less formidable. Franchisors must comply with the same local requirements as domestic businesses, and the franchise agreements must comply with local contract law, antitrust law, and trademark licensing law.

The populations in many foreign countries are young and like to try new products and concepts. In addition, more and more women everywhere are going to work outside the home. This trend not only increases the family's disposable income, which is good for franchisors in the service and consumer products business, but it also reduces the amount of time spent in the kitchen and increases the demand for food purchased away from home.

Foreign developed countries increasingly exhibit the same attributes that fostered the surge of service industries in the United States. These attributes include rising disposable personal income, growing demand for consumer goods and services, expanding urbanization, and high consumer mobility.

Canada continues to be the dominant market for U.S. franchisors, as shown in Figure 9–4. Of all U.S. foreign franchised outlets 30 percent are located in Canada. Japan continues to be the second largest market for U.S. franchisors; the United Kingdom ranks third.

CHAPTER HIGHLIGHTS

—— Franchising is a way of doing business that allows an independent businessperson (the franchisee) to use another firm's (the franchisor) operating methods, financing systems, trademarks, and products in return for payment of a fee.

—— Franchising is the fastest-growing segment of retailing and accounts for one third of retail sales. Franchising is forecasted to account for 50 percent of all retail sales by the year 2000.

—— Franchises are of two basic types: product and trade name franchises such as automobile dealers and gasoline outlets, and business format franchises in which firms that have developed a unique method of performing a service or of doing business decide to make a profit by selling the concept to others.

—— Sales by product and trade name franchises have declined since 1972. In contrast, the volume of sales and the number of units owned or franchised by business format franchises have been steadily increasing since 1972.

—— The most essential ingredient for a franchising program is a line of merchandise with high gross margins. High gross margins are necessary to cover the annual franchise fee, operating expenses, and profit.

—— The overriding advantage of a franchising program is the ability to quickly expand a store with limited capital.

—— Franchisors may grant individual franchises to businesspersons. Alternatively, they may sell master franchises. Some persons purchase area-development franchises which give them rights to an extensive territory in which they develop a large number of outlets.

—— The typical franchise contract gives the franchisee the right to sell a product or service under an arrangement that requires the individual to follow the franchisor's formula. The franchisor is typically paid an initial fee for the right to operate at a particular location and a franchisee fee based on monthly sales.

—— Information about a company and the franchises it sells is contained in a disclosure document required by federal law to be made available to interested buyers prior to buying a franchise. State laws also require the franchisor to register franchise offers with state authorities.

—— Some franchisees have established franchisee associations to represent individual owners in dealing with the franchisor. These associations allow the franchisees to exert greater power in dealing with the franchisor.

—— The primary advantage of franchising is the training programs that are available which allow an individual with no experience to enter a business. The franchisee can also benefit from the purchasing power of the franchisor. Equally important are the programs of research and development many franchisors have established to improve their product or service.

—— The major disadvantage of a franchise is the high initial fee. The franchisee also gives up some flexibility in return for the right to purchase a franchise. Complaints often arise over the nature of the franchise contract.

—— Some franchise contracts require buyers to purchase specified products in order to obtain other desired products. Such contracts are illegal under Section 3 of the Clayton Act if a substantial portion of the sales is in interstate commerce and if the effect of the restraint is to lessen competition.

—— Franchising can accurately be described as the "wave of the future." Business and personal service franchises are expected to grow rapidly over the next few years as are such other types of franchises as ice cream, yogurt, and popcorn outlets, video sales and rental outlets, and security systems.

—— U.S. franchisors are currently operating in most major countries or are engaged in serious negotiations for the purpose of entering foreign markets.

KEY TERMS

Arbitration The settlement of a dispute by a person or persons chosen to hear both sides of a dispute and come to a decision.

Area-development franchise An individual purchases an extensive territory and then opens a large number of franchises within the territory.

Business format franchising An ongoing relationship between a franchisor and franchisee that includes not only the product, service, and trademark but the entire business format.

Co-ownership and comanagement franchises Franchise arrangements in which a franchisor has an ownership interest in the operation.

Distributorships Franchise systems whereby franchisees maintain warehouse stocks to supply other franchisees. The distributor takes title to the goods and provides services to other customers.

Franchisee An individual who pays a fee for the right to use a franchisor's product, service, or way of doing business.

Franchisee association A situation in which individual franchisees join an organization to represent the individual owners in dealing with a franchisor.

Franchise contract A legal document that enables an independent businessperson to use a franchisor's operating methods, financing systems, trademarks, and products in return for the payment of a fee.

Franchisor An organization that has developed a unique product, service, or way of doing business and allows another firm to use the product, service, or business concept in return for payment of a fee.

Master franchise An individual buys the right to an extensive geographic area and sells the rights within the territory to individual franchisees.

Mobile franchise Business is done from a mobile vehicle.

Product and trade name franchising An independent sales relationship exists between a supplier and a dealer, but the dealer acquires some of the identity of the supplier. Primary examples are automotive and truck dealers, gasoline service stations, and soft-drink bottlers.

Service franchises Franchises in which franchisors license people to dispense a service under a trade name.

DISCUSSION QUESTIONS

1. What are the differences between product and trade name franchising, and business format franchising?
2. Discuss the ingredients of an ideal franchise program. What are the types of franchises that appear to be suited to the elements of such a program?
3. Write a brief essay on the cost elements that are typically included as part of a franchising contract.
4. What are the issues a prospective franchisee should evaluate in deciding whether to purchase a franchise?
5. What are the ingredients of a typical franchise contract?
6. Why would franchisees join a franchisee association?
7. Highlight the advantages and disadvantages of becoming a franchisee and of franchising as a way of doing business.
8. What are the legal restrictions on franchising?
9. Discuss the trends and outlook for franchising.

APPLICATION EXERCISES

1. Review the various sources cited in the chapter (these typically are found in your local library) to establish the initial opening costs for the following types of franchises: A national food franchise such as Hardee's, a personnel service franchise such as Snelling and Snelling, a preschool franchise such as Kinder Care, and a transmission repair business such as AAMCO.
2. Talk to the owner/managers of three fast-food franchises in your community and write an essay outlining the primary advantages and disadvantages they see in being a franchisee.
3. Interview the owner of a local automobile agency (an example of a product and trade name franchise) and the owner of a services franchise. What are the similarities and differences between the two types of franchises? Which type of a franchise is likely to generate the greatest loyalty to the franchisor?

CASES

1. Increasing the Number of Blacks in Fast-Food Franchises

McDonald's, Burger King, and other chains are risking civil-rights suits to open up shops in the inner city. Fast-food franchisors, both because of their own marketing projections that show a need for greater penetration of minority markets and because of pressures from civil-rights groups, are making aggressive efforts to sell their franchises to blacks. Some of the franchisors' actions are bringing them into potential conflict with civil-rights laws, but the companies believe the payoff is worth the risk.

Fast-food franchisors are making special financial arrangements with black franchisees that are not available to other franchisees. Burger King Corporation, for example, asks blacks for $25,000 in initial cash compared with the usual minimum of $125,000. The typical start-up cost for a Burger King franchise is $300,000. Burger King concedes that the company was pressured into its program by Operation PUSH (People United to Save Humanity), an activist group started by Jesse Jackson. The goal of PUSH is to increase the number of black employees and the level of purchases from black suppliers to a level that equals the percentage of sales to black customers.

Other companies are following Burger King's lead, though not necessarily as a result of pressure from operation PUSH. Pizza Hut, Inc. is actively searching for black franchisees as is Taco Bell, Baskin Robbins, Inc., and Kentucky Fried Chicken.

An enlightened social consciousness is not the only reason for the new programs. Management is hoping that the black franchisees will be able to open up inner city markets in a way that white franchisees would find impossible to do. Pizza Hut at this point, for example, has no franchisees in New York City, although it has more than 4,000 franchisees nationwide. Most of its franchises are concentrated in suburbs near the highways.

Questions

1. Why are franchisors especially interested in locating franchises in predominantly minority areas of communities?
2. What are the advantages of franchising that are likely to attract blacks (and other minorities) to franchising as a way of becoming an independent businessperson?
3. Are the programs outlined in the case primarily social responsibility or are they based on sound business decisions?

Source: Based on "The Push to Enlist Blacks in Fast-Food Franchises," *Business Week*, June 25, 1984, pp. 54–56.

2. Greyhound to Franchise Bus Routes

Beset by ongoing losses in its bus operations, Greyhound Corp. has come up with a novel plan to turn the worst of its business around: franchising. The company offered more than 200 people, including some of its own employees and representatives of other bus companies, the opportunity to operate their own routes under the Greyhound name and logo.

The 70 money-losing routes being offered, which Greyhound had planned to drop, comprise about 10 percent of the company's total route system. Its hope is that small, lower-cost owner/operators will be able to cover these territories profitably by offering services—passenger, package, and charter—at lower prices. Explaining the move, Greyhound Lines president Fred Dunikoski says: "When a passenger can fly cheaper than he can travel by bus, then the bus industry has to find a new growth niche, and we believe franchising is that better way."

Greyhound will charge franchisees a licensing fee from $5,000 to $20,000 depending on the territory, plus a percentage of annual revenues. In return, franchisees will have access to Greyhound's terminals, maintenance facilities, and telephone information system. The company also plans to offer insurance and financing arrangements and to provide driver training. Greyhound chairman John W. Teets estimates that the program will bring in more than $12 million in pretax profits in about two years.

Questions

1. What are the reasons the Greyhound Corporation would consider franchising its marginal bus routes?
2. Why would franchisees be attracted to the Greyhound bus routes? Why would the Greyhound Corporation believe that the franchisees could be successful even though the corporation has been unable to make a profit on the routes?
3. Does franchising of bus routes contain the necessary ingredients for an ideal franchise program, as discussed earlier in the chapter?

Source: Based on "Greyhound to Franchise Bus Routes," *Dun's Business Month*, May 1985, p. 23.

ENDNOTES

1. "Franchises to Ring Up Half of Retail Sales," *Marketing News*, February 28, 1986, p. 3.
2. These data are based on *Franchising in the U.S. Economy: 1983–1985* (Washington, D.C.: U.S. Department of Commerce, 1985).
3. For further reading, see Brenton Schlender, "Working on the Chain Gang," *The Wall Street Journal*, May 19, 1986, p. 14-D.
4. Philip D. White and Albert D. Bates, "Franchising Will Remain Retailing Fixture, but Its Salad Days Have Long Since Gone," *Marketing News*, February 17, 1984, p. 14.
5. *Franchising in the U.S. Economy.*
6. "Franchises Ring Up Half."
7. Ann Dorfman, "New Frenzy in Franchising," *New York*, March 3, 1986, p. 31; see also,
"Domino's: A Unique Concept Pays Off," *Dun's Business Month*, May 1986, p. 50.
8. For further reading, see "Here Comes McDentists," *Fortune*, February 21, 1983, pp. 135–39.
9. "The Scoop on Ice Cream Sales," *Business Week*, September 20, 1982, p. 73.
10. "Recipe for Success in the Fast-Food Game," *U.S. News & World Report*, November 21, 1983, pp. 58–59.
11. Ibid.
12. Adapted from *Franchising in the U.S. Economy;* Steven Golante, "Small Franchisors Put Accent on Growth in Markets Abroad," *The Wall Street Journal*, April 14, 1986, p. 31.

APPENDIX A

FRANCHISE CHECKLIST

A. Franchise—General

1. Is the product or service:

	Yes	No
a. Considered reputable.	___	___
b. Part of growing market.	___	___
c. Needed in your area.	___	___
d. Of interest to you.	___	___
e. Safe.	___	___
Protected.	___	___
Covered by guarantee.	___	___
f. Carry the name of a well-known personality.	___	___
Sound franchise without well-known personality.	___	___

2. Is the franchise:

	Yes	No
a. Local.	___	___
Regional.	___	___
National.	___	___
International.	___	___
b. Full-time.	___	___
Part-time.	___	___
Full-time possible in future.	___	___

3. Existing franchises:
   a. How long was the company in business before the first franchise was awarded? ___ years.
   b. What date was the company founded and what date was the first franchise awarded? Company founded ___. First franchise awarded ___.
   c. Number currently in operation or under construction? ___

SOURCE: Adopted from *Franchise/Index Profile,* Small Business Management Series No. 35 (Washington, D.C.: U.S. Small Business Administration).

4. Why have franchises failed?
   a. How many franchises have failed? _____ How many of these have been in the last 2 years? _____
   b. Why have franchises failed?

   Franchisor reasons: _____
   _____
   _____

   Better Business Bureau reasons: _____
   _____
   _____

   Franchisee: _____
   _____
   _____

5. Franchise in local market area.
   a. Has a franchise ever been awarded in this area? _____
      If so and if it is still in operation:
      Owner _____
      Address _____
      Date started _____ Date ended _____
      Reasons for failure _____
      _____

6. What product or service will be added to franchise package?
   a. Within 12 months _____
   _____
   b. Within 2 years? _____
   _____
   c. Within 2 to 5 years? _____
   _____

7. Competition?
   a. What is my competition? _____
   _____
   _____

8. Are all franchises independently owned?
   a. Of the total outlets, __ are franchised, and __ are company owned.
   b. If some outlets are company owned did they start out this way __ or were they repurchased from a franchisee __. Date of most recent company acquisition _____.
9. Franchise distribution pattern:
   a. Is the franchise exclusive __ or nonexclusive__.
   b. Is the franchise a distributorship __ or a dealership __. If it is a dealership who is the distributor in my area:
      Name _____
      Address _____
      How long has he/she been a distributor? _____

10. Franchise operations:
    a. What facilities are required, and do I lease or build?
    b. Getting started . . . who is responsible for what?

	Franchisor	Franchisee
Feasibility study	_____	_____
Design	_____	_____
Construction	_____	_____
Furnishing	_____	_____
Financing	_____	_____

B. Franchise Company

1. The company:
   a. What is the name and address of the parent company if different than the franchise company:
      Name _____
      Address _____
   b. Is the parent company public ___ or private ___ ?
   c. If the company is public where is the stock traded:

New York Stock Exchange	_____
American Stock Exchange	_____
Over the Counter	_____
_____	_____

2. Total franchise cost:
   a. How much money do I have to have to get started?

Item	Amount
Franchise start-up	$ _____
First year operating	$ _____
First year personal	$ _____
Total	$ _____

   b. What do I have to pay the franchisor to get started?
      $ _____
      Basis of cost:

Item	Amount
Franchise fee	$ _____
Services	$ _____
Product	$ _____
Real estate	$ _____
Equipment	$ _____
_____	$ _____

   c. Is any of the initial franchise cost refundable? _____
      If so, on what basis? _____
      _____

C. Financing

      a. Is part of the initial cost to the franchise financed? _____
         If so how much $\underline{\hspace{2cm}}$, this represents _____ percent
         of the total initial cost.
      b. What is the interest rate? _____ percent. When does
         financing have to be paid back? _____

1. Forecast of income and expenses:
    a. Is a forecast of income and expenses provided? _____.
      Is it:
      Based on actual franchisee operations? _____
      Based on a franchisor outlet? _____
      Purely estimated? _____
      If a forecast is provided does it:

	Yes	No
Relate to your market area	____	____
Meet your personal goals	____	____
Provide adequate return on investment	____	____
Provide for adequate promotion and personnel	____	____

2. Are all details covered in a written franchise contract?
    Yes _____ No_____ (get copy for lawyer and accountant review)
    a. What to look for—are these included?

	Yes	No
Franchise fee	____	____
Termination	____	____
Selling and renewal	____	____
Advertising and promotion	____	____
Patent and liability protection	____	____
Home office services	____	____
Commissions and royalties	____	____
Training	____	____
Financing	____	____
Territory	____	____
Exclusive versus nonexclusive	____	____

D. Training

1. Initial Training:
    a. Does franchisor provide formal initial training? _____.
      If so, how long does it last? _____.
    b. Cost

	Yes	No
Included in franchise cost	____	____
Includes all materials	____	____
Includes transportation	____	____

Includes room and board ____ ____

If not included in franchise cost, what is total $____ .
cost including all outlined above?

c. What does the training course include?

	Yes	No
Franchise operations	____	____
Sales	____	____
Finance	____	____
Promotion	____	____
Personnel	____	____
Management	____	____
Manufacturing	____	____
Training	____	____
_____	____	____
_____	____	____

d. How do you train your initial staff? Is a training program provided? _____. Does the franchisor make available a staff member from the home office to assist? _____. What materials are included in the staff training program? _____

_____

_____

2. Continuing training
   What is the continuing program? Is there any cost? _____. If so how much? $_____. Are there any special materials or equipment required? _____. If so what? _____. What is the cost to the franchisee? $_____.

E. Marketing

1. What is the national advertising program of the franchisor?
   a. What is the national advertising budget?
      $_____.
   b. What are the primary advertising media?
      Television _____
      Radio _____
      Outdoor _____
      Newspaper _____
      Magazine _____
      Direct mail _____

2. What kind of advertising and promotion support is available for the local franchisee?

	Yes	No
Is a packaged advertising program available?	____	____
Is there a co-op advertising program?	____	____
Is there a grand opening package?	____	____

3. Service departments:

	Yes	No
a. What service departments are available:	___	___
Finance and accounting	___	___
Advertising and promotion	___	___
Sales and marketing	___	___
Research and development	___	___
Real estate	___	___
Construction	___	___
Personnel and training	___	___
Manufacturing and operations	___	___
Purchasing	___	___
_____	___	___
_____	___	___

4. Field support:
   a. Is a field person assigned to working with a set number of franchises? _____
      Who would be assigned to my franchise? _____
      How many other franchises is the person assigned to? _____
      May I contact the person? _____

10

Making the Location, Site, and Building Decision

Irresistibles

John Doub and his wife, Karen, founded Irresistibles in 1977. They opened their first retail outlet in the Faneuil Hall Waterfront Center in Boston and sold primarily accessories and gift items. The single outlet has grown to a 10-unit chain of women's clothing and accessories stores. Doub has what he considers a near-scientific location formula. He notes that, "when you are only looking to open one or two locations a year, you don't have to take anything but the prime spaces."

The Doubs' location strategy has been to locate in upscale centers like Baltimore's Village of Cross Keys, Washington, D.C.'s exclusive Georgetown Park, and Boston's Copley Place.

The Doubs' merchandising strategy, combined with a commitment not to sacrifice location at any price, has made their concept successful in a geographic area ranging from Boston to Washington, D.C. Irresistibles as a private retail chain does not have to respond to stockholder pressures to see investments grow. The Doubs can simply wait for the right location to become available rather than moving aggressively ahead even if choice locations are not available. The Doubs insist on a high-quality combination of a shopping store mix and demographics. They seek prime, high-quality locations with a tenant mix that consists of outlets offering better price points. Their primary target is the working woman.

Future plans call for the chain to continue its growth over the next decade in the 500-mile

Source: Based on "Location Is Everything," *Chain Store Age Executive,* January 1986, pp. 41–42.

stretch between Boston and Washington, D.C. The Doubs have consciously stayed away from downtown New York because their target is not an impulse market. Rather, they say, "We are looking for the traditional retail outlet that will attract 90 percent repeat customers." They do not limit their locations to malls and will open free-standing outlets where appropriate. The Doubs have determined that in some instances, especially in metropolitan areas, their target market prefers to shop downtown as opposed to suburban malls.

*T*he Irresistibles retailing capsule illustrates the importance of location decisions for retailers. Outlets such as K mart can succeed in a stand-alone location. Other firms such as Sears seem to function best as an anchor tenant in a major shopping center. Small specialty firms, lacking the ability to attract customers on their own, often choose a high-traffic location in a shopping mall. Decisions on whether to build or lease are also important to an organization because such decisions affect cash flow and the ability of management to develop and execute a successful marketing plan. The Doubs believe that building upscale stores in prime locations is the key to serving their carefully targeted market.

LEARNING OBJECTIVES

After reading this chapter you will be able to:

1. Explain the strategic dimensions of the location decision.

2. Evaluate a trading area.

3. Determine the volume of business that can be done in a trading area.

4. Evaluate a store site.

The location decision is important because (1) opening a business costs a lot of money; (2) the retailer is committed to the location for a long period of time, even with a lease; (3) competition is getting tougher and a good location is one way to beat the competition; and (4) problems such as store saturation, an uncertain economy, and tough zoning laws are making good locations harder to find.

Simply estimating probable sales is not enough in a location decision. Retailers also have to pay attention to the types of customers who are candidates for the merchandise sold by the firm, the prospects for future growth in the trading area, customer lifestyles, and probable future competition.

STRATEGIC DECISIONS IN CHOOSING A GROWTH STRATEGY

Type of Market Coverage

Retailers should always think in terms of long-term growth when deciding on a location strategy. Three primary strategies are possible: (1) **regional dominance** (primarily for larger retail outlets), (2) **market saturation,** and (3) emphasis on smaller towns and communities. These decisions are important even when a retailer is opening an initial outlet because they indicate the path of the greatest growth over the years.

Regional Dominance
The retailer may decide to become the dominant retailer in a particular geographic area rather than locate the same number of outlets over a much wider geographic area. Examples of regionally dominant retailers include Rose in the South and Nordstrom in the Northwest. The advantages of regional dominance include:

1. Lower costs of distribution because merchandise can be shipped to all the stores from a central warehouse.
2. Easier personnel supervision.
3. The ability to better understand customer needs.
4. The likelihood of a strong reputation in the area.
5. Better economies in sales promotion since the outlets are concentrated in one region.

Market Saturation
This strategy is similar to regional dominance. However, saturation is often limited to a single metropolitan market. The advantages are the same in both instances. Dominance simply occurs on a larger scale than a single metropolitan market.

Smaller Communities

Why are smaller communities so popular in location decisions today? One reason is that building codes make it more difficult to build in large cities. Also, costs are higher and competition is tougher. The 300 largest metro areas are now served by at least one of the nation's 11 largest merchants.

Secondary markets, communities of 50,000 to 200,000, are often known as "midmarket" towns. Such areas are growing faster than larger cities. Why? (1) These communities often welcome new business, (2) the quality of life may be higher, (3) wage rates are lower, (4) unions are less of an issue, (5) the markets are easier to serve, and (6) competition is often less intense.[1]

Such major retailers as Sears, Wal-Mart, and Woolworth are now aggressively following a so-called small store strategy by opening smaller stores in secondary trading areas. Sears, for example, opened its first small store in Alma, Michigan, a 14,000-foot store with 8,300 feet of selling space.

Selecting the Community, the Trading Area, and the Site

After a retailer makes the overall strategic location decision in planning for growth, several other decisions need to be made. The decisions include:

1. Selecting the community in which to locate.
2. Defining the **trading area** for the outlet.
3. Selecting the best site.

Selecting the Community in Which to Locate

Key factors in choosing the community include:

1. The size and composition of the population.
2. The labor market.
3. Closeness to source of merchandise supply.
4. The media mix available.
5. The economic base of the community.
6. Existing and future competition.
7. Availability of store sites.
8. State, local, and federal regulations.

These issues are highlighted in Table 10–1. These factors must be considered with a preselected target market in mind.

Population characteristics are often a key in choosing a community. For example, a retailer needs to study the number of people; their education, income, ages, and family composition; as well as probable population increases in the area. Census data is a useful source of such information.

Labor availability can be a problem. Management talent is most readily available in larger areas, but is more expensive, as is clerical help. In smaller communities, local management talent may not be available, and outsiders may not want to move to the area. However, clerical labor is less likely to be a problem.

Population characteristics
  Total size
  Age and income distributions
  Growth trends
  Education levels
  Occupation distribution and trends

Competitive characteristics
  Saturation level
  Number and size of competitors
  Geographic coverage
  Competitive growth trends

Labor characteristics
  Availability of
    Management
    Clerical
    Skilled
  Wage levels
  Unions
  Training

Economic characteristics
  Number and type of industries
  Dominant industry
  Growth projections
  Financial base

Supply source characteristics
  Delivery time
  Delivery costs
  Availability and reliability
  Storage facilities

Location characteristics
  Number and type of locations
  Costs
  Accessibility to customers
  Accessibility to transportation
  Owning/leasing options
  Utility adequacy

Promotion characteristics
  Type of media coverage
  Media overlap
  Costs

Regulation characteristics
  Taxes
  Licensing
  Zoning restrictions
  Local ordinances

Distribution problems include the timing and frequency of delivery schedules to the store and the reliability of delivery.

The media mix issue includes the availability of newspapers, radio stations, and television coverage of the market. Also, good production facilities are needed to help ensure high-quality commercials.

The types of industries in the area are also important. Large manufacturing plants with highly skilled union workers provide better market potential than small plants which use unskilled labor and pay low wages. However, unionized firms are more subject to strikes that can hurt retail sales.

Service organizations such as hospitals and government offices provide a stable economic base, but pay low wage rates. Retailers ideally seek a community with a balanced economic base. They also look for a community with a history of growth and aggressiveness in seeking new industry. They tend to avoid a community with a history of labor problems or one that is losing population.

Pay attention to competition. Who are the likely competitors? Are any national retailers located in the area? How long have they been present?

STRENGTHS AND WEAKNESSES OF SELECTED LOCATION ALTERNATIVES

Type of Location	Strengths	Weaknesses
Regional shopping center	Large number of stores Drawing power of large anchor stores Parking availability Balanced tenant mix	Occupancy costs Some inflexibility (i.e., store hours, merchandise sold)
Community shopping center	Operating costs Shopping convenience Shared promotions	Poor tenant mix Facility condition High vacancy rate
Neighborhood shopping center	Shopping convenience Very low operating costs Distance from customer	Few tenants Susceptible to competition Facility condition
Central business district	Mass transit Urban redevelopment Business/work traffic generates exposure Rent costs	Parking Limited shopping hours Facility condition Surburban shift Rent costs
Solo location	Lack of close competition Lower rent More space for expansion Greater flexibility	Harder to attract customers Probably have to build instead of rent Higher promotion costs

Can the market support another retailer without taking too much business from competition?

Are decent locations available? Does the community have several shopping centers with vacancies? Does the downtown area look "alive"? Are plans under way to revitalize downtown? Is land available at reasonable prices for building a stand-alone location?

Finally, do not overlook regulations. Can a business license to operate be obtained, and how much will it cost? Can the firm be open on Sundays? Is the community aggressively seeking new retailers?

Choosing a Location within a Community

Where to locate in a community is one of the most important decisions for a retailer. The problem is to find the right location for the right undertaking because a location can make or break a business.

Different stores have different locational requirements. A retailer would not put a toy store in a retirement village or start a garden supply store in a rental apartment district. The customers served, the things they buy, the way they reach the store, the adjacent stores, the neighborhood—all bear upon the location. These factors must be related to the types and characteristics of possible locations when making the location decision.

Management typically has a choice between a (1) shopping center, (2) **central business district,** or (3) **solo location.** Table 10–2 shows the strengths and weaknesses of each type of location.

Shopping centers are a geographic cluster of retail stores collectively handling an assortment of varied goods that satisfy most of the merchandise wants of consumers within convenient driving time of the center.

Shopping centers may be either planned or unplanned. An **unplanned shopping center** is one that is built over time with little or no consideration for a balanced tenancy. **Balanced tenancy** means that management seeks to develop a store mix that will meet the needs of all shoppers in the trading area. Balanced tenancy, for example, means that management does not want six men's shoe stores and no drugstore in the center. In contrast, a **planned shopping center** is a development with planned tenancy, parking, and architecture.

Finally, a shopping center may be either a mall or a strip development. A *mall* is a climate-controlled, enclosed shopping center designed to shut out the weather. Open storefronts in the malls allow the display of merchandise across the full width of the store along the shopping corridors.

A *strip shopping center*, often called a **neighborhood shopping center,** contains a small group of stores and service establishments that primarily carry convenience goods. In contrast to a mall, the strip centers do not have an enclosed climate-controlled corridor that is shared by all the outlets. Rather, the entrance to each store is typically through exterior doorways which makes movement between the outlets more difficult and less comfortable than in an enclosed center.

What Are Shopping Center Strengths and Weaknesses?

The strengths of shopping centers, especially malls, are: (1) balanced tenant mix, (2) common store hours, (3) centerwide promotions, (4) controlled climate, (5) few parking problems, (6) longer store hours, and (7) a pleasant environment for attracting shoppers.

Small shopping center stores can take advantage of the traffic-drawing ability of large, mass merchandisers or outlets with national reputations. Often, people will shop in the small shops even though they came to the shopping center primarily to shop at the large, mass merchandisers.

Shopping centers also have weaknesses. The primary problems center around what the individual merchant can and cannot do. Specifically, tenants face restrictions on (1) what can be sold and (2) store hours. Also, the policies of the center are often dictated by the large **anchor tenant(s).** Finally, rent will be higher than in a stand-alone location.

What Are the Choices?[2]

Whether a retailer can get into a shopping center depends on the market and management. A small shopping center may need only one children's shoe store, for example, while a **regional center** may expect enough business for several.

In order to find tenants whose line of goods will meet the needs of the market to be reached, the developer/owner first signs prestige merchants as lead tenants. Then, other types of stores are selected that will complement each other. This bolsters the center's competitive strength against other centers, as well as supplying the market area's needs.

To finance a center, the developer needs major leases from companies with strong credit ratings. Lenders favor tenant rosters that include the triple-A ratings of national chains. When most spaces are filled, a developer may choose small outlets to help fill the remaining vacancies.

However, a person who is considering a shopping center for a first-store venture may have trouble. Financial backing and merchandising experience may be unproven. The problem is to convince the developer that the new store has a reasonable chance of success and will help the tenant mix.

Factors to Consider in a Shopping Center Choice

Suppose that the owner/developer of a shopping center asks a retailer to be a tenant. In considering the offer, the retailer needs to make sure of what he or she can do in the center. What rules will affect the operation? In exchange for the rules, what will the center do for the firm?

Even more important, the trade area, the location of competition, and the location of available space needs to be considered. These factors help to determine how much business can be done in the center.

The Center's Location.   In examining the center's location, look for answers to questions such as these:

1. Can the store hold old customers and attract new ones?
2. Would the center offer the best sales volume potential for the kind of merchandise to be sold?
3. Can management benefit enough from the center's access to a market? If so, can it offer the appeal that will make the center's customers come to the store?

A retailer should analyze the market the developer expects to reach. In this respect, money for professional help is well spent, especially when the research indicates that the center is not right for the type of firm planned.

Store Space.   Determine where the space will be. The location within a center is important. Does the store need to be in the main flow of customers as they pass between the stores with the greatest "customer pull"? What will be the nature of the adjacent stores? What will be their effect on sales of the planned firm?

The Amount of Space Is Also Important.   Using their experience, retailers should determine the amount of space needed to handle the sales volume expected. The amount of space will also determine the rent to be paid.

Total Rent.   Most shopping center leases are negotiated. Rental expense may begin with a minimum guarantee that is equal to a percentage of gross sales. While this is typically between 5 and 7 percent of gross sales, it varies by type of business and other factors.

Other charges are assessed in addition to the minimum guarantee. A retailer may have to pay dues to the center's merchant association and for maintenance of common areas. Rent, then, should be considered in terms of "total rent." If total rent is more than the present rent in an existing location, the space in the center will have to draw enough additional sales to justify the added cost.

Finishing Out. Generally, the developer furnishes only the bare space in a new center. The "finishing out" is done at the retailer's own expense. For example, a retailer pays for lighting fixtures, counter shelves, painting, and floor coverings. In addition, heating and cooling units may have to be installed.

An innovation in completing a new center is the "tenant allowance." According to this system, landlords provide a cost allowance to tenants toward completion of the space. The allowance is for storefronts, ceiling treatment, and wall coverings. Normally, the allowance is a percentage of cost and is spelled out in a dollar amount in the lease.

Some developers help tenants plan storefronts, exterior signs, and interior color schemes. They provide this service to ensure storefronts that add to the center's image rather than detracting from it.

Types of Shopping Centers

Because planned shopping centers are built around a major tenant, centers are classed, in part, according to the leading tenant. The classification includes three types: neighborhood, community, and regional. (See the illustrations on page 255.)

Neighborhood Center. The supermarket or the drugstore is the leading tenant in a neighborhood center. This type is the smallest in size among shopping centers and caters to the convenience needs of a neighborhood.

Community Center. Variety or junior department stores are the leading tenants in the next bigger type—the **community center.** Such centers also include some specialty shops, wider price ranges, greater style assortments, and more impulse-sale items.

Regional Center. The prestigious department store is the leader in the regional center—the largest type of shopping center. When a retailer finds that a second or third department store is also locating in such a center, he or she will know the site has been selected to draw from the widest possible market area. The smaller tenants were picked to offer a range of goods and services approaching the appeal once found only downtown.[3]

When considering a mall, retailers should weigh the benefits against costs. At the outset, it may be difficult to measure savings, such as the elimination of storefronts, against costs. For example, the cost of heating and air conditioning may be higher in the enclosed mall. In an enclosed mall center, tenant groupings include drugstores and supermarkets in a separate building at the edge of the parking area. Relatively high-priced women's goods stores tend to cluster together. Service and repair shops are located

In a neighborhood shopping center, the leading tenant is a supermarket or drugstore. The typical leasable space is 50,000 square feet, and the typical site area is 4 acres. The minimum trade population is 7,500 to 40,000.

In a community shopping center, the leading tenant is a variety or junior department store. The typical leasable space is 150,000 square feet, and the typical site area is 10 acres. The minimum trade population is 40,000 to 150,000.

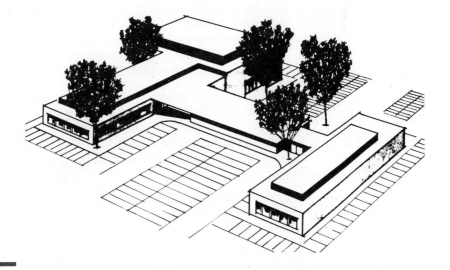

In a regional shopping center, the leading tenant is one or more full-line department stores. The typical leasable space is a minimum of 400,000 square feet, and the typical site area is 30 acres. The minimum trade population is 150,000 or more.

where customers have direct access from the parking lot for quick in-and-out pickup of goods.

A Downtown Location

Central business district (downtown) locations also offer several advantages:

1. Rents are lower than in many shopping centers.
2. Public transportation may be more readily available to downtown.
3. The locations are usually close to large office complexes which employ many people.

However, disadvantages can exist. They include the following:

1. Downtown stores are often not open in the evening.
2. Crime rates are often higher.
3. Traffic congestion is bad.
4. Downtown areas are often decaying and run-down.

A Solo Location

A retailer may want to locate in a free-standing location. Organizations such as K mart often choose to do this.

Stand-alone locations on heavily traveled streets have several advantages including:

1. The lack of close competition.
2. Lower rent.
3. More space for parking and expansion.
4. Greater flexibility in store hours and other methods of operation.

But, disadvantages also exist. For example:

1. Such stores may have difficulty attracting consumers because comparison shopping is not easy.
2. Advertising costs are often higher than if the firm were in a shopping center with other stores which would advertise together.
3. The retailer will probably have to build a store rather than rent one.

The most successful stores in stand-alone locations are those with a strong customer loyalty and a wide assortment of national-brand merchandise from which consumers can choose. After deciding on an acceptable general location, a retailer then assesses the economic potential of the trading area to determine whether it can support the planned store.

Making the Choice

Ultimately the choice of a location depends on the retailer's strategy for growth. The choice also depends on the market to be served, the characteristics of the customers who will be shopping at the outlet, the image of the firm, the current or projected competitive position of the retailer, and the growth objectives and capabilities of the firm.

An additional consideration is financial strength. Management has to decide if they can successfully underwrite an expansion. The capacity for expansion can be determined by an evaluation of cash flow, possible liabilities, and, if management already operates one or more existing businesses, secured assets, profits, and goodwill.

The image of the organization is also important. Management needs to determine whether the firm is strongest on customer service, convenience, or price in the eyes of consumers. Careful attention to the findings can help management identify the sites that are most consistent with the store's image.

Stand-alone locations are likely to be more successful in situations where consumers do not feel the need to make extensive comparisons of price and selection. Some specialty stores, in which the consumers will make a major effort to acquire a particular brand of merchandise, can function successfully in solo locations. Similarly, outlets such as 7-Eleven, which offer primarily fill-in, convenience merchandise for busy people, can succeed in solo locations with high traffic volume moving to and from suburban neighborhoods.

Management also has to decide whether they want to locate in proximity to the competition. Locating near competitors can encourage comparison shopping. Some areas of a community, for example, have a concentration of automobile dealers or furniture outlets for that reason.

HOW TO EVALUATE A TRADING AREA

Retailers differ from manufacturers because they have to be close to their target market since consumers typically shop at the nearest retail outlet that meets their needs. Techniques for measuring a trading area range from a simple "seat-of-the-pants" approach to complex mathematical models. Many retailers still think that they can simply drive by several sites and then decide how far customers will travel to reach an outlet. Such an approach can be disastrous.

Some stores watch what the "big boys" are doing and then follow them. For example, specialty outlets such as County Seat and Jeans and Things look at the shopping centers where mass merchandisers such as Sears, Montgomery Ward, or J. C. Penney are locating and follow them into the same centers. The smaller outlets rightly think that major outlets have done their homework and know they can draw customers to the center.

Information from Existing Stores
Retailers with existing stores have an advantage over a person seeking to open an outlet for the first time. The experienced retailers can use information they have obtained about their existing stores in making decisions about a planned new store. If the new store is similar to the old one, the sales generated are likely to be similar. Retailers must, however, make sure that the stores are alike in all key respects.

License Plate Analysis

One of the more common methods of measuring trading areas for comparable stores is auto license plate analysis. The retailer determines the addresses from public records of the vehicles in the parking lot of an existing store or one similar to the planned outlet. By plotting these locations on a map, it is possible to get a feel for the general nature of the trading area. This information can be used in planning for additional stores.

Check Clearance

Check clearance data can also be used to determine a store's trading area. However, this is based on the assumption that the distributions of cash customers and charge customers are basically the same. Plotting the addresses from the customers' checks makes it possible to determine the characteristics of the trading area for an existing store.

Credit Records

Credit records can be analyzed to determine the trading area of an existing store. A sample of charge accounts is selected, and customer addresses are plotted on a map.

Customer Spotting

Customer spotting is a frequently used technique for determining the location of target customers. The home addresses of the customers are spotted on a map and a circle is drawn to define the primary trading area of the outlet.

Driving Time Analysis

Driving time analysis can also be used to define a trading area by determining how far customers are willing to travel to reach an outlet. Trading areas typically are measured in terms of time instead of distance because of problems of congestion and physical barriers. A rule of thumb is that customers will travel no more than five minutes to reach a convenience outlet. Three fourths of the customers of a large regional shopping center normally will drive 15 minutes to reach the center.

Gravity Models

Retail **gravity models** are an improvement over other methods of trading area analysis. They are based on both population size and distance or driving time as the key variables in the models.

Reilly's Law is the oldest of the trading area models.[4] The model, as shown below, allows the calculation of a "breaking point" in retail trade between two communities.

$$D_b = \frac{D}{1 + \sqrt{\dfrac{B_a}{B_b}}}$$

where

$$B_a, B_b = \text{Population sizes of centers } a \text{ and } b$$
$$(b \text{ is the smaller community})$$
$$D_b = \text{Break-point distance of trade to center } b$$
$$D = \text{Distance between centers } a \text{ and } b$$

In applying the formula, assume the following information:

$$B_a = 200{,}000 \text{ population}$$
$$B_b = 50{,}000 \text{ population}$$
$$D = 25 \text{ miles}$$
$$D_b = \frac{25}{1 + \sqrt{\dfrac{200{,}000}{50{,}000}}} = \frac{25}{1 + \sqrt{4}} = 8.3 \text{ miles}$$

The breaking point between city a and city b is thus 8.3 miles. These break-points can be calculated between several cities and, when joined together, form a set of trading area boundaries for a community, as shown below.

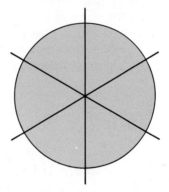

The formula can be modified in several ways including the substitution of driving time for distance, and square footage of retail floor space for population.

Reilly's law works satisfactorily in rural areas where distance has a major impact on the choice of a community in which to shop. Breaking points do not exist in metropolitan areas, however, because consumers typically have several shopping choices available within the distance they are willing to travel.

In essence, Reilly's Law states that the size of a trading area increases as population density decreases. For example, people may travel several miles to shop at a small rural village. However, the same people would only be willing to travel a few blocks in a major metropolitan area. Further, the use of Reilly's Law is appropriate only for communities of roughly similar size. Also, trade areas vary by type of good sought, a reality not reflected in Reilly's model.

Population Characteristics

Earlier we mentioned the importance of population in evaluating a community in which to locate. An analysis of population characteristics is even more critical when evaluating a trading area. Management needs to understand such features as the population profile of the trading area, population density, and growth trends. The population of a trading area may not change over time, for example, but the characteristics of the people in the area may change dramatically. Some older inner-city areas in recent years have experienced the return of young urban professionals (yuppies). Similarly, minorities can become the dominant force in a trading area and can change its suitability for a particular type of retailing.

Such variables as sex, occupation, education, and age are also important, as are family size and family life cycle. An outlet selling lawn supplies would be interested in the number of single-family homes in the vicinity. On the other hand, retailers seeking suitable sites for a day-care center would be more interested in the number of families with preschool children.

Analysis of Competition

The quality and intensity of competition is also important. One way to evaluate the strength of competition is to calculate an index of **retail saturation.** The index is based on the assumption that if a trading area is not already filled with competing stores, a new retailer has a better chance of success. The calculations can be made as follows:

$$IRS_1 = \frac{C_1 \times RE_1}{RF_1}$$

where

$IRS_1 =$ Index of retail saturation for area 1

$C_1 =$ Number of consumers in area 1

$RE_1 =$ Retail expenditures per consumer in area 1

$RF_1 =$ Retail facilities in area 1

Consider the following example of supermarket saturation in Market A:

The 100,000 consumers in market A spend an average of $5.50 per week in food stores. There are 15 supermarkets serving market A with a total of 144,000 square feet of selling area.

$$IRS = \frac{100,000 \times 5.50}{144,000} = \frac{550,000}{144,000} = \$3.82$$

The revenue of $3.82 per square foot of selling area measured against the revenue per square foot necessary to break even provides the measure of saturation in market A. The $3.82 figure is also useful in evaluating relative opportunities in different market areas.[5]

Published census data, though quickly outdated since it is published only every 10 years, can provide information on the number of potential customers within a trading area. The U.S. Bureau of Labor Statistics reports expenditure data by product category for households by income level. The number of competitors within the trading area can be determined by counting them, although square footage would have to be estimated.

Other conditions that can reflect an understored trading area include the limited availability of vacant buildings and a situation where people have to travel farther than they prefer to shop. An assessment of the quality of existing competition is also important. The number of stores alone does not indicate whether a market is saturated. Stew Leonards has over 93 competitors within a 10-mile radius of its Norwalk, Connecticut, store. Yet, Stew Leonards has sales in excess of $2,700 per square foot of selling space.

Customer Survey

A good way to determine a trading area is to conduct or sponsor a customer survey. The survey can be done by mail, telephone, or personal interview. Each method has its good and bad points, as shown in Table 10–3. The interviews can be conducted at the store if they are personal interviews. Alternatively, a sample of respondents can be chosen from customer records and called on the phone or mailed a questionnaire. Retailers may also be able to participate in surveys sponsored by the local chamber of commerce or a similar organization.

The customer survey can provide information on where people shop for items similar to the planned merchandise offering. For example, if a store interviews its own customers, the addresses can be plotted on a map to measure the store's trading area. Also, retailers can do a survey of noncustomers and establish trading areas for competitors. Drawing circles with a radius of one, two, and five miles makes it possible to see how far most customers travel to shop at the outlet. If a retailer is planning the first store, the information for an outlet similar to the one planned can be plotted.

A customer survey can provide other useful information as well. Such information might include: (1) *demographics* (e.g., age, occupation, number of children); (2) *shopping habits* (e.g., type of store preferred, how often consumers shop, area of town preferred); (3) *purchasing patterns* (e.g., who

---

T A B L E   10–3   STRENGTHS AND WEAKNESSES OF THE MOST FREQUENT MEANS OF RESPONDENT CONTACT

Issues	Mail	Telephone	Personal
Cost	Low	Low	High
Amount of time required	Large	Small	Medium
Response rate	Low	High	High
Ability to collect complex data	Good	Poor	Good
Control over response	Poor	Good	Good

does the family buying); and (4) *media habits* (e.g., radio, TV, and newspaper habits).

<hr>

HOW MUCH BUSINESS CAN BE DONE IN THE TRADING AREA?

Retailers need five sets of data to help estimate the amount of sales available in a trading area: (1) number of people in the trading area; (2) average household income; (3) amount of money spent each year by the households on the type of goods sold by the firm—that is, groceries, drugs, or apparel; (4) the total market potential; and (5) the share of the total market potential management can expect to get.

The number of people in a trading area can be obtained from an analysis of U.S. census data in almost any public library, as noted above. The data are reported by census tracts (small areas with 4,000 to 9,000 people) for all cities with a population of 50,000 or more. County data are reported in the Survey of Buying Power.

The average household income in each census tract is published by the U.S. Bureau of the Census every 10 years. The Survey of Buying Power also reports data annually on effective buying income (EBI) by county and metro area. EBI is equivalent to disposable personal income.

Information about the amount of money spent each year on various types of merchandise can be found in several places. Data published by the U.S. Department of Labor is probably the best source.

Multiplying average annual household income by the number of families in the trading area yields *total sales potential*. Multiplying total sales potential by the percentage of the average annual household income spent on each type of goods (for example, groceries) yields *total sales potential by type of good*.

Retailers then decide on the amount of the available sales potential they can get. One way to do this is by plotting competitors in the trading area on a map and trying to establish the sales levels of each. Indicators may be the number of checkouts, number of employees, square footage, and industry trade averages for sales per square foot as reported by the Urban Land Institute publication entitled *Dollars and Cents of Shopping Centers*. Retailers must also decide on the amount of business they need to make a profit. Then they decide on whether and how much business they can take from the competition. Table 10–4 shows this five-step process.

<hr>

SITE EVALUATION[6]

Evaluating a specific site is particularly important. In central and secondary business districts, small stores depend on traffic created by large stores. Large stores, in turn, depend on attracting customers from the existing flow

T A B L E   1 0 – 4   *ESTIMATING ANNUAL SALES IN A RETAIL STORE'S TRADING AREA*

Factor:	A		B		C		D		
Method:	Number of households in a census tract in retail trading area	×	Median annual income of the households in the census tract	×	Proportion of a household's annual income spent on items sold by store	×	Proportion of money spent on item that will be spent in store	=	Proposed store sales revenue from census tract
Census tracts in trading area:									
354XX	6,500		× $10,000		× .20*		× .10†		= $1,300,000
354XY	8,500		× 8,000		× .15		× .15		= 1,530,000
Total projected annual sales									$2,830,000

* The proportion of .20 means that 20 percent of the typical household's annual income of $10,000 is spent on merchandise sold by this store.
† The proportion of .10 means that management anticipates that 10 percent of the total merchandise purchased in this census tract will be purchased at this specific store.

of traffic. However, where sales depend on nearby residents, defining the trading area is more important than picking the specific site. The following factors are important in evaluating a site.

Customer Parking and Traffic Congestion

Customer parking and traffic congestion are often a problem in downtown areas and along busy thoroughfares. Consumers must make a major effort to shop in such areas. Merchant-sponsored parking which provides shoppers with either free or reduced-fee parking is often necessary.

The amount of parking needed depends on frequency of vehicle turnover, the type of merchandise sold, and peak parking requirements. However, peak parking should be evaluated in a "normal" period as opposed to a heavy shopping period such as Christmas. Otherwise, the retailer will find excess parking spaces sitting vacant most of the year.

Four to one is the typical ratio of selling space in shopping centers to square footage of parking. Some retailers also evaluate the relationship between the number of parking spaces and the square footage of selling area. The most frequently used ratio is seven parking spaces for each 1,000 square feet of selling area.

Type of Goods Sold

Merchandise can be classified as convenience, shopping, or specialty goods based on customer buying habits. Stores can be classified in the same way as shown in Table 10–5. Understanding how consumers perceive merchandise and stores can help in evaluating the adequacy of a site.

Convenience Goods

Convenience goods are often purchased on the basis of impulse at outlets such as 7-Eleven. The volume of traffic passing a site is thus the most important factor in selecting a site at which to sell convenience goods. Some convenience goods outlets such as card shops are often located close to major department stores in shopping malls and depend on the department stores to attract traffic for them.

Shopping Goods

Consumers purchasing **shopping goods** prefer to compare the offerings of several stores before making a buying decision. A clothing store such as Irresistibles is an example of a shopping goods outlet. Thus, consumers will travel farther in purchasing shopping goods than convenience goods, but will not make a special effort to reach an outlet if others are more easily accessible.

Specialty Goods

Specialty goods are items for which consumers will make a special effort to purchase a particular brand or shop at a given store. Such outlets generate their own traffic. As a result, retailers of such merchandise can choose a

		Stores		
		Convenience	Shopping	Specialty
Goods	Convenience	Consumers prefer to buy the most readily available brand and product at the most accessible store. 1	Consumers are indifferent to the brand or product they buy, but shop among different stores in order to secure better retail service and/or lower retail prices. 4	Consumers prefer to trade at a specific store, but are indifferent to the brand or product purchased. 7
	Shopping	Consumers select a brand from the assortment carried by the most accessible store. 2	Consumers make comparisons among both retail-controlled factors and factors associated with the product (brand). 5	Consumers prefer to trade at a certain store, but are uncertain as to which product they wish to buy and examine the store's assortment for the best purchase. 8
	Specialty	Consumers purchase their favored brand from the most accessible store that has the item in stock. 3	Consumers have strong preference with respect to the brand, but shop among a number of stores to secure the best retail service or price for this brand. 6	Consumers have preference for both a particular store and a specific brand. 9

SOURCE: Yoram Wind, *Product Policy: Concepts, Methods, and Strategy* (Reading, Mass.: Addison-Wesley Publishing, 1982), p. 71.

somewhat isolated site relative to outlets offering shopping goods or convenience goods.

EVALUATE THE FACTORS

As retailers obtain information on various areas, they should not limit themselves to data from only one source. Ask the same questions of many people and compare the answers. Some developers may tend to distort the picture of their areas, and retailers may find too late that the realities are quite different from what they anticipated. An excellent way to obtain facts is by talking with business owners who are established in the area under consideration. Some retailers, for example, complained that they were misled about the retail potential for the renovated Beale Street in Memphis, Tennessee. As a result, they found themselves in a high rent area that attracts relatively little pedestrian traffic. (Beale Street is where W. C. Handy wrote "Mr. Crump's Blues" in 1909 and gave birth to the "blues.")[7]

Consider the Future

Management should look ahead. Try to picture the situation 10 years from now. Try to determine whether the general area can support the firm as the business expands. Also, management must consider whether a site that fills its present needs will allow for future expansion. If management has to move a second time and the distance is too far, the firm is apt to lose a majority of its customers.

Use a Score Sheet

A score sheet can be useful in evaluating sites. Such an analysis will help show the strengths and weaknesses of each site being considered. The method can also help eliminate factors that are equal at all sites.

Make a Traffic Count[8]

Traffic counts can be of critical importance in evaluating the suitability of a site. The general objective of a traffic count is to count the passing traffic— both pedestrian and vehicular—that would constitute potential customers who would probably be attracted into the store. Data from traffic counts should not only show how many people pass by but also indicate what kinds of people they are. Analysis of the characteristics of the passing traffic frequently reveals patterns and variations not readily apparent from casual observation.

For counting purposes, the passing traffic should be divided into different classifications according to the characteristics of the customers who would patronize the business. Whereas a drugstore is interested in the total volume of passing traffic, a men's clothing store is more concerned with the amount of male traffic, especially men between the ages of 16 and 65.

It is also important to classify traffic according to its reasons for passing. A woman on the way to a beauty salon is probably a poor prospect for a paint store, but she may be a good prospect for a drugstore. The hours at which individuals go by are often an indication of their purpose. In the early morning hours, people are generally on their way to work. In the late afternoon, these same people are usually going home from work. When one chain organization estimates the number of potential women customers, it considers women passing a site between 10 A.M. and 5 P.M. to be the serious shoppers.

Evaluation of the financial bracket of passersby is also significant. Out of 100 women passing a prospective location for an exclusive dress shop, only 10 may appear to have the income to patronize the shop. Of course, the more experience a retailer has had in a particular retail trade, the more accurately the number of potential customers can be estimated.

In order to determine what proportion of the passing traffic represents potential shoppers, some of the pedestrians should be interviewed about the origin of their trip, their destination, and the stores in which they plan to shop. This sort of information can provide a good estimate of the number of potential customers.

The season, month, week, day, and hour all have an effect on a traffic survey. For example, during summer there is generally an increased flow of traffic on the shady side of the street. During a holiday period, such as the month before Christmas or the week before Easter, traffic is denser than normal. The patronage of a store varies by day of the week, too, as store traffic usually increases during the latter part of the week. In some communities, on factory paydays and days when social security checks are received, certain locations experience heavier-than-normal traffic.

BUILD, LEASE, OR BUY

No right answer exists to the question of build, lease, or buy. If management builds or buys, costs such as rent are eliminated. On the other hand, management may decide not to tie up working capital in a building, but try to keep money working in other ways. The advantages and disadvantages of each alternative are briefly outlined in Table 10–6.

Building a Facility[9]

If management must build its own facility, then it will need to consider a variety of factors.

Is a suitable site available in the general area where management has decided to locate or relocate? Management needs to consider whether the terrain is suitable and whether the foundations (the natural underlying base, such as limestone) are adequate. Can the necessary zoning be obtained? Is adequate water available? Adequate sewer service?

T A B L E   10–6 **ADVANTAGES AND DISADVANTAGES OF BUYING, LEASING, AND BUILDING ALTERNATIVES**

Alternative	Advantages	Disadvantages
Buy existing facility	Ownership Operating flexibility Quick occupancy Accessibility to traffic Asset appreciation	Long-term commitment Initial capital outlay Adaptability Initial facility condition Maintenance costs
Buy land and build	Ownership Operating flexibility Facility condition Asset appreciation Location flexibility	Long-term commitment Initial capital outlay Construction time Maintenance costs
Lease	Quick occupancy Relatively low initial costs Reduced commitments	Operating inflexibility Changing lease terms Initial facility condition Adaptability Lease nonrenewal

Community Interest

Whether the community or area wants the business is important. Some areas aggressively seek new firms. They are eager to eliminate many of the problems that hinder firms from locating in their community. The attitudes of other communities toward development range from passivity to open hostility. Management should concentrate on areas that show enthusiasm for the business.

Buy or Lease?

A final consideration in locating or relocating is whether to lease or buy the facility. The decision should be based on these factors:

1. Are business requirements going to change rapidly over the next few years? If they are, leasing should probably be considered.
2. Does management find itself in a very short supply of capital? Can the firm use available money better if it is not tied up in a building? What return can be expected from the funds if they are invested elsewhere? If capital is tight, leasing may be preferable.
3. Can management secure a favorable lease with an option to purchase from the owner of the building? Because of tax considerations, a property owner may prefer leasing property to selling it. In such a case, the owner is apt to make the lease price more attractive than the selling price.
4. An accountant can provide advice on the financial aspects of how leasing or purchasing might affect the firm's financial picture. If property can be bought at a favorable price and does not cause a shortage in working capital, then purchasing may be indicated.
5. Consider the resale value. Is the building one that can be readily resold? If so, to purchase may be wise. On the other hand, leasing may be better if there is a problem with the building (for example, little or no adjacent land for parking) which could limit resale of the property.

What Is a Lease?

A lease is a legal contract that conveys property from the landlord to the tenant for a specified period of time in return for an agreed-on fee. Leases can take several forms. Under a **fixed-payment lease,** the landlord charges the tenant a fixed amount each month. In a **variable-payment lease,** the retailer pays a guaranteed minimum rent plus a specified percentage of sales. The minimum rent typically covers the landlord's expenses such as taxes, insurance, and maintenance. The percentage-of-sales component of the rent allows the landlord to share in the profits the retailer makes as a result of being in a choice location.

The rent to be paid is determined by several factors. The primary factor is the sales per square foot which can be generated at the site. Retailers with high sales per square foot typically pay a lower percentage rent than retailers with lower sales per square foot. Outlets with high sales per square foot generate higher volumes of customer traffic and as a result are able to negotiate lower percentage rents because they are more desirable tenants.

RELOCATE FOR GROWTH?

Sometimes an owner/manager should consider relocating although the need for it is not apparent—even though the present space may seem adequate, and customers are being served without undue complaints.

If a facility has become a competitive liability, moving to another building may be the most economical way to become competitive again.

Retailers should keep in mind the danger of putting off relocating because they "can't afford it now." Some owner/managers find that as time goes by and their competitive position worsens, they can afford relocating even less. They learn the hard way that if a company stays too long in a location, it can die in that location.

The company that prospers is the one whose owner/manager chooses the best possible site and remains there only until the factors indicate that the present location's benefits no longer outweigh the advantages to be gained by moving.

When the firm has roots in a community, the retailer should look there first. The move to bring a firm up-to-date may be a move just down the road from the present building.

HELP IN CHOOSING A SITE

It is possible to get local assistance in choosing a site, and data can be secured from a number of sources. The electric, gas, or telephone company may have a person who is designated to help firms in their location decisions. Some banks and insurance companies also provide such service.

Thus, alternative sites can be evaluated after management (1) decides on the *importance* of selected factors in choosing a site and, (2) the *attractiveness* of the site based on the factors identified as important. Multiplying importance by attractiveness as shown in Table 10–7 yields a score for each variable. Summing the scores for each site allows management to compare alternative sites more objectively.

OVEREMPHASIZED FACTORS

When making decisions, many retailers overemphasize certain considerations. One is the initial cost of the property. This is a one-time charge, and if a retailer is buying a site, an additional $1,000 or so may not be significant when it is amortized over the years the business plans to remain at that site.

Factor	Importance to Management*	×	Management Attractiveness Ranking of Each Factor Considered†	=	Total Score
Future growth potential	2		1		2
Present size	6		4		24
Investment required	5		6		30
Strength of competition	4		5		20
Ability to meet the needs of the segment	1		3		3
Profit potential	3		2		6
Total					85

* 1 is most important.
† 1 is most attractive to management.

Also, a lower-priced property is not a bargain if the costs of operation from that site are higher than on a more expensive property.

Another overemphasized factor is tax considerations. Between communities, tax differences have tended to level off. Although some areas have gross volume taxes, and others income taxes, the net collected from most businesses tends to be the same. On rare occasions, some significant differences occur because of the peculiarities of some companies, but these are not necessarily permanent.

CHAPTER HIGHLIGHTS

— Location is a key factor in the retailing mix. Retailers should consider such a decision as carefully as pricing, promotion, and other elements of the marketing mix.

— Key factors in choosing a community in which to locate include its size, composition of the population, labor market, closeness to the source of merchandise supply, media mix available, economic base of the community, existing and probable future competition, availability of store sites, and state, local, and federal regulations.

— Choosing a location within a community is also important. Retailers can decide on a shopping center, downtown, or solo location. Shopping centers may be either planned or unplanned. The retailer has the choice of locating in a neighborhood center, a community center, or a regional center.

— Retailers can employ a variety of techniques in assessing the size of the probable trading area. These techniques include a study of existing stores, license plate analysis, check clearance analysis, an analysis of credit records, gravity models, and conducting a customer survey to help understand customer shopping behavior.

— After establishing the size of the trading area, management then has to determine the amount of business that can be done in the trading area. The amount of business is a function of the number of people in the trading area, the average household income, the amount of money spent each year by households on the type of goods sold by the firm, the total market potential available, and the share of the total market potential management expects to attract.

— Choosing a specific site involves assessing the adequacy and potential of vehicular or passenger traffic passing a site, the ability of the site to intercept traffic en route from one place to another, the nature of adjacent stores, type of goods sold, and adequacy of parking.

— The final decision is whether the retailer should build, lease, or buy a facility. In leasing, the retailer has the option of a fixed-payment lease or a variable-payment lease.

KEY TERMS

Anchor tenants The major tenants that serve as the primary consumer-attracting force in a shopping center.

Balanced tenancy A term that means that the types of stores in a planned shopping center are chosen to meet all of the consumers' shopping needs in the trading area.

Central business district The area of the central city that is characterized by high land values, high concentration of retail and service business, and high traffic flow.

Community center A shopping center in which the leading tenant is a variety store or junior department store. The typical leasable space is 150,000 square feet, and the typical site area is 10 acres. The minimum trade population is 40,000 to 150,000.

Convenience goods Frequently purchased items for which consumers do not engage in comparison shopping before making a purchase decision.

Fixed-payment lease A rental agreement in which rent is based on a fixed payment per month.

Gravity models Methods for trading area analysis that are based on population size and driving time or distance as the key variables in the models.

Market saturation A situation that occurs when such a large number of stores are located in a market that low sales per square foot, compared to the industry average, are the result.

Neighborhood shopping center A shopping center in which the leading tenant is a supermarket or drugstore. The typical leasable space is 50,000 square feet, and the typical site is four acres. The minimum trade population is 7,500 to 40,000.

Planned shopping center A shopping center developed with balanced tenancy, parking, and architecture.

Regional center A shopping center in which the leading tenant is one or more full-line department stores. The typical leasable space is 400,000 square feet, and the typical site is 30 acres. The minimum trade population is 150,000 or more.

Regional dominance A location strategy whereby a retailer decides to compete within one geographic region, for example, the Northeast.

Retail saturation The extent to which a trading area is filled with competing stores.

Shopping goods Merchandise for which consumers engage in a price and quality comparison process before making a purchase decision.

Solo location A location with no other retail stores nearby.

Specialty goods Merchandise with unique characteristics and/or brand identification for which consumers exhibit a strong preference and for which they are willing to make an extra effort to purchase the desired item.

Trading area The area from which a store primarily attracts its customers.

Traffic count A method used to determine the character and volume of traffic (both vehicular and pedestrian) passing a particular site.

Unplanned shopping center Typically a small group of stores and service establishments that have not been developed with a balanced tenancy in mind.

Variable-payment lease A situation in which the retailer makes a guaranteed monthly rental payment to the landlord in addition to a specified percentage of sales.

DISCUSSION QUESTIONS

1. Why is the location decision so important in retailing today?
2. Explain why regional dominance, market saturation, and emphasis on smaller towns and communities are seen today as the best three location strategies.
3. Why should a retailer consider the types of industries in the area when choosing a community in which to locate?
4. What do you consider to be the important factors in selecting a site for a fast-food outlet? How do these contrast, if at all, with your notion of the key factors for the location of an outlet selling stereo components?
5. In deciding whether to locate in a particular shopping center, what are the factors (questions) the retailer needs to consider?
6. Distinguish among the following: neighborhood shopping centers, community shopping centers, and regional shopping centers.
7. What are the advantages and disadvantages of a solo location?
8. What factors have led to the decline of downtown areas as desirable locations for many retail outlets? What can downtown areas do to better compete with suburban shopping centers?
9. Distinguish among the following techniques used by retailers to determine the size of a trading area: license-plate analysis, check-clearance analysis, gravity models, credit-records analysis, and customer surveys.
10. What are the various types of information a retailer needs to estimate the amount of likely sales within a trading area? What are some of the sources from which this information may be obtained?
11. Why is information about a retail store's target market an essential factor to consider when conducting a pedestrian traffic count?
12. What are the advantages and disadvantages of building one's own retail facility, leasing a facility, or buying an existing facility?

APPLICATION EXERCISES

1. Select a medium to large mall. Make a license plate survey of the cars on the lot (noting only the county and state symbols on the license plates) at three different times of the day as follows: midmorning, midafternoon, and evening. Make an analysis of your findings, including such things as percentage analysis of the count by county license plates and plot the locations on a map. Compare and contrast the results of your findings for the three different times of the day.
2. Devise a questionnaire to obtain the following information for the shopping center at which a sample of consumers most frequently shop:
   a. Distance traveled to the shopping center.
   b. Number of visits per week/month.
   c. Items usually purchased at this shopping center.
   d. Factors most liked about the shopping center.
   e. Dominant reason for shopping at the center.
   f. Opinion about the prices of merchandise.
   g. Opinion about the quality of merchandise.
   h. Opinion about selection of merchandise.
   i. Opinion about salespeople.
   j. Opinion about the convenience of location (open-end question).
   k. Amount spent here on the average per week/month.

   Expand this questionnaire to obtain similar information about the shopping center frequented second most. Using the data obtained from your questionnaire, do an analysis to isolate the factors that determine the choice of shopping centers. Which factors are the most important? Which are the least important? Are greater dollar amounts spent at the shopping center visited most frequently? What meaning does this have for the retailer? What are the similarities and differences in the reasons given for the shopping center visited most and second most?

3. A topic of interest in many cities is the future of the central business district (CBD). If you are in a city that has gone through a downtown revitalization program, arrange to have interviews with the public servants (and volunteers) who were responsible for getting the project going. Describe it; indicate the views of success; and indicate future directions. If you are not in such a situation, search the current literature for examples of cities which have done downtown revitalization jobs. Contact the chambers of commerce for information and indicate some of the national efforts along these lines.

4. Prepare a location and site analysis for a good-quality cafeteria (other types of service retailers or tangible goods establishments may be used) for your local community based on the information in the text. Assume that the cafeteria is a regional chain with excellent regional recognition and acceptance, but that it is not in your community. Prices are higher than fast-food outlets, but lower than service restaurants of comparable quality food.

CASES

1. Small Markets Looking Beautiful to Sears

Montgomery Ward recently shut its catalog mail order division and its 1,500 in-store catalog units. Sears saw the action by Wards as an opportunity to strengthen its small-town presence. Sears opened its first "small store" in Alma, Michigan, in early 1985. The 14,000-square-foot store has 8,300 square feet of selling space. At about the same time, Sears also opened a similar store in Monroe, North Carolina. The small stores have exceeded Sears' sales and volume projections. As a result, Sears plans to add at least 50 more stores in smaller markets over the next few years.

The small stores provide Sears with a rapid means of expanding into new and underserved markets without adding substantially to their administrative overhead. Previous research as part of its "Store of the Future" program had revealed to Sears management that an opportunity existed for a smaller store to serve markets of 20,000 to 100,000 people. Sears already had a presence in many of these markets because of its catalog stores. The chain believes that it can be competitive in small markets by opening smaller, less costly stores that would dominate the markets by offering a core merchandising mix of paint and hardware, consumer electronics, major appliances, and an automotive department.

Sears has targeted at least 300 communities as providing opportunities for expansion. Sears is also experimenting with a slightly larger version of the stores in markets with a population of 75,000–100,000 people. In essence, Sears has taken its traditional hardgoods strengths and fit them into 8,300 square feet of selling space. Their consumer electronics department, for example, is virtually the same as in the Sears store of the future. However, they have excluded home textiles, toys, housewares, stationery, and photo equipment from the smaller store.

Clearly, Sears has chosen hardgoods as its choice of weapons in the fight for market dominance.

Questions
1. What are the advantages to firms such as Sears and Woolworth in locating in small markets?
2. What are the problems that Sears and other retailers are likely to encounter in making the decision to locate outlets in smaller markets?
3. What steps can the independent retail outlet take to offset the threat from larger merchants constructing down-sized stores in small and mid-sized markets?

Source: Based on "Small Stores Looking Beautiful to Sears," *Advertising Age*, October 7, 1985, p. 76; "Small Stores Showcase Big Ideas," *Chain Store Age, General Merchandising Trends*, September 1985, pp. 19–20.

2. Instant Tradition—The Zehnder Family

Frankenmuth, Michigan, has a population of 2,300 and is located in the woods of central Michigan, at least two hours by car from Detroit. The town is a Norman Rockwell version of rural mid-America. The initial reaction is that in the world of restaurants and good eating, Frankenmuth will probably rate a 2 on a scale of 1 to 10. However, the 8th and 10th largest restaurants in the United States, Zehnder's of Frankenmuth and Bavarian Inn, both owned by the same local family, are in Frankenmuth. Big-league restaurants are usually located in major cities. The two largest in the United States are Windows on the World and Tavern on the Green, both in New York with magnificent views of Manhattan. Others include Anthony's Pier Four in Boston, Philip's Harbor Place in Baltimore, and New York's "21" Club and the Rainbow Room.

The basic Zehnder meal is an all-you-can-eat chicken dinner for $8.50 that includes a sizable plate of chicken, three kinds of bread, three kinds of potatoes, two vegetables, applesauce, and pie. The family, with their Bavarian upbringing, felt that blending the decor of the inn with a traditional American chicken dinner would be an effective contrast. They thus began to give people a total experience. Building on this concept, the family then started an annual Bavarian festival that now draws 250,000 people to Frankenmuth in the fall.

Near the restaurants, the Zehnders and their families have opened a variety of shops that sell everything from fudge to gifts. All of the names reflect the Teutonic theme: for example Tiffany Biergarten and Schnitzelbank Wood Carving Shop. They have even organized a 45-minute bus tour (Volkswagen) of the surrounding area. The result is that the community draws 2.5 million tourists a year. At least 2 million of them eat at the two restaurants. Each restaurant has its own gift shop. The family has opened a bakery to supply not only the two restaurants but also two large bake shops on the premises.

Questions

1. Speculate on the future of these two restaurants as America becomes an increasingly diet-conscious society that seeks low calories, but tasty meals. What can the Zehnder family do to ensure the continued growth of their restaurants?
2. A new generation of family members will soon be ready to enter the business. Should the Zehnder family consider building additional restaurants? If so, in what type of markets should they be built?
3. What are the secrets of the family success to date? Does the success of the businesses mean that location is secondary in retailing and that other dimensions of the marketing mix are more important?

Source: Reprinted by permission of *Forbes* Magazine, March 11, 1985. © Forbes, Inc., 1985.

ENDNOTES

1. "How Small-Town Retailers Make the Big Money," *U.S. News & World Report,* December 2, 1985, p. 62.
2. This material is condensed from J. Ross McKeever, "Factors to Consider in a Shopping Center Location," *Small Marketers Aid, #143* (Washington, D.C.: Small Business Administration); see also Eric Peterson, "Site Selection," *Stores,* July 1986, pp. 30–36; "Firm Anchors Secure Small Center Financing," *Chain Store Age Executive,* September 1986, pp. 52–57.
3. "Festival Market Places: Entertaining the Shopper," *Chain Store Age Executive*, October 1985, pp. 51–57.
4. William J. Reilly, *Methods for the Study of Retail Relationships*, Research Monograph #4, University of Texas Bulletin #2944 (Austin: University of Texas Press, 1929).
5. Bernard LaLonde, "The Logistics of Retail Location," in *Fall American Marketing Association Proceedings* (Chicago: American Marketing Association, 1961), p. 572.
6. For further reading, see Michael Poynor, "Finding the Right Site," *Retail and Distribution Management,* September-October 1985, pp. 7–11; Sofie Bowlby, Michael Breheny, and David Foot, "Store Location: Problems and Methods," *Retail and Distribution Management,* January–Feb-

ruary 1985, pp. 44–48; Sofie Bowlby, Michael Breheny, and David Foot, "Store Location: Problems and Methods," *Retail and Distribution Management,* March–April 1985, pp. 40–44.

7. "Renovated Beale Street Falling Short of Hopes," *Tuscaloosa News,* March 31, 1985, p. 4.

8. This information is condensed from James R. Lowry, *Using a Traffic Study to Select a Retail Site* (Washington, D.C.: Small Business Administration).

9. This information is condensed from Fred I. Webster, *Locating or Relocating Your Business,* (Washington, D.C.: Small Business Administration).

11

Recruiting, Selecting, Training, and Motivating Employees

Employers Respond to Two-Career Families

Each morning on her way to work at the Zale Corp. headquarters, Jean Barrow drops off her 11-month-old son at the day-care center. She's been doing it three days a week since he was two months old.

What's different about Barrow's situation and that of most working mothers is that Jamie Barrows spends the day literally yards away from his mother at the Zale day-care facility.

Zale is one of a number of retail companies addressing the needs of a changing work force. More than other industries, retailing is adjusting to today's two-career family.

Retailing is an industry dominated by women, albeit most are in nonmanagement positions. Many of these women are in their prime child-bearing years, but the stereotypical portrayal of women giving up their jobs to stay home and have babies is no longer a reality.

There are approximately 12 million married women with preschoolers; more than half of them are in the labor force. More than 15 million women aged 16 and over have children under the age of 6; 8.03 million are in the labor force, and 7.05 million are actively employed.

At the same time these women are picking up their briefcases, employers are adding benefits or instituting programs that bring the workplace a little closer to home—sometimes literally.

Source: Based on "Employers Respond to Two-Career Families," *Chain Store Age Executive,* July 1985, p. 11; see also Dana Friedman, "Child Care for Employees' Kids," *Harvard Business Review,* March–April 1986, pp. 28–34.

LEARNING OBJECTIVES

The unique success of well-known retail outlets such as Nordstrom's and Wal-Mart depend heavily on the skills, motivation, and dedication of their employees. Employees should not be regarded as throw-away assets. All dimensions of the human resources plan ranging from selection and placement to pay and performance appraisal should be structured to allow employees to feel they are a vital part of the organization. Sensitivity to the issues inherent in employee motivation and job enrichment are also important in progressive organizations, as demonstrated by the Zale Corporation.

After studying the materials in this chapter, you will be able to:

1. Evaluate the importance and content of personnel policies.

2. Determine needed job skills and abilities.

3. Recruit applicants.

4. Select employees.

5. Train employees.

6. Explain the essentials of an employee pay plan.

7. Plan employee benefits.

8. Develop an employee performance appraisal system.

9. Discuss the issues involved in employee motivation and job enrichment.

Management always faces the problem of recruiting, selecting, training, paying, motivating, and promoting good employees. All firms take risks when hiring new employees. However, the smaller the firm, the less it is able to afford the time and cost involved in hiring, and then firing, the wrong employee. Bigger companies have developed effective hiring techniques and procedures to lessen their risks. The owner/managers of small firms must employ some of the same techniques to manage their operations effectively.

THE JOB DESCRIPTION AND JOB ANALYSIS[1]

A manager looking for someone to fill a job should spell out in a job description exactly what he or she wants. Imagine an owner/manager advertising for a "salesclerk." What should the applicant be able to do? Just tally sales receipts accurately? Keep a customer list and occasionally promote products? Run the store while the manager is away? The job of salesclerk means different things to different people. Retailers should determine which skills the job requires, which skills an applicant can get by with, and what kind of training the employee needs.

Good **job descriptions** and **job specifications** are excellent tools, but they will not, by themselves, ensure the best possible selection and assignment of employees to jobs. Nor will they guarantee that the employees will be trained and paid properly. If good job descriptions and clear job specifications exist, however, selection, training, and salary decisions will be much easier and better.[2]

Job descriptions and job specifications are written from a **job analysis.**

Job Analysis

Job analysis is a method for obtaining important facts about a job. To create good job descriptions and job specifications, the job analysis must answer four major questions:

1. *What* physical and mental tasks does the worker accomplish?
2. *How* does the person do the job? Here the methods used and the equipment involved are explored.
3. *Why* is the job done? This is a brief explanation of the purpose and responsibilities of the job which will help relate the job to other jobs.
4. What *qualifications* are needed for this job? Here are listed the knowledge, skills, and personal characteristics required of a worker for the job.

A job analysis thus provides a summary of job:

— Duties and responsibilities.
— Relationships to other jobs.
— Knowledge and skills.
— Working conditions of an unusual nature.

EXHIBIT 11–1 *JOB ANALYSIS OUTLINE*

Full Service Gas Station Attendant

Duties
　Operates gasoline pump.
　Cleans windshields.
　Assists mechanics when requested.
　Takes end-of-day meter readings.
　Looks at tires.
　Cleans wrecker.
　Checks credit card list.
　Provides correct change to customer.
　Enforces no-smoking rule near gas pumps.

Education/Experience
　Read, write, add, subtract, give change.

Relationships
　Reports to manager every morning and at the end of the day.

Knowledge/Skills
　Operate gas pump.
　Check oil and fluids.
　Add oil and fluids.
　Operate cash register.
　Bill customer using credit card.
　Operate emergency safety equipment.
　Change a flat tire and check air.
　Replace windshield wiper blades.

Physical Requirements
　Capable of basic manual skills.
　Able to work on feet all day.

On-the-Job Hazards/Working Conditions
　Minimal danger of equipment-related hazards if safety rules and regulations are followed.

Conducting a Job Analysis

An easy way to begin a job analysis is to think about the various duties, responsibilities, and qualifications required for the position and jot them down on a notepad. The ingredients of a job analysis outline are shown in Exhibit 11–1. Management should chat with the job supervisor or a person who now holds a job to fill in the details about the job.

When conducting a job analysis, it is important to describe the job and the requirements of the job rather than the employee performing it. (The present employee may be overqualified or underqualified for the job or simply have characteristics irrelevant to the job.)

It is also a good idea to keep in mind the ultimate goals of job analysis: to simplify and improve employee recruitment, training, and development, and to evaluate jobs for determination of salary and wage rates.

Using the Job Analysis

After a job analysis has been conducted, it is possible to write a job description and job specification from the analysis. A job description is that part of a job analysis which describes the content and responsibilities of the job and how the job ties in with other jobs in the firm. The job specification is that part of a job analysis which describes the personal qualifications required of an employee to do the job.

The diagram below demonstrates the relationship of job analysis to job description and job specification.

In addition to their usefulness in explaining duties and responsibilities to the applicants, job descriptions and specifications can help with:

— *Recruiting*—Job descriptions and specifications make it easier to write advertisements or notices announcing the job opening, or explaining the job to an employment agency.

— *Interviewing applicants*—Since a job description provides a written record of the duties and requirements of a particular job, and a specification provides the qualifications needed for the job, they can be very helpful in planning an interview, especially as guidelines for asking the applicant questions about his or her abilities.

— *Training and development of new employees*—Having the duties of each job clearly defined can provide a basis for determining what knowledge and skills have to be taught to new employees and helps to plan training so that important skills are learned first and the training is comprehensive.

— *Coordination*—Job descriptions, when they are available, can help greatly to ensure that people know what is expected of them and that their activities are better coordinated.

— *Setting wage rates and salaries of employees*—By providing a better perspective of the relative amounts of work required and qualifications needed for different positions, fairer wage rates and salaries may be established.

— *Employee relations*—The information about the job in the description can ensure that fewer misunderstandings will occur about the respective duties and responsibilities of various jobs.

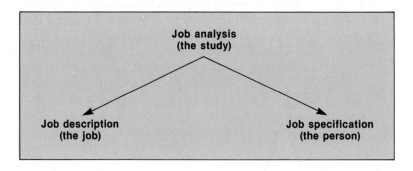

Job Description

A job description is a summary of the important facts about a particular job. It states in a concise, clear way the information obtained in a job analysis. A fully adequate job description should easily fit on one piece of paper. For instance, a job description for a car mechanic might appear as follows:

Job Description

Job Title: Car Mechanic   *Date:*

Statement of the Job
Inspects and services automobiles, repairs and/or replaces mechanically defective parts.

Major Duties

1. Inspects the mechanical, fluid, and electrical systems of the automobile to determine type and location of defect.
2. Services defective vehicles by repairing or replacing faulty parts:
   a. Major repairs such as motor or transmission replacements.
   b. Minor repairs such as brake lining, battery, carburetor, or hose replacements.
3. Performs major maintenance tasks such as tune-ups, brake adjustments, transmission overhaul.
4. Conducts routine maintenance such as lubrication, oil change, and transmission fluid changes.
5. Sees to proper care and maintenance of all garage equipment and the safekeeping of tools.

Relationships
The mechanic supervises a mechanic's helper and the station attendants who may, from time to time, be called upon for assistance. The mechanic reports to the station manager in the morning and afternoon to receive assignments of work.

Job Specification

A job specification, like a job description, is written from the job analysis and describes those personal requirements that should be expected of anyone who is placed on the job, as well as any unusual or hazardous environmental conditions the jobholder must be prepared to accept. A job specification thus describes the type of employee required for successful performance of the job. One way to prepare a job specification is shown here:

Job Specification

Job Title: Waiter/Waitress   *Date:*

Education: (List only that which is really necessary for the job, e.g., high school, college, trade school, or other special training.)
Three years high school or equivalent.

Experience: (The amount of previous and related experience a new employee should have.)
One year experience in a similar restaurant.

Knowledge/Skills: (List the specific knowledge and skills the job may require.)
Must know how to:

1. Cooperate with other waiters/waitresses when serving tables.

Job Specification (concluded)

2. Take customers' orders.
3. Carry food from kitchen to customer.
4. Properly serve customers.
5. Add up customers' bills.
6. Make change for customers.
7. Clean and reset table.
8. Follow procedures for handling customer complaints.

Physical and Mental Requirements: (Mention any special physical or mental abilities required for the job, e.g., 20/20 eyesight, availability for irregular work hours, ability to work under time pressure.)

Must have a pleasant personality, clean appearance. Must be well mannered and able to stand on feet all day.

RECRUITING APPLICANTS

When the owner/manager knows the kind of skills needed in a new employee, he or she is ready to contact sources that can help recruit job applicants.

Each state has an *employment service,* sometimes called Public Employment, Unemployment Bureau, or Employment Security Agency. All are affiliated with the U.S. Employment Service, and local offices are ready to help businesses with their hiring problems. The employment services will screen applicants by giving aptitude tests. Passing scores indicate the applicant's ability to learn a certain type of work. So, a retailer should be as specific as possible about the skills required for a job.

Private employment agencies can also help in recruitment. However, the employee or the employer must pay a fee to the private agency for its services.

Another method of recruiting is a "Help Wanted" sign in the front window. But there are drawbacks to this method: a lot of unqualified applicants may inquire about the job, and a retailer cannot interview an applicant and wait on a customer at the same time.

Newspaper advertisements are another source of applicants. They reach a large group of job seekers, and retailers can screen these people at their convenience, but retailers should think twice before listing the store's phone number in the ad. They may end up on the phone all day instead of dealing with customers.

Job applicants are also readily available from schools. The local high school may have a distributive education department, where the students work in the store part-time while learning about selling and merchandising in school. Many part-time students stay with the store after they finish school.

Retailers may also find job applicants by contacting friends, neighbors, customers, suppliers, present employees, local associations such as the Chamber of Commerce, service clubs to which they belong, or even a nearby armed forces base to find people who are leaving the service. There are, however, problems with such recruiting. What happens to the goodwill of these sources if somebody recommends a friend whom the firm does not hire, or if the firm fires the recommended person?

A combination of the many sources for job applicants may serve best. The important thing is to find the right applicant with the correct skills for the job, whatever the source.

Developing Application Forms

Some method of screening the applicants and selecting the best one for the position is needed. The application form is a tool that can be used to make the task of interviewing and selection easier. The form should have blank spaces for all the facts needed as a basis for judging the applicants. Retailers will want a fairly complete application so they can get sufficient information. However, the form should be kept as simple as possible.

The retailer must not abuse the information from the application in hiring. The Civil Rights Act of 1964 prohibits discrimination in employment practices because of race, religion, sex, or national origin.[3] Public Law 90-202 prohibits discrimination on the basis of age with respect to individuals who are at least 40, but less than 70. Federal laws also prohibit discrimination against the physically handicapped.[4] The **Equal Employment Opportunity Commission** oversees the enforcement of these laws and others summarized in Table 11–1.

SELECTING EMPLOYEES

The objective of the job interview is to find out as much information as possible about the applicants' work background. The major task is to get the applicants to talk about themselves, their skills, and their work habits. The best way to go about this is to ask each applicant specific questions, such as "What did you do on your last job? How did you do it? Why was it done?" A checklist of practices prohibited by one or more of the laws shown in Table 11–1 is included in Exhibit 11–2. Questions that have no relationship to the ability of a person to do the job in question cannot be considered in making a hiring decision.

As the interviews go along, evaluate the applicants' replies. Do they know what they are talking about? Are they evasive or unskilled in the job tasks? Can they account for discrepancies?

When conducting an interview, the following guidelines can be helpful:

1. *Describe the job in as much detail as is reasonably possible.* Give descriptions of typical situations that might occur and ask the applicant how he or she would handle them. "What would you say to a customer with a complaint?" "What color blouse would you recommend to complement a red plaid skirt?" The interviewer shouldn't expect responses to be as expert as his/her own, but training could make them so. Don't be discouraged or

TABLE 11–1   MAJOR FEDERAL FAIR-EMPLOYMENT-PRACTICES REGULATIONS

Regulation	General Coverage	Private Employer Jurisdiction	Basic Requirements
		Employment Practice	
Title VII of the Civil Rights Act of 1964, as amended in 1972 (Equal Employment Opportunity Commission).	Discrimination in employment on the basis of race, color, sex, national origin, or religion.	Employers with 15 or more employees.	Affirmative action may be included in a conciliation agreement or by court order.
Age Discrimination in Employment Act of 1967, as amended.	Age discrimination in employment of persons between the ages of 40 and 70.	Employers with 20 or more employees.	Affirmative action may be required after discrimination is found to exist.
Equal Pay Act of 1963, as amended in 1974 (Equal Employment Opportunity Commission).	Discrimination in compensation on the basis of sex.	Employers under coverage of the Fair Labor Standards Acts.	Affirmative action other than salary adjustment and back pay is not required.
Executive Orders 11246, 11375, and 11141.	Discrimination in employment on the basis of race, color, age, religion, sex.	Employers holding federal contracts or subcontracts in excess of $10,000.	Written affirmative action plans are required of federal contractors and subcontractors with contracts in excess of $50,000 and 50 or more employees.
Vocational Rehabilitation Act Amendments of 1973 and Executive Order 11914.	Discrimination in employment on the basis of physical or mental handicap.	Employers holding federal contracts or subcontracts in excess of $2,500.	Same as above.
Vietnam Era Veterans Readjustment Act of 1974.	Discrimination against disabled veterans and Vietnam War veterans, but more of an affirmative action order than antidiscrimination policy.	Employers holding federal contracts or subcontracts in excess of $10,000.	Same as above.

Regulation	General Coverage	Private Employer Jurisdiction	Basic Requirements
Pregnancy Discrimination Act of 1978, amending the Civil Rights Act of 1964.	Discrimination against pregnant women in hiring, promoting, or giving a wage increase.	Any firm with 15 or more employees.	Persons affected by pregnancy-related conditions must be treated in the same way as persons who have other disabilities.
Wage and Salary Guidelines			
Federal Wage and Hour Laws.	Employers engaged in interstate commerce or who have an effect on interstate commerce.	Any retail or service business with an annual gross sales volume of not less than $362,500 as of January 1, 1982.	Minimum hourly wages and wages, normally, time-and-a-half must be paid for work over 40 hours per week. Child labor laws must be complied with.
Employee Benefit Plans			
Employee Retirement Income Security Act of 1974 (ERISA).	Same as above.	All retirement and benefit programs.	Employee disclosure requirements, and funding, benefit accrual, and vesting rules are covered.
Safety Regulations			
Occupational Safety Health Act (OSHA).	Same as above.	All retailers with one or more employees who are not family members.	A business must provide each employee with a place of employment free from recognized hazards likely to cause death or physical harm.

SOURCE: Daniel Gallagher, "Fair Employment Practices Regulations Affecting Small Business Employee Recruitment and Selection," *American Journal of Small Business* 3 (January 1979), p. 7. Modified, updated, and expanded by the authors.

discouraging. Offer some praise such as, "That's a good way to go about it. If we hire you, we can teach you several other ways to handle situations such as that."

A detailed description lets the person know the expectations from the earliest stage. It also lets the person make a realistic personal judgment as to his or her ability to fill the job.

2. *Discuss the pluses and the minuses.* No job is without its drawbacks. If they are known initially, they are less likely to become obstacles later. If

EXHIBIT 11–2 *CHECKLIST ON THE HIRING INTERVIEW*

1. Don't ask the applicant's age.
2. Don't ask the applicant's date of birth.
3. Don't ask the applicant what church he/she attends or the name of his/her priest, rabbi, or minister.
4. Don't ask the applicant what his/her father's surname is.
5. Don't ask the female applicant what her maiden name was.
6. Don't ask the applicant whether he/she is married, divorced, separated, widowed, or single (but you may ask Mr., Mrs., Miss, or Ms.).
7. Don't ask the applicant who resides with him/her.
8. Don't ask the applicant how many children he/she has.
9. Don't ask the ages of any of the applicant's children.
10. Don't ask who will care for the children while the applicant is working.
11. Don't ask the applicant where a spouse or parent resides or works (although you may ask whether relatives of the applicant are or have been employed by the company).
12. Don't ask the applicant if he/she owns or rents his/her place of residence.
13. Don't ask the applicant whether he/she ever had his/her wages garnisheed.
14. Don't ask the applicant whether he/she was ever arrested.

SOURCE: *Checklist on the Hiring Interview* (New York: National Retail Merchants Association), p. 3.

the person is expected to work nights, weekends, or holidays, say so. This can prevent many misunderstandings later.

3. *Explain the compensation plan.* What is the salary? What fringe benefits are offered? What holidays are allowed? What is the vacation policy?

4. *Weigh all factors in reaching a decision.* Of all the factors just mentioned, no single one is overriding. Perhaps the most important characteristics to look for are common sense, an ability to communicate with people, and a sense of personal responsibility. Only personal judgment will tell the interviewer whether the applicant has these characteristics.

When the interviews are over, the applicants should be asked to check back later if the interviewers are interested in the applicant. The interviewers should never commit themselves until they have talked with all likely applicants.

Next, the interviewers should verify the information obtained. Previous employers are usually the best sources. Sometimes previous employers will give out information over the telephone that they might hesitate to put on paper for fear of being sued, but it is usually best to request a written reply.

To help ensure a prompt reply, retailers should ask previous employers a few specific questions that can be answered by a yes or no check, or with a very short answer. For example: How long did the employee work for you? Was his or her work poor, average, or excellent? Why did the employee leave your employment?

After the retailers have verified the information on all the applicants, they are ready to make the selection. The right employee can help the firm make money. The wrong employee will cost the firm much wasted time and materials, and may even drive away customers.

DEVELOPING AN EMPLOYEE PAY PLAN[5]

Pay administration may be another term for something management is already doing, but has not bothered to name. Or perhaps the organization has not been paying employees according to any system, but waiting until unrest shows up to make pay adjustments—using payroll dollars to put out fires, so to speak.

A formal pay plan, one that lets employees know where they stand and where they can go as far as salary is concerned, will not solve all employee-relations problems. It will, however, remove one of those areas of doubt and rumor that may keep the work force anxious, unhappy, less loyal, and more mobile.

What is the advantage of a formal pay plan for the firm? In business, it is good people who can make the difference between success and failure. Many people like a mystery, but not when it is about how their pay is determined. Employees under a pay plan they know and understand can see that it is equitable (fair) and equable (uniform), and that pay is not set by whim. They know what to expect and can plan accordingly. In the long run, such a plan can help to recruit, keep, and motivate employees. It can help build a solid foundation for a successful business.

Developing the Plan

A formal pay plan does not have to cost a lot of time and money. Formal does not mean complex. In fact, the more elaborate the plan is, the more difficult it is to put into practice, communicate, and carry out.

The foremost concern in setting up a formal pay administration plan is to get the acceptance, understanding, and support of management and supervisory employees. A well-defined, thoroughly discussed, and properly understood plan is a prerequisite for success.

The steps in setting up a pay plan are: (1) define the jobs as discussed earlier in the chapter, (2) evaluate the jobs, (3) price the jobs, (4) install the plan, (5) communicate the plan to employees, and (6) appraise employee performance under the plan.

Job Evaluation and Compensation

The question of how much to pay an employee in a particular position is an important but complicated matter. If management offers too little pay for a particular position, the good employee will leave to perform the same work elsewhere, and only the less motivated, less able employee will remain for the lower pay. On the other hand, management has very little to gain by paying an employee far more than what is being paid in other organizations for the same work.

Job evaluation is a method of ranking jobs to aid in determining proper **compensation.** The diagram that appeared on page 280 can now be used to demonstrate the relationship of these four basic personnel management tools.

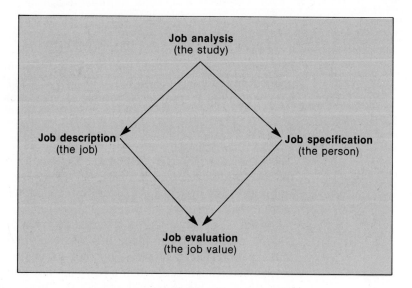

Thus, a job evaluation is obtained by evaluating both the responsibilities from a job description and the items on a job specification. The reason for job evaluation is to establish a fair method of compensating employees for their work.

In determining pay rates, it is important to take several principles into consideration:

— Equal pay for equal work.
— Higher pay for work requiring more knowledge, skill, or physical exertion.
— Reasonable pay, in comparison to pay for similar work in other organizations.
— Over-qualified employees are not paid more (or much more) than a qualified employee in the same position.
— After several years, very little or no extra pay for the length of time an employee has remained with your firm.
— Total earnings reflect, in some way, the employee's contribution to the organization.
— As much as possible, pay scales are known to employees.
— Fairness in application of these principles.

One general and effective rule of thumb to follow when determining salaries and wage rates is to pay the most important nonsupervisory job as well as or somewhat better than the job receives elsewhere and to do the same for the least important full-time job. Rates for all other jobs can then be set in a reasonable way, in between. Job descriptions are often helpful in finding similar positions in other businesses with which to compare pay rates.

Management can obtain information on competitive salaries from various sources, including:

— Local surveys conducted by business associations and organizations.
— Informal contacts, such as meetings with other owner/managers in social, civic, or community functions. Usually this information is useful only to get a general feel of things, since competitors may not wish to disclose salaries of jobs, and noncompetitive companies may be significantly different from your firm.
— Industry meetings and conventions.
— Job advertisements in local newspapers and trade journals.
— National surveys, if they exist.

It is not always possible to compare salaries with pay rates in other businesses. This is especially true if some of the jobs in a business are not standard or common jobs.

Another way, then, to establish salaries and pay rates for jobs is to evaluate the worth of the job to the business, so that more important jobs receive more pay. In this way, management is able to take into consideration all but one of the principles of salary administration discussed earlier. This principle concerns providing a reasonable pay level, in comparison to pay for similar work in other organizations.

There are two different ways to evaluate jobs. They are:

— Ranking—comparing a job against a job.
— Classification—comparing the jobs with the aid of a scale.

The Rank Method of Job Evaluation

Job ranking, possibly with the aid of job descriptions, is the simpler and usually more practical way to evaluate jobs. The most valuable and complex job is assigned a 1; the job that is second in complexity and importance, a 2; and so on until all jobs have been assigned a number. (Jobs that are equal in importance may be assigned the same number.) If management uses this method they know that the higher the job's position on the list, the more important the job is to the business, and can assign pay levels accordingly.

In creating new jobs, management can place them in their proper places in the ranking.

For example, suppose that a restaurant owner/manager who is looking for an assistant manager, a cook's helper, and a dishwasher has the following situation:

Job Rank	Job Title	Salary or Wage Rate
1	Manager	$20,000–$25,000/year
2	Assistant manager	
3	Cook 1	$12,000–$15,000/year
4	Cook 2	$4.50–$5.50/hour
5	Head waiter/waitress	$4.00–$4.50/hour
6	Cook's helper	
7	Waiter/waitress	Minimum wage and tips averaging $3.65/hour
8	Dishwasher	

In this case, then, the assistant manager should be paid more than a cook, but less than a manager, somewhere between $15,000 and $20,000/year. A cook's helper seems to fit in the range of less than $4.00 per hour, but more than $3.65 per hour. The dishwasher, being the least important job, would receive minimum wage or only a little above it.

The Classification Method of Job Evaluation

In **job classification,** jobs are evaluated and rated on two scales:

— *The complexity* of the various responsibilities and qualifications required on the job, and their respective importance to good performance.
— *The length of time* the respective responsibility and qualification are utilized during the average day.

For each responsibility and qualification, two rating numbers are assigned—one for the complexity and importance of the job, and the other one for the length of time during which it is used. For instance, if knowledge of computer programming is required on a job, it may receive a 7 for responsibility and qualification, but if that knowledge is required only a few hours out of each week, it may receive a 2 for length of time. These two numbers can then be multiplied and averaged with all other qualifications and responsibilities of that job to provide a classification number. Large numbers indicate the more difficult and important positions. The method of evaluating jobs based on classification is a complex one and cannot be adequately described in this book.

In general, a planned pay structure makes it possible to tie individual rates of pay to job performance and contribution to company goals. Table 11–2 shows the most frequently used retail sales pay plans.

Installing the Plan

At this point, employers have a general pay plan, but they do not, of course, pay in general. They pay each employee individually. They must now consider how the plan will be administered to provide for individual pay increases.

There are several approaches for administering the pay increase feature of the plan:

1. **Merit increases,** granted to recognize performance and contribution.
2. **Promotional increases,** given to employees assigned different jobs in higher pay levels.
3. **Tenure increases,** given to employees for time worked with the company.
4. **General increases,** granted to employees to maintain real earnings as required by economic factors and in order to keep pay competitive.

These approaches are the most common, but there are many variations.[6] Most annual increases are made for cost of living, tenure, or employment market reasons. Obviously, employers might use several, all, or combinations of the various increase methods.

FOUR COMMON RETAIL COMPENSATION PLANS (salespeople and sales-supporting)

Types	Basic Formula	Common Positions Covered by Such Plan	Primary Advantage(s)	Primary Disadvantage(s)
Straight salary	Paid for stipulated pay period.	Office employees and nontechnical sales areas.	Easily understood and easy to calculate and administer.	Lack of incentive.
Salary plus commission	Base salary plus small additional percentage.	Employees in areas where special effort might get "plus" sales (drapery, garden shop, etc.).	Incentive to sell more.	Somewhat complicated to deal with.
Quotas	Different dollar levels of goals established at which varying percentages of sales are paid.	Positions in selected big-ticket departments or departments in which money incentives usually produce extra effort. Examples—furniture, shoes, carpeting, etc.	Establishes a "target" for employees needing an incentive and can result in sales of higher markup, more sell-up merchandise.	Can become complicated to administer—especially substantiating factors in establishing quotas.
Straight commission	This is truly the incentive plan. Salary based on percent of sales—usually percent increases for goods that are more profitable	Positions in women's coats, men's suits, furniture, carpeting, outside drapery sales, major appliances, building supplies, etc.	Ties sales performance directly to sales results. From employees' point of view it is a true incentive; compensated directly for efforts made; easy to understand.	Salesperson often does not take care of "small-ticket" customer, and uses high pressure to close sales.

SOURCE: Adapted from C. Winston Borgen, *Learning Experiences in Retailing* (Santa Monica, Calif.: Goodyear Publishing, 1976), p. 124. Reprinted with permission.

Employers should document salary increases for each employee and record the reasons for them.

Updating the Plan

To keep the pay administration plan updated, the employer should review it at least annually. Adjustments should be made where necessary, and supervisory personnel should be retrained in using the plan. This is not the kind of plan that can be set up and then forgotten.

During the annual review, the owner/managers should ask themselves these important questions: Is the plan working? Are we getting the kind of employees we want or are we just making do? What is the turnover rate? Do employees seem to care about the business? What matters is how the plan helps employers achieve the objectives of the business.

PLANNING EMPLOYEE BENEFITS[7]

Employee benefits costs have greatly affected business expenses and profits since the enactment of the first workers' state compensation law around 1900 and passage of the Social Security Act of 1935.

Employee compensation includes wages or salary, commissions, incentives, overtime, and benefits. **Benefits** include holidays and paid vacations, insurance, health care, pensions, social security, disability payments, and services like credit unions, product or service discounts, legal assistance, travel clubs, and food services.

After productivity, employee compensation is the most difficult employee-relations issue for management. Employee benefits can help develop a stable and productive work force, but employers must have effective cost and administrative controls. Social security, workers' compensation, and unemployment compensation—which are the only legally required benefits—can be managed with minimal difficulty by keeping records, submitting forms to the proper authorities, and paying for the required coverage. When choosing and managing other types of benefits, however, employers should get professional advice in planning and setting up a program.

As the cost of benefits increases as a percentage of total compensation, the direct pay cost percentage decreases. Employers cannot recognize outstanding achievement with direct pay increases because funds for direct pay are diminishing as benefits spending gets bigger. As a result, unfortunately, the compensation differential between the mediocre employee and the outstanding achiever is narrowing. Managers need to recognize the advantages, limitations, and cost impact that employee benefits have on business operations and net profit.

Analyzing benefits costs can be accomplished by grouping them into the following categories:

— Legally required benefits (social security, workers' compensation, unemployment compensation).
— Pensions.
— Group insurance.
— Supplementary insurance.
— Payment for time not worked.
— Employee services such as day care.
— Perquisites such as employee discounts on merchandise.

Many employers now pay for most, if not all, of the employees' life, medical, and disability insurance. The rapid escalation of benefits costs, as compared to direct pay compensation, has caused managers to become more diligent in controlling these costs and in getting better employee relations.

*Selecting
Employee
Benefits*

Benefits should be designed with the help of an individual who is a competent planner and manager. Employers need an approach that allows them to offer employee benefits designed to meet the company's and employees' needs. For example, employees who are older and no longer have the responsibility of a family will have different requirements from those employees who have families. Also, employees whose spouses are employed and covered by another employer might be considered in such a way as to minimize double coverage.

EMPLOYEE PERFORMANCE APPRAISAL

Many retail employees are under a merit increase pay system, though most of their pay increase may result from other factors. This approach involves periodic review and appraisal of how well employees perform their assigned duties. An effective employee appraisal plan (1) achieves better two-way communications between the manager and the employee, (2) relates pay to work performance and results, (3) provides a standardized approach to evaluating performance, and (4) helps employees see how they can improve by explaining job responsibilities and expectations.

Such a performance review helps not only the employees whose work is being appraised but also the manager who gains insight into the organization. An open exchange between employee and manager can show the manager where improvements in equipment, procedures, or other factors might improve employee performance. Managers should try to foster a climate in which employees can discuss progress and problems informally at any time throughout the year.

Again, to get the best results, it is a good idea to use a standardized form of appraisal. A typical form includes job performance factors such as results achieved; quality of performance; volume of work; effectiveness in working with others in the store; effectiveness in dealing with customers, suppliers, and others; initiative; job knowledge; and dependability.

Employers can design their own forms, using examples in books on personnel administration, if necessary. The forms should be tailored to the jobs and should follow from job analyses as discussed earlier.

EMPLOYEE RELATIONS AND PERSONNEL POLICIES[8]

There are many ways to manage people. The manager can be strict or rigidly enforce rules. Communications can be one-way from boss to employee. The job might get done, but with fairly high turnover, absenteeism, and low morale.

Or the owner can make an extra effort to be a "nice guy" to everyone on the payroll. This may lead to reduced adherence to the rules, and employees may argue when they are asked to do work they do not like. Controlling the daily operation of the business may become more and more difficult. The business may survive, but only with much lower profit than if the owner followed more competent personnel policies. There is, however, another way, one in which employees feel a part of the firm, where manager and employees communicate effectively with each other, where rules are fair and flexible, yet enforced with positive discipline. The job gets done efficiently and profitably, and the business does well.

Large companies have a separate personnel department. Most managers of small firms view this "personnel function" as just part of the general job of running a business. It is good practice, though, to think of the personnel function as a distinct and separate part of management responsibilities—only then are personnel responsibilities likely to get the priorities they deserve.

The human resources function is generally considered to include all those policies and administrative procedures necessary to satisfy the needs of employees. Not necessarily in priority order, these include:

1. Administrative personnel procedures.
2. Supervisory practices based on human relations and competent delegation.
3. Positive discipline.
4. Grievance prevention and grievance handling.
5. A system of communications.
6. Adherence to all governmental rules and regulations pertaining to the personnel function.

Administrative Personnel Procedures

Favorable employee relations require competent handling of the administrative aspects of the personnel function. These include the management of:

— Work hours.
— The physical working environment, including facilities and equipment.
— Payroll procedures.
— Benefit procedures, including insurance matters, and vacation and holiday schedules.

Supervisory Practices and the Personnel Function

If a job satisfies an employee's needs, the employee responds more favorably to the job. Such employees tend to take their responsibilities seriously, act positively for the firm, and are absent from work only rarely.

The key point is that when a job satisfies needs, the employee may bring greater commitment to the job.

Five factors generally cause a deep commitment to job performance for most employees. These are:

1. *The work itself*—To what extent does the employee see the work as meaningful and worthwhile?
2. *Achievement*—How much opportunity is there for the employee to accomplish tasks that are seen as a reasonable challenge?
3. *Responsibility*—To what extent does the employee have assignments and the authority necessary to take care of a significant function of the organization?
4. *Recognition*—To what extent is the employee aware of how highly other people value the contributions made by the employee?
5. *Advancement*—How much opportunity is there for the employee to assume greater responsibilities in the firm?

These five factors tend to satisfy certain critical needs of individuals:

1. One need is the feeling of *being accepted* as part of the firm's work team.
2. Another need is for *feeling important*—that the employee's strengths, capabilities, and contributions are known and valued highly.
3. A third need is for the chance to *continue to grow* and become a more fully functioning person.

If the kinds of needs just described are met by paying attention to the five factors previously listed, management will have taken significant steps toward gaining the full commitment of employees to job performance. To do this, several practical strategies can be used, such as:

— Establishing confidence and trust with employees through open communication and the development of sensitivity to employee needs.
— Allowing employees participation in decision making that directly affects them.
— Helping employees to set their own work methods and work goals as much as possible.
— Praising and rewarding good work as clearly and promptly as inadequate performance is mentioned.
— Restructuring jobs to be challenging and interesting by giving increased responsibilities and independence to those who want it and who can handle it.

Positive Discipline

The word *discipline* carries with it many negative meanings. It is often used as a synonym for punishment. Yet discipline is also used to refer to the spirit that exists on a successful ball team where team members are willing to consider the needs of the team as more important than their own.

Positive discipline in a retail firm is an atmosphere of mutual trust and common purpose in which all employees understand the company rules as well as the objectives, and do everything possible to support them.

Any disciplinary program has, as its base, the concept that all of the employees have a clear understanding of exactly what is expected of them. This is why a concise set of rules and standards that are fair, clear, realistic, and communicated must exist. Once the standards and rules are known by all employees, discipline can be enforced equitably and fairly.

A good set of rules need not be more than one page, but can prove essential to the success of a business. A few guidelines for establishing a climate of positive discipline are given below:

1. There must be rules and standards, which are communicated clearly and administered fairly.
2. Rules and standards must be reasonable.
3. Rules should be communicated so they are known and understood by all employees. An employee manual can help with communicating rules.
4. While a rule or a standard is in force, employees are expected to adhere to it.
5. Even though rules exist, people should know that if a personal problem or a unique situation makes the rule exceptionally harsh, the rule may be modified or an exception may be granted.
6. There should be no favorites, and privileges should be granted only when they can also be granted to other employees in similar circumstances. This means that it must be possible to explain to other employees, who request a similar privilege with less justification, why the privilege cannot be extended to them in their particular situation.
7. Employees must be aware that they can and should voice dissatisfaction with any rules or standards they consider unreasonable as well as with working conditions they feel are hazardous, discomforting, or burdensome.
8. Employees should understand the consequences of breaking a rule without permission. Large companies have disciplinary procedures for minor violations which could apply equally well in small companies. They usually call for one or two friendly reminders. If the problem continues, there is a formal, verbal warning, then a written warning; and if the employee persists in violating rules, there is a suspension and/or dismissal. In violations of more serious rules, fewer steps are taken. It is not easy to communicate this procedure since it should not be so firm that it can be expressed in writing. If it is made clear to employees who violate a rule at the first reminder, the procedure soon becomes understood by all.
9. There should be an appeals procedure when an employee feels management has made an unfair decision. At the very least, the employee should be aware that management is willing to reconsider a decision at a later time.
10. Employees should be consulted when rules are set.

11. There should be recognition for good performance, reliability, and loyalty. Negative comments, when they are necessary, will be accepted as helpful if employees also receive feedback when things go well.

No matter how good the atmosphere of positive discipline in a business, rules are bound to be broken, by some people, from time to time. In those situations, corrective action is sometimes necessary. In some rare cases, the violation may be so severe that serious penalties are necessary. If an employee is caught in the act of stealing or deliberately destroys company property, summary dismissal may be necessary. In all other severe cases, a corrective interview is needed to determine the reasons for the problem and to establish what penalty, if any, is appropriate. Such an interview should include all, or most, of the following steps:

1. Outlining the problem to the employee, including an explanation of the rule or procedure that was broken.
2. Allowing the employee to explain his or her side of the story. This step will often bring out problems that need to be resolved to avoid rule violations in the future.
3. Exploring with the employee what should be done to prevent a recurrence of the problem.
4. Reaching agreement with the employee on the corrective action that should be taken.

Even in the best environment, though, employees will occasionally feel unhappy about something. They may not be paid on time, or may feel that the room is too hot, too cold, or too dark. They may feel that they deserve a merit increase, or that someone has hurt their feelings inadvertently. When this happens, good personnel policies require that employees know how they can express their dissatisfaction and obtain some consideration.

A written grievance procedure, known to employees, can be very helpful in creating a positive atmosphere. It informs employees how they can obtain a hearing on their problems, and it ensures that the owner/manager becomes aware that the problem exists. When employees know that someone will listen to them, grievances are less serious and hearing a complaint carefully often is half the job of resolving it.

A good grievance procedure begins with the manager making it a point to actively look for signs of possible sources of dissatisfaction, and by noticing changes in employee behavior which signal that a problem may exist. This often makes it possible to handle a situation when it is still easy to resolve.

JOB ENRICHMENT

Too many companies today treat employees as throw-away assets. The retail investment is too high to take such an approach. Forward-thinking managers

F I G U R E   11–1   REINFORCEMENT OPTIONS

Food Related	Prestige	Visual/Auditory	Tokens	Social	Privileges
Coffee-break treats	Wall plaques	Office with a window	Money	Friendly greetings	Job with more responsibility
Company picnics	Commendations	Piped-in music	Stocks	Informal recognition	Job rotation
	Rings/tiepins	Redecoration of work environment	Stock options	Formal acknowl- edgement of achievement	Early time off with pay
	Special assignments	Company literature	Vacation trips	Invitations to coffee/ lunch	Extend breaks
	Recognition in house organ	Popular speakers or lecturers	Coupons re- deemable at local stores	Solicitations of sug- gestions/advice	Personal time off with pay
		Feedback about performance	Profit sharing	Compliment on work progress	
				Pat on the back	
				Smile	

SOURCE: Julia R. Galosy, "Teaching Managers to Motivate: When Theory Isn't Enough." Reprinted with permission from the November 1983 issue of *Training*, The Magazine of Human Resources Development. Copyright 1983, Lakewood Publications Inc., Minneapolis, MN (612)333-0471. All rights reserved.

view the employee as a total person. They are concerned with what the employee does during working hours and during time off the job. They try to help employees get more education, sharpen job skills, and participate in worthwhile nonjob activities.

Keeping employees satisfied at work is more than a matter of salary. Employees want to feel they belong and that the company cares about them as total human beings.

Figure 11–1 highlights some of the reinforcement options that can help a person be self-fulfilled. Careful attention to these needs will contribute to higher employee productivity and a lower turnover rate.[9]

Motivation and job enrichment cannot be separated. Motivation is nor- mally related to work policies and supervisor attitudes. Motivated employees will devote their best efforts to company goals. As a result, management is recognizing the benefits of flexibility in work schedules, enrichment pro- grams, and building employee motivation. Yesterday's human resources so- lutions don't work with today's lifestyles. Programs such as **flex time, job sharing,** on-site day care, and quality circles have emerged in retailing in recent years as management has sought ways to increase productivity and enrich the job by reducing worker stress at home and at work.

Flex Time.   Flex time is a system by which workers can arrive and depart on a variable schedule. Flex-time programs contribute to improved employee morale, a greater sense of employee responsibility, less stress, and reduced turnover. Retailers with flex-time programs include J. C. Penney, Dayton- Hudson, and Sears Roebuck.

Job Sharing. Job sharing occurs when two workers voluntarily hold joint responsibility for what was formerly one position. In effect, two permanent part-time positions result from what was one full-time position. Job sharing differs from work sharing. **Work sharing** usually occurs in organizations during economic recessions where all employees are required to cut back on their work hours and are paid accordingly. Job-sharing programs are in place at such retailers as B. Dalton Booksellers and Chicago-based Walgreen Drug. Job sharing is a way to retain valuable employees who no longer want to work full-time. Management has found that the enthusiasm and productivity in such programs is high.

Child Care Programs. Young children pose a special problem for working mothers. More than half of all single mothers with preschool children are now in the work force. Zale Corp., as noted in the opening retail capsule, has responded to this trend by establishing its own child care center at corporate headquarters.

Employee Assistance Programs. Drug abuse and alcohol are two of the most obvious areas in which employers can provide counseling and assistance. Other programs include scholarships for children of employees and encouraging community volunteer work. Many retail firms such as Wards, Saks, and Gimbels now also participate in the National Merit Scholarship Program.

Quality Circles. **Quality circles** create situations in which workers at all levels have input into decisions that affect the company. Employees experience an increased sense of self-worth by taking part in the process. Also, management benefits from the ideas of dedicated workers at all levels in the organization. Managers and workers seek consensus on company operations instead of having orders simply passed down from above. Quality circles were initially started in the United States, popularized in Japan, and then reimported back into the United States. The benefits from such programs include higher productivity, less turnover, and less absenteeism.

CHAPTER HIGHLIGHTS

— Staffing a store with the right people is a critical part of the strategic plan for a retailer. Staffing needs vary depending on the type of merchandise carried, services the store will offer, the image management wants to project to customers, and the way in which the firm wants to compete.

— The initial step in developing a human resources plan for the firm is to develop descriptions of the jobs to be filled. Then job analysis is undertaken to determine the skills needed for the jobs.

— Recruiting, attracting the right people, is a critical element of the plan. Recruits may be sought either inside or outside the firm. Specific federal guidelines exist which management must follow in administering selection tests and in otherwise screening employees.

Simply hiring the right people is not enough. Training is often necessary for new employees and should be offered as an ongoing part of the personnel program. Employees need to know about their rights and responsibilities within the firm, the history of the firm, and specific information about their job responsibilities. Sales personnel may also need training in technical dimensions of the merchandise for which they will be responsible.

An equitable employee pay plan is a further important component of a personnel plan and can contribute to higher employee productivity and satisfaction. A wage survey within the surrounding area can determine the wages paid for comparable jobs. Retailers should make sure that employees understand how the pay plan was developed, how it will be administered, and how they will be evaluated for pay increases or promotions. Closely related to the pay plan is establishing the level and type of employee benefits to be paid.

Employee performance appraisal also needs to occur on a regular basis; normally employees are appraised annually. Standardized forms should be developed for this purpose. Ratings by supervisors should be discussed with the employees and suggestions should be given as to how the employees can improve their performance.

Finally, employee motivation and job enrichment are also important elements of the personnel plan. Management must recognize that employees have needs such as the desire for recognition and achievement which cannot be satisfied by money alone.

KEY TERMS

Benefits Holidays and paid vacations, insurance, health care, pensions, social security, disability payments, and various other forms of support for employees.

Compensation The amount of salary and fringe benefits to be paid for a particular job.

Employee compensation Wages for salary, commissions, incentives, overtime, and benefits.

Equal Employment Opportunity Commission An agency of the federal government with the responsibility to eliminate discrimination on the basis of race, sex, color, age, religion, or other variables in job hiring, retention, and promotion.

Flex time A system by which workers arrive at work on a variable schedule.

General salary increases Increases granted to employees to maintain real earnings as required by economic factors and in order to keep pay competitive.

Job analysis A method for obtaining important facts about a job.

Job classification Comparing jobs with the aid of a scale that evaluates job complexity and the length of time the respective responsibility and qualifications are utilized during an average workday.

Job description The part of a job analysis that describes the content and responsibilities of a job and how the job ties in with other jobs in the firm.

Job evaluation A method of ranking jobs to aid in determining proper compensation.

Job ranking Ranking jobs on the basis of how valuable they are to the organization and their complexity.

Job sharing A situation whereby two workers voluntarily hold joint responsibility for what was formerly one position.

Job specification The part of a job analysis that describes the personal qualifications required of an employee to do a job.

Merit increases Pay increases granted to recognize superior performance and contributions.

Motivation Getting people to do what is best for the organization.

Promotional increases Salary increases given to employees assigned a different job at a higher pay level.

Quality circles A situation in which workers of all levels within a retail firm have input into decisions that affect the company.

Tenure increases Pay increases given to employees for time worked with the company.

Work sharing A situation that occurs during economic recessions where employees are required to cut back on their work hours rather than face layoffs, and are paid accordingly.

DISCUSSION QUESTIONS

1. What are the key federal and state laws that affect recruiting, selection, and compensation of employees? What are the likely effects of these regulations?
2. Assume you are the manager of a men's clothing outlet located close to a major university campus. What would be the basic elements of a training program for the outlet? How might your program differ from the type of training offered for new employees who have been hired by Sears?
3. Briefly describe the steps that must be carried out in developing a formal compensation plan.
4. What is likely to be the most effective method for compensating (a) a retail salesperson, (b) an accountant, and (c) a department buyer?
5. Why should retail management institute an employee performance appraisal plan? What might be some of the performance factors evaluated?
6. Why should an employee grievance procedure and a procedure for handling disciplinary matters be established, even in the absence of a union?
7. What can retail management do to enhance job enrichment and motivation among employees?

APPLICATION EXERCISES

1. Devise a format and interview at least five people who have worked in the retailing industry in some capacity. Determine the individuals' honest views on wages, working conditions, superior-subordinate relationships, and so on. Prepare a report for class discussion on what you have discovered.
2. Secure an employee evaluation form from a local business. What specific criteria are used and for what purpose? Do you think that the criteria are valid? Can you suggest others?
3. Select several different retail companies (differing in organizational arrangement, number of stores and sales volume, and product line) and make an appointment with the executive responsible for the personnel functions. Describe the employment process of each (include selection, training, and benefits including compen-

sation) and draw comparisons among the group. See if you can explain the differences in apparent effectiveness of the programs. See if you can get them to discuss affirmative action.
4. Through your college or university placement office arrange to have a few minutes with all the recruiters coming to campus to interview people for retailing companies. Structure a questionnaire to administer to each recruiter to find out: what he or she is looking for in a student; how the interview on campus enters into the selection process; what kinds of questions are asked of the interviewee; what the recruiter expects the interviewee to know about the company; what variables are considered in evaluating the student; and what the subsequent steps are in the employment process.

CASES

1. Call Him Old-Fashioned

Who says nice guys finish last? In the tough world of supermarkets, George Jenkins's $3.2 billion (sales), closely held Publix Super Markets of Lakeland, Florida, is something of a legend. Jenkins's employees own 62 percent of the stock (he and his family own the rest) and get back 20 percent of the profits, right down to the bagboys.

A share of Publix stock bought in 1960 for $10 would be worth $400 today, and there are veteran Publix employees with a lot of it. C. L. Newsome, 56, Southeast Coast Division manager, for example, started as a bagboy 42 years ago and now owns 101,000 shares worth $1.6 million at its current price of $16 a share.

The result is workers who hustle. Wearing badges that say "I am a Publix stockholder," energetic stock clerks seem to be everywhere. When a *Forbes* writer visited stores in Miami to snoop around, he was stopped every few minutes by workers asking if they might help find something.

In turn, this helpful attitude keeps customers happy. Says one housewife: "This store is clean, and the people here are always polite. I drive by a Winn-Dixie that's closer to my house to come here."

It's worked so well that Publix, the 9th-largest supermarket chain by sales, has the fattest net profit margin of the 10 biggest chains. Its 2.36 percent is two-and-a-half times that of industry sales leader Safeway.

"Really, there's no secret to our success," says Jenkins, now 77. "We're not the only people who treat their people well, we just make a bigger deal out of it."

His own Horatio Alger life provides motivation, too. The son of a rural Georgia grocer, he came to Florida in 1927 and started as a stock clerk at a local Piggly Wiggly. By the age of 17 he was the store manager and at 20, having grown a mustache to look older, he borrowed $2,000 to start his own store across the street. By 1940 Publix was a going chain of 19 stores, and Jenkins has added an average of 6 every year since.

Not surprisingly, the way to the top at Publix is to start at the bottom. Jenkins doesn't hire from the outside except for an occasional computer programmer or other specialist. More than half his store managers started as bagboys—as did Publix President Mark Hollis, 51, and Jenkins's son, Howard, 34, vice president of research and development. "We feel that everyone is in management training," Hollis says.

While the founder never went to college, his second-generation managers are professionally trained. Hollis has a master's degree in supermarket distribution from Michigan State, Howard Jenkins majored in economics, and his cousin Charles Jenkins, Jr., vice president for real estate, has a doctorate in business from Harvard.

The new generation is bringing new ideas—like Publix's six new large combination stores, with pharmacies and more nonfood items like hardware, toys, and, soon, liquor. Publix was one of the first big supermarket chains to install bar-code scanners at checkout lanes. It had an automatic-teller cash machine network before Florida banks did, and is experimenting with debit card stations by the cash register in 16 stores. Hollis has also begun psychological testing of managers and issues a videotaped president's report every six weeks to all stores.

So far, the mix of old and new management techniques at Publix is working out pretty well. Major reason: George Jenkins himself approves just about every change, still shows up at every new store opening to bag groceries, and still watches everything like a hawk. Showing *Forbes* around a store in Lakeland, Jenkins eyes strawberries he thinks are too expensive, examines the floor for dirt, and stops almost every employee he meets. "I heard that somebody had to wait in line for 15 minutes here the other day," he tells them. Then to his visitor: "You know it all really begins and ends here in the store. Can't ever forget that."

Questions

1. How can Publix Supermarkets continue to expand and prosper when they have to share 20 percent of their profits with every employee in the organization? Why haven't other firms pursued this strategy?
2. What do you see as the ingredients in the success of Publix, other than profit sharing?
3. Can such persistence and attention to detail as shown by top management continue to be a part of retail strategy as the firm pursues an aggressive program of expansion? Is such attention to detail really necessary?

Source: Reprinted by permission of *Forbes* Magazine, October 26, 1985. © Forbes, Inc., 1985.

2. Do It Yourself

Among the spreading chains of hardware stores—now called home centers—that supply the tools of do-it-yourself home repair to America's suburbanites, fast-growing Payless Cashways Inc. does one thing better than the others, and that may be the secret of its success: It gives its store managers more autonomy and greater incentives.

The manager of any of 98 Payless Cashways or Furrow stores in the Midwest and Southwest controls the store's inventory, is responsible for pricing and local advertising, charts the store's own business plan and hands it to headquarters—not the other way around. He sets the net profit margin goals that govern the incentive bonus. The Payless Cashways managers—many of them with college degrees—earn salaries that range from $22,000 to $38,600, plus 3 percent of the store's pre-tax profits, and as much as 25 percent more if certain net margin goals are met.

Where did Payless come up with the incentives idea? It started in Pocahontas, Iowa (population 2,352), home of the first store opened in 1930 by company founder Sam Furrow. As Furrow opened more stores in Iowa and Minnesota, he gave his managers a piece of the ownership of each subsequent store. The incentives worked, and by 1969, when Payless went public, it had 16 stores with $18 million sales.

Furrow had a few other ideas that paid off. Payless, unlike most hardware or lumber companies, is strictly cash-and-carry. Why? "You have to remember the building environment after World War II," explains Chairman J. Stanley Covey, 52, whose first job in 1949 was as a yard worker in Furrow's second store in Early, Iowa (population 670—the store still offers free coffee). "Anybody in a retail business tied to construction had difficulty with accounts receivable. So we said, if we're going to eliminate accounts receivable, we have to replace it with a low cash-and-carry price." Payless caters to the homeowner, not the local builder.

A chain so dependent on the performance of individual managers is bound to come up short now and then. It happened to Payless when the chain ventured into the Houston market in 1979. Payless opened five stores in suburban Houston, appointed the store managers, and waited for the normal pattern of profitability in the first year. But the earnings lagged because store managers, though recruited from elsewhere in the chain, were new at their specific jobs and to metropolitan areas.

For the suburban homeowner, reluctant to pay the labor rates of professional plumbers and carpenters, the 30,000-square-foot Payless Cashways store—where all the necessary equipment comes with advice on such things as door hanging and faucet replacement—seems the answer to a prayer. And the Payless Cashways store managers know their customers. That is why they stock the shiny, expensive new faucets at eye level and the plainer, cheaper ones at floor level, where the customer must hunker down to reach them. The extra margin on the shiny faucet, after all, helps with the manager's incentive bonus, and helps keep Payless Cashways Inc. at the top of the do-it-yourself market.

Questions

1. What are the advantages and disadvantages of giving store managers as much autonomy as is done by Payless Cashways?
2. How does the compensation system at Payless Cashways differ from Publix Supermarkets? Might Payless Cashways be more successful if all employees, not just management, shared in the profits?
3. What are the employee characteristics necessary for success under the Payless operating philosophy? How do the characteristics you have identified differ from those of the typical retail store clerk?

Source: Reprinted by permission of *Forbes* Magazine, October 11, 1982. © Forbes, Inc., 1982.

ENDNOTES

1. The material on job analysis, job descriptions, and job specifications is reproduced, with modifications, from *Job Analysis, Job Specifications, and Job Descriptions,* a self-instructional booklet, No. 1020 (Washington, D.C.: U.S. Small Business Administration).

2. This material is reproduced, with modifications, from Walter E. Green, "Staffing Your Store," *Management Aid No. 5.007* (Washington: D.C.: U.S. Small Business Administration).

3. John P. Kohl, "How To Avoid Discrimination Charges," *The Cornell H.R.A. Quarterly,* No-

vember 1983, p. 86–93; also "Bare Trap: The Legal Pitfall of Requiring Scanty Costumes," *The Cornell H.R.A. Quarterly,* November 1985, pp. 78–82.

4. "Responsibilities and Benefits in Hiring the Handicapped," *The Cornell H.R.A. Quarterly,* February 1984, pp. 59–63.

5. This material is condensed from Jean F. Scolland, "Setting Up a Pay System," *Management Aid No. 5.006* (Washington, D.C.: U.S. Small Business Administration.)

6. See, for example, "Incentive Pay Is Catching On," *Chain Store Age Executive,* January 1986, p. 9.

7. This material is condensed from John B. Hannah, "Changing Employee Benefits," *Management Aid No. 5.008* (Washington, D.C.: U.S. Small Business Administration).

8. The material on employee relations and personnel policies is reproduced with modifications from *Employee Relations and Personnel Policies,* a self-instructional booklet, No. 120 (Washington, D.C.: U.S. Small Business Adminstration).

9. Julia R. Galosy, "Teaching Managers to Motivate: When Theory Isn't Enough," *Professional Trainer,* Spring 1984, p. 10.

PART 5

Positioning for Competitive Advantage

You are now at the point in the text where you can understand the environments facing the firm, the competitive strategy options available, and the resources needed to compete. Chapters 12–19 focus on developing merchandising and marketing plans in the . context of earlier decisions. This section covers such topics as merchandise and expense planning, buying and inventory management, pricing, and merchandise layout and presentation. Other topics covered include issues involved in physically handling and securing merchandise, developing a successful sales team, and developing the right sales-support services mix including credit, delivery, installation, and similar features.

The way in which the above decisions are structured depends on the positioning strategy of the firm, the level of resources available, the behavior of competitors, and similar factors. As an example, the merchandising and marketing plans of K mart are dramatically different from those of Neiman-Marcus.

12

Merchandise and Expense Planning

Inc., an operator of 310 mall toy stores (Playland, Playworld, and Circus World), decided not to compete head-on with warehouse-type stores in free-standing, highway locations, for example. The chairman said, "To buck them would take too much of the company's resources."

*H*igh-performance retailers such as Toys-R-Us are credited with having a "compelling competitive advantage." Consider also The Limited with its portfolio of businesses targeting specific market segments. Then there is Wal-Mart with its attention to secondary markets at discount prices. Stein Mart has captured the country's imagination with the off-pricing of upscale merchandise such as Liz Claiborne and Ralph Lauren in 40,000-square-foot stores from Denver to Jacksonville, Florida, where the company is headquartered. Each of these companies, differing in strategic approach, has carefully positioned itself to achieve a competitive advantage, which is the topic of this part of the text. In this chapter, we begin our discussion of competitive advantage by addressing merchandise and expense planning. Merchandise is the logical place to begin a discussion about competitive advantage in the marketplace, because without merchandise (or some offering), a retail establishment cannot exist. In addition to the merchandise-planning process, this chapter also includes a discussion of expense planning because the planning processes are interrelated and the purposes so similar.

LEARNING OBJECTIVES

After reading this chapter, you will be able to:

1. Define merchandise management.

2. Explain how merchandise strategies can be implemented to obtain competitive advantage.

3. Discuss merchandise management and develop an understanding of the mechanics of merchandise planning.

4. Describe expense planning as a way to balance income and outgo in a firm.

Dayton-Hudson is recognized as a leader in **merchandise planning and management** in the department store field (Dayton's is in Minneapolis and Hudson's is in Detroit). We are thus using that firm's concept of strategic planning within which merchandise management fits as an illustration.

Merchandise Management— The Management of Change

The Dayton-Hudson Corporation manages change through its strategic planning process. Management must recognize change and identify it in a way that is compatible with the firm's merchandising strategies.

Dayton-Hudson's corporate philosophy is based on providing value as defined by the customer. Management believes that customers look for the following five elements in deciding where to shop:[1]

1. *Dominance*—having the best assortment possible in the merchandise categories carried in the stores.
2. *Quality*—not only in the merchandise, but in the management, service, and shopping environment.
3. *Fashion*—change with timeliness and direction—applies to apparel, books, and, in fact, every item sold.
4. *Convenience*—respect for customers' time—easy-to-shop, hassle-free shopping.
5. *Price*—strive for competitive prices and to define what that means to customers.

Dayton-Hudson's merchandising philosophy is based on these five elements of customer value. An integral part of their merchandising process consists of five phases:

1. *Testing*—when buyers stock up on a small test quantity of a new item.
2. *Incoming*—when (and if) the test item starts catching on.
3. *Prepeak*—when the item's popularity is still growing.
4. *Postpeak*—when the rate of growth begins to decline.
5. *Outgoing*—when the customer has lost interest.

This process clearly indicates the importance of identifying merchandise trends and responding to them quickly. Retailers must be extremely alert to the particular phase of the merchandise trend so that inventories can be adjusted accordingly. In fact, merchandising planning is managing change, particularly meeting the changing needs (value changes) of customers, and interpreting the trends and adapting to the volatile elements of customer value.

A large part of this chapter is directed toward the merchandise plan at the department or classification level. The departmental buyer prepares six-month merchandise plans within the bounds of the firm's corporate mission and strategic plan. The technical nature of the plan, however, may cause students as well as practitioners to lose sight of the "big picture." We make this point to remind you of the strategic perspective that underlies merchandise planning.

The merchandise plan would be referred to as the "product plan" in perhaps all nonretailing companies. We may at times use the "product" designation, but tradition dictates the use of "merchandise" plan or planning. Practicing retailers do not speak of "product planning" as they prepare their plans. Still, merchandise management *is* the management of the product component of the marketing mix.

Merchandising Philosophies: Capitalizing on the Momentum of Change

The following examples illustrate major retailing efforts to understand, anticipate, and capitalize on the momentum of change through implementation of their individual merchandising philosophies.

Merchandise Composition Adjustments

Sears Roebuck & Co. Sears, in an attempt to turn around sagging retail sales, introduced over 100 new or improved items in 1986. Sears promoted these new items as "New Century" products, in conjunction with the company's 100th anniversary. A merchandising executive explained the move by saying that offering more of the same isn't good enough anymore.

The New Century products include a gel-like, no-splatter paint that turns to liquid when applied by roller, a line of men's socks that are guaranteed not to sag, and a projection television set that can be viewed from the side.[2]

K mart. Bernard M. Fauber, chairman of K mart, described the company's spirit as "change, adaptation, innovation." The publisher of *Chain Store Age* says that K mart is not only responding to, but in many ways is creating change as part of a competitive strategy for the 80s. K mart is making many changes in merchandising programs and operating strategies. Reports are that the changes have generated positive results. K mart is placing itself in a better position to cater to upscale customers with *upscale merchandise*. Concurrently, motivated as are most retailers by competition, K mart is emphasizing productivity of existing units and has committed a capital expenditure of $2 billion over five years which will include aggressive expansion of the following merchandise categories: home electronics centers; nutrition and health care departments; home centers; Kitchen Korners; bed and bath departments; wood and brass shops; and craft centers.[3]

B. Dalton Booksellers. B. Dalton, the 700-unit bookstore chain, is experimenting with a new merchandising program—a 1,500-square-foot, store-within-a-store computer software department. The merchandise-mix expansion initially will concentrate on software for the big four personal computers—Apple, IBM, Commodore-64, and Atari—in a downtown location which serves a broad demographic mix. Minneapolis was chosen as the pilot site. The B. Dalton stores have carried software for some time, but the new concept is a significant departure from anything the company has done in the past, according to the vice president of software marketing. Management investigated both free-standing stores and setting up departments in existing bookstores. Management is convinced that bookstores "present the best opportunity to be successful in this business because of their base in computer books and existing traffic base."[4]

Merchandising Philosophical Adjustments

Differing from the foregoing illustrations, the following represent changes in philosophical positions assumed by management.

Licensing

Licensing is an arrangement in which the *licenser* or owner of a "property" (the concept to be marketed) joins with a *licensee* (the manufacturer of the licensed product) and attempts to sell to retail buyers who offer the merchandise through retail organizations. Licensing is an important retail merchandising strategy.

Licensing is gaining widespread acceptance as a merchandising strategy among retailers because it provides the opportunity to capture a market whose customer is younger, richer, better educated, and willing to pay more than the average consumer for what he or she wants.[5] The challenge for the merchant working in the licensing markets is to choose the right ones, weed out the weak ones, and cut back on those that are always popular but may, from time to time, lose momentum.

When considering licensing as a merchandising strategy, retailers must evaluate the opportunity in terms of the partnership that must evolve. The licensee who offers the property must be strong, have a good product, and provide sufficient advertising and marketing effort for the offering. The industry cites Care Bears as an example of a phenomenal success which was supported by an extensive advertising program and sound plans for perpetuating demand via new product introductions over time.

Private-Label versus National-Brand Strategy

One of the most perplexing problems facing merchants today is the optimal balance between private labels and national brands. **Private labels** are owned by a retailer and are sold only by that owner. An example is Sears' Die-Hard Batteries. *National brands,* on the other hand, are often called "manufacturer" labels or brands and are owned by a manufacturer and can be sold to whomever the owner desires. General Motors' Delco Battery is a national brand. The issue is not limited to the general merchandise sector of retailing. The grocery and drug trades, for example, have struggled with such decisions for many years. In all merchandise categories and lines of trade, the position of the ideal mix is critical. Additionally, the drug and

National Brand. (Courtesy of Dillards)

National Brand. (Courtesy of Dillards)

Chapter 12 Merchandise and Expense Planning

grocery trade face the *generic* program issues. **Generics** are unbranded merchandise offerings which carry only the designation of the product type on the package, such as "salt." Retailers promote private-label programs to (1) defend themselves against off-price and outlet-store competition, (2) serve as a protection against fickle behavior of consumers as they react to changing acceptance of designer and/or manufacturer labels, (3) offer an alternative as the up-scale catalog companies feature virtually all competitive national labels, (4) guarantee some market exclusivity, (5) achieve a degree of control over merchandising programs, and (6) protect their profit margins.

THE MECHANICS OF MERCHANDISE PLANNING

This section of the chapter focuses on the planning component of merchandise management. The other element of the total management process is, of course, control. (We address the control aspect in Chapter 20 as a part of the evaluation of performance.) Merchandise planning includes those activities which are needed to ensure a balance between inventories and sales. Control efforts provide information on how effective the planning has been.

Essential Terms   Defining certain terms is necessary here. A *product* (or item) is what the retailer is selling—a physical object, such as a dress, or a service, such as dry cleaning. The **product line** includes all of the products or services offered by a retail firm.

Product lines are typically defined in terms of variety and assortment. **Variety** (also known as classifications or categories by some organizations) means the different kinds of merchandise (or services) in a product line. For example, the product line of a superstore would include such varieties as meat, bakery goods, dry groceries, frozen foods, paper products, and health and beauty aids among many others. No natural relationships necessarily exist among the classifications.

Assortment means the range of choices (selection) available for any given classification in a product line. Assortment can also be defined as the number of stock-keeping units (SKUs) in a category. For example a 1-pound can of Maxwell House coffee is one SKU; a 2-pound bag of Chock Full O' Nuts coffee is another SKU. Do not confuse, however, the number of items with an SKU. In other words, a food store might have 100 cans of the 1-pound Maxwell House coffee, but this represents only one SKU.

Merchandise (or inventory) **turnover** is the number of times the average inventory of an item (or SKU) is sold, usually in annual terms. Turnover can be computed on a dollar basis in either cost or retail terms. Turnover can also be figured in units.

The major focus of this section is merchandise assortment planning, the purpose of which is to maintain *stock balance*—a balance between inventories and sales. Figure 12–1 is a diagram of the merchandise planning

FIGURE 12–1 HOW TO UNDERSTAND THE MERCHANDISE-PLANNING PROCESS

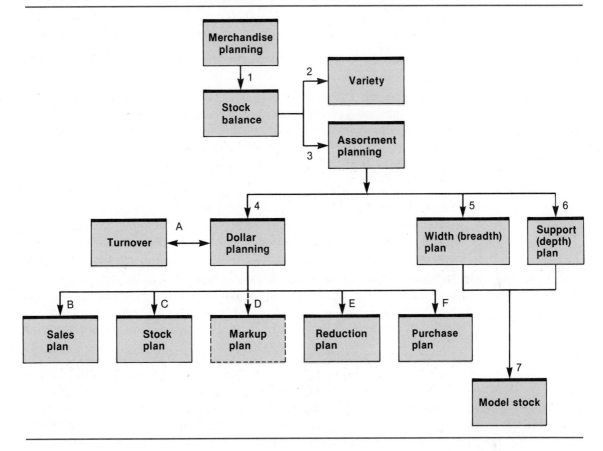

process. Reference will be made to this diagram throughout most of this chapter. (Note that points 2 and 3 have already been defined.)

Stock Balance

Retailers may consider merchandise assortment in three different ways, each of which requires a different kind of planning.

Ways to Look at Stock Balance

The three aspects of stock balance as shown in Figure 12–1 are: (1) width (or breadth), point 5; (2) support (or depth), point 6; and (3) total dollars, point 4.

Width (breadth). **Width** refers to the assortment factors necessary (1) to meet the demands of the market and (2) to meet competition. Referring to the coffee example used earlier, the following might be a width plan:

Brand		Types		Sizes	
(Folger's, Maxwell House, private)		(regular, instant, freeze-dried)		(3 in each kind of coffee)	
3 SKUs	×	3 = 9	×	9 = 81 SKUs	

Thus, 81 SKUs are needed to meet customer wants and what is offered by competition.

Support (Depth). Now that the number of SKUs has been decided upon, the next question is: How many units of merchandise are needed to support expected sales of each assortment factor? For example, how many 1-pound, Folger's, regular-grind cans of coffee versus 13-ounce, automatic-drip coffee cans are needed? The answer depends on the *sales importance* of each factor. If, for example, 10 percent of sales are in Folger's 1-pound, regular grind, the retailer may want 10 percent of **support** to be in that SKU. It sounds simple, but the art of merchandising enters here. Knowledge of the customer market, the image of the store and/or department, and other factors all enter into this decision. Only experience in planning the composition of stock will give retailers confidence in this activity.

Dollar Planning of Inventory. Assume that 1,000 cans of coffee are needed for the ideal stock level. This number, however, does not tell the manager how many *dollars* need to be invested in stock at any one time. Thus, the total dollar investment in inventory is the final way to look at stock balance.[6] Here *merchandise turnover* comes into play.

Figure 12–2 shows how to calculate turnover. For turnover goals to be meaningful, they must be based on merchandise groupings which are as much alike as possible. Planning on the basis of large, diverse merchandise groupings is unwise. Also, it is impossible to tell whether a particular turnover figure is good or bad unless it is compared to something. The retailer can compare turnover rates to average rates for various merchandise classifications or to the retailer's rates for past periods. The goal, however, is to have a turnover rate that is fast enough to give the retailer a good return on money invested in inventory, but not so fast that the retailer is always out of stock.

Figure 12–3 recaps what has been discussed thus far in the chapter. Students should understand the material before proceeding to the next section, which discusses how to set up a merchandise budget.

The Merchandise Budget

This section of the chapter focuses on merchandise planning in total dollars. Later sections look at planning in terms of width and support.

Approaches to Merchandise Planning

Traditionally, merchandise planning has been structured around either a *bottom-up* or a *top-down* approach. The bottom-up approach starts with

FIGURE 12-2 HOW TO UNDERSTAND STOCK TURNOVER

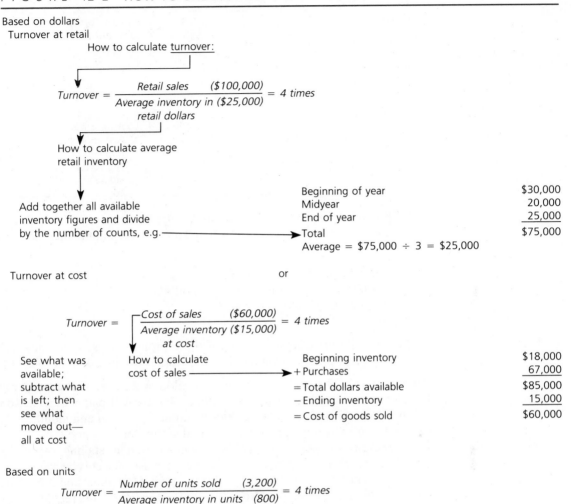

Based on dollars
Turnover at retail

How to calculate turnover:

$$Turnover = \frac{Retail\ sales \quad (\$100,000)}{Average\ inventory\ in\ (\$25,000)\ retail\ dollars} = 4\ times$$

How to calculate average retail inventory

Add together all available inventory figures and divide by the number of counts, e.g.

Beginning of year	$30,000
Midyear	20,000
End of year	25,000
Total	$75,000

Average = $75,000 ÷ 3 = $25,000

Turnover at cost   or

$$Turnover = \frac{Cost\ of\ sales \quad (\$60,000)}{Average\ inventory\ (\$15,000)\ at\ cost} = 4\ times$$

See what was available; subtract what is left; then see what moved out— all at cost

How to calculate cost of sales

Beginning inventory	$18,000
+ Purchases	67,000
= Total dollars available	$85,000
− Ending inventory	15,000
= Cost of goods sold	$60,000

Based on units

$$Turnover = \frac{Number\ of\ units\ sold \quad (3,200)}{Average\ inventory\ in\ units \quad (800)} = 4\ times$$

estimates at the classification level. These estimates are then combined into a departmental **merchandise budget** and finally into a total company plan. The top-down approach starts with a gross dollar figure established by top management. This dollar figure is then allocated to the various merchandise classifications. A third method of merchandise planning is the *interactive* approach. Interactive means that management sets broad guidelines, and the buying staff then follows the bottom-up approach with reviews by management. The interactive approach results in the most accurate merchandise plan.

FIGURE 12–3 **HOW TO LOOK AT STOCK BALANCE**

Ways to Look at Stock Balance	Examples	Things to Consider in Assortment Planning
Width (or breadth)	Number of brands, sizes, colors	1. What customers want.
		2. What competitors offer.
Support (or depth)	How many units are needed to support expected sales of each size, etc.	3. The sales importance of each size.
Total dollars	How many dollars are needed in inventory?	4. Look at turnover—
		a. Fast enough to get good return?
		b. Not so fast that out-of-stocks occur.

Items Included in the Merchandise Budget

The following items affect profit return and are included in the merchandise budget:

1. Sales: Figure 12–1, point 4B.
2. Stock (inventory): Figure 12–1, point 4C.
3. Reductions: Figure 12–1, point 4E.
4. Purchases: Figure 12–1, point 4F.

Figure 12–4 presents a diagram of these profit factors. Reference will be made to this diagram as each of these factors is discussed in more detail.

Sales planning. The beginning point in developing a merchandise budget is the sales plan. Note from Figure 12–4 that sales are first planned by season and then by month. In discussing sales planning by season and month, let's assume we are planning a merchandise budget for sporting goods.

By season. A *season* is the typical planning period in retailing, especially for fashion merchandise. Assume that the merchandise budget is being planned for the 1989 spring season (February, March, April, May, June, and July). The retailer would start planning in November 1988. The factors the retailer needs to consider in developing this seasonal plan are given in Figure 12–5.

In planning seasonal sales, the retailer begins by looking at last year's sales for the same period. Assume sales were $15,000 for the spring of 1988. Too many retailers at this point merely use the past period's figure as their sales forecast for the planning period. However, recent sales trends should be considered. For example, if sales for the 1988 fall season have been running about 5 percent ahead of fall 1987 and this trend is expected to continue, the retailer would project spring 1989 sales to be $15,750 ($15,000 × 1.05 = $15,750).

But the retailer cannot stop here. Now he or she must look at *forces outside the firm* which would have an impact on the sales forecast. For example, the retailer's projections would be affected if a new sporting goods store opened next door, carrying similar assortments (especially if this new

FIGURE 12–4 SCHEMATIC DIAGRAM OF MERCHANDISE BUDGET

	Components to Be Budgeted					
	Sales		Stock	Reductions		Purchases
	Season	Month		Season	Month	
Quantitative (factual) data						
Qualitative (subjective) data: trends and environmental factors						

FIGURE 12–5 DIAGRAM OF THE SALES BUDGET, 1989

	Sales	
	Season	By Month
Information available for planning	1. Sales for spring 1988. 2. Recent trends in sales. 3. Check trend against published trade data.	1. Sales percentages by month, 1988. 2. Check distribution against published trade data.
Judgment applied in certain issues	1. Factors outside the store such as new competition. 2. Internal conditions such as more space available.	1. Factors outside the store such as new competition. 2. Internal conditions such as more space available.

store was part of a national chain with excellent management), or a major manufacturer in the community were planning a large expansion. Next the retailer must look at *internal conditions* which might affect the sales forecast. Moving the sporting goods classification to a more valuable location within the store is an example of an internal condition.

Exact numbers cannot be placed on all of these external and internal factors. Retailers must, however, use judgment and incorporate all factors into the sales forecast. Assume that the retailer has decided sales should increase by 10 percent. The sales plan for the 1989 spring season is now $16,500 (15,000 × 1.10 = $16,500).

By month. The planned seasonal sales must now be divided into monthly sales. Figure 12–5 presents those factors which must be considered.

Again, the starting point is spring 1988. Assume the following sales distribution by month for this season: February—10 percent; March—20 percent; April—15 percent; May—15 percent; June—30 percent; and July—

10 percent. Further assume that the retailer has considered all internal and external factors that would affect this distribution and has decided that no adjustments need to be made. Based on this breakdown, the season's sales plan by month for spring 1989 would look like that in Figure 12–6.

Stock Planning. The next step in developing the merchandise budget is to plan stock (inventory) levels by month. In planning monthly stock needed to support monthly sales, several different techniques can be used depending upon the characteristics of the merchandise. For example, the **weeks-of-supply method** is a good approach to planning stock levels for staple goods. The **stock-to-sales ratio method** is used to plan monthly stock levels for fashion merchandise and for highly seasonal merchandise. The stock-to-sales ratio method could be used for sporting goods. Figure 12–7 is a guide to planning monthly inventory levels.[7]

To determine beginning-of-the-month (BOM) inventory, the retailer multiplies the month's planned sales figure by the month's stock–sales ratio figure. For example, as shown in Figure 12–6, planned sales for February are $1,650. If the retailer knows from past experience and industry trade data that 4.7 times more dollars in inventory than planned sales are needed, the beginning of the month inventory for February would be $7,755 ($1,650 × 4.7 = $7,755). The 4.7 figure is the stock–sales ratio figure for the month of February.[8]

To figure the average stock–sales ratio, divide the turnover figure into 12 (the number of months in a year). For example:

If Turnover Is:	Divide Turnover into 12 (number of months in year)	Then Average Stock Sales Ratio Is
4.0	12 ÷ 4.0 =	3.0
2.5	12 ÷ 2.5 =	4.8
30.0	12 ÷ 30.0 =	.4

As one can see, the *lower* the turnover rate, the *higher* the stock–sales ratio.

Figure 12–8 provides information on needed monthly BOM stock for spring 1989, using planned monthly sales for spring 1989 from Figure 12–6 and the monthly stock–sales ratios for past years. In reality, the retailer would use judgment in deciding whether to use last year's monthly stock–sales figures or whether any conditions exist that would require them to be changed.

One additional point. The end-of-the-month (EOM) inventory for a particular month would be the BOM inventory for the following month. Refer to Figure 12–8. The BOM inventory for February is $7,755. The EOM inventory for February would be $13,860 (the BOM inventory for March).

Reductions Planning. Reductions are anything other than sales which reduce inventory value.

SPRING SALES PLAN, 1989

Month	Percent of Total Season's Business in 1988	×	Season's Sales Forecast	=	Planned Sales for Months of 1989 Season
February	10		$16,500		$ 1,650
March	20		16,500		3,300
April	15		16,500		2,475
May	15		16,500		2,475
June	30		16,500		4,950
July	10		16,500		1,650
Total	100				$16,500

DIAGRAM OF INVENTORY BUDGET, 1989 (by month)

Concrete information available for planning	1. Stock–sales ratios based on past history 2. Trade stock–sales ratios or your own performance
Judgment applied to planning	1. Compare actual turnover with turnover goal

BOM STOCK, SPRING 1989

Month	Planned Sales	×	Stock–Sales Ratio	=	Planned BOM Stock
February	$ 1,650		4.7		$ 7,755
March	3,300		4.2		13,860
April	2,475		4.3		10,640
May	2,475		4.4		10,890
June	4,950		3.4		16,830
July	1,650		6.9		11,385
Total	$16,500				$71,360

Employee discounts are reductions. If an item sells for $100 and employees receive a 20 percent discount, the employee pays $80. The $80 is recorded as a sale. The $20 reduces the inventory dollar amount but is *not* a sale. It is an employee discount—a reduction.

Shortages (shrinkage) are reductions. A shoplifter takes a $500 watch from a jewelry department. Inventory is reduced by $500 just as if it were a sale. But no revenues come from shoplifting. If a salesperson steals another watch (internal pilferage), the results are the same. A $1,000 watch is received into stock and marked $500 by a clerical error. Fewer inventory dollars are in stock than the retailer thinks.

Markdowns are reductions, and are the only type of reductions we will focus on.[9] For example, assume a $25 tennis racket does not sell during the season and is marked down to $15. The $10 markdown is counted as a reduction of inventory and only $15 is counted as a sale.

Why plan reductions as a part of the merchandise budget? Note from Figure 12–8 that a planned BOM stock of $13,860 for March is needed to support March sales of $3,300 (with a 4.2 stock–sales ratio). However, suppose that the retailer's reductions during February amount to approximately $5,000. The EOM inventory in February (BOM-March) is $5,000 less than if no reductions had been taken. So, reductions must be planned and accounted for so the retailer will have sufficient BOM inventory to make planned sales.

Assume that reductions for the spring season in the department are planned at 8 percent or $1,320 ($16,500 seasonal sales × .08). Figure 12–9 shows how to plan the monthly reductions using historical monthly patterns. Reductions normally vary by month.

Planned Purchases. Up to this point, the retailer has determined planned (1) sales, (2) stock, and (3) reductions. The next step in developing the merchandise budget is to plan the dollar amount of purchases on a monthly basis. Planned purchases are figured as follows:

A. We *need* dollars of purchases to ——————→	Make sure we have enough retail EOM inventory to "be in business" the following month.
	Make sure we have enough to cover our sales plan.
	Take care of our planned reductions.
B. We *have* dollars to contribute to the above needs in the form of ——————→	Retail BOM inventory.

FIGURE 12–9 **PLANNED REDUCTIONS, SPRING 1989**

Month	Planned Sales	Planned Percentage Reductions (8 percent season)	Amount of Reductions
February	$ 1,650	20%*	$ 264
March	3,300	10	132
April	2,475	10	132
May	2,475	10	132
June	4,950	20	264
July	1,650	30	396
Total	$16,500	100%	$1,320

* 20% × $1,320 = $264, etc.

Stated more concretely:

$$\textit{Planned purchases} = \textit{Planned EOM stock} + \textit{Planned sales} \\ + \textit{Planned reductions} - \textit{Planned BOM stock}$$

To calculate planned purchases for March, look at Figures 12–8 and 12–9 to get the needed information.

Planned purchases	=	$10,640	(EOM March or BOM April)	(Figure 12–8)
		+ 3,300	(Planned sales, March)	(Figure 12–9)
		+ 132	(Planned reductions, March)	(Figure 12–9)
	=	$14,072	(Dollar *needs*, March)	
		− 13,860	(BOM March—what you *have*)	(Figure 12–8)
	=	$ 212		

One additional point. Purchases are planned in terms of *retail* dollars. However, when buying merchandise, the buyer must think in terms of the *cost* of merchandise. Thus, it is necessary to convert the planned purchase figure at retail to a cost figure. This conversion process will be explained in detail in Chapter 14. At this point simply remember: To convert retail dollars to cost dollars, multiply retail dollars by the complement of the initial retail markup. For example, assume that planned purchases for a given month are $1,000 at retail, and that the planned initial markup is 40 percent of retail. To convert retail dollars to cost dollars, multiply $1,000 by 60 percent, the complement of the planned initial markup. (100 percent − 40 percent = 60 percent.) Thus planned purchases at cost would be $600 ($1,000 × .60 = $600).

We have now worked through the dollar merchandise-planning process.[10] However, as Figure 12–1 shows, the retailer still needs to plan the width and support factors of stock balance (points 5 and 6). The following sections of the chapter describe how to plan these parts of the merchandise budget.

Planning Width and Support of Assortments

Now that the retailer knows how much to spend for stock, a decision still must be made on (1) what to spend the dollars for (width) and (2) in what amounts (support). The goal here is to set up a **model stock** (Figure 12–1, point 7). A model stock is the retailer's best prediction of the assortment needed to satisfy customers.

The Width Plan

Figure 12–10 is a model stock plan for a sweaters classification in a sporting goods department. Assume that only two customer-attracting features are important—synthetic and natural fibers. Even though the illustration is simple, it shows that to offer customers only *one* sweater in each assortment-*width* factor (in both synthetic and natural fibers), 270 sweaters (2 × 5 × 3 × 3 × 3) are needed (column 1 of Figure 12–10).

FIGURE 12–10 MODEL STOCK OF SWEATERS

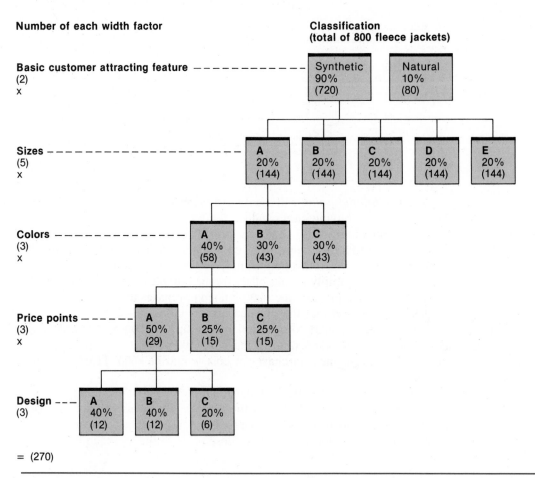

Column 1   Column 2

Number of each width factor   **Classification**
                                           (total of 800 fleece jackets)

Basic customer attracting feature — — — — — — — — — — | Synthetic 90% (720) | Natural 10% (80) |
(2)
x

Sizes — — — — — — — — — — — — — — — — — — | A 20% (144) | B 20% (144) | C 20% (144) | D 20% (144) | E 20% (144) |
(5)
x

Colors — — — — — — — — — — — — | A 40% (58) | B 30% (43) | C 30% (43) |
(3)
x

Price points — — — — — — | A 50% (29) | B 25% (15) | C 25% (15) |
(3)
x

Design — — — | A 40% (12) | B 40% (12) | C 20% (6) |
(3)

= (270)

Note: The percentage in each factor is the expected importance of that assortment factor. Numbers in parentheses represent the share of the 800-sweater total; for example, 90% × 800 = 720, 20% × 720 = 144, and so on.

The Depth Plan

The depth plan involves deciding how many sweaters are needed in each of the five assortment factors (Figure 12–10). Assume that 800 are needed for one turnover period. (If turnover is to be 3, then 800 sweaters are needed for 4 months—12 months divided by 3 = 4.) Also remember that the retailer is planning dollars at the same time as assortments. Thus, the amount of dollars will affect support.

If the retailer believes that 90 percent of sales will be in synthetic fibers then 720 sweaters will be needed (800 × .90 = 720). Following Figure 12–

10, one sees that the retailer will have 144 of size A, 58 in color A, 29 at price point A, and 12 in design A.

The Art of Planning. The foregoing illustration of the formulation of the width and support (model stock in units) appears to be a rather routine approach to planning. In fact, the decisions as to the percentage relationships among the various assortment factors are based on many complex factors relating to store objectives and to the merchandising "art" of retailing. Obviously, in planning the assortment width factors, the entire merchandising philosophy and strategic posture of management assume critical importance. The factors would be significantly different for a classification in a unit of Neiman-Marcus than for the same classification in a K mart outlet. The Neiman-Marcus merchandiser would consider the most unusual styles and fashion colors. Also, price points would greatly exceed those of K mart.

In other words, the total image management wants the store to project and the strategy assumed to accomplish the objectives affect decisions on width factors and the relative importance of each. Certainly the target market of the store affects planning decisions. Environmental conditions of the planning period will affect the factors as well. For example, as technological advances in textile fibers allowed more vibrant colorfast materials to enter the menswear industry, the width of offerings was expanded. The technology was, of course, a response to changing lifestyles, which dictated a more fashion-conscious male market for sportswear in general; also, changing styles of living and utilization of time for such activities as tennis and golf were reflected in sportswear offerings.

We have focused on the "how to" rather than the "what" and "why," because of the artistic and creative nature of merchandising, the immense variability among differing types of merchandise classifications, and especially because of the virtual impossibility of "teaching" the *art* of merchandising. Our major concern is that you appreciate how the operating and the creative aspects of merchandise planning relate.

EXPENSE PLANNING

The final objective of this chapter is to introduce expense planning following the analysis of merchandise planning. As noted, the reason for the inclusion of the former here is the close relationship and process of the two acts of budgeting. Expenses need to be forecast for a specific period just like the retailer would for the merchandise budget. The main purpose of merchandise budgeting is to maintain a balance between inventories and sales. The main purpose of expense budgeting is to balance planned expenses with planned income. Effective management of expenses can have a profound effect on profits.

Think of income as "maintained markup" (discussed in Chapter 14). The maintained markup must cover operating expenses and profits. Maintained markup is the difference between retail sales and the cost of sales. The following diagram shows these relationships.

Maintained markup covers:	
Expenses	$15,000
+	
Profit	5,000
Cost	$80,000

Sales $100,000

If expenses were $17,000, for example, instead of the planned $15,000, profits would be cut to $3,000. That would probably not be enough to satisfy the retailer as a return on investment. Thus it is important to plan and control expenses because of the impact they have on profits.

Expense Classification

Essential to the process of expense management is a system of expense classification. Ideally, the retailing industry should adopt a uniform method of expense classification, but this is not likely to happen. Philosophies differ, organizations are diverse in size, and merchandise varies. Major trade associations do, however, attempt standardization. The three major classifications are natural, functional, and expense center.

Natural

The Supermarket Institute recommends the following natural classification for its members:

— Labor expense.
— Advertising and promotion expense.
— Trading stamp expense.
— Store supply expense.
— Store occupancy expense (rent and utilities).
— Equipment depreciation or rental cost expense.
— Maintenance and repair expense.
— All other store expenses.

This system is appropriate for small retail stores wherein management is in continuous contact with all the operations and is involved with few transactions.

Functional

The functional system identifies the *purpose* of an expense, whereas the natural classification system focuses on its *nature*. The main functions promoted by the National Retail Merchants Association historically are:

— Administration.
— Occupancy.

— Publicity.
— Buying.
— Selling.

The medium-sized store, in particular, can benefit from a combination of the natural and functional systems.

Expense Center Accounting

Expense center accounting is a development of the mid-1950s. The appropriate natural expenses become a part of the expense center approach to classification. An example of the system promoted by the National Retail Merchants Association follows:

— Credit and collection (expense center).
  — Payroll.
  — Services purchased.
  — Bad debts.
  — Equipment costs.
  — All others.

Allocation of Expenses and Budgeting

The allocation of store expenses to various departments or classifications is critical if management is to know the profitability of specific subdivisions. Why isn't gross margin an adequate measure of operating effectiveness for a department or, for that matter, for the store? The reason is that departments with identical sales and margins may have different operating costs. For this reason, as many expenses as possible should be charged to a specific department.

The technical issue of expense allocation procedures is not addressed here. Our purpose, instead, is to stress that expense management is as important as merchandise management. Just as the retailer must plan for necessary merchandise, management must also plan for required expenditures. Expenses must be forecast for a specific period as is merchandise. The principal connection between the two budgets is that both are based on planned sales. The expense budget period coincides with the planning cycle of the merchandise budget.

Realistically, small stores seldom have even informal expense budgets, just as they seldom have formal merchandise plans. To the unsophisticated small retailer, expense management simply means "cut expenses."

Any merchant, however, regardless of size, is capable of utilizing trade associations, buying offices, vendors, noncompeting retailers, trade papers, and informed accountants as sources of the expense information needed for planning. The "reasons" for not planning expenses appear to be excuses, rather than realistic impediments.

The major purpose of merchandise management is to maintain a healthy balance between investments in merchandise inventories and planned sales. The major purpose of expense management is to balance planned income and planned expenses. Income, or maintained markup, must cover operating expenses and profit.

—— One major retailing company believes the following five elements are looked for by consumers in deciding where to shop: (1) dominance, (2) quality, (3) fashion, (4) convenience, and (5) price. They represent elements of customer value.

—— Merchandising planning is managing change, particularly meeting the changing needs of customers and interpreting the trends and adapting to the volatile elements of customer value.

—— Licensing is gaining widespread acceptance as a merchandising strategy among retailers because it provides the opportunity to capture a market whose customers are younger, richer, better educated, and willing to pay more than average consumers.

—— One of the most perplexing problems facing merchants is the optimal balance between private labels and national brands. The question affects all types of retailing.

—— The three aspects of stock balance (or ways to look at stock balance) are: (1) width or breadth, (2) support or depth, and (3) total dollars.

—— Merchandise planning can be structured around either a bottom-up or a top-down approach, and perhaps best by the interactive approach.

—— The following items affect profitability and are included in the merchandise budget: (1) sales, (2) inventory or stock, (3) reductions, and (4) purchases.

—— The main purpose of expense budgeting is to balance planned expenses with planned income. The three major expense classification systems are: (1) natural, (2) functional, and (3) expense center. Expense management is as important as merchandise management.

KEY TERMS

Assortment The range of choices available for any given classification in a product line or the number of stockkeeping units (SKUs) within a classification.

Generics Unbranded merchandise offerings carrying only the designation of the product type on the package.

Licensing A tool of marketing in which the licenser or owner of a "property" (the concept to be marketed) joins with a licensee (the manufacturer of the licensed product) and attempts to sell retail buyers.

Merchandise budget A plan of how much to buy in dollars per month by classification based on profitability goals.

Merchandise management The management of the product component of the marketing mix.

Merchandise planning Includes all the activities needed to plan a balance between inventories and sales.

Model stock plan A fashion merchandiser's best judgment about what demand will be at specific times of the year.

Product line All the products or services offered. (Also called merchandise lines.)

Private label (or private brand) The brand (or name or label) is owned by the retailer for exclusive use.

SKUs Stockkeeping units—the choices within an assortment (e.g., a pair of black hose, one-size-fits-all, is one SKU).

Stock/sales ratios Used in planning monthly stocks in relation to expected sales for the month.

Support The depth behind each assortment factor in a merchandise plan. Answers the "how many" question.

Turnover (also called stock or merchandise turnover) The number of times the average inventory is sold, usually in annual terms.

Variety (classification) The different kinds of goods that may be present in a product line.

Width The breadth of merchandise assortments; the choices available to the customer.

DISCUSSION QUESTIONS

1. By using examples, distinguish among the following: product, product line, variety, and assortment.
2. Describe the three points that go together in planning stock balance.
3. Explain "merchandise turnover"; indicate how it is useful in planning total dollars in inventory.
4. What factors must a retailer consider in deciding how many dollars to spend on inventory?
5. Discuss the following: sales planning, stock planning, reductions planning.
6. Explain the relationship between stock–sales ratios and turnover. How are stock–sales ratios used as a guide to stock planning in the merchandise budget?
7. What are reductions? Why should a retailer plan reductions as a part of the merchandise budget?
8. How does a retailer plan purchases? Give an example of the process.
9. Explain the difference in the purposes of merchandise budgeting and expense budgeting.
10. Discuss licensing and private label programs as merchandise strategies.
11. Explain SKUs.

PROBLEMS

1. If net sales for the season (6 months) are $48,000 and the average retail stock for the season is $21,000, what is the annual stock-turnover rate?
2. If cost of goods sold for the first four months of operation is $127,000 and average stock at cost for this same time period is $68,000, what is the annual stock-turnover rate?
3. Given the following figures, what is the stock-turnover rate for the season?

	Retail Stock on Hand	Monthly Net Sales
Opening inventory	$16,500	
End of: 1st month	16,450	$7,500
2nd month	16,000	6,900
3rd month	17,260	7,250
4th month	16,690	6,840
5th month	15,980	6,620
6th month	16,620	7,180

4. What is average stock if the stock-turnover rate is 4 and net sales are $36,000?
5. What is cost of goods sold if the stock-turnover rate is 2.5 and the average stock at cost is $8,700?
6. A new department shows the following figures for the first three months of operation: net sales, $150,000; average retail stock, $160,000. If business continues at the same rate, what will the stock-turnover rate be for the year?
7. Last year a certain department had net sales of $21,000 and a stock-turnover rate of 2.5. A stock-turnover rate of 3 is desired for the year ahead. If sales volume remains the same, how much must the average inventory be reduced (a) in dollar amount and (b) in percentage?
8. A certain department has net sales for the year of $71,250. The stock at the beginning of the year is $22,500 at cost and $37,500 at retail. A stock count in July showed the inventory at cost as $23,750 and at retail as $36,250. End-of-year inventories are $25,000 at cost and $38,750 at retail. Purchases at cost during the year amounted to $48,750. What is the stock-turnover rate (a) at cost and (b) at retail?
9. Given the following information for the month of July, calculate planned purchases:

Planned sales for the month	$43,000
Planned BOM inventory	60,250
Planned reductions for the month	1,200
Planned EOM inventory	58,000

10. Given the following information for the month of October, calculate planned purchases:

Planned sales for the month	$198,000
Planned EOM inventory	240,000
Stock–sales ratio for the month of October	1.2
Planned reductions for the month	3,860

11. Given the following figures, calculate planned purchases for January:

Stock on hand—January 1	$36,470
Planned stock on hand—February 1	38,220
Planned sales for January	21,760
Planned reductions for January	410

APPLICATION EXERCISES

1. Contact a local buyer of a line that interests you. If possible, do a full six-month merchandise plan for a specific merchandise classification. Utilize the text format for your process of planning. You will need to get information from the buyer. If such information is not available from the store, you may have to make certain assumptions to come up with your planned purchases.

2. Attention is given in the text to formal merchandise planning. Select some stores and find out how they handle this function. How much planning? Levels of sophistication? Does the degree differ by merchandise lines? See if you can develop some generalizations from your investigations.

CASES

1. Completing a Merchandise Line?

Philip North enjoys the best men's and boys' business in his community. His variety of merchandise includes suits and sportswear, as well as all furnishings (e.g., ties, shirts, and underwear). To complete his product line, he feels shoes are essential.

Question
1. Discuss the factors Philip must consider as he makes this strategic decision.

2. A New Product Category Grows into Separate Section?

"Travel irons, portable steamers, voltage converters, and compact personal care items are providing a passport to 'explosive' sales for some retailers and 'booming' successes for manufacturers." Retailers and manufacturers of the goods believe that the product category performs best in a section of its own. "There, impulse buying is encouraged and consumers shopping for a single item can be exposed to complete product lines that could otherwise have been overlooked if scattered throughout the housewares department."

At Dayton-Hudson, an entire travel department has been created to provide one-stop shopping for travel accessories. DH had such a fine Christmas season the prior year in travel-related items in the housewares department that the firm created an entire department with 26 to 80 square feet (depending on the size of the particular store in the organization) culled from products in the housewares department. Spokespersons from the firm are quick to explain that the new department is not an experiment in "cross-merchandising." (In cross-merchandising, products are duplicated in various departments.) Dayton-Hudson says that the look of the department continues to change as new fixtures are used and as new items are discovered to fit in. It is reported that the program is so popular that the stores have problems keeping sufficient stock on hand. The target market appears to be business travelers, vacation travelers, college students, and shoppers looking for that special gift for travelers. A representative from Norelco says, "Travel is booming." To meet that boom, Norelco has introduced color-coordinated, matching travel irons, steamers, converters, and adapters. Norelco believes that the yuppie is an important part of the market because of the lifestyle supported by significant disposable income and a preference for contemporary styling. A Sunbeam spokesperson indicated that their niche is working/traveling women in the 25-to-44 age group.

While the department store and manufacturers of travel-related products are enthusiastic, some discount store chains are less enthusiastic. They feel that a special travel section is not called for and have opted for adding more travel items to the housewares category, a conservative action.

Question

1. Refer to the discussion in the first part of this chapter entitled "merchandise management—the management of change" and see if you can relate the situation above to that discussion. Why do you think discount stores and department stores like Dayton-Hudson have differing opinions. Relate the issues in this case to products and product lines. Speculate as to why the merchants at Dayton-Hudson seemed to have trouble at the outset keeping the merchandise in stock. How can management make the decision about whether the expense associated with the new department is worth the effort involved?

Source: Based on "Sales in Travel Category Take Off," *Chain Store Age, General Merchandise Trends,* November 1985, pp. 38–39.

ENDNOTES

1. Kenneth A. Macke, "Managing Change: How Dayton-Hudson Meets the Challenge," *The Journal of Business Strategy* 4, no. 1 (1983), pp. 80–81; also George Lawson, Jr., Vice President, Corporate Development, Dayton Hudson Corporation, "Strategic Business Planning," National Retail Merchants Association 71st Annual Convention, January 1982.
2. Steve Weiner, "Sears Plans to Introduce New Products in Move to Reverse Retail-Sales Slump," *The Wall Street Journal,* August 22, 1985, p. 8.
3. Michael Bailenson, "Business Talk: K mart," *Chain Store Age, General Merchandise Edition,* June 1984, p. 7.
4. "B. Dalton Punches into Software Business," *Chain Store Age Executive,* May 1984, p. 14.
5. "Riding the Licensed Product Boom," *Chain Store Age, General Merchandise Edition,* April 1983, p. 31.
6. Obviously dollars invested in inventory relate to width and support. In fact, the dollars planned become the controlling decision. How many dollars the retailer has will determine investment in SKUs. But planning width, support, and dollars does not guarantee the optimal stock. Many of the questions about how well the planning is being carried out will be answered in Chapter 20—The Control Function.
7. Stock-to-sales ratios designate the amount of inventory necessary to support sales for a particular period of time (e.g., a month). This discussion assumes a "going concern" with "last year's" figures available. In a budget process for a new store, estimates/projections based on trade figures and/or experience are particularly valuable.
8. Readers may wonder why 4.7 times more dollars of inventory than sales is needed. This relates to the support factor. An example can help illustrate this point. If customers were individually predictable, that is if retailers needed only one jacket to satisfy each customer's demand, then they might get by with a one-to-one ratio. But people want to select from many colors, designs, fabrics, and so on. Thus, retailers need many more SKUs to support planned sales. The more fashion-oriented (or the less stable) the merchandise, the more stock is needed to support sales.
9. The planning of employee discounts and shortages is rather predictable, differing from markdowns. Retailers estimate the former based on historical data. Seldom will employee discounts and shortages vary from year to year in percentage terms as related to sales.
10. Chapter 20 discusses setting up a control system (open to buy) to measure how well the plan is working. Readers may want to look at that part of the book now.

13

Buying and Inventory Management

Liz the Whiz

The first commandment at Liz Claiborne, Inc. is "satisfy thy customer." The second is "support thy retailer." This philosophy has brought enormous success to Liz Claiborne, Inc. Liz Claiborne clothing is sold in more than 5,900 stores, including at least 200 department stores which account for 70 percent of the Claiborne business. Claiborne targets the working woman, that is, "the executive and professional career woman who is a little more updated in her taste level, as opposed to a very traditional customer who might wear structured suits and blouses with ties." Claiborne thoroughly understands her customer, her lifestyle, and the price she is willing to pay. The firm works closely with retailers to make sure the Claiborne clothing is effectively merchandised.

The retailer's first contact with the vendor is at the Claiborne showroom. All sales are made at that point. As many as 65 salespersons operate in the showroom. However, no sales force calls on store buyers. Claiborne is able to keep costs lower by not having a road sales force.

Frequent store visits are made by "travelers" who work with retail salespeople. The travelers seek to overcome the lack of experienced retail salespeople by holding seminars and clinics for store personnel to help them better understand Claiborne and its fashion point of view. Claiborne personnel, after visiting a store, submit a detailed report to the retailer indicating how they can improve the merchandising of the Claiborne line. They also provide detailed information that lists the names and style

Source: Based on Rayna Skolnik, "Liz the Whiz," *Sales and Marketing Management,* September 9, 1985, pp. 50–52.

numbers, by style groups, of every item in the line to help retailers in their merchandising efforts.

In the early 1980s, management started the Liz Claiborne Shops which retailers can install on their selling floors so that the items of clothing meant to be sold together can be displayed together. The self-contained shops are a time-saver for the customer.

*T*he retailing capsule illustrates the role of vendors and professional buyers in the retailers' success. Vendors can be a valuable source of information on market trends; they also can provide merchandising assistance, sales training, and assistance with inventory management. Buyers can be viewed as investment specialists. In their function, they invest at wholesale (cost) and plan to earn a profit on their investments (retail). Retail buyers can be responsible for literally millions of dollars in merchandise. They must be able to forecast demand for the merchandise, negotiate with vendors on a variety of issues such as price and transportation, and work as partners with the vendors to maximize the sale of the merchandise to the benefit of both the retailer and the vendor. This chapter discusses the roles of the buyer and vendor in retailer success and the responsibilities of the retailer in establishing strong vendor relationships.

After reading this chapter you will be able to:

1. Identify factors influencing the buying cycle.

2. List sources of merchandise for retailers.

3. Calculate desired inventory levels.

4. Describe alternatives in the selection of merchandise suppliers.

5. Explain how retailers negotiate price, discounts, datings, and transportation charges.

6. Discuss the key issues in inventory records management.

Because the responsibilities of the buyer are many and varied, buyers need certain qualifications to be good at what they do. The following quotation indicates some of the abilities a successful buyer must have:

Buyers must be merchandise *specialists*. They should be able to recognize quality, judge workmanship, and have knowledge regarding materials, color, and design. Although buyers should be able to appreciate the aesthetic appeal of merchandise, they must be prudent enough to buy what they think will sell rather than what might be in good taste in their opinion. . . . Experience plus a natural talent will aid buyers. . . .

Buyers must learn how to be traders. The profit margin of their departments will be bigger if they can negotiate low purchasing prices and take advantage of vendor helps as well. . . .

Buyers should be good managers. . . . Too often buyers get bogged down in paperwork or become too involved in the details of running their department. The ability to delegate authority . . . should be developed early in their careers. Otherwise they will soon find themselves on a treadmill leading nowhere.

A successful buyer must exhibit an uncommon amount of drive and a will to succeed. Buying is a highly competitive and exhausting job. Although the rewards are many, some persons cannot take the daily strain of meeting people, bargaining with vendors, placating customers, and pleasing superiors. Buyers are more subject to "ups and downs" than are persons in many other lines of endeavor. Buyers must be firm and decisive because quick decisions are part of their everyday lives. In order to cope with these tensions, buyers should enjoy conflict. People who are not aggressive and whose feelings are easily hurt will probably find that buying and merchandising are not for them.

Finally, buyers should possess personal integrity. Because they sign purchase orders amounting to hundreds of thousands of dollars, buyers are under great temptations to make "deals" with vendors. . . . Word quickly spreads if a buyer is on the "take," and professional reputations are easily ruined. High personal and business ethics cannot be measured in dollars and cents.[1]

THE BUYING FUNCTION[2]

The buyer is the operating manager in the merchandising division. This chapter focuses on the buying responsibility of this person. (The selling function is discussed in Chapter 17.)

Goals of Good Buying

For people not acquainted with retailing, the work of a buyer may seem to be a relatively simple one—finding and purchasing the needed merchandise at a good price. But there is more to buying than bargaining with vendors. Not only are there other functions to consider but good buying involves buying the right merchandise for customers:

— At the best price.
— In the right quantity.
— Of the right quality.
— From vendors who will be reliable and provide other valuable services.

Many considerations are involved in doing this thoroughly and competently. These are all described, in proper relationship, in the Buying Cycle.

THE BUYING CYCLE

1
Determining needs

WHAT do you need?
HOW much do you
    need?
Inventory, season,
    style, perishability

2
Select supplier

WHERE can you best
    obtain it?
Single vendor: No
    choice
Multiple vendors:
    Price, service,
    (delivery, credit,
    handling of
    problems, etc.)

4
Follow-up

HOW can I improve?
Review of present
    vendors
Search for new and
    better vendors

The Buying Cycle

3
Negotiate purchase

WHEN and HOW can you
    obtain it? and at
    WHAT price?
Purchase price, delivery
    date, single or
    multiple shipments,
    freight and packing
    expenses, guarantees,
    special purchases, etc.

The process of buying involves four major steps. They are:

1. *Determining needs.* The buyer must determine for each line of merchandise what will be needed until the next time the line is reviewed. Determining *what* is needed involves, for some items, merely looking at inventory and past sales. For other lines, it concerns risky decisions—*which* styles to select and *how much* of each to buy. One thing management doesn't want is a lot of merchandise in stock when a style is outmoded or the season is past.

2. *Selecting the supplier.* After determining the merchandise needs, the buyer must find a vendor(s) who can supply the merchandise. Some merchandise can be bought only from one vendor; in this case, the only decision to be made is whether to carry the line. For most merchandise, several suppliers are available. In these instances the buyer must evaluate price as well as service in terms of reasonable and reliable delivery, adjustment of problems, and help in emergencies and in other matters, such as credit terms, spaced deliveries, and inventory management assistance.

3. *Negotiating the purchase.* This crucial third step involves not only the purchase price but also quantities, delivery dates, single or multiple shipment deliveries, freight and packing expenses, guarantees on the quality of the merchandise, promotion and advertising allowances, special offers on slightly damaged materials or sell-outs, and so forth.

4. *Follow-up.* Finally, to improve service, the buyer must review the relationship with each vendor from time to time to determine if changes should be made. As necessary, a search for alternate or new suppliers should take place.

Determining Needs

Different types of merchandise require different techniques to determine what is needed. It is therefore important to recognize, for the various merchandise lines in the store, whether they are primarily *staples, seasonal items,* or *style* or *perishable items.* Most businesses carry some merchandise in each of these categories. Effective management of the buying function means planning the buying program and recordkeeping with the differences between these merchandise categories in mind.

The goal in each case, whether the merchandise is primarily staple, seasonal, style oriented, or perishable, is to establish or maintain inventory at the lowest possible level and still have a sufficient variety of colors, sizes, or models available from which customers can choose. Such a practice will minimize losses due to obsolescence and spoilage, while freeing capital which may be put to other worthwhile uses.

Forecasting Sales

Staples

Staple or semistaple **merchandise** is generally in demand year-round, with little change in model or style. Basic appliances, hardware, housewares, books, domestics, and basic clothing items like underwear and pajamas fall into this category. The staples in the store, even if the store is primarily a business of style or seasonal merchandise, not only bring extra profit but also serve as an incentive, bringing into the store customers who may then purchase some of the primary merchandise.

The important characteristic of staples is steady usage, enabling the buyer to order more of them whenever needed. Deciding how much to buy, therefore, concerns primarily:

1. *Sales trends.* If records are available which show how much of each staple sold during the past two or three months, and also how much of the same staple sold during the same period in the previous year, the buyer knows whether the item has increased in popularity or has remained the same. The buyer can then decide, if the trend is up, whether to buy more and increase average inventory, or whether to maintain the same sales trend without running out of stock.
2. *Profitability.* Items that bring a better return on investment in space and capital are the more desirable items to buy.
3. *Discounts.* These are usually available with quantity purchases.

The combination of these factors provides a general indicator of needs in staple merchandise.

Seasonal Merchandise

Seasonal merchandise, as implied, is in demand only at certain times of the year. Obvious examples include sleds, snow tires, bathing suits, sunglasses, lawn equipment, and patio furniture. Although some seasonal items can be secured during peak demand to replenish inventory, many are unavailable or cannot be obtained quickly enough at this time. Therefore, such merchandise is best bought well in advance of the season.

Because seasonal items are fast moving in season and slow moving or stagnant during the off-season, it is important to maintain the stock to satisfy this on-off movement. Determining needs for seasonal items (predicting, forecasting) relies heavily on *knowing* what customer demand for that item or merchandise line was in the past. One method of knowing previous customer demand on seasonal items is by maintaining a month-by-month tally of unit(s) sold, either by dollar value or amount (numbers). These records then can be examined on a yearly basis enabling the buyer to clearly see selling trends and make buying decisions accordingly.

One method of maintaining records is to use a separate sheet index card or computer record for *each* merchandise *item, group of items,* or the *entire line.* In the example below, note that in 1984 most of the sales on this item took place in April, and at the end of the season, 20 remaining items in inventory had to be sold below cost.

For the novice buyer who has no previous sales records to rely on, suppliers and their salespeople can serve as a good source of information for predictions.

Merchandise Item:	Sales Record				
	1984	1985	1986	1987	1988
January	—0—				
February	$50				
March	$700				
April	$2,200				
May	$1,000				
June	$300				
July through December	—0—				
Total units bought	300				
Sold below cost	20				

Where orders cannot be placed during the season, or where suppliers could delay shipments, good forecasting is of the utmost importance to help predict what quantity of each item will be needed for the season. Predictions can also include plans for a preseason sale which would entice customers to buy from the store rather than competitors. The forecast can also consider any end-of-season sales. If such late sales events are profitable, it may not be difficult to decide what quantities are needed. If such sales are not profitable, then the buyer has to estimate much more carefully so as not to be left with a large stock of slow-making or dead merchandise.

Unfortunately, there is no foolproof method of accurately predicting future sales. Usually, though, good prediction of future sales can be made from consideration of:

— Past experience with the movement of the merchandise.
— Records of previous sales.
— Length of the season.
— Planned selling price.
— Planned advertising and promotion effort, including sales.
— The extent to which there is an increase or decrease in competition.
— Predictions of consumer buying from trade journals.

These factors together can give a fairly good idea of the quantity of each item likely to sell during the upcoming season.

Style and Perishable Items

Items of style include such merchandise as fur coats, ladies' apparel, men's apparel, and sportswear. Stylish items are usually more expensive than staples and seasonals. Because the demand for any particular style tends to increase rapidly, then drop off rapidly, overbuying can have a disastrous effect on profits. Once a style is out, it is often difficult to sell it at a profit.

Style A

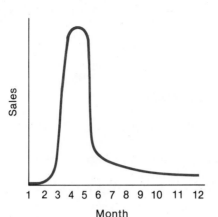

Style B

Style C

Style D

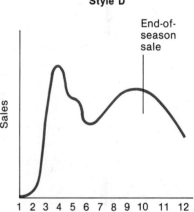

Perishable merchandise has similar characteristics. If management buys more than can be sold, some of it will begin to spoil and bring only a fraction of the normal price.

On those types of items where management has experienced sufficient difficulties in the past so that they feel they deserve detailed attention, management could plot the progress of different styles to see how they usually behave. A few examples of such graphs appear above. They can help to predict how much to buy and also when to buy.

When plotting graphs, it is important to note all special, significant events such as sales in the store and those of major competitors. These events also have to be planned or predicted and kept in mind when forecasting merchandise needs.

Although graphs may not predict sales very accurately, they usually will narrow the amount of buying error made on items on which they are used.

Sometimes, however, an overstock of nonseasonal goods occurs because of overbuying or because the items are either unstylish or of poor quality. In such a case, the amount of stock should be reduced as soon as possible to minimize the effect of any resulting loss.

Establishing Buying Guidelines

How much stock should be ordered? Why not enough merchandise for one month, two months, or even six months?

In some cases, product shelf life may be the determining factor. If the grocer stocked more than a two days' supply of muffins, the muffins would lose their freshness and the grocer would lose customers. Delivery is immediate. The grocer gives the order directly to the bakery truck driver, and the driver fills the order in minutes.

More often, there are many other factors to consider. Take the case of the retailer who may require two weeks to receive delivery from suppliers on most items. On an emergency basis, the retailer may be able to replenish inventory more promptly, but only by forfeiting quantity discounts or incurring extra delivery charges. For most items, it is better to accept normal delivery, taking full advantage of all available discounts and minimizing freight charges.

The length of time between order placement and receipt of goods is called **lead time.** If the lead time is two weeks, would it be sufficient to establish a minimum inventory level of a two weeks' supply? Probably not. If no order were placed until the supply of a certain item reached two weeks, there would probably be just enough stock on hand to cover expected sales until the order arrived. However, if anything went wrong (and it usually does), there would be a stockout before the order was received. An unexpectedly large request from a customer might not be filled because of insufficient inventory. A strike, shipping delays, manufacturing problems, or unforeseen weather conditions could seriously delay the arrival of the merchandise so that the stockout could last for several weeks. Therefore, most businesses maintain a **safety,** or cushion **stock** as protection against such occurrences.

The size of the safety stock will depend on the number and extent of the factors that could interrupt deliveries. Suitable guidelines have to be based on experience in the industry.

Additionally, many items require a **basic stock,** an amount sufficient to accommodate regular sales, offering customers a reasonable assortment of merchandise from which their selection can be made.

Assume that the lead time for a particular item is two weeks. The safety stock that the business wishes to maintain is four weeks' supply. Additionally, a one-week basic stock is required. The desired inventory level would be established as the sum of these factors:

	Lead time	2 weeks
+	Safety stock	4 weeks
+	Basic stock	1 week
=	Inventory level	7 weeks

What to Buy?

The desired inventory level should be considered an **order point.** Whenever the stock of an item falls below this point, it should be ordered.

For example, if a camera shop wishes to maintain a 10-week supply of film in inventory and average sales of a particular film type are 50 rolls per week, the order point is 500 (50 × 10 rolls). When inventory drops below 500 rolls, more film should be ordered.

How Much to Buy?

The quantity of film to purchase depends on the usual time between orders, called the **ordering interval.** In this way, sufficient supplies are maintained so that inventories between orders average out to the desired level.

A stock equal to expected sales during the camera shop's two-week order interval should be added to the order point to determine the **order ceiling.**

Order ceiling = Order point + Order interval sales
Order ceiling = 500 + (50 × 2)
Order ceiling = 600

An order quantity can then be determined as follows, assuming 450 rolls are on hand:

Order quantity = Order ceiling − Stock on hand
Order quantity = 600 − 450
Order quantity = 150 rolls

If an order for 50 rolls had already been placed, but had not yet been received, the present order should be *reduced* by the 50 rolls on order. The new order would then be 100 (150 − 50) rolls.

Review

Let us review the steps involved in establishing order quantities using a hardware store as an example. The store wants to maintain a basic tool stock equal to one week's sales and a safety stock of one week's sales for saws. Average weekly sales are three saws. Lead time for order placement and delivery is two weeks. Orders are placed every four weeks.

A desirable inventory level, or order point, is then calculated as follows:

Lead time	2 weeks
+ Basic stock	1 week
+ Safety stock	1 week
= Order point	4 weeks or 12 (4 × 3) saws

Whenever the supply of any tool drops to a four weeks' supply or below, an order should be placed.

To determine the order quantity, management must first calculate the order ceiling:

Order point	4 weeks
+ Order interval	4 weeks
= Order ceiling	8 weeks or 24 (8 × 3) saws

Assume that an order is being prepared for saws. Average weekly sales are 3 saws, and the stock on hand is 10 saws. This is below the order point of 12 (4 × 3) saws.

The order quantity would then be calculated as follows:

Order ceiling	24
− Stock on hand	10
= Order quantity	14

The hardware store should order 14 saws. If any are already on order, the outstanding order quantity should be subtracted.

SELECTION OF SUPPLIERS

Some suppliers may be excellent, some acceptable, and some less than desirable. The first step toward replacing undesirable ones, or selecting suppliers for new merchandise, is to obtain a list of those to consider. Awareness of available suppliers and their services will place the buyer in a position to choose the best one.

Sources of information concerning suppliers are plentiful. They include:

1. *Salespeople.* Salespeople of existing suppliers often provide excellent information concerning possible sources of supply. Many are well informed of alternative sources of noncompeting lines, and they can often suggest new services and new products. Since they call on many different businesses, salespeople are also a good source of information concerning merchandise selection of similar stores in different parts of their territories. All of this information is available to alert, openminded buyers who know how to obtain it without devoting too much time to vendor representatives who call on them.

2. *Trade magazines.* General and specialized trade journals often contain advertisements placed by suppliers and articles that provide clues to desirable new sources.

3. *Business contacts.* Often customers or other business contacts may be able to provide useful information concerning potential suppliers.

4. *Trade exhibits.* These provide an excellent opportunity to see a variety of new products and compare similar products of different manufacturers.

5. *Yellow Pages.* The Yellow Pages in the telephone directory contain listings of local suppliers.

How to Make Market Contacts

Vendor Contacts

Vendor contact may begin through catalogs and price lists. These documents are available to all potential retailers.

Another source of vendor contact is the sales representative who calls on the retailer. In such lines as groceries and drugs where item turnover is very fast, salespersons may call on the retailer almost weekly. For fashion lines, the representative will call on a seasonal basis.

The Central Market.   A **central market** is a place where a large number of suppliers concentrate. It may be a large, single building such as the Merchandise Mart in Chicago. New York City is still the primary central market for many types of merchandise, especially women's fashion goods. Chicago and High Point, North Carolina, are well known for furniture.

Not all central markets are permanent. For example, the fine-jewelry central market is held in New York periodically—in January and July. Such central market events are called trade shows.

Resident Buying Offices.   Resident buying offices are becoming more important and are located in central markets. Resident buyers are experts in market information and represent many retailers. They remain in constant contact with central market suppliers and know what is new, what is ''hot,'' and when prices are changing, as shown in Figure 13–1. They have market ''clout'' because they represent many buyers. The most common types of resident buying offices are shown in Table 13–1.

FIGURE   13–1

Halston, Garolini, Bernardo, Beene Bag, Anne Klein, Evan Picone—designer names; quality resources; a buyer-merchandising program. (Courtesy The May Department Stores Company)

TYPES OF RESIDENT BUYING OFFICES

Type of Office	Characteristics	Example
Cooperatively owned office	An office owned by the stores it serves with directors chosen from member firms	Frederick Atkins
Independent buying office	An office not owned by any retail store or group. It sets its own operating policies and often handles hard and soft goods	Felix Lilienthal & Co.
Divisional resident office	An office owned and operated by a retail chain or similar multi-unit retailer	Associated Dry Goods Corporation

The key role of resident buying offices is to provide advice and information, not only when the buyer is in the market but also when the buyer cannot be present. The offices range from one-person operations to large firms which may provide space and secretarial help for the buyer, and in fact become the buyer's "home away from home."

Selecting the Supplier

Factors to be considered in determining the best supplier are:

— Price and discounts.
— Quality.
— Reliability.
— Services.
— Accessibility.

1. *Price* is the most important consideration in the selection of a supplier, provided that quality and service are equivalent to that of other vendors. Price has many dimensions since it includes quantity discounts; special allowances; the chance to buy special lots, seconds, or sellouts; and dating of invoices.
2. *Quality,* and assurance that quality is always the same, is almost as important as price and closely linked to it. Obviously, in selecting a supplier buyers want to be certain that they will rarely, if ever, receive a poor-quality shipment.
3. *Reliability* of delivery from a supplier is important as unreliable delivery can create problems of stockout which result in sales loss. In addition, slow or unreliable delivery also requires the buyer to maintain larger average inventories which results in increased carrying costs. A good supplier will be reliable when the store has a sudden emergency and needs some quick supplies and will protect the store when there are shortages of material due to a strike or disaster.

4. *Services* suppliers might provide are many and include: spaced deliveries; allowing the buyer to purchase a larger quantity than the store may immediately handle, thus giving the advantage of **quantity discounts;** recycling of packaging to reduce overall freight and packing expenses; providing advertising and promotional materials and displays to help promote merchandise; and give-aways, such as literature and bags for the customers. In some industries, suppliers will offer inventory services to retailers. Usually these are provided for a small fee, but they can be quite valuable in helping the retailer manage inventory with greater efficiency.
5. *Accessibility* is another factor on which suppliers should be judged. It is often important to personally contact the supplier concerning special problems that may arise. A supplier difficult to contact is clearly not as desirable as one easy to reach.

Keeping these factors in mind can help to:

— Avoid mistakes in selecting suppliers.
— Compare vendors vying for the retailers' business.
— Provide a firm foundation for thorough negotiations.

Getting the Best Price from Vendors

Group Buying. **Group** (or cooperative) **buying** is the joint purchase of goods by a number of noncompeting, nonaligned stores such as independent department stores in different areas of a state. By combining their orders into one large order, the stores hope to get lower prices. These group arrangements can be beneficial in other ways, too, because the noncompeting buyers can share knowledge about markets, fashion trends, and so forth. Group buying can be arranged through resident buying offices.

Some buyers have difficulties entering into group buying. They give up some of their individuality, and that hurts. Fashion merchants, particularly, find cooperative buying difficult because they feel their customers are unique.

Central Buying. **Central buying** is most often practiced by chains. As branch-store organizations grow in size, central buying is also logical for them. Central buying means that one person handles the buying of goods for all stores in the firm.

In firms where central buying occurs, most of the authority for buying lies outside any one retail outlet. In some firms, store managers are given limited authority to purchase locally produced items. For example, in a food store, locally grown produce might be bought by the local store instead of by the central buyer.

Because they order in such large quantities, central buyers hope to get favorable prices. Technology is important in central buying, as the buyer must have adequate and rapid information from individual stores. Such information is necessary to make effective buying decisions.

Committee Buying. **Committee buying** is a version of central buying. It is a way to achieve the savings of central buying while having more than one person share the buying responsibility. This type of buying is common in firms selling staples, such as hardware stores.

Consignment. In **consignment,** suppliers guarantee the sale of items and will take merchandise back if it does not sell. The retailer assumes no risk in such an arrangement. Merchandise from an unknown supplier or a high-risk item might require such an arrangement. If a buyer has overspent the assigned budget, consignment can be attractive. But the buyer must be aware that most vendors would not offer consignment if the goods could be sold any other way.

Leased Departments. If retailers do not have the skills to operate a specialized department, they may choose to lease it. Shoe, camera, jewelry, and optical departments, as well as beauty salons and restaurants, are often operated under lease arrangements. By leasing to an expert, the retailer can provide customers with specialized items without fear of failure caused by inexperience.

Leased departments have been common in mass-merchandise stores. History has shown that after mass merchandisers learn how to run a department, however, they often take it over as a company-operated department.

Negotiations[3]

A good relationship between buyer and vendor may be one of the most important assets of the retail business. If a strong, friendly, yet professional, relationship exists with suppliers, negotiations can go smoothly. Of course, bargaining with vendors does not begin until the buyer is sure that the items are truly what are needed for the store.

The buyer should be prepared to sacrifice something during a negotiation. Then the buyer can ask the supplier, "What are you willing to give up?" Remember, the buyer is trying to get the best deal, while the vendor is trying to hold the price up to protect profits.

Buyers normally attempt to negotiate on the following elements:

1. Cost price of the items.
2. Discounts and datings.
3. Transportation charges.

Cost Price (List Price)

One area of negotiation is the cost, or list, price of the merchandise. Certain laws, however, affect the amount of dealing that can be done to get a good price from a vendor. Also, some vendors will not negotiate price.

After the gross wholesale list price has been negotiated and established, the buyer must turn to other areas for negotiation.

Discounts

Even though identical list prices may be offered by various vendors, they may offer different discounts and different provisions as to who will be responsible for paying transportation charges. An understanding of these purchase terms is necessary to negotiate the best price.

Trade. A **trade discount** is a reduction off the seller's list price and is granted to a retailer who performs functions normally the responsibility of the seller.

A trade discount may be offered as a single percentage or as a series of percentages off list price. If the list price on a sport shirt is $14.95, with a trade discount of 40 percent, the retailer will pay $8.97 ($14.95 − $5.98). The $5.98 ($14.95 × .40) is the trade discount. The same buyer might be offered an identical sport shirt from another manufacturer at a list price of $14.95 less 30 percent, 10 percent, and 5 percent. The net price in this case would be computed as follows:

$$
\begin{aligned}
\textit{List price} =\ & \$14.95 \\
-\ & \underline{4.48} \ (\$14.95 \times 0.30) \\
=\ & 10.47 \\
-\ & \underline{1.05} \ (\$10.47 \times 0.10) \\
=\ & 9.42 \\
-\ & \underline{0.47} \ (\$9.42 \times 0.05) \\
\textit{Net price} =\ & \$\ 8.95
\end{aligned}
$$

An alternative way of calculating the net price in the example above is to use the *complement* of the discount percentages. In this case, the net price would be calculated as: $14.95 × .70 × .90 × .95 = $8.95.

Quantity. A quantity discount is a reduction in unit cost based on the size of the order. Such discounts may be noncumulative, meaning the reduction is based on one order, or cumulative, meaning the reduction is computed over purchases for a specified period of time.

When deciding whether a quantity discount is worthwhile, the buyer must compare the money saved with the extra inventory carrying cost.

To determine the *value* of a quantity discount, use the following steps:

1. Determine the savings from the quantity discount.
2. Determine how much extra merchandise the store would have to carry in inventory, and for how long.
3. Multiply the average extra stock by the carrying charge (which is usually 20 to 25 percent) to obtain the additional cost of carrying the extra stock for a year.
4. Determine the additional carrying costs for the period of time it will take to work off the extra stock.
5. Compare the savings from the quantity discount with the cost of carrying the extra inventory and decide whether it is worthwhile to buy the larger quantity.

For example, if the buyer can save $500 by taking an extra $6,000 of merchandise into stock, and if it will take six months to work off the extra stock, the calculations are as shown below:

$$\text{Cost savings (discount)} = \$500$$

Extra inventory would be $6,000 in the beginning and zero six months later; therefore:

Average extra inventory = $3,000
Carrying costs of average extra = $3,000 × 25% × 1/2 year = $750
inventory   × 1/2 = $375
Actual savings = Cost savings − Carrying costs =
$500 − $375 = $125

Since the real savings from taking the discount would be only $125, this deal is worthwhile only if the store can work the extra inventory off in six months without getting stuck with any hard-to-sell merchandise.

Seasonal. A **seasonal discount** is a special discount given to retailers who place orders for seasonal merchandise in advance of the normal buying period.

Promotional Allowance. Vendors offer a **promotional allowance** to retailers as compensation for money spent in advertising particular items. This discount may also be given for preferred window- and interior-display space for the vendor's products.

Cash. A premium is often granted by the vendor for cash payment prior to the time that the entire bill must be paid. The three components of the cash-discount terms are: (1) a percentage discount, (2) a period in which the discount may be taken, and (3) the net credit period, which indicates when the full amount of the invoice is due. A **cash discount** stated as 2/10, n/30, means that the retailer must pay the invoice within 10 days to take advantage of the discount of 2 percent. The full amount is due in 30 days.

A cash discount may be taken in addition to a trade or another type of discount. Returning to the earlier example, the $8.95 net bill for the sport shirt, assume that the invoice is dated May 22. The retailer has 10 days to take the discount. Payment is due June 1 (9 days in May and 1 in June). If the invoice is paid within this time, the retailer will remit $8.77 instead of $8.95 ($8.95 × .02 = $.18; $8.95 − .18 = $8.77). If the retailer does not discount the invoice, the bill must be paid in full by June 21.

The 2 percent in the example represents an annual interest rate of 36 percent. Why? The full invoice payment is due in 30 days. Since the 2 percent cash discount can be taken if the invoice is paid within 10 days, the discount is allowed for paying the bill 20 days earlier than necessary. Since there are 18 20-day periods in the year (using 360 days as a year), this comes to 36 percent annually (18 × 2 percent).

Datings

The agreement between the vendor and the retailer as to the time the discount date will begin is known as dating.

Cash Datings. Technically, if the terms call for immediate payment, the process is known as **cash dating** and includes COD (cash on delivery) or CWO (cash with order). Cash datings do not involve discounts.

Two reasons may cause a negotiation to include cash terms. First, the seller may have a cash flow problem and must insist on cash on delivery (or with the order) in order to meet the bills incurred in the processing or distribution of the goods. Second, the retail buyer's credit rating may be such that the seller will deal with the firm only on a cash basis. In periods of "tight" money, retailers who must pay cash for orders may place themselves in a bad cash flow position. Retailers who are faced with COD or CWO terms should examine the supplier's reasons. They may be a symptom of much more serious problems in the future. The vendor, for example, may be in financial trouble.

Future Datings. The focus of this section is **future datings.** Future datings include end-of-month, date-of-invoice, receipt-of-goods, and extra dating.

End of Month (EOM). If an invoice carries EOM dating, the cash and net discount periods begin on the first day of the following month rather than on the invoice date. To allow for goods shipped late in the month, an invoice dated on or after the 25th of the month may be considered dated on the first of the following month. Thus, on a 2/10, n/30 EOM billing dated May 26, the 10-day discount period begins on July 1, not June 1. As a result, dating is further extended.

For example, if the $8.95 invoice for the sport shirt reads "2/10, n/30 EOM," and is dated May 22, the retailer has until June 10 to pay the invoice and take the 2 percent discount (that is, pay $8.77). If, on the other hand, the invoice is dated May 26 (within the same EOM terms), then the retailer has until July 10 to take the 2 percent discount.

Date of Invoice (DOI). DOI, or ordinary dating, is self-explanatory. Prepayments begin with the invoice date, and both the cash discount and the net amount are due within the specified number of days from the invoice date. The DOI method is not particularly favorable to the retailer. If the vendor is slow in shipping the merchandise, payment may actually be due before the merchandise arrives.

Receipt of Goods (ROG). Certain vendors are more distant from their customers than are their competitors. Rather than be at a competitive disadvantage with ordinary datings, they may offer receipt-of-goods (ROG) datings. With ROG datings, the time allowed for discounts and for payment of the net amount of the invoice begins with the date the goods are received at the buyer's place of business.

Extra. Extra datings allow the retailer extra time to take the cash discount. For example, 2/10–60 extra, n/90 means that the buyer has 70 days to take the cash discount instead of 10, and the net amount is due in 90 days.

Returning to the example of the sport shirt, if the invoice is dated May 22 with ordinary dating, payment is due (assuming 2/10, n/30) on June 1. However, with 2/10–60 extra, n/90, the retailer can take the 2 percent cash discount through August 1 (10-day discount period through June 1, 29 additional days in June, and 31 days in July).

Transportation Charges

The final aspect of negotiation relates to who will bear the responsibility for shipping costs. The most favorable terms for the retailer are *FOB (free-on-board) destination*. In this arrangement, the seller pays the freight to the destination and is responsible for damage or loss in transit. A more common shipping term is *FOB origin,* which means the vendor delivers the merchandise to the carrier, and the retailer pays for the freight.

Small retailers typically do not have the power to bargain with a vendor on discounts or the transportation charges. On the other hand, large retailers may be able to obtain price concessions from the supplier by bargaining on discounts even though the list price of the merchandise does not change.

FOLLOW-UP

The last step in the buying cycle is follow-up. Follow-up consists of continuous checking to find more desirable:

— Suppliers.
— Merchandise.
— Buying and merchandise control practices.

Finding better suppliers can be accomplished only by getting to know existing suppliers and being alert to information sources on new ones who may come into the market. Improving merchandise selection is a matter of merchandise management, as discussed in Chapter 12. Better buying practices evolve from experimentation with improved methods whenever a problem appears.

Lastly, maintaining good merchandise control practices, as described below, will ensure success while operating within the buying cycle.

RECORDING INVENTORY[4]

To manage inventory successfully, management should maintain accurate and up-to-date records of sales and stock on hand for every item. Inventory records tell you what you *have*. Sales records tell you what you *need*. Inventory records are used for making the following decisions:

— Purchases for inventory replenishment.
— Scrapping or clearing of obsolete items that are no longer in demand.
— Addition of new items to inventory.

Choosing a System

The best type of system for a retailer depends largely on the number of different items in inventory. A retail bicycle shop might carry 40 or 50 items in inventory, a bookstore might have a few hundred titles, and a plumbing supply house might carry several thousand different items in inventory.

Manual Inventory Control Systems

As a minimum, any retailer should have a manual inventory control system. Manual systems generally are based on an inventory control card similar to that shown here.

INVENTORY CONTROL CARD			
3648 Toaster			
Date	On Hand	In	Out
8/1	27		
8/2	26		1
8/4	38	12	
8/6	36		2
8/8	35		1
8/10	32		3

A separate record is maintained for each item in inventory. The stock status is shown for the end of each day. All changes in inventory are shown as in or out. In the "In" column, management would list all orders received from suppliers, returns from customers, and so forth. In the "Out" column, management would identify all sales, returns to suppliers, and similar changes.

Another useful inventory record is a sales summary. This information is needed for determining the adequacy of inventories and for order preparation. The sales summary can be compared periodically with stock on hand so that items that are not showing sufficient sales activity can be cleared through price reductions, scrapped, or otherwise disposed of. In this way, space and dollars invested in inventory are available for more active and potentially more profitable items.

SALES SUMMARY			
3648 Toaster			
Month	Sold	Ordered	Received
January	12	10	10
February	14	15	—
March	7	—	15
April	15	15	—
May	8	—	15
June	9	12	12
July	10	10	—
August			
September			
October			
November			
December			

Electronic Data Processing

When a large number of items are maintained in inventory, electronic data processing services are often desirable. These are available through local service bureaus. On a specified schedule, the business submits records of sales, receipts, and orders for the previous period so that the service bureau can update the inventory records. Depending on the type of business and the programs available from the service bureau, a sales analysis for each item can be provided which can guide inventory replenishment. Large retailers handle such an analysis on their own computer system.

Physical Inventory

A physical inventory should be taken periodically to be sure that the actual quantities on hand equal those shown on the inventory records. The inventory records must then be adjusted to reflect any difference between "physical inventory" and "book inventory," the quantities shown on the inventory records. The actual quantity of each item on hand must be counted and compared with that shown on the inventory record. Necessary adjustments should be made immediately.

Differences between book and physical inventory arise for many reasons. The most easily understood, of course, is pilferage. Any business naturally wants to maintain an inventory control system to detect this situation as early as possible.

Other reasons for inventory shortages are somewhat more subtle but equally damaging, if not worse. For example, if receiving procedures are faulty, a receiving clerk may not be counting actual quantities received and comparing them with those on the vendor's packing list or invoice. If the quantity actually received is less than that invoiced to the store, management is paying for the difference.

Merchandise may be sold to customers without being billed to them, through oversight or carelessness. In these cases, management will take a loss equal to their cost of the product and also lose the profit they should have earned on the sale.

Clerks may be accepting customer returns of merchandise that are no longer salable because of damage, stains, or packing defects. Management may be ignoring opportunities to return merchandise to vendors when it arrives in an unfit condition for resale.

Any of these factors can result in inventory shortages. While most businesses take careful steps to guard against theft, relatively few adopt serious procedures for protection from inventory shortages caused by such factors as poor receiving procedures, poor billing procedures, and merchandise damage.

CHAPTER HIGHLIGHTS

—— The buying cycle consists of determining needs, selecting suppliers, negotiating purchases, and following up after the purchase.

—— Buyers face different problems depending on whether the merchandise bought is primarily a staple, a seasonal item, or style or perishable merchandise. The goal in each instance is to establish or maintain inventory at the lowest level and still have a sufficient assortment from which customers can choose.

- The primary factors influencing the level of staples to be purchased include sales trends, profitability on various items, and discounts available.
- One way to establish buying levels for style and perishable items is to plot the progress of different styles in the past to see how they typically behave and use the resulting information as a guide in future purchasing decisions.
- A variety of factors determine what stock should be ordered. Product shelf life may be the determining factor for some items. The length of time between order placement and receipt of goods is also important. Most businesses maintain a safety, or cushion, stock as a protection against variation in demand and delivery.
- Sources of information on suppliers include salespeople, business contacts, trade registers and directories, trade exhibits, and the Yellow Pages.
- Contact with suppliers can occur in a variety of ways, including purchases made in a central market and use of resident buying offices.
- Factors to be considered in determining the best supplier include prices and discounts, quality, reliability, services, and accessibility.
- Group, or cooperative, buying is a joint purchasing of goods by a number of noncompeting, nonaligned stores. Other forms of buying include central buying and committee buying.
- Buyers normally attempt to negotiate on the following elements of the purchase price: the cost price of the item, discounts and datings, and transportation charges.
- Successful inventory management requires retailers to maintain an accurate and up-to-date record of sales and stock on hand for every item they sell. Inventory systems may be either manual or computer based.
- A physical inventory should be taken periodically to be sure that the actual quantities on hand equal those shown on the inventory records.

KEY TERMS

Basic stock The amount and assortment of merchandise sufficient to accommodate normal sales levels.

Cash datings Payment terms which call for immediate payment for merchandise. Cash datings include COD (cash on delivery) and CWO (cash with order). Cash datings do not involve cash discounts.

Cash discount A premium granted by the supplier for cash payment prior to the time the entire bill must be paid.

Central buying A method of buying in which the authority and responsibility for merchandise selection and purchase are vested in the headquarters office rather than in the individual store units that comprise the chain.

Central market The place where a large number of suppliers concentrate.

Committee buying A form of central buying where more than one person shares the buying responsibility.

Consignment A situation in which suppliers guarantee the sale of items and will take merchandise back if it does not sell.

Future datings A type of dating other than cash dating; includes DOI (date of invoice), ROG (receipt of goods), EOM (end of month), and extra datings.

Group buying The joint purchasing of goods by a number of noncompeting, nonaligned stores.

Lead time The length of time between order placement and receipt of goods.

Leased departments Departments of a retail business which are operated and managed by an outside person or organization rather than by the store of which it is a physical part.

Order ceiling A level of stock sufficient to maintain a minimum order point level of stock and one sufficient to cover sales between ordering intervals.

Order point The level of stock below which merchandise is automatically reordered.

Ordering interval The amount of time between merchandise orders.

Promotional allowance A discount from list price given by suppliers to retailers to compensate them for money spent on promoting particular items.

Quantity discount A reduction in unit cost based on the size of an order.

Safety stock The level of stock sufficient to maintain adequate inventory for accommodating ex-

pected variations in demand and variations in supplier delivery schedules.

Seasonal discount A special discount given to retailers who place orders for seasonal merchandise in advance of the normal buying period.

Seasonal merchandise Merchandise in demand only at certain times of the year.

Staple merchandise Items of merchandise generally in demand year round, with little change in model or style.

Trade discount A reduction off the seller's list price that is granted to a retailer who performs functions normally the responsibility of the vendor.

DISCUSSION QUESTIONS

1. Discuss the roles and responsibilities of a buyer.
2. In what ways can a buyer make market contacts?
3. What is a resident buying office? What are its functions? What are the various types?
4. Describe the different methods of buying.
5. Explain the types of discounts available to retailers.
6. Explain the types of datings available to retailers.
7. What are the most favorable transportation terms for the retailer? Explain your answer.
8. Discuss each element of the buying cycle.
9. What factors determine the desired inventory level for various types of merchandise?

PROBLEMS

1. A manufacturer of tables offers terms of 2/20, n/60. A furniture store places an order for a dozen tables at $27 each and receives an invoice dated July 2. The invoice is paid August 10. Failure to obtain the discount is equivalent to paying what annual rate of interest? (Use 360 days as a year.)
2. An invoice dated June 5 in the amount of $1,800, with terms of 3/10, n/30 EOM and a trade discount of 20 percent, arrives with the merchandise on June 8. The invoice is paid July 2. What amount is due the vendor?
3. An invoice dated January 3 in the amount of $12,200, with terms of 2/10, n/30 ROG and a trade discount of 10, 5, and 2 percent, arrives with the merchandise on January 10. The invoice is paid January 30. What amount is due the vendor?

4. A manufacturer of women's blouses quotes terms of 2/20, n/30 and grants retailers trade discounts of 10 and 5 percent. The list price of a blouse is $140 per dozen. A retailer receives an invoice dated July 7 for eight dozen of these blouses. The invoice is paid July 10. What is (a) the net cost per blouse and (b) the net amount of the cash discount taken?
5. A manufacturer of women's skirts quotes terms of 2/10, n/30 EOM and grants retailers trade discounts of 10, 5, and 2 percent. The list price of the skirts is $360 per dozen. A retailer receives an invoice dated September 16 for 10 dozen of these skirts. The invoice is paid October 2. What is the net cost per skirt to the retailer?

APPLICATION EXERCISES

1. To clarify the relationships between the buyer and the supplier, the text approaches the subject from the retail point of view. It may be valuable

to approach the subject from the other point of view. Make contacts with local suppliers (wholesalers, agents, or local manufacturers who sell to retailers), and see what they attempt to do to strengthen relationships with their customers. What problems do they incur in these relationships? What efforts do they make to "improve" the relationships?

2. Select a product line in which you are particularly interested. Spot merchants in your area who handle this line. Set up interviews after you have devised a questionnaire to determine how important the merchants believe relationships with suppliers are. Administer the questionnaires to the managers of the stores. Attempt to find out how these managers implement their "philosophy" of relationships with vendors. If you can get measurements of the various stores' success, see whether you can attribute some of that success to the "programs" for vendor relationships you discover. This will be a difficult project, but attempting to carry it out will be a beneficial experience, regardless of the outcome.

3. In interviews with retailers with whom you establish good rapport, attempt to find out: (a) what special problems have been encountered with vendors; (b) what kinds of special "concessions" are offered to the retailers; (c) whether any particular plans have been effective in improving relations; and (d) why vendors are dropped.

CASES

1. The Intermediary

The Handleman Company, based in the Detroit blue-collar suburb of Clawson, is getting rich selling top-of-the-pops records and is expanding dramatically into personal computer software sales. The company buys from manufacturers and stocks big retailers like K mart, Sears, and Wal-Mart with records and tapes, books, and personal computer software. Handleman accounts for 9 percent of all records sold in this country, including more than 3 million copies of Michael Jackson's all-time best seller, "Thriller."

The profits are dandy. On most records the Handleman Company gets about $1 each, and the retailer keeps about $2. On the biggest hits the margins are lower because the records are often used as traffic builders.

With thin margins like this, why doesn't the retailer cut out the middleman? Because records and tapes are risky, the most fickle and ephemeral changes in taste making the difference between a hot seller and scrap.

Obviously the customers think the Handleman Company earns its $1 per record. Handleman takes out much of the risk, projecting which of the recording groups will turn hot, which book might be a best-seller, and which company game will catch on. Once the company makes those picks, it buys big from the manufacturers and stocks the shelves of its retail customers.

Handleman also manages the advertising, the inventories, and the returns, which are no small chores.

Questions
1. Why do retailers rely on firms such as the Handleman Company instead of handling the record business themselves?
2. What are the functions that middlemen such as Handleman are able to perform more effectively than the retailer?
3. What are other lines of trade in which the risk taker is likely to be a valuable merchandising partner?

Source: Reprinted by permission of *Forbes* Magazine, July 16, 1984. © Forbes, Inc., 1984.

2. The Lyon's Den

The Lyon's Den had been a winner ever since Jane and Jim Lyon opened their gift shop in an old renovated home and moved in over it. The business was started in 1950. Over the years it had become "the" place for gifts and, eventually, decorating services in a city of some 70,000 and a trading area at least twice that size. Jane said on occasion that the Lyons had made it fashionable to live over the store. Their apartment was a showcase for the many lines of fine silver, china, crystal, and decorator furniture items that were carried in the shop. The Lyons made no pretense of using their home to display their wares—they felt that such items in use were virtually presold.

Over the years, their lines expanded. To the traditional gift lines they added cosmetics and linens.

Nothing in the shop was carried anywhere else in the trade area. Jane and Jim felt that exclusivity was a major advantage for The Lyon's Den.

Several years ago, Jane, who does the bulk of the buying (whereas Jim is the decorator and money man), felt that she had secured a market first for the area. She was able to acquire the finest and most prestigious lines of stainless Hensen. The name was not known in the market, but the quality was unsurpassed. Jane knew that, given an exclusive, she could develop a demand for the line that would make her a leading outlet for the merchandise. She had done this before; she knew merchandise and was a merchant with foresight—an entrepreneur who liked a challenge. The salesperson, whom she met at a regional trade show, assured her of market protection, and thus she set out to launch the new line.

She ran ads and invited special customers to attend a reception to meet the manufacturer. The market had probably never had such a dramatic introduction and perhaps never would again. After a year and a half, the line was one of the most profitable in the shop. Brides were convinced that, without Hensen from The Lyon's Den, marriage was out of the question. Jane had done what she set out to do—create a market demand for the line and bring in new customers because of it.

Just this morning, Jane got a phone call from the New York office of Hensen's. The national sales manager was on the phone with some distressing news for The Lyon's Den. Lucille's Table Top, a new market entrant carrying medium- to high-priced table accessories, had just been into the New York showroom and had bought the Hensen line. The sales manager felt that since Lucille's was in a shopping center some distance from The Lyon's Den, the competition would be negligible. In addition, the sales manager said that company policy was actually not to give exclusives in a market. The salesperson who originally opened the Lyon's account had not been aware of the policy.

Questions

1. What options are available to Jane?
2. What are the advantages and disadvantages to a supplier of granting a retailer the exclusive right to sell a line of merchandise?

ENDNOTES

1. Ralph D. Skipp, Jr., *Retail Merchandising: Principles and Application* (Boston: Houghton Mifflin, 1976), pp. 12–14.
2. The material on the buying function is based on, with modifications, *Business Basics: Retail Buying Function*, Self-Instructional Booklet 1010 (Washington, D.C.: U.S. Small Business Administration); for further reading, see Daniel Bello, "Retailer Buying Strategies at Merchandise Marts," in *1986 American Marketing Association Educators Proceedings*, ed. Terry Shrimp et al. (Chicago: American Marketing Association, 1986), pp. 178–81.
3. For further reading, see "Department Stores Put Squeeze on Small Vendors," *Chain Store Age, General Merchandise Trends*, August 1985, pp. 18–19; "New Breed of Discounter: More Wheeling and Dealing," *Chain Store Age, General Merchandise Trends*, September 1985, p. 17; "Where Have the Profits Gone for Power Merchants?" *Chain Store Age, General Merchandise Trends*, July 1985, pp. 15–16; "J. C. Penney Decentralizes Its Purchasing," *The Wall Street Journal*, May 8, 1986, p. 6; Hank Gilman, "Wholesalers Caught in a Squeeze by Retailers," *The Wall Street Journal*, May 29, 1986, p. 6.
4. With modifications, the material on inventory management is based on *Inventory Management: Wholesale/Retail*, Self-Instructional Booklet 1011 (Washington, D.C.: U.S. Small Business Administration).

14

Determin-
ing Retail
Prices

RETAILING CAPSULE

J. C. Penney and Halston: A Marriage on the Rocks?

The marriage between J. C. Penney and Halston seemed ideal when Halston agreed to design a fashion line for Penney in 1982. Penney management had decided to go after a new customer, the upscale professional woman with fashion sophistication and a relatively high level of disposable income. The Halston line, management hoped, would give the store the glamour it wanted in its fashion department.

Penney is pursuing a risky strategy with the Halston line. The prices are at least 15 percent higher than the rest of Penney's top-of-the-line apparel. In contrast, Sears introduced its Cheryl Tiegs line in a moderate price range compatible with its existing price structure.

Penney executives established the Halston price to undercut the prices of designer apparel in department stores. However, the market conditions softened and the department stores slashed their prices on designer apparel. The Halston line thus no longer has a price advantage, which makes Penney's price strategy difficult.

J. C. Penney's store managers have also complained that the line is priced too high for the traditional Penney customer. They contend that deep markdowns are necessary to move the merchandise. Some evidence exists that the line is only moving well when the merchandise is marked down by 50 percent.

J. C. Penney management and Halston are continuing to work to make their experiment a

Source: Based on Peggy Marion, "J. C. Penney: A Marriage on the Rocks?" *Ad Forum*, May 1985, pp. 49–50.

success. But doubts among some experts still exist about the long-term viability of the venture.

The difficulties experienced by J. C. Penney with its Halston line illustrate the crucial importance of price in retailing strategy. Pricing decisions must be compatible with the overall marketing strategy for the firm. Decisions must also be made on markdowns and markups and price points that are compatible with competition.

After reading this chapter you will be able to:

1. Explain how external factors affect the setting of retail prices.

2. Describe the store policies that affect pricing decisions.

3. Discuss the kinds of price changes that may be made after the original pricing decision.

4. Understand how to handle the arithmetic of pricing.

A merchant (buyer) is involved in the five "rights of merchandising." **Merchandising** means having the *right* merchandise, at the *right* place, at the *right* time, in the *right* quantities, and at the *right* price.

The retailer may have performed all other merchandising functions successfully, *but* if the price is wrong, it is like fumbling a football on the one-yard line. It is almost a touchdown, but no score is on the board. If the price is not right, no sale is made.

Setting retail prices is a vital part of the retail planning process. Pricing clearly is the most visible result of planning, at least from the customer's viewpoint. Pricing strongly influences the image of the retail outlet. Consumers can readily understand the merchandising strategy of Grand Union as shown in Figure 14–1, for example, based on its price emphasis.

FACTORS AFFECTING RETAIL PRICING

In setting the *right* price, the retailer must first consider those factors that affect the pricing decision. The retailer may not have set up these conditions; they may be the result of things the retailer or manager did in the past. But at the time of pricing, the factors still *do* exist.

Such factors include (1) type of goods carried, (2) store image, (3) level of profit desired, (4) level of customer demand, (5) market structure, (6) supplier policies, (7) economic conditions, and (8) government regulations.

Type of Goods

Pricing decisions depend on whether the products offered by the retailer are primarily *convenience, shopping,* or *specialty* goods. If products are viewed by consumers as convenience goods, prices are usually about the same in all stores. Consumers do not feel it is worth their time to shop around for a better price (or quality) for **convenience** goods since the savings are not likely to be worth the extra effort of comparison shopping. The retailer has only a little latitude in the pricing of these goods. A retailer has more leeway in setting prices for **shopping goods.** These are items consumers carefully compare for price and quality differences before making a purchase decision. The retailer has the greatest latitude in pricing **speciality goods** in comparison to convenience and shopping goods. Specialty items are products consumers know they want and are willing to make an effort to acquire. To them, price is not particularly important.

Store Image

Retailers must be familiar with their customers if they want to achieve profitable pricing. Customers may come to a store because of its quality image or because of its reputation for low prices. In the quality stores, customers expect to pay more, but also expect more service and a better environment (atmosphere). These "extras" cost money, and prices must cover them. The retailer's value equation ("what I pay, for what I get") in this context must not be out of balance. The retailer cannot survive for long by charging high prices, but offering lower quality merchandise and mediocre service is an unimaginative atmosphere.

Profit Desired

Prices must be high enough to cover *all* costs of doing business. This includes the original cost of the goods plus the expenses of doing business. Prices also must provide the level of profit the retailer wishes to earn. (This point is discussed further in the section on The Arithmetic of Retail Pricing.)

High prices do not necessarily mean high profits—the firm may have a high overhead or may have to discount merchandise to sell it. This problem has plagued J. C. Penney in recent years (see retailing capsule).

Customer Demand

If the retailer is selling an item where demand exceeds supply, a higher price can be charged. Objects of art are a good example. A fine painting by a well-known, deceased artist can be priced at whatever level the customer will pay. There is great pricing flexibility in this type of item.[1] Similarly, far less price negotiation typically occurs for high-quality or prestigious foreign automobiles than for less popular U.S. makes.

Market Structure

The degree of competition in the market will greatly affect pricing decisions. If little competition exists, pricing decisions are easier than if there is a great deal of competition. For example, a retailer with an "exclusive" on a brand in a market can probably price with greater freedom.

In addition, competitors' actions in the pricing area must be monitored. A good retailer is aware of prices being charged by competitive outlets.

A word of caution is in order, however. To focus too much on the competition means you're relying on them to do their marketing job right.

Supplier Policies

Suppliers will often suggest prices to retailers. If the retailer depends heavily on a particular supplier, then the supplier is likely to influence price decisions. Recently, retailers have gained more control over pricing decisions. Yet strong manufacturers have effectively suggested retail (or resale) price programs for some lines. In such cases, the retailer must give up pricing flexibility in order to carry the brand.

Economic Conditions

Retailers must be conscious of economic conditions and their impact on pricing decisions. During periods of inflation, increases in prices are expected (though not welcomed) by consumers. In times of recession, prices often go down. Retailers must be sensitive to economic changes since they often require price adjustments.

In addition, the retailer must be aware of any voluntary or required governmental price controls that can limit price decisions. Clearly, changing and uncertain economic conditions make pricing complex.

Government Regulations

Retailers have been restricted from certain kinds of pricing actions since the Sherman Act was passed in 1890. Chapter 3 presents a full discussion of legal impacts. The following discussion includes only some of the laws that affect pricing decisions.

The Sherman Act. Under the **Sherman Act,** price-fixing (different parties agreeing to certain prices) was declared illegal. But during the years since 1890, price-fixing has been interpreted differently.

For many years after the 1930s, **fair-trade** (or resale-price-maintenance) **laws** affected retailers' pricing decisions. Fair-trade laws allowed manufacturers to set minimum retail prices for their products. Store managers who attempted to sell designated items below the specific minimum price faced fines and prosecution. Thus, fair-trade laws allowed a form of *vertical* price-fixing. In 1976, the laws ceased to exist nationally for goods sold in interstate commerce (between states). President Ford signed federal legislation repealing the fair-trade laws. Vendors cannot "fix" a retail price at which a branded item must be sold.

Price-fixing between two or more retailers is referred to as **horizontal price-fixing.** Horizontal price-fixing is illegal under the Sherman Act. Thus, both types of price-fixing (vertical and horizontal) are illegal in interstate commerce.

Unfair Trade-Practices Acts. If retailers operate in one of the more than 20 states with unfair trade-practices laws, they will be required to charge a certain minimum percentage above cost.

Robinson-Patman Act. A merchant can legally receive favorable prices from vendors. But the Robinson-Patman Act requires that the vendors justify the savings in cost. In such situations, the retailer experiences lower merchandise costs and can perhaps undercut competition.

The factors discussed thus far affect the pricing decision, but are factors over which the retailer has little—and in some cases no—control. The following section focuses on store factors that impact the retailer's pricing decisions. These are store *policies* (guidelines for action) that management supports and that can be adjusted.

STORE POLICIES AFFECTING RETAIL PRICING

Price-Level Policy

The pricing decision is affected by the retailer's policy on the "price level" desired. The three choices are: (1) **at-the-market pricing,** (2) **below-the-market pricing,** and (3) **above-the-market pricing.**

Pricing at the Market Level. Most retailers are "competitive pricers." The prices they offer are roughly the same as their competitors'. When following such a policy, the retailer tries to make the store different in ways other than price.[2] This is called "nonprice competition." Superstores, for example, try to be competitive in prices with other superstores. But they may try to make themselves different by carrying more brands, having a better deli, and offering different services.

A department store or a general merchandise merchant such as Sears is typically a competitive, at-the-market pricer. Management attempts to meet discount store prices on identical merchandise. However, extra services may be offered by the department store that the discount store does not offer—for example, clothing alterations or merchandise delivery. If alterations or delivery are offered, then the department store will charge for these extra services, and the "total" product price may be higher.

FIGURE 14–2 DISCOUNT, BELOW-THE-MARKET PRICING STRATEGY

(Courtesy Revco)

Pricing below the Market Level. Off-price retailers, warehouse grocery firms such as Cubs, or other low-margin, high-turnover retailers typically price below the market.[3] Competition in these operations is almost entirely on a price basis as shown in Figure 14–2.

Pricing above the Market Level. Some firms price above the market without great concern for how customers are going to react.[4] Some of the reasons stores are able to follow this policy are: (1) they carry unique (exclusive) merchandise; (2) they cater to customers who are not price conscious and want the highest quality and/or style goods; (3) they offer convenience of location and time (convenience stores); (4) they provide many unusual services; (5) they take greater risks on credit terms; or (6) they have a prestige image customers are willing to pay for.

The Silver Palate Shop on Manhattan's fashionable Upper West Side is an example of a merchant with above-the-market pricing. The management has created a place where the highest quality foods are available in an atmosphere conducive to educating the public about the joys of fine food and cooking. Tortellini salad is sold at $3.40 a pound, a 7-ounce jar of mustard sells for $4.80, and a small jar of fruit preserves sells for $7.50.[5] Other well-known, above-the-market retailers that compete on the basis of atmosphere and image include Neiman-Marcus and Marshall Field's.

We cannot overemphasize the danger of price competition to retailers whose overhead structures make it impossible for them to compete on the basis of price in the long run (i.e., department stores attempting to match prices with warehouse clubs). Department stores and specialty stores must compete on nonprice bases. Otherwise, the margins on their merchandise would be reduced to such a level that the future of the firms would be in doubt. Such outlets have found that a more viable competitive strategy includes offering high-quality, private brands and excellent service in an exciting, vibrant, up-scale atmosphere.

One-Price versus Variable-Price Policy

The majority of retail firms in the United States offer goods at one take-it-or-leave-it price. Bargaining with customers is unusual. In other countries, such as Mexico and Italy, varying prices with "haggling" is expected. In the United States, some stores selling big-ticket items such as automobiles, appliances, and furniture do *not* follow a one-price policy. Bargaining occurs over the price paid for the product. If this practice is usual and expected, consumers may form a negative view of retailers who do not engage in this bargaining process.

Certain advantages exist in a store with a one-price policy. Customers do not expect to bargain, so salespeople and customers save time. Salespeople are not under pressure to reduce prices. Of course, self-service will not work where there is bargaining.

Retailers can follow a variable price policy even when they do not negotiate with consumers on the price itself. Negotiating over whether to charge for delivery and installation and varying the price of warranties can all result in a variable price policy.

Private-Brand Policy

Many retailers such as Sears, Montgomery Ward, J. C. Penney, and Safeway often have their own **private brands.** Wholesalers may also offer retail customers their private brands. Private brands (often called distributor brands) are *owned* by the retail or wholesale firm rather than by a manufacturer. The **manufacturer's brand** (often referred to as a national brand) is *owned* by a manufacturer as in the case of Johnson & Johnson in Figure 14–3. A private brand may be carried only by the owner or someone the owner allows. A manufacturer's brand may be carried by anyone who buys from the man-

(Courtesy Revco)

ufacturer of the brand. Bokar is a private brand of coffee owned by A&P. Maxwell House is a manufacturer's brand owned by General Foods Corp.

If private brands are featured, the retailer may offer them at below-the-market prices and still make a good profit. This is possible because the retailer can pay less for the private-brand merchandise than for a comparable manufacturer's brand. Consequently, the merchant has more freedom in pricing private-brand items.

Department stores and general merchandise retailers are increasingly turning to private-brand merchandise as a source of competitive advantage, especially in the face of the challenges posed by off-price retailers. Private brands, such as Cheryl Tiegs at Sears and Jaclyn Smith at K mart, are not subject to the massive price-cutting which is the norm for national (manu-

(Courtesy of Delchamps)

facturer brand) designer labels. Designer labels such as Calvin Klein at one time were available exclusively in better department stores. Over time, the manufacturers of the designer labels broadened their distribution base to include discount stores and off-price retailers. The result was that the labels lost their exclusivity and became price "footballs" for the discounters. The department stores, because of their overhead, could not meet the prices of the discount stores and off-pricers on the same merchandise. As a result, they turned to private labels as a way of maintaining greater control over their merchandise lines and protecting their store image.

The question of **generic merchandise** and pricing is important. Generics are "no-brand-name" goods as shown in Figure 14–4. For example, if a supermarket offers generic paper products, the identification might read *paper napkins*. Customers may be willing to accept lower quality in some types of goods in return for lower prices. They rely on the reputation of the store and figure, "If my supermarket has generics for sale, they must be OK for the price." More profits may be made on generics than on private brands, even though generics are priced lower.

Generics appear to have peaked in popularity. They are strongest in low-ego-involved merchandise such as paper products and other staples. Some supermarkets have gradually added their own generics such as the "Cost-Cutter" label at Kroger and the "Thrifty-Maid" label at Winn Dixie.

Psychological Pricing

A retailer can price merchandise too low. A blouse might not sell at $20, but marked up to $27, it might. The reason for this strange phenomenon is that, for some goods, customers believe that price reflects quality (or value).

Odd price endings are believed by many to have psychological value. Odd endings ($10.98 instead of $11.00) seem lower than even-ending prices. Some retailers, however, prefer the even endings, wanting the extra markup, even if it is only a few pennies. Many transactions of a few cents *could* be important over time.

Trade-In Allowance Policy

Trade-in allowances are similar to varying price policies discussed earlier. In certain merchandise lines (e.g., automobiles, tires, and batteries), customers expect trade-ins. If the customers are good bargainers, the retailer may actually take a lower price than desired. Thus, retailers who have a trade-in policy should plan their original prices very carefully.

Price-Line Policy

Retailers practicing **price-lining** feature products at a limited number of prices, reflecting varying merchandise quality. A price-lining strategy can be implemented either in the context of rigid **price points** or by the use of **price zones.** Using suits as an example, the merchant might establish a limited number of price points to indicate quality differences between merchandise. The "good" suits might be priced at $175, the "better" suits at $225, and the "best" suits at $300. Alternatively, the retailer may decide to use "price zones" instead of rigid price points. For example, prices for good suits might fall between $175 and $200.

Price-lining offers certain advantages. For example, many customers become confused and cannot make up their minds when they see too many prices. Price-lining makes shopping easier for consumers, since there are fewer prices to consider.

The merchant can offer a greater assortment of support and width with fewer price points. In addition, inventories can be controlled more easily.

The salesperson can also learn the stock more easily with price-lining. And it is much easier to explain differences between the merchandise when it is carefully planned and priced to show differences. In addition, the buyer may not have to shop at as many vendors if specific retail prices are sought.

Certain problems do exist in price-lining. The retailer may feel "hemmed in" by the price line and lose some flexibility. Also, selection may be limited. If wholesale prices rise and fall rapidly, it may be difficult to maintain rigid price points. This is a reason for the use of price zones.

Single-Price Policy

Small specialty stores may have **single-price policies.** A "$10 tie store" or a "$24.95 budget dress store" are examples. Clearly, with such a policy the variety of offerings is limited. Also, fewer assortments are possible. The real strength of such a policy is being able to "target" a specific customer group. These customers know what to expect in the store.

Leader-Pricing Policy

Some retailers use leader pricing with selected product categories. A less than normal markup or margin on an item is taken to increase store traffic. Some call this **loss-leader pricing.** The "loss" implies loss of the normal amount of markup or margin.

In using leader pricing, the retailer is trying to attract customers who will also purchase items carrying normal profit margins. If customers only buy the "leaders," the retailer is in trouble. Retailers often limit the quantity of leader items that can be bought at one time.

Supermarkets and mass merchandisers often use leaders. Typically, however, leader pricing does not occur for all items. The characteristics of the best price leaders are:

1. Well-known and widely used items.
2. Items priced low enough to attract numerous buyers.
3. Items not usually bought in large quantities and stored.

Grocery items that have proved to be good leaders are shortening, coffee, toilet tissue, and dishwashing liquid.

PRICING ADJUSTMENTS

In practice, retailers may raise or lower prices after the original pricing decisions have been made. These pricing adjustments may be (1) *additional markons (markups)* or (2) *markdowns*.

Additional Markons

In inflationary periods, additional markons may be needed. Such adjustments are made when the retailer's costs are increasing.

Markdowns

A **markdown** is a reduction in the original selling price of an item. Most retailers take some markdowns, since this is the most widely used way of moving items that do not sell at the original price. Other things a retailer *might* do instead of taking a markdown are: (1) give additional promotion, better display, or a more visible store position to an item; (2) store the item until the next selling season; (3) mark the item *up* (discussed in Psychological Pricing); or (4) give the goods to charity.

One of the most famous retail department store organizations in the United States is Filene's Basement in Boston. This firm made its name through its widely known "automatic markdown policy." The policy operates as follows: When an item has been in the store for 12 days, it is marked down to 75 percent of list; after 6 more days, it is reduced to 50 percent; when 6 more days pass, it is reduced to 25 percent; and after 30 days, it is given to charity. Very little merchandise is given to charity.

TABLE 14–1   MARKON TABLE

To use this table, find the desired percentage in the left-hand column. Multiply the cost of the article by the corresponding percentage in the "Markup Percent of Cost" column. The result, added to the cost, gives the correct selling price.

Markon Percent of Retail Price	Markon Percent of Cost	Markon Percent of Retail Price	Markon Percent of Cost	Markon Percent of Retail Price	Markon Percent of Cost
4.8	5.0	18.5	22.7	33.3	50.0
5.0	5.3	19.0	23.5	34.0	51.5
6.0	6.4	20.0	25.0	35.0	53.9
7.0	7.5	21.0	26.6	35.5	55.0
8.0	8.7	22.0	28.2	36.0	56.3
9.0	10.0	22.5	29.0	37.0	58.8
10.0	11.1	23.0	29.9	37.5	60.0
10.7	12.0	23.1	30.0	38.0	61.3
11.0	12.4	24.0	31.6	39.0	64.0
11.1	12.5	25.0	33.3	39.5	65.5
12.0	13.6	26.0	35.0	40.0	66.7
12.5	14.3	27.0	37.0	41.0	70.0
13.0	15.0	27.3	37.5	42.0	72.4
14.0	16.3	28.0	39.0	42.8	75.0
15.0	17.7	28.5	40.0	44.4	80.0
16.0	19.1	29.0	40.9	46.1	85.0
16.7	20.0	30.0	42.9	47.5	90.0
17.0	20.5	31.0	45.0	48.7	95.0
17.5	21.2	32.0	47.1	50.0	100.0
18.0	22.0				

SOURCE: *Expenses in Retail Business*, a publication of NCR Corporation, Dayton, Ohio.

Markdowns are also used for promotional reasons. The goods may not be slow moving, but markdowns create more activity. The next sections present illustrations of how smart merchants *plan* certain amounts of markdowns in order to protect profit.

Markdowns should be handled with care. Consumers normally do not expect large markdowns on luxury items, for example. Customers may question product quality if prices are slashed too much. Seasonal, perishable, and obsolete stock are exceptions. Further, excessive markdowns should be avoided. If markdowns are too high, the retailer should find out the reason. The causes can come from buying, selling, or pricing errors. A plan should be worked out to correct the errors once they have been determined.[6]

The Arithmetic of Retail Pricing

This section presents a simple plan to help you understand the arithmetic of pricing. Every retailer is faced with the issues explained in this section. Even though retailers may use "crutches," such as markon equivalent tables (see Table 14–1), it is important to understand the relationships discussed here.

THE CONCEPT OF SALES RETAIL

Original retail price	$1,000
Less reductions	− 200
Sales retail	$ 800

Concepts of Retail Price. Price can be looked at as shown in Table 14–2. The $1,000 **original retail price** is the first price at which an item (or a group of items) is offered for sale. The **sales retail price** of $800 is the final selling price, the amount the customer paid. Before the item was sold, a $200 reduction or markdown occurred. (In a classification of merchandise, reductions also include employee discounts and shortages or shrinkage. See Chapter 12, "Reductions Planning," for a review of these concepts.)

Concepts of Markon (Markup)

The diagram in Table 14–3 shows the various ways to look at markon. **Initial markon** is the difference between the cost of the merchandise and the *original retail price* ($102,000 − $80,000 = $22,000). Initial markon as a percentage of the *original retail price* is 21.6 percent ($22,000/$102,000). The concept of initial markon is used when planning a total classification or department (as discussed in Chapter 12 on merchandise planning).

    Maintained markon, shown in Table 14–4, is the difference between invoice cost and sales retail ($100,000 − $80,000 = $20,000). In percentage terms, maintained markon is related to *sales retail* and is $20,000/$100,000 = 20 percent. Maintained markon covers operating expenses and provides the retailer with a profit.

    Maintained markon and initial markon differ by the $2,000 reduction. For purposes of the present discussion, maintained markon can be considered the same as gross margin.

THE CONCEPT OF INITIAL MARKON

Original retail price	$102,000
Less invoice cost	80,000
Initial markon	$ 22,000

THE CONCEPT OF MAINTAINED MARKON

Original retail price	$102,000
Less planned reductions	2,000
Sales retail	100,000
Less invoice cost	80,000
Maintained markon	$ 20,000

Planning Required Initial Markon

Initial goals for margins are essential as are plans for sales and reductions. Assume that management has forecast sales of a merchandise line at $100,000, no reductions, expenses of $15,000, and a profit return of 5 percent of sales, or $5,000. The result is maintained markon of $20,000 or 20 percent. On the other hand, assume that management expects reductions such as markdowns and employee discounts to be 2 percent of sales, or $2,000. A planned initial markon of $22,000, or 21.6 percent ($22,000/$102,000), is necessary to maintain a markon of $20,000, or 20 percent ($20,000/$100,000). This type of planning requires management to consider all elements that can affect profit. For the formula oriented, the relationships discussed above can be shown as:

$$\text{Initial markon percentage} = \frac{\text{Expenses} + \text{Profit} + \text{Reductions}}{\text{Sales retail} + \text{Reductions}}$$

$$\text{Maintained markon percentage} = \frac{\text{Expenses} + \text{Profit}}{\text{Sales retail}}$$

A retailer cannot expect to have a uniform initial markon policy. That kind of policy suggests that every item brought into a department will carry the same initial markon. Too many external factors and store policies exist for a uniform markon to make sense. (These factors and policies were discussed in the first part of this chapter.)

The planned initial-markon figure becomes a good check. Actual performance in markon during an operating period can be checked against what has been planned.

Computations

Every merchandiser needs practice in computing some routine relationships among cost, initial markon, and original retail price. There is no need to memorize formulas, though formulas will follow examples for those who like them. Simply remember that *Cost + Initial markon = Original retail price*.

Given Cost and Retail. A color television costs the retailer $500. The original price charged is $800. What is the initial markon in dollars and percent computed on both cost and retail bases?

The difference between retail and cost is $300 ($800 − $500). Based on cost, the markon would be $300/$500 = 60 percent. Based on retail, the markon is 37.5 percent ($300/$800). Remember that markon percentage on cost = $ markup/$ cost, and markon percentage on retail = $ markup/$ retail.

Conversion of Markon—Retail to Cost. In working with pricing, the buyer is often confronted with the problem of converting a markon on retail to a markon on cost. If the buyer thinks in terms of cost and the vendor quotes in terms of retail, the buyer needs to know how to make the "switch." As noted earlier, conversion tables do exist (see Table 14–1).

Assume that a supplier quotes an initial markon of 42 percent on retail. What is the same markon on cost? The formula is shown below:

$$\text{Markup percentage on cost} = \frac{\text{Markup percentage on retail}}{100 \text{ percent} - \text{Markup percentage on retail}}$$

If the retail markon is 42 percent, then retail is 100 percent and cost must be 58 percent. So, markon as a percentage of cost is .42/.58 = .724, or 72.4 percent. In other words, 42 percent markon on retail is the same as 72.5 percent on cost. Clearly, markon on cost will always be larger than markon on retail, because the cost base is smaller than the retail base.

Conversion of Markup—Cost to Retail. Suppose a vendor quotes an initial markon of 60 percent on cost. What is the equivalent markon on retail? Use the following formula:

$$\text{Markup percentage on retail} = \frac{\text{Markup percentage on cost}}{100 \text{ percent} + \text{Markup percentage on cost}}$$

If the cost markon is 60 percent, then cost must be 100 percent, and retail has to be 160 percent. So, markon on a retail base is .60/1.60 = 37.5 percent. Or, 60 percent markon on cost is the same as 37.5 percent on retail.

Other Relationships. The following examples and results provide additional types of relationships the merchant will face.

1. A chair costs a retailer $420. If a markup of 40 percent of retail is desired, what should the retail price be?

If 60 percent = $420, then 100 percent = 420/0.60, or $700, the retail price needed to achieve the desired markup of 40 percent on retail.

Formula: Whenever the retail price is to be calculated and the dollar cost and markon percent on retail are known, the problem can be solved with the following:

$$\$ \text{ Retail} = \frac{\$ \text{ Cost}}{100 \text{ percent} - \text{Retail markup percent}}$$

2. A dryer retails for $300. The markup is 28 percent of cost. What was the cost of the dryer?

If 128 percent = $300, then 100 percent = $300/1.28, or $234.37, the cost needed to achieve the desired markon of 28 percent on cost.

Formula: Whenever the cost price is to be calculated and the dollar retail and markon percentage on cost are known, the problem can be solved as follows:

$$\$ \text{ Cost} = \frac{\$ \text{ Retail}}{100 \text{ percent} + \text{Cost markup percent}}$$

3. A retailer prices a sport jacket so that the markup amounts to $36. This is 45 percent of retail. What are the cost and retail figures?

If 45 percent = $36, then 100 percent = $36/0.45, or $80. If retail is $80 and markup is $36, then cost is $80 − $36 = $44.

Formula: Whenever the dollar markon and the retail markon percentage are known, the retail price can be determined as follows:

$$\$ \text{ Retail } = \frac{\$ \text{ Retail markon}}{\text{Percent retail markon}}$$

OTHER FACTORS AFFECTING RETAIL PRICES

Many factors can affect pricing decisions in addition to those discussed earlier.

Distributor Allowances

Zenith Radio Corporation has given special "promotional allowances" to distributors to help expand the sales of its television sets. These distributor allowances became common in the stereo equipment business as it entered the maturity stage of its life cycle in the late 1970s. A shakeout occurred as the manufacturers battled to maintain market share. SuperScope, which markets the Marantz line, and such other suppliers as U.S. Pioneer, Sony, Kenwood, JVC, Hitachi, Yamaha, and Technics offered distributors discounts of 15 to 20 percent and extended payment plans to encourage dealers to buy more stock. These situations allow retailers to lower prices to stimulate sales.

Consumer Rebates

Consumer rebates are a common practice when manufacturers want to increase the sale of slow-moving merchandise. Rebates, a financial transaction by the manufacturer with the consumer, are separate from the original purchase. Rebates of $400–$700 on some automobiles have been common in recent years. Technically, rebates do not affect the initial retail markon since they are given by the manufacturer. However, retailers may also lower their markon to further stimulate sales. Rebates, if sizable, are often accepted by retailers as a down payment on the item to be purchased.

Consumer Pressures

Consumer pressures for unit pricing, individual item pricing, and similar consumer shopping aids also affect pricing practices at the retail level. For example, some states now require retailers to price mark each item instead of shelf marking only. Such a requirement adds to their cost structure. Similarly, activist consumer groups often publish market basket prices, especially for food, of competing stores in efforts to force down prices.

Indirect Price Competition

Retailers are often hesitant to use price openly as a competitive weapon. They are more prone to use indirect methods of price competition which are not as likely to be followed by competitors. The following paragraphs discuss some types of indirect price competition practiced.

Scrambled Merchandising

The continued growth of **scrambled merchandising** has introduced a new dimension in retail pricing. For example, many drugstores have expanded their merchandise mix into non-health-related lines to take advantage of high markons. Supermarkets have also added nonfood lines for the same reason. Finally, home improvement items can be bought in many different types of outlets including hardware stores, home improvement centers, national chain outlets, and promotional chains such as K mart.

Multiple Distribution

Multiple distribution is widely practiced in major appliances retailing. Retailers who prefer not to use price as a competitive weapon often are at a significant disadvantage compared to promotional discounters. Thus, suppliers have responded by offering slightly different models under different brand names to various types of outlets. Each retailer can then maintain a preferred posture on price without a head-to-head battle with competition over identical merchandise.

Retailers also are increasingly developing a portfolio of different store types to remain competitive. For example, warehouse grocery outlets and limited assortment (box) stores may be owned by operators of conventional supermarkets, but are operated as separate divisions.

Variations in the Service Mix

Increasingly, retailers are competing in certain lines of business on a price and nonprice basis at the same time. For example, gasoline service stations have full-service pumps that sell gasoline for approximately 2 cents per gallon more than their self-service pumps. Arco has gone one step further and eliminated company-issued credit cards. They thus have eliminated the service fee on the cards. The lower costs are passed on to consumers in the form of lower prices. Some furniture outlets use a similar approach by charging for delivery and installation.

Cash Discounts

Cash discounts can be profitable if retailers have (1) a high proportion of credit sales, (2) a high proportion of credit customers who are willing to pay by cash or check as a result of a discount, and (3) large-ticket items or large-volume purchases. The Cash Discount Act allows retailers to offer unlimited discounts to encourage cash payments.

Frequent-Shopper Discounts

Some retailers are experimenting with frequent-shopper discounts, much like the frequent-flyer programs offered by the airlines, to generate greater sales volume and customer loyalty. Shoppers' cumulative purchases are tracked throughout the year, and bonuses are offered after shoppers reach a specified dollar volume of purchase. Additional bonuses are sometimes given to stimulate shopping on slow days or to clear out slow-moving merchandise.

Owl Supermarkets in Minneapolis generated a 10 percent increase in average sales through a frequent-shopper plan. The amount of the discount was determined by how much the shopper spent at the stores each month. Additionally, travel discounts were offered to those shoppers who reached certain participation levels.[7]

CHAPTER HIGHLIGHTS

— A variety of external factors affect retail pricing decisions. The factors include the type of goods carried, the type of store at which the merchandise is sold, the level of profit desired, the level of customer demand, the market structure, supplier policies, economic conditions, and government regulations.

— Primary government regulations affecting retail pricing decisions include the Sherman Act, various state unfair-trade practice laws, and the Robinson-Patman Act.

— Retail pricing decisions are affected by the retailers' policy on the price level desired. The three pricing levels are at the market, below the market, and above the market.

— The majority of retail firms in the United States offer goods at one "take it or leave it" price. Some stores such as appliance dealers, however, do not follow a one-price policy.

— Many retailers have their own private brands. Wholesalers may also offer retail customers their private brands. Alternatively, manufacturers may develop their own brand for selling to anyone who wants to buy it. Additionally, some retailers sell no-brand-name merchandise.

— Some retailers use leader pricing with selected product categories. The characteristics of the best price leaders are: (1) well-known and widely used items, (2) items priced low enough to attract numerous buyers, and (3) items not usually bought in large quantities and stored.

— In practice, retailers may raise or lower their prices after the original pricing decisions have been made. These pricing adjustments may be in the form of additional markups or markdowns.

— A variety of factors can affect pricing decisions in addition to markons and markdowns. These factors include distributor allowances, consumer rebates, and consumer pressure.

— Retailers often face indirect price competition. The most frequent means of pursuing a policy of indirect price competition include scrambled merchandising, multiple distribution by vendors, variations in the service mix, and offering price discounts for cash payment.

— The appendix to this chapter contains a checklist which includes many of the ideas discussed. Some new ideas are presented, as well. As such, this aid is a fine accompaniment to the material presented in this chapter and illustrates the type of information available to retailers from the Small Business Administration.

KEY TERMS

Above-the-market pricing A pricing strategy in which retailers set prices above the level of competitors.

At-the-market pricing A pricing strategy in which retailers set prices at the level of competitors.

Below-the-market pricing A pricing strategy in which retailers set prices below the level of competitors.

Consumer rebates A situation in which a manufacturer pays the consumer a sum of money in the form of a price reduction when a purchase is made.

Convenience goods Products for which consumers do not feel it is worth their time to shop around for a better price.

Distributor allowances Discounts and/or extended payment terms to retailers designed to encourage them to purchase additional merchandise from a wholesaler or manufacturer.

Fair-trade laws Federal legislation which allowed manufacturers to set minimum retail prices for their products. (The practice is now illegal.)

Generic merchandise Unbranded merchandise that is typically somewhat lower in quality than brand-name merchandise.

Horizontal price-fixing An agreement between two or more retailers to charge the same price for comparable merchandise.

Initial markon The difference between the cost of merchandise and the original retail price.

Loss-leader pricing A situation in which merchandise is sold with less than the normal markup or margin in an effort to increase store traffic.

Maintained markon The difference between invoice cost and sales retail.

Manufacturer's brand A brand, often referred to as a national brand, owned by a manufacturer who may sell to anyone who wants to buy the brand.

Markdown A reduction in the original selling price of an item.

Merchandising Having the right merchandise, at the right price, at the right place, at the right time, and in the right quantities.

Multiple distribution A situation in which suppliers offer slightly different models under different brand names to various types of retail outlets.

Original retail price The first price at which an item is offered for sale.

Price-lining Featuring products at a limited number of prices that reflect varying levels of merchandise quality. Price-lining may occur either in the context of rigid price points or price zones.

Price points Offering merchandise at a small number of different prices. For example, a merchant might price all "good" suits at $175, all "better" suits at $225, and "best" suits at $350.

Price zones Pricing strategy in which a merchant establishes a range of prices for merchandise of different quality. For example, prices for "good" suits might be between $175 and $200 while prices for "better" suits might be between $225 and $275.

Private brands Brands owned by a retail or a wholesale firm rather than by a manufacturer.

Sales retail The final selling price, or the amount the customer pays for the merchandise.

Scrambled merchandising A situation in which retailers diversify their merchandise mix to take advantage of higher markups on some merchandise lines.

Sherman Act Federal legislation which declares that price-fixing is illegal.

Shopping goods Items for which consumers carefully compare price and quality differences before making a purchase decision.

Single-price policy All merchandise in a store is sold at the same price.

Specialty goods Products that consumers know they want and that they are willing to make a special effort to acquire.

DISCUSSION QUESTIONS

1. Why is pricing such a vitally important part of the retail planning process?
2. Which external factors affect the prices a retailer charges? Discuss each of these factors.
3. Discuss the possible price-level policies available to the retailer. Give an example of a type of retail organization that follows each of the policy options.
4. How can a retailer offer private brands and generics at below-the-market price and still make a good profit?
5. Illustrate price-lining and evaluate the policy.

6. Explain and evaluate odd-price endings.
7. Evaluate the concept of a single-price policy.
8. Discuss the concept of a leader-pricing policy. What are the characteristics of products that are good price leaders?
9. Explain the kinds of pricing adjustments that may be made after the original price decision has been made.
10. Define the following terms: original retail price, sales retail, initial markon, and maintained markon.

APPLICATION EXERCISES

1. Devise a questionnaire to get consumer reaction to raising the price of goods already on display. (Grocers frequently do this by putting the higher price tag directly on top of the former price.) Do consumers feel this practice is fair or unfair? Why? Allow room for individual consumer comment on your questionnaire.
2. Devise a method for determining whether people perceive odd or even prices as being lower. This can be done, for example, by interviewing store managers or consumers, or by observing behavior in a store. Visit two types of stores, such as a hardware store and a clothing store; which pricing strategy does each follow? Why?
3. Assume that you are a management trainee for a major supermarket chain. Select a market basket of products which are available in all stores and easily comparable (e.g., no private brands), and compare prices (including specials) in a conventional supermarket, a "warehouse-type" outlet, and a convenience store (a 7-Eleven). Keep your record over a period of time, present your data in an organized format, and draw conclusions about the pricing philosophy of the different types of food operations.
4. Health and beauty aids are carried in many different kinds of retail establishments; for example, conventional drugstores, supermarkets, discount drugstores, and department stores. Often, each type of establishment promises lower prices, better assortments, and so on, to establish a differential. List selected items available in each store and group stores by type. Compare and contrast the items among the various types of stores. See what you find to be the "real" strategy of the competing stores in the market. Why is the lowest-priced store able to price as indicated? What are the specials? Are they similar for all stores?
5. Since meat is such an important item in a family budget, focus a project on the pricing strategy of competing food stores relative to key meat items. You will have to interview butchers to determine what kinds of meat items you should investigate to make your comparisons. Include different types of "image" stores, and see how meat prices follow the images projected by the stores. Charts comparing prices by type of meat item may show an interesting relationship. Watch for specials—try to use the regular prices for your comparisons. Come up with some strategy conclusions from your study.

PROBLEMS

1. If markup on cost is 36 percent, what is the equivalent markup on retail?
2. If markup on cost is 44 percent, what is the equivalent markup on retail?
3. If markup on retail is 18 percent, what is the equivalent markup on cost?
4. If markup on retail is 41 percent, what is the equivalent markup on cost?
5. A suit costs a retailer $36.80. If a markup of 43 percent on cost is required, what must the retail price be?
6. A lamp is marked up $168. This is a 61 percent markup on retail. What is (a) the cost and (b) the retail price?
7. The retail price of a ring is $7,800. If the markup on retail is 78 percent, what is the cost of the ring to the retailer?
8. The retail price of a picture is $48.50. If the markup on cost is 38 percent, what is the cost of the picture to the retailer?
9. Men's wallets may be purchased from a manufacturer for $300 per dozen. If the wallets are marked up 28 percent on cost, what retail price will be set per wallet?

10. Women's scarves may be purchased from a manufacturer at $81.60 per dozen. If the scarves are marked up 16 percent on retail, what is the retail price of each scarf?

11. What is (a) the initial markon percent and (b) the maintained markon percent in a department that has the following planned figures: expenses, $7,200; profit, $4,500; sales, $28,000; employee discounts, $450; markdowns, $1,200; and shortages, $225?

12. Sales of $85,000 were planned in a department in which expenses were established at $26,000; shortages, $2,200; and employee discounts, $600. If a profit of 6 percent of sales is desired, what initial markon percent should be planned?

13. Department Z has taken $600 in markdowns to date. Net sales to date are $22,000. What is the markdown percentage to date?

CASES

1. Waldenbooks Goes beyond Low Prices

The retail book business rings up sales of $11 billion a year. Waldenbooks and the B. Dalton Bookseller chain have 50 percent of the business. B. Dalton now discounts books that appear on the *New York Times* hard-cover best-seller list by 25–35 percent off the cover price and schedules nationally advertised book sales several times during each year. Their move is bad news for smaller discounters such as Barnes and Nobles Bookstores, Inc.

Waldenbooks began pursuing a similar, yet different, strategy after being acquired by K mart Corporation. Walden began testing a new store concept, called Readers' Market, that offers discounts ranging from 10 percent on paperbacks to 35 percent for hard-cover best-sellers. Readers' Market offers something other than low prices to distinguish it from other discounters. The emphasis is on best-sellers in hardback and paperback, but, in contrast to other discounters, they have not abandoned slower-selling categories like child care, nature and pets, sociology, and performing arts. Additionally, Readers' Market outlets sell Sine Qua Non classical music tapes and prerecorded movies, including the Kartes Video Classics. Management believes their merchandise mix gives them an edge over other discounters.

Readers' Market also attempts to differentiate itself in ways other than assortment. The stores offer all of the services of the regular Waldenbooks stores except the Waldenbooks Readers' Club, which allows customers to earn discounts by buying a specified number of books over a specified time period. Readers' Market will special order books for customers at discount prices and will accept credit cards for purchases.

Questions
1. Which elements of the Readers' Market merchandising strategy are designed to differentiate the firm from other discounters?
2. What are the risks in the Readers' Market strategy?
3. Is low price the primary weapon of Readers' Market? Why or why not?

Source: Based on "Waldenbooks Goes beyond Low Prices," *Chain Store Age, General Merchandise Trends,* March 1985, p. 21; Steven Weiner, "Dayton-Hudson's B. Dalton Subsidiary Signals Price War for Best-Seller Books," *The Wall Street Journal,* October 30, 1985, p. 10.

2. Off-Price Marketers on the Beam

Less than five years ago, off-price retailing began sending alarms through the retail industry. Such outlets sell national brand and designer label merchandise at prices below those offered by department stores and conventional discounters. However, they are now being hard pressed by deep discounters and traditional department stores which routinely run price-off sales each week. The result is that the off-pricers don't have the distinction of being off-priced anymore.

The off-price merchants have responded by following department-store selling tactics. They are abandoning their out-of-the-way locations, spartan buildings, and minimum advertising budgets. Now they are building upscale malls which include skylights, baby-sitting services, waterfalls, and other amenities. Brand-name merchandise is still being sold at deep discounts.

Questions
1. What, if anything, now differentiates the off-price merchants from the department stores and the conventional discounters?

2. What steps have the department stores taken to counter the actions of the off-price retailers?
3. Why were the off-price merchants able to achieve an initial high level of success when they entered the marketplace? Speculate on their future.

Source: Based on Pat Sloan, "Off-Price Marketers on the Beam," *Advertising Age,* November 4, 1985, p. 90; see also, "Off-Pricers Grab Growing Retail Market Share," *Marketing News,* March 13, 1987, p. 9.

ENDNOTES

1. Leonard L. Berry, "Multidimensional Strategies Can Combat Price Wars," *Marketing News,* January 31, 1986, p. 10.
2. "Forget Satisfying the Consumer—Just Out-Fox the Other Guy," *Business Week,* October 7, 1985, p. 58.
3. Steve Weiner, "Dayton-Hudson's B. Dalton Subsidiary Signals Price War for Best-Seller Books," *The Wall Street Journal,* October 30, 1985, p. 10; "Off-Pricers Grab Growing Retail Market Share," *Marketing News,* March 13, 1987, p. 9.
4. Janet Meyers, "Major Hotel Chains Discover How Suite It Is," *Advertising Age,* April 1, 1985, p. 12.
5. "At Silver Palate, Good Taste Is Priceless," *Chain Store Age, General Merchandise Trends,* April 1985, pp. 39–40.
6. "Wanted: A Few Courageous Leaders," *Apparel Merchandising,* December 1985, pp. 5–6.
7. "Frequent-Shopper Programs Help Deal with Retailing's 'Four Revolutions'," *Marketing News,* July 6, 1984, p. 6; "Frequent-Shopper Plan Builds Red Owl Volume," *The Supermarket News,* April 14, 1986, p. 4.

APPENDIX A

A PRICING CHECKLIST FOR RETAILERS

This aid is a checklist for the owner-manager of a retail business. These 52 questions probe the considerations—from markup to pricing strategy to adjustments—that lead to correct pricing decisions. You can use this checklist to establish prices in your new store, or you can use it to periodically review your established pricing policy.

A retailer's prices influence the quantities of various items that consumers will buy, which in turn affects total revenue and profit. Hence, correct pricing decisions are a key to successful retail management. With this in mind, the following 52-question checklist has been developed to assist small retailers in making systematic, informed decisions regarding pricing strategies and tactics.

This checklist should be especially useful to a new retailer making pricing decisions for the first time. However, established retailers, including successful ones, can also benefit from this aid. They may use it as a reminder of all the individual pricing decisions they should review periodically. And, it may also be used in training new employees who will have pricing authority.

The central concept of markup

A major step toward making a profit in retailing is selling merchandise for more than it costs you. This difference between cost of merchandise and retail price is called *markup* (or occasionally *markon*). From an arithmetic standpoint, markup is calculated as follows:

$$\text{Dollar markup} = \text{Retail price} - \text{Cost of the merchandise}$$
$$\text{Percentage markup} = \frac{\text{Dollar markup}}{\text{Retail price}}$$

If an item costs $6.50, and you feel consumers will buy it at $10.00, the dollar markup is $3.50 (which is $10.00 − $6.50). Going one step further, the percentage markup is 35 percent (which is $3.50 ÷ $10.00). Anyone involved in retail pricing should be as knowledgeable about these two formulas as about the name and preferences of his or her best customer!

Source: Bruce J. Walker, *Small Marketers Aid* no. 158, Small Business Administration (Washington, D.C.: U.S. Government Printing Office).

Two other key points about markup should be mentioned. First, the *cost of merchandise* used in calculating markup consists of the base invoice price for the merchandise, *plus* any transportation charges, *minus* any quantity and cash discounts given by the seller. Second, *retail price,* rather than cost, is ordinarily used in calculating percentage markup. The reason for this is that when other operating figures such as wages, advertising expenses, and profit are expressed as a percentage, all are based on retail price rather than cost of the merchandise being sold.

Target consumers and the retailing mix

In this section, your attention is directed to price as it relates to your potential customers. These questions examine your merchandise, location, promotion, and customer services that will be combined with price in attempting to satisfy shoppers and make a profit. After some questions, brief commentary is provided.

Yes *No*

1. Is the relative price of this item very important to your target consumers? ☐ ☐

   The importance of price depends on the specific product and on the specific individual. Some shoppers are very price-conscious; others want convenience and knowledgeable sales personnel. Because of these variations, you need to learn about your customers' desires in relation to different products. Having sales personnel seek feedback from shoppers is a good starting point.

2. Are prices based on estimates of the number of units that consumers will demand at various price levels? ☐ ☐

   Demand-oriented pricing such as this is superior to cost-oriented pricing. In the cost approach, a predetermined amount is added to the cost of the merchandise, whereas the demand approach considers what consumers are willing to pay.

3. Have you established a price range for the product? ☐ ☐

   The cost of merchandise will be at one end of the price range, and the level above which consumers will not buy the product at the other end.

4. Have you considered what price strategies would be compatible with your store's total retailing mix that includes merchandise, location, promotion, and services? ☐ ☐

5. Will trade-ins be accepted as part of the purchase price on items such as appliances and television sets? ☐ ☐

Supplier and competitor considerations

This set of questions looks outside your firm to two factors that you cannot directly control—suppliers and competitors.

		Yes	No
6.	Do you have final pricing authority?	☐	☐

With the repeal of fair-trade laws, yes answers will be more common than in previous years. Still, a supplier can control retail prices by refusing to deal with nonconforming stores (a tactic which may be illegal) or by selling to you on consignment.

		Yes	No
7.	Do you know what direct competitors are doing price-wise?	☐	☐
8.	Do you regularly review competitors' ads to obtain information on their prices?	☐	☐
9.	Is your store large enough to employ either a full-time or part-time comparison shopper?	☐	☐

These three questions emphasize that you must watch competitors' prices so your prices will not be far out of line—too high or too low—without good reason. Of course, there may be a good reason for out-of-the-ordinary prices, such as seeking a special price image.

A price-level strategy

Selecting a general level of prices in relation to competition is a key strategic decision, perhaps the most important.

		Yes	No
10.	Should your overall strategy be to sell at prevailing market price levels?	☐	☐

The other alternatives are an above-the-market strategy or a below-the-market strategy.

		Yes	No
11.	Should competitors' temporary price reductions ever be matched?	☐	☐
12.	Could private-brand merchandise be obtained in order to avoid direct price competition?	☐	☐

Calculating planned initial markup

In this section, you will have to look *inside* your business, taking into account sales, expenses, and profits before setting prices. The point is that your initial markup must be large enough to cover anticipated expenses and reductions *and* still produce a satisfactory profit.

	Yes	No
13. Have you estimated sales, operating expenses, and reductions for the next selling season?	☐	☐
14. Have you established a profit objective for the next selling season?	☐	☐
15. Given estimated sales, expenses, and reductions, have you planned initial markup?	☐	☐

This figure is calculated with the following formula:
Initial markup percentage

$$= \frac{Operating\ expenses\ +\ Reductions\ +\ Profit}{Net\ sales\ +\ Reductions}$$

Reductions consist of markdowns, stock shortages, and employee and customer discounts. The following example uses dollar amounts, but the estimates can also be percentages. If a retailer anticipates for a particular department $94,000 in sales, $34,000 in expenses, and $6,000 in reductions, and if the retailer desires a $4,000 profit, initial markup percentage can be calculated:

Initial markup percentage

$$= \frac{\$34,000\ +\ \$6,000\ +\ \$4,000}{\$94,000\ +\ \$6,000} = 44\ percent$$

The resulting figure, 44 percent in this example, indicates what size initial markup is needed on the average in order to make the desired profits.

16. Would it be appropriate to have different initial markup figures for various lines of merchandise or services? ☐ ☐

You would seriously consider this when some lines have much different characteristics than others. For instance, a clothing retailer might logically have different initial markup figures for suits, shirts and pants, and accessories. (Various merchandise characteristics are covered in an upcoming section.) You may want those items with the highest turnover rates to carry the lowest initial markup.

Store policies

Having calculated an initial markup figure, you could proceed to set prices on your merchandise. But an important decision such as this should not be rushed. Instead, you should consider additional factors which suggest the best price.

		Yes	No

17. Is your tentative price compatible with established store policies? ☐ ☐

   Policies are written guidelines indicating appropriate methods or actions in different situations. If established with care, they can save you time in decision making and provide for consistent treatment of shoppers. Specific policy areas that you should consider are as follows:

18. Will a one-price system, under which the same price is charged every purchaser of a particular item, be used on all items? ☐ ☐

   The alternative is to negotiate price with consumers.

19. Will odd-ending prices, such as $1.98 and $44.95, be more appealing to your customers than even-ending prices? ☐ ☐

20. Will consumers buy more if multiple pricing, such as 2 for $8.50 is used? ☐ ☐

21. Should any leader offerings (selected products with quite low, less profitable prices) be used? ☐ ☐

22. Have the characteristics of an effective leader offering been considered? ☐ ☐

   Ordinarily, a leader offering needs the following characteristics to accomplish its purpose of generating much shopper traffic: used by most people, bought frequently, very familiar regular price, and not a large expenditure for consumers.

23. Will price lining, the practice of setting up distinct price points (such as $5.00, $7.50, and $10.00) and then marking all related merchandise at these points be used? ☐ ☐

24. Would price lining by means of zones (such as $5.00–$7.50 and $12.50–$15.00) be more appropriate than price points? ☐ ☐

25. Will cents-off coupons be used in newspaper ads or mailed to selected consumers on any occasion? ☐ ☐

26. Would periodic special sales, combining reduced prices and heavier advertising, be consistent with the store image you are seeking? ☐ ☐

27. Do certain items have greater appeal than others when they are part of a special sale? ☐ ☐

28. Has the impact of various sale items on profits been □ □ considered?

Sale prices may mean little or no profit on these items. Still, the special sale may contribute to total profits by bringing in shoppers who may also buy some regular-price (and profitable) merchandise and by attracting new customers. Also, you should avoid featuring items that require a large amount of labor, which in turn would reduce or erase profits. For instance, according to this criterion, shirts would be a better special-sale item than men's suits that often require free alterations.

29. Will "rain checks" be issued to consumers who come in □ □ for special-sale merchandise that is temporarily out of stock?

You should give particular attention to this decision since rain checks are required in some situations. Your lawyer or the regional Federal Trade Commission office should be consulted for specific advice regarding whether rain checks are needed in the special sales you plan.

Nature of the merchandise

In this section you will be considering how selected characteristics of particular merchandise affect planned initial markup.

	Yes	No
30. Did you get a "good deal" on the wholesale price of this merchandise?	□	□
31. Is this item at the peak of its popularity?	□	□
32. Are handling and selling costs relatively great due to the product being bulky, having a low turnover rate, and/or requiring much personal selling, installation, or alterations?	□	□
33. Are relatively large levels of reductions expected due to markdowns, spoilage, breakage, or theft?	□	□

With respect to the preceding four questions, Yes answers suggest the possibility of or need for larger-than-normal initial markups. For example, very fashionable clothing often will carry a higher markup than basic clothing such as underwear, because the particular fashion may suddenly lose its appeal to consumers.

34. Will customer services such as delivery, alterations, gift □ □ wrapping, and installation be free of charge to customers?

The alternative is to charge for some or all of these services.

Environmental considerations

The questions in this section focus your attention on three factors outside your business: economic conditions, laws, and consumerism.

	Yes	No

35. If your state has an unfair sales practices act that requires minimum markups on certain merchandise, do your prices comply with this statute? ☐ ☐

36. Are economic conditions in your trading area abnormal? ☐ ☐

Consumers tend to be more price conscious when the economy is depressed, suggesting that lower-than-normal markups may be needed to be competitive. On the other hand, shoppers are less price conscious when the economy is booming which would permit larger markups on a selective basis.

37. Are the ways in which prices are displayed and promoted compatible with consumerism, one part of which has been a call for more straightforward price information? ☐ ☐

38. If yours is a grocery store, is it feasible to use unit pricing in which the item's cost per some standard measure is indicated? ☐ ☐

Having asked (and hopefully answered) more than three dozen questions, you are indeed ready to establish retail prices. When you have decided on an appropriate percentage markup, 35 percent on a garden hose for example, the next step is to determine what percentage of the still unknown retail price is represented by the cost figure. The basic markup formula is simply rearranged to do this:

$$Cost = Retail\ price - Markup$$
$$Cost = 100\% - 35\% = 65\%$$

Then the dollar cost, say $3.25 for the garden hose, is plugged into the following formula to arrive at the retail price:

$$Retail\ price = \frac{Dollar\ cost}{Percentage\ cost} = \frac{\$3.25}{65\%\ (or\ .65)} = \$5.00$$

39. Is the retail price consistent with your planned initial markups? ☐ ☐

Adjustments

It would be ideal if all items sold at their original retail prices. But we know that things are not always ideal. Therefore, a section on price adjustments is necessary.

	Yes	*No*
40. Are additional markups called for, because wholesale prices have increased or because an item's low price causes consumers to question its quality?	☐	☐
41. Should employees be given purchase discounts?	☐	☐
42. Should any groups of customers, such as students or senior citizens, be given purchase discounts?	☐	☐
43. When markdowns appear necessary, have you first considered other alternatives such as retaining price but changing another element of the retailing mix, or storing the merchandise until the next selling season?	☐	☐
44. Has an attempt been made to identify causes of markdowns so that steps can be taken to minimize the number of avoidable buying, selling, and pricing errors that cause markdowns?	☐	☐
45. Has the relationship between timing and size of markdown been taken into account?	☐	☐

In general, markdowns taken early in the selling season or shortly after sales slow down can be smaller than late markdowns. Whether an early or late markdown would be more appropriate in a particular situation depends on several things: your assessment of how many consumers might still be interested in the product, the size of the initial markup, and the amount remaining in stock.

46. Would a schedule of automatic markdowns after merchandise has been in stock for specified intervals be appropriate?	☐	☐
47. Is the size of the markdown ''just enough'' to stimulate purchases?	☐	☐

Of course, this question is difficult—perhaps impossible— to answer. Nevertheless, it stresses the point that you have to carefully observe the effects of different size markdowns so you can eventually acquire some insights into what size markdowns are ''just enough'' for different kinds of merchandise.

48. Has a procedure been worked out for markdowns on price-lined merchandise? ☐ ☐

49. Is the markdown price calculated from the off-retail percentage? ☐ ☐

This question gets you into the arithmetic of markdowns. Usually, you first tentatively decide on the percentage amount price must be marked down to excite consumers. For example, if you think a 25 percent markdown will be necessary to sell a lavender sofa, the dollar amount of the markdown is calculated as follows:

Dollar markdown = Off-retail percentage × Previous retail price
Dollar markdown = 25% (or .25) × \$500 = \$125

Then the markdown price is obtained by subtracting the dollar markdown from the previous retail price. Hence, the sofa would be \$375 after taking the markdown.

50. Has cost of the merchandise been considered before setting the markdown price? ☐ ☐

This is not to say that a markdown price should never be lower than cost: on the contrary, a price that low may be your only hope of generating some revenue from the item. But cost should be considered to make sure that below-cost markdown prices are the exception in your store, rather than being so common your total profits are really hurt.

51. Have procedures for recording the dollar amounts, percentages, and probable causes of markdowns been set up? ☐ ☐

Analyzing markdowns is very important since it can provide information that will assist in calculating planned initial markup, in decreasing errors that cause markdowns, and in evaluating suppliers.

You may be weary from thinking your way through the preceding sections, but don't overlook an important final question:

52. Have you marked the calendar for a periodic review of your pricing decisions? ☐ ☐

15

Physically Handling and Securing Merchandise

Effective Merchandise Distribution Cited as a Major Factor in Wal-Mart's Success

The Wal-Mart chain has grown from a small cluster of stores in Arkansas to a 22-state chain of 891 stores, selling more than $8.5 billion annually in discounted merchandise.

Chairman Sam Walton gives much of the credit for growth in sales and profitability to the Wal-Mart version of hub-and-spoke distribution marketing. Like most retailers, Wal-Mart endorses the first three guidelines to retail success—location, location, and location—but then comes a difference. Wal-Mart is primarily concerned with *warehouse* location. While other retailers build warehouses to serve existing outlets, Walton goes at it the other way around. He starts with a giant warehouse, then spots stores all around it. One large Walton warehouse serves a radius of 400 miles.

Today, some 80 percent of store needs are fulfilled from eight distribution centers in six hub cities. A typical 650,000-square-foot center serves 150 stores in a six-hour drive radius. All centers are highly automated, with on-line receipt of orders from store registers, automatic inventory control, and reordering on-line from 200 vendors. It is rare that store orders take more than 36 to 48 hours to be filled.

Still another hub-and-spoke system looms on the Wal-Mart horizon—satellite communication of voice, data, and video information—for faster, more efficient, less costly order transmission and delivery. The $16 million contract is expected to pay back quickly with reductions in major expense items such as the chain's $10 million annual phone bill.

Source: Based on "Wal-Mart Credits Deep Discounts to Hub-and-Spoke Planning," *Marketing News,* June 20, 1986, p. 18.

Wal-Mart's merchandise distribution system is constantly being fine-tuned although distribution costs now stand at a remarkably low 2 cents on the dollar. This figure is believed to be less than half the standard for the industry.

*T*he Wal-Mart example illustrates how an effective merchandise distribution system in a multiunit retail organization can be an important element of competitive strategy and can have a positive impact on profitability. The first part of this chapter focuses on multiunit firms and the issues involved in getting merchandise from consolidation warehouses/distribution centers to the individual stores. For purposes of discussion, the term **merchandise distribution** will be used to refer to this aspect of merchandise management. The second section of the chapter focuses on the *physical-handling* aspect of merchandise management including the receiving, checking, and marking of goods. The final issue of merchandise management in this chapter is stock shortages. Here attention is given to shoplifting and internal theft, with emphasis on how to detect and prevent such behaviors.

After reading this chapter, you will be able to:

1. Explain how multiunit retail organizations manage the movement of merchandise from consolidation warehouses/distribution centers to the individual stores.

2. Evaluate issues related to the management of physical handling activities.

3. Describe activities involved in the receiving and checking of merchandise.

4. Explain the various aspects of merchandise marking.

5. Discuss problems associated with shoplifting and employee theft and measures retailers can take to detect and prevent such behaviors.

MERCHANDISE DISTRIBUTION IN MULTIUNIT ORGANIZATIONS

Some multiunit retailers operate under a system whereby merchandise is shipped from vendors directly to the individual stores in the chain. Many chain operations, however, employ a merchandise distribution system involving the use of consolidation warehouses or distribution centers. Merchandise is shipped from vendors to the retail chain's distribution center(s) and from there is redirected to the individual store units. Many of these centers are computerized and highly automated, using the most recent innovations in merchandise handling and moving equipment. Scenes from such a facility are shown in Exhibits 15–1 and 15–2. These are pictures of a 72,000-square-foot distribution center opened in May 1986 by Younkers to serve the merchandise needs of its department and specialty-type stores.

Distribution centers provide advantages of better inventory control, quicker reordering of merchandise, and rapid movement of merchandise so as to increase turnover and margins at the stores. Central warehouses allow management to take advantage of the discounts offered by vendors for buying in larger quantities. Such facilities also simplify the accounts payable process since fewer purchase orders need to be paid. Vendors also pay more attention to large bulk orders which are moving to a central point.

Let's look at some specific advantages of using highly automated, computerized distribution centers. These examples illustrate how retail productivity and efficiency can be increased by using such centers effectively.

Greater Accuracy in Moving Merchandise to Individual Stores[1]

A common error in multiunit organizations is for individual stores to receive the wrong merchandise from the distribution center or receive the right goods, but in the wrong quantities. However, Rich's Department Stores, based in Salem, Massachusetts, has dealt with this problem and uses a computerized out-bound system which allows stores to know exactly what is on the way from the distribution center before it arrives at the stores.

When a store is scheduled to receive a shipment of merchandise from the distribution center, information concerning the shipment is put into a computer at the headquarters office located adjacent to the center. A printer generates peel-off, bar-code labels for the cartons of merchandise. Each bar code identifies a unique store, department, and warehouse transfer order. Warehouse personnel then pick the merchandise, affix the bar-code labels, and take the cartons to the shipping area. The cartons are then moved through a wanding station where an employee "reads" the bar codes with hand-held Telxon wands that have been programmed to accept only bar codes for a particular store. If an employee tries to scan a carton that has been mixed in with another store's shipment, the Telxon will emit a warning signal. Information concerning the contents of the shipment is then electronically communicated to the store. The system not only enables greater accuracy

EXHIBIT 15–1 **CHUTES AND ROLLERS ZOOM STORES-BOUND GOODS TOWARD YOUNKERS' TRUCKS**

EXHIBIT 15–2 **GRAVITY BRINGS GOODS TO OPERATOR, THEN TAKES THEM AWAY AT YOUNKERS, ON GARR-INSTALLED E-Z FLOW INCLINED ROLLER CONVEYOR SYSTEM**

in the movement of goods to individual stores but also has led to reduced paperwork and labor savings at the store level.

Faster Movement of Merchandise to Stores Leads to Higher Margins[2]

Highly automated, computerized distribution centers enable faster movement of merchandise to the individual stores, which results in higher margins being earned. Such advantages were apparent to Decelle, a seven-unit off-price retailer based in Braintree, Massachusetts, after moving into a new, automated merchandise-handling facility in May 1985.

Before moving into the new facility, the chain was often backlogged up to four weeks in deliveries of merchandise from its warehouse to stores. The backorder situation was so bad that the company was forced to mark down $150,000 to $200,000 worth of merchandise because it could not get the merchandise into the stores fast enough.

In the new facility, employees process 45 percent more merchandise than in the old one. Turnover time that was up to two weeks has now been reduced to as little as two days from distribution center to store rack. Company executives believe the quicker turnover will mean a 20 percent increase in store sales.

The major component of the new distribution center is the way in which hanging garments are handled. The company is now processing 50 percent more hanging merchandise per hour, which is important since 60 percent of company sales come from this merchandise category. Previously, the garments had to be unpacked from cartons, checked, ticketed, and repacked in cartons, only to be unpacked again later in the store. The new facility has a 26-line monorail system for handling hanging garments, similar to the one shown in Exhibit 15–3. The merchandise arrives hanging and remains hanging as it is checked, ticketed, separated by store, and moved out for store delivery.

Refined Merchandising Strategy through Assortment Expansion[3]

Adding a measure of sophistication to its merchandise distribution process enabled closeout retailer Ira Watson to refine its merchandising strategy by expanding assortments. Watson, headquartered in Knoxville, Tennessee, has many stores located in rural areas. The chain used to ship only full-case loads of merchandise to its stores. This system limited each store's merchandise mix, but the firm did not want to load stores with large quantities of slower-moving items.

Watson then improved its distribution system to handle less than case quantities. The chain immediately began increasing assortments, filling in its existing merchandise mix with lines that had not sold quickly enough to be included when the distribution center shipped only full cases. The change enabled the company to give its customers more merchandise choices, but without the chain having to handle more merchandise through its distribution system.

PHYSICAL-HANDLING ACTIVITIES

As stated earlier, **physical handling** involves receiving, checking, and marking merchandise. While these activities are often performed in distribution centers, the following sections focus on these activities being performed in the retail store. Before discussing each of the activities, however, let's talk about several issues related to managing the physical-handling process.

Managing the
Physical-
Handling
Activities

Several issues are related to managing physical-handling activities. One is the question of who is responsible for carrying out the activities. A second issue involves the location of physical handling within the store. Finally, procedures for controlling the process must be established.

Assigning Responsibility for the Physical-Handling Process

In a small retail store, the entire physical-handling process is simple. Probably a single individual such as a buyer or salesperson performs all the functions.

In a large retail firm where the volume of goods handled may be quite large, specialized personnel perform the physical-handling functions. These personnel are included under the operating division rather than the merchandising division of the retail firm. Several reasons exist for having the physical handling performed by specialists rather than by buyers or salespeople. Salespeople may resent having to do jobs other than selling and thus may be careless and negligent. Also, salespeople are likely to be more efficient at selling if they do not have additional nonselling responsibilities. Specialized personnel, on the other hand, do a better job of performing operational functions. Controls are better. Also, specialization normally results in a better, more efficient job.

Location of Physical-Handling Activities

Except in the very small store, physical-handling activities are normally located in a part of the store that is not used for selling. Even though the structure of the building affects the placement, several factors should be kept in mind when deciding the location of the physical-handling activities:

1. The merchandise must be received from transportation carriers, so the receiving area needs to be easily accessible to delivery vehicles.
2. The value of the space should be low in terms of traffic generated. "Expensive" space should be used for selling. An upper floor is often used in a large store. Of course, vertical movement facilities are then needed to get the goods to the receiving, checking, and marking stations.
3. Depending on the kind of goods, the retailer may want to locate the receiving, checking, and marking area close to the sales floor or the stockrooms. Handling costs are high, and ways must be considered to keep the costs to a minimum.

One merchant opened a ready-to-wear boutique and allocated no space to physical handling when planning the store's layout. The washroom was soon being utilized for these activities. Even though the store was small, moving goods from the remote washroom to the selling floor was inefficient. This example illustrates that planning and organizing are essential management functions, regardless of the size of the business.

Controlling Physical-Handling Activities

Every company strives to select the best method for controlling the physical-handling functions. Many variations exist, but the essential information must be collected by all retail managers. The J. C. Penney system is explained for illustrative purposes. The company, of course, is large, but what is done there must be done by all retailers. Only those elements of the system that can be adapted by the management of any type or size store are discussed.

The basis of the Penney system is the purchase-order form. Every retail company should have its own purchase order form. Using a supplier's form will diminish the control of physical-handling functions. The simplest control feature of the purchase order is a discrete number—in this case, 02973, as shown in Exhibit 15–4.

Important information is contained on this form. Immediately above the supplier's name and address, the buyer will place the supplier's number—another control feature. Each supplier has a specific number. The terms of sale (payment period and credit terms) are specified in the box labeled ''terms.''

The box labeled "mail" tells the mailroom whether the original and/or duplicate should be sent to the supplier or to a distribution point within the company. The remainder of the purchase order is fairly clear. Obviously, the "company retail" price will not be filled in on the original, which goes to the supplier. The triplicate, or office copy, is for accounts payable. The receiving copy is utilized in the receiving, checking, and marking activities. If back orders or incomplete shipments exist, the purchase order will be kept open. If the shipment is complete, the receiving copy of the purchase order is sent to the office for payment.

The issues just discussed all relate to managing the physical-handling process. Let's turn our attention now to a discussion of each of the activities comprising the process.

The Receiving Activity

Receiving is that phase of physical handling in which the retailer takes possession of the goods and then moves them to the next phase of the process. Certain operations are necessary as part of the receiving function. When the goods reach the store, packing cartons must be inspected for damages. After the cartons are opened, individual packages in the cartons must also be inspected for damages. A receiving record, an essential part of the procedures, must also be prepared. This record normally includes date and hour of arrival, weight, form of transportation, number of cartons, receiving number, invoice number, condition of packages, delivery charges, name of deliverer, amount of invoice, and department ordering the goods.

The receiving department's layout depends on the system used in handling the items received. Four methods are widely used: stationary tables, portable tables, bins, and mechanical conveyor belts or roller conveyors.

The following ideas can help improve the effectiveness of the receiving department:

1. Plan for the straight-line movement of all materials with as little backtracking as possible.
2. Plan the movement of all material through the shortest possible distance and with the fewest possible motions.
3. Plan for maximum machine operation and minimum hand operation.
4. Determine the most efficient methods for performing specific repetitive operations. Standardize these methods.
5. Pay careful attention to working conditions.
6. Practice the careful selection and training of personnel.
7. Maintain adequate supervision.
8. Have sufficient equipment.
9. Purchase standby equipment.
10. Maintain enough records for adequate control.[4]

The Checking Activity

Checking means matching the store buyer's purchase order with the supplier's invoice (bill), opening the packages, removing the items, sorting them, and comparing the quality and quantity of the shipment with what was ordered. Let's focus on the activities of quality and quantity checking.

Quality Checking

The decision to "check or not to check" for quality resides with the buyer. When quality checking is considered to be important, the responsibility is assumed by the buying staff. Remember—buyers are merchandise specialists; checkers are not.

Quantity Checking

Four accepted methods of quantity checking exist:

1. The **direct check**—The shipment is checked against the vendor's invoice. The goods under this system cannot be checked until the invoice arrives. This method is simple, but may cause carelessness in checking. The system can result in items accumulating in the checking area if invoices have not arrived.
2. The **blind check**—This system is designed to avoid carelessness and merchandise accumulation problems associated with the direct check. The checker lists the items and quantities received without the invoice in hand. The system is slower than the direct check, because the list prepared by the checker must then be compared to the invoice.
3. The **semiblind check**—The checker is given a list of the items in a shipment, but the quantity is omitted. The checker's job is to indicate quantities on the prepared list. The time saved in the checking process may be offset somewhat by the time required to prepare the list.
4. The **combination check**—This system is a combination of the blind and direct checks. It attempts to establish an accurate count of the goods received and to speed up the movement to the sales floor. If the invoices are available when the goods arrive, the direct check is used. If the invoices have not come in, the blind check is used.

The Marking Activity

Marking is putting information on the goods or on merchandise containers to assist customers and to aid the store in the control functions.

Various methods are used for establishing the price information to be marked on the goods. One common method is **preretailing.** Under this system, the buyer places the retail price on the store's copy of the purchase order at the time it is written. The buyer may also **retail the invoice.** In this practice, the buyer places a retail price on the copy of the invoice in the receiving room.

Goods can be marked either within the store or by a vendor. In **source marking,** the vendor rather than the retailer marks the merchandise. Source marking involves the use of codes such as the Universal Product Code (UPC) in the supermarket industry and the OCR code in the general merchandise field. This technology was discussed in detail in Chapter 5.

Retailers may use a number of different marking practices. Some of these include bulk marking, nonmarking, and remarking.

Bulk Marking

In **bulk marking,** items are not price marked until they reach the selling floor. Items that sell at very low prices and are subject to rapidly changing prices are typically bulk marked. The shipping carton is marked when the goods arrive; prices are placed on individual items when they are moved to the sales floor. This system is sometimes referred to as "delayed marking."

Nonmarking

Nonmarking is the practice of not price marking individual items of merchandise. Usually the display fixture will indicate prices. In some instances, the person at the checkout counter is supplied with the prices of the goods. Nails, for example, are rarely, if ever, individually price marked.

Remarking

Remarking is the practice of changing the prices marked on merchandise to reflect price changes. The retailer must consider store image when deciding how this practice will be handled. Some store managers, for example, insist on new price tickets rather than merely marking through the old prices.

CONTROLLING SHOPLIFTING AND EMPLOYEE THEFT

An important part of merchandise management is controlling for merchandise shortages. Merchandise shortages are caused by a variety of factors, as determined by a survey among managers of mass merchandise, department, and specialty stores. The retailers attribute approximately 44 percent of inventory shrinkage to employee theft, 30 percent to customer shoplifting, 22 percent to poor paperwork control, and 4 percent to vendor theft.[5] Figure 15–1 presents percent losses by store type. Because the greatest percentage of merchandise losses are due to shoplifting and employee theft, the following sections will focus on these two areas to provide an understanding of how they occur and what actions can be taken to control and prevent them.

Shoplifting

Shoplifting is the largest monetary crime in the nation. Annual losses have been estimated by *Forbes* at $16 billion nationally and as high as 7.5 percent of dollar sales.[6] But what does a shoplifter look like? The following section provides a description.

Who Are Shoplifters?

Shoplifters are male or female, any race or color, as young as 5 or well into their 80s. Fortunately for retailers, many shoplifters are amateurs rather than

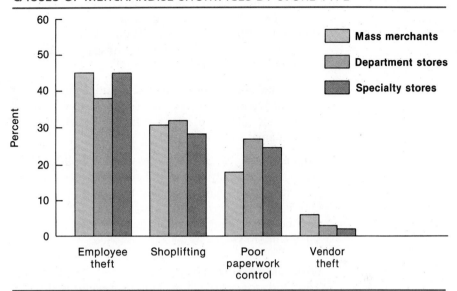

SOURCE: *6th Annual Study of Security and Loss Prevention Procedures in Retailing 1984* (New York: National Mass Retailing Institute and Arthur Young, 1984), p. 9.

professionals. Thus, they are not difficult to spot, and with the right kind of handling, they may never try petty thievery again. Let's look at the various types of shoplifters.

Juvenile Offenders.   Several studies have revealed that juveniles make up the largest percentage of shoplifters, accounting for approximately 50 percent of all shoplifting. A recent study surveyed over 7,000 students ages 7 to 19 to gain further insight into the shoplifting problem. Some of the key findings were:

1. Approximately one out of three juveniles said they had shoplifted.
2. Among teenagers ages 15 to 19, about 43 percent had shoplifted.
3. Male youths shoplift more than females; approximately 41 percent of males and 26 percent of females surveyed reported having shop-lifted at some time.
4. Motives for shoplifting are primarily social rather than economic, especially among girls.
5. Shoplifting done by juveniles is primarily unplanned; four times out of five it is done on impulse.[7]

Impulse Shoplifters.   Many "respectable" people fall into this category. Their thefts are not premeditated, but a sudden chance (such as an unattended dressing room or a blind aisle in a supermarket) presents itself, and the shopper succumbs to temptation. The shoplifting usually occurs while purchasing other merchandise. Items taken are generally for personal use.

Alcoholics, Vagrants, and Drug Addicts. Abnormal physical needs can drive people to theft, as well as to other crimes. These criminals are often clumsy or erratic in their behavior and may be easier to detect than other types of shoplifters. The store owner should remember, however, that people under the influence of drugs or with an obsessive physical need may be violent and may be armed as well.

Kleptomaniacs. Kleptomaniacs are motivated by a compulsion to steal. They usually have little or no actual use for the items they steal and in many cases could well afford to pay for them. Experts believe there are few real kleptomaniacs.

Professionals. Since the professional shoplifter is in the business of theft, he or she is usually highly skilled and hard to spot. Professionals generally steal items that can be quickly resold to an established "fence." The pro may case a store or department well in advance of the actual theft. They take no unnecessary chances and often work in pairs or organized teams. They seldom return to hit a store twice.

Controlling Shoplifting

Time and money are better spent in preventing shoplifting than in prosecuting the offenders. There are several areas where retailers can take actions to control shoplifting.

Educate Employees. Retailers know that salespeople are the first line of defense against shoplifting. However, some salespeople hesitate to "get involved" because of their fear of a possible confrontation. However, management can do a number of things to use salespeople more effectively as a way of controlling shoplifting. Here are five key points:[8]

1. *Create awareness and concern.* Managers must communicate their concern about shoplifting and keep employees constantly aware of the problem. For example, shoplifting and its effects should be discussed periodically at staff meetings.
2. *Provide employee training.* Salespeople will respond to shoplifting only when they feel comfortable in doing so. Thus, they need to be taught to recognize shoplifters and how to respond to the situation. Exhibit 15–5 presents some points on how to recognize shoplifters.
3. *Motivate salespeople to get involved.* Store managers should remind salespeople that shoplifters cost them personally. Salespeople must be aware that shoplifting affects their paycheck and benefits (averaging $1,500 per employee per year in many stores). Shoplifting makes the salesperson's job more difficult and diverts time from customers who are buying merchandise.
4. *Support the salesperson.* Salespeople need to know they are not alone in controlling shoplifting. Management needs to support salespeople's efforts by giving them the tools and devices they need to detect shoplifters and by providing backup assistance when needed.

EXHIBIT 15–5 HOW TO RECOGNIZE SHOPLIFTERS

Be on the lookout for customers carrying concealment devices such as bulky packages, large pocketbooks, baby carriages, or an oversized arm sling.

Be on the lookout for shoppers walking with unnatural steps—they may be concealing items between their legs.

Employees should be alert to groups of shoppers who enter the store together, then break up and go in different directions. A customer who attempts to monopolize a salesperson's time may be covering for an associate stealing elsewhere in the store. A gang member may start an argument with store personnel or other gang members or may feign a fainting spell to draw attention, giving a cohort the opportunity to steal merchandise from another part of the store.

Shoplifters do not like crowds. They keep a sharp eye out for other customers or store personnel. Quick, nervous glances may be a giveaway.

Sales help should remember that ordinary customers want attention; shoplifters do not. When busy with one customer, the salesperson should acknowledge waiting customers with polite remarks such as, "I'll be with you in a minute." This pleases legitimate customers—and makes a shoplifter feel uneasy.

Salespeople should watch for a customer who handles a lot of merchandise, but takes an unusually long time to make a decision. They should watch for customers lingering in one area, loitering near stockrooms or other restricted areas, or wandering aimlessly through the store. They should try to be alert to customers who consistently shop during hours when staff is low.

5. *Show appreciation.* Salespeople need positive feedback; they need to know that their efforts are meaningful and recognized by management. Salespeople should be provided with periodic information on progress being made toward controlling shoplifting. Individual performance should be recognized by certificates of merit, monetary awards, notations on personnel evaluations, and similar means.

Plan Store Layout with Deterrence in Mind. Retailers should maintain adequate lighting in all areas of the store and keep protruding "wings" and end displays low. In addition, display cases should be set in broken sequences and, if possible, run for short lengths with spaces in between. Small items of high value (film, cigarettes, small appliances) should be kept behind a counter or in a locked case with a salesclerk on duty. Display counters should be kept neat; it is easier to determine if an item is missing if the display area is orderly. If fire regulations permit, all exits not to be used by customers should be locked. Noisy alarms should be attached to unlocked exits. Unused checkout aisles should be closed and blocked off.

Use Protective Personnel and Equipment. Protective devices may be expensive, but shoplifting is more expensive. Table 15–1 presents information related to retail use of shrinkage control devices. The table shows frequency of use of selected devices as well as the effectiveness of the devices according to retailers.

Electronic tags are judged by retailers to be the most effective protective device. Retailers using such devices, however, should be sure that salespeople and cashiers are diligent in their use. If an employee forgets to remove the tag and the customer is falsely accused, the retailer could be held liable.

T A B L E 15–1 *SHRINKAGE CONTROL DEVICES*

Devices by Frequency of Use	Devices Judged to Be Most *Effective*	Devices Judged to Be Least *Effective*
Mirrors	Electronic tags	Mirrors
Limited-access areas	Guards	Visible TV cameras
Lock-and-chain devices	Point-of-sale systems	Guards
Guards	Observation booths	Observation booths
Point-of-sale systems	Visible TV cameras	Concealed TV cameras
Observation booths	Fitting-room attendants	Lock-and-chain devices
Electronic tags	Limited-access areas	Fitting-room attendants
Visible TV cameras	Lock-and-chain devices	Limited-access areas
Concealed TV cameras	Concealed TV cameras	Point-of-sale systems
Fitting-room attendants	Mirrors	Electronic tags

SOURCE: *6th Annual Study of Security and Loss Prevention Procedures in Retailing 1984* (New York: National Mass Retailing Institute and Arthur Young, 1984), p. 18.

Guards are also considered by retailers to be powerful visual deterrents to shoplifters.

While mirrors are the most frequently used device, they are judged by retailers to be the least effective. The nearest runner-up in lack of effectiveness is visible TV cameras.

Use Audible and Subaudible Messages. Some stores have developed a mix of audible and subaudible announcements which are broadcast over their internal public address systems. An audible announcement may say, "Security, please respond to Section D3." The store actually may not have a security staff, but such a statement may very well deter a prospective shoplifter.

A subaudible message uses spoken words which are repeatedly transmitted below the threshold of normal hearing on special equipment designed for this purpose. Such messages are often referred to as subliminal messages. Such a message may be, "I am honest, I do not steal." A recent study concluded that subaudible messages can be used effectively to deter retail theft when used properly. Even though audible messages are more powerful, subaudible messages do not disrupt normal store activities and do not require constant monitoring.[9]

Apprehending, Arresting, and Prosecuting Shoplifters

To make legal charges stick, retailers must be able to:

1. See the person take or conceal the merchandise.
2. Identify the merchandise as belonging to the store.
3. Testify that it was taken with the intent to steal.
4. Prove the merchandise was not paid for.

If retailers are unable to meet all four criteria, they leave themselves open to countercharges of false arrest. False arrest need not mean police arrest; simply preventing a person from conducting normal activities can be deemed false arrest. Furthermore, any physical contact, even a light touch on the arm, may be considered unnecessary and used against the retailer in court.

In general, store personnel should never accuse customers of stealing, nor should they try to apprehend suspected shoplifters. If they observe suspicious behavior or an apparent theft in progress, they should alert store management, the store detective, or the police.

It is wisest to apprehend shoplifters outside the store. The retailer has a better case if it can be demonstrated that the shoplifter left the store with stolen merchandise. Outside apprehension also eliminates unpleasant scenes that might disrupt normal store operation. However, retailers may prefer to apprehend a shoplifter inside the store if the merchandise involved is of considerable value or if the thief is likely to elude store personnel outside the store premises. In either case, verbal accusation of the suspect should be avoided. One recommended procedure is for store employees to identify themselves, then say, "I believe you have some merchandise you have forgotten to pay for. Would you mind coming with me to straighten things out?"

Some organizations have control files on shoplifters who have been caught. The local retail merchants' association can supply information about the services available in the area. These files can be checked to see whether the person has a prior record. Unless the retailer gets positive identification and files the shoplifter's name with the police and local retail merchants' association, the "first offender" may claim this status each time he or she is caught shoplifting.

Naturally, each situation must be handled individually, and good judgment is required. Retailers, for example, may wish to release elderly or senile shoplifters and not press charges if there is some indication that the person could honestly have forgotten to pay for the merchandise. Juvenile shoplifters require special handling. A strict, no-nonsense attitude often makes a lasting impression on the young offender and may deter future theft.

Prosecution is in order if the shoplifter is violent, lacks proper identification, appears to be under the influence of alcohol or other drugs, or appears to be a professional. If the theft involves merchandise of great value or management suspects a prior record, prosecution is essential.

Employee Theft
Employee theft is a major problem facing retailers. A study by the University of Minnesota revealed that the large majority of dishonest employees steal only occasionally. The study also found that 10.6 percent of dishonest employees steal at a weekly frequency or more and that these individuals are responsible for nearly 79 percent of total theft incidents.[10]

Another study among managers of mass merchandise, department, and specialty stores revealed that apprehensions of female employees are slightly more prevalent (54 percent) than those of male employees (46 percent). Retailers apprehend young-adult employees more frequently than other age

T A B L E 15–2 CATEGORIES OF EMPLOYEES APPREHENDED

	Mass Merchants	Department Stores	Specialty Stores	All Participants
Cashiers	49%	21%	27%	37%
Selling floor personnel	22	59	40	35
Management	9	3	17	10
Distribution center/store backroom	13	11	15	13
Other	7	6	1	5

SOURCE: *6th Annual Study of Security and Loss Prevention Procedures in Retailing 1984* (New York: National Mass Retailing Institute and Arthur Young, 1984), p. 16.

groups. This same study found that more than 70 percent of all reported employee apprehensions were attributed to cashiers (37 percent) and selling floor personnel (35 percent). Table 15–2 shows the percentage of employees apprehended by job category for each type store.[11]

How Do Employees Steal?

Statistics emphasize discount abuse as the leading form of retail theft by employees. Most frequently employees will purchase merchandise for friends and relatives who are not eligible for a discount. The amounts of merchandise purchased often exceed limits set by company policy. Employees may purchase merchandise at a discount and then have it returned by a friend for full value.[12]

Some employee theft is carried out in collusion with customers. A Midwest supermarket chain discovered that a cashier was paying off her baby-sitter by undercharging her for groceries. Instead of running all the items over the electronic scanner, the cashier lifted most of the items over the glass scanner so they wouldn't register. The cashier admitted to giving her baby-sitter more than $1,100 worth of groceries over a period of time.[13]

Working in collusion with a vendor is another way employees steal. The receiving clerk for one East Coast chain was signing for many more cases of cookies than were actually being delivered. The phantom cases added up to $15,000 before the employee was caught.[14] Read Case 2 at the end of the chapter for other examples of theft occurring in a distribution center.

Theft of merchandise and cash also occurs. Sales personnel who work directly with merchandise and cash may steal. However, one retailer discovered that the cleaning crew was stealing merchandise. The employees were caught stuffing merchandise into their cleaning buckets and vacuum cleaners.

Even though this is not a comprehensive treatment of the topic, the previous examples show that employee stealing can occur in a variety of ways. Because of the magnitude of the problem, retailers must establish prevention and detection procedures for controlling internal theft.

Controlling Employee Theft

Some of the ideas discussed earlier for controlling shoplifting, such as use of guards and detection devices like mirrors and TV cameras, also serve to detect and prevent employee theft. This section thus looks at some of the things retailers are doing specifically to control employee theft.

Obviously the greatest deterrent to internal theft is to hire honest people. Traditionally, retailers have used the polygraph in employee screening. Now, however, they are turning to written honesty tests and better background checks because of some controversy surrounding the use of polygraph tests. Some retailers are using the Reed report which consists of 90 psychologically oriented questions whose yes/no answers classify a person as prone or not prone to theft.

Another way to cut employee theft is to run awareness programs. Such programs show how employees can hurt themselves by stealing. Through awareness programs, management points out the store's policy on dealing with employee theft and how important honesty is to job security and to a good reference when an employee changes jobs. Letting employees know that management cares about them is an effective way to prevent theft.

Peer pressure and use of a reward system can be effective. For such a system to work, however, management must assure employees that confidences will be respected and anonymity ensured—that their efforts in helping catch employee thieves will not place them in danger of termination, retaliation, lawsuits, or reputation as a "snitch." Giant Food Inc., for example, uses a special phone line for anonymous tips from workers about dishonesty. The company gets more than one call a week.[15]

Other deterrents to internal thievery include use of (1) employee identification badges; (2) restriction on employee movement within the store before, during, and after selling hours; (3) regular internal audits; (4) surprise internal audits; and (5) tight controls over petty cash, accounts receivable, payroll, and inventory.

CHAPTER HIGHLIGHTS

— Many chain operations have merchandise distribution systems that involve the use of consolidation warehouses/distribution centers. Merchandise is shipped from vendors to the retail chain's distribution center(s) and from there is redirected to individual store units. Many of these centers are highly automated and computerized. Distribution centers provide several advantages and, when used effectively, can enhance retail productivity and efficiency.

— The physical handling process involves receiving, checking, and marking merchandise. Issues related to managing the physical handling process include who is responsible for carrying out the activities, the location of the activities within the store, and establishing procedures for controlling the process.

- Receiving is that phase of the physical handling process which involves taking possession of the goods and then moving them to the next phase of the process. Packing cartons and individual packages must be inspected for damages. A receiving record should also be prepared.
- Checking means matching the store buyer's purchase order with the supplier's invoice, opening the packages and removing the items, sorting them, and comparing the quality and quantity of the shipment with what was ordered. Quality checking, if done, should be performed by the buying staff. Four accepted methods of quantity checking are the direct check, the blind check, the semiblind check, and the combination check.
- Marking is putting information on the goods or on merchandise containers. Various methods may be used for establishing the price information to be marked on the goods. Goods can be marked either by vendors or by the retailer. Retailers may use a number of different marking practices.
- Shoplifting is the largest monetary crime in the nation. Retailers, however, can take a number of actions to detect and prevent shoplifting.
- Employee theft is also a major problem retailers face. Because of the magnitude of the problem, retailers must establish prevention and detection procedures for controlling internal theft.

KEY TERMS

Blind check A checking method in which the checker lists the items and quantities received without the invoice in hand and then compares the list to the invoice.

Bulk marking A merchandise marking practice (used for items that sell at very low prices and are subject to rapid price changes) whereby items are not marked until placed on the selling floor.

Checking A phase of the physical handling process that involves matching the store buyer's purchase order with the supplier's invoice (bill), opening the packages, removing the items, sorting them, and comparing the quality and quantity of the shipment with what was ordered.

Combination check A checking method that is a combination of the blind and direct checks—if the invoices are available when the goods arrive, the direct check is used; if the invoices have not come in, the blind check is used.

Direct check A checking method whereby the shipment is checked against the vendor's invoice.

Kleptomaniacs Persons motivated by compulsion to steal.

Marking A phase of the physical handling process that involves putting information on the goods or on merchandise containers to assist customers and to aid the store in the control functions.

Merchandise distribution An aspect of merchandise management in multiunit organizations related to getting merchandise from consolidation points/distribution centers to the individual stores.

Nonmarking The practice of not price marking individual merchandise items; usually the display fixture will indicate prices.

Physical handling Activities involved in receiving, checking, and marking merchandise.

Preretailing The practice of determining merchandise selling prices and writing these prices on the store's copy of the purchase order at the time it is written.

Receiving A phase of the physical handling process that involves taking possession of the goods and then moving them to the next phase of the process.

Remarking The practice of changing the prices marked on merchandise in order to reflect price changes.

Retail the invoice The practice of determining merchandise selling prices and writing these prices on the copy of the invoice in the receiving room.

Semiblind check A checking method whereby the checker is provided with a list of the items in a shipment, but the quantities are omitted; the checker's job is to indicate quantities on the prepared list.

Source marking The practice of the vendor rather than the retailer marking the goods.

DISCUSSION QUESTIONS

1. Describe the advantages of a multiunit retail organization employing a distribution system involving the use of consolidation warehouses/distribution centers.
2. What are the specific dimensions of the physical handling process? Briefly describe each.
3. Comment on the validity of the following statement: The buyer should always be responsible for the physical-handling functions.
4. Discuss the factors a retailer should consider in deciding on the location of the physical-handling activities within the store.
5. What is involved in the receiving function of the physical-handling process? Is there anything the retailer can do to improve the effectiveness of the receiving activity? If so, what?
6. Typically, what information does the receiving record contain?

7. Comment on the validity of the following statement: Physical-handling specialists should assume the responsibility of merchandise quality checking.
8. Explain the four accepted methods of quantity checking.
9. Define the following terms: preretailing, retail the invoice, source marking, bulk marking, nonmarking, and remarking.
10. What are the various types of shoplifters? What can retail managers do to control shoplifting?
11. What are some points retailers must remember regarding the apprehension, arrest, and prosecution of shoplifters?
12. What things can retailers do to control employee theft?

APPLICATION EXERCISES

1. Arrange a trip to a distribution center or several centers. Seek as much information as possible on the mechanization of the centers and the roles computers play.
2. Visit several different types of retail operations (varying in size and type of merchandise carried) and interview the people in charge of the physical-handling activities. Write a report comparing the procedures in the different stores. For each store, diagram the movement of goods through the physical-handling process.
3. Interview managers of several retail firms concerning actions being taken in their stores to control shoplifting and employee theft. Be sure to select a variety of types of stores, such as a supermarket, a discount department store, and a specialty store. Write a report comparing the actions being taken by the firms.

CASES

1. Merchandising Decisions Impact Distribution Costs

Sometimes the activities of buyers are at cross-purposes with those performing the firm's merchandise distribution functions. One reason for this is the lack of understanding of how distribution adds to or subtracts from profitability. Another reason stems from the intensive nature of competition in retailing, especially among hard goods retailers.

Buyers, for example, are often unwilling to pull back on promotions even when the constant promotional emphasis at some chains exhausts distribution systems and creates increases in distribution expenses which offset profit gains. The result is what James Guinan, chairman and chief executive officer of Caldor stores, calls a "handful" of gross margin dollars for a "hatful" of effort.

In an attempt to deal with this problem, Caldor uses a series of matrixes to measure increases in distribution costs the firm can expect from merchandising strategies designed to generate added sales. In its matrix for increased sales produced by advertising, Caldor generally expects a 1 percent increase in distribution costs. Guinan says, however, that while some products can bear a large percentage increase in distribution costs, other products cannot. For a product that has a gross margin of only 5 percent, 1 percent may be too high. However, for products with a 35 percent gross margin, a 3 percent increase in distribution costs may not be too much.

While Guinan says the matrixes help Caldor do a better job of judging how a buyer's merchandising decisions add to distribution costs, the difficulty of using such matrixes demands a staff to work them out. As a $1 billion company, Caldor can afford this investment in staff; smaller companies may not be able to do so.

According to Stephen Kennedy, vice president of operations at Crowley's, a Detroit-based department store chain, what is needed is a concrete way of determining the retail cost of merchandise distribution. Without such a tool, Kennedy feels that the added expenses of a particular merchandising move may outweigh the gross margin dollar gains.

Questions
1. Explain how merchandising activities designed to increase sales can lead to an increase in merchandise distribution costs.
2. What are some things retailers can do to provide greater coordination between the merchandising and distribution functions and personnel?

Source: "The Same Company, Different Goals," *Chain Store Age*, February 1986, p. 24.

2. Thieves' Center

The loss-prevention director of a chain in the Southwest began to think employee theft might be the problem in its distribution center when merchandise transfers to the chain's 11 stores began turning up short. An outside security consultant was called in to study the situation.

The consultant noticed several things. Employees were entering and leaving the center through the loading-dock door instead of the employee entrance. Employees at the center were allowed to buy damaged merchandise, but no one checked packages as employees left the building. Also, employees were carrying out the trash with no one checking it. Employees were allowed to park their cars and trucks close to the loading docks. The distribution center had no security fence so there was no way of controlling who entered or left the area around the center.

Acting on these concerns, the loss-prevention director interrogated and polygraphed the employees one at a time. It was discovered that three fourths of the center's 45 employees had engaged in thievery by some means. One supervisor, for example, led a group of six or seven employees in hiding merchandise in empty packing cases and trash bags. They carried them out with broken pallets to a truck waiting to carry trash to a dump. The truck driver dropped off the merchandise at an employee's home on the way to the dump.

Another supervisor would come in very early in the morning before the center opened. He would turn off the alarm, unlock the doors, and load whatever he wanted onto his truck parked at the loading dock. He then reset the alarm, locked up, drove home and unloaded the merchandise, and returned to the center to open for the day.

While the company fired all employees involved in thievery, it was able to file charges against only a few of the employees who had sold merchandise locally. The rest had traded the stolen merchandise in Mexico in exchange for drugs. The company was unable to get this merchandise back and could not prosecute without evidence to go along with the confessions.

Questions
1. Summarize the company's security-system problems that enabled employees to steal from the firm.
2. Recommend some things the company should change or initiate to prevent employee theft.

Source: Taken from *6th Annual Study of Security and Loss Prevention Procedures in Retailing 1984* (New York: National Mass Retailing Institute and Arthur Young, 1984), p. 39.

NOTES

1. Taken from "What You See Is What You Get," *Chain Store Age Executive,* February 1986, p. 43.
2. Taken from "Junking the Model T," *Chain Store Age Executive,* January 1986, p. 75.
3. Taken from "The Same Company, Different Goals," *Chain Store Age,* February 1986, p. 24.
4. Gerald Pintel and Jay Diamond, *Retailing* (Englewood Cliffs, N.J.: Prentice-Hall, 1971).
5. *6th Annual Study of Security and Loss Prevention Procedures in Retailing 1984* (New York: National Mass Retailing Institute and Arthur Young, 1984), p. 9.
6. "The Juvenile Shoplifter," *The Marketing Mix* 10, no. 1 (Winter–Spring 1986), p. 1.
7. Ibid.
8. "Five Key Steps to Reducing Shoplifting," *Shrinkage Control,* September 1985, pp. 1–2.
9. "New Study Supports Use of Subliminal Messages to Deter Retail Theft," *Shrinkage Control,* September 1985, p. 3.
10. "Facts Continue to Show that Shoplifting Exceeds Employee Theft," *Shrinkage Control,* September 1985, p. 1.
11. *6th Annual Study of Security and Loss Prevention,* pp. 15–16.
12. "Number One Form of Employee Theft," *Shrinkage Control,* March 1986, p. 7.
13. *6th Annual Study of Security and Loss Prevention,* p. 50.
14. Ibid., p. 20.
15. "Employee Pilfering Rockets in Some Industries, Which Toughen Controls," *The Wall Street Journal,* January 28, 1986, p. 1.

16

Store Design and Layout and Merchan- dise Presen- tation

A New Store Design for A&P Futurestores

A&P stores across the country are being transformed into crisp, sparkling, black-and-white, trend-setting supermarkets. The store design program was undertaken as part of the company's revitalization efforts to provide A&P with a completely new image. The new store design project included every aspect of the store, from planning and architectural design, to lighting and fixture design, graphic design, and the development of electronic display techniques.

The whole interior is on display from outside the store, as shown in Exhibit 16–1 on page 410. Customers can see clearly to all parts of the store from the mounds of fresh fruit and vegetables at the front to the large pictorial images of fresh meat and seafood at the very back.

The black-and-white design was based on the belief that the supermarket must be focused on the people who use it and the merchandise they buy. The only color in the store is provided by the merchandise and the people. The black-and-white environment creates an ideal counterpart to the brightly lit shelves, trays, and cases of colorful fresh and packaged products, and the A&P staff in their bright red coats.

Each department has its own distinct character with appropriate architectural forms and graphic symbols. A giant slice of cheese arches over the cheese counter. The floral department

Adapted from a press release and used by permission of Robert P. Gersin Associates, Inc. of New York City which was responsible for creating the complete design for the A&P Futurestore. This included space planning, architectural, lighting, and store fixture design, and the entire in-store visual communication system.

is reminiscent of a greenhouse. Shown in Exhibit 16–2 (page 411) is a special coffee and tea section.

The black-and-white theme is animated by the use of over 250 pictorial symbols. The large pictograms on the walls provide a billboard of products that can be seen from anywhere in the store. These pictograms, which are used to highlight departments, are repeated on aisle directories and even on the smallest point-of-sale sign. The huge fish mural turns up on the point-of-sale sign on the haddock; the chicken, cabbage, or grapes can be found in daily advertisements in local newspapers.

*T*he A&P example illustrates how store layout and design and merchandise presentation are critical elements of a firm's positioning strategy. It also shows that firms may need to redesign their stores' interiors and exteriors as part of a new image projection for the organization. For A&P, the new design provides a unique, exciting, functional, and appropriate store identity. The new design creates a store that invites customers to shop, makes them feel comfortable, helps them find the merchandise, and increases their satisfaction. The major goal of store design and layout and merchandise presentation is to get the shopper into the store to spend as much money as possible on a given shopping trip. In many instances, identical merchandise can be found in directly competing stores. Thus, it is critically important for any given store to create a general atmosphere and specific presentations that will trigger buying decisions on its own salesfloor rather than that of competitors.[1]

LEARNING OBJECTIVES

This chapter focuses on planning and evaluating store design and layout and merchandise presentation. The end goals are to show how effective layout and presentations can lead not only to increased sales levels but also to greater space productivity. After reading this chapter, you will be able to:

1. Discuss the role of atmospherics in the store.

2. Describe typical store arrangements.

3. Explain how to allocate space to selling departments and nonselling activities.

4. Explain how to measure selling-space productivity.

5. Evaluate factors to consider in locating selling departments and sales-supporting activities within the store.

6. List the essentials of merchandise display.

SOURCE: Robert P. Gersin Associates Inc. of New York City was responsible for creating the complete design for the A&P Futurestore. This included space planning, architectural, lighting and store fixture design, and the entire in-store visual communication system.

In order to more easily discuss the important physical environment of a store, a few terms should be defined. **Store planning** includes exterior and interior building design, the allocation of space to departments, and the arrangement and location of departments within the store. **Store design** refers to the style or atmosphere of a store that helps project an image to the market. Store design elements include such exterior factors as the storefront and window displays and such interior factors as colors, lighting, flooring, and fixtures. **Store layout** involves planning the internal arrangement of departments—both selling and sales supporting—and deciding on the amount of space for each department. Figure 16–1 shows the relationships among these three terms.

STORE DESIGN

Store design is a reflection of two elements: (1) the interior design, which includes everything within the store such as walls, floor, ceiling, lighting

EXHIBIT 16-2   COFFEE AND TEA SECTION OF A&P FUTURESTORE

SOURCE: Robert P. Gersin Associates Inc. of New York City was responsible for creating the complete design for the A & P Futurestore. This included space planning, architectural, lighting and store fixture design, and the entire in-store visual communication system.

fixtures, colors, scents, and sounds, and (2) exterior design. The interior and exterior designs should be in harmony with the store's merchandise and customers. For example, bold colors, flashing lights, and eye-popping displays might be very appropriate for a store catering to young people, but inappropriate for a store focusing on older, conservative shoppers.

Exterior Design

All stores depend, in varying degrees, on walk-in customers, and the decision to enter a store depends partly on a customer's impression of its exterior. A store located in a shopping center usually abides by the rules for store

FIGURE 16–1 *THE STORE PLANNING PROCESS*

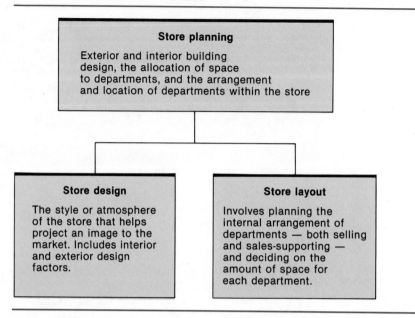

fronts established by the developer. In stores not located in a shopping center, retailers have more flexibility and can be quite creative in the use of painting, awnings, or flower boxes. The creative use of a distinctive outdoor sign which is tasteful and easily read can also help create a favorable image. However, many cities have zoning laws that require both sign permits and design approval.

Interior Design   Consumers respond to more than a tangible product or service. Retailers, thus, must consider the psychological effects of their outlets on consumer purchasing behavior. As has been observed:

> A subtle dimension of in-store customer shopping behavior is the environment of the space itself. Retail space, i.e., the proximate environment that surrounds the retail shopper, is never neutral. The retail store is a bundle of cues, messages, and suggestions which communicate to shoppers. Retail store designers, planners, and merchandisers shape space, but that space in turn affects and shapes customer behavior. The retail store . . . does create moods, activates intentions, and generally affects customer reactions.[2]

Some retailers view the interior of their stores as a stage in a theater and realize that theatrical elements can be used to influence customer behavior. They feel the customer should be entertained and excited.

EXHIBIT 16–3 L.L. BEAN—INTERIOR DESIGN IMPARTS A SENSE OF THE OUTDOORS

Men's apparel surrounds the trout pond in L.L. Bean's Freeport, Maine, store's addition, designed by Retail Planning Associates. The pond makes use of unmerchandisable space under the circular stairs and provides a focal point for the store, which seeks to impart a sense of the outdoors. Used with permission of Retail Planning Associates.

An excellent example of the store as a theater is the Hard Rock Cafe in New York City. The interior of the restaurant is an "adolescent's romper room." At one time the rear portion of a 1960 Cadillac was suspended over the front door. The 40-foot bar is shaped like a guitar. Rock memorabilia are also on display: a hat that Jimi Hendrix once wore, Jerry Lee Lewis's shoes, the guitars played by Eric Clapton, George Harrison, and Peter Townshend, and a drum played by Ringo Starr.[3]

Another example of the store as a theater is the L.L. Bean store located in Freeport, Maine. The store's interior is a theatrical presentation of the outdoors. Large windows and skylights contribute to the out-of-doors feeling as do the stuffed black bear and the duck decoys. One of the most dramatic elements in the store's interior design is a trout pond—an 8,500-gallon pond which supports about 16 trout. As shown in Exhibit 16–3, the pond makes use of unmerchandisable space under the circular stairs and provides a focal point for the store.[4]

Many fast-food outlets are undergoing interior design changes as a way of attracting customers in an intensely competitive environment. Many feel that a more upscale design will attract a broader range of customers. Customers will see less plastic, metal, and bright primary colors. Typically, operators are now aiming for subtler lighting and are using pastel colors, marble, mirrors, brass, wood, and greenery to create a warm, earthy environment.[5] See Case 2 at the end of the chapter for a further discussion of design changes in fast-food operations.

The store's interior design should be based on an understanding of the customer and how design contributes to the strategy for reaching the target market. Fanny Farmer Candy Shops Inc., for example, have renovated all of their stores based on preferences revealed in a consumer survey conducted by the company. The survey found that 75 percent of the firm's customers are women, 50 percent are aged 22–40, and the majority have annual earnings of more than $30,000. This profile dictated the move to a more contemporary look. The renovated shops will create an environment that is warm and feminine yet contemporary and upscale.[6] Exhibit 16–4 shows the interior of their store in Rockefeller Center.

STORE LAYOUT

Store layout is a very important element of store planning. Layout not only affects customer movement in the store but also influences the way merchandise is displayed. The following elements are part of layout planning:

1. The overall arrangement of the store.
2. Allocation of space to selling departments and sales-support activities.
3. Evaluation of space productivity.
4. Location of selling departments and sales-supporting activities within the store.

Arrangement of the Store

Typical layout arrangements are the grid, the free-flow or open plan, and the boutique concept. Let's look first at the grid layout.

Grid Layout

In a **grid layout,** merchandise is displayed in straight, parallel lines, with secondary aisles at right angles to these. An example is shown in Figure 16–2. A supermarket typically uses a grid layout.

The grid arrangement is more for store efficiency than customer convenience, since the layout tends to hinder movement. Customer flow is guided more by the layout of the aisles and fixtures than by the buyer's desire for merchandise. For example, 80 to 90 percent of all customers shopping in a supermarket with a grid layout pass the produce, meat, and dairy counters. Fewer shoppers pass other displays, because the grid forces the customers to the sides and back of the supermarket.

In department stores, a grid layout on the main floor usually forces traffic down the main aisles. Thus, shoppers are less likely to be exposed to items along the walls. Shopping goods (highly demanded merchandise) should be placed along the walls, and convenience goods should be displayed in the main part of the store. Customer traffic then is drawn to otherwise slow-moving areas.

SOURCE: Courtesy of the Fannie Farmer Company.

FIGURE 16-2 GRID LAYOUT

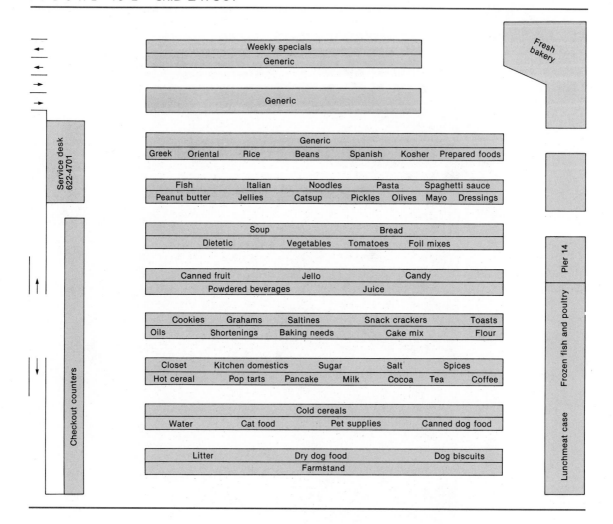

Free-Flow Layout

In a **free-flow layout,** merchandise and fixtures are grouped into patterns that allow an unstructured flow of customer traffic, as shown in Figure 16–3. The free-flow pattern is designed for customer convenience and exposure to merchandise. Free-flow designs let customers move in any direction and wander freely, thus encouraging browsing and impluse purchasing. The layout, however, is more costly and uses space less efficiently than the grid layout.

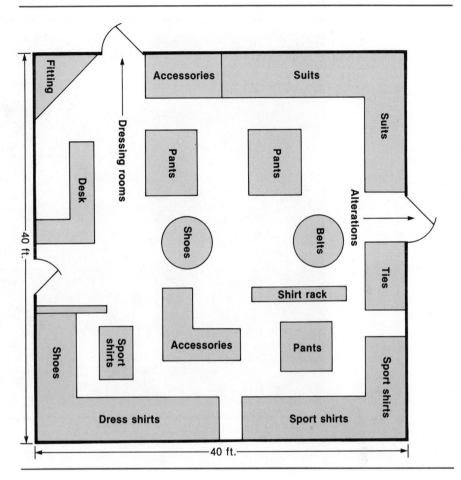

Boutique Layout

A variation of the free-flow layout is the **boutique layout** where merchandise classifications are grouped so that each classification has its own "shop" within the store. The boutique concept is an outgrowth of lifestyle merchandising wherein a classification is aimed at a specific lifestyle segment often featuring merchandise from a single designer or company, as shown in Exhibit 16–5.

Each shop has its own identity, including color schemes, styles, and atmosphere. Even though greater flexibility is possible with this arrangement, construction costs and security costs are higher. As a result, the concept is used in high-status department stores and other outlets where the sale of higher priced merchandise allows absorption of the increased costs.

(Courtesy The Parisian Company)

Allocation of Space

Dividing total space between selling and sales-supporting areas is the first step in space allocation. As a general rule, retailers—other than specialty or fashion outlets—devote as much space to the sales area as possible. However, the amount of sales space varies by size and type of store. In a very large department store, selling space may account for roughly 65 percent of total space. Jewelry stores need almost no sales-supporting space. A home improvement center, however, may use more space for warehousing and storage than for selling. In general, the larger a store, the higher its ratio of sales-supporting space to selling space.

Management can use three basic methods for allocating selling space:

1. Industry averages by type of merchandise.
2. Sales productivity of product lines.
3. The build-up (model stock) method.

Industry Averages

Management can use the national average percentage of selling space that a particular merchandise line occupies in a certain type of store. For example, assume that the health and beauty aids department accounts for 4 percent of total selling space as an average in a superstore. Thus, in a superstore with 36,000 square feet of selling space, management would set aside 1,440 for the health and beauty aids department (36,000 × .04 = 1,440).

Sales Productivity Method

Sales productivity is measured by sales per square foot of selling space. Assume that the planned sales for health and beauty aids is $144,000. If the national average sales per square foot for this department is $100, then management would allocate 1,440 square feet to the department ($144,000/$100 = 1,440).

Build-Up (Model Stock) Method

Let's use a ladies' blouse department to illustrate this space allocation method. The build-up method would proceed as follows:

1. What is the ideal stock balance necessary to achieve expected sales volume? The merchant, based on past experience, may believe that sales of $30,000 per year are obtainable. Trade sources indicate that in the price line planned, three turns per year are realistic. Within the price-line structure, the average price of a blouse is $15. Given these assumptions, approximately 666 blouses will be needed as a normal offering during each turnover period ($30,000/3 = $10,000 in merchandise; $10,000/$15 = 666 blouses). Normally, 666 blouses must be in stock. However, the merchandise planner may vary from this number during high- and low-sales-volume months. Under this method, planning ties merchandise needs to actual seasonal variations rather than yearly averages. For example, Mother's Day might be the yearly peak sales period and should be considered in layout planning.

2. How much merchandise should be kept on display, and how much should be kept in reserve stock? How many of the 666 blouses should actually be displayed? Ideally, 100 percent should be on display, because goods do not sell if they are not seen. Since this is not realistic and since the decision is arbitrary, assume that two thirds of the stock, approximately 444 blouses, will be displayed and one third will be in reserve.

3. What is the best method of displaying the merchandise? This decision depends on the merchandise display equipment available and the affordable opportunities for display. Let's decide that we will hang the less expensive blouses on circular steel racks that have a glass top for display purposes. The most expensive blouses will be displayed in glass cases where they can be accessorized with jewelry, scarves, and other small items. Reserve stock will be stored in drawers beneath the display cases. Only one of each style will be displayed.

4. How many display racks and cases are necessary to display the items? The physical size and capacity of the fixtures must be determined to answer this question. Scale models of fixtures are often placed on floor plans to assist in the layout planning process.

5. What is the best way to handle the reserve stock? We have already determined that the reserve stock for the expensive blouses will be maintained under the display cases. Space can be allocated for the remaining items in special storage fixtures on the selling floor or in a stock area as close to the selling area as possible.

6. What service requirements are necessary for the department? Fitting rooms and a point-of-sale terminal or register will be needed. Likewise, depending on the nature of the operation, space for packaging may be required. Finally, all departments need aisles.

7. What are the total space requirements? The total space needs can be determined in steps 4, 5, and 6.

Evaluation of Space Use

Good use of space involves more than creating an aesthetically pleasing environment, although such a goal is important. Effective use of space can also translate into additional dollars of profit. Thus, retailers must evaluate whether store space is being used in the most effective way. Management can use a variety of measures to evaluate space utilization. The gross-margin-per-square-foot method is discussed below to illustrate one method retailers can employ.

To determine whether a department can "afford" the space it occupies, the gross margin per square foot of the department should be measured. Big-ticket items may ring up more sales than lower priced goods, yet the ratio of gross margin to square feet may be smaller for high-priced merchandise.

As shown in Figure 16–4, three calculations are involved in evaluating space utilization by the gross-margin-per-square-foot method. Sales per square foot less cost of merchandise sold per square foot yields the gross margin per square foot figure.

With this gross-margin-per-square-foot figure, departments of varying sizes selling different types of goods can be compared. Gross margin per square foot can show management which departments are doing well, which are not, which might improve if expanded, and which can be reduced in space allotment.

For example, based on the calculations shown in Figure 16–4, management might be tempted to decrease the selling space allocated to department A and increase the selling space devoted to department B. However, the decision to reallocate space is not a simple one. Advertising and selling costs may rise when selling space is increased. After the reallocation, the merchandise mix may change which can result in either higher or lower gross margins. Management thus needs to simulate the likely changes in the three

Three calculations are involved in figuring gross margin per square foot:

$$1. \frac{\text{Total sales}}{\text{Total square feet}} = \text{Sales per square foot}$$

$$2. \frac{\text{Cost of merchandise sold}}{\text{Total square feet}} = \text{Cost of merchandise sold per square foot}$$

3. Sales per square foot − Cost of merchandise sold per square foot = Gross margin per square foot

Example

	Department A	Department B
Sales	$50,000	$70,000
Cost of merchandise sold	$30,000	$35,000
Square feet of space	500 square feet	700 square feet
Sales per square foot	$100	$100
− Cost of merchandise sold per square foot	60	50
= Gross margin per square foot	$ 40	$ 50

variables used in the calculations as a result of possible shifts in space allocation and determine whether reallocations are likely to increase the overall profitability of the firm.

An evaluation of space utilization may not only lead to a reallocation of space among selling departments. Some stores are converting unproductive retail space to other uses. For example, G. Fox and Company reduced its 11-story downtown store in Hartford by closing the 3 upper flooors so that the space could be devoted to office space by other companies.[7] See Chapter 22 for a discussion of space reduction as a future trend in retailing.

Locating Departments and Activities

Management must decide where to locate selling and sales supporting activities within the store. Several guidelines are available to retailers to aid in making these decisions.

Locating Selling Departments

The convenience of customers and the effect on profitability are the primary concerns of management in locating selling departments within the store. With these factors in mind, the following suggestions are offered:

1. *Rent-paying capacity.* The department with the highest sales per square foot is best able to pay a high rent. Thus, this department should be placed in the most valuable, highly trafficked area of the store. If a number of departments are equally good, the decision should be made based on the gross margins of the merchandise.

2. *Impulse versus demand shopping.* **Impulse merchandise** is bought on the basis of unplanned, spur-of-the-moment decisions. Departments containing impluse merchandise normally get the best locations in the store. **Demand merchandise** is purchased as a result of a customer coming into the store to buy that particular item. Departments containing demand merchandise can be located in less valuable space because customers will hunt for these items.

3. *Replacement frequency.* Certain goods, such as health and beauty aids, are frequently purchased, low-cost items. Customers want to buy them as conveniently as possible, so the department should be placed in an easily accessible location.

4. *Keep related departments together.* Similar items of merchandise should be displayed close together. In a superstore, for example, all household items—such as paper products, detergents, kitchen gadgets—should be placed together, so customers will make combination purchases. Similarly, the men's furnishings department—such as shirts, ties, and underwear—should be placed near the suit department in a department store. A customer wanting a new suit often needs a matching shirt and tie as well. Combination selling is easier when related items are close together. Location of related goods is even more important in a self-service store because no salesperson is around to help the customer.

5. *Seasonal variations.* Items in some departments are big sellers only a few months or weeks of the year. Toys and summer furniture are examples. Management might decide to place these departments next to each other. When toys expand at Christmas, extra space temporarily can be taken from summer furniture, and vice versa.

6. *Size of departments.* Management also may want to place very small departments in some of the more valuable spaces to help them be seen. A very large department could use a less desirable location in the store because its size will contribute to its visibility.

7. *Merchandise characteristics.* In a supermarket, bakery products (especially bread) should be near the checkout. Customers avoid crushing these items in the carts by selecting bakery products at the end of their shopping. Products such as lettuce are usually displayed along a wall to allow more space and to better handle wiring for cooling.

8. *Shopping considerations.* Items such as suits and dresses are often tried on and fitted. They can be placed in less valuable locations away from heavy traffic. Also, they are demand, not impulse, items and can be placed in out-of-the-way areas since shoppers will make an effort to find them.

9. *New, developing, or underdeveloped departments.* Assume management has added a new department such as more "nonfoods" in a superstore. Management may want to give more valuable space to the new department to increase sales by exposing more customers to the items.

Locating Sales-Supporting Activities

Sales-supporting activities, such as credit departments, can be thought of in several ways:

1. Activities that must be located in a specific part of the store—Receiving and marking areas should be located near the "dock" area, usually at the back of the store.
2. Activities that serve the store only—Such activities are office space and personal services for employees of the store. These departments can be located in the least valuable, out-of-the-way places.
3. Activities that relate directly to selling—Cutting areas for fresh meat need to be close to the refrigerators. Both refrigeration and cutting need to be close to the display cases. Drapery workrooms in department stores need to be close to the drapery department.
4. Activities with direct customer contact—In a supermarket, customers often want to check parcels, cash a personal check, or ask for information about an item. Credit departments and layaway services are needed in department stores. Such activities can be located in out-of-the-way places to help increase customer movement in the store.

MERCHANDISE PRESENTATION

Merchandise displays are part of the so-called silent language of communication. They can be used to excite, entertain, and educate consumers. If effectively used, they can have a profound influence on consumer behavior. For example, Rich's in Atlanta was selling only two pink Sony television sets a week. A designer then set up an elaborate display of pink cameras, TVs, tape players, and telephones held aloft by pink robots with whirring lights for eyes. Thanks to the merchandise display, the stock of pink equipment sold out in five days.[8]

Often entire courses are devoted to the technical aspects of merchandise display. Because of space limitations, however, we must limit our discussion and will provide a brief overview of the following topics: the essentials of display, window displays, interior displays, and shelf-space allocation.

Principles of Display

Customers in a retail store stop at some merchandise displays, move quickly past some, and smile at others. Shoppers are professional display watchers and know what they like. However, customers usually do not consciously judge displays. So the job of the retail manager is to "prejudge" for the purchaser. Managers need to be clever and creative enough to affect behavior by display. Displays should attract attention and excite and stimulate customers. An illustration of such a display is seen in Exhibit 16–6. The creative use of TV screens as mannequins' heads was used by L.S. Ayers in Indianapolis to attract customers' attention.

In spite of the basically artistic and creative flair needed for display, some principles do exist. The following basic principles have been developed from years of experience:

1. Displays should be built around fast-moving, "hot" items.
2. Goods purchased largely on impluse should be given ample amounts of display space.
3. Displays should be kept simple. Management should not try to cram them with too many items.
4. Displays should be timely and feature seasonal goods.
5. Color attracts attention, sets the right tone, and affects the very sense of the display.

6. Use motion. It attracts attention.
7. Most good displays have a theme or story to tell.
8. Show goods in use.
9. Proper lighting and props are essential to an effective display.
10. Guide the shopper's eye where you want it to go.

Window
Displays

Window displays were downplayed during the 1970s and early 1980s because of increased cost cutting and energy consciousness among retailers. Also, during this period emphasis was placed on building stores in malls; thus, attention was focused more on interior merchandise presentations than on window displays.

Today, however, there is a renewed interest in store window displays, especially among department stores and higher-priced retailers and especially in cities where walking and window shopping are still in style. Window displays may be used to enhance store image, to expose would-be shoppers to new products, or to introduce a new season.

Much art is involved in developing window displays. Principles of good design—balance, proportion, and harmony—are all essential. Errors retailers sometimes make are using too much or too little merchandise, inappropriate props and lighting, or simply not changing a display frequently enough with the result that it loses its special significance.

A city that has some of the most creative and attractive store windows in the country is New York. Some stores' window displays rival stage sets in a Broadway production. One such store is Bloomingdale's which uses its store windows to reinforce its advertising. The merchandise is advertised in the newspaper, is put in the window displays, and then there is usually a point-of-sale display in the department.[9]

Saks-Fifth Avenue in New York City has 31 window displays. The store presents about 1,200 different windows a year, including the toy-stuffed Christmas productions that inspire five-deep holiday crowds. The 14 windows facing Fifth Avenue are changed every week; the remaining 17 on the side streets are replaced every two weeks. The allocation of windows generally correlates with departmental sales.[10] The 10-foot-by-10-foot windows showcase new fashions, introduce innovative designs, and are even used to head off possible sales erosions in vulnerable departments. For example, when the gift department was moved from the ground floor to the ninth floor, the department manager feared that sales would erode. She managed, however, to get the best of her merchandise into an eye-catching Fifth Avenue window the week the department was moved. Sales increased 20 percent![11]

Management can evaluate the results of window displays by (1) the number of people passing the window in a certain period, (2) the number of passersby who glance at the window, (3) the number that stop, and (4) the number that enter the store after looking at the window display.

| Interior Displays | Interior displays can take a variety of forms, depending on the type of merchandise and image to be projected by the firm. While space does not permit an in-depth discussion of the principles of interior display, we do offer several guidelines for planning the effective arrangement of merchandise in departments. Also see Chapter 22 for a discussion of future trends in interior display of merchandise. |

Consider the following suggestions regarding interior merchandise display:

1. Place items so that choices can readily be made by customers. For example, group merchandise by sizes.
2. Place items in such a way that "ensemble" (or related-item) selling is easy. For example, in a gourmet food department, all Chinese food components should be together. In a women's accessories department, handbags, gloves, and neckwear should be together to help the customer complete an outfit.
3. Place items in a department so that trading up or getting the customer to want a better-quality, higher-priced item is possible. Place the good, better, and best brands of coffee, for example, next to each other so customers can compare them. Information labels on the package help customers compare items displayed next to each other.
4. Place merchandise in such a way that it stresses the wide assortments (choice of sizes, brands, colors, and prices) available.
5. Place larger sizes and heavy, bulky goods near the floor.
6. If the firm carries competing brands in various sizes, give relatively little horizontal space to each item and make use of vertical space for the different sizes and colors. This arrangement exposes customers to a greater variety of products as they move through the store.
7. Avoid locating impulse goods directly across the aisle from demand items that most customers are looking for. The impulse items may not be seen at all.
8. Make use of vertical space through tiers and step-ups, but be careful to avoid displays much above eye level or at floor level. The area of vertical vision is limited.
9. Place items in a department so that inventory counting (control) and general stockkeeping is easier.
10. Finally, make the displays as attractive as possible.

| Shelf-Space Allocation | A very important merchandise presentation issue is determining the amount of space that should be allocated to individual brands or items in a product category. A number of rules have been devised for allocating facings to competing brands. One rule frequently stressed by major consumer goods manufacturers is that shelf space should equal market share. Thus, a brand with 20 percent market share in a category takes 20 percent of shelf space. |

For a retailer, however, this rule makes little sense. It takes no account of the profit margins or direct costs associated with each item. Some retailers, thus, allocate space according to gross margin. Other retailers apply the concept of direct product profit (DPP). DPP is the remainder when the direct costs of ordering, receiving, stocking, displaying, selling, and transporting a product are subtracted from gross margin. The problem is that most retail management accounting systems are not sophisticated enough to be able to assign these costs directly to items. However, where this is achievable, more space should be allocated to brands/items with greater DPP.

Computer applications for shelf-space allocations are becoming more widespread. With the aid of software, retailers can determine optimum formulas for deciding how much shelf space each item should be allotted.[12]

A particularly thorny problem is how to assign space to new products. Some manufacturers, having conducted test markets, are able to recommend facing levels. The new-item problem is simpler for a line extension. A new flavor of potato chips, for example, is invariably located with existing products in single-carton quantities until increased sales demand otherwise. In the case of a completely new category, facings can only be provided by creating new space or by destocking one or more lines from another category. Some firms tackle the new-item problem by allocating it a special display until demand has stabilized at a predictable level of trial and repurchase.

CHAPTER HIGHLIGHTS

— Store layout and design and merchandise presentation are important aspects of a firm's positioning strategy. The major goal of store design and layout and merchandise presentation is to get the shopper into the store to spend as much money as possible on a given shopping trip.

— Store design is a reflection of two elements: the interior design and the exterior design. Both should be in harmony with the store's merchandise and customers. Some retailers view the interior of the store as a theater and realize that theatrical elements can be used to influence customer behavior.

— Store layout is a very important part of store planning. One aspect of store layout is the arrangement of the store. Typical arrangements are the grid, the free-flow or open plan, and the boutique concept.

— Another element of store layout is space allocation. Dividing total space between selling and sales-supporting areas is the first step in space allocation. Management can use three basic methods for allocating selling space: industry averages by type of merchandise, sales productivity of product lines, and the build-up (model stock) method.

— Effective use of space can translate into additional dollars of profit. Thus, retailers must evaluate whether store space is being used in the most effective way. The gross-margin-per-square-foot method is one method retailers may use.

— Management must decide where to locate selling and sales-supporting activities within the store. Several guidelines are available to aid in making these decisions.

—— Merchandise displays can be used to excite, entertain, and educate consumers. If effectively used, they can have a profound influence on consumer behavior. In spite of the basically artistic and creative flair needed for merchandise display, some guidelines and principles do exist.

—— Today, there is a renewed interest in window displays, especially among department stores and higher-priced retailers and in cities where walking and window shopping are in style. Window displays can be used to enhance store image, to expose shoppers to new products, or to introduce a new season.

—— Interior displays can take a variety of forms, depending on the type of merchandise and image to be projected by the firm. A number of guidelines to the use of interior merchandise displays are offered.

—— An important aspect of merchandise display is determining the amount of space that should be allocated to individual brands or items in a product category. Some retailers allocate shelf space according to gross margin; others use the concept of direct product profit. Some retailers use computer software packages to determine optimum formulas for deciding how much shelf space each item should be allocated.

KEY TERMS

Boutique layout Merchandise classifications are grouped so that each classification has its own "shop" within the store.

Demand merchandise Merchandise purchased as a result of a customer coming into the store to buy that particular item.

Free-flow layout Merchandise and fixtures are grouped into patterns that allow an unstructured flow of customer traffic.

Grid layout Merchandise is displayed in straight, parallel lines, with secondary aisles at right angles to these.

Impulse merchandise Merchandise bought on the basis of unplanned, spur-of-the-moment decisions.

Store design Refers to the style or atmosphere of a store that helps project an image to the market.

Store layout Planning of the internal arrangement of selling and sales-supporting departments, and deciding on the amount of space for each department.

Store planning Includes exterior and interior building design, the allocation of space to departments, and the arrangement and location of departments within the store.

DISCUSSION QUESTIONS

1. Define store planning, store design, and store layout.
2. What are the decision areas that comprise layout planning?
3. Compare the following layout arrangements—the grid layout, the free-flow or open plan, and the boutique concept.
4. Describe the three methods retailers can use for allocating selling space in a store among the various departments.
5. Explain the gross-margin-per-square-foot method of evaluating space use.
6. What various factors do retailers need to consider in deciding where to locate selling departments and sales-supporting activities within the total store space?
7. Discuss the guidelines retailers can use relative to interior display of merchandise.
8. What information can retailers use in making the shelf-space allocation decision?

APPLICATION EXERCISES

1. Select three different types of stores (e.g., a traditional department store, a discount department store, a specialty apparel shop) and carefully observe their displays, fixturing, appearance—all the elements that make up the interior design of the stores. Write a report describing differences between the stores and how these differences relate to image projection and market segmentation.

2. Visit the following types of stores: a multilevel department store, a supermarket, a national chain such as J. C. Penney, a national specialty chain outlet, and a discount department store. Describe the overall arrangement of the stores (e.g., grid, free-flow, boutique). Evaluate the layout of each store and comment on the impact of each layout on the general image of the outlets. What changes, if any, would you suggest and why?

3. Visit several department stores and interview store management. Determine the method(s) used to allocate selling space to the various departments and how management evaluates space use. Based on what you learned in the chapter, evaluate the location of selling departments and sales-supporting activities within each store.

CASES

1. Cosmetic Companies Fight over Space

Behind the rosy glow of rouge and the scent of perfume in any department store cosmetics floor, some fierce fights are taking place. Many cosmetic companies are locked in battle for better retail locations and space. The reason for the situation is the ever-increasing numbers of new products being introduced into the market. In 1985, for example, 41 new perfumes were introduced.

Even though new products have multiplied, space has not. Bloomingdale's, for example, restyled its 1,600-square-foot cosmetics display area, adding marble and new lighting, but no new space. Thus, for a newcomer to fit in the sales floor, an old-timer must be moved or removed.

The cosmetics floor is so competitive because it is so profitable. A recent study found that cosmetics averaged sales of $350 per square foot, compared with between $80 and $120 per square foot for clothing. On each sale, the store earns a gross margin of 40 percent, which is substantially higher than most other types of merchandise. Thus, it is understandable that retailers parcel out space to manufacturers who can provide the best return for the real estate.

Cosmetic manufacturers thus have to maintain their volume to keep their space in the store. Aware of this, manufacturers are now attempting to make their products "must-haves" long before they enter the department store. Christian Dior's perfume, Poison, for example, was not introduced into American stores until after more than a year of expensive European promotion. The company felt that Poison would become so popular overseas that U.S. retailers would eagerly clear shelf space for the product. In 1982, Giorgio pioneered the mail-order plan, advertising its product with scent strip inserts in national magazines and providing a toll-free number for potential customers. The strength of sales became leverage for better retail floor space.

Questions

1. What types of information would retailers want to evaluate in making decisions as to the amount of space to be allocated to each cosmetics line?

2. Based on what you have learned about the location of departments in a store, where would you expect to find the cosmetics department in a department store?

Source: Lisa Belkin, "Cosmetic Companies Fight over Space," *The Tuscaloosa News*, November 3, 1986, p. 6.

2. Store Design in Fast-Food Operations

Many fast-food chains have embarked on major redesign programs to be completed in the next few years. Typically, operators are aiming for warm, earthy environments reminiscent of the "fern" bars that overtook urban areas about 10 years ago with their exposed-brick walls and abundant greenery. Thus, bright primary colors, plastic, and metals are being replaced with pastel colors, wood, brass, and mirrors.

One goal is to give the restaurants more individual style than they had in the past. For example, a Wendy's located in the French Quarter in New Orleans is painted gray and has red awnings, wrought-iron stairs and balconies, columns, and a stained-glass ceiling inside. In Round Rock, Texas, a Wendy's located on the Chisholm Trail is built of native limestone and rough-hewn cedar. It has a porch and is supposed to look like an 1850 central Texas country farmhouse.

A second goal of the more upscale design is to attract a broader range of customers. Management feels they will attract people that they didn't in the past—people who used to eat only in sit-down restaurants.

Just the opposite strategy as that discussed above is being followed by other fast-food companies. More than a dozen young fast-food operations—primarily in the southern states—are returning to the days when hamburger restaurants were simple affairs.

They are building tiny restaurants with stripped-down menus and take-out-only service. These fast-food operations are not stressing the ambiance of the firms discussed above. Rather, these no-frills restaurants rely almost exclusively on drive-throughs, two of them on opposite sides of a small kitchen. Most don't have walk-up windows; none offer indoor seating. They also keep the menu simple, typically offering only hamburgers, fries, and soft drinks.

Questions

1. Describe what you think are the target markets of these two versions of fast-food operations.
2. Discuss how the positioning strategies of these two types of operations differ.
3. Explain why the menu prices of the no-frills operations are lower than the prices of the more upscale operations.
4. How might the more upscale design features of the fast-food operations discussed in the case impact the turnover rates of these firms? What are the advantages and disadvantages of the more leisurely dining atmosphere?

Adapted from Trish Hall, "At Fast-Food Restaurants, Plastic Is Out, and Marble, Brass, and Greenhouses Are In," *The Wall Street Journal*, December 2, 1985, p. 33; and Stephen P. Galante, "Some Hamburger Restaurants See Their Future in the 1950's," *The Wall Street Journal*, September 8, 1986, p. 31.

ENDNOTES

1. Lewis A. Spalding, "Getting Visual," *Stores*, June 1984, pp. 22–23.
2. Rom J. Markin, Charles M. Lillis, and Chem L. Narayana, "Social Psychological Significance of Store Space," *Journal of Retailing*, Spring 1976, p. 43.
3. "Ballad of a Mad Cafe," *Forbes*, November 19, 1984, p. 288.
4. "Design Lends Sense of Theater to Mail-Order Firm's Home Town Store," *Marketing News*, February 1, 1985, p. 26.
5. Trish Hall, "At Fast-Food Restaurants, Plastic Is Out, and Marble, Brass, and Greenhouses Are In," *The Wall Street Journal*, December 2, 1985, p. 33.
6. "Consumers Give Fanny Farmer the Recipe for Sweet Comeback," *Marketing News*, January 31, 1986, p. 12.
7. For additional reading, see Isadore Barmash, "Spaced Out," *Stores*, July 1982, pp. 26–28.
8. Anthony Ramirez, "Department Stores Shape Up," *Fortune*, September 1, 1986, p. 52.
9. Holly Klokis, "Store Windows: Dynamic First Impressions," *Chain Store Age Executive*, November 1986, p. 108.
10. Lisa Gubernick, "Through a Glass, Brightly," *Forbes*, August 11, 1986, p. 98.
11. Ibid.
12. For additional reading, see Susan Zimmerman, "Computerized Shelf-Space Management Works Wonders," *Supermarket News*, November 24, 1986, p. 18; and "Space-Managing Program Offered Auto Aftermarket," *Marketing News*, October 24, 1986, p. 31.

Children's World at Hess's in Poughkeepsie, New York,
is an exuberant display of neon and lively colors.
(Both photos reprinted with permission from The Best of
Store Designs 2, PBC International, Glen Cove, New York.)

DESIGN AND LAYOUT

"In the ever-changing retail world of today, individuality is that special ingredient which sets one store apart from another. Some call it atmosphere or environment." So say the professionals who use design and layout to differentiate stores. These pictures are an indication of why Hess's of Poughkeepsie, New York, received the first award for full-line department stores in the store interior design competition. Winners of the competition, which was conducted by the Institute for Store Planners and the National Retail Merchants Association, are pictured in *The Best of Store Designs 2*, 1987.

Left: An eye-catching merchandising display at Hess's demands attention.

DAYTON'S MODERNIZED NICOLLET MALL STORE

Dayton's, Dayton Hudson Department Store Company's flagship store in Minneapolis, is the major anchor of Nicollet Mall, one of the earliest of the revitalization efforts in a major metropolitan central business district. Dayton's exemplifies the dramatic impact that modernization can have on an old, downtown property if done with great expertise. Nicollet Mall is famous for its skyways, which connect Dayton's to high-rise office complexes in the city center; Dayton's is a lively focal point in this development.

Dayton's main floor.

Above: Dayton's stuffed bear display is an example of classification dominance.

Right: A boutique layout.

(All photos courtesy of Dayton Hudson Department Store Company.)

Dayton's men's department.

This pillow display is another example of classification dominance.

A room setting.

The sweeping curves and dramatic angles of the ceiling cover emphasize the unique layout of the tabletop department in Bloomingdale's, New York.

Above: At Personal Eyes in Beverly Hills, California, a unique diagonal axis makes the store's 600 square feet appear larger.

Left: The predominance of white paint highlights architectural details in this Richardson Place store in Burlington, Vermont. Note the use of rare between-floor merchandising space.

(All photos reprinted with permission from The Best of Store Designs 2, PBC International, Glen Cove, New York.)

17

Keys to Successful Selling

wrench on the shiny flagstone patio next to the accessory boutique. A 1936 Mercedes 500K Cabriolet and Schimmel grand piano accent the showroom, where cars are bathed in the rainbow light from the giant stained-glass window, also starred with Mercedes emblems.

The combined effect is almost religious, with a noise level appropriate to a funeral parlor. Here, big-ticket auto sales are achieved through the ultimate in soft sell. A few old-time car hustlers remain, but "Smilin' Sam" need not apply.

Mr. Sumser typifies the new breed. He eschews polyester clothing, avoids white shoes and belts, and never slams a door or kicks a tire. His suits are wool; his ties are silk. A graduate of Hartford College with a degree in marketing, he seriously considered becoming a stockbroker. Now, he says, "A lot of them try to sell me stock, and I try to sell a lot of them cars; usually, I'm the successful one."

One way to create strong customer loyalty is to offer a superior sales force as a complement to good merchandise and strong price/value relationships. Creative selling differs dramatically from the image of the huckster or clerk that too many people have in mind when they think of retail sales.

Steve Sumser is a new breed of retail salesperson who looks upon selling as a lucrative career. He is professional in every sense of the word and is a high achiever in a very competitive job setting. This chapter provides a framework for developing salespeople with the same professional outlook as Mr. Sumser.

LEARNING OBJECTIVES

After reading this chapter you will be able to:

1. Define the types of selling needed in retailing.

2. Name the steps in the selling process.

3. List ways to increase sales-force productivity.

4. Discuss the need for sales-training programs.

5. Explain how to help people in buying.

6. Discuss the use of management by objectives in retail sales programs.

7. Describe opportunities for motivating retail salespeople.

To the customer, the salesperson often is the business. The salesperson is the only human being with whom the customer has contact. The salesperson encourages the customer to buy or, through a hostile or indifferent attitude, drives the customer away—forever. Salespeople can act as "sales prevention managers" by their rudeness or indifference.[1]

Building Sales and Profit

Salespeople can help build a business for greater sales and profit. They can:

— Sell skillfully to realize maximum sales and profit from each customer attracted to the firm.
— Provide customers with useful selling suggestions that will build sales and improve customer satisfaction.
— Ensure that customers' needs are met so that returns are held to a minimum.
— Develop a loyal following of customers who will return to the store and will send their friends.
— Follow store policies and procedures so that losses through billing oversights, failure to secure credit approvals, and acceptance of bad checks are held to a minimum.

Personal selling in retailing is essentially matching customers' needs with the retailer's merchandise and services. In general, the more skillfully this match is made, the better the personal selling. If salespeople make a good match, not only is a sale made, but a satisfied customer is created (or maintained). Thus, a long-term, profitable relationship can be established. Figure 17–1 helps to illustrate this process.

In retailing, the top producers far outsell the average. The more top producers in a store, the more profitable it will be. Retailers cannot expect salespeople to become top producers by accident. There is no magic wand to wave or button to push to make this happen. However, there are a number of positive actions that can be taken to attract people with potential and, once hired, develop that potential so that maximum performance is achieved.

BASIC DECISIONS

Self-Service or Full Service?

The key to a good sales force is creating the right interaction between (1) the merchandise, (2) the customer, and (3) the salesperson. Some items, such as groceries, can be sold by self-service. A fully staffed store is needed when selling items such as expensive furs. A third possibility is a combination of self-service and full staffing. This is the policy of most stores.

When Are Salespeople Needed?

A salesperson is needed when: (1) customers have little knowledge about the product they plan to buy; (2) price negotiation is likely, as when buying a car; and (3) the product is complex—for example, stereo equipment.

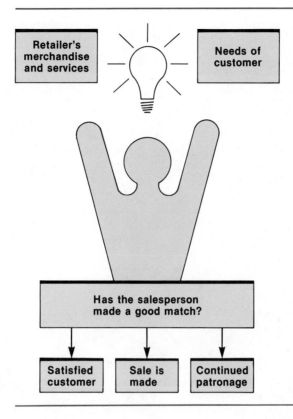

The sales force represents the store. In many respects, the image projected by salespeople is one of the most important elements of the retail operation. But far too often, the key role of the retail salesperson is not acknowledged.

What Are the Types of Retail Selling?
Several types of selling occur in retailing. A different type of person and different skill levels are needed for each type.[2]

Transaction Processing. The easiest selling task is **transaction processing.** Employees simply serve as checkout clerks or cashiers and do little selling, as shown in Figure 17–2. Typical examples are personnel in discount department stores or supermarkets.

Routine Selling. **Routine selling** involves more product knowledge and a better approach to the sales task. Often, people in routine selling are involved in the sale of nontechnical items such as clothing. These salespeople assist the shopper in buying by giving them confidence in their judgment and answering simple questions.

Venture quality-discount stores offer customers wide assortments of merchandise at value prices in a self-service format. (Courtesy The May Department Stores Company)

Personnel involved in routine sales should also be trained in the techniques of **suggestion selling,** as shown in Figure 17–3. For example, a salesperson might be taught to suggest a shirt and tie to go with the suit a customer is trying. Salespeople should then be monitored closely to make sure they practice the concepts they have learned. Such techniques may increase sales by 10 percent or more, and additional sales are almost pure profit since they add little, if anything, to the cost structure of the firm.

(Courtesy The Parisian Company)

Sales Consultant.   Creative selling requires the use of salespeople who have complete information about product lines, product uses, and technical features. These people are often called sales consultants and may, for example, work as interior designers in a furniture store. Creative selling occurs when the product is highly personalized.

Regardless of the type of selling involved, salespeople have a key role in the communications plan for a firm. Many extra sales can be made by creative sales efforts. The cost of retail selling is high, in spite of the low wages paid to sales personnel, and these costs must be offset by high productivity. A well-trained sales force can be a major advantage for a firm. Competing firms may duplicate price cuts and promotion, but may have difficulty in developing a quality sales force. Differences in the three types of selling are summarized in Table 17–1.

An Overview of Personal Selling

A basic concept in retail sales is that a sale must first occur in the mind of the buyer. The job of the salesperson is to lead the customer into a buying situation. A successful salesperson should think of selling as a process consisting of the steps shown in Table 17–2.

Prospecting

Prospecting involves identifying and qualifying possible customers. Promotional, telephone, and direct-mail programs often attract potential cus-

TABLE 17–1 *TYPES OF PERSONAL SELLING IN RETAILING*

Criteria for Comparison	Transaction Processing	Routine Selling	Sales Consultant
Purpose	Assist in checkout	Suggestion selling	Creative selling
Training required	Clerical training	Sales training	Indepth product knowledge
Source of sales	Impulse purchases	Maintain sales volume plus "add-on" accessories	Creation of new sales volume
Type of products	Simple, convenience items	Standardized with new options	Complex and customized
Primary activity	Order processing	Suggestion selling	Creative problem solving

TABLE 17–2 *STAGES IN THE SELLING PROCESS*

Stage	Purpose	Key
Prospecting	Identify prospects	Referrals, walk-ins, telephone contacts, responses to advertising
Approaching	Stimulate interest	Offer service or merchandising assistance
Determining needs and wants	Decide how to meet customer needs	Ask questions, listen, show, or demonstrate a variety of merchandise choices
Demonstrating and handling merchandise	Create a desire for the product or service	Involve the customer
Answering questions and meeting objections	Overcome objections	Seek to determine whether the problem is price, quality, service, or other features
Closing the sale	Obtain a purchase commitment	Ask for the purchase by using trial or assumptive closing
Following up	Ensure continuing customer satisfaction	Resolve any problems facing the consumer

tomers to the firm. Likewise, word of mouth can be effective when satisfied customers refer friends to the store.

Salespeople should try to know as much about their customers as possible before approaching them. This may seem difficult at first, but the concept of market segmentation discussed earlier may aid in identifying customers. The type of promotion program featured by the store is also a key. For example, most customers shopping at K mart expect good price/value relationships and normally buy on the basis of price. These customers are often presold on products through national-brand advertising and do not expect many services. On the other hand, the customers of an exclusive dress shop expect personalized attention, a high level of product knowledge by the salesperson, and a wide variety of services.

Some firms keep lists of their good customers' likes and dislikes. Salespeople often call these customers when a new shipment of merchandise arrives.

Approaching the Customer

The initial approach is crucial in getting the sale. When approaching the customer, the salesperson should quickly (1) gain the customer's attention, (2) create interest, and (3) make a smooth transition into a presentation. Various approaches to customers are possible. Commonly used approaches are the **service approach** and the **merchandise approach.**

The Service Approach. The service approach ("May I help you?") is weak if a customer is simply browsing. The customer is given an opportunity to quickly say no. However, this greeting is useful when (1) the customer has apparently made a selection, (2) the customer clearly needs a salesperson to explain something about the merchandise, or (3) the customer needs someone to ring up a sale. Above all, sales personnel should always make the customer feel welcome. The customer needs to know that the salesperson is willing to serve him or her, and that the salesperson is knowledgeable about the merchandise.

The Merchandise Approach. This approach begins with a statement about the merchandise, such as, "The style you are looking at is very popular this year." The salesperson waits until a potential customer seems to have decided on an item before approaching the individual. The salesperson then begins talking to the customer about the merchandise without asking whether the person would like to be waited on.

Table 17–3 outlines 12 basic types of customers that salespeople are likely to meet in their day-to-day activities. The information in the table describes their characteristics and explains how to respond to their behavior and actions.

T A B L E   17–3   *RECOGNIZING CUSTOMERS OF ALL TYPES*

	Customer			Salesperson
Basic Types	*Basic Characteristic*	*Secondary Characteristics*	*Other Characteristics*	*What to Say or Do*
Arguer	Takes issue with each statement of salesperson	Disbelieves claims; tries to catch salesperson in error	Cautious; slow to decide	Demonstrate; show product knowledge; use "yes, but . . ."
Chip on shoulder	Definitely in a bad mood	Indignation; angry at slight provocation	Acts as if being deliberately baited	Avoid argument; stick to basic facts; show good assortment

	Customer			Salesperson
Basic Types	Basic Characteristic	Secondary Characteristics	Other Characteristics	What to Say or Do
Decisive	Knows what is wanted	Customer confident his choice is right	Not interested in another opinion—respects salesperson's brevity	Win sale—not argument; sell self; tactfully inject opinion
Doubting Thomas	Doesn't trust sales talk	Hates to be managed	Arrives at decision cautiously	Back up merchandise statements by manufacturers' tags, labels; demonstrate merchandise; let customer handle merchandise
Fact-finder	Interested in factual information—detailed	Alert to salesperson's errors in description	Looks for actual tags and labels	Emphasize label and manufacturers' facts; volunteer care information
Hesitant	Ill at ease—sensitive	Shopping at unaccustomed price range	Unsure of own judgment	Make customer comfortable; use friendliness and respect
Impulsive	Quick to decide or select	Impatience	Liable to break off sale abruptly	Close rapidly; avoid oversell, overtalk; note key points
Look-around	Little ability to make own decisions	Anxious—fearful of making a mistake	Wants salesperson's aid in decision—wants adviser—wants to do right thing	Emphasize merits of product and service, zeroing in on customer-expressed need and doubts
Procrastinator	"I'll wait 'til tomorrow"	Lacks confidence in own judgment	Insecure	Reinforce customer's judgments
Silent	Not talking—but thinking!	Appears indifferent but truly listening	Appears nonchalant	Ask direct questions—straight forward approach; watch for buying signals
Think it over	Refers to desire, but needs to consult someone else	Looking for another adviser	Not sure of own uncertainty	Get agreement on small points; draw out opinions; use points agreed on for close

SOURCE: From C. Winston Borgen, *Learning Experiences in Retailing* (Santa Monica, Calif.: Goodyear Publishing), p. 293. Copyright © Goodyear Publishing Company. Reprinted by permission.

Determining Customers' Needs and Wants

Salespeople should quickly discover the customer's needs and wants after the greeting. Good listening skills are the key. Once the salesperson has the customer's attention and understands his or her needs, the salesperson can quickly move the customer into the interest and desire stage and on to the buying stage. Motives for buying generally are either emotional or rational.

One way to develop information on customer needs and desires is to ask the customer about his or her planned use for the merchandise. This knowledge will help the salesperson better understand the buying problem and how the merchandise can help solve the problem. Such information can also provide insight into the price, styles, and colors a customer may prefer.

Good listening is more than giving the other person a chance to talk. It means giving the person your undivided attention. Getting a prospect to talk is important because it is the only way to find out the person's special problems, interests, and needs. Then, when making the sales presentation, the salesperson is in a position to stress the things that are important to the prospect and to talk specifically about the situation.

Knowing the *importance* of listening and actually doing it are two different things. Many salespeople keep planning what to say next instead of listening. A salesperson who is wrapped up in the sales pitch cannot hear the prospect. A good listener concentrates on what is being said. A good salesperson learns the attitudes and problems the customers have. Learning what is important to the individual may be important in selling *to* the individual.

By visualizing the person's problems, the salesperson can understand a customer's motivation. Eye contact is important. Salespeople should make a special effort to be attentive, without letting the mind wander to other subjects.

To keep the prospects talking, salespeople should acknowledge that they are listening by prompting with nods or commenting "I see" or "I understand." Asking a question now and then helps. Salespeople should not worry about what to say next. If they listen carefully, their next move will usually be obvious. It is not easy to be a good listener, but it is important. Top salespeople listen to a prospect, show that they understand, and remember what is said.[3]

Demonstrating and Handling Merchandise

Good listening helps determine which merchandise to show the customer and which features of the merchandise will help solve the buying problems the customer faces. Good salesclerks have a mental outline they follow when presenting the merchandise. This mental outline differs from a canned sales presentation in which the salesperson repeats exactly the same statements to each customer. The salesperson is free to deviate from a fixed statement, but still keeps key points from the outline in mind as a checklist. A mental guide should include the following points:

1. *Begin with the strongest features of the product.* These features might be price, durability, performance, and so forth.

2. *Obtain agreement on small points.* This helps the salesperson establish rapport with the customer.
3. *Point out the benefits of ownership to the customer.* Salespeople should try to identify with the customer in making these points.
4. *Demonstrate the product.* A demonstration helps the customer make a decision based on seeing the product in action.
5. *Let the customer try the product.* Good salespeople get the customer involved as much as possible. The involvement pushes the customer toward the sale.

Other useful techniques include testimonials of customers who have used the product, discussion of research results, and discussion of product guarantees and case histories.

Answering Questions and Meeting Objections

Customers may object to a point during the sales process. When that occurs, the salespeople should try to find the real reason for the objection, which may be based on price, quality of the product, service available, or various other reasons. The salespeople should try to get the customers to see the situation in a different way. They should acknowledge that they can understand why the customers hold a particular view. But they also should try to provide information that can overcome the objection. For example, an objection to a high price might be overcome by pointing out that the purchase is really an investment. Also, the salespeople might point out that the price of the product has not gone up any more than other items that consumers have recently purchased.

Above all, the salespeople should consider a customer's question as an opportunity to provide more information about the product or service. They should welcome objections as providing a way for overcoming obstacles to a sale. The key to handling objections is *timing,* as explained in Exhibit 17–1.

Transition to the Close

Salespeople often have a problem with the close. Too often, they simply wait for shoppers to buy instead of trying to close the sale. The customers often give signals to alert salespeople that a buying decision is at hand. Such signals may include questions about the use of the item, delivery, or payment. Facial expressions may also indicate that the customer is close to the buying stage. More frequently, it's up to the salesperson to bring up the closing question.

Trial Closes.[4] An easy way to do this is through *trial closes.* A trial close is a question that is asked to determine the prospect's readiness to buy. The following is an example of such a question: "Are you satisfied that our product will help you reduce your maintenance costs?" If the answer is negative, the salesperson can re-emphasize how the product reduces maintenance costs or can ask the prospect to be more specific about the cause of his or her doubt.

Knowing *when* to answer an objection is almost as important as being able to answer it.

Timing is crucial! In general, it's wise to answer as many objections as you can *before* the prospect brings them up.

Putting the answers to objections into the sales talk saves time. But more important, when a salesperson, rather than the prospect, mentions an objection, the issue seems less important. It also makes the customer feel you're not trying to hide anything.

Sometimes a customer may hesitate to bring up a particular objection because he doesn't want to embarrass you. You can save the day by getting it out in the open, showing the customer you understand his or her concerns.

Another reason for discussing as many obvious objections as possible is that you avoid an argument. If the prospect brings up an objection, you may have to prove he's wrong in order to make the sale. That's a situation to avoid if you possibly can.

On the other hand, what if the customer *does* bring up an objection before you get to it? If you can give a satisfactory reply without taking attention away from your sales point—answer it immediately.

Sometimes you should delay your answer to a customer's objection. For example, you may not even need to answer if there's a good chance the objection will diminish in importance as you continue your presentation.

It's also best to delay answering if you would seem to be flatly contradicting the prospect. Rather than do this, wait and let the answer become clear as you proceed with your presentation. This gives the prospect a chance to save face.

There are some objections that it's best not to answer at all. If the prospect's statement is simply an excuse, or a malicious remark, don't bother trying to answer. This will only put you on the defensive.

Having good answers to objections and presenting them to the customer's satisfaction is important. But so is timing. Choosing the right time and the right way to handle objections keeps you in control of the selling process.

SOURCE: *On the Upbeat*, June 1982, pp. 11–13.

Seeking Agreement.   If the prospect agrees with the salesperson on a series of points, it becomes difficult to say no when the salesperson asks for the order. However, the prospect who disagrees on a number of points will probably defend this position by also saying no when the salesperson asks for the order.

The salesperson should seek agreement on a number of points such as:

— "Don't you think the self-defrosting feature of this refrigerator is a real convenience, Mr. Baker?"
— "You probably need a larger refrigerator than your present one, don't you?"

The salesperson probably knows the points to which the prospect will agree. The idea is to summarize them and ask them consecutively to establish a *pattern* of agreement, one that will make it difficult for the prospect to say no when the salesperson asks for the order.

Above all, salespersons should:

1. Not make exaggerated claims.
2. Use honest facts and figures to back up the claims they do make.
3. Demonstrate and prove their points whenever possible.
4. Use solid, legitimate testimonials the prospect can check.
5. Not promise what they cannot deliver.

Critical skills

Good listening to establish needs and to develop basic information.
Demonstrating how a product or service can meet an identified need.
Establishing rapport with customers.
Skillfully handling objections or negative attitudes.
Summarizing benefits and actions required in closing the sale.

Common errors

Talking instead of listening.
Not seeking critical information from a customer by failing to ask crucial questions.
Failing to match customers' needs with product benefits.
Failing to handle objections.
Not knowing how or when to close the sale.

6. Back promises in writing and in performance.
7. Show sincere interest in every customer's problems.
8. Consistently and conscientiously put the customer's interest ahead of their own.[5]

Table 17–4 summarizes the critical skills needed and common errors to avoid in the personal selling process.

Benefit Summary. Another effective transition is a statement that summarizes product benefits, such as the following:

> Ms. Perkins, I think you'll find that the Brand X washer has everything you're looking for. A partial load cycle saves you water, energy, and money. Temperature controls protect your fabrics. And Brand X's reputation for quality assures you that this machine will operate dependably for a long time with little or no maintenance.

Closing the Sale

Now let us look at the most vital factor in the selling process—*closing the sale*. All previous steps have been taken with one purpose in mind—to close the sale, to get the prospect to buy.

Various Techniques

A variety of techniques can be used to close the sale. The best approach often depends on the salesperson's individual selling style, the prospect, the product or service that is offered, and the salesperson's earlier success in convincing the prospect of the advantages of the product and the benefits that it offers.

Direct Close. The direct close assumes that the prospect is ready to buy. In closing, the salesperson asks a direct question such as the following:

— "We can deliver your sofa next week. What is the address that we should ship to?"
— "You want this in green, don't you?"
— "Will this be cash or a charge?"
— "Would you like to put this on a budget plan?"

Assumptive Close. The **assumptive close** is a modification of the direct close. The salesperson assumes that the prospect is ready to buy, but asks less direct questions, such as:

— "Which color do you prefer, red or green?"
— "Which model do you prefer, the standard or the deluxe?"
— "Have you decided where you would like the machine installed?"
— "Shall I call an electrician to arrange the installation?"

Open-Ended Close. In the open-ended close, the salesperson asks open-ended questions that imply readiness to buy, such as:

— "How soon will you need the sofa?"
— "When should I arrange for installation?"

The prospect's answer to these questions leads to an easy close. If the prospect needs the sofa in three weeks, the salesperson can respond, "Then I'll need an order right away, to assure you of delivery on time."

Action Close. The salesperson takes some positive step toward clinching the order, such as:

— "I'll write up the order right now and as soon as you sign it, we can deliver."
— "I'll call the warehouse and see if they can ship immediately."

Urgency Close. The salesperson advises the prospect of some compelling reason for ordering immediately.

— "That's a pretty tight schedule. I'll have to get an answer from you very quickly if we are going to be able to meet it."
— "That item has been very popular and right now our inventory is running pretty low."
— "Our special price on this product ends the 15th of the month."

Dealing with Delay

Not all closing attempts are immediately successful. The prospect may delay, unable to make a decision. If so, the salesperson should ask the reason for the delay. The reason will often help the salesperson plan the next course of action in reestablishing the presentation of the product or service.

For example, the prospect might say: "I think I'll stick with my present machine a while longer." If the salesperson has properly qualified the prospect earlier, he or she might respond: "But didn't you say that repair costs were running awfully high? Isn't it worth a few dollars to know that you will save on maintenance costs, and not have to worry about a breakdown at a critical time?''

Choosing the Closing Technique

The choice of closing techniques will depend on the salesperson, the salesperson's style, the customer, and the facts. Regardless of the technique chosen, the most important thing to remember is to pursue some closing technique so as not to avoid this critical step.

Following Up

Salespeople should make sure that the merchandise is delivered on time, that it arrives in good condition, and that installation, if needed, is satisfactory. The salesperson should take this opportunity to try to sell the customer an extended warranty, for example, if this was not done initially.

Above all, the salespeople should think back over the sale to determine what they learned that will help them in their future sales efforts. Also, they should think about why some sales were not made and what might have been done to overcome the lack of a sale. Salespeople should always seek to identify ways of achieving future sales by satisfying their customers.

What Can Be Done to Increase Sales Force Productivity?

Developing a strong retail sales force is not a matter of luck. Training is needed. Adequate incentives must exist to motivate personnel to high levels of performance. And supervision is necessary. Above all, management of the sales force means planning for increased sales. With selling expenses around 8 percent of sales, and assuming pre-tax profits of 4 percent, a 10 percent increase or decrease in the selling expense ratio can affect pre-tax profits as much as 20 percent! Also, selling costs are the most flexible payroll expense item in the short run.

The level of selling expense varies by store. The expense even varies by department because of differences in merchandise and customer services needed. Regardless, the goal should always be to hold down selling costs without reducing sales.

What are the ways of increasing sales productivity? The typical activity of salespeople is as follows: 35 percent selling, 25 percent sales-support, 20 percent delay-idle, and 20 percent out of assigned sales areas.[6] The percent of selling time thus can be increased. How? One way is to avoid overscheduling employees and knowing how many salespeople are needed at a given time. Management should consider having less overtime and more part-time personnel. They should avoid having too little personnel available at periods such as lunchtime and think about split schedules to cover these busy periods. Also, salespeople should be used for selling only. Such tasks as wrapping and shelf stocking can be done by nonselling personnel.

Details on these and other points for increasing sales-force productivity are in Appendix A at the end of this chapter.

Better Employee Selection[7]

Finding good salespeople is a problem for both large and small retailers. What retailers fail to realize is that much of the problem is of their own making. They may not define clearly what they mean by "good" salespeople or specify what qualities they are seeking.

An effective way to avoid this problem is to use *job descriptions* as discussed in Chapter 11. A job description is a written statement, often no longer than one or two paragraphs, spelling out the requirements for a particular job. For example, a job description for a retail sales position in a sporting goods store might appear as follows:

Type of Job:
Retail sales of sporting goods.

Requirements of the Job:
This job involves mainly in-store sales of a full line of sporting goods ranging from items of low-unit value (such as golf balls) up to higher-priced merchandise (such as complete sets of golf clubs and skiing equipment). The emphasis is on big-ticket items. Telephone follow-up selling is expected, and there is occasional stock work.

The job description forces the retailer to be more explicit about what a job requires and provides a guide for appraising the capabilities of prospective employees. For example, since the job discussed above emphasizes big-ticket items, the retailer should look for people who have this kind of experience. There are many instances of salespeople who can do an excellent selling job on low-unit-value merchandise, but have trouble closing sales on the big-ticket items. Job specifications help to avoid such problems.

Sales Training Programs

Many people wonder why training salespeople is necessary, since their turnover is often so high. But effective training can increase employee sales levels, lead to better morale, and produce higher job satisfaction and lower job turnover. Training or retraining gives employees more knowledge about the items they sell and may make them feel more a part of the firm. Much training occurs on the job for the purpose of skills enhancement as shown in Figure 17–4 for K mart.

Retailers should budget dollars for training just as they budget dollars for hiring staff members, since training is a way to increase sales. Most people really want to succeed, but no one can succeed without adequate training. Customers will show their appreciation by increased levels of buying. And add-on sales as a result of employee training are almost pure profit since they add little or nothing to expenses.

Unfortunately, when the word *training* is mentioned, the retailer typically associates it with formalized programs conducted by large department stores and national chains. However, sales training by smaller retailers does not have to be a formal and structured program. Actually, any conscious effort the retailer makes to improve the basic skills needed for effective retail selling is a form of sales training.

Here are several examples of sales training methods used by retailers.

FIGURE 17–4

K mart's "K Care" mechanic and service manager in training check engine timing, as national automotive service manager observes. (Courtesy K mart Corporation)

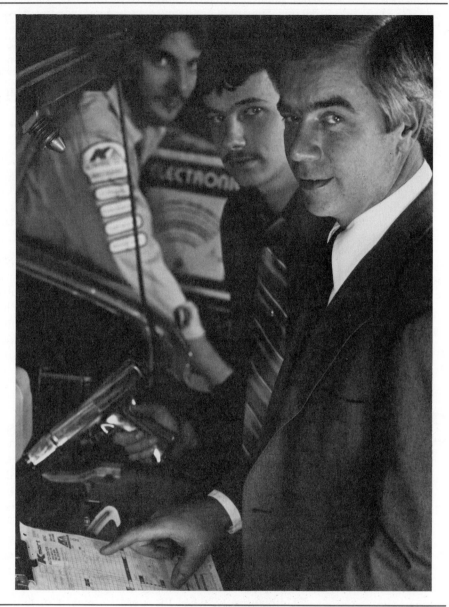

Role Playing

Role playing is an excellent method for developing a salesperson's skills at learning customer needs. In role playing, one person plays the part of the customer, while the other plays the part of the salesperson. Next time around, they reverse the roles. Role playing enables salespeople to see various sales situations from the customer's point of view. The skill necessary to quickly "size up" customers (learn about their needs) is rapidly sharpened through role playing.

Sales Meetings

Knowledge of the merchandise and service can be improved with regularly scheduled *sales meetings*. Sales meetings offer an excellent opportunity to discuss the features of new products, changes in store policies, new merchandising strategies, or other matters relating to the store's merchandise and services. Sales meetings do not have to be formal and precisely scheduled events. Instead, they can be conducted right on the sales floor during slack periods or shortly before the store opens for business.

What is important is that management holds the meetings regularly and frequently (once per week at a minimum) and each has a specific theme or focus. For example, at one meeting, management might discuss the features of a new line of products the store is now carrying and how to introduce them to the customer. The next meeting might focus on changes in the store's merchandise return policy. At another meeting, management might talk about the sales strategies for the upcoming inventory clearance sale. If meetings are held regularly, management may be pleasantly surprised at how much better informed salespeople will be about the store's merchandise and service offerings.

Seminars

Training aimed at improving the ability to convince customers that a store's merchandise and service offering is superior is perhaps the most difficult. Some people believe that an individual either has this skill naturally or does not, and hence training makes little difference. While there may be some truth in this position (people do differ in their natural communication abilities), training can still make a difference. Such training can range from encouraging salespeople to take a formal course in salesmanship, to informal *sales seminars* organized by the store. These seminars may be no more elaborate than sitting down with salespeople for half an hour over a cup of coffee and discussing ways that merchandise and service offerings can be better communicated to customers.

If conducted informally (but regularly), these sessions may foster a constructive interchange of ideas about selling. For example, a salesperson may have developed a good argument that can be used successfully to close a sale when it looks as if the customer is ready to walk out. "Good salespeople do like to talk about and share their success stories and can contribute to a sales development program."[8]

1. *Information about the company.* Who started the company? How long has it been in business? What lines of merchandise are sold?
2. *Expectations of the salesperson.* A training program should outline such things as dress code, job skills expected, goals to be met, and how performance will be measured.
3. *Basic training in selling techniques.* Will the personnel need special technical skills? Management should also help employees to understand their nonselling duties.
4. *The company's promotion and fringe-benefit policies.* Management should explain promotion opportunities. Does the company pay for education for the employees? Also, what are the sick leave and annual leave policies? What benefits, such as health and life insurance, does the company provide?
5. *Training in telephone selling.* Salespeople may call a list of regular and preferred customers when new merchandise arrives. Table 17–5 shows the basic rules of telephone courtesy.

Finally in Exhibit 17–2, we have included an example of the policies, rules, and standards of conduct from the Neiman-Marcus handbook entitled, "You're What We're Famous For." Each new employee receives it as part

---

T A B L E 17–5 **TELEPHONE COURTESY**

If used correctly, the telephone is one of the most effective tools for public relations, customer service, and clientele development. The following points will help you in establishing the Neiman-Marcus image when communicating over the telephone.

Answer promptly. No one likes to be ignored.

Greet the caller. Identify yourself and your department. Speak clearly so the caller can understand you.

Do whatever you can to help the caller. If you take a message, make it complete: who called, for whom, the caller's telephone number, date and time of the call, and your name.

Place the call on hold rather than placing the receiver on a table or POS terminal. What you talk about in the stockroom is not always what you would want the customer to hear.

Answer with a smile. Since the caller cannot see your face, you must communicate your smile through your voice. You are talking to a person, not an object. You can say all of the right things, but if the pleasant tone of voice is missing, the Neiman-Marcus image is shattered.

Offer to transfer the call if the caller has not contacted the correct area. Do not tell the customer to call back and ask for the correct extension.

Indicate a call-hold or transfer to the caller. Otherwise the caller may think you have disconnected the call.

Complete the call properly. Thank the person for calling and invite him/her to call again.

All of your actions on the telephone not only affect the image of Neiman-Marcus in the caller's mind, but also in the minds of walk-in customers.

SOURCE: "You're What We're Famous For," Neiman-Marcus handbook.

EXHIBIT 17–2 RULES AND REGULATIONS—NEIMAN-MARCUS

Professional Standards

Whether you are in a selling or sales-supporting department, you represent Neiman-Marcus to our customers. Be conscious of maintaining a high level of professionalism at all times. Customers judge you by your conduct, attitude, and appearance. In order to maintain quality customer service, all employees are required to follow certain standards of professionalism:

1. Treat each customer as you would a guest in your home. Avoid personal conversation with your fellow workers and friends in the presence of customers. They come to the store for a purpose and deserve your attention.

2. Address your co-workers as "Ms.," "Mrs.," or "Mr." and not by first names when in the presence of customers.

3. If you are helping a customer at closing time, take the additional time to finish the transaction properly.

4. Do not allow the store to look disorderly. Stock work is a part of your responsibility—return stock to its proper place as soon as possible.

5. Do not make any promises to a customer without the proper approval. Check with the receiving department before promising an early delivery date or the alterations department before promising an early completion date.

6. Chewing gum, eating, and smoking are prohibited on the selling floor.

7. Store business matters are highly confidential. Purchases made by any customer are private transactions between that individual and the store.

8. Purchasing Neiman-Marcus merchandise at a discount is a privilege extended to all employees. Failure to adhere to the discount regulations is a serious violation of store policy.

9. Guard against destruction or damage of all store property. A sale can be lost because of damaged merchandise.

10. Enforcement of security regulations in regard to yourself, associates, and customers is for your protection. If you suspect someone of shoplifting, do not try to apprehend the person yourself: report it to the security department.

11. Wearing merchandise is restricted to the modeling staff. Employees may not wear apparel or accessories from stock.

12. Neiman-Marcus has a "no-solicitation" rule barring agents, collectors, or other employees not engaged in store business from approaching you in a Neiman-Marcus facility at any time during working hours. If such a person should approach you, report this to your supervisor. Written permission from the personnel manager is required for collection of money from employees or distribution of literature on company property.

13. Never leave your assigned area during working hours without informing your supervisor. Sign-out sheets are kept in some departments. Whatever the method used in your department, notify your supervisor.

Standards of Conduct

Among the causes of discipline, which may include immediate discharge, are the following:

1. Any act of dishonesty, including theft or misappropriation of money, time, or merchandise.

2. Any act which questions one's integrity, such as falsification of company records and documents, competing in business with the company, divulging trade secrets, or engaging in conduct which may adversely affect the company or its reputation.

3. Any act which may create a dangerous situation, such as carrying a concealed weapon on company premises, assaulting another individual, or disregard of property and safety standards including violation of smoking regulations.

4. The use of intoxicating liquors, narcotics, or drugs while at work or reporting to work while under the influence of the same or otherwise in a condition unfit for work.

5. Refusal to perform a job assignment or reasonable request of supervision, unprovoked insubordination, or discourteous conduct toward customers, associates, or supervisors.

6. Failure to adhere to attendance or timekeeping regulations (including excessive absenteeism or tardiness).

7. Violation of the company's no-solicitation rule.

8. Failure to adhere to work rules and regulations or other serious violations of company policy.

9. Failure to perform satisfactorily after prior notification of substandard performance.

Should you have a question concerning the above rules and regulations, or if you are in doubt about certain conduct being permitted, please consult your personnel department.

SOURCE: "You're What We're Famous For," Neiman-Marcus handbook.

of the training program. All employees must sign a statement indicating that they have read the booklet and understand its contents. The example is representative of information given to new employees in many stores.

Teaching Selling Skills[9]
Teaching selling skills consists of the three following steps:

— *Customer communications*. Developing a courteous approach to greeting customers and discussing their buying needs. This permits the salesperson to assist customers in their product selection and describe products in terms that show how they fulfill the customers' buying needs.
— *Feature-benefit relationship*. Understanding the reasons why customers buy, relating products or services to those reasons, and describing the products or services to the customers accordingly.
— *Suggestion selling*. Using customers' original purchase requests to develop suggestions for related or additional sales in which the customers might be interested.

Customer Communications

Customer relations is the foundation of a successful selling effort, not simply because a courteous approach to selling is "nice," but because it can build sales and profit. In small businesses, it is particularly important because the customers of small retailers generally expect more personal service than they find in a major department or discount store. The personal service could be advice on the color, quality, or use of certain products. Or it might be just a friendly greeting and the confidence that comes with knowing that they are buying from people who are interested in them and their business.

The salesperson should try to know as much about the customer's buying interest as possible. This is done by asking questions such as:

— "Are you looking for a fall or a winter coat?"
— "How long has your daughter been playing tennis?"
— "How often do you need a power saw?"

The answers to these questions will help the salesperson direct the customer to the right product—perhaps the winter coat, the expert model tennis racket, or the most durable saw. The salesperson will be performing a service for the customer by matching the customer's needs to the right product and will be increasing the chances of closing the sale.

As in the hiring interview, *the most effective questions are those that cannot be answered yes or no*. Instead, the salesperson should try to use open-ended questions that require a more complete answer. These are usually questions that begin with *why, what, how,* or offer a choice for the customer to make.

Even an apparently negative response can be useful. The customer who likes the style of a skirt but dislikes the color can be shown another skirt in a color she may prefer. The customer who objects to the price of an appliance can be shown a lower-priced model, or can be shown how the particular appliance justifies the apparently high price. Unless the salesperson is aware of the customer's objections, nothing can be done to overcome them.

Salespeople are responsible for *selling* products and services. Customers have *no* responsibility to *buy* them. It is up to the salesperson to find out what the customer wants and match a product or service to those wants.

Feature-Benefit Relationship

Whenever a salesperson describes the product or service to a customer, it should be described in terms of the **feature-benefit relationship.** Features and benefits are defined as follows:

— A *feature* is any tangible or intangible *characteristic* of a product or service.
— A **product benefit** is the customer's *basic buying motive* that is fulfilled by the feature.

For example, a salesperson says, "These all-leather hiking boots have waterproof seams. They are our highest-priced line, but the leather will last a long time, look good, and keep you dry even on wet trails." The salesperson mentioned two features, "all-leather" and "waterproof seams." The benefits that the owner can expect to derive from these features were also mentioned as follows:

— "Last a long time." Although they are higher priced, they represent value because they won't have to be replaced frequently.
— "Look good." People want things that they wear to look good.
— "Keep you dry." People are naturally interested in comfort and in preserving their health.

People's buying motives vary widely, as noted earlier. In fact, two people buying the same product might be looking for altogether different benefits. One man buys an expensive suit because of the status it confers upon him. Another man buys the same suit because its superior tailoring will make it more durable and long-lasting. A third buys it because he likes the styling.

The following are some typical benefits, as noted in Table 17–6, that people seek from the things they buy:

— *Safety*. The desire to protect their lives and property.
— *Economy*. Not just in the initial purchase price but in long-run savings through less frequent replacement or, in the case of certain products, lower maintenance and operating costs.
— *Status*. People buy things to be recognized. The woman buying an evening dress may consider the designer's name all-important. A 12-year-old boy might consider the brand of blue jeans or the autograph on a baseball bat to be equally important.
— *Health*. People buy exercise equipment, athletic equipment, and outerwear because they wish to preserve their health.

Rational	Emotional
Price	Lifestyle image
Convenience	Adventure and excitement
Warranties	Pleasure
After-the-sale service	"Keeping up with the Joneses"
Economy	Good provider for family
Length of service	Pride
Health and safety	Fantasy fulfillment
Quality	Status

— *Pleasure*. People attend theaters, go to athletic events, eat at restaurants, and buy books and objects of art because they expect to derive personal pleasure from these pursuits.

— *Convenience*. People buy many things to make the routine chores of life easier. For example, the cook buys a cake mix because it is far more convenient than mixing the individual basic ingredients.

The list could go on indefinitely. The important question to consider is the *customer benefits* that are provided by the goods or services to be sold. Knowing these benefits, salespeople can describe products to customers in terms of the benefits that the customers can derive from them. *Relatively few customers are interested in the technical or design details of a product.* Customers are primarily interested in what the product will do for them. The principal reason for a salesperson to describe features of a product or service is to *prove the benefits* that the person can expect from it. For example, a salesperson might describe insulating material to a customer as follows: "This insulating material creates a thermal barrier." Impressive words, perhaps, but the statement tells the customer little or nothing about the reasons for buying.

Suggestion Selling

In suggestion selling, the salesperson tries to build on the customer's initial request in order to sell additional or related merchandise. For example, the salesperson might suggest that a woman buy two blouses to take advantage of a weekend special. If a man buys a dress shirt, the salesperson should suggest a complementary tie. With a tablecloth, a salesperson might suggest napkins that go well with it. With a stereo receiver, a skilled salesperson could suggest a pair of speakers matched to the output of the receiver.

The opportunities for suggestion selling are endless. Frequently, the *benefit* that a customer might derive from one product could be used to develop suggestions for others. Young parents buying one safety product for a baby would be interested in seeing others. Or the man who buys a designer necktie for status reasons could be persuaded to buy a belt, shirt, or eyeglass frames from the same designer.

Even a "no sale" or a return can become a sales opportunity through suggestion selling. The customer who is looking for a shirt to buy as a gift may not find the right shirt, but could be persuaded to buy something else, perhaps a necktie or a sweater. The man who returns a raincoat because it doesn't fit properly still needs a raincoat and could be sold one if the salesperson takes advantage of the opportunity for a suggestion sale.

Involvement and Feedback[10]

When training people in sales skills, it is relatively easy to get their involvement and the feedback needed to evaluate their progress to better shape the training needed. Instead of telling salespeople how *you* would sell a certain product, ask them how *they* would do it, and what they would say to a customer.

After hearing the salespeople's presentations, management can explain any other features that should have been mentioned and any other benefits that are important. Then let the person try again, perhaps reviewing the basic technique of features and benefits if necessary.

Similarly, management can list a number of products that the store offers and have the salesperson write down a related product that could be suggested to every customer. In so doing, management will be gaining the trainee's active involvement and securing necessary feedback so they can see where review or correction is necessary. Management will also learn of the employee's strengths and weaknesses and can perform a more effective supervisory job.

Criteria for Successful Training

Regardless of the training method used, there are two key elements for success. These are as follows:

— *Trainee participation*. The training process should *directly involve* the trainee. Listening to a person talk has little value. Few can absorb it. The passive role of reader or listener is seldom helpful in understanding and remembering. Reading a book or hearing a speech is fine for entertainment or intellectual stimulation, but these activities are seldom effective in a training environment. People learn by doing things. When new personnel are taught how to prepare an invoice or credit memo, it is not enough to tell them how or show them how. It is far more important to have them do it.

— *Feedback*. Feedback is what a person learns by testing the employee's understanding of the facts that are being taught. It permits the trainer to measure the employee's progress at each step. Through feedback, management can recognize problems when they arise. Through early recognition of misunderstandings, they can correct them as soon as possible so that training can progress. Feedback helps direct training efforts since management then knows those things that give the employee particular difficulty, such as arithmetic or trade terminology. In the re-

_____ Explain:
_____ Company purpose
_____ Company image
_____ Kind of clients catered to

_____ Introduce to other employees and positions

_____ Explain relationship between new employee's position and other positions

_____ Tour the building:
_____ Working areas
_____ Management office
_____ Rest facilities
_____ Records
_____ Employee locker room or closet
_____ Other relevant areas

_____ Explain facilities and equipment

_____ Review the duties and responsibilities of the job from the job description

_____ Introduce to emergency equipment and safety procedures

_____ Questions and answers

mainder of the training effort, management can then be particularly careful and painstaking in teaching anything that involves trade terminology or arithmetic skills.

Job Orientation

A job description and job specification can simplify the process of providing an orientation or introducing a new employee into the business. An orientation will make the new employee feel at ease and better able to begin work. It is important to note, however, that a job orientation only explains the job to the employee and does not train her or him to do it. A typical job orientation checklist is shown in Exhibit 17–3.

After the period of formal job training and orientation are completed, management still faces the task of helping the salesperson perform successfully. One way to do this is a program of **management by objectives** that helps the person work to achieve tangible goals.

MANAGEMENT BY OBJECTIVES[11]

Direction and Evaluation

Goals give direction to one's efforts and permit an evaluation of progress. Through an evaluation of progress, people can detect inefficiencies so that corrective actions can be taken. Similarly, when people achieve objectives, they know that they have done the job properly and can continue to do it in the same way.

Criteria for
Objectives

This concept is perfectly valid in setting goals for the performance of retail salespeople. To be effective, however, objectives must meet certain criteria, as follows:

— Objectives must be *specific* so that the person responsible for meeting them will understand clearly what is expected. An objective such as "Take better care of customers" is vague and can be interpreted in a number of ways. The same objective, however, can be translated into more specific terms such as: "Advise every lawn mower buyer of the break-in procedures" or "Offer every customer a credit application."

— Objectives must be *measurable*. Objectives such as "Make a better selling effort" or "Be sure that customers get the right size" could be achieved with a minimal increase in effort or efficiency. A more useful statement would be "Improve sales by 10 percent" or "Reduce the *rate* of returns to 2 percent."

— Goals must be *attainable*. There is no sense in setting a goal for a salesperson to increase sales by 25 or 30 percent if the owners of the store plan no action to increase the flow of traffic through the store. A goal that is beyond the person's capabilities will soon be ignored and therefore will have little impact.

— Objectives must be *consistent with the owners' goals*. Any objective set for salespeople is simply one segment of the total goal of building sales and profit. There is little point in setting an objective for a person to achieve unless realization of the objective helps the owners realize a greater goal.

— Objectives must be *agreed upon* with the person responsible for meeting them. Unless the owners can explain the goal to the employee's satisfaction and work with the employee to develop a plan for accomplishing it, the objective will soon be ignored. When the employee's performance is reviewed and compared with the objective, the discusssion will focus on the reality of the initial objective rather than the more important issue of how performance can be improved to achieve it.

— Objectives must be used as a basis for *performance review*. Employees must realize that they are responsible for meeting the objectives to which they have agreed. They must be advised on a regular basis whether they have achieved the objective. Further, any failure to meet the objective must be accompanied by a discussion of proposed corrective action that can be taken so that it can be realized in the future.

Joint Effort

A successful program of management by objectives requires a joint effort by owners and employees. Working together, they must arrive at agreeable, realistic solutions for performance improvement. It is not enough to say, "You'll have to work harder next month." It is far more productive to ask the employee, "What can *we* do so we can get sales up to the objective that we are looking for?"

Authority and Control	Goals must be consistent with the person's authority and responsibility. There is little value in setting objectives with a person if the person has no control or authority.

Retailing Objectives	Frequently, the role of the retail salesperson is minimized. As a result, people often overlook opportunities for setting specific performance objectives. However, there are a number of areas in which objectives can be set for the performance of retail sales personnel.

Measurable Objectives	At first glance, it may be difficult to see how the job of the retail salesperson can be expressed in specific, measurable terms. However, consider the following examples:

— *Sales in dollars.* The owners can set sales objectives for each retail salesperson based on expectations of the department in which the person is employed and performance in previous periods.

— *Average sale per customer.* If the owner expects the salesperson to suggest related sales or to upgrade customer purchases, the average dollar value of each sale becomes a meaningful criterion for evaluating performance.

— *Returns as a percentage of sales.* There is little value in making a sale if the item is later returned. Frequently, the cause of a return can be the fault of the salesperson. The salesperson fails to give the customer the correct size or suggests the wrong tool for a certain job. The dollar value of returns can be compared with the dollar value of sales and an objective set for performance.

— *Time for fulfillment of certain tasks.* A salesperson may be responsible for stocking or arranging displays. A specific deadline can be set for completing this task each day. On a longer-range basis, salespeople expected to read instructional literature concerning products they sell could have a specific time limit set for completion.

Performance Review

Performance review and comparison with objectives should be as frequent as realistically possible. *Shorter review periods* are generally more effective since the objective is constantly in front of the employee, convincing the employee of the owners' full intention of attaining it. Short review periods also permit prompt corrective action before a problem becomes too serious or too many dollars are lost through inattention. Similarly, short-term review reinforces employees' efforts for jobs well done. The employee can then continue to apply the same success techniques that were proved effective.

MOTIVATION[12]

Historically, the concept of **motivation** has evoked heroic images of fearless leaders whose courage, dedication, rhetoric, and charisma inspired their followers to ignore their own self-doubts and overcome overwhelming odds.

This view of motivation makes great movies, but does the concept a disservice. It makes motivation appear to be an unattainable goal in itself, one that can't be reached by ordinary mortals. Yet, the motivation of people is an everyday function of retail management.

The task of motivation can be described in simple terms without epic overtones. Motivation is simply a matter of *getting people to do what's best for the business*.

In an earlier, more authoritarian society, the task was relatively simple. *Fear* was the motivator. The turn-of-the-century coal miner knew that failure to meet his daily quota meant not only the loss of his job but also the loss of his home.

In today's society, fear is no longer a valid motivator. In retailing, the salesperson motivated solely by fear would not be likely to project the ideal image for the business.

To realize the type of performance expected, management wants people to be motivated on a higher plane than that of fear.

Motivating the Employee

In a working environment, people are motivated by demonstrating to them that a job well done satisfies certain basic *human needs*. By satisfying these needs, the manager will be motivating the employees to do the job expected, in the way that is expected.

Security Needs

Security needs are filled through compensation, benefits, job availability, and advancement opportunities. In some parts of retailing, economic rewards are somewhat limited. The retail salesperson is often employed at a wage at or near the legal minimum. There are exceptions, such as appliance sales, automotive sales, and door-to-door sales, where midlevel five-figure incomes are commonplace and six-figure incomes can be achieved. Similarly, service personnel in popular restaurants often realize incomes well above the national average. However, in most retail businesses, narrow profit margins restrict the owners' ability to pay attractive wages.

This presents the management of a retail establishment with a serious dilemma. The retailer must compete with more profitable businesses to attract effective personnel. Frequently, the business owner has higher expectations of salespeople's performance, relying heavily on personal service as a way of attracting customers. Since retailers cannot compete effectively in providing economic rewards, they must take full advantage of other motivators to offset the effects of inferior salaries and wages.

The retailer's competitive disadvantage in offering security rewards is not limited to salaries alone. Without the natural chain of command through which the talented and motivated individual can progress, advancement opportunities are limited. To some extent, opportunities for advancement can be made available. Better sales personnel can assume new responsibilities such as assisting with buying, training, and supervising. They can also participate in sales and profit growth and expansion, assuming new and more rewarding responsibilities—perhaps managing a new branch, location, or department.

Recognition

Beyond the security need, people also need *recognition*. This social need is a natural desire to be part of the group, to have one's efforts recognized by those with whom the person comes in contact—customers or fellow employees. In this respect, praise for good performance is even more important than the reprimand for poor performance. Employees' behavior is often reinforced by management's reaction toward it. If management ignores a mistake or an oversight, they reinforce it by their inattention. If they neglect to praise a job well done, the employee may feel unappreciated. Therefore, the employee will not repeat the good work, particularly if it required any extra effort.

By recognizing good performance when it occurs, management reinforces good behavior so the employee will be more likely to perform well again.

Often, it is the best employee who is uncertain about his or her own performance. Having set high personal standards for performance, the employee may often have doubts as to whether or not performance is satisfactory.

Self-Fulfillment

To many people, the ultimate achievement is self-fulfillment, the satisfaction realized from a job well done. The self-fulfillment of the athlete, the entertainer, the poet, or the author is easily recognized. Yet it exists at other levels of endeavor. The teacher is rewarded by the progress of pupils, the accountant is rewarded by the error-free trial balance, and the landscaper is rewarded by the beauty of the plantings. In each of these cases, the person's self-esteem is fulfilled by the knowledge of a job well done.

This same type of self-esteem can be developed within the retail environment so that employees look upon their jobs as something more than "another day, another dollar." Let us take a look at some of the personal achievements that can be realized by a retail salesperson that could fulfill the need for self-esteem.

— A personal daily sales record.
— Leading all other salespeople for a week or a month.
— Selling the "unsellable" customer.

— Discovering a new and effective selling technique.
— Knowing that his or her selling efforts solved a customer's problem.
— Achieving a record of zero customer complaints.

CHAPTER HIGHLIGHTS

- The trend today is toward more self-service. Improved signing, displays, packaging, and store layouts all make self-service possible. But retailers still need salespeople to answer customers' questions about the technical dimensions of products, to reassure customers about items of fashion apparel, and to help customers fit items such as shoes.
- The key to a good sales force is the right interaction between the merchandise, the customer, and the salesperson. A salesperson is needed when customers have little knowledge about the merchandise they plan to buy, when price negotiation is likely, and when the product is complex.
- The easiest type of selling is transaction processing. This means that employees simply serve as checkout clerks or cashiers and do little selling. Routine selling involves more product knowledge and a better approach to the sales task. Creative selling requires the use of creative sales skills by salespeople who need complete information about product lines, product uses, and technical features.
- The job of the salesperson is to lead the customer to a buying situation. Successful salespeople normally think of selling as a process consisting of the following steps: prospecting (preapproaching), approaching, determining needs and wants, demonstrating and handling merchandise, answering questions and meeting objections, closing, and following up.
- Developing a strong sales force is not a matter of luck. Training is needed; adequate incentives must exist to motivate personnel to high levels of performance; and supervision is necessary. Above all, management of the sales force means planning for increased sales. Sales per person can be increased by: better employee selection, training, and supervision; improved departmental layout; more self-selection by customers; streamlining sales processing; improved merchandising and promotion; making sure salespeople are fully knowledgeable about the products they're selling; and following up where necessary after the sale (e.g., with the service department).
- Retail sales managers should set up performance standards and let salespeople know what they are. Nonselling activities should be included if they are also expected to be performed by the employee. Finally, management should decide how to reward employees who exceed the established standards.
- Management by objectives can help in the personal selling process. Objectives established by such a process give directions to the salespeople's efforts and can permit them to evaluate their progress. The objectives must be specific, measurable, attainable, consistent with the owners' goals, agreed upon with the person responsible for meeting them, and serve as a basis for performance review.

— Measurable objectives for the salesperson can include sales in dollars, average sale per customer, returns as a percentage of sales, and time for fulfillment of certain tasks.
— Motivation means getting people to do what's best for the business. Salespeople can be motivated by demonstrating to them how a job well done can satisfy their human needs. Basic human needs include the need for security, recognition, and self-fulfillment.

KEY TERMS

Assumptive close A sales closing technique that asks a question about preferred colors, method of payment, or type of delivery. It helps the salesperson determine quickly whether a customer is ready to make a purchase.

Creative selling A type of higher-level selling in which the salesperson needs complete information about product lines, product uses, and the technical features of products.

Feature-benefit relationship Understanding the reasons why customers buy, relating products to those reasons, and describing the products or services to the customers.

Management by objectives Goals established with salespeople which give direction to their efforts and permit them to evaluate their progress.

Merchandise approach A retail sales approach that begins with a statement about the merchandise.

Motivation The process of getting people to do what's best for the business.

Product benefit A customer's basic buying motive that is fulfilled by a product feature.

Role playing A sales training situation in which one person plays the part of the customer, while another person plays the part of the salesperson.

Routine selling A type of selling that involves the sale of nontechnical items.

Service approach A weak approach in personal selling in which salespeople simply ask if they can be of assistance to a potential customer.

Suggestion selling Using a customer's original purchase decision as a basis for developing suggestions about related or additional items in which the customer might be interested.

Transaction processing A situation in which employees serve as checkout clerks or cashiers and do little selling.

DISCUSSION QUESTIONS

1. What are the various types of retail selling? How do the skills required vary by type of selling?
2. What is the difference between the service approach and the merchandise approach?
3. Under which conditions is the presence of sales personnel most essential in a retail store?
4. What are the various ways a salesperson can determine customer needs and wants?
5. Comment on the following statement: The best way for a salesperson to deal with a customer objection is simply to ignore it and continue with the sales presentation.
6. In closing a sale, how does an assumptive close differ from that which might be used during a special-sale event?
7. Why is sales-force productivity so important? How can it be increased?
8. Why is self-selection and self-service becoming more common in retailing?
9. Assume that you have been asked by a retail store manager to describe what an effective sales training program should include and what sales training methods can be used. How would you respond?
10. Why should performance standards be established for sales personnel? List examples of performance standards for salespeople.

APPLICATION EXERCISES

1. Visit with the personnel manager of the leading department store in your community and discuss briefly their training programs for salespeople. Find out their major problems with sales personnel. Do the same thing with the manager of a fast-food franchise. Be prepared to discuss the differences you find.

2. Interview 10–15 of your student friends and find out their overall impression of salespeople in your community. Are they satisfied? If yes, why? If not, why not? Get their thoughts on what can be done to improve the quality of service in retail outlets. Now, talk to several of your friends who have worked for or are working as part-time salespeople. Prepare a report based on their experiences. Get them to talk about their reaction

to most customers in the stores where they work, their likes and dislikes about their jobs, and what could be done to make their jobs easier.

3. Visit three of the new-car dealers in your community and act as a serious buyer. Develop a list of questions ahead of time about such things as miles per gallon of the auto, service requirements, and warranty and safety features. Compare and contrast the results you get in talking to the different salespeople about each of these points. Find out if they have what you consider the necessary knowledge for selling the product. Do they conduct themselves in the way you would expect from persons who are selling items valued at $10,000–$20,000? If not, make suggestions for improving their quality of service to customers.

CASES

1. Well-Trained Personnel Can Whip Up Sales Totals

Surrounded by the glittering displays of one of Manhattan's most prestigious department stores, a saleswoman slumps by the cash register in the bath department. She is a study in inertia until a young woman disturbs her.

"Could you help me?" the customer asks. "I'm looking for a shower curtain called Springtime."

"What's that?" the saleswoman demands.

"Well, I saw it in here two weeks ago. It's a fabric curtain in jade and yellow."

"Springtime?" the saleswoman repeats.

"Yes."

"I never heard of that," declares the saleswoman. "I can't keep up with all these names. Where was it?"

The customer leads the saleswoman to the fabric curtains where she looks aimlessly through the displays for several minutes. She returns to her post empty-handed. The customer vanishes.

This example is lifted from a store praised for its effective selling. But it is no more an aberration here than throughout the retail industry, one pocked by horror stories of rudeness, apathy, and ignorance among sales staff. In an industry grounded on repeat

business—where the sales floor is the production floor—experts find a pervasive neglect of the selling function.

Selling plays a lowly role in most retail operations. Expenditures for sales training are "extremely minimal," with a $50,000 investment considered large, says one source, whereas millions are spent on advertising, design, and remodeling to lure a customer into the store.

Questions
1. Why does the selling function receive only limited attention in most retail outlets?
2. What can be done to upgrade the quality of sales personnel in retail stores?
3. What type of compensation would be most effective for department store retail salespersons? Provide a rationale for your answer.

Source: Portions quoted from "Well-Trained Personnel Can Whip Up Sales Totals," *Chain Store Age Executive,* November 1983, p. 15. Reprinted with permission.

2. Low Morale among the Sales Staff

Bart Crowder moved up the executive ladder rapidly. He is now buyer for 20 Whizmart promotional department stores in a major metropolitan area in the Midwest. His progress was not unexpected to management, as he had been hired after receiving an MBA from a very prestigious university in the East and had been promised a "fast track." The company had not previously stressed college degrees, let alone MBAs. But the second generation of management was changing the philosophy, and rather than hiring away employees from other companies after they had undergone a period of training and experience, it was rapidly implementing a policy of promotion from within after its own training program was completed. Bart was the first MBA to be hired in the fast-track program, and from all indications management was pleased. After all, he now bought for three classifications (linens, domestics, and art needlework) and was responsible for $3 million in annual retail sales volume.

Bart had gone through 13 weeks of intensive training along with others hired in the Junior Executive Training (JET) program. He was assigned initially as the manager of the Fashion Fabrics Department in an inner-city store catering to first-generation families of primarily Polish and Italian heritage. Sales associates in that store were expected to speak both Polish and Italian, but in actuality most of them spoke only one of these languages. The sales associates were hired from the neighborhood, and those of Italian or Polish extraction spoke the language of their homeland.

Bart was from a small southern city and had attended college in the East. Finding himself in this environment was different, to say the least. He considered his initial training quite good and felt that the company's philosophy, though in transition, was adequately presented. He had learned systems; had acquired a good grasp of the company's target market (though he felt that there were some problems with the many varied types of micromarkets in which stores were located); and had trained with good store managers and buyers. Although he was a senior buyer now, he thought back on a situation which was, at the time, untenable.

His first assignment as the department manager in Fashion Fabrics had provided him with some of the best training possible. But the composition of his department and the policies he inherited had caused great problems. He had two full-time sales-people; one person who worked three-fourths time (Crystal); and three part-time women who worked the busy hours during the week. Crystal was the only person in the department who spoke, in addition to English, Polish and Italian. Her hours had been worked out with the store manager some years previously, and they were the best hours for business. She was the only person in the department on a straight commission. The two full-time women were on a salary plus 1 percent commission on net sales; the part-timers were on straight salary.

Bart hadn't been in the department a month when the two full-time saleswomen asked for a conference. They were vehement, and their complaints were as follows: (1) Crystal "hogs" all sales and ties up a dozen customers at a time, and we can't make a penny extra without small commissions. (Bart was not sure whether they knew of the straight commission arrangement, but he certainly was not going to open that up for discussion.) (2) Since Crystal speaks all the languages, she is able to say things we don't understand, and we know she's talking about how good she is and how inefficient we are—she's careful to speak the "other" language when one of us is around. (3) The stock work in a fabrics department is tremendous: you always have to be folding bolts, straightening remnants, etc. Crystal *only* folds her own sales and won't straighten out anything else, so we're always doing stock work while she's grabbing customers. (4) Crystal sells so much and runs such a good book that we look bad. Even the commissions she "steals" from us don't bother us as much as how we must look to you and others. (5) Crystal is so "sweet" when any of you are around, but when it's just us and customers, she's a real witch.

Bart remembers, with clammy hands, what a difficult position that short conference put him in.

Questions

1. Is Crystal so valuable that her reactions must be considered?
2. Is it typical to find varying compensation plans within a single department?
3. Are the salespersons' complaints legitimate or emotional?
4. What should Bart do?

ENDNOTES

1. "Tuning in to the Time Efficiency Factor," *Chain Store Age, General Merchandise Edition*, February 1984, p. 149.
2. This material, including Figure 17–1, is reproduced from Bert Rosenbloom, *Improving Personal Selling* (Washington, D.C.: Small Business Administration), pp. 1–3.
3. *On the Up-Beat* A, no. 7A (1980), pp. 12–13.
4. The material on closing the sale is reproduced with modifications from *Marketing Strategy,* self-instructional booklet 1009 (Washington, D.C.: U.S. Small Business Administration).
5. *On the Up-Beat*, p. 23.
6. Steven Cron, "Control of Retail Selling Costs," *Retail Control,* August 1976, p. 60.
7. Rosenbloom, *Improving Personal Selling*, p. 4.
8. Ibid.
9. This material is reproduced, with modifications, from *Managing Retail Salespeople,* self-instructional booket 1019 (Washington, D.C.: U.S. Small Business Administration).
10. The material on involvement and feedback, criteria for successful training, and job orientation is reproduced, with modifications, from *Job Analysis, Job Specifications, and Job Descriptions,* self-instructional booklet No. 120 (Washington, D.C.: U.S. Small Business Administration).
11. *Managing Retail Salespeople,* pp. 35–39.
12. This material is reproduced, with modifications, from *Employee Relations and Personnel Policies,* self-instructional booklet No. 123 (Washington, D.C.: U.S. Small Business Administration).

A P P E N D I X A

A CHECKLIST FOR RETAIL SELLING ACTIVITIES

Retail selling activities are all brought together when the salesperson asks the customer, "May I help you?" To ensure that sales personnel are effective, you must plan the training, scheduling, supervision, and positioning of the selling staff. Numerous opportunities exist for reducing costs and improving productivity in this area.

The following questionnaire examines selling activities in relation to sales personnel and customer service.

Questionnaire and work guide

Scheduling of the sales forces

	Yes	No
1. Have daily traffic patterns been analyzed by transaction counts showing peak hours for:		
a. Day of the week?	☐	☐
b. Individual departments?	☐	☐
c. Selling zones?	☐	☐
2. Is the daily/weekly sales force scheduled for each department or selling zone according to:		
a. Identified traffic patterns and total selling hours required?	☐	☐
b. Promotional and seasonal requirements?	☐	☐
3. Has a determination been made of the minimum number of sales personnel required per department or selling zone?	☐	☐
4. Do designated selling supervisors have the authority to shift sales personnel to other areas as required?	☐	☐
5. Are support personnel (i.e., nonsales personnel) used during peak selling periods?	☐	☐

Using part-time employees effectively

	Yes	No
1. Is part-time work scheduled according to:		
a. Forecasted peak and slack customer-traffic patterns?	☐	☐
b. Maximum floor coverage?	☐	☐
c. Minimum floor coverage?	☐	☐
d. Promotional and seasonal staffing needs?	☐	☐

Source: Coopers and Lybrand, *Profit Improvement Opportunities for Retailers.*

	Yes	No

2. Is adequate supervisory coverage scheduled for part-time employees? ☐ ☐

3. Do part-time personnel receive adequate training in merchandise information, store systems, and procedures? ☐ ☐

4. Do part-time schedules attract the kind of part-time employees the store requires? ☐ ☐

5. Are recruitment techniques (e.g., display/classified ads, inserts to charge customers, in-store signs, radio/TV ads, and bus signs) periodically evaluated in terms of:
   a. Cost? ☐ ☐
   b. Results? ☐ ☐

Training sales personnel

1. Are sales personnel trained to be:
   a. Alert to customer needs? ☐ ☐
   b. Enthusiastic about merchandise? ☐ ☐
   c. Knowledgeable about what they have in stock? ☐ ☐
   d. Familiar with selling points of individual items? ☐ ☐
   Sales personnel have the most direct contact with customers. They represent the retailer to the buying public, and the success of a retail organization can depend on the competence and attitude of the sales force.

2. Are supervisors directly responsible for on-the-job training of sales personnel? ☐ ☐
   Supervisors can provide efficient and thorough training based on the department's specific selling requirements.

Defining selling zones

1. Is each store divided into control centers or zones that are related to cash registers and logical merchandise groupings? ☐ ☐

2. Have time requirements for all customer service and support work been determined by selling zone? ☐ ☐

3. Are staffing requirements for each selling zone based on an analysis of sales patterns and the desired level of customer service? ☐ ☐

4. Are selling costs periodically evaluated in relation to gross margin when setting departmental/zone selling-cost percent goals? ☐ ☐

5. Have departments been identified where these selling costs are excessive? ☐ ☐

Scheduling by selling zones

	Yes	No
1. Are customer-service assignments issued by selling zones that correspond with identified traffic patterns?	☐	☐
2. Are sales personnel who are assigned to a particular zone during peak hours moved to stock-related activities in another zone during slow periods?	☐	☐
3. Are stock-support assignments made to cover larger areas (floorwide or storewide)?	☐	☐
4. Are certain clerks assigned full-time to stock support activities?	☐	☐

Interselling concepts

1. Does the main store practice interselling on an extensive basis?   ☐   ☐
   Interselling provides improved customer service and greater selling productivity potential without increasing personnel.
2. Is the sales register capacity adequate to cover extensive interselling?   ☐   ☐
   Assign sales personnel a selling area number rather than a selling department number.
3. Are departmental sales forces familiar with the merchandise in other departments?   ☐   ☐
   Sales personnel should receive training in product information, selling techniques, and forward and reserve stock locations for merchandise in their selling area.
4. Do variable commission rates among departments make interselling undesirable to sales personnel?   ☐   ☐
   Shifting to straight-salary basis (except on "big ticket" items) will facilitate implementation of interselling.
5. Can department floor plans be adapted to accommodate interselling?   ☐   ☐
   Changing fixtures, opening aisles, and removing physical barriers are methods of adapting space for interselling.

18

Advertising, Promotion, and Publicity

Humor and Subtlety Supplant Hard Sell in Retailers' TV Ads

Funnyman Harry Anderson wants to talk turkey, frozen turkey that is. "With the right dressing, the turkey can become an attractive addition to anyone's table," he tells TV viewers as he holds up one of the birds and flips it over to reveal a red necktie and pocket handkerchief. In another spot, the subject is eggs, which Mr. Anderson describes as "the hobby of chickens." Chickens, he says, "can't drive recreational vehicles or water-ski, so in their spare time, they lay eggs. Please buy 'em; otherwise we're going to have chickens hanging out in pool halls."

What gives here? The food gags sound like a nightclub routine, but they're actually part of a new series of TV commercials for Tom Thumb–Page, a Texas supermarket chain.

Flashy commercials also are important these days because department stores face increased competition from specialty and discount stores, while supermarkets find themselves up against new bargain warehouse stores. To stand out, some stores try to project "a personality." Take, for example, Bayless Markets in Arizona, a stodgy food retailer that decided to pursue the many young people relocating to the Sun Belt. One approach: An ad that shows only a mayonnaise jar and a hand beating on it as if it were a bongo drum. The only sound is a voice chanting, "may-o, may-o."

Another spot is nothing but white space for about 15 seconds. An announcer apologetically explains: "Yes, we have no kumquats, but yes, we do have bananas." Says Bruce Fowler, the company's ad director: "We want to establish an image that's both friendly and intelligent."

On the department-store side of retailing, Jordan Marsh of Boston has segmented its audience much as automobile and cigarette marketers do. Last fall, it ran three commercials, all romantic in tone, but each aimed at a different age group. For young married couples, one ad showed a father hurrying his son off to bed while the mother put on a slinky new nightie. Another spot tried to appeal to the over-50 set by depicting a gray-haired woman modeling a new dress for her flirtatious husband. "You can't be everything to everybody," says Don O'Brien, marketing director. "We tried to create situations our target customers could identify with."

*P*romotion is the primary retailer-dominated source of communication with consumers. Promotion includes the creative use of advertising, sales promotion, and publicity in communicating information to consumers. The purposes of communication may be to inform the consumers of short-term price promotions, to help establish and maintain a desired image, or to accomplish a variety of other tasks. Developing promotion plans, establishing budgets, and evaluating the effectiveness of promotions are critical issues in the success of any retail firm. Retailers are constantly seeking new and creative ways of communicating with the consumer, as shown in the retailing capsule.

After reading this chapter you will be able to:

1. Explain the requirements for good promotion plans.

2. Establish budgets.

3. Allocate a budget.

4. Describe media options available.

5. Determine the effectiveness of media.

6. Measure the results of advertising.

7. Decide when to use an ad agency.

8. Evaluate the essentials of a good advertisement.

9. Discuss the role of sales promotion and publicity in the retail firm.

As individuals, we communicate in different ways. Retailers similarly have a variety of ways for communicating with consumers. One role of retail communication is to *inform,* by providing information on store hours, brands carried, services available, and so forth. Retailers may also seek to *persuade* individuals to do a variety of things, such as to make a merchandise purchase during a reduced-price sale. Communication only takes place when the individuals with whom the retailer is attempting to communicate attach to the communication a meaning similar to what was intended by the retailer.

The **source** in the communication process is the originator of the message, normally the retailer. The **message** is the idea to be transmitted. The message must be right for the audience and for the purpose of the promotion. A careful analysis of the individuals who constitute the target audience will help the retailer to better understand how the ideas can be most effectively communicated to achieve the desired effect.

The next decision after message content selection is how to *transmit* the message in a communicable form. The message can be transmitted by such media as radio, television, newspaper, direct mail, or other means of message transmission. Market segmentation plays a particularly important role in this process because segmentation ensures that the message is targeted at a relatively homogeneous audience.

The **promotion** plan starts with the goals of the firm. Retailers must decide (1) who they want to reach, (2) the message they want to get across, and (3) when and how often their message should reach the audience. Answers to the following questions can help in making such decisions.[1]

1. What business am I in?
2. What quality of merchandise do I sell?
3. What kind of image do I want to project?
4. How do I compare with competition?
5. What customer services do I offer?
6. Who are my customers?
7. What are their tastes?
8. What are their income levels?
9. Why do they buy from me?

Retailers cannot be all things to all people. They must segment their messages, markets, and merchandise. Understanding the customer is the key in all such decisions. Sears, for example, makes its pitch to one family member at a time, informing Dad of a new electronic tool or trying to convince Mom or the kids that Sears apparel is fashionable. Sears carefully targets individual niches with product-oriented ads that allow the firm to make very specific statements, sometimes using moods or techniques that might not seem appropriate in its total store ads.[2]

Some people define promotion to include advertising, personal selling, and displaying merchandise. Personal selling was discussed in Chapter 17, and display and layout were explained in Chapter 16. Our definition of promotion in this chapter includes mass-media advertising, publicity, and promotions such as coupons, trading stamps, and premium offers.

ADVERTISING

The basic goals of advertising can include:

— Communicating the total character of the store.
— Getting consumer acceptance for individual groups of merchandise.
— Generating a strong flow of traffic.
— Selling goods directly.

These goals can be combined with merchandising and store image objectives into the following framework:

How much to spend	Advertising budget
What to advertise	Merchandise
When to advertise	Timing
Where to say it	Media
How to say it	Technique
Whom to reach	Audience
How to provide balance	Planning[3]

How to Set an Advertising Budget

Why Have an Advertising Budget? A budget helps retailers plan their promotions. This step alone can go a long way toward better campaigns. Why? (1) A budget forces retailers to set goals so they can measure the success of the promotions; (2) retailers are required to choose from a variety of options; and (3) budgets are more likely to result in well-planned ads.

What Should Be in the Budget?[4] Promotion is a completely controllable expense, and the function of the budget is to control expenditures. By comparing the budget with actual financial reports coming from business activities of the firm, it is possible to compare planned activities with actual events. This can be done through a monthly tabulation as shown in Table 18–1. With this record, danger signals flash when the budget becomes overextended. The accounts listed in the table are not comprehensive. They serve only as examples.

What retailers would like to invest in advertising and what they can afford are seldom the same. Spending too much is obviously an extravagance, but spending too little can be just as bad in terms of lost sales and diminished visibility. Costs must be tied to results. It is necessary to be prepared to evaluate goals and assess capabilities. A budget will help do this.

The budget can help retailers choose and assess the amount of advertising and its timing. The budget also will serve as the background for next year's plan.

Methods of Establishing a Budget[5]

Each of the ways to establish an advertising budget has problems as well as benefits. No method is perfect for all types of businesses—nor is any combination of methods.

PROMOTION BUDGET

Account	Month Budget	Month Actual	Year to Date Budget	Year to Date Actual
Media				
Newspapers				
Radio				
TV				
Literature				
Other				
Promotions				
Exhibits				
Displays				
Contests				
Advertising expense				
Salaries				
Supplies				
Stationery				
Travel				
Postage				
Subscriptions				
Entertainment				
Dues				
Totals				

Here, concepts from several traditional methods of budgeting have been combined into three basic methods: (1) percentage of sales or profits, (2) unit of sales, and (3) objective and task. Management needs to use judgment and caution in settling on any method or methods.

Percentage of Sales or Profits

The most widely used method of establishing an advertising budget is to base it on a percentage of actual sales. Advertising is as much a business expense as the cost of labor and should be related to the quantity of goods sold for a certain period.

The percentage-of-sales method avoids some of the problems that result from using profits as a base. For instance, if profits in a period are low, it might not be the fault of sales or advertising. But if retailers base the advertising budget on profits, they will automatically reduce the advertising allotment when profits are down. There is no way around it: 2 percent of $10,000 is less than 2 percent of $15,000.

If profits are down for other reasons, a cut in the advertising budget may very well lead to further losses in sales and profits. This in turn will lead to further reductions in advertising investment, and so on.

In the short run, it may be possible to make small additions to profit by cutting advertising expenses. But such a policy could lead to a long-term deterioration of the bottom line. By using the percentage-of-sales method,

Industry	SIC no.	Ad Dollars as Percent of Sales	Ad Dollars as Percent of Margin	Annual Growth Rate (percent)
Retail—lumber and building material	5211	2.2	8.5	12.2
Retail—mobile home dealers	5270	.8	4.0	13.5
Retail—department stores	5311	3.3	13.5	9.9
Retail—variety stores	5331	2.2	8.0	8.6
Retail—grocery stores	5411	1.4	6.0	5.9
Convenience stores	5412	.4	2.2	10.5
Retail—auto dealers and gas stations	5500	1.6	5.7	8.2
Retail—apparel and accessories store	5600	2.0	5.2	12.5
Retail—women's ready to wear	5621	2.0	6.1	16.7
Retail—shoe stores	5661	2.0	5.5	4.4
Retail—furniture stores	5712	7.1	18.2	12.1
Retail—household appliance stores	5722	5.7	19.0	15.3
Retail—radio, TV and music stores	5730	4.1	12.1	27.8
Retail—eating places	5812	3.7	15.8	13.9
Retail—drug and proprietary stores	5912	1.6	6.1	11.5
Retail—jewelry stores	5944	6.2	15.9	5.7
Retail—sewing and needlework	5949	4.0	7.9	11.1
Retail—mail-order houses	5961	15.3	38.8	8.5
Retail—auto merchandising machine operations	5962	8.3	20.7	14.1
Retail—fuel and ice dealers	5980	.6	2.7	−44.2
Retail—computer stores	5995	3.7	12.6	34.7
Retail—stores NEC	5999	3.4	8.7	9.8
Service—motion picture theatres	7830	4.1	19.8	7.8
Service—automotive repair and service	7500	2.5	6.1	5.0
Hotel-motels	7011	2.6	9.7	8.6

SOURCE: *Advertising Age*, July 15, 1985, p. 39. Reprinted with permission. © Crain Communications, Inc., 1985.

it is possible to keep advertising in consistent relation to sales volume. Sales volume is what advertising should primarily affect. Of course, gross margin, especially over the long run, should also show an increase if advertising outlays are properly applied.

How High Should the Percentage Be? The choice of a percentage-of-sales figure can be based on what other businesses in the line of trade are doing. This is easy to do since these percentages are fairly consistent within a given category of business. The information can be found in trade magazines and association publications, Census and Internal Revenue Service reports, and financial reports such as those published by Dun & Bradstreet and Robert Morris Associates. Sample percentages are shown in Table 18–2.

Knowing the ratio for a particular industry helps assure retailers that they will be spending proportionately as much or more than competitors. But remember, these industry averages are not gospel. A particular situation may dictate that a business advertise more than or less than its competition.

Average may not be good enough. It may be necessary to out-advertise competitors and be willing to cut into short-term profits to do so. Growth takes investment.

Retailers should not let any method bind them. The percentage-of-sales method is quick and easy, and ensures that the advertising budget is not out of proportion for the business. It is a sound method for stable markets. But if retailers want to expand market share, they will probably need to use a larger percentage of sales than the industry average.

Which Sales? The budget can be determined as a percentage of past sales, of estimated future sales, or as a combination of the two:

1. *Past Sales.* The base can be last year's sales or an average of a number of years in the immediate past. Consider, though, that changes in economic conditions can make the figure too high or too low.
2. *Estimated future sales.* The advertising budget can be calculated as a percentage of anticipated sales for next year. The most common pitfall of this method is an optimistic assumption that the business will grow. General business trends must always be kept in mind, especially if there is the chance of a slump. The directions in the industry and in the firm must be assessed realistically.
3. *Past sales and estimated future sales.* Future sales may be estimated conservatively based on last year's sales. A more optimistic assessment of next year's sales is to combine both last year's sales with next year's estimated sales. It is a more realistic method during periods of changing economic conditions. This method allows management to analyze trends and results thoughtfully and predict more accurately.

Unit of Sales

In the unit-of-sales method, retailers set aside a fixed sum for each unit of product to be sold. This figure is based on their experience and trade knowledge of how much advertising it takes to sell each unit. For example, if it takes 2 cents' worth of advertising to sell a case of canned vegetables, and the object is to move 100,000 cases, management will plan to spend $2,000 on advertising. If it costs X dollars to sell a refrigerator, management will need to budget 1,000 times X to sell a thousand refrigerators. Managers simply base the budget on unit of sales rather than dollar amounts of sales.

Some people consider this just a variation of percentage of sales. The unit-of-sales method, however, does permit a closer estimate in planning what to spend for maximum effect. This method is based on a retailer's experience of what it takes to sell an actual unit, rather than an overall percentage of the gross sales estimate.

The unit-of-sales method is particularly useful where product availability is limited by outside factors, such as the effect of bad weather on crops. The owners estimate the number of units or cases available to them. Based on a manager's experience, they advertise only as much as it takes to sell the products. The unit-of-sales method works well with specialty goods, but it is not very useful in sporadic or irregular markets or for style merchandise.

Objective and Task

The most difficult (and least used) method for determining an advertising budget is the objective-and-task approach. Yet this method is the most accurate and best fulfills what all budgets should accomplish. It relates the appropriation to the marketing task to be achieved.[6] This method correlates the advertising money to the volume of sales, so profits and reserves will not be drained. To establish a budget by the objective-and-task method, it is necessary to have a coordinated marketing program. This program should be set up with specific objectives based on a thorough survey of markets and their potential.

The percentage-of-sales method first determines the amount retailers will spend with little consideration of a goal. The task method establishes what must be done to meet company objectives. Only then is the cost calculated.

It is best to set specific objectives, not just ''increase sales.'' For example, a retailer wishes to ''sell 25 percent more of product X or service Y by attracting the business of teenagers.'' First, the manager determines which media best reaches the target market. Then the retailer estimates the cost to run the number and types of advertisements it will take to get the sales increase. This process is repeated for each objective. When these costs are totaled, the projected budget is available.

Of course, retailers may find that they cannot afford to advertise as they would like to. It is a good idea, therefore, to rank objectives. As with the other methods, managers should be prepared to change plans to reflect reality and to fit the resources available.

How to Allocate the Budget

Once the advertising budget has been determined, management must decide how to allocate the advertising dollars. A decision to use institutional (image) advertising, illustrated in Figure 18–1, or promotional (sales) advertising must be made. After setting aside money for the different types of advertising, retailers can allocate the promotional advertising funds. Among the most common breakdowns are: (1) departmental budgets, (2) total budget, (3) calendar periods, (4) media, and (5) sales areas.

1. Departmental Budgets. The most common method of allocating advertising to departments is on the basis of their sales contribution. Those departments or product categories with the largest sales volume receive the biggest share of the budget.

In a small business, or when the merchandise range is limited, the same percentage can be used throughout. Otherwise, a good rule is to use the average industry figure for each product.

By breaking down the budget by departments or products, those goods that require more promotion to stimulate sales can get the required adver-

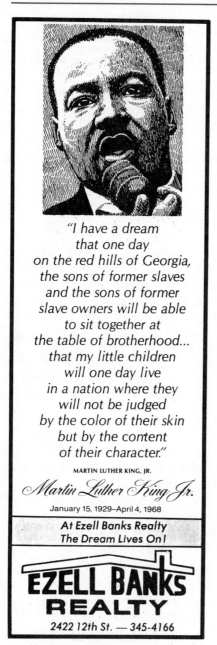

(Note the absence of any information designed to directly stimulate sales) (Courtesy Ezell Banks Realty)

tising dollars. The budget can be further divided into individual merchandise lines.

2. Total Budget. The total budget may be the result of integrated departmental or product budgets. If the business has set an upper limit for the advertising-expense percentage, then the departmental budgets might be pared down.

In smaller businesses, the total budget may be the only one established. It, too, should be divided into merchandise classifications for distribution.

3. Calendar Periods. Most executives usually plan their advertising on a monthly, or even a weekly, basis. Even a budget for a longer planning period, however, should be calculated for these shorter periods as well. This permits better control.

The percentage-of-sales methods are useful to determine allocations by time periods. The standard practice is to match sales with advertising dollars. If February accounts for 5 percent of sales, it might get 5 percent of the budget.

Sometimes, retailers adjust advertising allocations downward in heavier sales months in order to boost the budget in poorer periods. This is done only when a change in advertising timing could improve slow sales, as when competition's sales trends differ markedly from those of the firm.

4. Media. The amount of advertising placed in each advertising medium—such as direct mail, newspapers, or radio—should be determined by past experience, industry practice, and ideas from media specialists. Normally, it is wise to use the same sort of media that competitors use. That is most likely where potential customers will look or listen.

5. Sales Areas. Retailers can spend their advertising dollars in established customer areas or use them to try to stimulate new sales areas. It is wise to do the bulk of advertising in familiar areas. Usually, it is more costly to develop new markets than to maintain established ones.

Dividing the budget by line of goods is not easy, as suggested earlier. One way is by percentage of total sales of a department or merchandise line. Sales can vary by month, so the allocations should also vary.

Monthly percentages of annual sales differ by store type and region. Also, economic conditions can affect budget plans. Other ways for allocating funds focus on the traffic-drawing power of some items or on the growth potential of key lines. Sales variations by month normally have the largest effect on advertising. Almost three fourths of the advertising budget by boating retailers, for example, is spent during the March–July period. In contrast, over 20 percent of the advertising budget for jewelry is spent in the month of December. Garden supplies retailers spend over 50 percent of their advertising budget between March and June. December is the largest advertising month for appliance dealers, bookstores, department stores, retail furniture dealers, hardware dealers, music stores, and shoe stores.

Cooperative advertising is a situation in which a manufacturer pays part of the retailer's advertising costs under specific conditions. Many manufacturers and wholesalers state that a significant part of the reserves they set up for cooperative advertising are not used by their retailers. This is surprising. Cooperative advertising substantially lowers the cost for the retailer, since manufacturers or wholesalers pay part of the advertising cost.

For their own legal protection and to ensure the greatest return from their investment, manufacturers set up specific requirements to be observed in cooperative advertising. The retailer must also be aware of the procedures to follow to apply for and receive payment.

Cooperative advertising as a percentage of total advertising is approximately 50 percent for department stores, shoe stores, and clothing stores, and approximately 75 percent of the total advertising budget for food stores and electrical appliances, radio, and TV outlets, for example.[7]

EVALUATING MEDIA OPTIONS

Each medium has its strengths and weaknesses. Retailers normally use a media mix to give them the strengths of each. Media choices include, among others, radio, newspapers, TV, magazines, direct mail, and billboards. The characteristics of each medium are shown in Table 18–3.

Radio follows the listener everywhere: in the home and on the highway. Radio advertising is characterized by comparatively low rates, few or no production costs, and immediacy in scheduling.

Basic rates depend on the number of commercials contracted for, the time periods specified, and whether the station broadcasts on AM and/or FM frequencies. Usually, FM broadcasting is more localized and offers wider tonal range, for technical reasons.

The strengths of radio are its ability to: (1) direct ads to target audiences; (2) reach people at home, in their cars, on the beach, and almost anywhere else; (3) advertise at relatively low cost; and (4) work with short lead time.

The disadvantages of radio are: (1) no pictures; (2) short messages; (3) the need to use several stations in large cities to reach a large target audience; (4) production problems, since most programming is local; and (5) large, wasted audiences for small local retailers.

Radio advertising is used to convey and reinforce distinctive images that draw shoppers to retail outlets. Such advertising typically is institutional, stressing features retailers believe customers are looking for. Humor, ad-lib dialog, catchy music, and jingles increasingly are used to create bright images in radio advertising. Retailers prefer institutional advertising over price advertising because they believe that price/item advertising gets "lost" on the air. Retailers typically spend 12–15 percent of their advertising budget on radio.[8]

	Advantages	Disadvantages
Newspapers	Good flexibility Timeliness Good local coverage Broad acceptance High believability	Short life Poor reproduction quality Small pass-along audience
Magazines	Good geographic and demographic selectivity Good credibility and prestige High-quality reproduction Long life Good pass-along readership	Long production lead time Some waste circulation Poor position guarantee
Radio	Mass use audience Good geographic and demographic selectivity Low cost	Audio presentation only Lower audience attention than TV Nonstandardized rate structure Fleeting exposure
Television	Appeals to many senses Commands high attention levels High reach	High absolute cost High clutter Fleeting exposure Less audience selectivity Long production lead time
Direct mail	Best audience selectivity Good flexibility No clutter Good personalization	Relatively high cost Sometimes poor image
Outdoor	Good flexibility High repeat exposure Low cost Low competition	Poor audience selectivity Limited creativity

Buying Radio Time

Radio advertising time is typically sold in blocks of 10-, 30-, or 60-second slots. The 60-second slots tend to be most popular. The price of advertising time varies by time of day, size of listening audience, and length of the spots.

Radio rate schedules vary by stations, as does the system of discounts. The most expensive time is known as "drive time," between 6 and 10 A.M. and 3 and 7 P.M. on weekdays. Advertising is very inexpensive between midnight and 5 A.M., since few people are listening to the station. Weekend rates often differ from weekly rates, depending on the composition of the audience.

Other factors affecting cost include the frequency of advertising during a given week, the number of weeks the ad is aired, and the time of year the spot is on the air. The station may select the air time or the retailer may choose a more costly fixed-time slot. If the slots are part of a package, they probably consist of different time slots and frequencies for an extended period of time.

Television

TV has the visual impact of print and the sound impact of radio, plus color, motion, and emotion. People now spend as much time viewing TV as radio, newspapers, and magazines combined. Problems include the high cost of time and high production costs. Most people view TV at night after stores are closed. Infrequent summer viewing is also a disadvantage as is the increasingly fragmented audience because of cable services such as Cable News Network, Showtime, and others.

Local TV stations carry the programs of major networks. These programs include ads bought by national retailers such as Sears. The stations sell local ad time during station breaks. Management probably should plan on using daytime, news program times, and early evening hours before TV prime time.

TV ads are costly. The cost for a 30-second ad in prime time (8 P.M.– 11 P.M.) may cost more than $100 in a small local market and several thousand dollars for a local ad in a major market.

Cost per viewer is the lowest for a national audience. However, few retail firms other than Penney's, Ward's, Sears, and K mart have enough outlets to justify national TV ads. Use of local TV by large retailers is increasing, but no more than 4 percent of retail budgets go to TV today.

Few retailers feel that TV is the best overall medium by which to reach their audience. However, they are more prone to use television to reach a specific target audience, like youth, which has been weaned on TV. Chains such as Merry-Go-Round, Target, and K mart advertise on cable shows such as MTV to reach teens. In doing so they promote selected departments, not the entire chain. Target and K mart only advertise their record departments on MTV spots. Similarly, Foley's and The Broadway limit their spots to those aimed at junior and young men's back-to-school merchandise. Cable TV does not yet have a sufficiently large audience, particularly in major markets, to attract many national advertisers. Cable was initially developed to provide better reception for viewers outside major market areas. Thus, cable penetration is higher in secondary markets. Chains like Wal-Mart, whose stores are primarily in smaller rural markets, could use cable TV more effectively than stores whose primary targets are major metropolitan areas.[9]

Buying Television Time

Television time is normally sold in 10-, 30-, and 60-second time slots, with the 30-second slot being the most popular. The cost of television depends on the size of the audience, which can be described in terms of *ratings* and **shares.**

A **gross rating point** *(GRP) is 1 percent of all homes with television sets in a market area.* A program with a GRP of 10 is reaching 10 percent of the television homes. In contrast, *a share is the percentage of television sets in use that are tuned to a given program.* Thus, a program may have a GRP of only one, for example, at 4 A.M. on Sunday morning, but it may also have a share of 56.

Newspapers   About 70 percent of all retail ad dollars go to newspapers. Most markets have some type of newspaper, and newspaper ad supplements are a popular advertising medium. **Supplements** are preprinted pages of ads that are inserted into the papers. Sunday papers are usually full of supplements, and local department stores are heavy users.

Newspaper ad rates are quoted for short-term advertisers as weekly insertion rates, as monthly rates, and as yearly rates. Newspapers quote local retailers a *retail rate* that is below the **general rate** charged to agencies for national advertisers.

Newspaper personnel speak in terms of column inches when quoting prices. A **column inch** is one column wide and one inch deep. Special rates are set for supplements, and color rates are higher than black-and-white rates.

The strengths of newspapers include: (1) broad market coverage; (2) short lead time for ads; (3) a large number of items can be advertised together; (4) wide readership; (5) high graphic potential; and (6) assistance in ad preparation (important for a small retailer).

Newspapers have their weaknesses, too. They include: (1) problems in reaching the younger market and children; (2) the chance that many readers will miss an ad; (3) accelerating ad rates; (4) limited ability to segment readers; and (5) lower suburban coverage by big-city papers.

The newspaper office can be helpful in planning the copy and layout. Many small retailers have few skills in these areas and rely on the newspaper professionals to provide the needed services.

Shoppers

Shoppers go by many names, including "shopping guides," "penny savers," or "advertising newspapers." These papers are quite different from the traditional newspaper. They normally carry very little news. Virtually all news is syndicated feature material as opposed to local news, and shoppers are distributed on a free basis.

They offer retailers the opportunity for almost total coverage of a market area. Since they are primarily an advertising medium, the people who read them are already in a buying mood and seeking specific information. Still, the fact that the papers primarily contain advertising may cause some customers not to read them, and wasted advertising can occur.

More and more merchandisers are demanding the services of shoppers, however, since they want better market coverage. Some publishers of shoppers can be quite selective in the market areas they cover. For example, they can provide retailers with total coverage of only selected streets or blocks.

Each shopper has its own advertising rate schedule, and costs are often quite low. Some suppliers of shoppers in large metropolitan areas may have a dozen or so different shoppers. Each will cover only a selected portion of the metropolitan area, such as a specific suburban community.

Special-Purpose Papers

There are newspapers for special-interest groups such as colleges, the military, and ethnic groups. These media are especially desirable advertising outlets for retailers who are seeking to reach highly specific audiences.

Magazines

Until recently, the only retailers using magazines were national firms such as Penney's or Sears. However, local retailers can now place ads in regional editions of such magazines as *Time* and *Newsweek*.

Magazine strengths include: (1) carefully defined audiences, (2) good color, (3) long ad life because they are not thrown away as quickly as newspapers, and (4) low **cost per thousand.** The primary problems are: (1) high cost, (2) long closing dates (ads must be submitted several weeks before publication for monthly magazines), and (3) slower response.

Buying Magazine Advertising Space

Advertising space is typically sold in pages or fractions of pages, such as one half or one sixth. The rates charged depend on the circulation of the magazine, quality of the publication, and type of primary audience. Rates are higher for magazines with higher circulation. Magazines typically offer discounts for advertising depending on the bulk and frequency of advertising. Higher prices are normally charged for special positions in the magazine and for special formats.

Direct Mail

Direct mail is the most selective form of retail advertising, but the cost per person reached is high. According to retailers, direct mail is among the top three forms of retail advertising today.

Most retailers use some form of direct mail.[10] Typical examples are shown in Figure 18–2. The strengths include: (1) the high response rate by consumers, (2) the ability to send material to a specific person, (3) not being bound by media format (it is possible to use as much space as needed to tell the story of the product and use colors or other creative effects as the budget allows), and (4) the message does not have to compete with other editorial matter.

The weakness of direct mail is its high cost compared to other media. The cost per thousand is many times higher than for other media.

There are good reasons for the popularity of direct mail. Direct mail includes bill stuffers (which are about 70 percent of direct mail), catalogs, flyers for store openings, sales letters, and everything we normally call "junk mail."

The Procedure for Direct Mailing

Mailing lists can be rented from mailing houses. The list can be selected according to consumer tastes on a variety of bases including, for example, model of automobile, family income, tendency to buy through mail-order compa-

nies, and ZIP code or census tract. A typical mailing list will cost between $30 and $50 a thousand. An occupant list (no personalized name) of all households in a designated area may cost as little as $5 per thousand. Understandably, the more precise and well-defined the list, the higher the cost.

The frequency of mailing depends on the purpose of the campaign. However, to generate new sales leads, one consulting firm recommends one mailing every other month for continuity and long-term effectiveness, or four mailings six weeks apart for maximum short-term impact. But one annual mailing may be sufficient for a seasonal operation or for a firm that occasionally needs a limited amount of new business.[11]

Catalogs

More than 5,000 merchants now operate catalog sales departments. Sales through mail catalogs are growing at an annual rate of 15 percent.

Catalogs are a special form of direct-mail promotion and rank third, behind radio and newspaper, as the advertising medium used most frequently by department and specialty stores. More than three fourths of all department stores with sales of $500 million now have Christmas catalogs.

The following are trends in catalog marketing:

1. New and better design.
2. Emphasis on "lifestyle" merchandising, although the term itself is defined in almost as many different ways as there are catalogs.
3. A stepped-up search for cost-cutting techniques, including charging a "subscription" to a series of catalogs, or offering the catalog, via magazine advertising, at a charge to noncustomers.
4. Growth of separate catalog operations, with full responsibility for inventory and controlling direct mail business.

The typical department store catalog has a life of about six weeks. Twelve catalogs per year is not uncommon for many stores, and many are talking about 20 or more "specialogs." For example, Macy's New York produces 11 catalogs, almost like a magazine publication. The emphasis in all of the stores is on "target mailing"—the use of catalogs to sell separate categories of merchandise. Stores are increasingly using computers to target prime customers instead of blanket mailings.

Directories

Every retail business normally advertises in one or more directories. The most common is the Yellow Pages in the telephone directory. Directories, however, are published by various trade associations and groups, and they reach more prospective customers than virtually any other medium. Consumers have normally already made a decision to purchase before turning to a directory for help in deciding where to buy. Also, directories have a longer life than most advertising media.

Most directories are published for a minimum of 12 months, which can serve as a drawback. Retailers do not have the option of changing the advertisement in any way until the appearance of a new directory. Thus, the advertisements can become obsolete rather quickly.

Costs are reasonable for ads such as the Yellow Pages advertising in a telephone directory. A half-column display ad can vary from $20 a month in an area with 14,000–18,000 residents to $200 a month or more in an area of 950,000.

Transient Advertising

Transient advertising includes signs placed on taxis, buses, subway cars, and commuter trains, as well as advertising placed in the terminals, platforms, and stations for such vehicles.

Transient advertising has a captive audience in the people using the vehicles. For example, the average transit rider spends 22 minutes inside a vehicle on each ride and takes 24 rides a month.[12] Outdoor transient advertising (ads on the outside of the vehicle) is especially effective for certain types of retailers. The vehicles carrying the advertising normally travel through the business area of a community and have a high level of exposure to prospective consumers.[13] Transient advertising is typically a media option only for retailers in large metropolitan areas. Small areas normally do not have public transportation.

Outdoor Advertising

Outdoor advertising signs are among the oldest form of advertising. Most retailers have signs outside their business even if they don't use billboards.

Outdoor advertising signs have a large number of advantages, one of which is a high exposure rate. People tend to see the same outdoor billboard 29 times a month because they tend to follow the same traffic patterns each day.[14] The signs are inexpensive, but are heavily read by travelers and other customers seeking specific information.

The disadvantages are the relatively small amount of information that can be placed on a billboard, the large amount of display space needed, and the competition with other billboards in a community.

Buying Outdoor Advertising

Outdoor billboard advertising usually is bought from companies that specialize in leasing sign space to merchants. The typical billboard size is 12 feet by 25 feet. Outdoor advertising signs are bought in terms of **showings.** *A 100 showing in a market means that advertising space was purchased on enough posters to reach 100 percent of the audience in an area at least once each month.*

Nonstandard signs are normally those erected by the retailer. No standard size exists for such billboards. The retailers arrange with each individual landowner for the space they want to lease. They have to be careful not to violate local regulations on the placement and construction of the signs, however. Billboards are becoming increasingly controversial in many communities because of concerns over quality of life and aesthetics.

Video Technology

We discussed video technology in Chapter 5 and are highlighting it again as a reminder of its growing impact on promotion plans. Video involves promoting directly to the consumer by the use of cable TV, teletext, or video-discs. Technological advances in two-way interactive cable are making shop-at-home services more feasible. The primary drawback still is the high cost per purchase. Nevertheless, merchants are looking at the new technologies as ways of expanding their profit centers.

The "Shopping Channel," a continuous cable-television program, is one of the most ambitious experiments in video shopping. The "Home Shopping

Show'' is transmitted to some 3.5 million households by Modern Satellite Network, a cable TV service based in New York. Neiman-Marcus has used the channel to advertise items costing up to $500 for china and silver candlesticks. Shopping channel viewers order displayed merchandise by means of a toll-free number.

Viewtron is a joint venture of Sears Roebuck and Knight-Ridder newspapers and American Telephone & Telegraph. Viewtron enables viewers to ''call up'' a catalog text and pictures on a specially adapted TV set. Sears, J.C. Penney, and local merchants in a Coral Gables, Florida, test market area offer merchandise via the Viewtron system. Indax is a similar experiment by Cox Cable Communications. The firm advertises merchandise from about 30 retailers ranging from big department stores to a lumberyard.

Specialty Advertising

Specialty advertising uses gifts to customers as the advertising medium. Examples include matchbooks, fountain pens, calendars, and key chains. The gifts typically contain the name of the firm, company address, and perhaps its logo or slogan. The business endeavors to build goodwill among customers by providing useful items that will remind customers of the firm each time they use them. The specialty items chosen should match the type of merchandise sold by the firm. For example, wallpaper and paint stores often will provide a tape measure. But specialty advertising is more useful in retaining present customers than in attracting new ones.

Visual Merchandising

Visual merchandising is often viewed as a form of nonmedia advertising. Visual merchandising was introduced in Chapter 16, but we want to remind you again of its critical role in communicating store image to consumers. Good displays inform the consumer about the merchandise offered and help to entertain and delight the consumer in such a way as to differentiate the outlet from competitors. As such, visual merchandising is part of a total store focus for communicating a unified image.

EVALUATING THE EFFECTIVENESS OF MEDIA

Media effectiveness is usually measured in terms of (1) cost per thousand and (2) reach and frequency. The most common method of evaluating media is the cost of reaching 1,000 members of a desired audience (CPM). The CPM is measured by dividing the cost of an ad by the number of households or persons reached. The formula is:

$$CPM = \frac{Ad\ cost}{Audience\ or\ circulation\ (in\ thousands)}$$

For example, radio station A provides 100,000 impressions (the audience reached by each spot in the schedule) weekly and costs $500. The cost per 1,000 impressions is $5.

$$\frac{\$500}{100} = \$5$$

This formula is useful only for intramedia comparisons, for example, for comparing one newspaper to another. Intermedia comparisons such as radio and a newspaper are less useful.

Broadcast schedules are often planned in terms of reach and frequency. **Reach** is the number of different persons exposed at least once to a message during an ad campaign. Reach is often expressed as a percentage of the total audience. **Frequency** is the average number of times a person will be exposed to a message during the advertising period.

Remember, (1) CPM for *cost* plus (2) reach and frequency for *audience* are the most common *quantitative* measures of media effectiveness. But it is necessary to relate the measures to media strengths and weaknesses, as discussed above. The strengths and weaknesses are the *qualitative* dimensions. For example, radio may have lower CPM and higher reach and frequency than a newspaper. But a firm may need to present the merchandise product visually, and this cannot be done by radio.

MEASURING THE RESULTS OF ADVERTISING

Sales response to ads can be checked daily during the ad period. The effects of image ads are harder to measure. It is not always possible to tie a purchase to image advertising. However, the message may stay in the minds of people who have heard it. Sooner or later, it may help trigger a purchase. Research is needed to measure the success of image advertising.

Tests for Immediate Response Ads[15]

In weighing the results of the *immediate* response to advertisements, the following measurements should be helpful: *coupons brought in.* Usually, coupons represent sales of a product. Where coupons represent requests for additional information or contact with a salesperson, management may ask if enough leads were obtained to pay for the ad. If the coupon is dated, it is possible to determine the number of returns for the first, second, and third weeks.

Requests by Phone or Letter Referring to the Ad. A "hidden offer" can cause people to call or write. For example, included in the middle of an ad is a statement that the product or additional information will be supplied on request. Results should be checked over periods of one week through 6 months or 12 months, because this type of ad may have considerable carryover effect.

Testing Ads. Retailers can prepare two ads (different in some way that they would like to test or for different stations or broadcast times) and run them on the same day. Management can identify the ads by the message or with a coded coupon so they can tell them apart. They can ask customers to bring in the coupon or to use a special phrase. Broadcast ads can be run at different times or on different stations on the same day with varying "discount phrases." Newspapers can provide a "split run"—that is, to print "ad A" in part of its press run and "ad B" in the rest of the run. The responses to each can then be counted.

Sales Made of a Particular Item. If the ad is on a bargain or limited-time offer, retailers can consider that sales at the end of one week, two weeks, three weeks, and four weeks came from the ad. They may need to make a judgment as to how many sales came from in-store display and personal selling.

Checks of Store Traffic. An important function of advertising is to build store traffic. Store traffic also results in purchases of items that are not advertised. Pilot studies show, for example, that many customers who were brought to the store by an ad for a blouse also bought a handbag. Some bought the bag in addition to the blouse, while others bought it instead of the blouse.

Testing
Attitude
Advertising

When advertising is spread over a selling season or several seasons, part of the measurement job is keeping records. Retailers' records of ads and sales for an extended time should be compared.

An easy way to set up a file is by marking the date of the run on tearsheets of newspaper ads (many radio stations now provide "radio tearsheets," too), keeping log reports of radio and television ads, and keeping copies of direct-mail ads. The file may be broken down into monthly, quarterly, or semiannual blocks. By recording the sales of the advertised items on each ad or log, management can make comparisons.

In institutional (image-building) advertising, individual ads are building blocks, so to speak. Together they make up the advertising over a selling season. A problem is trying to measure the effects of the ads, since they are designed to keep the name of the store before the buying public and to position the outlet in a way that harmonizes with overall marketing strategy. In contrast to institutional advertising, product advertising is designed to cover a short period of time and increase sales.

One approach to testing is making the comparisons on a weekly basis. If a retailer runs an ad each week, management can compare the *first* week's sales with sales for the same week a year ago. At the end of the second week, managers can compare sales with those at the end of the first week, as well as year-ago figures, and so forth.

DEVELOPING THE COPY

Copy can be either rational or emotional. The rational approach focuses essentially on the merchandise and various facts about it. The emotional appeal addresses the psychological benefits that one can obtain by using the product. Normally, a combination of the two possibilities is very effective. For example, product benefits could be both rational (economy) and emotional (appearance). Headlines in the ad can focus on benefits, promises, or even news.

The text of the advertisement can do many things, including "(1) stating reasons for doing something (buying the product, patronizing the store), (2) making promises or giving testimonials, (3) publicizing the results of performance tests, (4) telling a story, (5) reporting a real or imaginary dialogue, (6) solving a predicament, or (7) amusing the audience."[16]

The elements of good copy are sometimes summarized in the term: AIDCA. This is, attract *Attention,* develop *Interest,* arouse *Desire, Convince* the reader, and get *Action.* For effective copywriting, readers should make each word count and avoid unnecessary words. Retailers should keep sentences short, put action in words, use terms the reader will understand, and not use introductions. It is important to get right to the point of the message.

The Role of the Ad Agency

The function of an agency is to plan, produce, and measure the effectiveness of advertising. Larger retailers with outlets in several communities are more likely to use an ad agency's service. An agency helps them avoid the complication of having to deal with a variety of media in each community.

Advertising agencies typically earn their incomes from commissions. As an agent for the retailer, the agency will buy space in a medium. The agency then will bill the retailer for 100 percent of the cost and pay the medium, such as a newspaper, 85 percent. The 15 percent is the normal agency commission. Agencies may also take on the accounts of small retailers on a fee basis if the normal commission of 15 percent is too small to make the project worthwhile. Also, in situations such as preparing direct-mail advertising, the agency may charge a percent of the cost involved.

SALES PROMOTION

The American Marketing Association defines **sales promotion** as "marketing activities other than personal selling, advertising, and publicity that stimulate consumer purchasing and dealer effectiveness, such as displays, sales and exhibits, and demonstrations." Perhaps the best way to introduce the varied nature of sales promotion possibilities is to highlight trends in sales promotion activities by retailers. One of the popular promotions in recent years, as shown in Figure 18–3, is the sale of a Christmas Bear at a greatly reduced

THE SALE OF A CHRISTMAS BEAR AT A GREATLY REDUCED PRICE WITH A DOLLAR MINIMUM MERCHANDISE PURCHASE HAS BEEN A POPULAR PROMOTION IN RECENT YEARS

price provided the customer purchases a minimum dollar amount of other merchandise.

Promotion Device Trends[17]

1. More couponing. Although coupon fraud and misredemption are serious problems, couponing continues to be a very popular promotion device to introduce new products, stimulate trial, and increase purchase frequency.

More in- and on-pack coupon usage is likely, as is continued use of retailer in-ad coupons (retailer coupons paid by manufacturers), and more combination promotions with other devices—premiums, sweepstakes, and refunds. More interesting and creative applications are also likely.

2. More Sampling. Use of sampling is increasing, especially to new users or nonusers. Quite a few services now provide selective sampling.

Retailers prefer salable samples because they make a profit on them. Retailers don't profit from free samples. Salable samples are good for manufacturers too because they save distribution costs.

3. Fewer Cents-Off Bonus Packs. Retailers generally resist these promotion devices because they necessitate additional stock-keeping units. They can also be quite costly to marketers because of the required special labeling and/or packaging.

The advantages are that the benefit is passed on to the consumer, and the consumer readily sees the value in them.

4. More Premiums. Retailers are lukewarm to premium offers. This is especially true when they are used alone, rather than in combination with other promotion devices, such as coupons. In- and on-packs, special containers, and other forms of package-related or in-store premiums are sometimes resisted because of pilferage and handling problems. Nevertheless, consumers like these types of promotions.

Retailers prefer premium offers that do not require their involvement, but add excitement and impact to a promotion, create consumer interest, and generate increased product movement.

The general trends are toward more expensive self-liquidators, free premiums with multiple proofs-of-purchase, and brand-logo premiums that are product or advertising related.

5. More Selective Point-of-Purchase Material. Typical point-of-purchase (p-o-p) materials include end-of-aisle and other in-store merchandising and display materials. Retailers like and want p-o-p material, but generally feel that the material provided by manufacturers does not meet their needs. Retailers are highly selective in their use of p-o-p material and prefer displays that: merchandise an exciting and interesting promotion theme, support other promotion devices, adapt to storewide promotions on a chainwide and individual store basis, harmonize with the store environment, sell related products, provide a quality appearance, install easily, are permanent or semi-permanent, and guarantee sales success.

Some retailers develop and produce displays in accordance with the manufacturer's budget and guidelines. Some retailers rent floor space to manufacturers.

6. More Refunds/Rebates. These devices, similar in intent and nature, continue to grow in popularity and use. Refunds and rebates are usually handled as mail-ins with proofs of purchase. They are very effective promotion tools and will be used in more creative ways. Increasingly popular are rebates as charitable donations that show social concern, and higher-price refunds for multiple products.

7. Fewer Contests and More Sweepstakes. Sweepstakes are generally more popular than contests and are growing in use and importance. Retailers like them especially when they bring traffic into the store to look at product packages and obtain entry blanks. Table 18–4 highlights the conclusions about the effectiveness of sales promotion research based on 15 studies in recent years.

Staple products exhibit the highest degree of price elasticity and are thus the most responsive to point-of-purchase displays. Sugar, vinegar, ketchup,

1. Sales promotions are most effective for new product introductions or unfamiliar brands. However, except for new introductions, substantial doubt has been raised about the ability of deal offerings to attract new consumers who will be loyal following deal retraction.

2. For immediate effects, sales promotions can induce substantial brand switching and when coupled with advertising can have a synergistic effect on total sales.

3. Repeat purchase probabilities appear higher for food than nonfood products; package coupons appear most effective for maintaining current brand franchises.

4. Consumer deal proneness is positively correlated with venturesomeness, media exposure, and gregariousness and inversely related to brand loyalty.

5. For those brands which do not dominate competing brands on a critical product attribute, sales promotions provide an alternative for attracting purchasers of other brands.

6. Means of distribution and value associated with promotion can significantly impact campaign success and coupon redemption rates.

7. Future applications of sales promotions will undoubtedly increase in response to increasing consumer price-consciousness and in efforts to fight advertising clutter and to encourage retailer support.

SOURCE: William O. Bearden, Jesse E. Teel, and Robert H. Williams, "Consumer Responses to Cents-Off Coupons," in *The Changing Marketing Environment,* ed. Kenneth Bernhardt, et al. (Chicago: American Marketing Association, 1981), p. 62.

coffee, and canned/powdered milk are all in the top 10 price-elastic product categories for human consumption.[18] Figure 18–4 shows the effects of in-store displays when used with other dimensions of promotion strategy.

Suppliers often advertise directly to retailers and inform them of upcoming national campaigns so the retailer can stock sufficient merchandise to meet consumer needs and coordinate local advertising with the national advertising program, as shown in Figure 18–5, for the H.J. Heinz Company.

Cooperative Promotions

Manufacturers offer co-op funds for promotions in the same way they offer co-op dollars for advertising. Suppliers often advertise directly to retailers informing them about promotion allowances available for a product line, as shown in Figure 18–6. Suppliers then seek a commitment from the retailers for an increased volume of purchases, because of the accelerated promotional program for the product line.

PUBLICITY AND PUBLIC RELATIONS

The American Marketing Association defines **publicity** as "any nonpersonal stimulation of demand for a product, service, or business unit by planting commercially significant news about it in a published medium or obtaining favorable presentation of it on radio, television, or stage that is not paid for by the sponsor." Publicity and public relations are known by various names. Regardless, such activities normally fit into three categories: merchandising, entertainment, and education or community service.

PROMOTION

DAYTON'S BLEACHED BLUES CAMPAIGN

Promotion is an integral part of a firm's total merchandising process. Retailers can create unique images for their outlets through astute promotional plans. Promotion includes careful blending of such activities as advertising and display. Here, Dayton's of Minneapolis provides a helpful example with the integrated promotion campaign for "Bleached Blues."

Setting up a display.

A Dayton's window display.

An interior display.

Planning the ad.

(All photos courtesy of Dayton Hudson Department Store Company.)

Faux pearl and goldtone
jewelry. Oversized round
lace collar.

Jewelry and Accessories

"This season, bikinis will
make news wherever
they go!"

Women's Sportswear Buyer

CONTEMPORARY ADVERTISING

Parisian used these elegant photographs to create a fashion image in a spring insert and mailer. Such advertising supports the Parisian slogan, ''The Parisian Point of View. And it's in everything we do,'' and dramatizes the regional fashion department store's positioning strategy.

''Remember how your mom used to dress you up? She did it to show you off.''

Children's Buyer

''The pouf dress has a reputation for being a flirt.''

Dress Buyer

(All photos courtesy of Parisian Incorporated.)

''We look for topflight designs that put you at ease.''

Woman's Sportswear Buyer

Christmas in Oz—a Fortnight selection for unusual Christmas ornaments and trimmings.

Neiman's patterned the Koala Blue Boutique after the Los Angeles shop founded by Olivia Newton-John and Pat Farrer, and included an Aussie Milk Bar.

(Both photos courtesy of Neiman-Marcus.)

A SPECIAL EVENT

NEIMAN-MARCUS AUSTRALIAN FORTNIGHT 1986

Special events have been defined as "something happening that will bring people into a store—whether they are shopping or not." Special events should have a reason for being, however, and should be an integral part of a store's strategy. Neiman-Marcus Fortnight was one of the most successful special events ever staged. Each year, the firm's downtown Dallas store saluted a particular country, using the merchandise and culture of that country as a framework for a major promotional happening.

FIGURE 18–4
TOPICAL REPORT ON TRADE PROMOTIONS: AVERAGE CATEGORY
RESPONSE TO TRADE PROMOTIONS

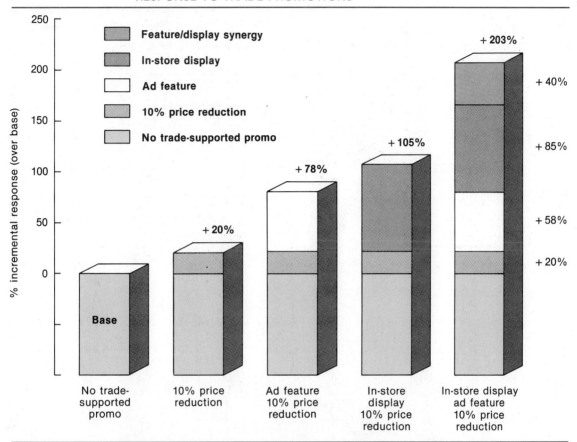

SOURCE: "Price and Promotion Strategies for Impact at Retail," *Marketing Communications*, October 1985, p. 70.

Merchandising Events

Special events create publicity. Often they may be featured in the editorial section of a newspaper, may result in an interview on a talk show, or generate other free promotion. Merchandising events require careful coordination between merchandising, advertising, and publicity. Such events can include fashion shows, bridal fairs, cooking demonstrations, celebrity authors, cartoon characters, or sports heroes. They can include exhibits of art, costumes, antiques, or rarities. Merchandising events may also be staged in conjunction with designers such as Gloria Vanderbilt or sports figures such as Mary Lou Retton.

Princess Diana and Prince Charles, for example, made a promotional visit to a J.C. Penney store in a suburb of Washington, D.C., on behalf of the chain's $50 million line of British merchandise, as shown in Figure 18–7. The visit attracted thousands of people to the store and generated substantial free publicity for J.C. Penney.[19]

Entertainment

Retailers seek to build goodwill, store image, and name awareness through entertainment programs. The results of such activities are hard to measure. Macy's Thanksgiving Day Parade, highlighted in Figure 18–8, is shown on national television and is known nationwide. Free publicity from such events can be worth hundreds of thousands of dollars.

Education or Community Service

Retailers often sponsor education or community service activities. Macy's, for example, sponsors a "Women Mean Business" week that is held every spring and fall and attracts capacity crowds. Activities are provided free of

FIGURE 18–6

Advertising & Merchandising Notices

IMPORTANT NOTICE TO RETAILERS

Scott periodically makes available **Performance Allowances** on special short-term promotions of specific Scott products.

Payments are made for advertising in newspapers or handbills; special price features; displays; extra trading stamps; store coupons; and other consumer directed promotions. Merchandising materials consisting of display material, newspaper mats, repros, etc., are also made available. Such services and materials are designed so that one or more of them may be used by all retailers.

For details, contact your supplier, local Scott Representative or write directly to:

SCOTT PAPER COMPANY
DEPARTMENT C – PROMOTION
SCOTT PLAZA I
PHILADELPHIA, PA. 19113

SCOTT

PROCTER & GAMBLE NOTICE TO THE TRADE

ATTENTION STORE MANAGER:

We offer Cooperative Merchandising Agreements, promotion allowances and merchandising materials which are practical and usable by all retailers regardless of size.

Payments are made for newspaper or handbill featuring, display, and consumer directed promotion. Details are set forth in specific agreements. Proof of performance (e.g. tear sheets) and proof of delivery (jobber's invoice) are required for payment of allowance. Our merchandising materials consist of display material, newspaper mats and proofs etc.

If you would like to receive specific information on offers available to you, send your name, address and telephone number to Procter & Gamble, Box 162, Cincinnati, Ohio 45201. Please specify, if possible, the Division in whose brands you are interested.

Packaged Soap & Detergent Division
Beauty Care Division
Health & Personal Care Division
Paper Products Division
Food Products Division
Bar Soap & Household Cleaning Products Division
Coffee Division

For additional information about this special section call:
JUDY NAPOLEON
212-714-4013

IMPORTANT NOTICE TO RETAILERS

Periodically, the Consumer Products Group, Norwich Eaton Pharmaceuticals, offers promotional discounts and/or special allowances for displaying, advertising, and promoting its line of products, which include:

PEPTO-BISMOL®
ENCARE®
UNGUENTINE®
CHLORASEPTIC®
NECTA SWEET®
BPN® OINTMENT
NORFORMS®
NP-27®
NORWICH® ASPIRIN
NORWICH®
  GLYCERIN
  SUPPOSITORIES
HEAD & CHEST™

For full details on offers currently available to you, contact your local Norwich Eaton Consumer Products Group Sales Representative or write to:

Sales Promotion Department
Consumer Products Group
Norwich Eaton
  Pharmaceuticals
17 Eaton Avenue
Norwich, New York 13815

Limited buyer's name items are also available. For information, contact the above address

Beecham Products

Beecham Products periodically makes available advertising and promotional allowances. These allowances are available to all retailers regardless of size.
For further information, contact your wholesaler or Beecham representative, or write:

Beecham Products
Division of Beecham Inc.
P.O. Box 1467
Department 5
Pittsburgh, Pa. 15230

NOTICE TO GROCERY OPERATORS

ATTENTION STORE MANAGER:

The Birds Eye Division from time to time offers merchandising payments, assistance, and materials to all Retail Customers.

Currently selected Birds Eye brand items are offering a merchandising allowance to all Retail Customers in parts of the country. For details of this program, please write at once to General Foods Corporation, (Birds Eye Division Sales Manager), 250 North Street, White Plains, New York 10625.

charge during lunch hours. Other retailers offer fashion advice, career counseling, and even evening college courses, all on the store premises.

Similarly, McDonald's sponsors an All-American high school basketball team and an All-American high school band. McDonald's also makes sub-

FIGURE 18–7 *PRINCESS DIANA AND PRINCE CHARLES VISIT A J.C. PENNEY STORE TO PROMOTE THE CHAIN'S $50 MILLION LINE OF BRITISH MERCHANDISE*

(Courtesy of the J.C. Penney Company)

stantial pledges to the Muscular Dystrophy Association and sponsors the Ronald McDonald houses as places of residence for families of seriously ill children who are being treated at nearby hospitals.

CHAPTER HIGHLIGHTS

- Promotion should be viewed as a sales-building investment and not simply as an element of business expense. When promotion is executed correctly, it can be an important factor in the future growth of a business.
- Promotion is communication from the retailer to the consumer in an effort to achieve a profitable sales level. Promotion includes, among others, mass media advertising, coupons, trading stamps, premium offers, point-of-purchase displays, and publicity.
- Promotion is a key element of the marketing mix. All promotion should be in harmony with pricing, product lines, and store-location decisions (place). Inattention to these factors may result in a poor image for the firm.
- Promotion plans begin with the goals of the firm. Retailers must decide on whom to reach, the message to get across, the number of messages to reach the audience, and the means of reaching the audience.

FIGURE 18–8 MACY'S PARADE—AN IMAGE-CREATING PROMOTIONAL EVENT

(Courtesy Macy's)

- Numerous options exist for retail advertising, and each medium has its strengths and weaknesses. Media choices include, among others, direct mail, magazines, billboards, transient ads, newspapers, radio, and television.
- Media effectiveness is normally measured in terms of cost per thousand and reach and frequency. Results tests for immediate response ads can be in terms of coupons redeemed, requests by phone or letter referring to the ad, sales made of a particular item, or an analysis of store traffic.
- Advertising copy can be either rational or emotional. The rational approach focuses on the merchandise, while an emotional appeal focuses on the psychological benefits of using the product. Headlines in an ad can concentrate on benefits, promises, or news.
- Many retailers use an advertising agency. The function of an agency is to plan, produce, and measure the effectiveness of advertising. Agencies earn their commissions on advertisements placed for the retailers.
- Retail sales promotions include such activities as couponing, product sampling, cents-off bonus packs, premiums, point-of-purchase materials, refunds or rebates, contests and sweepstakes, and trade-in allowances.
- Publicity includes media exposure that is not paid for by the sponsor. Such activities normally fit into three categories: merchandising, entertainment, and education or community service.

KEY TERMS

Column inch Newspaper advertising space that is one column wide and one inch deep.

Cooperative advertising Promotional programs in which wholesalers or manufacturers pay a portion of the retailers' advertising cost under specified conditions.

Cost per thousand (CPM) A measure of the relative cost of advertising which is determined by the number of households or persons reached.

Frequency The average number of times a person will be exposed to a message during an advertising period.

General rate The advertising rate charged to agencies for national advertising.

Gross rating point One percent of all homes with television sets in a market area.

Message The development of an idea in transmittable form.

Promotion Any form of paid communication from the retailer to the consumer.

Publicity Any nonpersonal stimulation of demand for a product, service, or business unit by planting commercially significant news about it in a published medium or obtaining a favorable presentation about it on radio or television, or in other ways that are not paid for by the sponsor.

Reach The number of persons exposed at least once to a message during an ad campaign.

Sales promotion Marketing activities other than direct selling, advertising, and publicity that stimulate consumer purchasing. Examples include displays, sales, exhibits, and demonstrations.

Share The percentage of television sets in use that are tuned to a given program.

Shoppers Newspapers that carry primarily advertising and very little news. They are distributed free to the homes of consumers.

Showing A term that describes the way in which outdoor advertising space is bought or sold. A 100 showing in a market means that advertising space was purchased on enough posters to reach 100 percent of the audience in an area at least once each month.

Source The originator of the promotion message.

Supplements Preprinted pages of ads that are inserted into newspapers.

DISCUSSION QUESTIONS

1. Is it possible to increase advertising expenses as a percentage of sales, yet increase the profitability of the firm?
2. Comment on the following statement: The only goal of advertising is to increase sales and profitability.
3. Discuss the following approaches to establishing an advertising budget (be sure to include in your discussion the advantages and disadvantages of each): the percentage-of-sales method, the unit-of-sales method, and the objective-task method.
4. What are the reasons a retailer should consider using a multimedia mix?
5. Evaluate the following media in terms of their strengths and weaknesses: billboards, radio, television, newspapers, transient advertising, and magazines.
6. What is specialty advertising, and how is such advertising of benefit to the retailer?
7. Why should a retailer consider the use of cooperative advertising funds?
8. What are the various ways by which retailers can measure advertising results?
9. The text states that the elements of good advertising copy are summarized in the term *AIDCA*. What does this statement mean?
10. How does advertising differ from publicity and from sales-promotion tools and techniques?

APPLICATION EXERCISES

1. Imagine you work for the promotion division of a department store and have been told that you are to prepare a campaign for a new product. Select your own "new product." Plan the campaign, select the media, and prepare the message.
2. Choose any currently popular product. Determine how many different ways it is advertised. What are the differences and similarities among the methods?
3. Make contacts with dealers in a specific product line (e.g., automobiles) which have definite differences in product image, price, quality, and so on. Through interviews with the dealership managers, attempt to determine the allocation of the advertising (promotional) budget among the various media. Compare and contrast among the dealers. If actual dollars of promotional expenditures are not available, then utilize percentage allocations. Additionally, collect national and local ads for the same dealerships/brands and evaluate the differences and similarities noted.
4. Select several automobile dealerships that seem to project differing public images. Interview management of each to determine their particular image perceptions of themselves and perhaps of their competition. Prepare a portfolio of ads of each dealership and also of the national ads of that same dealership's make of auto. Compare the images that seem to be projected by the local versus the national promotions. Attempt to reach certain strategy conclusions from your investigation.

CASES

1. Stop and Shop Refuses to Carry P&G's Gem-in-Package Items

Stop and Shop Supermarket Co. doesn't think Procter & Gamble's idea of putting garnets, diamonds, sapphires, and emeralds inside soap-product packages is such a gem of a promotion.

A Stop and Shop spokesperson said the 114-unit chain would not carry the products in which the gems are packed, but would continue to stock the same items without the gems.

The gem promotion is being used for the 600-sheet roll of scented or unscented Bounce fabric softener, the 16-oz. and 27-oz. No-Rinse Spic and Span, and the three-bar packs of Camay and Safeguard soap. According to the manufacturer, 13 million packages have been shipped to stores.

Aside from the stones, 1.6 million pairs of 14-karat gold-plated, self-setting pierced earring posts have been made available free to customers at the checkout. Customers can write for additional gem settings to a post-office box assigned by Procter & Gamble and divulged to the stores.

Procter & Gamble claims the retail value of the gems in circulation is $86 million. Every box shipped contains a garnet (retail value $5), sapphire ($50), emerald ($250), or diamond ($500).

Stop and Shop turned down a similar but smaller-scale Procter & Gamble promotion last year. At that time, even though the Spic and Span packages containing stones were not on the shelves, shoppers opened boxes of the product, the spokesperson said.

"This is the reason we're not participating, because people come into the stores and rip open the boxes, looking for the gems."

Last year's Procter & Gamble promotion offered customers a chance to find either a one-third carat diamond or cubic zirconia in one of 500 boxes of Spic and Span. Procter & Gamble said the promotion increased monthly sales by $8 million during the three-month period. More than 2 million boxes of Spic and Span were sold.

A spokesperson for Procter & Gamble said it never received any complaints from Stop and Shop regarding the promotion.

Questions

1. Do the risks from not participating in Procter & Gamble's gem-in-package sales promotion outweigh the advantages of participating? Why or why not?
2. Why do you think Procter & Gamble chose the gem-in-package sales promotion strategy instead of relying on advertising to stimulate product demand?
3. What types of publicity, if any, is Procter & Gamble likely to achieve as a result of the sales promotion?

Source: Quoted from "Stop and Shop Refuses to Carry P&G's Gem-in-Package Items," *Supermarket News*, February 10, 1986, p. 4. Reprinted with permission.

2. Jewel Food Stores Handles a Crisis

Jewel Food Stores faced hundreds of lawsuits as a result of 16,000 cases of salmonella contracted by consumers in six midwestern states from drinking contaminated milk. Some stores lost up to 25 percent of their volume in the earliest weeks of the crisis. The outbreak was associated with Jewel's Hill Farm dairy plant which was closed until the exact cause of the outbreak could be pinpointed and corrected.

Jewel hired a public relations firm to develop a plan for handling any future crises involving product removal or consumer problems related to products distributed by Jewel. Industry analysts indicated that, because a plan was being formulated, Jewel had not been prepared for the outbreak and did not move quickly enough to reassure consumers. Jewel quickly ran a public service advertising campaign, including an open letter from Jewel's president and 30-second TV commercials to replace scheduled price-item ad spots. The company also established a hotline for consumers to call for information regarding salmonella and for filing their claims. Jewel also moved quickly and substituted Dean's Dairy Products for its own line of dairy products.

Questions

1. Should firms such as Jewel have a plan prepared in advance for responding to company crises? What should be the key ingredients in such a plan?
2. What parallels, if any, do you see between the actions taken by Jewel and the actions taken by Tylenol following the accidental deaths of several people from consuming cyanide-contaminated Tylenol capsules?
3. What other steps, if any, do you think Jewel should have taken in responding to the crisis? What types of advertising and sales promotion would have been appropriate over the long term to reestablish confidence in Jewel's line of dairy products?

Source: Based on Patricia Natschke, "Jewel Sales Off 6–8%; Crisis Plan Set," *Supermarket News*, June 17, 1985, p. 1.

ENDNOTES

1. Ovid Riso, "Advertising Guidelines for Small Retail Firms," *Small Marketers Aid, No. 160* (Washington, D.C.: U.S. Small Business Administration), p. 4.
2. "Ad Strategy: Divide and Conquer," *Chain Store Age, General Merchandise Edition,* December 1985, p. 30.
3. Marvin J. Rothenburg, "Retail Research Strategies for the '70s," in *Combined Proceedings,* Editor, Ed Mazze (Chicago: American Marketing Association, 1975), p. 409.
4. Riso, "Advertising Guidelines."
5. The material on establishing and allocating the budget is based on Stewart Henderson Britt, "Plan Your Advertising Budget," *Small Marketers Aid, No. 164* (Washington, D.C.: U.S. Small Business Administration).
6. Thomas A. Petit and Martha R. McEnally, "Putting Strategy into Promotion Mix Decisions," *The Journal of Consumer Marketing* 2, no. 1 (Winter 1985), pp. 41–47.
7. William L. McGee, *A Marketing Approach to Building Store Traffic with Broadcast Advertising* (San Francisco: Broadcast Marketing Co., 1978), p. 170.
8. "Use of Radio Ads Is Growing for Retailers' Image Building," *Supermarket News,* May 27, 1985, p. 3.
9. "Medium Gets Message to Youth Market," *Chain Store Age, General Merchandise Trends,* April 1985, p. 23; "Advertising on Cable Television," in *Marketing, Sales Promotion, and Advertising Plan Book* (New York: National Retail Merchants Association, 1986), pp. 64–65.
10. For further reading, see Lewis A. Spalding, "Strategies for Selling by Mail," *Stores,* September 1982, pp. 23–28.
11. "Advertising Small Business," *Small Business Reporter* (San Francisco: Bank of America, 1981), p. 13.
12. Ibid., p. 14.
13. Ellen Paris, "Follow the Moving Sign," *Forbes,* September 9, 1985, p. 116.
14. "Advertising Small Business," p. 14.
15. This material is condensed, with modifications, from Elizabeth Sorbet, "Do You Know the Results of Your Advertising?" *Management Aid, No. 4, 020* (Washington, D.C.: U.S. Small Business Administration).
16. William Haight, *Retail Advertising: Management and Techniques* (New Jersey: General Learning Press, 1976), p. 357.
17. For further reading, see "Inside Report: Sales Promotion," *Marketing News,* June 7, 1985, p. 12; Marc Schnapp, "War Games 'In Retailing Promotions'," *Marketing Communications,* June 1985, pp. 85–88; "Retailers Bullish on Bears," *Marketing News,* March 13, 1987, p. 18.
18. "Price and Promotion Strategies for Impact at Retail," *Marketing Communications,* October 1985; see also, "Sign of the Times: Singles' Night Shopping," *Supermarket News,* September 22, 1986, p. 1.
19. "Prince, Di Paying Visit to J.C. Penney," *The Tuscaloosa News,* November 11, 1985, p. 1.

19

What Remains?— Customer Support Functions

Car Dealers Opt for Psychology in Repair Shop

"I brought this car in four times for the same problem and you haven't done anything to fix it," Gary Clark barks at Mark Robbins, an auto service manager. "It shudders driving uphill at 45 miles an hour. What are you going to do about it?"

Mr. Robbins quietly asks the car's age and mileage and suggests a shop foreman take a ride with Mr. Clark. But that won't do. "I have to get to work," he says. "I've wasted too much time on this car already."

"OK," says Mr. Robbins, "we'll give you a car to use while we fix it."

Mr. Robbins sounds too good to be true, and in a way he is. He and Mr. Clark are both auto service managers, and they improvised this scene in a class where they and colleagues from four Pennsylvania dealerships were learning to do a better job of keeping customers happy.

When it comes to customer satisfaction, American car makers and dealers are struggling to catch up with foreign competition. The most recent report by J.D. Power & Associates, a Westlake, California, market-research firm, shows only four U.S. makes—Lincoln, Mercury, Cadillac, and Ford—among the top 16 in customer satisfaction for year-old 1985-model cars.

A more pleasant experience in the service department, some dealers hope, may help close the gap. Says Joseph A. Kordick, general manager of Ford Motor Co.'s parts and service division, "There's no question that the treatment a person receives in a dealership service department goes a long way in determining whether that customer continues to do business with that dealer—and even that model."

The problem, says Harry Woehr, a Philadelphia industrial psychologist who runs the course here, is that most service personnel are former mechanics, more comfortable with cars than people. These individuals tend to prefer brief, pointed conversations intended solely to find out about the car. "They don't deal with the feelings of the customer at all," he says. "Until you deal with their feelings, you are not going to satisfy them."

*C*ustomer support services include such functions as credit, layaway, delivery, personal shopping programs, and a variety of other activities designed to attract new customers and to strengthen relationships with existing ones. Customer support services are a primary way for retailers to differentiate their own outlets from those of competitors. Many retail outlets offer essentially the same merchandise at the same price with similar merchandising programs. Services provide the opportunity to create a unique image in the minds of consumers, as shown in the retailing capsule. Services are expensive, however, and many retailers do not agree on what services should be offered. Some are even reducing the number of services they offer.

LEARNING OBJECTIVES

After reading this chapter, you will be able to:

1. Describe the strategic role of customer support services in the retailer's overall marketing plan.

2. Name the various types of retail credit.

3. List the various types of retail credit cards.

4. Explain the laws affecting customer support services.

5. Discuss customer support activities such as shopper services, educational programs, delivery, and extended shopping hours.

Many customers now bag their own groceries, price mark goods at warehouse outlets, serve themselves in restaurants, handle their own deliveries, and pump their own gas. Shifting these functions to customers is the result of efforts by retailers to lower their costs and increase profit margins, but retailers cannot eliminate all **basic services** if they want to stay in business. Such services include credit, repair, warranty service, and others (depending on the merchandise sold). No service should be offered, however, unless it contributes directly or indirectly to profit.

A high-fashion store appealing to the upper-income shopper will usually offer more services than a discount store. Also, two different stores may offer wide variations in the same service. For example, a discount store may accept a bank credit card as the only means of payment other than cash, but a department store may also accept the store's credit card, a travel and entertainment card such as Diner's Club, or offer a customer charge plan. Department stores may deliver large items such as furniture free of charge, whereas a warehouse furniture store may charge extra for delivery.

A full-service specialty outlet such as Motherhood Maternity shops offers a full array of customer services, often through special promotions. In contrast, a discount outlet such as K mart may offer identical merchandise at reduced prices, but without supporting services. The use of services is thus part of the positioning strategy by merchants in targeting key market segments, as discussed in Chapter 2.

STRENGTHENING RELATIONSHIP RETAILING

The purpose of customer support services is to strengthen customer relationships. **Relationship retailing** includes all activities designed to attract, retain, and enhance customer relationships.[1]

Management can increase sales by attracting new customers, making more sales to existing customers, or reducing the loss of existing customers. Building relationships with existing customers costs less than efforts to attract new ones.

"The foundation of relationship retailing is quality of service. No customer wants a relationship with a retail company that is unreliable, unresponsive, incompetent, or otherwise inefficient on the quality-of-service dimensions. The heart and soul of relationship retailing is personal attention: to treat the customer as a client, rather than as a face in the crowd, individualizing service, tailoring it, adding a touch of grace, making the client feel special."[2] Numerous examples of efforts to strengthen relationship retailing exist, including personalized shopper services, special credit cards for uniquely valuable customers, and other services ranging from multilingual signing to bridal registries. Getting close to the customer is the critical ingredient in learning how to use service as a way of enhancing customer relationships.[3] The essence of a good customer service support program is captured by a sign in Nordstrom's, a retailer in the Northwest, which says

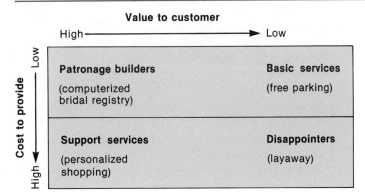

SOURCE: Based on Albert D. Bates and Jamil G. Didion, "Special Services Can Personalize Retail Environment," *Marketing News*, April 12, 1985, p. 13.

it all: "The Only Difference Between Stores Is How They Treat Their Customers."

STRATEGIC DIMENSIONS OF SERVICES

Management's goal is to provide a package of services that generates the greatest customer benefits at the lowest cost. In this context, services can be analyzed on two dimensions—value to customers and cost. Four categories of services emerge from such an analysis, as shown in Figure 19–1: support services, disappointers, basics, and patronage builders.[4]

Support Services

Support services directly support the sale of the retailer's merchandise. They have high value to consumers, but also a high cost to the retailer. Such services include home delivery, child care, gift wrapping, and personalized shopper services.

Disappointers

Disappointers include layaway and parcel pick-up. These services require high labor effort, but return little value to the customer. They are candidates for elimination from the services offered by some retailers. An alternative possibility is to restructure them in such a way as to reduce their cost and increase their value to customers.

Basic Services

Customers take some services for granted. An example is free parking. Retailers often provide such services without giving much thought to their cost content, particularly if they are a competitive necessity.

Patronage builders *are the services that receive the most strategic attention from retailers.* They include such services as birthday reminders and gift certificates. The services have high consumer value and can be provided at nominal cost. As such, they provide the opportunity to increase the store's customer base, especially if competitors are unable to provide comparable service at the same price. Computers have thus allowed retailers to shift some services from the high-value/high-cost category to one of high consumer value but low cost. Computerized bridal registries, for example, can be accessed from multiple store locations, and purchases can be entered on a real-time basis.

Management may want to charge for support services, eliminate disappointers, and use patronage builders as a way to expand the customer base. Regardless, management needs to periodically reevaluate services and make sure that patronage builders do not drift into the support services category.

A SERVICES AUDIT

A services audit can help management evaluate the firm's services offerings relative to competition and on the basis of value to customers, as discussed above. The end result likely will be a more customer-driven services program. Identifying what services consumers *really* value is no simple task, partly because consumers may have difficulty articulating their preferences. Additionally, customers often form opinions about the quality and quantity of services by using competitors as a reference point.

Customer services cannot be an afterthought. A quality services program can help to differentiate the firm from competition, generate new sales leads, discourage consumers from switching to alternative retail outlets which may offer the same merchandise, and reinforce customer loyalty. Asking questions such as those listed below helps management integrate services as a strategic element of its customer support plan:

1. What are the company's customer service objectives on each service offered—to make a profit, break even, or, in order to remain competitive, to sustain the loss?
2. What services does the company provide (i.e., customer education, financing arrangements, predelivery preparation, complaints handling, repair service)?
3. How does the company compare with the competition on the customer services provided?
4. What services do customers want?
5. What are the customer service demand patterns?
6. What trade-offs in terms of cost versus service are customers prepared to make?
7. What level of service do customers want and at what price? For example, is an 800 telephone number adequate or is a salesperson necessary?[5]

T A B L E 19–1	HOW MUCH WOULD IT INFLUENCE YOUR DECISION WHERE TO SHOP IF YOU WERE CONFIDENT OF . . . ?	
Quick checkout		52.8%
Background music		8.5
Sales assistance		43.3
Giftwrap		19.7
Women's restroom		50.7
Store charge card		37.0
Phone orders		24.6
Money-back satisfaction		77.9
Convenient parking		61.0
Private fitting rooms		43.8
Advance notice of sales/events		45.9
Someone in the store knows you by name		19.5
Low-cost home delivery		21.1

SOURCE: "Service: Retail's No. 1 Problem," *Chain Store Age, General Merchandise Trends*, January 1987, p. 19.

Effective implementation of the services program is critical after the completion of the audit. Services response systems should be standardized whenever possible, and a pricing policy should be established in those situations where management decides to charge for various services.

The value of a services audit can be seen in Table 19–1. The information is based on interviews with more than 1,000 female shoppers in five major metropolitan areas to determine the types of services that most influence their decision on where to shop. As shown, money-back satisfaction was ranked more important than any other factor. Convenience factors such as available parking close to the store, quick checkout, and restrooms were the other services that would sway 50 percent of the women to change their shopping habits. It may come as a surprise that merchants could restore a large chunk of their total service package simply by making sure such mundane things as restrooms meet customer expectations.[6]

Today's shopper is busy, so it should also come as no surprise that 45 percent would shop a certain store if they were notified in advance of sales and other events. Also important to over 40 percent of the women were private fitting rooms and quality sales assistance.

Let's now look at the range of services offered by many retailers to see how they fit into a customer support program.

RETAIL CREDIT

The average American credit user now has seven cards for credit or check cashing.[7] The most popular cards in the United States are shown in Table 19–2. Understandably, credit in one form or another is one of the most basic customer support services many retailers can offer.

T A B L E 19–2 CREDIT CARDS IN U.S. (in millions)

Visa	86.4
MasterCard	64.9
American Express	15
Sears store cards	60
Diner's Club and Carte Blanch	2.5
Citicorp Choice	1.2
Amoco MultiCard	1

SOURCE: Bill Richards and Steve Weiner, "Credit-Card Battle Spurs Issues to Offer New Incentives to Holders," *The Wall Street Journal*, September 4, 1985, p. 27. Reprinted by permission of *The Wall Street Journal*, © Dow Jones & Company, Inc., September 4, 1985. All rights reserved.

Advantages and Disadvantages of Internal (Store) Credit

Credit is expensive. Still, many retailers believe that granting credit is necessary. Consumers apparently feel the same way since they often shop only in stores where various credit cards are honored.

Some of the major advantages of internal (store) credit are:

1. Credit customers are more store-loyal than noncredit customers.
2. Retail outlets often have a more personal relationship with customers to whom they have granted credit, particularly in-house credit.
3. The use of credit can lead to "plus" sales which can help the return on investment, since the extra sales can be made at little or no additional cost to the firm.
4. Credit account records can provide retailers with a mailing list for announcing special sales and other promotional efforts.
5. Credit helps spread sales evenly throughout a time period because people do not have to wait for payday.
6. Credit tends to make customers less price conscious.[8]

However, retailers also need to weigh some disadvantages of internal credit. These include the following:

1. Higher overhead costs are necessary for handling the opening of new accounts, mailing out statements, collections, and similar activities.
2. The business ties up working capital because of the delay in receiving payment for credit purchases.
3. Bad debts create problems. Write-offs are very costly to management. As shown in Table 19–3, retailers with a 2 percent profit margin need an additional sales volume of $12,500 to break even on a bad debt write-off of $250.
4. Customers are more likely to abuse the privileges of returning goods and taking goods on approval when they have store credit accounts.

What Types of Internal Credit Should Be Offered?

Management has five choices in offering internal credit: (1) installment payments, (2) open-charge credit, (3) revolving credit, (4) deferred billing payment, and (5) layaway.

EVERY DOLLAR YOU "WRITE OFF" REQUIRES A FORTUNE IN NEW BUSINESS TO BREAK EVEN!

Your Profit Percent	Write-Offs of							
	$250	$500	$1,000	$2,000	$3,000	$5,000	$7,500	$10,000
	Equivalent to sales of							
2	$12,500	$25,000	$50,000	$100,000	$150,000	$250,000	$375,000	$500,000
3	8,333	16,666	33,333	66,667	100,000	166,667	249,975	333,333
4	6,250	12,500	25,000	50,000	75,000	125,000	187,500	250,000
5	5,000	10,000	20,000	40,000	60,000	100,000	150,000	200,000
6	4,165	8,333	16,667	33,333	50,000	83,333	124,950	166,667
7	3,572	7,143	14,286	28,571	42,857	71,429	107,145	142,857
8	3,125	6,250	12,500	25,000	37,500	62,500	93,750	125,000
9	2,778	5,556	11,111	22,222	33,333	55,556	83,340	111,111
10	2,500	5,000	10,000	20,000	30,000	50,000	75,000	100,000

Example: If you decide to write off $2,000 in bad debts and are averaging 6 percent profit, you must sell an additional $33,333 to recover that $2,000.

SOURCE: I.C. System, Inc., St. Paul, Minnesota.

Installment credit (a monthly payment account) means that a customer pays for a product in equal monthly installments, including interest. Automobiles and major appliances are often paid for in this way.

Open-charge credit means that the customer must pay the bill in full when it is due, usually in 30 days. Credit limits are set which the customer cannot exceed; also, part payments on the account are not allowed.

Revolving credit means that a customer charges items during a month and is billed at the end of that month on the basis of the outstanding balance. Such a plan allows the customer to purchase several items without having a separate contract for each purchase.

A business can also offer **deferred billing credit.** Deferred billing occurs when a retailer allows customers to buy goods and defer payment for an extended time with no interest charge. Many stores advertise during the Christmas season, "No down payment, and first payment not due for 90 days."

A **layaway plan** is another type of credit. This plan allows a customer to make a small deposit, perhaps two or three dollars, to hold an item. The retailer retains possession of the item until the customer completes paying for it. The advantage to customers is not having to worry about whether the item will be in stock when they need it. And retailers do not have to worry about collection problems.

What about a Charge Card?

Most retailers today honor some type of credit card. Businesses have two basic choices with credit cards. They can (1) have their own card or (2) participate in a third-party program.

Third-party credit can consist of (1) a *bank card* such as Visa or MasterCard, (2) a **private label credit card** for the store which is issued by a third party such as a bank, (3) an **umbrella shopping card** which can be used at all stores in a specified shopping center, or (4) *travel and entertainment cards* such as American Express or Diner's Club.

Why Have a Store Card?

Several advantages exist in having a store card as part of the internal credit function as discussed earlier, but *disadvantages* also exist. Specifically, (1) maintaining a store credit card program is expensive, (2) management has the hassle of trying to collect unpaid bills and getting money from slow payers, (3) employees have to do creditworthiness checks, and (4) management may lose sales because potential customers have a bank card, but not a store card.

Today, independent department stores are practically the only stores that have internal credit operations. These stores believe they get a strong marketing advantage from in-house credit. Many have added bank credit card plans to their programs, primarily to take advantage of out-of-town business. But in-house credit probably is on its way out for many merchants.

Some merchants, however, are turning to special store cards to maintain a unique relationship with their customers.[9] Bloomingdale's selects those customers who are consistently large spenders and gives them a Gold Card. The company's philosophy is "This is a special kind of a card and we're recognizing you." Management hopes the salespeople realize they are dealing with customers who are special and that possession of the Gold Card will raise the strength of the personal relationship between the customer and the store. Bloomingdale's does not offer any "perks" with the card, although they do advertise certain sales that are exclusively for this customer segment.

Rich's in Atlanta offers a program similar to Bloomingdale's for its special customers, but also offers free check-cashing privileges. The customer also receives a special number for the store's personal shopping service and free downtown parking. Outlets such as Neiman-Marcus, Weinstock's in Sacramento, and Palais Royal in Houston are also more aggressive in the perks that accompany their card. They offer such benefits as free gift wrapping, special notices of upcoming special events, private sales, and special opportunities for social events. The idea for the program is to establish strong identification by the customer with the merchant.

Third-Party Credit

Bank credit cards or travel and entertainment cards such as Diner's Club are not controlled by the merchant. Rather, the bank or the entertainment company receives applications and issues cards and is responsible for customer billing and collection. The firms then bill the merchants accepting the card at a flat percentage of all credit sales.[10]

A more recent version of the third-party card is the private label card. One example is the General Electric Credit Corporation (GECC) customer credit program now used by many retail firms. GECC works with each merchant to tailor a package to the store's needs. Sometimes the GECC maintains an office in the store to handle credit processing and collection. Often, customers are not aware that they are dealing with an outside agency.

In a third-party program, banks handle (1) credit applications, credit processing, and authorization; (2) customer inquiries; (3) promotion; and (4) issuing each customer a card with the name of the participating store on it. Recently, Visa has gone this route and will place a store name on the face of their card. The advantage is that the retailer gets more loyal customers plus the wide acceptability of Visa.

Another version of third-party credit is the *umbrella shopping center card*. A bank normally sponsors the program which operates the same way as any regular bank credit card program, but the card is honored only by the participating merchants in the shopping center.

Sears Discover card is the latest example of third-party credit.[11] The Discover card should not be confused with the traditional Sears credit card which is limited to use in Sears stores. The Discover card can be used at thousands of retail outlets including Dayton-Hudson, Montgomery Ward, Ace Hardware, Radio Shack, Genesco Shoes, American and Eastern airlines, Denny's, Pizza Hut, and others.

Sears promotes the Discover card as a financial services card that combines spending, saving, and investment possibilities in a single card. Ultimately, Sears expects to deliver a broader array of credit, banking, brokerage, and insurance services by using the card as part of the Sears financial network.

In summary, more and more retailers are dropping in-house credit as a service. Many are (1) going to a private-label third-party system, (2) honoring bank cards such as Visa, (3) honoring travel and entertainment cards, or (4) structuring a program to encourage the use of checks and cash. Some retailers, for example, give discounts of 3 to 5 percent on cash purchases. This discount is the equivalent of what merchants pay the banks for the right to allow customers to make purchases with a bank credit card such as Visa.

Managing Internal Credit	Most firms issuing credit use an application form (see Figure 19–2). The application requests information that allows the firm to decide whether the person should be granted credit. The forms may ask for such information as the size of savings and checking account balances, extent of debts, and various other personal information (see Table 19–4). Often information on the creditworthiness of the applicant is obtained from a credit bureau.[12]
Credit Scoring	Many firms use **credit scoring** in screening credit applicants. This method gives points about various types of personal information concerning the applicant. The points are determined through a study of information obtained from other good and bad accounts. An example of a credit scoring system for screening accounts is shown in Table 19–5. Depending on the number

Charge Application

Account Number	Credit Office Use Only
	Limit	Auth. By

READ INSTRUCTIONS BEFORE COMPLETING APPLICATION FORM

INSTRUCTIONS TO APPLICANT: (1) If married and you are applying for credit based on individual credit worthiness, do not complete the section for a joint account. (2) If married and you wish to use your spouse's credit worthiness in the evaluation, you must complete the joint account section. (3) Payments from alimony, child support, and maintenance need not be reported as income unless you are relying on such payments in this application. (4) If married and the type of account is marked "JOINT", the credit history of both applicant and spouse will be reported to credit reporting agencies. PRINT CLEARLY. APPLICATION MUST BE SIGNED.

PLEASE OPEN A JOINT ACCOUNT ☐ OR AN INDIVIDUAL ACCOUNT ☐ IN THE FOLLOWING NAME

Name, First	Second	Last	Social Security No.
Home Address, Street	City	State	Zip	How Long Yrs. Mos.
Home Phone No.	Monthly Mtg./Rent	Resident ☐ Own ☐ Rent ☐ Other		Date of Birth
Previous Address		Yrs. at Prev. Address	Employer Phone
Employer (Give Full Name)		How Long (3 Yrs. Required)	Position
Employer's Address	Monthly Salary $	Other Income - Source(s) $	
Former Employer		How Long	
Name of Relative or Personal Reference	Address	Phone	Relationship

JOINT ACCOUNT

Name of Joint Applicant	Social Security No.	Date of Birth
Employer (Full Name)	How Long (3 Yrs. Required)	Position	Employer Phone No.
Employer's Address	Monthly Salary $	Other Income - Source(s) $
Former Employer	How Long	

CREDIT REFERENCES

Do you presently have or have you ever had an account with _____ ☐ Yes ☐ No
Account No. _____ Date Opened: _____ Amount Owing $ _____

Name of Creditors	Important Account Numbers	Exact Name in Which Account is Held	Date Opened	Balance Owed

(SIGNATURE OF AUTHORIZED BUYER OTHER THAN APPLICANT) **X**

The undersigned affirm(s) that the information furnished to _____ by the undersigned in connection with this transaction is true and correct and hereby authorizes _____ to investigate my credit record, and to verify my employment and income references.
The undersigned further agree(s) that if this application is accepted and a Credit Card issued that any use of the card will be governed by the terms and conditions accompanying the card, and the undersigned assume(s), if more than one jointly and severally, liability for all charges incurred in any such use.
Upon approval you will receive a copy of the _____ Charge Agreement to keep.

SIGNATURE IN FULL OF APPLICANTS	**X**	Date	Dr. Lic. No.
	X	Date	Dr. Lic. No.

notice: *The Federal Equal Credit Opportunity Act requires that all creditors make credit equally available to all creditworthy customers without regard to sex or marital status. The federal agency which administers compliance with this law concerning this store is Federal Trade Commission, Washington, D.C. 20580.*

Any holder of this consumer credit contract is subject to all claims and defenses which the debtor could assert against the seller of goods or services obtained pursuant hereto or with the proceeds hereof. Recovery hereunder by the debtor shall not exceed amounts paid by the debtor hereunder.

---

of points received, a person may be given a credit limit or may be rejected. Table 19–6 shows how the result of an application might look based on the information contained in Table 19–4. Experience can help decide on the minimum number of points necessary to approve an application.

The Equal Credit Opportunity Act (1977).   Many retailers are going to credit scoring because of the federal **Equal Credit Opportunity Act** (1977). The act

Telephone at home	Telephone at work
Own/rent living accommodations	Bank savings account
	Bank checking account
Age	ZIP code of residence
Time at home address	Age of automobile
Industry at which employed	Make and model of automobile
	Geographic area of United States
Time with employer	Finance company reference
Time with previous employer	Debt to income ratio
	Monthly rent/mortgage payment
Type of employment	Family size
Number of dependents	Telephone area code
Types of credit reference	Location of relatives
	Number of children
Income	Number of other dependents
Savings and loan references	Ownership of life insurance
Trade union membership	
Age difference between husband and wife	

SOURCE: Noel Capon, "Credit Scoring System: A Critical Analysis," *Journal of Marketing* 46 (Spring 1982), p. 85.

states that a person who is denied credit can demand a written statement of reasons for denial. Thus, businesses now are under more pressure to operate with objective and consistent credit approval policies. Scoring gives the retailer the following advantages: (1) better control over credit, (2) ease in training new personnel, (3) lower cost of processing loan applications, and (4) a more legally defensible way of granting or denying credit.

Exhibit 19–1 gives more specifics on practices that are illegal under the Equal Credit Opportunity Act.

The Fair Debt Collection Practices Act (1978). Management also needs to study the requirements of the federal **Fair Debt Collection Practices Act** to make sure its collection practices are legal. The act prohibits abusive, deceptive, and unfair debt collection practices by debt collectors. The law will not permit debt collectors to use unjust means in attempting to collect debt, but does not cancel debts consumers owe. Further details are shown in Exhibit 19–2. Figure 19–3 shows a typical sequence of collection letters which can be used by management to help collect on overdue accounts.

The retailer also needs to decide how credit will be verified when a credit purchase is made. Some firms still have *manual credit verification,* where a clerk calls the credit department when a sale is made and gives the account number and the sale size and asks for approval.

Some stores set a limit, say $50, above which all credit charges must be approved. All sales less than the amount are approved on the floor. The

MAJOR NATIONAL RETAILER'S FINAL SCORING TABLE FOR
APPLICATION CHARACTERISTICS

ZIP code		Teacher	41
ZIP codes A	60	Unemployed	33
ZIP codes B	48	All other	46
ZIP codes C	41	Not answered	47
ZIP codes D	37	Time at present address	
Not answered	53	Less than 6 months	39
Bank reference		6 months–1 year, 5 months	30
Checking only	0	1 year, 6 months–3 years, 5 months	27
Savings only	0	3 years, 6 months–7 years, 5 months	30
Checking and savings	15	7 years, 6 months–12 years, 5 months	39
Bank name or loan only	0	12 years, 6 months or longer	50
No bank reference	7	Not answered	36
Not answered	7	Time with employer	
Type of housing		Less than 6 months	31
Owns/buying	44	6 months–5 years, 5 months	24
Rents	35	5 years, 6 months–8 years, 5 months	26
All other	41	8 years, 6 months–15 years, 5 months	31
Not answered	39	15 years, 6 months or longer	39
Occupation		Homemakers	39
Clergy	46	Retired	31
Creative	41	Unemployed	29
Driver	33	Not answered	29
Executive	62	Finance company reference	
Guard	46	Yes	0
Homemaker	50	Other references only	25
Laborer	33	No	25
Manager	46	Not answered	15
Military enlisted	46	Other department store/oil card/major credit card	
Military officer	62	Department store only	12
Office staff	46	Oil card only	12
Outside	33	Major credit card only	17
Production	41	Department store and oil card	17
Professional	62	Department store and credit card	31
Retired	62	Major credit card and oil card	31
Sales	46	All three	31
Semiprofessional	50	Other references only	0
Service	41	No credit	0
Student	46	Not answered	12

SOURCE: Noel Capon, "Credit Scoring System: A Critical Analysis," *Journal of Marketing* 46 (Spring 1982), p. 85.

approval limit is often raised in the busy seasons of the year to handle more customers.

Credit authorization is now often done electronically. The clerk enters the account number and the amount of the sale at the cash register. The system then automatically checks the accounts receivable information stored in the computer and indicates whether a credit charge should be approved.

HYPOTHETICAL SAMPLE APPLICANT AND THE ASSOCIATED CREDIT SCORE

Applicant Characteristics	Allotted Points
Home phone	36
Rents	0
No other finance company debt	0
Bank credit card	29
Farm worker	3
Both checking and savings accounts	19
Age 48	8
Same job for 18 years	18
	113

SOURCE: Gilbert Churchill, et al., "The Role of Credit Scoring in the Loan Decision," *The Credit World*, March 1977, p. 8. Reprinted with permission of *The Credit World*, official publication of the International Consumer Credit Association, St. Louis, Mo.

E X H I B I T 19–1 *EQUAL CREDIT OPPORTUNITY ACT*

The E.C.O. Act was enacted by Congress to give consumers important rights when applying for and using credit. A major provision of the law gives married women the right to establish their own credit records based on jointly held accounts. Other important provisions state that in evaluating an applicant's creditworthiness, a creditor must not:

Consider sex, marital status, race, national origin, religion, or age (with limited exceptions).

Refuse to consider reliable public assistance income (such as Social Security or Aid to Families with Dependent Children).

Discount or refuse to consider income derived from part-time employment or from a pension, annuity, or retirement benefit program.

Discount income because of sex or marital status, or assume that a woman of childbearing age will stop work to raise children.

Refuse to consider consistently received alimony, child support, or separate maintenance payments in the same manner as other income, if the applicant wants this income considered.

The act does not guarantee that an applicant will get credit. Creditors may still determine creditworthiness by considering economic factors such as income, expenses, debts, and previous bill-paying habits.

For further information write: Director, Office of Bank Customer Affairs, Federal Deposit Insurance Corporation, Washington, D.C. 20629. Ask for their publications entitled "Equal Credit Opportunity for Women," and "Equal Credit Opportunity and Age."

Promoting Credit	In spite of the possible losses from a credit operation, many retailers aggressively promote their credit plans because they can result in increased merchandise sales. College students are often special targets. They are perceived as upwardly mobile, soon-to-be-young-professionals with high income potential. Many independent retailers also offer credit applications through "Welcome Wagon" services. The population turnover in a community can easily equal 15 percent per year, and an ongoing program of credit promotion is necessary to maintain a strong customer base for a retail outlet.

EXHIBIT 19–2   Fair Debt Collection Practices Act

What types of debt collection practices are prohibited?

A debt collector may not harass, oppress, or abuse any person. For example, a debt collector cannot:

Use threats of violence to harm anyone or anyone's property or reputation.

Publish a list of consumers who refuse to pay debts (except to a credit bureau).

Use obscene or profane language.

Repeatedly use the telephone to annoy anyone.

Telephone any person without identifying the caller.

Advertise one's debt.

A debt collector may not use any false statements when collecting any debt. For example, the debt collector cannot:

Falsely imply that the debt collector represents the U.S. government or any state government.

Falsely imply that the debt collector is an attorney.

Falsely imply that a person committed any crime.

Falsely represent that the debt collector operates or works for a credit bureau.

Misrepresent the amount of the debt.

Represent that papers being sent are legal forms, such as a summons, when they are not.

Represent that papers being sent are *not* legal forms when they *are*.

Also, a debt collector may not say:

That a person will be arrested or imprisoned if he or she fails to pay a debt.

That he will seize, garnish, attach, or sell your property, or wages, unless the debt collector or the creditor intends to do so and it is legal.

That any action will be taken against anyone which cannot legally be taken.

A debt collector may not:

Give false credit information about anyone.

Send a person anything that looks like an official document which might be sent by any court or agency of the United States or any state or local government.

Use any false name.

A debt collector must not be unfair in attempting to collect any debt. For example, the debt collector cannot:

Collect any amount greater than the debt amount, unless allowed by law.

Deposit any postdated check before its date.

Make anyone accept collect calls or pay for telegrams.

Take or threaten to take property unless there is a present right to do so.

Contact anyone by postcard.

Put anything on an envelope other than the debt collector's address and name.

Even the name cannot be used if it shows that the communication is about a debt collection.

What control do you have over specific debts?

If you owe several debts, any payment made must be applied as you choose. And, a debt collector cannot apply a payment to any debt you feel you do not owe.

What can you do if a debt collector breaks the law?

You have the right to sue a debt collector in a state or federal court within one year from the date the law was violated. You may recover money for the damages suffered. Court costs and attorney's fees can also be recovered.

A group of persons may sue a debt collector and recover money for damages up to $500,000.

Who can you tell if a debt collector breaks the law?

You should contact the proper federal government enforcement agency. The agencies use complaints to decide which companies to investigate.

Many states also have debt collection laws of their own. Check with your state attorney general's office to determine your rights under state law.

Where should you send complaints and questions?

Unless your complaint is about collection practices by banks and other financial institutions, write to: Federal Trade Commission, Debt Collection Practices, Washington, D.C. 20580.

To find out more:

If you have any general questions about the Fair Debt Collection Practices Act or you wish to complain about collection practices by creditors, write to the Federal Trade Commission, Debt Collection Practices, Washington, D.C. 20580, or to one of its regional offices.

At the time . . .

your account was reviewed recently, your statement showed an overdue balance.

Of course, you may have sent us this payment since the date the account was reviewed. If you have, please disregard our notice and accept our thanks.

If you haven't already mailed us your check, we are sure you will appreciate this reminder.
Cordially,

Past due notice

Several days have elapsed since we notified you relative to the payment which is past due on your account; however, we are still without remittance from you. Your future credit with us will be determined by your present payment record. It is essential that this matter be taken care of without further delay.
Cordially,

Time flies . . .

and another month has almost slipped by without a payment on your account.

When you miss a payment, or pay less than our minimum terms, the overdue payment grows larger and reflects on your credit standing with us.

We are sure that you are concerned about your past due account and will send us a check by return mail.
Cordially,

We are willing to make allowances . . .

for any emergency which may have arisen that made it impossible for you to meet our credit terms, but, for a lack of a reply, we must assume that you do not intend to pay.

UNLESS YOUR PAYMENT HAS ALREADY BEEN SENT, WE MUST HEAR FROM YOU IN THE NEXT FIVE DAYS, SO WE WILL NOT HAVE TO SEND THIS ACCOUNT TO OUR COLLECTION DEPT.
Credit department

If . . .

you realized that your continued disregard of the many notices we have sent has made your account 90 days or more overdue, we are sure your check would have been sent to us before the date we reviewed your account.

We cannot continue to hold this account in our hands without positive action on your part to make your account current.

Your credit is a valuable asset—we are sure you realize this and will send your check today before it is too late. If it has been mailed in the last few days, please accept our thanks.
Collection department

We have had no response . . .

to our recent notices to you concerning the overdue amount on your charge account.

Silence is golden except where your failure to reply is certain to affect your credit record with us.

If a check hasn't already been sent, enclose it in the attached envelope and mail it to us today . . . before you forget again.
Collection department.

Reluctantly . . .

WE ARE CLOSING YOUR ACCOUNT TO ALL FURTHER PURCHASES. This means that your account cannot be used again without the specific permission of the office.

To protect your credit record, we are giving you the consideration of a 10-day period to pay your delinquent balance before turning this account over to an outside collection agency.
Very truly yours,

FIGURE 19–3 (concluded)

Your continued purchases . . .

ON YOUR SERIOUSLY OVERDUE ACCOUNT FORCE US TO RELUCTANTLY CLOSE YOUR AC-
COUNT AT ONCE, AND TO NOTIFY OUR STORES TO DISCONTINUE ANY FURTHER CREDIT
TO YOU.

We are still willing to discuss arrrangements on your account. But any further attempt to
purchase will result in stringent collection action.

To avoid the embarrassment of having our collection agent call in person to pick up your
charge plate, your plate must be returned to our office within four days from the postmark
of this letter.

Collection department.

HANDLING CHECKS

Historically a customer with a checkbook at the head of a checkout line was
sure to bring moans and grumblings from customers waiting in line. The
process of paying by check can easily take 5 to 10 minutes and create great
customer frustration.

Stores are now turning to on-line check acceptance services which make
payment by check as simple as using a credit card and just as quick. Sage-
Allen and Company, Inc., a department store based in Hartford, Connecticut, operates with such a system. Before going to a check acceptance service, it could take a customer as long as 15 or 20 minutes to pay by check
at the outlet if the purchase was for a large dollar amount. Now, the payment
system is on-line as part of the firm's electronic point-of-sale terminals.
Typically, approval for a check comes back within 10 seconds. The entire
process of approval normally takes no more than 90 seconds.

Many retail customers still prefer to pay by either cash or check. Making
it easy for them to pay by check generates customer goodwill and a substantial amount of "plus" business.

SHOPPING SERVICES

Retailers are always trying to make it possible for customers to buy goods
without having to spend an extended time in the store. Shopping services
thus are making a comeback. The most common shopper services are (1)
telephone shopping, (2) in-home shopping, and (3) personal shopping.

Telephone Shopping

Telephone shopping is pushed by retailers because many people have less
time for shopping. Often, the store will issue a catalog to the consumer.
After looking at the catalog, the customer calls the store, orders the merchandise, and charges the goods to an account or credit card. The goods

are then delivered to the shopper's home by the United Parcel Service or a similar organization.

Some retail outlets also offer toll-free 800 service as a way of increasing sales. Harrod's Department Store in London, England, was the first store in Europe to join AT&T's international 800 service. U.S. shoppers were able to order goods during the store's post-Christmas sale by dialing direct—even before the store opened for business to Londoners.[13]

In-Home Shopping
In-home demonstrations remain popular for such services as home decoration. Employees bring samples of draperies, carpeting, and wallpaper to a customer's home and the customer can then see how the materials look under normal lighting conditions.

Personal Shopping Services
Personal shopping is one of the fastest-growing services. Some firms, such as Dayton-Hudson (Minneapolis), Barney's (New York), Foley's (Houston), and Garfinkel's (Washington, D.C.), specialize in assembling wardrobes for working women and men. The customer goes to the store and provides a list of needed measurements, style and color preferences, and lifestyle information. After that, the person can call the store and indicate the types of item wanted. The store personnel then assemble several choices and have them ready at the customer's convenience.[14]

OTHER CUSTOMER SUPPORT SERVICES

Warranties
Most services are designed to help sell merchandise and are offered at no extra cost. But retailers can offer some additional services for which customers may gladly pay. An example is *extended warranties* or service contracts. The store agrees to extend a manufacturer's warranty for a period of time, commonly a year or so. The customer does not have to pay a repair bill during the agreed period of time regardless of how much the repair service may cost. Extended warranties are common on major household appliances and television sets.

Retailers should be aware of truth-in-warranty legislation, however, when offering extended warranties. Satisfaction guaranteed is a phrase often heard, but today such a statement is more of a contract than a courtesy. Specifically, management needs to be aware of the provisions of the *Magnuson-Moss Warranty Act* (discussed in Chapter 3), Federal Trade Commission rules, and state and county laws that may affect warranties offered to customers.

Some laws also determine where and how warranty information must be displayed. Many retail catalogs inform consumers that warranty information is available by mail before purchasing from the store.

Educational Programs	Some retailers have been successful in attracting customers by offering sewing lessons, cooking lessons, and sessions on interior decorating.[15] Cooking sessions help sell microwave ovens and have been very popular in recent years.
	Retailers can turn these programs into money makers or at the very least make them pay for themselves. For example, they can limit the classes to people who have purchased the products being promoted. Spreading the classes over several different time periods and days can keep customers coming back to the store and increases the chance of making additional sales.
Delivery	Delivery can be a large expense item for "big ticket" items such as furniture and household appliances. Stores are often pressured not to charge extra for delivery.
	Retailers can help their image as full-service retailers by having their own trucks for delivery. The delivery schedule can then be more flexible, but the cost of having delivery trucks is high.
	Another method of delivery is to use parcel post and service express. Retailers may want to use these services in addition to independent delivery services. Parcel post is a good way to deliver small packages to customers who may live a long distance from the store. Mail-order retailers often arrange delivery in this way.
Extended Shopping Hours	More and more retailers are offering consumers longer shopping hours, either late night or 24-hour shopping. Utility charges are about the same since the equipment runs most of the time anyway. Additional sales generated by longer hours can help spread the fixed costs over a larger sales base.
	Merchants may do very well with such a service since in many communities only a few stores are open 24 hours a day. But it is important to study such a move carefully before making a decision. Retailers will have to pay overtime to employees or add part-time workers. The chance of being robbed is greater, and energy bills will go up somewhat.
	Retailers should also remember that **blue laws** (laws against opening on Sunday) are enforced in some areas. Such laws are particularly prevalent in the Southeast and Southwest. Enforcement is spotty, but a retailer can wind up in jail if a pressure group pushes the police to enforce the law. Blue laws are likely to be a thing of the past in the next few years since most consumers seem to want Sunday shopping.
Automatic Bill Payment	Retailers are increasingly offering bill-payment programs that allow bills to be paid by telephone, by preauthorization, or by electronic terminals as an alternative to paying by check. Businesses such as J. C. Penney, Montgomery Ward, Foley's, Dayton-Hudson, and others are experimenting with automated bill payment procedures.

The advantages of such systems include (1) the elimination of bad checks, (2) lower labor costs to the retailer, (3) lower check processing fees because of a smaller check volume, and (4) reduced postage.

The disadvantages include (1) the loss of direct contact with the consumer, (2) the loss of the opportunity to send stuffers with monthly statements, (3) misunderstandings with consumers over the timing of the payments, which can lead to loss of goodwill, and (4) the loss of an audit trail which would help in catching dishonesty and fraud. Automated bill paying is likely to increase in popularity in the future because consumers react positively to saving time by this means of payment.

Customers with Special Needs

Special opportunities exist to meet the needs of "special" consumers, including those who don't speak English, the aged, and the infirm (including people who are deaf, blind, or confined to wheelchairs). More than 36 million people have physical or sensory disabilities.

Section 504 of the Rehabilitation Act (1973) mandated the push toward barrier-free environments in education, employment, and nonemployment situations. Now many states also have legislation requiring architectural compliance in developing barrier-free environments. Some progressive stores offer programs to assist and inform handicapped and aged shoppers. Examples of such services include the following:

1. Sears installed an experimental teletype ordering system that would allow deaf customers in Los Angeles to place catalog orders.
2. Braille menus have been built into the counters of selected Mc-Donald's locations.
3. Merchants at the South Town Mall in Rochester, New York, volunteered for sign-language training to better communicate with hearing-impaired and deaf customers.
4. Giant Foods has had a teletypewriter network installed specifically to accommodate deaf shoppers.

Large retailers in such metropolitan markets as Miami, New York, and Los Angeles offer multilingual signing to attract and serve foreign tourists. They also maintain lists of employees with foreign language ability. In addition, store directories and information pamphlets are sometimes printed in foreign languages. For example, Zayre Corporation prints a booklet outlining store policies in four languages. Saks-Fifth Avenue has had its International Shopping Service for more than 50 years, which is offered free to make shopping easy for tourists.

Registries

Computerization gives department stores a convenience and flexibility in their registry system that was previously unavailable. These retailers have seen broadbased benefits in a computerized bridal registry. The most obvious advantage is in access and updating capabilities. Because a complete registry can be printed from the computer within a matter of minutes, stores on the system can provide customers with an instant "shopping list" for a betrothed couple—a list they can carry with them from department to department as they make their selections.

Perhaps of most interest to store executives is the merchandising aspect, providing buyers and merchandise managers with complete, up-to-the-minute sales information, right down to details on vendor, patterns, size, or color of each gift purchased.

Neiman-Marcus is known worldwide for its unique services available to customers. We have chosen to highlight some of their services in Table 19–7 to illustrate the range of customer support services offered by retailers.

HANDLING COMPLAINTS AND RETURNS

Retailers need a policy for dealing with customer complaints and merchandise returns. Customers are allowed to return items in most stores, and some retailers feel the customer should be satisfied at any price. Almost all retailers, while not guaranteeing satisfaction, do try to be fair to the customer. There may be many problems in addition to returns, including complaints about products, poor installation, problems with delivery, damaged goods, errors in billing, and so forth.

Complaints and returns can be handled on either a centralized or decentralized basis. Stores with a *centralized policy* handle all issues at a central level in the store; in this way they can be sure that a standardized policy is followed for all departments. In a *decentralized approach,* problems are handled on the sales floor by the person who sold the item, and the customer gets greater personal attention.

Stores normally prefer not to give a cash refund when handling a complaint or return. Most retailers try to get the customer exchanging an item to accept a slip (a due-bill) which allows them to purchase an item at the same price in the future. This policy is designed to keep the customer coming back to the store. Some retailers may feel, however, that the consumer should be given a refund. They believe this better satisfies customers and builds better customer relations.

Stores also have to make a decision in handling complaints and returned merchandise about whether to put the emphasis on the customer or the store. Again, a cost-benefit analysis is required. Providing an elaborate system for handling complaints and returns is costly, especially when the consumer wants money instead of merchandise upon returning an item. Still, stores may be better off viewing returns primarily from the viewpoint of the consumer and generating goodwill by going out of their way to have a liberal returned-goods policy.

These types of policies have problems even under the best of circumstances. For example, what will be the store policy on merchandise returned after Christmas? The merchandise was probably purchased at full price when

Our clientele system requires each salesperson to develop a personal interest in each customer by recording individual taste and merchandise preferences in a clientele book. This record allows the salesperson to use the purchase history to better serve each customer. With this information on file, a customer can keep his/her wardrobe updated without coming into the store. Initiated by Stanley Marcus, the clientele system offers the personalized attention and customer service that make Neiman-Marcus famous.

The *"one fitting room" service* enables the professional salesperson to fulfill all the customer's shopping needs. Creative selling techniques allow everything—from apparel to the appropriate accessories—to be brought to one fitting room.

The travel service, available in most of our stores, will plan an unforgettable itinerary and take care of the details in order to allow the customer the enjoyment and the adventure of the trip.

The Bridal Salon makes that special day perfect by aiding in the selection of the wedding and bridesmaids' gowns, answering questions of etiquette, and personally coordinating all wedding activities.

The bridal registry offers assistance in the selection of the china, silver, and items for the home based on a couple's needs and lifestyle. The registry maintains a record of all gifts purchased for each couple. This is a wonderful way to prevent duplication of wedding gifts.

The Neiman-Marcus restaurants offer a fine selection of delectable foods. Customers enjoy the excellent standard of food service and the opportunity to relax during a hectic shopping day.

Personal shopping services, available to all customers, provide expert fashion advice concerning travel, wardrobe coordination, and gift selections. They specialize in being knowledgeable about merchandise from all areas of the store.

Public relations informs our customers about upcoming events at Neiman-Marcus. They take reservations for fashion shows, coordinate special events, and aid salespeople in communicating with customers.

Mail order is the answer for those who wish to shop by mail. Many mail-order customers have never been to a Neiman-Marcus store, but are well aware of our worldwide reputation and our fine, quality merchandise. Direct mail order, for our charge customers, offers the latest in direct mail literature including catalogues, charge-statement inserts, and special mailers.

The Hosiery Club offers a wide selection of Neiman-Marcus exclusive hosiery and is a wonderful way to stay well-stocked. A predetermined number of pairs is sent to the customer on a specified schedule.

Gift wraps designed for Neiman-Marcus are world famous. Unique and attractive paper, ribbons, and ornaments convey seasonal themes. Often, recipients are as intrigued with the package as they are with the contents.

The alterations department provides expert alterations on all Neiman-Marcus merchandise.

Fur storage is available at all Neiman-Marcus stores. Upon arrival at fur storage, each fur or fur-trimmed garment is thoroughly sterilized. Alterations such as new linings, repair of worn areas, or a total redesign can be done at this time. There is no charge for estimates, and all work is done in our supervised workrooms.

Local delivery service is provided by UPS at all Neiman-Marcus stores. If specific information is needed, check with the receiving department.

it was bought, and the customer probably will bring the merchandise back to the store after Christmas when the store is running an after-Christmas markdown sale. Assuming the person wants cash, should the customer receive the regular price of the merchandise or the sale price at the time the merchandise is returned? Will the store allow consumers to return such items as formal wear or perhaps swimsuits after they have been worn a time or two? Customers have been known to buy formal wear for a special occasion and then return the items the next day for a full refund, even if the merchandise has been smudged or perhaps stained. Many stores exclude made-to-order goods, swimwear, mattresses, bedding, pierced earrings, millinery, and foundations from their return policy for health reasons. Finally, will proof of purchase be required before returned merchandise is accepted?

EVALUATING THE COST-EFFECTIVENESS OF SERVICES

All services offered cost the firm money. Employees may need to be added to offer certain services. The cost must be balanced against anticipated revenues or the loss of goodwill if the services are not offered.

It is not possible to determine precisely the revenue-generating effects of each service. Also, if certain services are offered by competition, the firm may have to offer them to remain competitive.

Many factors must be considered in deciding to offer or discontinue a service. The same is true when the retailer is deciding whether to charge for a service. Let's consider the issue of credit. Management must balance the additional revenue from additional customer sales against the cost of offering credit. For example, interest is lost because the funds are not available to management.

Outside costs of credit include the discounting of receivables such as when a financial institution buys the credit accounts from a retailer at a discount. The advantage to the retailer is that the cash is immediately available and no risks of collection are assumed. Still, the discount paid to get quick access to the funds can result in lower net profit. Other outside costs include the time salesclerks spend in charging a sale to a bank credit card or a travel and entertainment card.

CHAPTER HIGHLIGHTS

—— Many features of a store affect how customers view it and whether they will continue to shop at the outlet. The kind and quality of services are a key factor.

—— Retailers face a variety of decisions in deciding whether to offer credit. They can offer in-store credit or have credit handled by an outside agency such as a bank by honoring bank credit cards. They may also issue a store credit card of their own or have a card with their name on it, but have the bank handle the administrative details. The pressure for retailers to accept bank credit cards is increasing, and most stores now honor them.

— Most types of credit are offered by the retailer at a loss. However, credit normally is a necessary customer service.

— Retailers can offer a variety of other services as part of the customer support mix. These include extended hours and Sunday openings, delivery, services such as baby sitting, interior-design counseling, nonstore shopping opportunities, appliance installation, and an almost endless variety of other services. However, it is important to try to balance likely revenue against the cost of the services.

— Retailers should closely monitor the legal issues relating to many of the services they offer. The laws include, among others, the Equal Credit Opportunity Act, the Fair Debt Collection Practices Act, and the Magnuson-Moss Warranty Act.

KEY TERMS

Basic services Services that customers expect to have available at all retail outlets. An example is free parking.

Blue laws State laws that prohibit retailers from opening on Sundays.

Credit scoring A method used by retailers to screen credit applicants based on various types of personal information about the applicant.

Deferred billing credit A payment plan in which a retailer allows customers to buy goods and to defer payment for an extended period of time with no interest charge.

Disappointers Services offered by a retailer which have a high labor content and return little value to the consumer. An example is layaway.

Equal Credit Opportunity Act Federal legislation which states that a person who is denied credit can demand a written statement of the reasons for denial.

Fair Debt Collection Practices Act Legislation designed to prohibit abusive, deceptive, and unfair debt collection practices by debt collectors.

Installment credit A payment plan in which a customer pays for a product in equal monthly installments, including interest.

Layaway plan A situation in which a customer can make a small deposit which ensures that the retailer will hold the item until the customer is able to pay for it.

Open-charge credit A charge account in which the customer must pay the bill in full when it is due, usually in 30 days.

Patronage builders A classification of services that provide high customer value and can be provided by the retailer at nominal cost. An example is a computerized bridal registry.

Personal shopping service A situation in which a retailer will assemble wardrobes for men and women at their request and have the items ready for inspection when the customer comes to the store.

Private label credit card A credit card that is imprinted with the name of the issuing retail outlet, but for which the administrative details of the credit transaction are handled by a third party such as a bank.

Relationship retailing The process of attracting, retaining, and enhancing customer relationships.

Revolving credit A customer is billed at the end of a month on the basis of an outstanding credit balance.

Support services Services offered by a retailer which directly support the sale of the retailer's merchandise. Examples include home delivery or gift wrapping.

Third-party credit A situation in which a customer uses a card such as Visa or MasterCard to charge merchandise purchased at a retail outlet.

Umbrella shopping card A credit card for which use is restricted to all the stores in a particular shopping area.

DISCUSSION QUESTIONS

1. What might be the major reasons for a retailer to offer selected services? Why are many retailers cutting down on the number of services they offer?
2. Why should a retailer offer a store's own card for credit? What problems or disadvantages exist for a store having its own card?
3. Explain the differences between the following terms: installment credit, open-charge credit, revolving credit, deferred-billing credit, and a layaway plan.
4. Explain the differences among the following terms: bank credit card, private label credit card, umbrella card, and travel and entertainment card.
5. What are some retailers doing to encourage customers to pay cash for purchases?
6. What are some of the methods retailers use to determine to which applicants credit should be extended?
7. What impact does legislation such as the Equal Credit Opportunity Act and the Fair Debt Collection Practices Act have on retail credit operations?
8. What are the advantages and disadvantages of offering customers automatic bill-payment programs?
9. What are some of the things retailers are doing to be more responsive to customers who have special needs?
10. What are the advantages and disadvantages of a centralized versus a decentralized procedure for handling consumer complaints?

APPLICATION EXERCISES

1. Talk to the credit manager at a couple of the local department stores in your community and to the loan officer at a couple of banks to determine how they evaluate customer applications for credit. Try to get a copy of the forms they use, if possible. Find out if they use credit scoring. If not, what do they do in order to be objective in their evaluations? Find out if they are reasonably current on the regulations about granting credit to women.
2. Visit several different types of stores in your community including supermarkets, department stores, and specialty stores. Find out the nature of their check-cashing policies. Specifically, what sorts of identification are required? Check-cashing policies are likely to vary by type of store. Think about the reasons why the policies are different and be prepared to discuss them.
3. Ask for an interview with the credit manager of a large department-type store in your community. Find out the types of credit offered in the store and how the decision whether to extend credit is made. Finally, see if you can get a copy of the credit application form used.
4. Interview a group of students at random and select a department store, supermarket, discount store (e.g., K mart), and national chain like Sears. Develop a list of services the stores might offer (from the text listing). Then have each student check the services which they perceive are offered by each type of store chosen. Write a report on the findings and suggest what they mean to you in terms of the material included in the chapter.
5. Make a list of the key services noted in the chapter. Then make an appointment with managers of the types of stores noted above. Get the impressions of each manager as to the importance of each service and summarize your findings in a brief report. Do you see any trends in the information collected?
6. Discuss with several friends complaints which they may have had against a store or stores. Describe how each was handled by (1) the customer and (2) the store. Evaluate the process you discover in this project.

CASES

1. Japan's Got Us Beat in the Service Department, Too

My husband and I bought one souvenir the last time we were in Tokyo—a Sony compact disk player. The transaction took seven minutes at the Odakyu Department Store, including time to find the right department and to wait while the salesman filled out a second charge slip after misspelling my husband's name on the first.

My in-laws, who were our hosts in the outlying city of Sagamihara, were eager to see their son's purchase, so he opened the box for them the next morning. But when he tried to demonstrate the player, it wouldn't work. We peered inside. It had no innards! My husband used the time until the Odakyu would open at 10 to practice for the rare opportunity in that country to wax indignant. But at a minute to 10 he was preempted by the store ringing us.

My mother-in-law took the call, and had to hold the receiver away from her ear against the barrage of Japanese honorifics. Odakyu's vice president was on his way over with a new disk player.

A taxi pulled up 50 minutes later and spilled out the vice president and a junior employee who was laden with packages and a clipboard. In the entrance hall the two men bowed vigorously.

The younger man was still bobbing as he read from a log that recorded the progress of their efforts to rectify their mistake, beginning at 4:32 P.M. the day before, when the salesclerk alerted the store's security guards to stop my husband at the door. When that didn't work, the clerk turned to his supervisor, who turned to his supervisor, until a SWAT team leading all the way to the vice president was in place to work on the only clues, a name and an American Express card number. Remembering that the customer had asked him about using the disk player in the United States, the clerk called 32 hotels in and around Tokyo to ask if a Mr. Kitasei was registered. When that turned up nothing the Odakyu commandeered a staff member to stay until 9 P.M. to call American Express headquarters in New York. American Express gave him our New York telephone number. It was after 11 when he reached my parents, who were staying at our apartment. My mother gave him my in-laws' telephone number.

The younger man looked up from his clipboard and gave us, in addition to the new $280 disk player,

a set of towels, a box of cakes, and a Chopin disk. Three minutes after this exhausted pair had arrived they were climbing back into the waiting cab. The vice president suddenly dashed back. He had forgotten to apologize for my husband having to wait while the salesman had rewritten the charge slip, but he hoped we understood that it had been the young man's first day.

My Tokyo experience contrasts sharply with treatment I've received at home. In late July, without explanation or apology from Bloomingdale's, a credit of $546.66 appeared on my American Express statement for china ordered January 12, paid for April 17, and never received.

Back in mid-February, the saleswoman who had promised delivery in three weeks knew nothing; it was up to Customer Service to resolve the problem. In Customer Service a Ms. X could tell me nothing either, but took all of the relevant information and said someone would get back to me. "When?" I asked. "In three weeks," she said.

Three weeks and no word from Bloomingdale's. Later, I called Customer Service and asked for Ms. X. I was told that customers cannot request to speak to a particular person in Customer Service, but have to speak to whoever happens to answer their call. How many people were employed in Customer Service? "I can't tell you that," she said. So I recounted my American Express card number, sales slip reference code, date, amount, name, and address and agreed to mail new copies of the paper work to this new person. How long would it take to put this "retracer" on the first "tracer"? "Three weeks."

This time I had the nerve to ask just what could take so much time. "We have to put it through a process," she said. What process? The only description I could elicit was of a labyrinthine, slow internal communications system linking, through shuffling couriers, every video terminal and desk to the Bloomingdale's mailroom. Hoping to be helpful, I offered to deliver the paper work in person. "You can't do that!" she barked. "Customers cannot see anybody in Customer Service."

On May 10, I received a letter from Ms. Y in Merchandise Adjustments, who informed me that I had taken the purchase with me on January 12, and that she hoped this clarified the matter. I looked at the copy of the sales slip she had attached as proof. It was mine, but it wasn't for the china to be delivered. The amounts, reference codes, and sales slip number for the taken merchandise didn't jibe with those of the china in question. The only similarities, in fact, were my name, the date, and the department. I pointed this out to Ms. Y on the phone. She told me to resubmit all of the documentation so she could put it through the "process" once again. Could I deliver it to her in person? "No." But if I insisted, I could leave it at the regular credit window, where it would be routed to her via the mailroom. . . .

Every employee I dealt with implied that it was my fault the store had both my money and the china. I shouldn't have paid my American Express bill, said one. I must have given Customer Service the wrong information, said another.

I'm sure this isn't a problem unique to Bloomingdale's. As I sit here, listening to my compact disk player and eating off my old china a half-year after the ordeal began, I'm struck that buyers in the United States cannot afford to assume a common interest with the seller, but must be ready to take up an adversarial position.

In all the current hysteria over our $37 billion trade deficit with Japan, it is often overlooked that the United States still enjoys a considerable surplus in trade in services with that country. It would be naive to assume this comparative advantage is permanent, however. U.S. and European pressure on Japan to liberalize its economy is drawing it into direct competition with us over this last piece of turf as well. American consumers will eventually turn to the best product (or service). Walter Mondale once warned Americans that the only jobs left for us will be "working at McDonald's and sweeping up around Japanese computers." But no nation can guarantee its people any job, even those.

Questions
1. Compare and contrast the efforts between Odakyu Department Store and Bloomingdale's in responding to a customer problem.
2. What are the elements of customer relationship building which Bloomingdale's could pursue to strengthen its customer support services?
3. Which form of customer service is likely to cost the most in out-of-pocket expenditures? Which one is likely to yield the greatest return on the money invested? Why?

2. Warren's on the Hill

The following situations are real problems faced by Warren's on the Hill, a fine jewelry company located in a major metropolitan area.

Mrs. Peck Is Furious
Tom Davis has been a store manager for 15 years at Warren's on the Hill, a guild jewelry store. His firm was one of approximately four with similar market positioning strategies in a major metropolitan market. His branch was in a high-income area, and his familiarity with the customers was a matter of pride to him. He worked hard at knowing as many as possible of the "regulars."

Recently, Mrs. G. T. Peck came into the store visibly furious. Davis approached her and greeted her as usual, attempting not to recognize her displeasure. (She came in relatively frequently and was considered a "good" customer.) After the greeting, Mrs. Peck lashed out in a virtual monologue—voice shaking; face flushed; words rehearsed!

"Mr. Davis, I can't tell you how mortified I am. My son and his new bride were in the store awhile ago. They had been working in their yard and were in their work clothes. I can tell you they didn't look too terrific. But they came in here with the specific purpose of completing their silver. My daughter-in-law has never been into this store of yours; my son never goes into jewelry stores unless someone pulls him in. My husband and I agreed to buy for them all the pieces they needed for 12 place settings and the serving pieces they needed. Most of their friends don't have sterling, but I think it's important. Well it's important, but I can assure you, neither they nor I will ever set foot in this store again—not any of your snobbish stores! They came in, mind you, with money to buy—a snippy salesperson, without even a courteous greeting, continued working on some forms, and when Cindy said she wanted to discuss an International silver pattern, the salesperson merely handed her a brochure and said, 'All of International's patterns, prices, and descriptions are in this catalog. See if you can find what you want.' Can you imagine? She hardly looked up—only long enough to see two young people very casually attired. You and everyone else carries International silver. Please close my account at once. I shall pay the balance now. I don't want to deal with people who are so rude and thoughtless.''

Michael Overstreet Is Frustrated

Michael Overstreet's wife, Helen, received a lovely 14-karat gold overlay chain with a lifetime guarantee (so the ads say) in a Superior chain box from her aunt for her birthday. Helen was delighted. She had heard of the name and, more importantly, anything which came from Warren's on the Hill had a mystique for her. She knew it wasn't solid gold, but her aunt always gave nice gifts, and in today's market, even overlay probably was expensive. And Superior was, after all, superior!

One evening at dinner at the club, Helen's chain seemed to ''fall apart'' as Michael remembered it. Luckily, Helen's dress had a cowl collar which managed to catch the chain intact—it was all there. Helen was also delighted that she had saved the Superior box and Warren's as well. Mike said he'd drop it off at the store on the way to work the next day.

As usual, Michael was running late. He dropped into Warren's in a rush and hurriedly approached the first salesperson he saw. It was early, and the entire staff appeared to be sleepwalking. Mike explained what had happened; the unsmiling salesperson took the chain in hand, examined it, and said, ''This isn't a Superior chain. And if it isn't, we have no responsibility for the guarantee. The manager is running late, but when he comes in I'll check with him. Can I have your phone number?''

Michael thanked the ''rigid'' salesperson and asked to be called as soon as possible, so that the problem could be solved and Helen satisfied. The salesperson nodded, Mike thought to stay awake. He noticed the salesperson's name as he left. That was fortunate, he thought later, since he received no call from Mr. Davis that day, nor had he received a call two weeks later. Michael called Nancy, the identified salesperson, who said that they were checking and would definitely call.

Three weeks later, Michael Overstreet is frustrated. He has heard that Warren's is top flight. He now wonders. He calls Tom Davis, the store manager, direct. When Mike begins his story, Tom says he has never heard about the problem. He apologizes. Mike thinks something ''smells'' and implies as much to Tom. Mike, who never gets angry, says that Mr. Warren and he are members of the same Rotary Club and have been acquaintances for some years. ''Shall I call Mr. Warren?'' Mike asks Tom Davis.

Mr. Strickland's Wife Is Displeased

Tom Davis wonders how he always ''gets the hard ones.'' Recently Warren's on the Hill ran an ad for their inventory sale—everything in the store was marked down appreciably, and all sales were ''final.'' Tom worked for some time with Strick Strickland whose wife was at La Costa in California shedding those excess pounds, and Strick supposed she was having a miserable time. He wanted to remember his wife on their anniversary when she was away and wanted it to be something important. He was a man who loved a bargain, and when the word *discount* was promoted, he knew that important jewelry pieces were being offered at great savings; he knew the anniversary gift was in hand!

A particularly dramatic (but as Tom admits privately, rather flashy-tacky) necklace was on sale at $3,500, regularly priced at $7,000. Tom did not ''hard sell'' the necklace as he was not at all sure Mrs. S. would like it; she had displayed exquisite taste, he thought, and was typically with her husband when anything important was being purchased. Tom also carefully stressed the final nature of this type of sale.

Mr. Strickland loved the piece and the price. The gift was mailed to La Costa, and then the phone started ringing—at both the Strickland's and Warren's. Mrs. Strickland loved her husband and his thoughtfulness, but she hated the necklace. Mr. Strickland called Tom and said, ''I know what you said about the sale being final, but since I'm such a good customer, I'm sure you'll make an exception in my case.'' Davis said he'd check with management. He did. The buyer said that under no circumstances could any exception be made to the established policy.

Tom wondered if he should call Mr. Warren. What would that do to the decision? Would he tell the buyer to make an exception? Would Mr. Strickland remain a customer under the existing decision? What a problem!

The Bride's Mother Sees Red

Ellen Bright's wedding was a social smash. Her paternal grandparents were ''social register,'' and when Mrs. J.T.V. Bright came into Warren's on the Hill with Ellen to register, Tom Davis, though expecting it, was delighted. It would be a special registration for his store.

Warren's had the kind of clientele which called the store, asked for Tom or one of the ''old timers,'' and placed bridal orders via phone.

Ellen was the kind of bride who had an everyday bone china and a dinner-special occasion china registered; and got lots of each (or expected to!). Her everyday china was Noritake and her good china was Spode.

Aunt Agatha Bright, Ellen's great-aunt, a very important customer for years, called and ordered a place setting of the Spode and was quoted the price of the Noritake by mistake. Agatha paid the billed price when she received it. She thought that she was giving Spode, but was unknowingly paying for Noritake.

Mrs. J.T.V. and Ellen made a date with Tom Davis to "do their exchanges" after the wedding. Everything was going smoothly until Aunt A's gift card, which indicated the place setting of Spode, was checked against the price paid. It was found that indeed she had been quoted the incorrect price and Ellen would be given the Noritake instead.

Ellen and her mother slightly bristled during the episode, but being ladies to the end left after perfunctory thanks. En route to their car, Mrs. Bright said that she was horrified at the behavior of the manager relative to Agatha's gift. Ellen, as always, agreed with her mother. They parted, and each felt the situation had been handled rather shabbily. After all, Warren's had gotten an enormous amount of business from the wedding, and the family had been outstanding customers over the years. It was the store's fault; it was not Agatha's or the bride's.

After hearing the story, Mr. Bright called the store manager, whom he had known for some years, and said they did not like the way the china mistake was handled. Mr. Davis said that he was sorry they felt that way, but after all, Aunt A's gift, regardless of the gift card and her intentions, was only enough for the Noritake. The Brights were not pleased—Tom could feel it.

Feeling a big uncomfortable, Tom called Mr. Warren for an opinion. His conversation with Mr. Warren was in fact a defense of his own actions.

The Decanter Isn't Ours

Sally Grayson was a bride of note, and Warren's on the Hill had registered her silver, china, and crystal. They also had gift items listed. Sally's grandmother was a personal friend of the Warren family and a superb customer. Sally and her husband would make their home within the Hill's market area.

As Sally was showing her grandmother her latest gifts, Granny Grayson noticed that a very attractive decanter was badly chipped. Sally said that she had noted it when the package was opened and that it had come from Warren's on the Hill. Granny said that she was going home via the Hill and would be pleased to drop the broken decanter off at the store. They'd credit the account and Sally wouldn't have to make an extra trip. Grandmother didn't like to see a chipped item displayed!

Mrs. Grayson rushed into the store; deposited the decanter in the Warren box with the gift card in it from Mrs. C. D. Revel at the service desk; asked that their account be credited; and departed. Tom Davis was in the vicinity of the desk and when Granny departed, went over to see what was being returned. When the decanter was being unwrapped and observed, Davis knew immediately that it was not from Warren's. He at least suspected where it had come from; Mrs. Revel was not a customer of Warren's, at least not a charge customer. He did not know her; none of the salespeople knew her.

Rita Smart, noticing the activity at the service desk, walked over and said, "That decanter is being featured at Service Merchandise right now; there must be thousands of them in stock. It's really a good buy at $10. Why is it here?"

Tom's suspicions were verified. He asked Rita to call Mrs. Revel and inquire about the decanter. When Mrs. Revel heard Rita say that she was calling from Warren's about a decanter, Mrs. Revel immediately hung up.

Here was Tom Davis standing with a $10 decanter which had been returned by an outstanding customer who wanted her account credited, and the gift hadn't even been purchased at Warren's. Decision time!

ENDNOTES

1. Len L. Berry and Larry B. Gresham, "Relationship Retailing," *Business Horizons,* November–December 1986, p. 43.

2. Ibid., p. 46.

3. "Staying Close to Your Customers," *Chain Store Age, General Merchandise Trends,* January 1987, pp. 20–21.

4. Albert D. Bates and Jamie G. Didion, "Special Services Can Personalize Retail Environment," *Marketing News,* April 12, 1985, p. 13.

5. Hirotaka Takeuchi and John A. Quelch, "Quality Is More than Making a Good Product," *Harvard Business Review,* July–August 1983, pp. 139–45.

6. Larry Forester, "Service Ain't What It Used to Be," *Chain Store Age, General Merchandise Trends,* January 1987, p. 5; "Pul-eeze! Will Somebody Help Me?" *Time,* February 2, 1987, pp. 48–57.

7. "Should You Go for the Gold?" *U.S. News & World Report,* January 19, 1987, p. 67.

8. For further reading, see Jules Abend, "Making Plastic Pay," *Stores,* February 1986, pp. 43–46.
9. Ibid.
10. See David P. Schultz, "Plastic Practices," *Stores,* October 1986, pp. 34–39.
11. For further reading, see "Sears' Discover Card Starts to Find Its Way," *Business Week,* September 15, 1986, p. 166; Steve Weiner, "Sears' Discover Passes a Hurdle to Introduction," *The Wall Street Journal,* August 5, 1985, p. 5; "Dayton-Hudson Signs Pact for Discover Card," *Chain Store Age Executive,* November 1985, p. 12; "Discover Launches Early," *Chain Store Age Executive,* February 1986, p. 39; "Sears Credit Card Goes National—With Clout," *Stores,* February 1986, pp. 50–51.
12. For further reading, see "Coping with Growing Personal Bankruptcies," *Stores,* April 1986, p. 47.
13. "London's Harrod's Department Store," *Sales and Marketing Management,* January 13, 1986, p. 83.
14. See "Career Dressing," *Stores,* January 1987, pp. 51–56.
15. "Move over, Julia Child," *Chain Store Age Executive,* September 1986, pp. 180–82.

PART 6

Evaluating Competitive Actions

By this point in the text you have been exposed to the environmental factors affecting the development of strategy, issues in selecting markets in which to compete, methods for securing the resources necessary to compete, and ways of using the retailing mix variables for competitive advantage.

Chapter 20 reviews the essence of retail control systems as a way of measuring actual performance against planned performance. Chapter 21 reviews the importance and contents of an accounting system for retailers. A good accounting system can solve problems of cash flow, can assist in taking timely discounts on merchandise, and can signal problems within the firm before they become difficult to address.

20

Evaluation of Merchandise and Expense Planning: Control

RETAILING CAPSULE
Inventory Tracking

"Less expensive PCs and more versatile, easier-to-use software packages are making automation—and specifically inventory management systems—increasingly attractive to the medium-size and smaller specialty store."

In the opinion of experts, these retailers have no choice but to get on with inventory planning and control. There is no other way to compete with the "giants." For the fearful retailer who feels the store is too small or management not adept enough to use these tools in-house, the alternative is to utilize a service organization to provide timely information.

In the recent past, the number of companies offering software for inventory tracking and automatic balancing (replenishing based on forecasting demands) has grown significantly. PC-based point-of-sale capability to tie in is becoming increasingly available. The retailers must take the initiative now. A spokesman for a big eight accounting firm says, "In the next economic downturn, retailers who have inventory management under control through automated systems are going to have a substantially better chance of surviving than those who haven't." He believes that firms with automated systems that can track inventory are much more sensitive to changes in the marketplace and to their inventory levels. It is clear that these merchants can move quickly to adjust to these changes—more quickly than those who do not have such assistance. He further states that retailers so prepared will be able to do much more aggressive pricing and

Based on Jules Abend, "Inventory Watch," *Stores*, August 1985, pp. 25–29.

promotion. The less prepared competitors will be floundering.

A good merchandise planning and control system allows the retailer to monitor what's going on so that better decisions can be made to attain a productive investment in inventory (i.e., not too much or too little).

*T*he foregoing capsule stresses the importance of merchandise management to competitive survival in today's marketplace. The capsule focuses on existing technology which assists in monitoring the management process. Automation is significant to sophisticated management activity, but this chapter places more emphasis on the basics of the control of merchandise and expense management. We are interested primarily in the evaluation of planning activities through the control efforts, however maintained. Planning, discussed in detail in Chapter 12, was presented as an effort to obtain competitive advantages in the marketplace. The merchandise and expense budgets were noted as key plans utilized by management to reach specific objectives. This chapter is a companion to the Chapter 12 material since it approaches the evaluation of these plans to achieve certain objectives. Planning is useless unless retailers monitor operating results to determine whether goals are being met. If plans are not being followed, corrective action must be taken to improve the situation. The monitoring process is the *control* aspect of retail management. Without control, planning is wasted effort.

After reading this chapter, you will be able to:

1. Explain the relationship between planning and control.

2. Illustrate how to establish a dollar control and open-to-buy system to control dollar merchandise investment.

3. Explain unit control of inventory investment.

4. Understand expense control.

THE RELATIONSHIP BETWEEN
PLANNING AND CONTROL

The relationship between planning and control is essential, direct, and two-way. As shown in the following diagram, control records are needed to develop plans. And once a plan is developed, control records are needed to determine how well the retailer is doing.

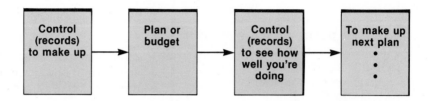

In Chapter 12, the merchandise plan was discussed in terms of developing the following aspects of stock balance: (1) dollars, (2) width, and (3) support. A merchandise budget in dollars and a model stock were developed for planning the width and support factors. In this chapter, attention is given to the systems used to control these aspects of the merchandise plan. Figure 20–1 illustrates the relationships between the merchandise planning and control systems.

Note from Figure 20–1 that two systems are used for controlling the merchandise plan. **Dollar control** is the way of controlling dollar investment

FIGURE 20–1   FROM PLANNING TO CONTROL

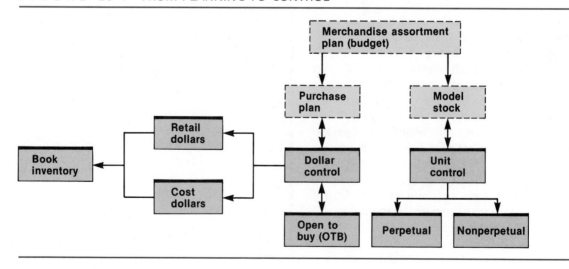

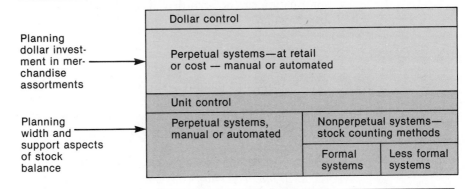

in inventory. **Unit control** is used to control the width and support aspects of stock balance. Figure 20–2 shows how these two types of control—dollar and unit—work together.

Dollar Merchandise Inventory Control

Dollar control is important to retail management as a way of controlling dollar investment in inventory. To control dollar inventory investments, the retailer must know the following:

1. The beginning dollar inventory.
2. What has been added to stock.
3. How much inventory has moved out of stock.
4. How much inventory is now on hand.

A more detailed statement appears later in this section. But the following illustration shows the basic facts that the retailer must know to control dollar inventory investments.

1.	Inventory at the beginning of the period	$10,000
+2.	Total additions to stock	2,000
=	Available for sale during the period	$12,000
−3.	Total deductions	2,500
=4.	Inventory at the end of the period	$ 9,500

To determine the value of inventory at the end of the period (4 in the illustration above), the retailer may (1) take a *physical inventory* (actually count all of the inventory on hand) or (2) set up a **book inventory** *or perpetual inventory system*. It is impractical to take a physical inventory every time the manager wants to know how much inventory is on hand. Thus, retailers set up a book inventory system. This enables them to know the dollar value of inventory on hand without having to take a physical inventory.

To have efficient and effective dollar control, a book inventory system is needed. Information must be collected and recorded continually. The information can be recorded in retail dollars or in cost dollars, manually or by computer.

Retail Dollar Control

Figure 20–3 includes the typical items in a retail-dollar control system. The system is a perpetual one and provides answers to the following questions:

What dollar inventory did the retailer start with? The BOM (beginning of month) inventory dated 3/1 gives the answer to this question. This March BOM inventory figure is the EOM (end of month) February figure.

What has been added to stock? The additions to stock are purchases, transfers, and additional markups which add dollars to the beginning inventory.

How much inventory has moved out of stock? The deductions from stock are sales, markdowns, and employee discounts, which reduce the total dollars of inventory available for sale.

How much inventory is on hand now? The EOM inventory, dated 3/31, is the difference in what was available and what moved out of stock. This is the book inventory figure.

The explanations in Figure 20–3 should be studied carefully since it is important to fully understand the items that affect retail book inventory. The information in Figure 20–3, however, should not be confused with an accounting statement (discussed in Chapter 21, "Evaluation through an Accounting System"). The information in Figure 20–3 comes from accounting data, but it is for control purposes only.

Note in Figure 20–3 the notation "including shortages" at the end of the illustration. Since these are "book" figures, a chance for error exists. The only way to determine the accuracy of the book figure is by taking a physical inventory.

The retail book figures indicate the value of on-hand inventory to be $9,300. Assume that when a physical inventory is taken, the retail value of on-hand stock is $9,000. This situation represents a **shortage** of $300. Shoplifting, internal theft, short shipments from vendors, breakage, and clerical error are common causes of shortages. If, on the other hand, the physical inventory had indicated the value of stock on hand to be $10,000, then the retail classification has incurred an **overage** of $700. In retailing, an overage situation is usually caused by clerical errors or miscounts.

Open-to-Buy

One of the most valuable outputs of a retail dollar control system is **open-to-buy** (OTB) (see Figure 20–1). OTB exists to "control" the merchant's utilization of the planned-purchase figure (see Chapter 12, section on planned purchases). Dollar control provides the essential information to set up an OTB system. These essentials are the BOM and EOM inventories.

If we assume the following, OTB as of February 15 can be illustrated:

Items Affecting Dollar Value of Inventory during Month				Necessary Explanations of Certain Items	Where Do You Get the Information
BOM inventory, 3/1			$10,000		EOM February inventory
Additions to stock:					
Purchases	$2,000				Purchase records or invoices
Less—vendor returns	(100)			Goods go back to resource	Vender return records
Net purchases		$1,900			
Transfers in		$ 200		In multistore firm goods transfer from one store to another	Interstore transfer forms in multistore firm
Less—transfers out		(100)			
Net transfers in		100			
Additional markups		300		Price increase after goods in stock	Price change forms
Total additions			2,300		
Total available for sale			$12,300		
Deductions from stock:					
Gross sales	$2,500				Daily sales report
Less—customer returns	(100)				Return forms
Net sales		$2,400			
Gross markdowns	$ 500			Reduction from original price	Price change forms at start of a sale
Less—markdown cancellations	(100)				Price change cancellation at end of sale to bring prices back to regular
Net markdowns		400			
Employee discounts		200		Employee pays less than merchandise price	Form completed at sale
Total deductions from stock			$ 3,000		
EOM inventory, 3/31 (Including shortages)			$ 9,300	A book inventory figure so actual amount is somewhat different (physical inventory necessary for actual)	Derived figure from additions and deductions from BOM inventory

Planned purchases = $25,000 (*EOM February or BOM March at retail*)
+ 2,500 (*Planned sales—February*)
+ 600 (*Planned reductions—February*)
= $28,100 (*Dollars needed*)
− 24,000 (*BOM February at retail*)(*EOM January*)
= $ 4,100 (*Planned purchases*)

Commitments against
  planned purchases
  during the month of
  February:
On order to
  be delivered
  in February: $1,000
Merchandise
  received as of
  February 15: $1,500 − 2,500 (*Commitments against planned purchases*)
OTB as of February 15 = $1,600 (*Note: The $1,600 figure is in retail dollars and must be converted to cost to use as a buying guide in the market.*)

As illustrated above, OTB is determined by deducting from planned purchases "commitments" which have been made. The two commitments are: (1) merchandise on order that has not been delivered and (2) merchandise that has been delivered. Remember, planned purchases relate to *one* particular month (in the case above, to February). So, OTB relates to only one month. If, for example, merchandise was ordered in January to be delivered in March, that amount would not be a February commitment and would not affect OTB for February.

FIGURE 20–4 EXAMPLE OF AN OPEN-TO-BUY REPORT

Open-to-buy report (1)	Department (2)	(3)	(4)	Classification (5)	(6)	Date prepared (7)	February 15 (8)
Last month (January)							
Sales		**Stock**				**Sales**	
Actual last year	Adjusted plan this year	Actual this year	Adjusted plan EOM this year	Actual EOM this year	Actual last year	Adjusted plan this year	Month to date this year
				24,000		2,500	

From the illustration, one can see that as of February 15, the buyer has $1,600 (in retail dollars) to spend for merchandise to be delivered in February. At the beginning of any month with no commitments, planned purchases and OTB are equal. Assume, however, that by February 20 all of the OTB has been used up and that, in fact, the buyer has overcommitted by $100. This situation is called "overbought" and is not a good position to be in. This leads to another point that must be made about OTB.

OTB must be used only as a guide and must not be allowed to actually dictate decisions to the merchant. A merchant, however, always wants to have OTB to take advantage of unique market situations. The system must also allow for budget adjustments. If the buyer needs more OTB for certain purposes, management must be convinced. This can be done by: (1) convincing management of the importance of a contemplated purchase and obtaining a budget increase for planned sales; (2) increasing planned reductions or taking more markdowns than have been budgeted; or (3) increasing the planned EOM inventory in anticipation of an upswing in the market. Each of these is a legitimate merchandising option and indicates that the OTB control system is flexible, as any budget control system must be.

Figure 20–4 presents a sample open-to-buy report form. Of course, this form would vary by company based on what the retailer feels is needed for decision making. By using this form, OTB could be derived by: *Column* 11 + *Column 7* + *Column 14* − *Column 5* = *Planned purchases* − *Column* 17 = *OTB* (*Column* 18). (Figures from prior example.)

Cost Dollar Control

Retail dollar control is used more often than cost dollar control. The major problem in using cost versus retail control is "costing" each sale. Costing means converting retail dollars to cost dollars after a sale has been made.

(9)	(10)	(11)	(12)	(13)	(14)	(15)	(16)	(17)	(18)
This month (February)									
Stock				Markdowns				On order to be received and received to date	Open-to-buy
Balance of month this year	Actual EOM last year	Adjusted plan EOM this year	Actual as of this report	Actual last year	Adjusted plan this year	Actual as of this report	Balance of month this year		
		25,000			6,000			2,500	1,600

FIGURE 20–5 PERPETUAL COST DOLLAR CONTROL

Date	BOM Inventory	Cost of Items Received	Cost of Items Sold	Net Change
March 1	$15,000	$1,500	$1,000	+ $ 500 ($1,500 − $1,000)
March 2	15,500	—	2,000	− 2,000
March 3	13,500	400	1,200	− 800 (+ $400 − $1,200)
March 4	12,700			

Because of this costing problem, a cost dollar control system is used only when (1) merchandise is of an unusually high unit value and (2) there are relatively few transactions. With merchandise such as furniture or automobiles, cost-dollar control is practical. However, for merchandise classifications such as our sweat suit illustration, retail dollar control is used. Figure 20–5 shows the kind of information needed for a perpetual cost control system. When using a cost dollar control system, it is not possible to record additional markups and reductions such as markdowns and employee discounts, because all of the figures are in cost dollars.

Unit Merchandise Inventory Control

Unit control is the system used to control the width and support aspects of stock balance (see Figures 20–1 and 20–2). Unit control is simpler than dollar control since fewer factors affect units than affect dollars invested. The difference is that the price changes do not affect units carried. As Figures 20–1 and 20–2 indicate, the two types of unit control are perpetual and nonperpetual (or stock-counting) systems.

Perpetual Unit Control

Perpetual unit control, like perpetual dollar control, is a book inventory. Figure 20–6 provides an illustration of perpetual unit control.

Note in Figure 20–6 the notation "including shortages," which appears at the end of the illustration. As with dollar control, this is a book figure; thus, there is chance for error. Again, the only way to determine the accuracy of the book figure is to take a physical inventory. The concepts of shortages and overages apply here just as they do in dollar control. The only difference is that shortages and overages are expressed in terms of number of units rather than in dollars.

A perpetual book inventory for unit control is the most sophisticated of the unit systems. Since perpetual book systems require continuous recording of additions and deductions from stock, they are expensive to operate and involve a great deal of paperwork. The technology of point-of-sale systems offers great potential. It costs less and saves time in collecting the information needed for a perpetual unit control system. If the system is *manually* maintained, sales information can be recorded by:

FIGURE 20–6 ILLUSTRATION OF PERPETUAL UNIT CONTROL—SWEAT SUITS—FOR MONTH OF MARCH

BOM inventory			1,000
Additions to stock:			
Purchases	250		
Less—vendor returns	(40)		
Net purchases		210	
Transfers in	41		
Less—transfers out	(20)		
Transfers in		21	
Total additions			231
Total available for sale			1,231
Deductions from stock:			
Gross sales	225		
Less—customer returns	(8)		
Net sales		217	
Total deductions from stock			217
EOM inventory, 3/31 (including shortages)			1,014

1. Writing on a sales check and having the information recorded in the back office.
2. Detaching a part of a sales ticket to be counted later.
3. Deducting items sold from a tag on a floor sample.

Nonperpetual Unit Control

Nonperpetual unit control systems are also called stock-counting methods. These include *formal* and *less formal* systems.

Stock-counting systems are *not* book-inventory methods. Thus, the retailer will not be able to determine shortages or overages since there is no book inventory against which to compare a physical inventory.

Formal systems. The requirements of *formal, nonperpetual systems* are:

1. A planned model stock.
2. A periodic counting schedule.
3. Definite, assigned responsibility for counting.

The tie classification is an example. Every tie in stock might be counted once a month. The retailer might select the first Tuesday of each month for the count schedule. Based on the stock on hand, the stock on order, and the stock sold, the buyer will place a reorder as the information is reviewed each count period. Figure 20–7 is an example of a type of count sheet that might be used.

A nonperpetual system for unit control is actually a compromise. Perpetual control is better and the retailer gets more and better information. But sometimes the benefits simply do not justify the cost. Under certain conditions, however, the formal system that is nonperpetual can work quite successfully. The rate of sale of the items being controlled must be predict-

Department:_____ Classification:_____ Stock number:_____

Item description:_____ Fabric:_____ Style:_____

Design:_____ Cost:_____ Retail:_____ Vendor number:_____

Miscellaneous:_____

Date of count:_____ On hand:_____ On order:_____

Received:_____ Sold:_____

able. For example, the retailer can predict quite well the sales behavior of a seasonal item such as beach towels. The formal system *does* account for items on order (which the less formal system does not). The items controlled by this system should not be of such a fast-moving, fashionable nature that the retailer needs to know the status of stock more often than the periodic count schedule will permit. Of course, the alert merchant will spot-check between count dates to catch any "out of stocks" that occur.

Less formal systems. Some kinds of merchandise can be controlled with a less formal system. If immediate delivery of goods is possible, there is no need to account for merchandise on order. The retailer still must, however, have a planned model stock and a specific time for visually inspecting the stock.

Under this less formal system, there will be a minimum stock level (e.g., shelf level or number of cases in the stockroom) which the stock must not go below. When the stock reaches that level, a reorder is placed. In the canned goods department in a supermarket, this system might be used quite effectively.

Expense Control

The final objective of this chapter is to introduce expense control. In Chapter 12, we discussed the development of the expense plan (budget). As with the merchandise plan, retailers must control the expense plan. They must look at expenses on a routine basis to see how actual expense commitments compare with planned expenses. If differences are found, action can be taken.

An expense report is similar to an open-to-buy report in merchandising. The expense report, however, is referred to as an **open-to-spend report.** An example of an expense control form is presented in Figure 20–8.

FIGURE 20–8

ILLUSTRATION OF OPEN-TO-SPEND REPORT BASED ON EXPENSE BUDGET FOR _____ SEASON FOR _____ CLASSIFICATION*

Expenses†	January	February . . . Total
Plan	$1,000	
Committed	400	
Open-to-spend	600	
Actual at end of month	‡	

* As of January _____
† Other expenses handled similarly.
‡ Actually put in at end of month.

CHAPTER HIGHLIGHTS

— Planning is useless unless retailers monitor operating results to determine whether goals are being met. If plans are not being followed, corrective action must be taken to improve the situation. The monitoring process is the control aspect of merchandise and expense management.

— The relationship between planning and control is essential, direct, and two-way. Control records are needed to develop plans, and plans are evaluated by these control data.

— Two systems are used for controlling the merchandise plan: *Dollar control* for controlling dollar investment and *unit control* for controlling the width and support aspects of stock balance.

— To control dollar inventory investments, the retailer must know: (1) the beginning dollar inventory, (2) what has been added to stock, (3) how much inventory has moved out of stock, and (4) how much inventory is now on hand.

— To have efficient and effective dollar control, a book inventory system is needed and can be maintained in retail or cost dollars as well as manually or by computer (automated). Less expensive PCs and more versatile, easier-to-use software packages are making automation (computerization) increasingly attractive to the medium-sized and smaller specialty store.

— One of the most valuable outputs of a retail dollar control system is open-to-buy (OTB) which exists to control the retailer's utilization of the planned purchase figure.

— Retail dollar control is used more often than cost dollar control because of the problems of ''costing'' each sale for the latter system.

— Unit control is the system used to control the width and support aspects of assortments and is simpler than dollar control since fewer factors affect units than affect dollars invested. Price changes do not affect units.

The two types of unit control are perpetual and nonperpetual (or stock-counting systems); the latter can be formal or less formal.

The expense budget demands control just as investment in merchandise. The open-to-spend report is a valuable assistance in this management task.

KEY TERMS

Book inventory Recording of all additions to and deductions from a beginning stock figure to continually have an ending inventory figure. (Also called perpetual inventory.) The book inventory must be compared to the actual physical inventory to determine shortages or overages.

Dollar control A system for controlling the dollar investment in inventory. To work, the system must record the beginning dollar inventory, what has been added to stock, how much inventory has moved out of stock, and how much inventory is now on hand. Involves perpetually recording additions and deductions at retail or cost.

Nonperpetual unit control (Also called stock-counting methods). This is *not* a book-inventory method. A nonperpetual unit system requires the retailer to have a planned model stock, a periodic counting schedule, and definite, assigned responsibility for counting. The beginning and ending inventories are counted and the differences are the sales (and shortages).

Open-to-buy A control system devised to "control" the retailer's utilization of the planned purchase figure. Dollar control provides the essential component of the system. OTB records the commitments made against the planned purchases amount.

Open-to-spend A report recording commitments against planned expenses for a period.

Overage The physical inventory (either in dollars or units) is larger than the book inventory.

Shortage The physical inventory (either in dollars or units) is smaller than the book inventory.

Unit control System used to control the width and support aspects of stock balance. The system records (perpetual) beginning inventory and all additions and deductions to stock to obtain the ending inventory. (See Nonperpetual unit control for the other system in use.)

DISCUSSION QUESTIONS

1. Explain the relationship between *planning* and *control*.
2. What is dollar control? What is its value to retail management?
3. What is the relationship between dollar control and book inventory?
4. Distinguish between *shortages* and *overages*. How are they determined?
5. Explain open-to-buy. How can a buyer who is "overbought" make adjustments to get more open-to-buy? Why should a retailer always attempt to have open-to-buy available?
6. What is the major problem faced in cost dollar control (versus retail)? When is a retailer likely to use cost dollar control?
7. Compare the mechanics of maintaining a dollar versus a unit control system.
8. Compare the formal and less formal systems of nonperpetual unit control systems. Can a retailer determine shortages in a nonperpetual unit control system? Explain your answer.
9. What is the difference between an "open-to-buy" report and an "open-to-spend" report?

PROBLEMS

1. Given the following data for a certain department as of June 10, calculate (*a*) planned purchases and (*b*) open-to-buy:

Planned sales for the month	$47,000
Planned reductions for the month	1,500
Planned EOM inventory	52,550
Planned BOM inventory	47,800
Merchandise received to date for June	14,980
Merchandise on order, June delivery	6,850

2. The following data are for a certain department as of January 20. Calculate (a) planned purchases and (b) open-to-buy:

Planned sales for the month	$142,000
Planned BOM inventory	177,000
Planned reductions for the month	4,200
Planned EOM inventory	165,000
Merchandise received to date for January	130,000
Merchandise on order, January delivery	4,200
Merchandise on order, February delivery	2,000

3. Given the following data for a certain department as of September 20, calculate (a) planned purchases and (b) open-to-buy:

Planned sales for the month	$ 9,200
Planned reductions for the month	100
Planned BOM inventory	14,600
Planned EOM inventory	15,500
Merchandise received to date for September	9,800
Merchandise on order, September delivery	500

4. Given the following information for the month of July, calculate (a) planned purchases and (b) open-to-buy:

Planned sales for the month	$27,000
Planned reductions for the month	650
Planned EOM inventory	36,000
Stock-sales ratio for July	1.5
Merchandise received to date for July	13,800
Merchandise on order, July delivery	5,250

5. Find open-to-buy for March given the following figures:

Stock on hand, March 1	$72,500
Planned stock on hand, April 1	80,000
Merchandise on order for March delivery	49,875
Planned sales for March	63,500

6. Given the following information for November, calculate open-to-buy (a) at retail and (b) at cost:

Planned sales for the month	$24,600
Planned reductions for the month	300
Planned EOM retail stock	32,300
Planned BOM retail stock	30,800
Merchandise received for the month of November	16,300
Merchandise on order, November delivery	4,000
Merchandise on order, December delivery	2,575
Planned initial markup at retail	35%

7. Given the following information for August, calculate open-to-buy (a) at retail and (b) at cost:

Planned sales for the month	$57,000
Planned reductions for the month	1,200
Planned EOM retail stock	72,000
Stock-sales ratio for the month of August	1.2
Planned initial markup at retail	42%
Merchandise received for the month of August	35,000
Merchandise on order, August delivery	16,400

APPLICATION EXERCISES

1. If you have a friend who is a retailer, make an appointment with that person and ask to see: (a) the types of controls which are used in the store and (b) what they are used for. Report your findings to the class.
2. Visit a local grocery store. See if they have "scanning" equipment at the checkout. If they do, ask to see the manager and tell that person you are a student and want to ask him/her a few questions. Design your questions so you can find out if information received from the new equipment is being used for control. If not, what is it being used for?
3. If you can, find a person who sells to retailers. Ask that person what he or she knows about retailers' "open-to-buy." Report your findings to your class.
4. Make an appointment with a merchandising executive at a department store or rather large specialty store in your community. Ask to be allowed

to see the forms used to prepare the dollar control, open-to-buy, perpetual inventory, and unit control figures. If possible, ask the executive to let you have a "real" report for a past season and trace through all the procedures discussed in this chapter. The forms may differ a bit, but the information obtained will be quite similar. It is difficult to arrange such a project. If you know someone to contact, it is advisable. The retailer will be helpful if you make it clear it is for learning purposes. Remember, a person always likes to talk about his or her business!

CASES

1. What Should Joe Do about Dollar Control?

Joe Williams has recently been hired as assistant buyer for menswear in Oak's Department Store. Oak's is actually a limited-line, junior department store, located in a new community mall in a medium-sized southern city. The downtown store was recently closed, and plans for a new branch in another planned mall are on the drawing boards.

For three years, Williams had worked as assistant store manager of Beck's, a small, family-owned men's store in the deteriorating downtown area. He had previous, similar experience for two years at another downtown men's store. Virtually all the stores in the central business district have either branched to shopping centers or closed their downtown sites and moved to a center, making, in effect, the mall store their "main" store.

Ransom Reese, the buyer for Oak's men's department, has run the store's profitable men's area for over 30 years. Ransom, as he admitted, "ran the whole show out of his hip pocket." Future plans for expansion and Reese's age caused management to insist that an assistant be hired in the large department, which included furnishings, clothing, and sportswear. Ran had never been interested in clas-

sification merchandising; he did not have any real controls, either dollar or unit. The controller of Oak's was pushing to put in some systems.

Joe's first assignment was to prepare the department for classification or dissections and to make a report within a month as to what would be needed to set up a unit control system for each established classification. Reese didn't know much about dollar control, he had no open-to-buy, even though some departments were experimenting with the system. Ran asked Joe to make a recommendation about that, too, since he was working on all the merchandise.

Joe was somewhat shocked and frightened. He had been good at personnel relations in his prior jobs, and he kept a neat, clean store! But this—he was beside himself and really didn't know where to start.

Questions
1. Advise Joe carefully and make his job easier.
2. Prepare the report and recommend what should be done about dollar control.

2. An Overage in Fashion Fabrics

Bart Crowder was facing his first inventory since having been made manager of the fashion fabrics department. He had been warned that once you have gone through an inventory in fabrics, you'll never forget it. How correct!

Bart reflected on the enormous technological advances that had been made to assist in keeping good records at the point of sale and beyond, and about how sophisticated the inventory control systems, both in dollars and units, were throughout the store. But in fabrics—it was impossible. His company had not gone to wanding for input at the point of sale,

but the electronic cash registers (ECRs) were capable of doing some remarkable things in the future. His department did have an ECR, and he had rather good dollar-control data for his OTB and dollar-inventory information. Instinctively, however, he knew that something was not right with his EOM inventory statements, and thus his profit.

Bart's first inventory had been a disaster, and as he thought about it, the question of what should have been done was still haunting him. First of all, two weeks before the inventory date (the Wednesday evening, after store closing, when the entire store's inventory would be taken) the sales staff began counting all yardage and tagging the bolts or rolls with the number of yards on them. When a sale was made from a tagged bolt, the salesperson was supposed to deduct the number of yards sold from the "counted amount." Since Bart had never done an inventory in fabrics before, he pitched in and counted, tagged, and sold-deducted when his managerial duties allowed such activities. He found himself frustrated at the system. The task of using a measuring machine and counting all the yards on a bolt or roll was bad enough, but rerolling and tagging was so time-consuming. As his frustration grew, he began watching the salespeople, particularly the part-timers, and found some interesting situations. On occasion he saw a salesperson say that a particular bolt of cloth did not have enough material on it to bother with the tedious job ahead. He also noted that often, after a sale was made, the clerk failed to deduct the yardage sold from the tag.

Bart also observed a condition which he thought was sheer insanity—but he found out that it was store policy. For out-of-season goods stored in a remote stock area, counts had to be made in advance of the two-week inventory-counting period, as some of these goods were stocked in large quantities and the floor stock was almost too much to count in the time allotted. Bart was a sales-oriented person, and it disturbed him to see the obvious customer inconvenience during the counting period. But he was tremendously frustrated when he heard a salesperson say to a customer who wanted an item in the stockroom, "I'm sorry, but that material has been counted for inventory and cannot be sold until after the inventory date." Bart was told by store management that once the stockroom had been completely counted, it was sealed and could not be opened to make a sale. Bart wondered what the marketing concept really meant.

The final inventory debacle occurred some days prior to "the day." A big, preinventory sale was going on. Almost all seasonal fabrics were reduced, and, just to create an atmosphere of excitement, even staples had been reduced. The floor was busy; the ECR was clicking; and customers were walking out with bargains. Fashion fabrics, like almost all departments, was on the retail method of account-

ing. Markdowns were planned and built into the retail deductions from stock. Price change forms were used routinely throughout the store. But the situation in fabrics was different. When Bart assumed the manager's position, he was told that in his department salespeople would tally the yardage of each type of fabric on sale and markdowns would be taken after the sale. The normal procedure is to count items (e.g., dresses) before a sale, take a markdown on all the items, recount the items after the sale, and take a markdown cancellation to bring them back up to the original price. The logistical problem of counting thousands of yards before and after a sale was insurmountable; consequently, the system of tallying was used. Bart watched the process during the busy preinventory sale and saw salespeople forget to tally, and then estimate later in the day or forget it altogether.

Knowing something about recordkeeping and retail accounting, Bart became frightened about his first inventory. If the markdowns were not taken properly, it was obvious his department would show a large shortage when the physical inventory was taken. What to do? Bart decided to take the clerks' tallies and double the amount they recorded. After all, he had observed the procedures of his people and felt that this decision would be wise and make his operation look much healthier.

Inventory day came and went. The physical counts and the operating statements were available for analysis. The fashion fabrics department showed a very large overage. Bart was speechless. Management was not pleased. Yes, he'd never forget his first inventory.

Question

1. As an outside observer, note all the problems you see in the situation just described. What kinds of technological innovations could have helped? Given the circumstances and the systems of his store, was Bart wrong to do what he did? Why was management not pleased? How would you have explained the overage to management? Check with fabric retailers, and see whether these problems are normal. What is being done to overcome such conditions?

21

Evaluation of Perfor-mance through an Accounting System

RETAILING CAPSULE

Strategies for Success in Department Store Retailing

The department store—"She ain't dead yet," says James Zimmerman, chairman of Atlanta-based Federated division, Rich's. This firm is one of the few companies in the department store sector which has not only survived the long series of closings in the industry but has also managed to be profitable.

As the retailing world has been rocked by news of the departure from the scene of such department stores as Gimbel's, Alexander's, and Orbach's in New York, the attention of the critics has been on such "winners" as Rich's, Bloomingdale's, Macy's, and Little Rock-based Dillard's. Dillard's has been de-scribed by Merrill Lynch as "a growth com-pany in a maturing industry."

The success of the firms noted above prompted *Fortune* to address the reasons for the success of the winners—those organiza-tions who are beating back competition from specialty shops and are learning to put excite-ment into the humdrum business of shopping. The following strategies were cited as being common to those firms:

— *Find a strong chief executive.* Analysts cite strong chairmen like Macy's Edward Finkel-stein, Bloomingdale's Marvin Traub, and the Nordstrom family in Seattle.
— *Invest in computers.* Dillard's built a cen-tralized, $20 million computer system that links 115 stores (at the time of writing) and tracks all operations including inventory from the point of sale.

Based on Anthony Ramirez, "Department Stores Shape Up," *For-tune,* September 1, 1986, pp. 50–52.

— *Buy out competitors.* Because of dwindling locations due to sluggish shopping-center construction throughout the nation, acquiring weaker rivals is a common way to gain new locations.

— *Develop a clear image.* Sears is still having trouble because of a "fuzzy" image, while Bloomingdale's is clearly the "yuppie emporium" and doing well.

— *Build medium-size stores and fill them with strong departments.* The successful department stores concentrate on high margin and rapid turnover. Wallets and wristwatches, for example, move faster than dishwashers and provide better markups while taking up less space.

— *Spend money on staff.* Dillard's has saved money with their computers and has hired more and better-trained salespeople.

— *Change displays monthly and remodel the entire store every three to five years.* The *Fortune* investigation ends by stating flatly that the "biggest single problem in America is boredom. That's why people shop."

*U*nderlying the strategies for success in retailing is a need for performance appraisal leading to action. In the previous chapter we addressed control information necessary to take proper action relative to merchandise and expenses. We indicated that the tracking data came from the accounting function of the organization. In this chapter we focus entirely on that accounting function as it relates to actions taken not for control purposes but for appraisal of the firm's profitability.

After reading this chapter, you will be able to:

1. Review the key financial statements.

2. Utilize the strategic profit model (SPM) as a framework for monitoring performance results.

3. Explain how inventory turnover affects profitability (performance) by utilizing the concept of gross margin return on inventory investment.

4. Examine the problems that management faces in determining the cost and value of merchandise inventory.

5. Understand the accounting practices that assist management in value decisions.

KEY FINANCIAL STATEMENTS

The balance sheet, the income statement, and the various ratios derived from them give management the information needed to evaluate the effectiveness of strategy in financial terms.

The Balance Sheet

Figure 21–1 lists the components of the **balance sheet**—assets (**current** and **fixed**), liabilities, and net worth. The simplest expression of the balance sheet equation is: Assets = Liabilities + Net worth. Net worth is the owners' claim on the assets of the business—that is, the owners' investment or equity. Figure 21–2 is an example of a balance sheet.

The Income Statement

While the balance sheet is a snapshot of a business's financial health on a specific date, the **income statement** is more like a moving picture of the firm's financial performance over time. The income statement shows whether investments in assets and the implementation of strategy were successful during a particular time period. (See Figure 21–3.)

Analysis of this statement shows (1) how much gross margin was made ($85,645), (2) how much was spent on total expenses ($70,655), and (3) how much profit (after taxes) has been made ($10,040). *Gross margin* is the difference between net sales and cost of goods sold. Cost of goods sold is computed as follows:

> Beginning inventory
> \+ Purchases
> = Goods available for sale
> − Ending inventory
> = Cost of goods sold

Notice that the key elements of the income statement are also stated in percentages. For example, the gross margin percentage is calculated by dividing gross margin dollars by net sales dollars (or $85,645 divided by $192,300 = 44.54 percent). Percentages help the manager compare present performance with performances (1) in prior periods or (2) of similar stores.

Information from the income statement assists the manager in making any adjustments deemed necessary. For example, if expenses are higher than in the past and higher than in similar stores, the manager may decide that corrective action is needed. In general, the income statement is a valuable tool for measuring the results of operations.

THE STRATEGIC PROFIT MODEL

The second purpose of this chapter is to utilize the **strategic profit model** (**SPM**) as a framework for monitoring performance results. The SPM is

Assets What the business itself owns.	**Liabilities** This side of the balance sheet shows the claims on the assets by both creditors and owners of the business. The claims of creditors are debts of the business—the *liabilities*. The owners' claim is their investment in the business—the *net worth*.

Assets
What the business itself owns.

Current assets: In varying states of being converted into cash within the next 12 months.
  Cash: Money on hand, in the bank.
  Accounts receivable: What the customers owe the business for merchandise or services they bought.
  Inventory: Merchandise on hand.

Fixed assets: Used in the operation of the business. Not intended for resale.
  Real estate: Land and buildings used by the business. Listed at original cost.
  Leasehold improvements: Permanent installations—remodeling or refurbishing of the premises.
  Machinery, equipment, vehicles: Used by the business. Listed at original cost.
  Less accumulated depreciation: These assets (except land) lose value through wear, tear, and age. The business claims this loss of value as an expense of doing business. The running total of this expense is the accumulated depreciation.
  Net fixed assets: Cost of fixed assets − Depreciation = Present value.

Liabilities
This side of the balance sheet shows the claims on the assets by both creditors and owners of the business. The claims of creditors are debts of the business—the *liabilities*. The owners' claim is their investment in the business—the *net worth*.

Current liabilities: Debts owed by the business to be paid within the next 12 months.
  Notes payable: IOU bank or trade creditors.
  Accounts payable: IOU trade and suppliers.
  Income taxes: IOU government.

Long-term liabilities: Debts owed by the business to be paid beyond the next 12 months.
  Mortgage: On property.
Net Worth: Owners' (or stockholders') assets of the business; owners' investment; owners' equity in the business.
For proprietorship or partnership:
Owner, capital: Owners' original investment plus any profit reinvested in the business.
For corporation:
Capital stock: Value assigned to the original issue of stock by the directors of the corporation. If the stock sold for more than the assigned value, the excess will show as:

Surplus, paid-in: The difference between the assigned value and the selling price of the original issue of stock. (The subsequent selling price of the stock does not change the assigned value.)
Retained earnings: Profits reinvested in the business *after* paying dividends.

Balance sheet equation: Assets = Liabilities + Net worth

SOURCE: Reprinted with permission from "Understanding Financial Statements," *Small Business Reporter* 7, no. 11, copyright © Bank of America, San Francisco, 1974.

FIGURE 21–2 **BALANCE SHEET DECEMBER 31, 19____**

Assets

Current assets:

Cash	$15,000	
Accounts receivable	24,000	
Merchandise inventory	84,000	
Prepaid expenses	10,000	
Total current assets		$133,000

Fixed assets:

Building	$85,000	
Furniture and fixtures	23,000	
Total fixed assets		108,000
Total assets		$241,000

Liabilities and Net Worth

Current liabilities

Accounts payable	$20,000	
Wages payable	18,000	
Notes payable	32,000	
Taxes payable	5,000	
Interest payable	3,000	
Total current liabilities		$ 78,000

Fixed liabilities

Mortgage payable	$75,000	
Total fixed liabilities		75,000
Total liabilities		$153,000

Net worth

Capital surplus	$80,000	
Retained earnings	8,000	
Total net worth		88,000
Total liabilities and net worth		$241,000

derived from information obtained in the balance sheet and the income statement. The SPM provides the essential ratios for performance evaluation needed here, and is illustrated below:

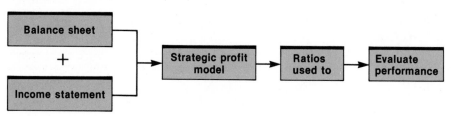

The object of all retailing is to make a profit, but exactly what does "making a profit" mean? Perhaps the most common way to describe profit is net profit after taxes—the bottom line of the income statement. Profit performance is often evaluated in terms of sales volume—that is, profit as a percentage of sales. For stra-

FIGURE 21–3 **INCOME STATEMENT YEAR ENDING DECEMBER 31, 19___**

Gross sales		$208,600	
Less: Returns and allowances		16,300	
Net sales		$192,300	100%
Cost of goods sold:			
Opening inventory	$ 21,650		
Net purchases	113,500		
Goods available for sale		$135,150	
Less: Closing inventory		28,495	
Cost of goods sold		106,655	55.46
Gross margin		$ 85,645	44.54
Expenses:			
Rent	$ 19,400		
Payroll	32,950		
Advertising	8,825		
Insurance	1,475		
Travel	2,160		
Utilities	5,265		
Miscellaneous	580		
Total expenses		70,655	36.74
Profit before taxes		$ 14,990	7.80
Income tax		4,950	2.57
Net profit after taxes		$ 10,040	5.22%

tegic purposes, the most valuable way to view profit, however, is in terms of a return on investment (ROI). So, what does this mean?

The two ways of looking at ROI from a strategic point of view are: (1) return on assets (ROA) and (2) return on net worth (RONW). The ROA reflects all funds invested in a business, whether they come from owners or creditors. The RONW is a measure of profitability for those who have provided the net worth funds—that is, the owners.

Purposes of the SPM

Figure 21–4 diagrams the SPM. Boxes 1 through 5 provide the basic ratios (derived from the key financial statements) which comprise the model. A simple algebraic representation of the model would look like this:

$$\underset{(1)}{\frac{\text{Net profit}}{\text{Net sales}}} \times \underset{(2)}{\frac{\text{Net sales}}{\text{Total assets}}} = \underset{(3)}{\frac{\text{Net profit}}{\text{Total assets}}} \times \underset{(4)}{\frac{\text{Total assets}}{\text{Net worth}}} = \underset{(5)}{\frac{\text{Net profit}}{\text{Net worth}}}$$

Figure 21–4 also indicates the various paths to profitability and indicates what each component of the model measures. Specifically, the SPM:

1. Emphasizes that a firm's principle financial objective is to earn an adequate or target rate of return on net worth (RONW).
2. Provides an excellent management tool for evaluating performance against the target RONW and high-performance trade leaders.
3. Dramatizes the principal areas of decision making—*margin management, asset management,* and *leverage management.* A firm can im-

FIGURE 21–4   THE STRATEGIC PROFIT MODEL

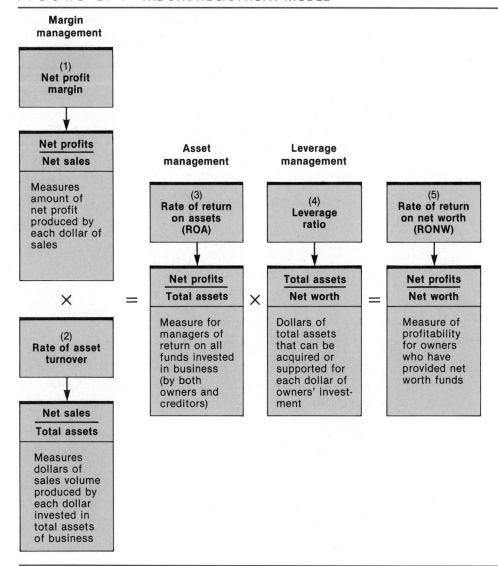

prove its rate of RONW by (1) increasing its profit margin, (2) raising its rate of asset turnover, or (3) **leveraging** its operations more highly.

The Impact of Turnover on Profitability

The concept of turnover (either stock or merchandise) was discussed in Chapter 12 in some detail. The SPM shows that a basic path to profitability is asset management. In this discussion we focus on how inventory turnover affects profitability. *Managing turnover* helps management achieve the return

FIGURE 21–5 AVERAGE ANNUAL TURNOVER BY PRODUCT CLASS OF FOOD
PRODUCT INVENTORIES

Product Class	Average Annual Turnover
Fats and oils	27.3
Condiments/dressings	18.6
Breakfast foods	16.5
Flour, cake mixes, etc.	17.0
Canned goods	14.9
Beverages	12.4
Household products	18.3
Paper products	24.5
Pet foods	22.4

SOURCE: "Inventories and Stock Turns, How Do They Balance?" *The Nielsen Researcher* (Northbrook, Ill.: A.C. Nielsen Company, November 3, 1982), pp. 2–11.

on investment targeted. Through accounting systems, management is able to *monitor turnover* as an evaluation tool for performance. If the performance is less than planned, then corrective action can be taken. (We are not addressing margin or leverage management here. The attention is on asset management.)

To be meaningful, turnover goals must be planned for homogeneous merchandise groupings. Planning for large, diverse categories is unsound. Today's computer technology allows classification planning and thus better turnover information for managing that asset.

No one can say whether a particular turnover figure is good or bad, or whether a particular ratio is efficient. Figures 21–5 and 21–6 indicate average stock turnover rates for various kinds of product classes. They show that turnover goals must be related to a particular operation and that a "raw"

FIGURE 21–6 AVERAGE ANNUAL TURNOVER BY PRODUCT CLASS OF HEALTH AND
BEAUTY AID (HBA) PRODUCTS: FOOD VERSUS DRUG VERSUS MASS
MERCHANDISER

Product Class	Average Annual Turnover		
	Drug	Food	Mass
Remedial products*	3.8	5.3	5.0
Men's products	4.1	5.8	5.4
Women's products	4.4	6.9	6.0
Oral hygiene	6.5	9.9	7.3
Miscellaneous[†]	5.3	10.7	6.6

* Includes multiple vitamins, cold tablets, headache and/or sinus remedies, topical antiseptics, and stomach remedies.

[†] Includes disposable diapers, foot remedies, shampoo, and deodorants.

SOURCE: "Inventories and Stock Turns, How Do They Balance?" *The Nielsen Researcher* (Northbrook, Ill.: A.C. Nielsen Company, November 3, 1982), pp. 2–11.

turnover figure is virtually meaningless. Comparisons within and among the various kinds of businesses illustrate the range of performance results. For example, in Figure 21–5, annual turnover in food products varies from a low of 12.4 for beverages to a high of 27.3 for fats and oils.

Figure 21–6, which shows turnover in health and beauty aids (HBA), illustrates that different types of stores can experience varying turnover rates for the same merchandise line. Oral hygiene products vary from 6.5 turns in drugstores, to 7.3 in mass merchandisers, to 9.9 in food stores. Management in the HBA business can find these figures very useful in targeting turnover goals.

If, for example, management of a food store experienced a turnover of 22.0 on paper products, the performance is below the Nielsen average of 24.5 (Figure 21–5) and might indicate a problem for profitability. The relationship between turnover and profitability is addressed in the following section.

Gross Margin Return on Inventory Investment (GMROI)

Gross margin return on inventory (GMROI) can be stated as follows.

$$\text{GMROI} = \frac{\text{Gross margin dollars}}{\text{Average inventory investment}}$$

This single ratio does not indicate clearly the focus we want to emphasize—that of the important relationship between profit return (margin) and sales-to-retail stock (which is inventory turnover). Consequently, it is more useful to express GMROI as follows:

$$\text{GMROI} = \frac{\text{Gross margin dollars}}{\text{Total sales}} \times \frac{\text{Total sales}}{\text{Average inventory investment}}$$
$$\text{(expressed in retail dollars)}$$

We must emphasize that gross margin return on *retail* inventory investment is *not* a real measure of return on investment because investment is in *cost* dollars. But many retail managers with a planning focus maintain retail book inventory figures. Thus, *retail* value GMROI can be calculated more frequently using the more common and more easily obtainable turnover component. Sales-to-cost inventory ratios are more accurately ROI ratios. In this particular discussion, however, the value of utilizing retail GMROI outweighs the somewhat different terminology. Our intent is to focus on the impact of turnover on profitability; thus, retail value is important.

The value of the turnover and margin components of the GMROI concept can be seen in Figure 21–7. Three hypothetical retail classifications each produce the same GMROI, although they have differing gross margin percentages and turnover components. This indicates the impact that turnover and margin management has on the return on each dollar invested in inventory. For illustration, let's keep the gross margins constant at 40.0 percent and change only the turnover ratios, as in Figure 21–8.

This hypothetical illustration dramatically indicates how turnover can affect profitability and stresses the importance of turnover goals.

FIGURE 21–7 **EXAMPLES OF DIFFERING RETAIL OPERATIONS, MARGINS, AND TURNOVERS RESULTING IN IDENTICAL GMROI**

Type of Store	Gross Margin × (percent)	Turnover = Ratio	GMROI (percent) (retail)
Discount store sport shirt classification	25.0	4.0	100.0
Specialty store sport shirt classification	40.0	2.5	100.0
Department store sport shirt classification	33.3	3.0	100.0

FIGURE 21–8 **EXAMPLES OF IMPACTS IN CLASSIFICATIONS WITH CONSTANT GROSS MARGINS AND VARYING TURNOVER RATES**

Type of Classification	Gross Margin (percent)	×	Turnover Ratio	=	GMROI (percent)
A	40.0		4.0		160.0
B	40.0		2.5		100.0
C	40.0		3.0		120.0

DETERMINING COST AND VALUE OF INVENTORY

The focus of this section is on the importance of merchandise inventory in performance evaluation and the problems that arise in determining its cost and value. The importance of merchandise inventory is reflected in several ways. As previously noted, merchandise inventory is typically the largest current asset on the balance sheet. The cost of merchandise sold, reported on the income statement, is critical in determining gross profit. Thus, an error in determining the inventory figure will cause an equal misstatement of gross profit and net income in the income statement. The amount of assets noted on the balance sheet also will be incorrect by the same amount. The effects of understatements and overstatements of inventory at the end of a period are demonstrated in Figure 21–9, which includes an abbreviated income statement and balance sheet.

Determining Inventory Cost

A major problem in determining inventory cost arises when identical units of a product are acquired over a period of time at various unit cost prices. Consider purchases of sport shirts during the spring season:

	Knit Sport Shirts	Units	Unit Cost	Total Cost
February 1	Inventory	50	$ 9	$ 450
April 15	Purchases	40	13	520
May 1	Purchases	30	14	420
Total		120		$1,390
Average cost per unit				$11.58

Income Statement—19___			Balance Sheet—19___	
Net sales		$200,000	Merchandise inventory	$ 20,000[a]
Beginning inventory	$ 30,000		Other assets	80,000
+ Purchases	110,000		Total	$100,000
= Available for sale	140,000		Liabilities	30,000
− Ending inventory	20,000[a]		Net worth	70,000
= Cost of goods sold		120,000	Total	$100,000
Gross profit		80,000		
− Expenses		55,000		
= Net profit		$ 25,000		
Net sales		$200,000	Merchandise inventory	$ 12,000[b]
Beginning inventory	$ 30,000		Other assets	80,000
+ Purchases	110,000		Total	$ 92,000
= Available for sale	140,000		Liabilities	30,000
− Ending inventory	12,000[b]		Net worth	62,000
= Cost of goods sold		128,000	Total	$ 92,000
Gross profit		72,000		
− Expenses		55,000		
= Net profit		$ 17,000		
Net sales		$200,000	Merchandise inventory	$ 27,000[c]
Beginning inventory	$ 30,000		Other assets	80,000
+ Purchases	110,000		Total	$107,000
= Available for sale	140,000		Liabilities	30,000
− Ending inventory	27,000[c]		Net worth	77,000
= Cost of goods sold		113,000	Total	$107,000
Gross profit		87,000		
− Expenses		55,000		
= Net profit		$ 32,000		

[a] Ending inventory correctly stated.
[b] Ending inventory understated $8,000 (thus income, assets, capital also).
[c] Ending inventory overstated $7,000 (thus income, assets, capital also).

In some departments and/or classifications, it may be possible to identify units with specific expenditures. This can occur when assortments and varieties of merchandise carried and the sales volume and transactions are relatively small. More often, however, as in the sport shirt classification, specific identification procedures are too complex to justify their use.

Consequently, one of the two accepted costing methods, each approved for income determination by the Internal Revenue Service, may be adopted to simplify the problem of inventory costing.

The assumption of the **first-in, first-out (FIFO)** method of costing inventory is that costs should be charged against revenue in the order in which they were incurred—that is, the first shirts purchased are the first ones sold. Thus, the inventory remaining at the end of an accounting period is assumed to be of the most recent purchases as follows:

February 1	Inventory:	50 shirts @ $ 9 = $ 450
April 15	Purchases:	40 shirts @ 13 = 520
May 1	Purchases:	30 shirts @ 14 = 420
October 1	Purchases:	100 shirts @ 16 = 1,600
Available for sale during year		$2,990

Let's assume that the physical inventory at the end of the fiscal year (January 31) is 130 shirts. Based on the assumption that the inventory is composed of the most recent purchases, the cost of the 130 shirts is as follows:

Most recent purchases (October 1)	100 shirts @ $16 =	$1,600
Next most recent (May 1)	30 shirts @ 14 =	420
Inventory, January 31	130 shirts	$2,020

If we deduct the end-of-period inventory of $2,020 from the $2,990 available for sale during the period, we get $970 as the cost of merchandise sold. FIFO is generally in harmony with the actual physical movement of goods in a retail firm. Thus, FIFO best represents the results that are directly tied to merchandise costs.

The costing method known as **last-in, first-out (LIFO)** assumes that the most recent cost of merchandise should be charged against revenue. Thus, the ending inventory under LIFO is assumed to be made up of earliest costs. Referring to the previous example:

February 1	50 shirts @ $ 9 =	$ 450
April 15	40 shirts @ 13 =	520
May 1	30 shirts @ 14 =	420
October 1	10 shirts @ 16 =	160
Inventory, January 31	130 shirts	$1,550

If we deduct the inventory of $1,550 from the $2,990 of merchandise available for sale during the accounting period, we get $1,440 as the cost of merchandise sold.

In comparing FIFO and LIFO:

	FIFO	LIFO
Merchandise available for sale	$2,990	$2,990
Inventory, January 31	2,020	1,550
Cost of merchandise sold	$ 970	$1,440

FIFO yields the lower cost of merchandise sold and thus yields higher gross profits and higher inventory figures on the balance sheet. On the other hand, LIFO yields a higher figure for cost of goods sold and lower figures for gross profit, net income, and inventory.

In periods of inflation, most companies experience increases in inventory investment. Those companies which value inventories at current costs (using FIFO) will have higher inventory valuation and thus higher taxable income and income taxes. Increased taxes require almost immediate cash outlays, and "inventory paper profits" are tied up in inventory and are not available for investment in other assets or for the payment of dividends. LIFO will usually give an ongoing firm a financial statement showing a lower income before tax and lower inventory values. This lower income will also result in lower tax payments and increased cash flow. LIFO is inflation-oriented.

Given the technicality of LIFO/FIFO issues, retailers need qualified advisers to help them know when to stay with or change to the last-in, first-out method of valuing inventories.

Conservative Valuation of Inventory

Cost or Market, Whichever Is Lower. Another problem in determining the cost of merchandise inventory is placing a conservative value on the inventory—that is, at cost or market, whichever is lower. This approach is an alternative to valuing inventory at cost. With either course, it is first necessary to determine the cost of inventory. *Market* means the cost required to replace the merchandise at the time of the inventory, whereas *cost* refers to the actual price of merchandise at the time of its purchase.

Figure 21–10 demonstrates the impact on profits of valuing the ending inventory at (1) actual cost, (2) depreciated value, and (3) appreciated value. In addition, it provides a rationale for the acceptance of the conservative practice of valuation—at cost or market, whichever is lower. At any given time, some merchandise in stock may not be valued at the amount originally paid for it. The merchandise may have declined in value because of obsolescence, deterioration, or decreases in wholesale market prices. It may have increased in value because of inflation, scarcity of materials, and the like. The first column in Figure 21–10 indicates that the profit is $5,000 after the valuation of inventory at its actual cost (determined by one of the methods discussed earlier). The second column indicates that, if the retailer were to replace the same inventory at the time of valuation, it would be depreciated to $4,000 (a $6,000 decline in value from the actual cost); instead of a $5,000 profit, a $1,000 loss has been incurred. The information in the third column reflects a $12,000 valuation of the ending inventory resulting in a $7,000 profit, rather than a $5,000 profit based on actual cost.

The depreciated ending inventory value relative to the actual cost results in an increased cost of goods sold and thus reduces gross profit. The appreciated ending inventory relative to the actual costs results in a decreased cost of goods sold, an increased gross profit, and, with the same expense amount, an increased net profit. Comparing each method with the actual cost, the conservative rule would dictate that the inventory value should be taken at the depreciated value [column (2)] and at actual cost [column (1)] when compared with market increase. Let's investigate the logic of such a practice.

FIGURE 21–10 THE IMPACT ON PROFITS OF VALUATION OF ENDING INVENTORY AT ACTUAL COST, OR DEPRECIATED OR APPRECIATED MARKET VALUE

	(1) Actual cost		(2) Depreciation		(3) Appreciated	
Net sales		$100,000		$100,000		$100,000
Merchandise available for sale	$70,000		$70,000		$70,000	
Ending inventory	10,000		4,000		12,000	
Cost of goods sold		60,000		66,000		58,000
Gross profit		$ 40,000		$ 34,000		$ 42,000
Expenses		35,000		35,000		35,000
Net profit		$ 5,000		$ (1,000)		$ 7,000

Rationale for the Conservative Rule

If management values the ending inventory at $4,000 rather than the cost of $10,000, the loss resulting will be taken in the period in which it occurs. This is logical, because the ending inventory of one period becomes the beginning inventory of the next. Thus, by placing a realistic depreciated market value on ending inventory, the lowered figure, which will be the next beginning inventory value, will give the merchant the opportunity to reflect a proper beginning inventory cost in the next period. This lets the merchant show realistic, and perhaps profitable, performance in the next period. This ending inventory figure also becomes an asset item on the balance sheet.

A realistic valuation reflecting declining value is wise because otherwise the assets, and consequently the net worth of the firm, will be overstated. Finally, if the market value were declining and the inventory were taken in at cost, the firm would show a profit, as illustrated in Figure 21–10. Income taxes would be paid on "paper profits."

To emphasize the concept of "paper profits," consider what the results would be if the inventory were valued at an appreciated value [column (3)] of $12,000, rather than a cost of $10,000. The $7,000 profit, rather than the $5,000, represents anticipated profits on merchandise that has not been sold and thus should not be reported.

In summary, retail inventories should be valued at cost or market, whichever is lower. As with the method chosen for the determination of inventory cost (LIFO or FIFO), the method elected for inventory valuation (cost, or lower of cost or market) must be consistent from year to year.

METHODS OF VALUATION OF INVENTORY

The final objective of this chapter is to introduce the accounting practices that assist management in valuation decisions. Retailers invest large sums of money in merchandise and must know at all times the value of this inventory investment. The information is needed for tax reasons, to compute gross margins as measures of performance, and to make day-to-day decisions. How *is* a value placed on inventory in retailing? Basically the two ways are (1) *the cost method* and (2) *the retail method*.

The Cost Method

The *cost method* provides a book evaluation of inventory and the system uses only cost figures. All inventory records are maintained at cost. When a physical inventory is taken, all items are recorded at actual cost including freight. The cost of sales and cost of markdowns (depreciation) are deducted from the total merchandise available to provide the book inventory at the lower of cost or market value, which can be checked by means of a physical inventory. The limitations of the cost method are: difficulty in determining depreciation; difficulty for large retailers with many classifications and price lines; daily inventory is impractical; and costing out each sale, allocating transportation charges to the cost of the sales, and reducing markdowns to cost are extremely difficult. The cost method is appropriate in operations with big-ticket items, where there are few lines and few price changes, where the rate of sale is rapid, and/or management has very sophisticated computer expertise.

Because of the limitations in the cost method, the *retail method* of inventory was created early in this century.

The Retail

Advantages of the Retail Method

The *retail method* of inventory is a logical extension of a retail book (perpetual) inventory utilized for dollar control (see Chapter 20). The advantages of the retail method are:

1. Accounting statements can be drawn up at any time, especially with the new technology. Income statements and balance sheets are normally available once a month.
2. Shortages can be determined. The retail method is a book inventory, and this figure can be compared to the physical inventory. Only with a book inventory can shortages (or overages) be determined.
3. The retail method, through its book inventory, serves as an excellent basis for insurance claims. In case of loss, the book inventory is good evidence of what *should* have been in stock. Records should be kept in a safe, fireproof vault, or cabinet. This reason and the two just mentioned are advantages that exist because the retail method is a perpetual, book inventory method. The following two advantages are uniquely related to the system of the retail method of inventory.
4. The physical taking of inventory is easier with the retail method. The items are recorded on the inventory sheets at *only* their selling prices, instead of their cost and retail prices.
5. The retail method gives an automatic, conservative valuation of ending inventory because of the way the system is programmed. This

means that the retail method gives a valuation of ending inventory at cost or market, whichever is lower.

The retail method is in actuality an income statement that follows certain programmed steps in the final determination of net profits. These steps are illustrated in Figure 21–11. The methodology provides a format for computing net profit. The steps are described next.

Steps of the Retail Method

1. Determine the Total Dollars of Merchandise Handled at Cost and Retail. As indicated in Figure 21–11, we start with a beginning inventory that we assume is an actual, physical inventory from the end of the previous period. To this figure we add purchases (minus vendor returns and/or allowances), any interstore or departmental transfers, and transportation charges (at cost only). The price change, which is a part of step 1, is additional markups. Suppose the retailer has a group of sport shirts in stock which were recently received. They are carried in stock at $14.95. Wholesale costs have increased since the delivery, and the wholesaler suggests that we take an additional markup of $3.00 per unit, bringing the retail price to $17.95. We take a physical count and find we have 700 shirts in stock; thus, we take an additional markup of $2,100 to accommodate the price increase. Immediately after processing the price change, we find that the count was incorrect, or the amount of the additional markup was too high due to a misunderstanding. At any rate, the retailer wants to cancel $600 of the additional markup so that the mistake can be corrected. (See Step 1 in the statement for the handling of this situation.) Cancellation of an additional markup is *not* a markdown, which reflects market depreciation. Cancellation is rather a procedure for adjusting an actual error in the original additional markup. Summing all the items that increase the dollar investment provides the total merchandise handled at cost and retail ($270,000 and $435,000, respectively).

2. Calculate the Cost Multiplier and the Cumulative Markon. As indicated in Figure 21–11, the computation of the cost multiplier (sometimes called the cost percentage or the cost complement) is derived by dividing the total dollars handled at cost by the total at retail (that is, $270,000 ÷ $435,000 = 62 percent). This is a key figure in the retail method and in fact involves the major assumption of the system. This cost multiplier says that for every retail dollar in inventory, 62 percent—or 62+ cents—is in terms of cost. The assumption of the retail method is that if cost and retail have this relationship in goods handled during a period, then that same relationship exists for all the merchandise remaining in stock (that is, the ending inventory at retail).

The *cumulative markon* is the complement of the cost multiplier (that is, 100.00 − 62.069 = 37.931) and is the control figure to compare against the planned initial markup. (See Chapter 14, where this planned figure is

FIGURE 21–11   STATEMENT OF RETAIL METHOD OF INVENTORY

Calculations	Step	Items	Cost	Retail	Cost	Retail	Percent
	1	Beginning inventory			$ 60,000	$105,000	
		Gross purchases	$216,000	$345,000	207,000	330,900	
		Less: Returns to vendor	(9,000)	(14,000)			
		Transfers in	3,000	4,800			
		Less: Transfers out	(4,500)	(7,200)	(1,500)	(2,400)	
		Transportation charges	4,500		4,500		
		Additional markups		2,100			
		Less: Cancellations		(600)		1,500	
		Total merchandise handled			270,000	435,000	
($270,000 ÷ $435,000)	2	Cost percent/cumulative markon					62.069/37.931
	3	Sales, gross		309,000		300,000	
		Less: Customer returns		(9,000)			
		Gross markdowns		12,000		10,500	
		Less: Cancellations		(1,500)			
		Employee discounts				1,500	
		Total retail deductions				312,000	

($435,000 − $312,000)		Closing book inventory @ retail		123,000	
	4	Closing physical inventory @ retail		120,750	
($123,000 − $120,750)		Shortages		2,250	0.75
($120,750 × 0.62069)		Closing physical inventory @ cost	74,949		
($270,000 − $74,949)	5	Gross cost of goods sold	195,051		
($300,000 − $195,051)	6	Maintained markup	104,949		34.9
		Less: Alteration costs	(3,000)		
		Plus: Cash discounts	6,000		
($104,949 + $3,000)		Gross margin	107,949		35.9
		Less: Operating expenses	75,000		25.0
		Net profit	32,949		10.9
	5	Gross cost of goods sold	195,051		
		Less: Cash discounts	(6,000)		
		Net costs of goods sold	189,051		
		Plus: Alteration costs	3,000		
		Total cost of goods sold	192,051		
($300,000 − $192,051)	6	Gross margin	107,949		35.9
		Less: Operating expenses	75,000		
		Net profit	32,949		10.9

discussed.) For example, let's assume that the planned initial markup is 37 percent. If our interim statement shows, as ours does, that our cumulative markon is 37+ percent, then management will consider that operations are effective, at least as they relate to the planned markup percentage. The initial markup is planned so as to cover reductions (markdowns, employee discounts, and shortages) and provide a maintained markup (or gross profit or margin) at a level sufficient to cover operating expenses and to assure a target rate of profit return.

3. Compute the Retail Deductions from Stock. Step 3 includes all the retail deductions from the total retail merchandise dollars handled during the period. Sales are recorded and adjusted by customer returns to determine net sales. Markdowns are recorded as they are taken.

As an example, let's assume that during this period a group of 1,200 sport shirts retailing for $25.95 are put out for a special sale at $15.95. We would thus take a markdown of $12,000 before the sale. After the sale, we want to bring the merchandise back to the regular price; an additional markup is not appropriate since we are merely cancelling an original markdown. Consequently, we put a markdown cancellation through the system for the remaining number of shirts—in this case, 150 that were not sold, making a cancellation of $1,500, which will reestablish the original retail price of $25.95. Employee discounts are included as deductions because employees receive, for example, a 20 percent discount on items purchased for personal use. If a shirt retails for $19.95, the employee would pay $15.96. If the discount were not entered as a separate item in the system, the difference between the retail price and the employee's price would cause a shortage. Recording employee discounts as a separate item also gives management a good picture of employee business obtained and affords a measure of control over use of the discount.

4. Calculate the Closing Book (and/or Physical) Inventory at Cost and Retail. The statement thus far has afforded us a figure for the dollars at retail that we had available for sale ($435,000) and what we have deducted from that amount ($312,000). Thus we are now able to compute what we have left ($435,000 − $312,000), or the ending book inventory at retail—$123,000. We are assuming, in this particular illustration, that this is a year-end statement and that we have an audited, physical inventory of $120,750. Consequently, we can now determine our shortages by deducting the amount of the physical inventory from the book inventory ($123,000 − $120,750 = $2,250)—0.75 percent of sales.

Let's assume that we were working with an interim statement rather than a fiscal-year statement. If this were the case, we would include in our retail deductions from stock (Step 3) an *estimated* shortage figure, which would give us as accurate a figure as possible for total deductions, and thus a figure for closing book inventory at retail. If we have an interim statement, then the cost multiplier is applied to the book inventory at retail to determine the cost value: if there is a physical retail inventory figure, as in Figure

21–11, then we use that figure for cost conversion, since the physical inventory figure is accurate.

The key to the retail method, as noted, is the reduction of the retail inventory to cost by multiplying the retail value by the cost multiplier ($120,750 × 0.62069). In our illustration, we get a value of $74,949. We can now go to the next step with this figure.

5. Determination of Gross Cost of Goods Sold. Since we know the amount of the merchandise handled at cost ($270,000) and know what we have *left* at cost ($75,949), we can determine the cost dollars that have moved out of stock ($195,051).

6. Determination of Maintained Markup, Gross Margin, and Net Profit. Two procedures may be followed at this step. (We prefer the first method because of the emphasis given to the concept of maintained markup in Chapter 14.) The gross margin and net profit figures in either case are identical; slightly different accounting philosophies are the determining factor, and the justification of either method is neither appropriate nor valuable here. We simply show the two ways to let you see the differences between them. Gross cost of goods sold is deducted from net sales to determine maintained markup ($300,000 − $195,051). Alteration costs (or workroom expenses) are traditionally considered in retailing as merchandising, nonoperating expenses and in this first method are offset by cash discounts earned (nonoperating income). The net diffference between the two is added or subtracted from the maintained markup to derive the gross margin ($104,949 − $3,000 + $6,000 = $107,949), from which operating expenses are deducted to calculate net profits before taxes ($107,949 − $75,000 = $32,949). The various percentages appearing on the statement are all based on net sales (with the exception of the cost percentage and the cumulative markon).

The second process for determining gross margin and net profit differs in that cash discounts earned are deducted from gross cost of goods sold ($195,051 − $6,000) to derive *net* cost of goods sold ($189,051). Alteration costs are added to that figure to obtain *total* cost of goods sold ($189,051 + $3,000 = $192,051). Total cost of goods sold is deducted from net sales ($300,000 − $192,051) to obtain the gross margin figure of $107,949.

Evaluation of the Retail Method

Determination of profits using the retail method of inventory is not a new system, and over the years has been criticized. A major complaint is that it is a "method of averages." This refers to the determination of the cost multiplier as the "average relationship" between all the merchandise handled at cost and retail, and the application of this average percentage to the closing inventory at retail to determine the cost figure. Such a disadvantage, more real in the past than today, can be largely overcome by classification merchandising or dissection accounting—that is, breaking departments into small subgroups with homogeneity in terms of margins and turnover. The new technology in point-of-sales systems affords unlimited classifications and thus allows the homogeneity necessary for implementation of the retail method, giving management a good measure of the actual effectiveness of operations.

The retail method of inventory is not applicable to all departments within a store. For example, unless the purchases can be "retailed" at the time of receipt of the goods, the system will not work. The drapery workroom could not be on the retail method. Consequently, there are certain "cost" departments within many establishments. Such a condition does not lessen the value of the system where it is appropriate.

Finally, the retail method is easily programmed for computer systems and has proved most effective for management decisions. All accounting entries into the system can be automated, and the management reports that can be "called" are virtually limitless.

CHAPTER HIGHLIGHTS

—— Accounting systems are essential in monitoring the performance of a retail firm.

—— The strategic profit model (SPM) dramatizes the principal areas of decision making—margin, asset, and leverage management—and is the framework for profitable retail management.

—— Inventory turnover has a direct impact on profitability. The gross margin return on inventory investment (GMROI) concept effectively illustrates this impact.

—— Deciding whether to use FIFO or LIFO as a method for inventory costing is a technical issue that calls for professional advisers; in simple terms, LIFO has advantages in inflationary periods.

—— Inventories should be valued at the lower of cost or market. The retail method of inventory valuation provides this information.

KEY TERMS

Assets, current Primarily cash, accounts receivable, and inventory. They are in varying states of being converted into cash within the next 12-month period.

Assets, fixed Used in the operation of the business; they are not intended to be resold. They include real estate, leasehold improvements, machinery, equipment, and vehicles.

Balance sheet The financial statement which expresses the equation: Assets = Liabilities + Net worth. (Net worth is the owners' equity or claim to the assets of the business.)

FIFO (first-in, first-out) An inventory costing method which assumes that costs should be charged against revenue in the order in which they were incurred; in other words, the first items purchased are the first ones sold. The method is generally in harmony with actual movement of goods.

GMROI (gross margin return on inventory investment) Expression of the relationship between margin and sales-to-retail stock (turnover), stated to effectively indicate the impact on profitability as:

$$\frac{\$GM}{\$Sales} \times \frac{\$Sales}{\$Average\ inventory\ investment}$$

Income statement Operating results of a period indicating if investments in assets and strategy have been successful and if a profit has resulted.

Leveraging When assets worth more than the amount of capital invested by the owners are acquired. Leveraging is the ratio of total assets to net worth. The higher the ratio, the higher the amount of borrowed funds in the business.

LIFO (last-in, first-out) An inventory costing method that assumes that the most recent cost of merchandise should be charged against revenue. LIFO yields a higher figure for cost of goods sold than FIFO and thus lower figures for gross profit, net income, and inventory. LIFO is popular during inflationary periods.

Strategic profit model (SPM) A model from the basic ROI model which focuses on the firm's primary profit paths—margin, assets, and leverage.

DISCUSSION QUESTIONS

1. Distinguish between the balance sheet and the income statement. Illustrate an advocated format for each.
2. Explain the problems related to defining the terms *profit* and *investment*.
3. What are the significant purposes of the strategic profit model (SPM)?
4. Discuss the practical value of the strategic profit model.
5. Discuss your reaction to the following statement made by the manager of a large, full-line department store: "I am very pleased that my store had a 3.6 turnover rate for 1986."
6. Discuss the impact that turnover and margin planning have on the return of each dollar invested in inventory using a GMROI format.
7. Why is it difficult to determine cost of ending inventories? How do (a) FIFO and (b) LIFO relate to this problem? Explain the assumptions of and contrast the two methods.
8. Explain the effects on net profits of a correct statement, an understatement, and an overstatement of the period's ending inventory.
9. Explain the conservative method of inventory valuation and discuss the rationale of accountants who support this "rule."
10. Describe the cost method of inventory valuation. What are the limitations of the cost method? Under what conditions would this method be more appropriately used?
11. Explain in simple terms what the retail method of inventory is. What is the relationship between "the retail method" and a retail book inventory?
12. Describe in detail the steps of the retail method.
13. What are the advantages of the retail method?
14. What are the disadvantages of the retail method?

PROBLEMS

Use the retail method of accounting. Prepare a well-organized statement and determine for each of the three problems the following sets of figures (see p. 574):

a. Cumulative markon percentage.
b. Ending inventory at retail
c. Ending inventory at cost.
d. Maintained markup in dollars and percent.
e. Gross margin of profit in dollars and percent.
f. Net profit in dollars and percent.

1. Item	Cost	Retail
Beginning inventory	$20,000	$ 35,000
Gross purchases	72,000	115,000
Purchase returns and allowances	3,000	4,700
Transfers in	1,000	1,600
Transfers out	200	400
Transportation charges	1,216	
Additional markups		700
Additional markup cancellations		400
Gross sales		111,000
Customer returns and allowances		11,000
Gross markdowns		4,500
Markdown cancellations		1,000
Employee discounts		500
Estimated shortages, 0.4 percent of net sales		
Cash discounts on purchases	1,600	
Workroom costs	800	
Operating expenses	16,000	

2. Item	Cost	Retail
Additional markup cancellations		$ 620
Estimated shortages, 0.05 percent of net sales		
Gross markdowns		8,000
Workroom costs	$ 500	
Sales returns and allowances		12,000
Transportation charges	2,094	
Beginning inventory	44,000	64,000
Purchase returns and allowances	2,200	5,200
Markdown cancellations		1,200
Gross purchases	65,600	105,240
Gross additional markups		2,480
Gross sales		102,000
Employee discounts		1,400
Cash discounts on purchases	1,500	
Operating expenses	11,000	

3. Item	Cost	Retail
Gross sales		$ 27,200
Beginning inventory	$14,300	20,100
Sales returns and allowances		200
Gross markdowns		2,200
Gross additional markups		650
Transportation charges	418	
Purchase returns and allowances	830	1,720
Employee discounts		500
Gross purchases	17,200	27,520
Markdown cancellations		300
Operating expenses	3,800	
Cash discounts on purchases	200	
Additional markups cancelled		150
Alteration and workroom costs	300	
Ending physical inventory		16,500

APPLICATION EXERCISES

1. Check with your library and see how many publications of retail trade associations are represented in its collection (e.g., NRMA—National Retail Merchants Association; Men's Wear Retailers of America; Jewelers of America). Look for operating data and conclusions that may be drawn about the most recent operating results. Summarize your findings in a short paper. What assistance can such information provide management?

2. With clearance from your instructor, interview at least three types of retailers, such as managers of department stores or catalog showrooms. Discuss the issue of LIFO versus FIFO methods of inventory valuation. See if they understand the advantages and disadvantages of each. Do not attempt to teach them; merely appraise their knowledge of the issue. Summarize their perceptions and degree of sophistication. Try to draw some conclusions from this exercise.

3. Interview several small retailers and perhaps a large one (e.g., several dress shops, men's stores, and a department store). Ask if you could speak with the person in charge of the accounting records. Find out if any of them is using the retail method of accounting. If not, find out how they operate the cost method. How do they determine shortages? Try to strike up a conversation about the subject of this chapter; report back your findings.

4. Secure an annual report of a retail firm and construct (to the best of your ability) an SPM for that organization.

CASES

1. Ratios and Decision Making

Bobbie's Fashiontique is a small, family-operated store staffed by Mr. and Mrs. Townsend (in their late 50s) and their daughter Bobbie. Bobbie's parents started the business for her when she left her job as an elementary school teacher. The Townsends had been employed by a large department store throughout their careers until opening Bobbie's. Mr. Townsend was the manager of warehouse and traffic and delivery at the department store when he left. Previously, he had been in charge of receiving and marking. Mrs. Townsend had been in charge of alterations and fur storage. At one time she also ran a customer adjustment department.

The Townsend family had no real merchandising or control background. Consequently, whenever they faced an accounting problem, they ignored it or turned it over to the accounting firm that did their routine bookkeeping and tax returns.

Realizing that the family's management sophistication was limited, Bobbie joined the state retail association and went to a seminar on financial management. After the conference, she was confused and frustrated. She didn't even know whether the store was making any money. She was certain the family had to obtain more information, especially about operating ratios. Bobbie called her accounting firm and talked to Tom Maden. She asked him to calculate key ratios and to tell her what they meant.

Tom took the latest balance sheet and operating statement of the Fashiontique and came up with these figures for Bobbie's firm and similar companies:

Ratio	Bobbie's Fashiontique	Trade
Net profit margin	4.8%	10.2%
Rate asset turnover	1.7x	1.5x
Return on assets	8.16%	15.3%
Leverage ratio	4.0x	2.8x
RONW	32.64%	35.1%

Questions

1. You are Tom Maden. Report to Bobbie Townsend and interpret the data for her. Point out the strengths and weaknesses for Bobbie's Fashiontique and the areas that need particular attention.

2. Inventory Cost Determination in a Volatile Market

Mr. Richard Edwards, who has worked for many years for Zale's Jewelry Company, has taken a lease in a new regional mall in his hometown. He is coming home to open a fine, guild-type jewelry store. He is opening with approximately 1,000 square feet of space and a very limited merchandise mix compared with some of the competitors in his market. He has learned, however, from his Zale's experience that the "action" is in gold jewelry and diamonds. "No 'table-top' goods for me," Dick told a friend. "Every discount house and catalog showroom carries silver flatware, china, and crystal. I can't compete with them with the service I'll give and the rent I have to pay in the mall."

When Edwards was with Zale's, they changed from FIFO to LIFO. He was a store manager and knew how to perform under the "new" method, but didn't feel comfortable in deciding which was best for him. He was watching prices of gold and diamonds skyrocket (with some sharp drops now and again, too), and knew that LIFO had great advantages in periods of rising prices. But he really didn't understand the logic.

Questions
1. Assume you are Richard Edwards. Prepare questions and answers that must be reached before a sound decision can be made. What should he do at the time you are preparing this case?

PART 7

Retailing Issues and Outlook

This final chapter in the text allows you to assess the significance of the material you have learned and to speculate about trends that can affect retailers in the near-term future. The chapter covers changing social issues, emerging retailer responses to changes in the environment, the social responsibility of retailers, issues inherent in consumerism, and quality-of-life issues that can be important in making retail decisions. Of all executives, retailers have the closest day-to-day contact with consumers. They have a special opportunity to be of service to society while at the same time earning a sound profit by providing good price and value relationships for goods and services.

22

Retailing: Trends, Social Dimensions, and Prospects

Super Warehouses 'Chomp' into the Food Business

Food retailers are discovering that discount—or off-price—will attract retail customers. This lesson has long been known to other sectors of retailing. Cub Foods, a division of Super Value Stores, Inc. is pioneering the super warehouse discount concept. Competitors are scrambling to copy the format.

The typical super warehouse food outlet is twice the size of a normal supermarket, but operates on smaller margins and generates more than six times the sales of conventional supermarkets. These outlets should not be confused with the no-frills, big-volume warehouses of the late 1970s or with conventional supermarkets. Conventional warehouse supermarkets stock fewer items than warehouses, carry no fresh produce, cheese, or meats and limit the number of brands they stock. Many shoppers do not like their limited selection and dingy appearance although they are attracted to the low prices.

The super warehouse, in contrast, offers a wide array of food, including high-quality produce, fresh vegetables, and bakery items as well as meats and deli items, all at discount prices. Cub Stores, for example, sells an average of a million dollars a week in food compared to approximately $150,000 a week for a conventional supermarket. The Cubs are able to achieve these volumes because shoppers will spend an average of $45 per trip in such outlets, more than twice the national average. Management is able to operate on a high-volume, low-overhead format by taking direct

Based on "Super Warehouses 'Chomp' into the Food Business," *Business Week*, April 16, 1984, p. 72.

shipments of goods from the manufacturers, often displaying goods in the manufacturers' original cartons, and by stocking the items to the top of 24-foot ceilings. Customers also pack and carry their own groceries which reduces labor costs by almost 50 percent. As a result of these innovations, the Cub units are able to operate on margins of 14 percent, a substantial reduction from the 22 percent which is typical in the industry.

*T*he emergence of Cub Food Stores is an example of the constantly changing nature of the retailing structure which occurs as management seeks ways to meet consumer needs effectively. Retailers, because of their closeness to the consumer, often face greater and more rapid changes in the environments than other sectors of the business community. As a consequence, retailing strategies are constantly changing in response to shifts in the external environments and as new forms of competition, such as the super warehouse described in the retailing capsule, emerge. This chapter highlights some of the many changes occurring today.

This chapter is a projection into the future. After reading this chapter, you will be able to:

1. Discuss the meaning of a shift from a merchandising to a marketing orientation in retail strategy development.

2. Describe key merchandising trends.

3. Explain how the changes occurring in the external environments can affect retail strategy.

4. Evaluate retailing strategies that are emerging in response to changes in the external environments.

5. Discuss the rapid growth of services retailing.

6. List the key issues in the consumerism movement and management responses to consumer dissatisfaction.

The environments retailers face are changing at an ever-faster rate. *What is in store for retailing in the future?* More than ever, managing changes will be the key to success. Consider the changes of the past 20 years. The 1960s were a time of high growth in population, income, employment, and profits. Consumers thought in terms of "bigger" and "better." In contrast, the 1970s brought an energy crisis, inflation, high unemployment, high interest rates, a recession, and, for many people, a loss of confidence in the future.

What has been the nature of the decade of the 1980s for retailers and their customers? Some issues are clear. Retailers have operated in an environment of decreasing inflation, fluctuating interest rates, and an increasingly global economy. An accelerated information explosion brought about by the personal computer and video technology has introduced other changes. The tenor of the remainder of the decade and the early 1990s is still unclear, but continuing adjustment to economic uncertainty seems likely as does continuing change in operating philosophy as competition continues to accelerate.

CHANGING FROM A MERCHANDISING TO A MARKETING ORIENTATION

Evidence indicates that retail management's focus will continue to shift from merchandising to marketing. **Merchandising** means that the primary focus of the firm is to have the right merchandise at the right place, at the right time, in the right quantities, and at the right price. *Marketing* means that all of the retailer's activities support an integrated marketing strategy with a strong consumer focus. This shift does not lessen the importance of the merchandising function within retailing. Rather, it means that merchandising is no longer *more* important than other functions.

Today, finding the right goods and creatively displaying them no longer assures that a retailing firm will grow and prosper. Management can no longer simply "mind the store"; it must "run the business" with a constant eye on the consumer. Historically, retailers have felt that profitability and market share would follow if they presented consumers with the right goods at the right price. Under such a philosophy, financial systems and business operations were merely necessary housekeeping chores.

Today, firms ranging from J. C. Penney to Macy's are creating new types of retail organizations to meet changing consumer needs. The shift has created a major reorganization within the firms. Merchandising experts no longer automatically rise to the top roles in their organizations. These changes have extended managers' planning horizons well beyond one season, which is the standard for a firm with a merchandising orientation.

Today, more and more firms are looking at the long term. They are developing a strategic view of the business and are focusing on such issues as market positioning, changing consumer lifestyles, and competitive strategies.

As a result, management is no longer content to respond to competitive pressures simply by changing displays, pricing, layout, or promotion. Instead, they are more likely to reexamine the entire business concept in a search for new growth opportunities. Part of this change has come about as retailers have been rudely awakened from a period of rapid growth to find themselves confronted with slow growth, market saturation, stronger competition, and more demanding consumers. Successful retailers today are reorienting their organizations toward:

1. Questions about themselves: What business are we in? How are we positioned competitively? Have we tried to be all things to all people? Would we be more successful if we tried to be something specific to someone specific? How can we distinguish ourselves from our competitors in the minds of our target customer? Who is our target customer? Why does it matter?
2. A broader business perspective that examines the impact of each functional specialty on others and strives for excellent, effective business decisions at all levels.
3. Increased financial sophistication and skill in asset management to ensure optimum financial results.
4. Skill in working through people to achieve effective implementation, encourage creativity, and retain valued employees with changed lifestyle expectations.[1]

Management today is starting to recognize that merchandising genius must be combined with sound management systems, good staff development, and information processing systems to achieve targeted returns on investments. Such persons have a willingness to abandon old formulas of success and create new ones that are more likely to ensure success in today's environment. The new planning enables retailers to determine how and where to improve their businesses with methods that are more reliable than the planning approaches used in earlier years.

Significant changes in merchandising are also occurring. Many of these trends are discussed in the following section.

MERCHANDISING TRENDS

Productivity Improvement

Retailers are seeking productivity improvements through an improved merchandise mix, cost reductions, and increased margins.

Improved Merchandise Mix

Many department stores are reducing the number of marginal lines carried. Department stores are vulnerable in consumable items, health and beauty aids, and various houseware categories because they compete with every discounter in the city, every drugstore, and every mass merchandising outlet.

In specific merchandise categories, fashion areas are where department stores perform best: fashion apparel, accessories, jewelry, and cosmetics.

Department stores are dropping lines subject to heavy discounting and low margins. In the process, many are becoming less of a full-line outlet and more like higher-margin fashion stores. Major appliances in particular offer little return relative to their space and inventory costs. Retailers are realizing that consumers have no special inclination to shop for these products at department stores, no matter how favorable a store's image.

Cost Reductions

Many firms are also focusing on cost reductions as a way to increase productivity. Costs are either fixed or variable. *Fixed costs,* such as those for a building, do not vary with the level of sales. *Variable costs,* such as labor costs, do vary with the level of sales. Variable costs are the easiest to reduce in the short run.

Keys to reducing variable costs include self-service, reduction of store hours, and better use of part-time help. The long-term effects of cost reductions lead to increased profit margins and firms which can be more effective competitors. Competition is accelerating not only by domestic retailers but also by foreign-based retailers, such as Benetton, Laura Ashley, and Ikea.

A potential problem which will confront retailers seeking to pursue further cost reductions is the forecasted slow growth rate of the teen population which will reduce the pool of part-time labor available to retailers looking to reduce their human resources costs. The smaller pool of teenagers may be offset, however, by a growing number of retired persons seeking part-time employment. Such persons are likely to provide a more skilled labor pool than the teenagers.

Margin Increases

Higher-than-normal prices on low-visibility items or infrequently purchased items are being implemented. Charging for services such as repair or installation is also occurring more frequently. Some firms charge a stiff fee for delivering merchandise, for example. Banks also have started to vary their service charges to customers based on account balances. Customers with small balances often have to pay a monthly service charge and a check-processing fee.

Merchandise-Assortment Planning

Retailers are beginning to take a leadership role in identifying the kinds of merchandise that should be added to their assortments. Drugstores, for example, increasingly are adding auto parts and supplies since these are sought by many of their mainstream customers. No longer are retailers relying primarily on suppliers to suggest new merchandise lines, particularly as retailers begin to understand more about market segmentation and the role of research in helping to plan product assortments.

Space Reduction	Management is moving aggressively to convert unproductive retail space to other uses. The move is accelerating among department stores, large specialty stores, discount stores, mass merchandisers, and even shopping centers. More productive use of space must be found when land costs, taxes, and rentals become so high that sales productivity drops below a minimum level, often $50 per square foot or so. Conversions or cut-backs to smaller space allow the retailer to save on staff, inventory, and energy. Renting to outsiders in some situations can be more profitable than retailing.[2]
Vertical Merchandising	The trend in many outlets is also toward vertical merchandising, the so-called cube effect, and away from displaying merchandise in low horizontal formats. Vertical merchandising lowers construction costs and increases space productivity, making smaller stores possible. However, without creativity, vertical merchandising can be boring. Another problem is that management can build up excessive inventory by the use of vertical merchandising. During slack demand and periods of high inventory carrying costs, inventory is likely to be lower. Vertical merchandising can thus make a store look as though it is going out of business.
Classification Dominance	**Classification dominance** means displaying and arranging merchandise in such a way that the consumer is convinced the firm has the largest assortment in the city of merchandise in that category. Normally, management will display all different sizes and colors of the items for which they want to make a dominance "statement." Often, all reserve stock will be displayed to give a strong impression of the depth of the merchandise available. Large amounts of space are required for classification dominance. Clearly, management must be careful in selecting the merchandise lines with which it will use this display technique. Management may decide to eliminate some marginal product lines or categories to continue classification dominance.[3]
Flexible Fixturing	Many stores today are using more flexible, movable, low-cost fixtures as opposed to high-cost, permanent fixtures. The initial investment in the fixtures is less and the decor in the store can be easily changed to reflect changing consumer tastes and seasons. New innovations in flexible fixturing are occurring as management continues to look for ways of reducing construction costs and increasing space productivity.
Coordinated Graphics	Accelerated use of self-service to increase store productivity has made in-store consumer information and communications more important than ever. Management is seeking less labor-intensive, less costly, but more effective means of communicating the store image and messages to customers. Graphics play an important role in this effort. Clear, consistent, informative graph-

EXHIBIT 22–1

Safeway's supermarket of the future uses enormous photomurals to identify departments along the store walls in Arlington, Texas. (Courtesy The Doody Company)

ics should begin externally with advertising and continue throughout the store. All aspects of communication, including promotional signs, point-of-sale graphics, departmental identification, and institutional messages are most effective when coordinated. An example of the trend in coordinated graphics is shown by Safeway in Exhibit 22–1.

Signs. Informative signs are important. Many customers want to inform themselves about merchandise before making a purchase. Sales clerks are often unavailable and may lack technical knowledge about sophisticated products. Careful explanations about product use, warranties, and technical dimensions of the product can be facilitated by the careful use of informative signing.[4]

Increasing Emphasis on Theatrics

Retailers also are realizing that not only must they make a major statement in a particular category of merchandise but they must also present it in a powerful, visual way. Design and layout are thus becoming an increasingly important factor in attracting consumers. Product demonstrations; lectures by well-known designers; and use of music, art, and other visual means of communication will be an increasingly important part of retail merchandising.

Changes in the external environments facing the firm can also be powerful forces in affecting both marketing strategy and merchandising trends. The next section of the chapter highlights the external forces which are likely to affect retail strategy development and implementation.

THE EXTERNAL ENVIRONMENTS

What are some of the specific uncertainties for the next few years? *First*, economic uncertainty will be a prime issue. This uncertainty means retailers will need to develop multiple strategies depending on which economic forecasts they believe. Flexibility will be the key to avoid being trapped by the wrong strategy.

Second, strong price awareness and consumer sensitivity will continue to be major issues. Shoppers will be increasingly price oriented because of pressures on their incomes. Such innovations as warehouse retailing and generic foods will continue to have a marketplace advantage with consumers for this reason.

Third, the level of investment in retailing will have to increase sharply. Land and building costs are up, as are fixture and equipment costs. However, sales in real dollars have been flat in recent years. This will require the investment of large sums of money in fixed assets.

The Consumer

Consumers will be more careful users of information in their choices among *products and services*. They will have more of the information they need to make wise choices. Smart retailers will be able to take advantage of this trend by adjusting their offering to specific groups of consumers.

The right information presented in the right way will more than ever go a long way toward helping retailers beat the competition. The focus will be on serving the *information* needs of the consumer whose *products* needs management wants to satisfy.

Expect Technology Shifts

Technology changes will continue to occur at an ever-faster rate. Electronic funds transfer systems will be installed in rising numbers of retail outlets by the end of the decade. These systems will allow consumers to instantly transfer funds from their checking accounts to the accounts of the merchant. Universal vendor marking (UVM) in nonfood retailing will also continue to make progress. Once UVM reaches the 70 percent level in nonfood retailing, major increases in productivity will appear.

The use of scanners will also continue to make major inroads into such areas of retailing as drugs. In the past they have not been factors of major importance. Conversion to the metric system will continue to slowly increase as will the use of two-way interactive cable TV systems.

Institutional Reliance

During the past two decades, government has sought to legislate remedies for virtually every issue facing the American public. The consumer and environmental movements of the 1970s brought about a variety of new government agencies. The Environmental Protection Agency (EPA), and the Occupational Safety and Health Administration (OSHA) are among these federal agencies. The Consumer Product Safety Commission sets standards for more than 10,000 different consumer goods. The Equal Employment Opportunity Commission (EEOC) constrains the hiring practices of retailers. Those agencies have added to the cost of retailing without helping to increase productivity.

Recent trends suggest that Americans are moving away from **institutional reliance** to self-reliance. Deregulation of the trucking and airline industries manifests this change. The shifting of tax dollars by the federal government back to the states is another indication.

Similarly, Americans are divorcing the corporate life. Self-employment and entrepreneurial activity are accelerating. Educational self-help is growing and many persons are rebelling against institutionalized medicine. Instead, they are seeking to solve their problems through diet and exercise.

Employee Rights

Employees are increasingly pushing for a greater influence on management action in the United States. In European firms, employees already have more rights. They are increasingly insisting on an input into company decisions and on lifetime employment contracts. These pressures are coming at the same time that many retailers are struggling to survive in a slow-growth economy, often in mature or declining markets.

Growth of the Upscale Market

The population is aging and a larger share of the wealth will be distributed among fewer people. The result is a growth in the importance of the upscale market, partly occurring because of the increasing number of working women.[5] Merchandise lines such as those offered by Liz Claiborne and Laura Ashley are rapidly growing in importance as a result of the more upscale market opportunities, as are designer furniture outlets, innovative department stores, and specialty stores.

Continuing Slow Growth

Retailers can no longer get long-term profit growth by adding stores. As a result, competition for customers will become murderous. Apparel sales, for example are expected to increase by only 1–2 percent a year until at least 1990.[6] Stores will continue to increase their market share primarily by taking business away from competitors.

Consumer Resistance to Prices

The operating costs of retailers are continuing to increase at the same time that consumers are less willing to pay higher prices. Consumer price resistance has led to the growth of **off-price retailers,** especially apparel stores which sell branded and designer labels at 20 percent to 40 percent below normal retail prices. Markdowns are also becoming increasingly frequent. Consumers are now witnessing a virtual epidemic of fictitious pricing in which high "normal" prices are established, quickly followed in a week or two by 40–50 percent markdowns. Sales lose their impact when everyone is having them. Retailers will have to return to strategies based on all elements of the marketing mix, not just price.

Decline in Consumer Loyalty

Consumers today know that most merchants carry essentially the same brands. The result is that shopping patterns are no longer predictable and merchandising alone will not be sufficient to retain consumer loyalty.

Continued Overstoring

Some experts estimate that the U.S. market contains as much as 20 percent excess retail space. Still others contend that the problem is not primarily one of overstoring but more of a failure to differentiate one retailer from another in meeting customer needs. In any event, "copy cat" retailing will not suffice in the overcrowded market that will characterize retailing for the next decade.

The Liability Explosion

The increasing concern over shareholder lawsuits accompanying the wave of merger and acquisition activity in retailing will continue to create a boom in directors' and officers' liability insurance among retailers.[7] The potential for such exposure was illustrated when the shareholders of Marshall Field sought $200 million in damages for the chain's rejection of a merger offer from Carter Hawley Hale Stores, Inc. Suits against retailers include: (1) suits brought by shareholders on behalf of the corporation; (2) suits by shareholders on their own behalf; and (3) claims brought by outside individuals or firms. Common charges include:

— Failure to honor employment contracts.
— Manipulation of financial statements.
— Unfair labor practices.
— Antitrust violations.
— Collusion or conspiracy to defraud.
— Improper expenditures.
— Imprudent expansion that results in a loss.
— Conflict of interest.
— Unfair or illegal marketing practices.
— Misleading statements and forms filed with the Securities and Exchange Commission.

Skyrocketing Insurance Costs

The nation is in the midst of an unprecedented liability crisis. Juries are returning million-plus dollar verdicts against retailers. Liability suits filed in state courts have jumped by 20 percent or more over the past seven years. To cope, insurance companies have been raising premiums since the mid-1980s, sometimes as much as 1,000 percent or more per clip. Some retailers are abandoning selected lines of business, operating without insurance, or raising their prices to cover premium costs. Many bar owners have been forced to go without insurance coverage because they cannot afford the premium insurers demand in such a high-risk business.[8]

EMERGING KEY RETAILING STRATEGIES

Some trends are becoming evident in retailing strategies as a result of the environmental changes discussed. These trends reflect the diversity in retailing and indicate the creativity and innovativeness of merchants as they seek to find ways to meet the needs of consumers in the midst of constant change.

Expect More Niching in the Future

Such firms as Claire Stores, The Limited, and Benetton have carved out a unique position in the marketplace and offer customers something different. These retailers have discovered niches of specialization which offer high potential. Claire Stores are devoted entirely to selling popular-priced jewelry. The concept of extremely targeted formats (**niching**) is also evident in The Limited. Their niche operations include Limited Express Stores, Lane Bryant, and Victoria's Secret. Benetton, the Italian knitwear retailer, is able, through its manufacturing capability, to tailor its stores' merchandise mix directly to the customers in the surrounding marketplace.

Expect Continued Success in Commodity Retailing

Commodity retailers count on dominance in the marketplace. Such stores include membership warehouse clubs, home-center warehouse stores, and supermarket mega-stores. The outlets make a strong statement in the merchandise categories they carry. They are sufficiently strong to attract customers from great distances and may do over $1,000 a square foot in sales.

Continued Strong Growth in Small and Middle Markets

Small and middle markets are currently the most underserved in America. Retailers who have found success in such markets include Family Dollar Stores, Wal-Mart, Ames Department Stores, and Hess's Department Stores. Secondary markets are also coming to the attention of major retailers such as Sears.[9]

Shopping Center Mix Changes	Signs of overstoring will continue. As a result, shopping centers are now leasing space to such tenants as exercise studios, auto parts stores, and individuals seeking office rentals. Such tenants could not get into shopping malls until recent years. The number of shopping centers to be built will also decrease sharply in response to the overstored condition.
Expect Continued Growth of Power Retailers	**Power retailers** are merchants with sufficient financial strength, marketing skill, and price/value relationships to enter a market, regardless of how saturated, and make a profit. Examples include Dayton-Hudson and Macy's. Such retailers contend that strong markets always exist for merchants offering excellent service and good price/value relationships.
Increased Emphasis on Inventory Control	Computerized inventory controls allow merchants to do a better job of reordering goods as they need them instead of placing an order for an entire line at the beginning of a season. The more efficient inventory management also allows retailers to use less space and achieve a higher return on their space.
Research Will Be More Important	Data on demographics, psychographics (measures of attitudes), and lifestyles are increasingly being fed into retailers' computers. This enables management to make decisions based on actual customer spending patterns and to estimate inventory needs with less risk. Computer-based scanning services at checkout counters are making such data more readily available. Research is becoming increasingly vital for sales analysis, sales forecasting, traffic pattern studies, and advertising impact measurement.
Return to Private Labels	Apparel retailers increasingly are seeking to develop **private labels** as a way of attracting and maintaining customer loyalty. Designer labels lose their attractiveness when they are available in too many outlets. Successful private brand lines help the retailers to avoid such problems. Sears' Cheryl Tiegs line is an example. Similarly, The Limited has created its own designer labels such as Forenza (a fictitious Italian designer). Their other brands such as Hunters' Run and Cassidy are also well-known national names. The ratio of private labels to branded merchandise is now as high as 40 percent in some department stores.
Smaller Stores	*Stores for the remainder of the decade and into the 1990s will be smaller than in the 1960s and 1970s.* Higher productivity is easier to obtain in smaller stores. Space for malls and for new, large, free-standing stores is getting harder to find.

The 1990s will continue to be the era of specialty shops that appeal to narrow market segments. Few stores will try to be all things to all people. The ultimate in segmentation is a New York store called Just Bulbs, which stocks 2,500 types of light bulbs. More than ever, management is thinking in terms of different store sizes to better serve diverse markets. Also, more previously used space is being purchased and refinished to hold down costs.

Characteristics of High Performance Retailers

In summary, successful retailers in the future will share several common characteristics:

1. *Attention to detail.* Winners not only do the right big things, they do the little things right.
2. *Constant communication with customers and employees.* Getting close to the customer is more than just an expression. Understanding and responding to customer needs requires close continuing contact as exemplified by such superior retailers as Stew Leonard's in Connecticut and Nordstrom's in the Northwest.
3. *Market drive.* Progressive retailers will continue to be preoccupied with offering strong price/value relationships. Such firms will continue to offer greater value, fashion, and convenience that will induce customers to spend less time and money at competing outlets.
4. *Strategic planning.* Successful retailers, as we have seen throughout the text, are ones who are committed to a clearly defined purpose and mission that indicates what they want to be and where they want to go.
5. *Technological leadership.* Retailers will continue to accelerate their moves to an integrated management information system that will link outlying retail outlets and distribution centers with the headquarter's buying and financial functions.

Listening, planning, and technology will be the key priority words for success in the foreseeable future.

SERVICES RETAILING

Services retailing is becoming such an important part of the U.S. economy that we are devoting a separate section of this chapter to the subject. Growth in services retailing exceeds growth in other sectors of the economy. By the year 2000 the service sector of the economy is forecast to provide four out of every five jobs.[10] Services retailing includes health spas, legal clinics, educational institutions, hair stylists, dental clinics, law firms, and so forth. This incomplete list helps to show the diversity that characterizes services retailing.

Problems in Services Retailing

Despite the importance of services retailing to the economy, less attention has been given to the unique problems of services retailers than to those of tangible goods firms. The differences between the two types of retailing pose specific marketing and merchandising problems for service retailers.[11]

Perishability

One problem is that many services are essentially perishable. If a hotel room is empty for an evening, the revenue is lost forever. Tickets to a symphony performance are only good at the time of the performance. Similarly, dentists, physicians, attorneys, and beauticians cannot recover revenue lost because of an unfilled schedule.

Lack of Transportability

The inability to transport services means that services normally must be consumed at the point of production. The services of a physician typically are available only at the physical location of the outlet, for example. House calls are possible, but are an inefficient way of service delivery.

Lack of Standardization

Standardization in service quality is difficult to achieve. Fast-food restaurants, which offer a combination of tangible goods and services, are an exception. A related problem is the difficulty consumers have in judging the quality of a service. How does one objectively decide which attorney or CPA is the most qualified, for example?

Labor Intensity

The labor intensive nature of services retailing is another factor which prevents such outlets from easily achieving economies of scale. The output of a hair stylist cannot easily be increased since the service is personally produced and tailored to the needs of each individual client. Services retailers as a result have difficulty establishing large market shares which means that competitors can quickly enter the market.

Demand Fluctuations

The demand for services also is often more difficult to predict than for tangible goods. The demand for some services can fluctuate strongly during a month, the day of the week, or even the hour of the day. Management has difficulty forecasting the demand for visitors to museum exhibits, ballet performances, or such theme parks as Disney World or Six Flags over Georgia, for example.

Planning the Services Offering

Planning the services offering is in many ways similar to planning a tangible goods offering. The question ultimately is one of what people are buying. The *core service* is the primary benefit customers seek from a services firm.

Peripheral services are secondary benefits sought by customers. The core service for a motel is a clean, comfortable room. Peripheral services could include a swimming pool, Showtime or HBO service, restaurants, or a golf driving range. Management often seeks to integrate core and peripheral services into a coherent competitive strategy.

Distribution

Distribution is an important aspect of services retailing, even though many services are intangible. As noted above, most services are provided directly by the retailer to the end user, without an intermediary. Still, some indirect channels are used in services retailing. An example is the acceptance of bank credit cards by retailers. Banks extend credit to retail customers who use the bank's credit card. The bank is a third party to any transaction which the customer has with the retail outlet.

Promotion

Effective use of promotion often is more difficult for services retailers than for tangible goods retailers because services are more difficult for consumers to evaluate than tangible goods. Increasingly, however, services retailers are using a variety of promotional tools and techniques to communicate information. Advertisements for dental health services offered by dental chains for example, often include a pricing schedule in much the same way a person would expect to find price quotations in tangible goods retailing ads. The advertisements also often focus on specific attributes of the service to be performed in an effort to make services more tangible.

Pricing

Pricing, although a key part of a service retailer's marketing plan, traditionally has been a "hush-hush" topic. Managers have been reluctant to talk about the prices of their services, and instead tend to refer to price as "admission" for entertainment events, or a "fee" for the services of an attorney. Pricing is becoming a more open subject, however, as more and more service firms go aggressively into marketing.

Some service retailers have long used pricing strategies to smooth demand. Resort hotels offer lower prices during the off-season. Airlines offer reduced rates for customers who fly during low demand, "red eye," periods such as midnight to six A.M. Banks have different fee structures to accommodate various customer segments.

CRITICAL CONTEMPORARY ISSUES

A text on retailing would be incomplete without a focus on consumerism and other contemporary social issues of importance to retail strategists.

	Frequency of Occurrence (percent rating)				
Offense or Practice	Very Frequent	Frequent	Sometimes	Infrequent	Very Infrequent
False or misleading advertising	17.5	30.7	41.3	7.4	2.6
Failure to honor warranties or provide service	3.2	22.2	43.4	22.2	7.4
Deceptive price comparisons	14.3	33.9	36.0	12.2	2.1
Failure to clearly reveal credit terms	5.3	26.6	33.0	23.9	8.5
Selling defective or damaged merchandise	2.6	9.0	39.7	37.6	10.1
High-pressure selling tactics	16.4	37.0	24.9	7.9	2.6
Not having advertised merchandise available	13.8	18.1	42.6	20.7	4.3

SOURCE: Ronald J. Adams and John M. Browning. "Correlates and Dimensions of Consumer Dissatisfaction with Deceptive Retail Practices." Paper presented at the 1982 annual meeting of the Southwestern Marketing Association.

Consumerism

Retailers, in analyzing the economic and social environments and their effects on strategy, would be remiss if they failed to recognize the continuing influence of consumerism. **Consumerism** *is an organized expression of dissatisfaction with selected business practices.* The consumer movement of the 70s and 80s is continuing into the 90s, but in a quieter, more mature context.

Many of the issues consumers first rallied around are now being addressed, if not remedied, in retailing. Consumer concerns that still persist, however, include complaints about false or misleading advertising, deceptive price comparisons, and high-pressure selling tactics. These concerns are reflected in Table 22–1.

One manifestation of the new consumerism is the increasing number of mandatory bottle deposit laws for beverages.[12] The laws mark a continuing fundamental shift in society away from an energy and materials intensive system toward one that is more heavily focused on recycling. Some retailers understandably are unhappy with such trends because of the costs involved.[13]

For the foreseeable future, local organizations that can provide direct tangible benefits to consumers will likely be more effective vehicles for change than national groups. An example of a local organization's success was the Massachusetts-based animal welfare group that pressured McDonald's and Burger King to boycott Canadian fish products in protest of that nation's seal hunting.[14] In another example, Albertson's agreed to stop selling *Playboy, Penthouse,* and *Playgirl* magazines in its western Washington stores. Similarly, Fred Meyer's, Inc. banned the magazines in all 66 of its stores in Washington, Oregon, Montana, and Alaska. 7-Eleven has taken similar action.[15]

We also cannot overlook the darker side of consumerism—the era of the consumer who cheats.[16] Problems range from insurance fraud to supermarket theft. Coupon fraud by consumers, another major problem, includes redemption of coupons for items not purchased, the purchase of different products sharing the same brand name, or purchase of an item that violates the size, quantity, expiration date, or other terms of the coupon.[17]

Voluntary Responses by Management to Consumer Dissatisfaction

Most retailers would probably agree with a former chairman of the FTC who observed that "providing for customer satisfaction . . . is good business." He contends that "the benefits from responding to consumer dissatisfaction are higher sales and profits."[18] Thus, retailers in recent years have taken various steps to lessen consumer dissatisfaction.

Home Warranties

The National Association of Home Builders (NAHB) now sponsors the Home Owners Warranty (HOW) program to help resolve consumer complaints. One of every four houses built carries a HOW warranty. About one third of the NAHB builders offer the program in 45 states and the District of Columbia. Warranties for varying periods cover structural defects and other problems caused by faulty workmanship or materials in violation of the program's building standards. The cost of a typical HOW warranty is around $2 per $1,000 of the sales price, or $150 for a $75,000 home.

Consumer Advisers

Forward-thinking retailers have appointed consumer advisers to bridge the communication gap between the shopper and management. Such persons make sure that customer complaints and questions are handled quickly and honestly. They represent management to the consumer and the consumer to management. Their job is to keep people happy by giving them straight answers and by allowing management to keep a constant finger on the pulse of the shopper.

Corporate Consumer Professionals

Corporate consumer affairs has also become a profession in recent years as retailers have made major investments in professionally trained personnel to respond more effectively to consumer concerns. These persons represent the interests of consumers in corporate councils. Probably the first corporate consumer affairs professional was Esther Peterson, who was hired by Giant Foods in the early 1970s. Giant Foods personnel indicated that Peterson's efforts required a restatement of what business is all about—"satisfying and winning over customers."

Third-Party Arbitration

Third-party arbitration *is a process by which two parties agree to have an impartial third party or panel resolve their difficulty with a final and* *binding decision*. Montgomery Ward has initiated an arbitration program in its Chicago retail stores and mail-order outlets. Sears has a program in selected outlets, as does J. C. Penney. General Motors also offers such an option to consumers. In addition to generating consumer goodwill, the programs offer management a way to resolve complaints without resorting to litigation. The program also gives merchants protection against irresponsible consumers. Such programs are often sponsored by local Better Business Bureaus.

Advisory Boards

Consumer **advisory boards** are also experiencing a revival in popularity as retailers seek more effective programs for communicating with consumers. Such boards comprise a cross section of community citizens, including senior citizens, men, women, and representatives of various ethnic groups. The new boards reflect a broadening and maturing of the public interest concept.

Voluntary Certification

Such agencies as the National Institute for Automotive Service Excellence (NIASE) are being created as independent nonprofit corporations for the primary purpose of improving the quality of skilled workers. The NIASE was established in 1972; since that time it has certified thousands of mechanics. The tests of competence are developed and administered by the Educational Testing Service of Princeton, New Jersey. In addition, the NIASE publishes a directory entitled "Where to Find Certified Mechanics for Your Car."

Quality of Life

Consumerism is concerned with more than the satisfaction of consumer needs in the marketplace, as we observed earlier. Consumers are also becoming increasingly concerned about quality of life in a broader sense. These concerns are evident in consumer protests about endangered wildlife species and vegetation, air and water pollution, beautification, and a host of similar issues.

Consumers clearly expect the retailing community to protect and preserve the environment and our natural resources in addition to operating in an economically efficient manner. Many of the quality-of-life concerns of consumers have culminated in federal and state regulations covering such issues as open space, land use, historic preservation, job safety and health, and much more.

In recent years, consumers have also been pressing for greater privacy. Thus, the postal authority and other groups must remove consumers from so-called junk mailing lists if they ask to be removed. Consumers are also often frustrated over telephone sales calls, especially when the call is a prerecorded message, and they are less willing to respond to market research interviews which they often consider an annoyance.

FUTURE CERTAINTIES

Regardless of the changes occurring, we can safely make the following observations about the future:

— Retailing will continue to grow in importance as a way of facilitating exchange.
— Retailing, to be successful, must continue to anticipate and respond to changes in the environments.
— Retailing will continue to offer exciting, rewarding, and diverse career opportunities. Job opportunities will continue to abound in promotion, personal selling, distribution, research, and various other dimensions of retailing, including competitor analysis, sales management, and corporate training.

Wouldn't you like to be a part of the phenomenal success of firms such as The Limited, Benetton, or The Gap? Or maybe you want to be on the team helping to rewrite competition in the financial services industries as Sears has done as a result of deregulation, or part of the A&P team which is working to develop a store of the future, or to help make McDonald's more of a world competitor. Perhaps your primary interest is retailing in your hometown, or helping to broaden the public's awareness of the beauty of ballet, or helping to bring more excitement to professional sports. Whatever your interests and career aspirations, retailing can play a vital role in your success. We urge you to get on board! You can begin by discussing the specifics of career options with your instructor and by investigating other marketing or retailing courses at your university. Good Luck!

CHAPTER HIGHLIGHTS

— The focus of management will continue to shift from merchandising to marketing as a key to strategy development.
— More and more firms are looking to the long term in developing a strategic view of the business and are focusing on such issues as store positioning, changing consumer lifestyles, and unique competitive strategies.
— Numerous changes are also occurring in merchandising as retailers seek to respond to a constantly shifting environment. The key changes include modified merchandise mixes, better merchandise-assortment planning, stringent cost reduction programs, increased use of classification dominance and vertical merchandising, flexible fixturing, an increased use of coordinated graphics and informative signing, and more emphasis on theatrics.
— Changes in the external environments are also affecting strategy. Key shifts include stronger price awareness by consumers and less store or brand loyalty, accelerating technology shifts, growth of the upscale market, increasing

time pressures on consumers, slow growth in many market segments, continued overstoring, and growth in small and medium-sized markets. The accelerating liability explosion is also impacting retail strategy because of rising insurance costs.

—— Retailers are choosing to respond to the changing environments in a variety of ways. The key trends include niching by specialty stores, continued strong success of commodity retailing in selected categories such as food, a strong return to private labels, and continued growth of power retailing.

—— Greater responsiveness to the social consciousness of society will continue to impact retailing strategies, as will consumerism. Consumer concerns about false or misleading advertising, deceptive price comparisons, and high-pressure selling tactics still persist.

—— Management has taken a variety of voluntary steps in helping to alleviate consumer dissatisfaction. The steps include the use of in-store consumer advisers, corporate consumer professionals, third-party arbitration, and consumer advisory boards.

—— Quality-of-life issues continue to be important as reflected in consumer concerns about air and water pollution, beautification, and a host of similar issues. Consumers clearly expect the retailing community to protect and preserve the environment and its natural resources.

KEY TERMS

Advisory boards A cross section of community citizens appointed by a retailer to offer advice and council to management on a variety of issues.

Classification dominance Displaying and arranging merchandise in such a way that psychologically the consumer is convinced the firm has a larger assortment of merchandise in the category than competitors.

Consumerism An organized expression of consumer dissatisfaction with selected business practices.

Institutional reliance A belief that members of society should turn to government for solutions to their problems.

Merchandising An operating philosophy in which the primary focus of the firm is on having the right merchandise at the right place, at the right time, in the right quantities, and at the right price.

Niching A strategy whereby a retailer carves out a narrow marketplace position that offers high potential and then specializes in meeting the needs of the consumers in that segment.

Off-price retailers Outlets offering well-known brands of merchandise at substantial discounts compared to conventional stores handling the same products.

Power retailers Merchants with sufficient financial strength, marketing skill, and price/value relationships to enter a market, however saturated, and make a profit.

Private labels Labels that are under the exclusive use and control of a retailer.

Third-party arbitration A process by which two parties agree to have an impartial third party or panel resolve a difficulty with a final and binding decision.

DISCUSSION QUESTIONS

1. What changes are expected in the future relative to store size, layout, and design?

2. What does it mean to say that retail management is shifting its emphasis from a merchandising to a marketing orientation?

3. Summarize the major changes projected for the 1990s in the competitive structure of retailing.
4. Highlight the major competitive strategies that are emerging among retailers as keys to success in the 1990s.
5. What are the most common charges against retailers in law suits brought against them by different groups?
6. What are the factors which led to the emergence of consumerism as a major market force?
7. What have been some of the voluntary retailer responses to consumer dissatisfaction?
8. Why should retailers be concerned about quality-of-life issues?

APPLICATION EXERCISES

1. A major discussion in this chapter relates to the questions, "What are the likely future operating environments?" and "What are some of the specific changes in operations methods likely to be?" List these changes. Then interview several retailers in your community and see if they agree. If they believe other things are likely to be as important, ask why they feel this way. You might work with a classmate, make a table showing your results, and present your findings to the class.
2. Prepare a short questionnaire, one page or so, based on the various trends in the economic and social environments that will affect retailing in the 1990s. Interview a cross section of retailers in your community to determine the strengths of their beliefs about the likelihood of these trends occurring or continuing in the near future. Prepare a short paper based on your findings.

3. Prepare a short questionnaire to be administered by telephone to a representative group of households in your community. Seek to find out (a) the effects of working wives on the household, (b) the effects of changing social values on the household, and (c) the effects of the inflation and deflation of recent years.
4. Select a given type of retailing such as a specialty retail jeweler or a convenience food outlet. Assume you are preparing a report for management which will help shape their planning for the next several years. Highlight the trends you think will most likely affect this type of retailing. Additionally, make recommendations to management for ways of responding to the changes you foresee.

CASES

1. Sears Is Exploring Ways It Can Enter Business of Selling Merchandise on TV

Sears Roebuck & Co. is exploring ways to enter the fast-growing business of selling merchandise on television.

A major Sears focus, trade sources said, is C.O.M.B. Co.'s Cable Value Network, which reaches about seven million cable television subscribers with programs oriented toward the sale of mostly close-out, surplus, and liquidation merchandise. Among other things, Chicago-based Sears and Minneapolis-based C.O.M.B. are said to be discussing sales of first-quality merchandise and of Sears' financial, insurance, and travel services, possibly tied into the company's new Discover credit

card. Pilot programs have been produced to test various formats; trade sources said.

C.O.M.B. wouldn't comment, and Sears wouldn't be specific about its plans. Joseph H. Batagowski, senior executive vice president of Sears' merchandise group, said the retailer is weighing a variety of options.

"We're looking at the business intensely," Mr. Batagowski said. "We've been interested in the business from the beginning." Among other things, he said, televised sales could be a quick way to reach thousands of homes at comparatively low cost. "The companies that are in it are doing some attractive volumes," Mr. Batagowski said.

Boost for Industry

A Sears entry into television shopping could provide an important boost to that fledgling industry, which is led by hard-selling, high-profile Home Shopping Network of Clearwater, Fla. Much of the merchandise sold by that largely cable television network and competitors, like Cable Value Network, consists of close-out items. Such merchandise of good quality is becoming increasingly difficult to find, and although some networks sell many items made to their specifications, none has consistent supplies of the quality and reputation offered by Sears.

But the benefits to Sears aren't as clear. Some of the existing formats use high-pressure sales techniques foreign to the retailer. It is impossible to predict the size or interest of television audiences, and televised sales of Sears merchandise might hurt the company's catalog business and chain of 110 close-out stores, some believe.

"Sears has plenty to do as it is beefing up its existing businesses. It doesn't need a distraction," said Edward A. Weller, an analyst with E. F. Hutton & Co. Still, he noted, televised shopping may produce $1 billion in sales this year. "Sears has seen a lot of changes go by and failed to respond; maybe they should respond to this one very aggressively," he said.

Major retailers like Sears and J. C. Penney Co. have toyed with electronic shopping forms for years, seeking a high-technology way to reach customers accustomed to shopping by catalog in their homes. Most of the operations have failed because they cost too much, were too cumbersome to operate, or required equipment like computers to function.

Two-Minute Commercials

Sears has experimented recently with "infomercials," two-minute-long commercials with an informational tone for goods that aren't easy to sell in a typical 30-second spot. In one such test, Sears marketed a vacuum and cleaning machine, Mr. Batagowski said. Results suggest "it's worth continuing to look at" such sales techniques, he said.

The shopping networks have built a following by generating a sense of bargains and excitement. Home Shopping Network, with its game-show environment, is available to an estimated 10 million cable television customers and to viewers of UHF television stations in some major markets where cable penetration is low. Cable Value Network has relied on a comparatively low-key sales patter in its programming, making it a more suitable vehicle for Sears.

Questions

1. What are the reasons Sears would consider selling merchandise on television?
2. What are the risks to Sears of such a strategy?
3. Should Sears consider affiliating with an existing channel or develop its own program format and merchandising strategy?

2. General Nutrition Centers

General Nutrition Centers has grown from virtually no retail stores in 1970 to more than 13,000 on the basis of strong aggressive marketing strategies. Critics contend that the company's sales have been built primarily by always promoting the latest health fad and making sensational claims in its more than 17 million mail-order catalogs which are distributed each year.

As long ago as 1969, the Federal Trade Commission brought false-advertising charges against the company over its Geri-Gen "therapeutic tonic" and Hemotrex vitamin supplements. FDA records further show enforcement actions in eight of the past nine years against the organization. In 1980, for example, the FDA seized quantities of a powdered milk promoted by GNC as a cure for arthritis. In 1981, they moved to halt GNC's distribution of brochures that claimed that lysine was a cure for genital herpes. Over the years, competing retailers and manufacturers have accused the company of trademark infringements. Independent stores and small regional chains have also accused GNC of unfair tactics designed to drive the competition out of business.

General Nutrition has proved to be a formidable competitor to government regulators and private prosecutors. For example, postal service complaints have had to be rewritten as many as 15 times to "catch the nuances in GNC advertising." One of the latest controversies surrounds the alleged promotion by GNC of Oil of Evening Primrose as a drug to treat diseases ranging from hypertension and multiple sclerosis to manic-depressive psychosis and heart disease. Recently, GNC was under fire for deceptive advertising tied to the company's marketing of Health Greens. The product is made from dehydrated vegetables and was introduced after the National Academy of Sciences indicated a dietary link between green vegetables and lower incidences of cancer. The Food and Drug Administration contended that GNC made claims for cures or risk reduction in diseases without competent scientific evidence. Over the years, GNC has paid millions of dollars in settlements, in court costs, and in legal fees defending itself against the various allegations.

Questions

1. What danger, if any, do you see in a retailer such as GNC promoting various products as a cure for a variety of ailments based on preliminary scientific evidence?
2. What are the ethical or social responsibility issues at the heart of the firm's marketing strategy?
3. Suggest an alternative marketing strategy for the retail outlet built around premises other than controversial advertising and fad products.

ENDNOTES

1. Debra J. Cornwall, "Say Good-Bye to the Merchant Mystique," *Business Horizons*, September–October 1984, p. 82. © 1984 by the Foundation for the School of Business at Indiana University. Reprinted by permission.
2. For further reading, see "Space Exploration: With Retail Rents in the Stratosphere, the Challenge Is to Use Every Inch," *Chain Store Age Executive, General Merchandise Trends*, March 1986, p. 13.
3. For further reading, see "Crowley's Light Motiff: A Delicate Balance," *Chain Store Age Executive, General Merchandise Trends*, March 1986, p. 86.
4. For further reading, see "Department Stores Score on Price Signs," *Chain Store Age Executive, General Merchandise Trends*, March 1986, p. 18.
5. Aimee Stern, "Retailers Restructure," *Dun's Business Month*, February 1986, p. 28; "Last Year It Was Yuppies—This Year It's Their Parents," *Business Week*, March 19, 1986, pp. 68–72.
6. Jeremy Main, "Merchants' Woe, Too Many Stores," *Fortune*, May 13, 1985, p. 62; see also Jim Osteroff, "Updating Present Stores Seen Economizing Trend," *Supermarket News*, November 3, 1986, p. 1.
7. See, "Retailers Warned of Liability in Product Tampering Suits," *Supermarket News*, January 24, 1983, p. 21.
8. For further reading, see "Sky High Damage Suits," *U.S. News & World Report*, January 27, 1986, pp. 36–37; "Insurance Costs Reach Crisis Level: Distributors," *Supermarket News*, February 10, 1986, p. 1.
9. "Rural Retailing: The Last Frontier," *Chain Store Age Executive*, March 1986, pp. 18–22.
10. David A. Collier, "Managing a Service Firm: A Different Management Game," *National Productivity Review*, Winter 1983–84, p. 36.
11. Leonard L. Berry, "Retail Businesses Are Service Businesses," *Journal of Retailing* 62 (Spring 1986), pp. 3–6; "When Marketing Services, the Four P's Are Not Enough," *Business Horizons*, May–June 1986, pp. 44–50.
12. "Push Voluntary Recycling, Retailers Urged," *Supermarket News*, February 13, 1984, p. 17.
13. "Bottle Losses Mount in New York Metro Areas," *Chain Store Age Executive*, April 1985, p. 17.
14. Desmond Smith, "McDonald's, Burger King Pressed to Join Fish Boycott," *Advertising Age*, March 26, 1984, p. 40.
15. "Two N.W. Chains Drop Three Nudie Magazines," *Supermarket News*, August 6, 1984, p. 11; "No More Adults," *Time*, April 21, 1986, p. 62.
16. Paul Bernsten, "Cheating—The New National Past Time?" *Business*, October–December 1985, p. 24; "A Nation of Liars?" *U.S. News & World Report*, February 23, 1987, p. 54.
17. P. Rajan Varadarhaan, "Coupon Fraud: A $500 Million Dilemma," *Business*, July–September 1985, p. 23.
18. "Customer Gripe Funnel Urged," *Supermarket News*, July 17, 1981, p. 7.

Careers in Retailing

RETAILING CAPSULE
The Rebirth of Retail

The retail field is one of the most important growth areas of the mid-'80s. Buoyed by dual-income families, larger discretionary incomes, and a general desire on the part of the American public to achieve a better lifestyle, the retail field is experiencing a boom like none in recent years. If today's retail customers were to adopt a motto, it would be, "When the going gets tough, the tough go shopping." In a word, retail is hot.

If you simply looked at the number of new stores in operation, you might not be very impressed. According to Audits and Surveys Inc., a New York-based market-research firm, there were 1,804,150 stores in operation last year, only 3.5 percent more than the 1980 figure. But, points out Solomon Dutka, Audits and Surveys' CEO, "While the long-term trend to larger stores continues, there has been strong growth in new types of specialty stores."

Convenience centers, small drive-up shopping centers that host a variety of specialty and food stores, have sprung up virtually overnight in the hopes of satisfying the spending needs of a busy, increasingly affluent public. "The convenience centers will see a significant increase in the next 5 to 10 years because of the time constraints on the American consumer," says Fred E. Winzer, Jr., an analyst with Alex, Brown & Sons in Baltimore, Maryland.

In addition, the emergence of some important demographic groups has redefined the opportunities available in retail. America is experi-

Susan Sachs, "The Rebirth of Retail," *Entrepreneur*, August 1986, p. 33.

encing population increases on both ends of the spectrum. The children of the Baby Boomers, a sort of Baby Boomlet, are proving to be a rapidly emerging group, both in numbers and influence.

A survey conducted by the Childrenswear Manufacturers Association in New York noted that the Boomlet generation's parents, aged roughly 25 to 34, represent the first generation of parents who "are better educated, dual-earners, and more affluent than the nation as a whole."

The other emerging group is the 55-and-over set. By the year 2030, the population is expected to include 33.6 retirees for every 100 active workers. (Compare this to 1975, when there were only 18.9 retirees for every 100 workers.) This creates a huge, previously overlooked area of opportunity for retailers. Sociologist Lynette Miller at U.S. International University in San Diego has coined this group "Sippies," or "Senior Independent Pioneers." Says Miller, "They have money to burn."

While the population as a whole may not quite have money to burn, many are enjoying higher wages than their predecessors, and most have shown an increased willingness to spend money on things they perceive will improve the quality of their lives—or their children's lives, in the case of the Baby Boom parents. People who work hard feel they deserve some of the finer things one can buy, particularly if those items in some way relieve some of the stress of a busy life. These include the latest in high-tech gadgetry as well as some of life's simpler things. Home entertaining is enjoying a renaissance as are writing and gift-giving, leading to an increase in stores that carry cards, gifts, party goods, and cookware.

One unexpected retail offshoot of this trend that has reached prominence is the modern novelty store, a place where adults can purchase nostalgia and novelty items. Stores of this type are enjoying increased popularity as the Baby Boom set has displayed a desire to relieve stress and have a good time, along with a penchant for looking back.

Specialization is another buzzword when it comes to retail, particularly in the area of clothing. As successful retailers of large-size women's apparel like The Forgotten Woman have found, there are entire groups of people who have previously felt ignored. They provide excellent opportunities for people who wish to cater to large-sized people, petites, or children.

Businesswear is another specialty area that some people are profitably getting in on now, and sportswear and leisurewear promise continued growth to correspond with America's unrelenting interest in fitness. With over half of U.S. adults regularly participating in some type of physical-fitness activity, health-and-fitness-related businesses that meet their needs are doing well.

It seems that leisurely shopping, once considered a luxury of the very rich, has become a new American pastime, with people regularly flooding the large, indoor malls and rediscovering the downtown shopping areas in addition to frequenting the convenience centers. For many people, disposable income is at an all-time high, as is concern about image and lifestyle. Even those who do not have expendable cash appear to be increasingly willing to extend their credit to buy something they can enjoy NOW.

The message for potential retailers is this: Find a specialty that is linked to a current trend and jump in.

The retailing capsule focuses on timely opportunities to become a retailing entrepreneur. We encourage budding entrepreneurs to consider the field of retailing as a likely, long-term choice for one's own business. We hasten, however, to encourage all students *not* to go into retailing immediately following an educational experience, regardless of how many years this experience has involved. We are strong believers in "making mistakes for someone else" before investing one's own capital in any business, especially retailing. *If* a student has been intimately involved in retailing management decision making prior to or during his or her educational life, *and* if the experience has continued over several operating periods, then we would admit that this person has a chance of succeeding.

Admitting our biases, we thus look on this Appendix as addressing the concerns of the average college students who will probably go into the job market to seek a job with someone else. Consequently, the purposes of this Appendix are to:

1. Focus your attention on career orientation.
2. Describe the characteristics of retailing careers.
3. Review the job skills needed to succeed in retailing.
4. Provide some tangible tips on:
   a. The value of internships/experience.
   b. Preparing a game plan for job finding.
   c. Interviewing dos and don'ts.
   d. Reviewing questions you can ask in an interview.
   e. Getting together an up-to-date resumé.
   f. Common mistakes job hunters make.
5. Illustrate typical training programs and career paths that exist in retail organizations.
6. Offer suggestions for career progress and success.

Students considering retailing as a career possibility probably have a particular type of retailing in mind because of personal knowledge. They may not realize where the jobs really are. Department stores, for example, although highly visible, are just one source of entry-level opportunities. Probably because of the college-recruiting of department stores, they seem to be the major opportunities for entry-level job aspirants. Retailing, of course, takes place in many kinds of operations—specialty stores (The Limited), off-price (T. J. Maxx), and discount firms (Wal-Mart); the so-called national chains (Sears and Penney's); national, regional, and local food organizations (Safeway, Kroger, and Cub); the specialty chains (Toys-R-Us); and many other types of firms. Students interested in retailing careers must consider as well resident buying officers in a central market; direct sellers (Mary Kay and Tupperware); shopping center developers and managers (Rouse Company); mail-order firms (Spiegel); and services retailing (Century 21 and Delta Airlines). This is quite a list, though still incomplete, to add to Macy's and Bloomingdale's.

Students must recognize that retailing is not without disadvantages. Retailing suffers from an image problem that affects the success of recruiters on college campuses throughout the country. Some of the image problems relate to the long hours that must be spent in the beginning, particularly during evenings and weekends. A young person expecting to get ahead in retailing must no doubt endure these long hours. Retailing trainees also can expect to do some menial tasks as part of the learning process.

Still, the skills gained in retailing will be transferable to just about any field. Retailing can be a wonderful experience for anyone who enjoys buying and selling merchandise. If you are excited about "making your day"—seeing how well you did compared to the same day in the previous year—retailing can be a challenge. If you like to sit at a desk, retailing is not for you. A retail management trainee and potential manager/merchandiser is on the go all the time. Retailers travel, share experiences, meet interesting people, and enjoy immediate feedback on their efforts. If you are prepared to work hard and long, the payoffs can be very gratifying—and the remuneration excellent.

Not everyone who studies retail management wants a career in the field. For those of you who are curious about retailing opportunities, however, this Appendix can help you discover what to expect after graduation.

CAREER DEVELOPMENT

Students are at various stages of career development. The continuum below suggests the degrees of career development or orientation that you may be experiencing. You probably have friends who are at each phase. A student who is "career disoriented" may not have given any thought to the future; the student may be less disoriented than unconcerned. This apparent casual attitude may seem immature, and indeed this may be the case. Career development is, after all, part of total human development.

$$x\text{―――――}x\text{―――――}x$$

Disoriented   Initial orientation   Definitive orientation

We encourage you to seek career counseling at all phases of your career development, especially when a concern about careers surfaces. If you are uncertain about your career path, do not despair. Get to work on helping yourself. Do not confuse "getting a job" with "career development." We suspect that a great deal of early attrition in first jobs results from both a desire to get a job simply to earn money and uncertainty about a career. A job without a career direction is likely to prove unsuccessful in the long run.

The following sections offer information on careers in retailing and on careers in general to assist you in finding the right direction for *your* career.

CHARACTERISTICS OF RETAILING CAREERS

Employment in retailing exceeds 14 million persons in over 1.9 million establishments. The diversity of opportunities is staggering and can fulfill almost every kind of ability, ambition, and desire. Retail establishments are located in the smallest rural village and the most sophisticated metropolitan area.

Security
Security in a job is important to many people. Retailing offers a high degree of job security. Even during periods of economic stagnation, retailing suffers fewer employment declines than manufacturing or wholesaling. The reason is that consumers must continue to buy merchandise regardless of the state of the economy.

Decentralized Job Opportunities
No matter where they live, people must purchase merchandise on a regular basis to maintain their standards of living. This means you can have a successful career in retailing even if you do not want to move far from home. On the other hand, people who want to move frequently can find the opportunity for employment in retailing wherever they go.

Opportunities for Advancement
Many executive positions exist because of the large number of retail establishments in the United States. Retailing is continuing to expand, and positions in management are being created on a basis proportionate to this expansion. The *Occupational Outlook Handbook* (U.S. Department of Labor) predicts that the number of managerial positions in retailing will grow about as fast as the average for all occupations through the 1980s.

Reward for Performance and Entrepreneurship
Retailing offers a daily performance measure because sales and profits can be read and evaluated daily. For high performers, such tangible measures are a delight; for the nonperformers, each day is painful. Obviously, not everyone is right for retailing (and the same can be said for all career options). A college graduate who performs may become a buyer for a high dollar volume department in a large department store organization within two or three years. As a buyer responsible for producing a profit in the department, such an achiever will really be acting as an entrepreneur in the security of an established firm.

Women in Retailing
A recent survey found that the retail industry offers women good opportunities for advancement. Women have moved into all middle-management positions and beyond. In the 1980s women hold top management positions—president,

general merchandise manager, and divisional merchandise manager—and in numbers which give evidence that rather dramatic changes are taking place. Women were locked into advertising, publicity, fashion coordinating, or personnel training 15 or 20 years ago. "Though women in retailing haven't yet made it to the top in equal numbers as men, by the end of the decade we expect they will earn genuine parity with their male counterparts."[1]

Promotion-from-within Policies

Progressively managed retail firms promote from within. The Broadway, for example, promotes about 87 percent of all management positions from within—a big change from the past decade. Management attributes the firm's improved stability partly to strong recruiting and better training, but perhaps just as much to paying more attention to improving compensation and to *retention*—a key word for the 80s.

Salaries in Retailing

Starting salaries for college graduates entering retail training programs vary widely—from $17,000 to $23,000 annually. The contrast in starting salaries reflects the variation in training programs, location, cost of living, and the competitive market for trainees.

Nonmonetary Rewards

A person's ability and effort—or their absence—are quickly recognized in retailing. The position of store manager appeals to persons with the ability to organize and direct the activities of others. As store manager, you set your own sales and profit goals as well as control expenses, compensate employees, and perform other vital management functions. In effect, you have the opportunity to manage your own business with someone else's money. A management career in retailing also offers the opportunity to work with ideas. Managers create ways of increasing sales and profit through imaginative use of the retail mix.

Working Conditions

Working conditions in retailing are comparable to those in many areas of employment. The typical workweek is 40 hours with some overtime at peak periods. Work in the evenings and on weekends is common.

JOB SKILLS NEEDED IN RETAILING

Cashiers and salesclerks are the positions many people imagine when retailing is mentioned. These jobs are only two of the many available. A substantial number of "behind the scenes" jobs exist in all retail settings.

The different types of job opportunities in retailing can be grouped into five employment categories. These five areas of employment are common to most retail firms.

Retailing demands creative merchandising ability. (Courtesy Dillards)

Creative people design exciting displays. (Courtesy Dillards)

Merchandising. Merchandising is buying and selling goods. Merchandising is one of the most important areas of employment. Trainees often start out in this area, because it is the heart of the store. Buyers work with suppliers in acquiring goods for the outlet. They also help coordinate advertising and display, and may travel worldwide to acquire the latest fashions. An ambitious and successful buyer may become a merchandise manager, which means overseeing several buyers.

Exhibit A–1 is an interesting discussion of the role of a buyer at Neiman-Marcus in Dallas. You will find the source of the material interesting as well.

Operations. Operations means sales support. The jobs include store management, warehousing, receiving, delivery, security, and customer service.

Sales Promotion. Sales promotion is closely related to merchandising. Sales promotion involves advertising, display, publicity, and other sales promotion

---

E X H I B I T A–1   *THE ROLE OF A BUYER AT NEIMAN-MARCUS*

Pat Barker was born in San Antonio, Texas. After changing his major several times, he received his bachelor's degree in public relations from the University of Texas. With no career plans upon graduation, he moved to Dallas where he worked as a waiter. On the advice of several employees he applied for and was hired for work at Neiman-Marcus.

Barker demonstrated his creative capabilities first by dressing and designing windows in the display department for three years and then as display manager for two more. When a gift buyer's position became available, he was offered the job. Says Barker, "I had no merchandising experience, but I was familiar with the store, and it was a lot easier to teach me about buying than it would have been to hire someone from the outside."

Now, his official title is "fashion director for the gift division and group buyer of executive accessories." On a buying trip he may travel to the Philippines, Hong Kong, Bangkok, Southern Italy, and London. On these trips he must make quick decisions.

Idea Generation

Pat Barker began his job as buyer with a fundamental understanding of what to buy. After having worked at Neiman-Marcus for five years, he could empathize with both his customers' needs and the company's mission. Armed with these basics, Barker uses several methods to find clues to exciting merchandise. In-house information is always a good starting point. Barker explains, "Because everything is computerized, I can look back and see how prior products have done. Using the past as a guide, we can make judgments about the present as well as the future. Before we buy, we have to know what we can earn on the money we spend." Basically, Neiman's looks at last year's sales as a financial guide. Although management cannot sell the same merchandise as the previous year, they could sell the same category, such as tapestries or American folk art.

The computer system is quite elaborate. The Neiman-Marcus merchants may use it to examine financial data, place orders, receive reports, and even send intracompany memos. Unlike some buyers, Barker does not buy with his budget in mind; rather he buys, then sees how his purchases fit the budget. Here, a computer is useful. With 22 stores and 22 different budgets, the computer is essential to see how the purchases fit the budgets and if he needs to buy less, buy more, or even change the budgets. Completely flexible, the budgets may be rearranged to accommodate the merchandise and the regions' needs.

Because Neiman-Marcus must constantly change and update its merchandise, Pat Barker cannot depend on last year's financial data for new ideas. The buyer must draw not only upon his environment but also upon his creativity. According to Barker, new ideas for merchandise come from everywhere and from seeing everything. All it takes is looking around a lot and seeing something new. Keeping up with what is happening in the world is a matter of pride with Barker.

Careers in Retailing

At the time of this writing, the Neiman-Marcus buyers were looking at antiques because the national mood was conservative and favored traditional goods. Buying in themes is not unusual. For example, the 1960s era is now in vogue. Therefore, buyers can look to music and clothing for gift ideas. Nothing is absolutely original; however, at Neiman-Marcus, management must "try to do it first." Because Neiman's does it first, their products are more expensive.

When asked if the recent buy-American trend affected him, Barker said that people are now interested in American crafts and their heritage. He believes, however, that a product's origin should have no effect on his purchase decision. Barker says he buys "because of what the item is."

New vendor contacts are not a problem for Neiman-Marcus; large suppliers and individuals alike actively solicit the elegant store. Buyers always respond to inquiries, even though they may buy from only one of 10 unknowns. It is important always to be courteous—that little supplier may have a friend who is very good.

Shipping

Once purchases have been negotiated, shipping arrangements must be made. If the goods must be imported into the United States, shipping may become a problem. "Purchasing goods from abroad can be very tricky," explains Barker. "It can take from 8 to 10 months between the time you order something and receive it. The goal is to have the merchandise shipped in one piece, in excellent condition." In this respect, shipping is a constant battle. Because the store has an agency that handles shipping in each country, Barker does not deal directly with the shipper. In terms of safe shipping strategies, he said that they just ship it and see how it goes.

Sometimes the shipping costs amount to more than the original price of the item. At the U.S. port of entry, the tariff duties must be added to the cost of the goods. Before the goods reach that point, Barker should have a general knowledge of the tariffs.

Other Duties

Between buying seasons, Pat Barker spends a lot of time on the phone dealing with everyday operating concerns. Keeping up with what is and is not selling, identifying any problems that exist, ironing out such problems, explaining his purchases to the sales arm of the company and the stores, and communicating with all involved parties are a few of the things that occupy Barker's day.

He must keep involved store employees motivated, even though that is more the job of store management. Sometimes motivation comes through a vendor, who might offer a bonus to the salespeople, all of whom work on commission at Neiman's.

It is important for him to spend time in the stores telling stories and providing information, because as he explains, "It's unreasonable to assume that everyone is going to be as excited as I am about a product."

Performance Evaluation

As with most management-level executives, the typical buyer's performance is measured by how much he or she makes for the store. Because Barker has responsibilities other than buying, he is also evaluated on creativity. For example, it is good if he starts an interesting trend. In other words, he must make money with style and creativity.

Buying Careers

Pat Barker had several observations to make. He feels that in his job he must be interested in the fashion industry and not be afraid of hard work. He says that one has to enjoy working with people. A good buyer must enjoy seeing change and movement, be aware of world trends and events, and be both flexible and aggressive. He reflects on his lifestyle. He is single, and says that when he started, he ran himself crazy putting in long days on the road as well as at the store. He's now learned to delegate and works conventional days. He tries to do what he knows he can do well and he delegates the rest.

For those people desiring a career as a buyer, Barker suggests accepting a department store job after college in order to discover areas of interest. There is a place for talented and ambitious learners. He says, "A lot of talented people who have moved up through the ranks at the company have almost written their own job descriptions. Filling needs that didn't exist created new jobs."

SOURCE: From a class paper written at The University of Alabama by Melissa Provost who was inspired by (and used some of) Bob Weinstein, "What I Do on the Job, Retail Buyer," *Business Week's Careers*, September 1986, pp. 130–31. Ms. Provost was so interested in the article that she called Mr. Pat Barker in Dallas and conducted an extensive telephone interview, which became a source for her paper and in turn for this exhibit.

activities. Creativity and originality are needed for these jobs; for example, writing and artwork skills are important in advertising. Jobs include copywriter, decorator, and art director.

Control. Persons working in the control area manage the company's assets. Knowledge of statistics, accounting, or data processing are needed for these jobs. Credit, accounts payable and receivable, auditing, and data processing are some of the jobs found in this area.

Personnel. Jobs in personnel involve recruiting, selecting, and training employees. People in this area also work with employee compensation and other benefits, and they handle union problems.

TANGIBLE CAREER TIPS

For this discussion to be meaningful, we must assume that you have moved along the career orientation continuum to at least the initial orientation phase. We also want to note here that this section is rather "generic." We think the tips herein are valuable even if retailing is not your career objective.

Get a Head Start

"Across the country, innovative work-learn programs are providing new solutions to an old dilemma for thousands of college students. You can't get a job without experience, and you can't get experience without a job."

Work-learn programs go by other names: internships, experiential education, or perhaps just salaried jobs. These programs can be at either the undergraduate or the graduate level, full- or part-time, and for as many as 12 semester hours credit, or no credit at all. These programs are available in the public as well as the private sectors, and for profit and nonprofit organizations. The time frame is flexible—for a month or perhaps for a year. They all have one thing in common: "They are intended to help you learn while you work. . . ."

The cooperative education (co-op) programs differ from the internships, but the former certainly serve the essential purpose of learning and working. The co-op programs, from their inception, were viewed as long-term projects which allow students to alternate between work and school; they were originally intended to offer financial aid in "technical" fields and thus tend to attract students with a higher level of skills who see their work as "hands-on" practice for the real world. On the other hand, internships are more exploratory and are designed to give students a feel for the job rather than develop their skills. In point of fact, the differences are blurred today, and both give the students a valuable headstart.

In some fields (retailing being one of them) some kind of work experience is becoming virtually a job requirement. The more competitive the field, the more important this requirement is.

Here are four proven strategies that will help you in your job quest.

— Develop a game plan. Think about the kind of job you want. Where do you want to work? How do you plan to approach the job search? What information do you need? Where can you get it? Who are the resource people who can help you?

— Organize your job search. Work as hard at getting a job as you would on the job. Plan job search activities on a daily basis. Set goals. Keep detailed records. Maintain deadlines.

— Utilize all available resources. Go to the placement center, employment agencies, and community organizations. See what services they offer. Learn what their strengths and weaknesses are. Respond to want-ads, and use personal and direct contacts. Go to lectures, workshops, and seminars. Attend professional meetings and conferences. The more resources you utilize, the better your chances are for success.

— Continually evaluate your game plan. If your strategy isn't working, look realistically at what you're doing. Get help if you need it. Remember that the job search is a process, not an outcome. Nothing is irreversible. Resumes can be rewritten. Interviewing techniques can be improved. What is most important is that you remain flexible at all times.

SOURCE: *Business Week's Guide to Careers,* Spring–Summer 1984, p. 65.

Internships are viewed by many as mere stepping-stones to a real job in the future. Experts believe, however, that the enhanced self-confidence and the introduction to professionalism they provide may be invaluable in the long run to the students. After all it is an investment in the future.

Job Finding Game Plan

We urge you to develop a "job-finding game plan" with which you can live. We cite Figure A–1 which includes four proven strategies you will find very helpful.

Questions to Ask in an Interview[2]

"If you really want the job, you ask probing, intelligent questions." The following 10 questions are suggested by *Business Week's Careers:*

— How would you describe a typical day on the job?
— When was my predecessor promoted?
— What kind of training can I expect in the first three months?
— What specific skills or experience would help someone do well in this job?
— Do most managers have advanced degrees? If so, which ones?
— When will the first job performance evaluation take place?
— To whom would I report?
— Will I have a chance to meet people who would be my co-workers?
— Would I be assigned to a specific department or rotate throughout the organization?
— Does the company anticipate changing the current structure soon?

Have a Good, Up-to-Date Resume

Check with the college placement office for ideas, but above all, make sure that the resume is neat, has no spelling errors, and points out your skills and

INTERVIEW DOS AND DON'TS

Ninety-nine out of 100 bright-as-a-penny candidates who are wearing their best dressed-for-success outfits and have all the credentials necessary to impress St. Peter at the gate of heaven won't make the effort necessary to answer the following typical interview questions:

— How did you happen to select X as a career choice?

— What are the qualities necessary for success in X?

— What do you consider your chief strengths in this profession?

— What are some of the weaknesses that might hinder your success?

— Why should we hire you rather than one of your equally competent classmates?

— What are your long-term career objectives at this point?

— Why do you think you would like to work for our company?

There's no way you can answer these questions without also revealing whether or not you have done your homework about yourself, your career decisions, and the company.
Here is sound advice from Sydney Reynolds, New York City Executive Search Consultant:

Do:

— Anticipate probing questions about any obviously difficult career episode on your resume, such as a job briefly held, or a summer job that did not result in a permanent offer.

— Control your desire to run the interview. Instead, concentrate on adopting a pleasant and cordial tone throughout.

— Be succinct.

Don't:

— Oversell and make promises you will live to regret once you are actually on the job.

— Project a self-centered perspective, such as "What's in this for me?"

— Be negative about any employer or company. Don't blame others in the course of explaining situations.

Allan Sarn, a New York-based executive search consultant who sees the mistakes that experienced candidates make while interviewing for executive jobs, emphasizes that candidates must know the following about the company before an interview:

— The dollar volume of the company's annual business.

— The number of employees who work for the company.

— The products manufactured or services provided by the company.

— The names of the top executives in the company.

— The scope of the business—whether domestic or international.

— The general content of the company's most recent annual report as well as information contained in major articles written about it.

SOURCE: Reprinted from the Spring/Summer 1984 issue of *Business Week's Guide to Careers* by special permission © 1984 by McGraw-Hill, Inc. All rights reserved.

work-related background. Focus on the jobs you have held and on your skills, talents, and interests. Figure A–3 shows you the organization of a typical resume for a person in college seeking retailing employment. Exhibit A–2 is a checklist for dos and don'ts in resume preparation. Other useful tips are found in Figure A–2, the interview "dos and don'ts" presented along with typical interview questions to contemplate in your initial career search activities—the job interviewing process.

J. B. Delbridge
Post Office Box 123
Main City
State ZIP
(111) 222-2222

Objective

Retail management—Aiming for employment with a retail firm where a strong sense of responsibility, strong technical skills, and a willingness to learn and grow are valued characteristics.

Retail experience

September 1989 (present)—Part-time salesperson, home furnishings department, Green's Department Store, Riverview City

Summer 1989—Intern to Mr. G. S. Green, Owner/Manager of Green's Department Store, Riverview City

Summer 1988—Worked in the receiving and marking department at Woolbright Discount Stores, Anycity

Summer 1987—Cashier at Woolbright Discount Stores, Anycity

Education

B.S., The University of Riverview

Major: Marketing with a concentration in Retail Management
Grade Point Average: B overall and in major

Activities/Honors

College: Collegiate Retailing Association (president and treasurer); The Marketing Club (membership chairman); Student Government Association (senator); Member of the Student Executive Council of the College of Commerce and Business Administration; Retailing Achievement Award, Dean's List (3 semesters)

High School: Valedictorian; Student Council Vice President; Beta Club; Society of Outstanding American High School Students

References

Available upon request.

Common Job-Hunting Mistakes[3]
"You'll find a job faster and more easily—and even enjoy the quest—if you steer clear of these frequently made errors."

— Not knowing what you want to do.
— Not taking initiative.
— Going to too few prospects.
— Not viewing employment from the employer's perspective.
— Asking too directly for a job.
— Not targeting the people with whom you would be working.
— Approaching prospects in an impersonal way.
— Having an unfocused resume.

1. Give your resume an informative heading worded for the appropriate degree of "selling."
   a. Identify your name, type of work desired, and (preferably) the company to which addressed.
   b. Be sure you apply for work, not a job title.
2. For appropriate emphasis, ease of reading, and space saving:
   a. Balance the material across the page in tabulated form.
   b. Use different type and placement to affect emphasis and to show awareness of organization principles.
   c. Use centered heads that carry emphasis and help balance the page.
   d. Capitalize the main words in centered heads and underline the heads unless in solid caps.
   e. If you have to carry over an item, indent the second line.
   f. Remember to identify and number pages after the first.
3. Lead with whatever best prepares you for the particular job, but account for the chronology of your life since high school. (Gaps of more than three months may arouse suspicion.) When older and extensively experienced, such complete coverage is less necessary.
4. Education details should point out specific preparation.
   a. Show the status of your education early: degree, field, school, and date.
   b. Highlight courses which distinctively qualify you for the job. Listing everything takes away emphasis from the significant and suggests inability to discriminate.
   c. In listing courses, give them titles or descriptions which show their real content or briefly give specific details of what you did.
   d. Give grade averages in an understandable form (letters, quartiles, or percentages; GPA systems vary too much).
   e. Avoid belittling expressions like "theoretical education."
5. Experience: for jobs listed,
   a. Give job title, duties, firm or organization name, full address, specific dates, *responsibilities,* and immediate superior's name.
   b. If experience is part time, identify it as such.
   c. Consider reverse chronology or other arrangement to emphasize the most relevant and important.
   d. Use noun phrases and employ action verbs that imply *responsibility.*
6. If you include a personal details section, it should present a clear, true picture. (Though law prevents employers from asking, no law prohibits you from volunteering information about race, religion, age, health, and marital status.)
   a. Tabulate, but try combining ideas to save words:

Born in East Lansing,	Married, no children
Michigan, 1960	Member of (list appropriate
5'11'', 185 lbs.	organizations)
Good health, glasses	Like fishing and
for close work	reading

   b. Give your address(es)—and phone(s) if likely to be used—in minimum space where easily found but not emphasized.
7. List or offer to supply references. When you list references (to conclude your resume or supply later on request):
   a. Give the names, titles, full addresses, and telephone numbers of references for all important jobs and fields of study listed.
   b. Unless obvious, make clear why each reference is listed.
8. Remember these points about style:
   a. A resume is ordinarily a tabulation; avoid paragraphs and complete sentences.
   b. Noun phrases are the best choice of grammatical pattern.
   c. Items in any list should be in parallel form.
   d. Keep opinions out of resumes; just give facts. Use impersonal presentation, avoiding first- and second-person pronouns.

SOURCE: C. W. Wilkinson, Peter B. Clarke, and Dorothy C. M. Wilkinson, *Communicating through Letters and Reports* (Homewood, Ill.: Richard D. Irwin, 1980), p. 343.

— Overlooking selling points.
— Not following through.

TRAINING PROGRAMS AND CAREER PATHS

Thus far, the Appendix has focused on career orientation, the characteristics of retailing careers, the job skills needed to succeed in retailing, and some generic, tangible career tips. This concluding section is concerned with training programs and career paths.

Training Programs

Training programs involve rotation among the various departments/functions within a firm until the trainee is familiar with the operations. Programs vary in detail, but the following example we believe is typical and representative of the general philosophy of organizations with formalized programs.

Macy's New York[4]

Macy's is a worldwide name in retailing. They have operating divisions serving the East, South, Midwest, and West. They also operate the world's largest store, in New York. Macy's bureau of standards is still the only one of its kind in a department store. Each Macy's division has its own management, buying staff, and merchandising approach consistent with the market it serves.

For the average American, when the name Macy's is mentioned, the New York division comes to mind, particularly the Herald Square flagship store. The following information is for the Macy's New York store.

Do You Have What It Takes? Can you compete in a fast-paced, demanding atmosphere? You can—if you are energetic, imaginative, and dedicated. Of course we know we're not the only ones looking for talented graduates with those characteristics, but we also know not every industry offers the kind of immediate responsibility, rapid advancement, and financial reward that department store retailing can.

Consider for a moment the 24-year-old-buyer of a multimillion dollar business who travels the world seeking new items of merchandise and enjoys almost immediate feedback on the validity of the decisions made. Think about the 30-year-old store manager of a 330,000 square foot unit with total responsibility for profit, the excitement, and color within those four walls.

We'll Train You. Our Executive Development Program enjoys a nationwide reputation for excellence. We combine a comprehensive introduction to department store retailing with extensive on-the-job training assignments which provide the opportunity to apply your understanding of merchandising and management procedures. Where else can you test those newly acquired skills, then return to the classroom to share experiences with your colleagues and learn from each other's successes? Completion of the program brings immediate responsibility in one of our 15 stores. Career advancement is based on performance and accomplishment.

Career Paths   A career path can be thought of as the route taken *within a particular company* as is illustrated in Figure A–4 (Macy's corporate headquarters). The pattern of advancement is typical of department store retailing in general, and is not atypical of other sectors of retailing. The progression through a retailing organization depends at least in part on the organizational structure. For example, in a highly centralized structure, more executive-level opportunities exist in the corporate or division headquarters. In a more decentralized operation, where most of the necessary functions are at the local level, additional opportunities may exist in the individual stores.

Career paths differ from the department store model of course, but the variation at this point in time is not significant. Within food chains, the national specialty chains, and other sectors of retailing, patterns of movement will vary; names of functions will differ; but the basic philosophy remains.

A career path can also be viewed as a "life-time pattern" of advancement. This longer time frame will undoubtedly involve multiple organizations; different industries; and apparent total changes in direction. To prove this point, and also to indicate that success is not necessarily directly tied to a one-track career path, the following paths of former students, selected for their differences are cited:

Student	Year Graduated	College Major	First Job	Subsequent Jobs	Present Position
Male 1	1965	Marketing	Trainee, national discount chain	Facilities management	Director, world-class convention center
Female 1	1970	Retailing	Trainee, New York upscale department store	Corporate buyer, New York department store group; merchandise manager, garment manufacturer	Owner, direct marketing firm
Female 2	1975	Retailing	Trainee, major New York department store; assistant buyer	Bank marketing	Assistant vice president, major stock brokerage firm, New York
Male 2	1980	Marketing	Trainee, southern fashion department store group	Sales manager; assistant buyer same firm	Buyer, same firm

Store Management

Sales Manager → Group Manager → Merchandise Manager → Store Manager → Senior Vice President

Buying

Trainee → Assistant Buyer → Buyer → Merchandise Administrator → Senior Vice President for Merchandising

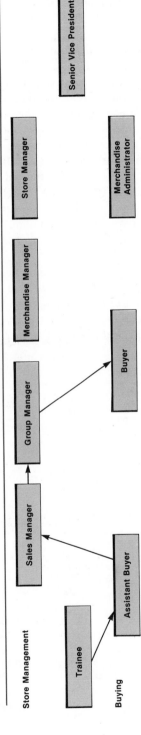

Trainee
General orientation to the retailing industry and the specifics of our operations through both classroom work and extensive on-the-job experience.

Sales Manager
Responsible for running a complete selling area in a store, including merchandise presentation, supervision of sales personnel, customer service, inventory control, and all other aspects of running a business.

Assistant Buyer
Learning to be a Buyer through assisting a Buyer in planning, acquiring, pricing, distributing, and promoting a category of merchandise for all stores of a division.

Group Manager
Responsible for executing merchandising plans for several departments in a store and reaching sales goals; supervises, trains, and develops sales managers.

Buyer
Responsible for planning, selecting, acquiring, pricing, distributing, and promoting merchandise for all stores of a division. With experience, buying responsibilities increase.

Merchandise Manager
Similar to Group Manager's position but with responsibility for expanded merchandise categories; coordinates the efforts among different departments; acts as major liaison between store executives and buyers.

Store Manager
Responsible for the total operation of a store, including merchandising, operations, and personnel; responsible for community relations, overall image of the store, and providing leadership in planning and goal setting.

Merchandise Administrator
Administrator responsible for conceptualizing and planning overall buying in several related merchandise classifications for a division; coordinates, develops, and evaluates the work of buyers, with responsibility for profits.

Senior Vice President for Merchandising Responsible for developing and overseeing divisional objectives and policies in buying, merchandise planning, advertising, promotion, and systems for large sectors of the business; direct responsibility for the overall profitability of those sectors.

Conclusions   We do not believe it is our role to *sell* you on a retailing career. We have presented information for you to think about. Retailing career paths are rather definite and understandable, and can result in high-level performance for the right person. Retailing offers many excellent training programs. You must evaluate them in terms of your own career aspirations. We do encourage you to consider retailing as a career possibility—we ask no more.

APPENDIX HIGHLIGHTS

— Retailing offers many diverse opportunities, but suffers from an image problem as far as a career is concerned.

— Students are at various stages of career development or orientation—from disoriented, through initial orientation, to definitive orientation. Students are encouraged to become oriented as soon as possible.

— Characteristics of retailing careers are: high degree of job security; decentralized job opportunities; opportunities for advancement growing about as fast as the average for all occupations; daily performance measures with tangible rewards; good opportunities for women; progressive firms promote from within; salaries, although varying, are basically competitive at the entry level; and working conditions are essentially comparable to those in other fields, but often do require evening and weekend work.

— The different types of job opportunities can be grouped into the following areas of employment: merchandising, operations, sales promotion, control, and personnel.

— The following career tips are useful: get a head-start through some kind of experiential learning activity; create a job-finding game plan; prepare carefully for interviews; have a good, up-to-date resume; and avoid the 10 common job-finding mistakes.

— Retailing training programs and career paths are rather definite and understandable and can result in high performance for the right person.

DISCUSSION QUESTIONS

1. Why do you think the job status of retailing appears to be low? What can be done to improve the situation?
2. Why are starting salaries low in retailing? Should salary be a major factor in choosing a career?
3. What are the employment possibilities for women in retailing? What are the reasons women should consider a career in retailing? Are the reasons different for men? Explain your answer.

4. What are the major types of jobs in retailing? What are the skills needed to work in each of these areas?
5. What is the typical advancement in a training program for a large department store?
6. If you are planning to own your own retail business in the future, what types of experience should you first have?
7. What recommendations would you give someone for preparing for a job interview?

APPLICATION EXERCISES

1. Write to several retail organizations and ask for any "career information" they have. Then make up a summary chart contrasting and comparing the various "career components" a potential trainee in retailing would want to evaluate. Try to get information on beginning salaries, promotional paths, career options, and so on.

2. Assume you have been out of school for several years. You have been in a nonretailing position (assume anything you desire) and want to change career patterns. You look at retailing as a career possibility. Outline the steps you might go through to assist you in your decision. Assume you decide on retailing as a career. What sources are available in your job search? Do an inventory of steps you will take and information you can develop. Then do a *marketing job* on yourself and prepare to offer your services to the firm you believe offers a good future.

3. Many companies do not recruit college graduates in the college placement office, if one exists. Thus, in your local community, find out the different choices that exist in the retail field for college graduates. Find out the entry level for college grads; kind and length of training program, if one exists; steps up the management ladder; and, if possible, beginning salaries and chances for promotion in each firm. Prepare a "career chart" for the city as a result of your findings.

CASES

A–1. A Family Affair

Henderson's is located in a very small community of 17,000 people within an SMSA of some one million population. The 40th anniversary of Henderson's had been celebrated recently. Mr. Henderson, Sr., was approaching 80 years of age and was wondering about what the future held for him. He encouraged Eric, his grandson, to consider coming back home, as the family business would be his. Eric's father was a successful doctor in the central city and, for the past 25 years, Eric's mother had done most of the buying and book work for the company. In actuality, the oldest Henderson was very tired and skeptical about the future.

Eric was not sure he wanted to leave college and go directly into the family business, but was very interested in the opportunity because he eventually wanted his own business. He thought it was very important to get experience that could be helpful in his own business later, so he took a job with a major department store some 200 miles from his home. He went through the training program at the department store and was placed in the furniture department as an assistant buyer. His commitment was to learn fashion merchandise since the family business was predominately apparel. At the time,

he was unhappy in his placement. Consequently, he entered the job market after three or four months as an assistant buyer and got a very interesting position with an off-price retailer in the same city. He is currently serving as a department manager in a unit of the off-price, multiple-unit organization and feels he is learning a great deal about merchandising and management.

At a recent family meeting, Eric, who is engaged to be married in a few weeks, wanted some commitments from his grandfather about Eric's entering the family business. Eric thinks that after about a year he will be ready to take over the business. His grandfather is not so certain that the time frame is acceptable. The grandfather believes that approximately three more years would be better. Eric, in his own mind, realizes that his grandfather is afraid of retiring and wants to work as long as he possibly can.

Questions
1. Comment on Eric's career objectives. Is the time frame which Eric has set for himself realistic, or is the grandfather being more realistic? What do you think will happen in the long run?

A–2. Joan Has a Career Decision to Make

It was a very exciting day for Joan White, as she had just received job offers from the two leading department store organizations in the state's major metropolitan area. The opportunities were similar, but, of course, different in that one of the outlets was a full-line department store and the other was a more limited-line apparel store. Each organization had multiple units operating throughout the state. Joan was having a difficult time making a decision about which organization to join, as they were so similar. The initial salary was identical for both organizations and the fringe benefit packages were as well. It was impossible to judge which company would offer the most rapid promotion up the ladder of management, but Joan suspected there was little difference. As she was contemplating how she could make a choice, she went to the post office to check her mail. In that delivery was a letter from Neiman-Marcus of Dallas. She was invited for a second interview at that prestigious, specialty chain. She was elated and excited, but had a problem. She had been told that she must let the other two stores know about her decision within the week. She felt obligated to go to the second interview with Neiman-Marcus because it was an opportunity that could not be ignored.

Questions

1. Can Joan ask for a delay from the two stores with whom she has been negotiating? What if neither one will give her an extension; should she risk not having an offer at all? If Neiman-Marcus offers her a job, should she accept "on the spot" or should she go back to her home environment, think about it, and negotiate further with the other two stores? Is this a typical kind of problem that college seniors face?

ENDNOTES

1. Janice Harayda, "Internships: Getting a Head Start," *Business Week's Careers*, September 1986, pp. 21–23.
2. Marilyn Moats Kennedy, "Questions You Can Ask the Interviewer," *Business Week's Careers*, September 1986, pp. 26–30.
3. Robert B. Nelson, "10 Common Mistakes Job Hunters Make," *Business Week's Careers*, November 1986, pp. 91–93.
4. This section is quoted from "We've Got News in Store for You" Macy's New York, Executive Personnel.

INDEX

Employees—*(Cont.)*
 job orientation, 456
 job sharing, 296–298
 job skills in retailing, 607–8
 job specification, 279–80, 298
 motivation of, 459–62
 pay plan for, 285–90
 performance appraisal, 291
 recruitment of, 280–81
 rights of, 586
 selection of, 281, 283–84, 447
 and store image, 145
 and theft, 401–3
 training of, 447–48, 450, 452–56
Employers and two-career families, retailing capsule, 274–75
Employment in retailing, 27
Employment Retirement Income Security Act, 283
End of month (EOM) dating, 345
Entertainment, publicity, 496
Entrepreneurship and performance rewards, retailing, 606
Environmental dynamics, 82
Environmental Protection Agency (EPA), 586
Equal Credit Opportunity Act, 71, 75, 514–15, 517, 527
Equal Employment Opportunity Commission (EEOC), 281, 298, 586
Equal Pay Act, 282
Establishment types, extremes in, 90
Ethical standards, 73
Evaluation and control, 55–56
Exclusive dealing, 68, 75
Exclusive territories, 69, 75
Executive Orders, 11246, 11375, 11141, 282
Expense categories, retail outlet, 197
Expense center accounting, 323
Expense control, 544–45, 548
Expense planning, 321–24
Express warranties, 70, 75
Extended shopping hours, 522
Exterior design, store, 411–12
External environment and retailing, 585–88
External factors, 45, 58
Extra dating, 345
Extreme segmentation, 46–47, 58

F
Fact-finder, customer type, 440
Failures, retail, 186–88, 192

Fair Credit Billing Act, 71, 75
Fair Credit Reporting Act, 71, 75
Fair Debt Collection Practices Act, 72, 75, 515–16, 518, 527
Fair trade laws, 358–59, 373
False advertising, 68
Family Affair, case, 620
Family size, decrease in, 170
Faneuil Hall Marketplace, Boston, 15
Farmer-owned stores, 24
Feature-benefit relationship and sales training, 453–54, 462
Federal fair-employment-practices regulations, 282–83
Federal Trade Commission (FTC), 65, 68, 75, 229, 521, 594
Federal Trade Commission Act, 65, 76
Fee, franchising, 227–29
Feedback and sales training, 455–56
Female-male roles, changes in, 171
Festival markets, 15–19
Fictitious trade name, 71
Financial risk, 139, 157
Finishing out, shopping center, 252
First-in, first-out (FIFO) method of costing inventory, 562–63, 572
Fixed liabilities, 554, 572
Fixed-payment lease, 266, 269
Flexible fixturing, as retailing trend, 583
Flex time, 296, 298
Foley's Answers Back, case, 158–59
Followers, and lifestyle analysis, 173
Follow-up, and buying, 346
Food and Drug Administration (FDA), 70
Forms of ownership, retail, 188, 189, 206
Forward-integrated stores, 23
Forward integration, 89, 95
Franchisee associations, 231, 235
Franchising
 advantages of, 220
 costs of, 227–28
 disadvantages of, 221–22
 elements and forms of, 225–26
 evaluation of, 229–31
 franchise contract, and franchisor and franchisee, 220–22, 230–31, 235, 238–43
 franchisor perspective and legal restrictions, 222
 Greyhound Company and, 237
 growth and importance of, 220–21
 identifying opportunities for, 228

P